DON PEDRO CALDERÓN

Don Pedro Calderón de la Barca (1600–1681) is Spain's most important early modern dramatist. His varied career as a playwright, courtier, soldier and priest placed him at the heart of Spanish culture, and he reflected on contemporary events in his plays, most famously *La vida es sueño* (*Life is a Dream*). In the first scholary biography of Calderón in English, Don W. Cruickshank uses his command of the archival sources and his unparalleled understanding of Calderón's work to chart his life and his political, literary and religious contexts. In addition, the book includes much fresh research into Calderón's writings and their attributions. This elegant, erudite work will bring Calderón to a new audience both within and beyond Spanish studies. With illustrations, extensive notes and detailed indexes, this is the most comprehensive English-language book on Calderón, and it will long remain the key work of reference on this important author.

DON W. CRUICKSHANK is Emeritus Professor of Spanish at University College, Dublin. He has published widely on Calderón and on Spanish literature and has edited several editions of Calderón's works.

Juan de Alfaro, *Don Pedro Calderón*, ?*c*. 1675 (Biblioteca Nacional de España, Madrid)

DON PEDRO CALDERÓN

DON W. CRUICKSHANK

CAMBRIDGE UNIVERSITY PRESS
Cambridge, New York, Melbourne, Madrid, Cape Town, Singapore, São Paulo, Delhi

Cambridge University Press
The Edinburgh Building, Cambridge CB2 8RU, UK

Published in the United States of America by Cambridge University Press, New York

www.cambridge.org
Information on this title: www.cambridge.org/9780521765152

First published 2009

Printed in the United Kingdom at the University Press, Cambridge

A catalogue record for this publication is available from the British Library

ISBN 978-0-521-76515-2 Hardback

To the Memory of
Edward Meryon Wilson
1906–1977

Contents

Illustrations

FIGURES

Preface

> For *interpretation* if not *assessment* of a work biographical knowledge is often useful and sometimes most valuable.
>
> (David Daiches, *Critical Approaches to Literature*)

Not so long ago, one branch of critical theory held that the identity of the author was irrelevant: what mattered was the text. Had its proponents carried this point of view to its logical conclusion, they should have remained anonymous. The contrary view, that the facts of authors' lives and the events they lived through as they wrote, can help us interpret their texts, is inherently more plausible. That view is the basis of this biography. We can justify the view from the way Calderón composes his work: we shall find it harder to penetrate the allegory of *La segunda esposa* (1649) if we know nothing of Philip IV's second marriage. Contemporary events provided sources of inspiration and points of reference, and the plays are full of allusions to them and to other works, from Classical to contemporary, including the poet's own.

Producing a biography of Calderón is a daunting task, especially in the light of the unlucky precedents. Don Juan de Vera Tassis, Calderón's first editor, who published nine volumes of his plays, had planned to publish ten, and even supplied titles of the plays to be contained in the tenth: he listed fourteen of them in the *Novena parte* of 1691. But although he was still alive in 1716, and although his second edition of the *Verdadera quinta parte* (1694) benefited from his continuing efforts to find better texts, the *Décima parte* never saw the light. No doubt good texts, or any texts at all, had proved elusive for some plays, but he must have had several of them, since printed editions of a few still existed in the eighteenth century. Only one of the fourteen, *El acaso y el error*, survives today. Referring to Calderón's works in the *Verdadera quinta parte* of 1682, Vera Tassis wrote that 'sus obras las venera, y guarda la Libreria del Colegio Mayor de Ouiedo en Salamanca' ('his works are reverenced and preserved by the library of the Colegio Mayor de Oviedo in Salamanca'). Whether these were manuscript or printed, they should have been transferred, with the college's other holdings, to the university's main library. No trace of them has been found so far.

After Vera Tassis, the first attempt to produce a critical edition of Calderón's plays was made by Juan Jorge Keil, who explained in a prospectus how he intended to provide textual variants and commentary for all of the plays, including those not printed by Vera Tassis. Keil managed to produce a complete edition, in four volumes, of the 108 plays in Vera Tassis's nine *partes* (1827–30), but the original grand plan was never realised.

The first scholar to prepare the way for a serious Calderón biography was Cristóbal Pérez Pastor, the author of *Documentos para la biografía de don Pedro Calderón de la Barca* (1905). The title-page proclaims that this is Volume I, and Don Cristóbal's prologue explains that so many documents have turned up since the book was sent to press that 'hemos decidido reservar los datos últimamente encontrados para un segundo tomo que además llevará las ilustraciones necesarias para aclarar algunos puntos dudosos' ('we have decided to keep the data recently discovered for a second volume, which will also include the illustrations needed to clarify some doubtful points'). Volume II never appeared; Don Cristóbal died in 1908. We may take comfort from the likelihood that many of the documents referred to have since been discovered by others, and that those which have not still await rediscovery.[1]

The first biographer to take advantage of Pérez Pastor's unfinished work was Emilio Cotarelo y Mori, in his *Ensayo sobre la vida y obras de D. Pedro Calderón de la Barca* (1924). One is alarmed, but by this time not entirely surprised, to discover the words 'Parte Primera' on the title-page. Cotarelo had planned four volumes: the *Biografía*, the *Fama póstuma*, the *Crítica* and a *Bibliografía*. Only the first was published. Now, over eighty years later, all four would be out of date, but they would have been enormously useful to later *calderonistas*.

In 1960 (to judge from the dates of the works he cites), the late Edward Wilson began to write a biography of Calderón. He produced eighty pages of typescript, two chapters, around 20,000 words, which ended in 1651. Although it was clearly his intention to continue to 1681, he apparently wrote no more after 1960: the handwritten revisions do not extend to a work which appeared in 1961, and which he saw prior to publication. As Wilson's literary executor, I still have that typescript. While my biography is very different from the one he planned (it is bound to be, with half a century of published Calderón research to help), I have found the typescript enormously useful from the point of view of references. Wilson had numerous friends and contacts in the world of Hispanic studies, and the amount of information he received from them indicates that his preparation for what he wrote extended back for years.[2] One cannot thank a long-dead mentor, but I dedicate this book to his memory, in recognition of the fact that it could not have been written without his work on Calderón, the vast majority of which he did publish.

Calderón's huge output has certainly contributed to the difficulties of his biographers, but these misfortunes have extended even to his mortal remains. In his will, Calderón had asked to be buried in the church of San Salvador, and this was done, in the manner in which he had specified.[3] Cotarelo provides a list, in the last chapter of his *Ensayo*, of the five occasions on which the remains were moved, beginning in 1841 and ending in 1902 in San Pedro, near the Glorieta de Quevedo. San Pedro was one of the churches sacked in the Civil War, and the remains were never recovered.

This biography tries to avoid promising too much: it deals mainly with Calderón's secular career, the first half of his writing life, up to 1650, when he took the first steps to becoming a priest. It is also an old-fashioned, traditional biography. That is, it tries to set the subject in his political and cultural context, while dealing with the events of his life, and significant events which happened during that life, in chronological order. The chronology also extends to his writings, to the development of ideas and techniques, as far as the known facts allow. If this old-fashioned approach requires justification, it lies in the fact that the traditional biography of Cotarelo has been badly in need of revision for many years. Cotarelo was wealthy enough to conduct research on a full-time basis, and his favourite topic was the drama of the Golden Age. Modern scholars owe a great deal to him. Since 1924, however, much new research has been done on Golden-Age drama in general, and on Calderón in particular, thanks in large measure to the stimulation provided by two centenaries within twenty years (1981, 2000). The new research has revealed new documents, new facts and new dates, but only one scholar has attempted to draw the information together to write a new Life: Felipe Pedraza Jiménez, in his *Calderón: vida y teatro* (2000). His stated aim, in his 'Declaración de intenciones', is very similar to my own:

> Mi trabajo se ha limitado a contar la vida, tal y como puede deducirse de los documentos que conservamos, a intentar perfilar el carácter, sin juicios previos, y a ir pasando las páginas de sus dramas, comedias, autos y piezas menores.
>
> (My work has been limited to recounting the life, to the extent that it can be inferred from the documents we possess, to attempting to sketch the character, without prejudgements, and to going through the pages of his dramas, comedies, *autos* and minor pieces.)[4]

Pedraza's book is very useful, but despite this usefulness and the similarity of intention, the result is rather different. Here, there are pictures, notes, and an index. That is, I want readers to see, as far as possible, what the people and places referred to looked like, the physical appearance of the documents quoted, as well as the sources of information and conclusions. When necessary, I have gone back to documents which were known, as well as looking for new ones. Finally, I want this to be a reference book, in which readers searching for information about a single play, or a single character, can find it without having to guess at my estimate of the play's date of composition.

Pedraza quotes Ángel Valbuena Prat's famous remark that Calderón's life-story is 'la biografía del silencio' ('the biography of silence'), but rightly points out that this remark is really true only when we compare his with that of Lope de Vega (p. 11). Lope was an egotist, an emotional extrovert who not only left behind some 500 personal letters, but constantly used his own life as a source for his art, most notably in the *Dorotea*; he even created a character, Belardo, to be his mouthpiece in his plays. In Calderón, we may complain, there is none of this. But there is none of this in Shakespeare, in Marlowe, in Tirso, in Luis Vélez, in Corneille … In fact, we know far more about Calderón than we do about Tirso or Marlowe, more even than about Shakespeare, although no author has been more thoroughly investigated. Lope is unique: it is Calderón who is typical. We should remember, too, that his work is full of personal references: there are self-mocking jokes about poets, advertisements for his other plays, remarks about studying in Salamanca, and so on. There are, indeed, scores of occasions when national or personal events provide certain or plausible inspiration, either for whole works, for scenes or for passages. What we do not find is an obvious mouthpiece for the author, and we soon learn that remarks which may seem autobiographical need to be supported from other sources.

Calderón's first biographers were Don Juan de Vera Tassis (in his edition of Calderón's *Verdadera quinta parte*, 1682) and Gaspar Agustín de Lara (in his *Obelisco funebre, pyramide funesto que construia a la inmortal memoria de D. Pedro Calderon de la Barca*, 1684). Vera Tassis's reference to himself as the dramatist's 'mayor amigo' ('greatest friend') has often been derided. There is evidence, though, that he discussed with Calderón his plans to publish a complete edition of Don Pedro's plays, and that Calderón supplied him with information and perhaps even some texts. Vera Tassis's chief defect as a biographer was akin to his shortcomings as an editor: excessive intervention. Not, unlike his subject, a *madrileño* (he calls Salamanca 'amada patria mía' ('my beloved homeland') in the *Verdadera quinta parte*), Vera Tassis was born much later, probably in the 1630s. There is no evidence that he met Calderón until the 1670s, but he was unwilling to leave blank those areas about which his information was scanty. As for Lara, he evidently recalled personal information contributed by Calderón; his information, when we can check it, is accurate. However, there is no evidence, in either case, for any ordered attempt to supply (on Calderón's part) or to record (on the part of Vera Tassis and Lara) such details as might be used in a biography. Vera Tassis did consult Don Pedro's sister Dorotea, but the only piece of information attributed to her is the remark that she had often heard her parents say that her brother had cried three times while still in the womb: evidence, supposedly, of precocity. Not until the *Documentos* of Pérez Pastor was there any systematic effort to gather information about the dramatist. Pérez Pastor was a priest and a 'doctor en ciencias' who spent much of his life hunting through archives for information about the classical theatre of Spain. His volume is the starting-point for this biography. As was normal a century ago, his transcriptions of documents tend to modernise; occasionally one finds minor errors, and it has often been necessary to check documents which he merely summarises. Without his preliminary labours, however, the amount of research required simply to discover material would have been enormous.

As the words 'secular career' suggest, this study not only deals with the writer's life before he became a priest, but also concentrates on his secular works. The *autos* are not ignored, especially when they are based on *comedias* or on current events, or when there is reliable information about their date of composition. However, the *autos* present more dating problems than the plays, particularly before 1650, as well as less biographical information.

My thanks are due to the Irish Research Council for the Humanities and Social Sciences, for the funding which enabled me to devote a complete academic year to this project; to the staffs of the Archivo de Villa, Madrid; the Archivo del Ayuntamiento de Santillana del Mar; the Archivo del Ayuntamiento de Yepes; the Archivo Histórico de Protocolos, Madrid; the Archivo Histórico Nacional, Madrid; the Audio Visual Centre, University College, Dublin; the Bayerische Staatsbibliothek, Munich; the Biblioteca Apostolica Vaticana, Rome; the Biblioteca Histórica Municipal, Madrid; the Biblioteca Nacional de España, Madrid; the Biblioteca Universitaria, Universidade de Santiago; the Bodleian Library, Oxford; the British Library; Cambridge University Library; the Hispanic Society of America; the Museo Arqueológico Nacional, Madrid; the Museo Nacional del Prado, Madrid; the Museum of Fine Arts, Boston; the Österreichische Nationalbibliothek,

Vienna; the library of Trinity College, Dublin; the Wellington Museum, Apsley House, London; to Linda Bree, Tom O'Reilly and Maartje Scheltens of Cambridge University Press and to their two anonymous readers for their numerous helpful suggestions; to my copy-editor Jo Bramwell; and to my colleagues in Hispanic and Lusophone Studies in University College, Dublin, for the tolerance with which they have looked on my obsession. Colleagues there and elsewhere who deserve special mention for sending information and helping to solve problems are John C. Barnes, Martin Cunningham, Charles Davis, Victor Dixon, Sara Ferraro, Meg Greer, David Hook, Luis Iglesias Feijoo, Giulio and Laura Lepschy, John O'Neill, George Peale, José Luis Ramos González, Alison Ribeiro de Meneses, María Ana Rodríguez Villaumbrales, Pepe Ruano de la Haza, Jeremy Squires, Alejandra Ulla Lorenzo and Germán Vega García-Luengos; and I thank Professor R. R. Bakalski for granting permission to quote from his doctoral thesis. Finally, I am particularly grateful to Don Rafael Atienza y Medina, Marqués de Salvatierra, for allowing me to examine the portrait of Calderón preserved in his house in Ronda.

Abbreviations

AHN	Archivo Histórico Nacional, Madrid
AHP	Archivo Histórico de Protocolos Notariales, Madrid
AL	*Anuario de Letras*
BAE	Biblioteca de Autores Españoles
BBMP	*Boletín de la Biblioteca Menéndez y Pelayo*
BCom	*Bulletin of the Comediantes*
BH	*Bulletin Hispanique*
BHS	*Bulletin of Hispanic Studies*
BM	*Burlington Magazine*
BNE	Biblioteca Nacional de España, Madrid
BRAE	*Boletín de la Real Academia Española*
BRAH	*Boletín de la Real Academia de la Historia*
BSS	*Bulletin of Spanish Studies*
CSIC	Consejo Superior de Investigaciones Científicas
FMLS	*Forum for Modern Language Studies*
Hisp	*Hispania*
HR	*Hispanic Review*
IEM	Instituto de Estudios Madrileños
JHP	*Journal of Hispanic Philology*
MLN	*Modern Language Notes*
MLR	*Modern Language Review*
MP	*Modern Philology*
NRFE	*Nueva Revista de Filología Española*
PMLA	*Publications of the Modern Language Association of America*
PQ	*Philological Quarterly*
RABM	*Revista de Archivos, Bibliotecas y Museos*
RBAM	*Revista de la Biblioteca, Archivo y Museo del Ayuntamiento de Madrid*
RBPH	*Revue Belge de Philologie et d'Histoire*
RCEH	*Revista Canadiense de Estudios Hispánicos*

RevHisp	*Revue Hispanique*
RFE	*Revista de Filología Española*
RHMC	*Revue d'Histoire Moderne et Contemporaine*
RLit	*Revista de Literatura*
RQ	*Renaissance Quarterly*
RR	*Romanic Review*
ZRP	*Zeitschrift für Romanische Philologie*

Note on measurements, currency, translations and dates

The *pie castellano* (Castilian foot) was about 28 centimetres, or 11 inches. References to money in Golden-Age Castile mention *maravedís*, *reales*, *escudos* and *ducados*. The *ducado*/ducat was a money of account: with 34 *maravedís* per *real* and 11 *reales* per ducat, there were supposedly 374 *maravedís* in a ducat, but to make calculation easier, the ducat was often reckoned as 375 *maravedís*. The *escudo* was a real coin, but its relationship to the others varied. Minsheu (1599) rated it at 11¾ *reales* (400 *maravedís*), or 5/10½d in English money (for him, a *real* was sixpence); in Spain, after 1609, it was reckoned at 440 *maravedís*. Since inflation and currency manipulation caused the purchasing power of Castilian coins to vary hugely in the seventeenth century, readers will find it easiest to think of *escudos* and ducats as roughly equal. Translations are supplied for all quotations, in whatever language. Translations of all Calderón titles referred to are given in the Appendix. All dates are New Style, unless followed by the abbreviation OS.

CHAPTER I

The birthplace: Madrid in 1600

En Madrid, ¿qué quietud
hay como el ruido? y ¿qué cuadros,
aunque con más tulipanes
que trujo extranjero mayo,
como una calle que tenga
gente, coches y caballos,
llena de lodo el invierno,
llena de polvo el verano ... ? (*El agua mansa*)

(In Madrid, what peace is there like noise? What flowerbeds are there, though they have more tulips than were ever brought by foreign May, like a street with people, coaches and horses, full of mud in winter, full of dust in summer?)

When Don Pedro Calderón de la Barca Henao y Riaño was born in Madrid on 17 January 1600, the city had been the capital of Spain for less than forty years, since May 1561; until then, the court had been peripatetic, following the monarch from place to place. At the time when Philip II chose the city as his seat of government, the court was in Toledo; before that, it had been in Valladolid. All three cities are in central Castile, but it has often been alleged that Philip chose Madrid in particular because the city was at the centre of the Iberian peninsula. When we hear the allegation, and consult a map, with Madrid equidistant from the sea in every direction, the apparently cold logic seems plausible enough. It is at least as likely, though, that Philip was motivated by centrality on a smaller scale. Madrid was in the middle of a circle containing his favourite resorts and palaces, some of which he had ordered refurbished as early as the 1540s: Valsaín (near Segovia, modified and added to in the 1540s and 1550s); the Casa de Campo (just to the west of the city, on land bought by Philip in 1556, although reconstruction began only in 1562); El Pardo (just north of Madrid, re-roofed in the Flemish style in 1559); Aranjuez (south-east of the city, on the Tagus: regularly used by Philip as a retreat in the 1550s, although the residences and magnificent gardens were developed in the 1560s and 1570s); and Aceca (also on the Tagus, near Toledo, ordered to be rebuilt in 1556). Philip's most famous palace, the Escorial, was not ready to be lived in until 1566, and not completed until September 1584, but the site, some 27 miles west of the city in the foothills of the Guadarrama mountains, was chosen in 1561, soon after the decision to move to Madrid.[1] Quite probably, too, Valladolid was tainted in Philip's eyes by the discovery of a Protestant group there in 1558. Philip's choice, then, may have had more of an emotional content than the common explanation suggests. Besides, Madrid had several advantages. The climate, at 2,300 feet above sea level, was dry and healthy. There were reliable sources of good water and of firewood, at least at first. There was a suitable palace (Plate 1), a squat unhandsome *alcázar* of Moorish brick, situated pleasantly enough at the top of the rise on the western outskirts, with a view of the Manzanares river, the uncultivated countryside of scrub and evergreen oak, and, in the distance, the Gredos and Guadarrama mountains. Philip liked the view, and chose the western façade for his apartments to take best advantage of it; he also supervised major improvements and extensions, including the new Torre Dorada, on the south-west corner.[2]

The river Manzanares, compared with the Seine or the Thames (or indeed the Tagus or Guadalquivir), left a good deal to be desired, especially in summer, when it was reduced to a muddy trickle, provoking many jokes. In 1561 there was no stone bridge. The Puente de Segovia (Plate 2), the first to be constructed, by Juan de Herrera, Philip's principal Escorial architect, was the only stone bridge in Calderón's lifetime,[3] but at least it was impressive, even disproportionately so: 'No eres río para media puente' ('You're not a river for half a bridge'), Góngora imagined people saying to the river, while the bridge 'es puente para muchos mares' ('is a bridge for many seas').[4] Lope de Vega imagined the river pleading with Madrid's councillors to take away the bridge, or bring it another river: '¡Quítenme aquesta puente que me mata, | señores regidores de la villa …! | … tráiganle sus mercedes otro río' ('Take away this bridge that's killing me, sir aldermen! Bring it another river, your worships').[5] Even Calderón joined in:

> Que para ser la 'Florida'
> estación de todo el orbe
> la más bella, hermosa y rica,
> solo al río falta el río. (II, 1249a)[6]

(For La Florida to be the most beautiful, pretty and exquisite situation in the whole world, all the river needs is the river.)

Nevertheless, the Manzanares was a favourite spot for picnics, for washing clothes, and even, in hot weather, for bathing.[7] Moreover, Madrid did have a royal history. It had been captured from the Moors in 1083 (or 1085, according to some sources) by Alfonso VI. The palace had been refurbished by King Peter. Henry III had been crowned there, in 1390. It was one of the favourite residences of Henry IV; Juana, 'La Beltraneja', the daughter of Henry's queen (and perhaps of Henry himself) was born there in 1462, and Henry himself died in it, indeed, in December 1474, and was buried in the city. The palace was also chosen, in 1525, as the prison of King Francis I of France, captured at the battle of Pavia in February; he remained there and in the Torre de los Lujanes (Plate 3) until the signing of the Treaty of Madrid in January 1526. The palace had also been one of several to be restored, in the 1540s, by Philip and his father, the Emperor Charles V. While the court was still peripatetic, Philip had occasionally stayed there, for example between 1551 and 1553. On the other hand, even by sixteenth-century standards, the city's population prior to 1561 was pretty modest for a capital: by some accounts, as few as 9,000 in mid century, with only 16,000 even by the end of 1561, after the court had arrived.[8] Growth was very rapid thereafter: by the time of Philip's death in 1598, the population was around 75,000; by 1617, 150,000.[9] In *El hombre pobre todo es trazas* (1627), the *gracioso* Rodrigo refers to Madrid's rapidly changing urban geography:

> [¿]En Madrid, no es cosa llana,
> señor, que de hoy a mañana
> suele perderse una calle?
> Porque, según cada día
> se hacen nuevas, imagino
> que desconoce un vecino
> hoy adonde ayer vivía. (II, 201b)

(Is it not obvious, sir, that in Madrid a street gets lost between today and tomorrow? Because, given how they make new ones every day, I suppose that today a resident can fail to recognise where he lived yesterday.)

This rapid growth was achieved by immigration, and the poorest immigrants lived in the outskirts, in wooden shacks of one or two storeys, not unlike the *favelas* of modern Rio de Janeiro. It was still possible, however, even in 1600, to walk across the city in little more than half an hour.

Perhaps we should think of Liverpool in Victorian times: an old but originally modest settlement, its ancient past swamped by a later influx of immigrants, most of them living in the squalor of jerry-built tenements which have had to be demolished since. An air of bustle, an appearance of prosperity: a great city in a vast empire. In the side streets, poverty, filth, disease; and waiting unseen, largely unguessed-at in the future, horrendous wars, recession, decline from greatness, loss of empire. Largely unguessed-at: for even in 1600 González de Cellorigo, writing in the aftermath of the plague outbreak of the 1590s, was in no doubt about the decline from greatness, or that its cause lay in contempt for

las leyes naturales, que nos enseñan a trabajar, y que de poner la riqueza en el oro y la plata, y dexar de seguir la verdadera y cierta, que proviene y se adquiere por la natural y artificial industria, ha venido nuestra República a decaer tanto de su florido estado.

(the natural laws, which teach us to work, and that our country has come to decline so much from its prosperous state due to placing wealth in gold and silver, and to abandoning the pursuit of true and certain riches, which arise and are acquired through natural and applied industry.)

Anticipating Adam Smith by nearly two centuries, he argued that 'la verdadera riqueza no consiste en tener labrado, acuñado o en pasta mucho oro, y mucha plata' ('True wealth does not consist in possessing much gold and silver, whether it has been worked or coined or is in bullion').[10] But the bookstalls were full of the pamphlets of 'projectors'. The Spanish term, *arbitristas*, soon acquired derogatory connotations, and few people, including those in government, were capable of distinguishing the perceptive from the lunatic, or of enforcing appropriate laws. Since the 1570s the Cortes had been calling for legislation to control extravagant consumption, and in 1623 the Olivares regime, conscious that the possession of 'much gold and silver' manifested itself in ostentatious dress and huge retinues of servants, would introduce a series of sumptuary laws, in which the government would set an example. Government officials and civil servants were to be reduced to a third; the king would halve his household expenses; nobles would cut down on servants and clothes, and spend eleven months a year on their estates, administering them personally, and employing their former court servants on their lands. Yet the only obvious casualty of these new laws was the old starched linen ruff, which was replaced by the simple collar called the *golilla*.

In 1561 Madrid was still, technically at least, a walled city, although some of the surviving walls were of mud brick, with many buildings already outside them. The centre of the city was not, as at present, the Puerta del Sol, which was then the city's eastern administrative gateway;[11] even the splendid Plaza Mayor did not take on its present shape until the reign of Philip III, whose equestrian statue now stands in the middle.[12] Most of the old buildings were *mudéjar* (built by Moors living under Christian rule).

The original dwelling-houses were mostly of one storey, of whitewashed brick or adobe, as can still be seen in many small towns in Spain. Since the city was not yet a diocese (not until 1885), it had no cathedral. The main church was Santa María de la Almudena, supposedly once a mosque, at the junction of the present Calle Mayor and Calle de Bailén: it was pulled down at the end of the nineteenth century, when work was begun on the modern cathedral, a little to the south-west. The story was that an image of Our Lady, hidden in the defensive wall just before the city fell to the Moors in the early eighth century, was miraculously rediscovered nearly 400 years later. (The word *almudena* derives from Arabic *almudayna*, 'fortress', but it has often been thought to derive from *almud*, a measure of grain, and so to mean 'grain market', 'grain store'. This is the meaning Calderón gives it in his *auto*, *El cubo de la Almudena*, written for 1651. He also wrote two plays on the subject, *Nuestra Señora de la Almudena*, parts I and II, but they are lost. We can guess, though, that they resembled his *Origen, pérdida y restauración de la Virgen del Sagrario* (?1629), which tells a similar story of an image in Toledo.) Surviving examples of *mudéjar* architecture can be found in the churches of San Nicolás de los Servitas in the Plaza de San Nicolás, and San Pedro el Viejo, in the Costanilla de San Pedro. Both have impressive *mudéjar* towers, that of the former dating from the twelfth century. Other *mudéjar* details are visible in the original part of the Monasterio de las Descalzas Reales (in the square named after it), founded by Charles V's daughter Juana in 1559, in the building in which she had been born, or in the Torre de los Lujanes in the Plazuela de la Villa. Buildings outside the old walls included the churches of San Jerónimo el Real, in the present Calle de Ruiz de Alarcón, founded by Ferdinand and Isabella just before the queen's death in 1504, and Nuestra Señora de Atocha, founded by the Dominicans in 1523. The image of Our Lady of Atocha, supposedly carved by St Luke himself, had, according to legend, been hidden from the Moors like that of La Almudena, and miraculously rediscovered at the reconquest of the city.

Buildings which have not survived from this period include Madrid's two public theatres, the Corral del Príncipe and the Corral de la Cruz. The site of the former, on the east side of the Calle del Príncipe, is now occupied by the Teatro Español, which faces the statue of Don Pedro across the Plaza de Santa Ana. The site of the Cruz, a few hundred yards away on the corner of the Calle de la Cruz and the Calle de Espoz y Mina, is now marked only by a plaque. As the name *corral* indicates, both had originally been yards, open spaces surrounded by tenement buildings. By 1600, some twenty years into their life as theatres, the yards had acquired high apron stages at one end, as well as arrangements to allow part of the audience to sit, but they remained open to the elements.[13] Even Philip IV, the first Spanish monarch to be a true patron of the theatre, had to take part in this improvisation, sometimes attending these public playhouses, sometimes (from about 1623) using spaces in the *alcázar*, notably the *salón* (from 1640, the *salón dorado*), for performances.[14] Not until 1640 and the completion of the Coliseo del Buen Retiro did Madrid acquire a purpose-built theatre with movable perspective scenery and artificial lighting. The new design made possible new kinds of play, but a species of nostalgia for the old public theatres meant that some of their features were preserved, including their general layout. Thus, although the Coliseo was part of the new Retiro palace complex, it was opened to the public, and 'efforts were made to simulate for the amusement of the king and queen the kind of atmosphere to be found in the public theatres'.[15]

While Philip IV's predecessors had not been notable theatre patrons, they had presided over the development of a major new art-form. The first 'plays' to be printed in Spanish, in 1496, were the eclogues of Juan del Encina, eight of them, probably written for the ducal court of Alba in the previous decade. Encina is called the father of Spanish drama, but the father of the commercial theatre was Lope de Rueda, a Sevillian whose touring company brought theatre to the ordinary public, among them, around 1560, the young Miguel de Cervantes. Cervantes remembered the experience half a century later, and perhaps many young members of an audience first encountered literature in this way, an encounter that in some cases inspired them to become writers themselves. Whatever the exact nature of the inspiration, there was no shortage of it: the latest catalogue of seventeenth-century Spanish dramatic works contains about 10,000 titles, which can be compared with the 838 entries in Sir Walter Greg's *Bibliography of the English Printed Drama to the Restoration*.[16] By 1623, the year of Don Pedro's earliest known plays, Lope de Vega had been writing them for forty years, and had probably written over 700: an average of a play every three weeks, for four decades! It took the book trade thirty years to comprehend that printing plays no longer needed to be the sporadic affair it had been in the sixteenth century: by the time the booksellers had realised that Lope had made possible the printing of plays in numbered volumes of a dozen each, many of his early ones were lost.

Printing had come to Madrid only in 1566, nearly a century after Spain's first books were printed in Segovia (1472). The late start meant that Madrid never came to dominate the book trade as London did in England; and the delay was only one symptom of the gradual nature of the process of transformation from a minor town into a cultural capital. Before 1561, Spanish writers and artists were likely to pursue their careers in, or close to, their place of birth. This situation changed only gradually. Thus Cervantes, born in Alcalá in 1547, well before Madrid became the capital, settled there definitively only in 1606; Góngora, born in Córdoba in 1561, moved to Madrid in 1617; Mira de Amescua, born in Guadix in 1574, moved to Granada as a student, and settled in Madrid in 1606; Luis Vélez de Guevara, born in Écija (just over 50 miles east of Seville) around 1579, joined the service of the Archbishop of Seville, and eventually settled in Madrid in 1607; Zurbarán, born at Fuente de Cantos (70 miles north of Seville) in 1598, spent most of his life in Seville, but moved to Madrid in 1658; Velázquez, born in Seville in 1599, made an attempt to find patronage in Madrid in 1622, and moved there in August 1623. The Count-Duke of Olivares, a *sevillano* born in Rome, was the main instigator of this Seville–Madrid connection. Another migrant whose career was affected by it was Alonso Cano, born in Granada in 1601, who studied in Seville, and moved to Madrid in 1638. Even Cano's teacher, Juan Martínez Montañés (born in Alcalá la Real, near Jaén, in 1568), the most esteemed sculptor of his age, had to visit Madrid in 1635–6 to model the head of Philip IV, a stay recorded by Velázquez's portrait.

* * *

In addition to its surrounding circle of royal palaces and hunting lodges, Madrid was conveniently close to Toledo, once the seat of the Visigothic kings and by this time the ecclesiastical headquarters of Spain; close, but far enough for a monarch who wanted to keep the princes of the church firmly in their place, since 44 miles – less than an hour in a modern car – was two days' journey by mule, the normal ecclesiastical form of transport. Alcalá de Henares (Complutum in Latin), around 20 miles away to the north-east (and now a dormitory suburb for the capital), provided a handy university, opened in 1508 and made famous by the great Complutensian Polyglot Bible, planned by the university's founder, Cardinal Cisneros, and completed in the year of his death, 1517. The university moved to Madrid in 1836 and became the Universidad Complutense; the present University of Alcalá is a modern foundation (1977).

The climate of the Castilian meseta has been described as three months of winter (*invierno*) and nine months of hell (*infierno*). In Madrid, however, the weather is pretty mild for much of the year, and the winter months do not always bring frost and snow. Even in the hottest months, July and August, the climate was more bearable then than now, when the hot exhausts of hundreds of thousands of vehicles and air-conditioning units increase the humidity, the pollution and the temperature. Not that the air of

Madrid was pure in 1600: as in many early modern cities, the sanitation arrangements involved emptying everything into the streets (sewerage was not introduced until the eighteenth century). Theoretically, this took place only at night, preceded by the euphemistic warning '¡Agua va!' ('Gardyloo!'), but the state of the streets in the early morning, or all day during the less dry months, is better not imagined in detail. In *Dar tiempo al tiempo* (by 1650), Chacón, following his master along a darkened Madrid street, falls into a muddy pothole; as he is trying to clean off the mud, a maid pours liquid from above, with the cry 'Agua va'. 'Mientes, picaña', says Chacón, 'que esto no es agua' ('Water away!' – 'That's a lie, you hussy, this is not water': II, 1332b).

This scene reminds us that even pre-industrial societies produced huge amounts of pollution, rubbish and effluent. There were horses, mules and donkeys everywhere, and their droppings littered the streets, while cleanings from their stables were piled wherever it was convenient, and sometimes where it was not; pigs and chickens roamed freely, since many citizens kept farm animals in their city property (even cows, as was the practice, occasionally, until at least the 1960s); butchers and fishmongers produced large amounts of offal; and some industries, such as tanning, although confined to the Ribera de Curtidores, in the southern part of the city, produced odours and refuse on a scale that would never be tolerated now. Then, people were more tolerant of smells: they had to be. Modern Spanish cities use huge quantities of water, for cleaning the streets, washing the pavements, watering the lawns and flowerbeds, and the frequent showering of the inhabitants in warm weather. Then, not only was the environment smellier for lack of washing: so were those who lived in it, and for the same reason. Yet even then, when germs were undiscovered, there were complaints that effluent from the slaughterhouses and tanneries was polluting drinking water. There were attempts to keep the streets clean; there were even workmen permanently assigned to the task, but repeated complaints about their failure to do the job properly, or about the failure of the authorities to enforce such legislation as there was, show that the battle was not being won.[17] In this respect, Madrid's reputation was international: Robert Burton could write in 1628: 'Some find the same fault [carrion lying in the streets] in Spain, even in Madrid, the king's seat; a most excellent air, a pleasant site, but the inhabitants are slovens, and the streets uncleanly kept.'[18]

Not surprisingly, disease was widespread, including many ailments that modern science has almost eradicated. Since no one imagined that bubonic plague was carried by fleas living in the fur of rats, it was endemic, and there was no way of preventing regular outbreaks. No single epidemic was as severe as that of two-and-a-half centuries earlier, the Black Death, which had killed a third of Europe's population (and, in Spain in particular, in 1350, King Alfonso XI, the only reigning monarch to die of the disease); but in 1599–1600, hundreds of thousands succumbed in Castile to an outbreak which may have killed 15 per cent of the inhabitants, that is, the entire population growth of the sixteenth century.[19] Fifty years later (1647–52), there was another major outbreak, affecting several Iberian cities, particularly Seville, where '200,000' died (an exaggeration, but one which points to a very high figure), Valencia (where one third of the population of 50,000 supposedly succumbed) and Barcelona.[20] Madrid got off lightly, as it had largely done in 1599, but only by establishing 'plague guards', to keep travellers from infected areas from entering the city. In *El agua mansa*, Eugenia (or Mari Nuño, in the printed version) wonders how the obnoxious Don Toribio, who has just arrived in Madrid, managed to get past the plague guards.

The twenty-first century has 'plagues' (AIDS and SARS come to mind) which never troubled our forebears; the difference is that, while some cures may remain elusive, we know how diseases work, and what we should do to preserve health. Then, health was much more precarious, and the average life expectancy half of what it is now. Not all of the illnesses that afflicted our forebears four centuries ago are readily identifiable. Some of the 'tertian agues' or 'quartan agues' they complained of were certainly malaria, but the Madrid area had few suitable breeding-grounds for mosquitoes, and the citizens suffered less than elsewhere. When Calderón wrote in 1648 from the palace of the Duke of Alba in Alba de Tormes that he was 'en una cama con unas grandes tercianas' ('in bed with a severe tertian fever'),[21] we cannot assume, without more details, that he was suffering from malaria, or draw conclusions about where he might have contracted it. Practised medical observers were sometimes capable of usefully accurate accounts of symptoms. Thus, an experienced doctor like Alonso López de Corella could describe (1574) those of 'tabardillo' in sufficient detail for us to recognise what we call typhus.[22] Yet López and his colleagues never suspected that this disease was spread, like bubonic plague and malaria, through insect bites. Similarly, if there were doctors able to distinguish the symptoms of what we call typhoid from those of typhus, they did not realise that typhoid was spread through contaminated food or drinking water. For the non-specialist, there were catch-all terms: *fiebre* or *calentura* might be used for any illness that made the patient feverish, while any malady involving the retention of fluid was *hidropesía*, dropsy (some of the symptoms of 'dropsy' might point to diabetes). Where causes were not understood, treatment was frequently inappropriate. Ailments which are now controlled, or controllable, but which then were potentially fatal, included influenza, smallpox, leprosy, tuberculosis, asthma, measles, whooping-cough and diphtheria (*garrotillo*). Malnutrition was widespread, both through sheer ignorance about diet, and through shortages of famine proportions, as in the 1590s and around 1650:[23] two of Calderón's *autos sacramentales, La semilla y la cizaña* and *El cubo de la Almudena*, both performed in 1651, were written against a background of grain shortage and bread riots.[24] The Spanish language is full of proverbs about bread, and bread still plays an important part in Spanish meals. In the seventeenth century, in a society which was still largely agricultural, the role of bread was fundamental. We cannot know how often grain was affected by ergot, the then uncomprehended fungus which made bread poisonous, but the title of a lost *auto* attributed to Calderón, *La peste del pan dañado*, suggests that outbreaks were frequent enough to be significant. The same scientific ignorance meant that even normal, non-pathological physical events such as pregnancy and parturition were extremely life-threatening, even to women who had already borne several children: Calderón's mother was one such woman.

Experience, rather than real understanding, showed that some of the remedies prescribed for the unwell, particularly herbal ones, were genuinely useful; thus infusions of willow-bark, described by Laguna in his great edition of Dioscorides as useful for earache (I, cxv, p. 89), contain aspirin; camphor (I, lxxi, pp. 55–6: 'mitiga el dolor de cabeça procediente de causa caliente', 'lessens headache proceeding from a warm cause') is still used as a decongestant; feverfew (III, cxlix, p. 362: described by Culpeper as 'very effectual for all pains in the head', p. 140) is still used for migraine – and for insecticides!); peppermint (*menta piperita*, cf. *hierbabuena*, III, xxxvii, p. 290; Culpeper, p. 235), used then and now to aid digestion, is a source of menthol; caraway seed oil (III, lxii, pp. 306–7; Culpeper, pp. 78–9) is still a remedy for indigestion; St John's Wort (*hypericum perforatum*, III, clxv–clxviii, pp. 371–2: Culpeper tells us that 'a tincture of the flowers in spirit of wine, is commended against melancholy', p. 203), is still – controversially – used as an antidepressant; rhubarb (III, ii, p. 263; Culpeper, pp. 292–4) is still recognised as a purgative, and so on; finally, Laguna's remark about the ambiguous benefits of the opium poppy, the source of laudanum, morphine and heroin (IV, lxvi, p. 415; Culpeper, pp. 290–2), might have been made by a practitioner today: 'no deuemos administrarle, sino quãdo son los dolores tan inclementes, que à ningun otro beneficio obedecen' ('we should not administer it except when the pains are so severe that they respond to no other benefit'). Other remedies, while not now generally recognised as appropriate for the ailments for which they were then prescribed, were largely beneficial. Thus saffron, which is not normally taken today for urinary and digestive problems (I, xxv, pp. 31–2; Culpeper, pp. 308–9), is at least rich in vitamin B2 (riboflavin); and while we could hardly imagine prescribing lettuce because it 'increases milk in nurses' (II, cxxv, pp. 220–1; Culpeper, p. 212), it can have done no harm, and perhaps a little good, to those to whom it was administered.[25] Some remedies, however, were useless, or worse than useless. The remedy most commonly prescribed for almost all ailments was bleeding. 'Bad' blood was removed, in quantities of anything up to 20 ounces, usually from a vein in the wrist, although the seventeenth century saw a sterile controversy about the virtues of letting blood from the ankle. The nature of the controversy was the only sterile feature of the treatment, which was likely to introduce infection, wherever it was carried out.

One consequence of all this was that the profession of doctor, one of the most highly respected in present-day society, was then much less highly thought of, as the outrageous barbs of writers like Quevedo suggest. As for other professions, foreign travellers to Madrid were often struck by the large numbers of men and women in religious orders: Spain is reckoned to have had the highest proportion in Europe at this time.[26] Inevitably, many of these people must have joined without a true vocation, although a greater respect for religion (reinforced by the Inquisition) meant that they were treated with deference. Contrariwise, it is appropriate to remember that although Madrid drew artists (whether writers, painters, sculptors or musicians) from all over Spain, the status of the artist in early modern society was lower than it is now, despite efforts to improve it, some of them Calderón's, as in his play *Darlo todo y no dar nada* (1651), or in his *Deposición a favor de los profesores de la pintura* (1677).[27] Writers in particular could not survive without patrons, partly because the high rate of illiteracy made their potential readership much smaller. One calculation puts the overall rate of literacy in Spain in 1600 at only 20 per cent.[28] In rural Castile, over 90 per cent of the population was illiterate; even in Madrid, in the first half of the seventeenth century, half of the inhabitants could not read or write.[29] Lope de Vega is perhaps the first writer who could, if necessary, have survived on the income from his work alone; but where his plays were concerned, the greater part of his audience was illiterate.

Even in a modern, supposedly literate, society, we easily forget the enormous role played by images, whether moving, as in television and film, or static, in printed form, as in magazines and newspapers, advertisement hoardings or the packaging of items offered for sale. In terms of the role played by images, *madrileños* of 1600 were not completely different from today's. The difference was as much a reflection of the available technology as it was of culture, of a culture in which religion was dominant: from *autos sacramentales* and religious processions, through the multitude of religious buildings, of religious images, three-dimensional and two-dimensional, down to the simple crosses painted in dark corners of the public streets to discourage people, in those days before public lavatories, from urinating in them.

The Spanish legal system may have had little power against the merely antisocial, but for those who broke the law, it appeared intimidating enough: the *Recopilación de las leyes destos reynos* (the '*Nueva recopilación*'), published in 1567 by direction of Philip II, filled two massive folio volumes.[30] Enforcement of these laws was another matter. In an effort to end the anarchy which had prevailed during the reign of Henry IV, 'the Impotent', Ferdinand and Isabella had increased the number of *corregidores*, and by the end of the sixteenth century seventy towns in Castile had one of these: Madrid's first dated from 1475. Under these were the *regidores* (aldermen), assisted by judges, *alcaldes* and a host of minor officials including market-inspectors and tax-collectors. Enforcement on the ground, however, came down to the *alguaciles*, the 'constables'. Of the *alcaldes* (who were often simply referred to as the *justicia*), some were elected, like Pedro Crespo in *El alcalde de Zalamea*, while others were chosen by the Crown; like Crespo, they could be respected. They could also be bought, at least in fiction: in *La gitanilla*, the grandmother of Preciosa was arrested three times, but 'de la una me libró un jarro de plata, y de la otra una sarta de perlas, y de la otra cuarenta reales de a ocho' ('a silver jug got me off one, a string of pearls off another, and forty pieces of eight off the third').[31] *Alguaciles* seem to have been universally unpopular, and were regularly complained about or satirised, for example in Quevedo's *El alguacil alguacilado* (1607). In Calderón, whether during the day or in their night patrols, their officiousness leads them to provide sword-fodder for dashing male protagonists. Often their cowardice saves them, but sometimes they are wounded and, in *Luis Pérez el gallego*, killed.

When the law passed judgement, sentences might be brutal and, to a modern eye, arbitrarily administered, although some law-enforcers would try to distinguish between offences committed against the common weal and those committed against individuals. This meant, for example, that the relatives of a man killed in a 'fair' sword fight were given the option of prosecuting or settling for an agreed amount of compensation. Calderón's plays are full of examples, based in part, no doubt, on the brothers' own experiences in 1621.

We certainly have the impression that in Golden-Age Spain there may have been more crime, but there was also more use of legal services (and, one suspects, more litigation). Nowadays, for example, we do not need a notary public to witness a hire purchase agreement; pressed for cash, we use a card when, then, we might borrow it from a colleague or friend, providing a duly witnessed IOU as guarantee. When we use these documents as sources of information, we need to remember that they were produced hundreds of years before the invention of electronic transaction records, in a very different society.

CHAPTER 2

The family background

¡Oh, sencillez de mi patria,
cuánto de hallarte me huelgo! (*El agua mansa*)

(Oh, artlessness of my homeland, how I rejoice to find you!)

Given Madrid's small population when it became the capital, it was inevitable that many of its seventeenth-century inhabitants should be descended from immigrants. The Calderón de la Barca family was in this category. They seem to have originated in the village of Viveda, in the modern province of Cantabria. Present-day Viveda has a population of about a thousand, and lies just to the west of the main Santander–Torrelavega road: the nearest sites familiar to the modern tourist are Santillana del Mar and the caves of Altamira, which are about 3 miles to the west; just to the north of the Santillana–Viveda road is an area of hillside called La Fuente de Calderón. The ancestral home now stands empty, but is more or less intact. In 1924, Emilio Cotarelo y Mori, the poet's most systematic biographer, published two photographs and a plan of a large, rambling building, consisting of a series of annexes to a square tower, originally built for defensive purposes, and which he thought might date from the late twelfth or early thirteenth century (Plate 4a).[1] Modern houses have come uncomfortably close, but little else has changed since Cotarelo. The origin of the name Calderón is obscure, and early coats-of-arms show only a tower and two cauldrons, a simple word-play; it was, and to a degree still is, a common surname (Plate 4b). As for de la Barca, Cotarelo suggests that it reflects a franchise granted to the family for ferrying travellers across one of the nearby rivers.[2] Eguía Ruiz prints documents which support this theory, and which show that the family was prepared to go to law to protect its fishing rights in the Saja and Besaya rivers.[3] This may not seem a lot on which to base a claim to nobility, but the Calderón family was clearly the principal one in Viveda.

By 1548, one member of the family, Diego Calderón de la Barca, was living in Boadilla del Camino, in the province of Palencia. Boadilla del Camino (to distinguish it from other Boadillas, and to signify its place on the Santiago pilgrimage route) is about 4 miles east of Frómista and about 16 miles north-north-east of Palencia itself; now, its importance diminished, it has barely 200 inhabitants. There, on 31 January, Pedro, Diego's second son, was baptised in the village's only parish, that of Santa María. The church, mostly of the sixteenth century, still survives, as does its fine Romanesque font.[4]

Pedro was absent at the time of his father's death in 1573, having left to better himself. A document compiled in Boadilla on 5 April 1575, when he was twenty-seven, notes that he was still absent, but describes him as a 'Procurador en Corte [*sic*] de Su Magd', a delegate in the Cortes ('parliament'), although it is not clear how he obtained this position.[5] By then, too, he must have been married to Isabel Ruiz de Blasco, daughter and sister of two famous Toledo swordsmiths, both named Francisco. Presumably he spent some time in Toledo around 1570, a city where he had relatives. As we have seen, the court had left Toledo for Madrid in 1561; Pedro must have followed it there by 1575. Cotarelo suggests that it was during this deduced period in Toledo that he met Isabel Ruiz, and acquired the expertise necessary to become a civil servant, possibly by working as assistant to an *escribano*, that is, a notary.[6] As the Ruiz family were artisans, not *hidalgos*, Pedro had – technically at least – married beneath himself. However, a swordsmith, particularly a skilful one working in Toledo, the centre of the industry, earned a great deal of social prestige – and money. It was a marriage of mutual advantage to the two parties, reminding us of the point made by Nuño to his master Don Mendo in *El alcalde de Zalamea*: that social rank was carried by the male line, while the large dowry was brought by the wealthy commoner bride.

By 1582, Pedro was one of the secretaries to the Treasury (secretario del Consejo y Contaduría mayor de Hacienda). As Cotarelo explains (and subsequent events in the poet's life confirm), such posts were bought and sold, and, once bought, could be passed, for a fee, to a son, like any property.[7] Pedro could have bought the post either outright, with money conceivably supplied by his father-in-law, or by instalments; that is, by agreeing to do the work on behalf of the post's real owner, to whom he paid a portion of the income, with the arrangement that it would eventually become his own. A report prepared for the king in 1581 noted that a post of *regidor* (alderman) in Madrid might cost a buyer as much as 1,200–1,400 ducats (450,000–525,000 *maravedís*), while a new one created by the king might cost 800 ducats (300,000 *maravedís*). Ana Guerrero Mayllo, who quotes this report, points out that if an aldermanship also incorporated the post of *procurador en Cortes* (the post Pedro held by 1575), it might involve truly important sums.[8] While we do not know what Pedro had to pay to become a *procurador*, or, later, a *contador/secretario*, we can assume that a substantial sum of money was involved in both cases. In his will of 1615, Pedro's son Diego valued the secretaryship at 20,000 ducats, but this figure probably reflects inflation.[9] Details of the relationships between the various departments in the Consejo de Hacienda, what their jobs involved, and the names of those who held the important ones in 1623, are provided by Gil González Dávila.[10] By that time there had been changes in personnel, rather than in the *modus operandi*.

The evidence for Pedro's status in 1582 comes from a document concerning the sale of two houses and their yards in the Calle del Príncipe. The document, of 24 February, names the owners of the adjoining houses, including that of the *contador* ('accountant') Pedro Calderón. The buyers were the Cofradías de la Pasión y de la Soledad, who were buying the properties to convert them into a theatre, the Corral del Príncipe.[11] As noted above, the Corral site is now occupied by the Teatro Español. The Calderón property faced into the Calle del Lobo (now the Calle de Echegaray), leaving the owner a brisk twenty-minute walk to his place of work on the ground floor of the northern façade of the royal palace, where the royal councils had their offices. Appropriately enough, the site of the Calderón property also forms part of the modern Teatro Español complex.

In 1585, to confirm and benefit from his now established position, the *contador* Calderón obtained an *ejecutoria*, a document confirming his status as an *hidalgo*, a status which was passed on to his descendants. Cotarelo explains that the *ejecutoria* was as much an insurance policy as anything else: no *hidalgo* could be imprisoned for debt, or be held liable for various taxes and duties to which lesser mortals were subject; and it opened the way to various important careers. Traditionally, the attorney-general opposed the granting of the *ejecutoria*, to which the individual had to prove his right, at his own expense. The need for proof obliged the *contador* to return for documents to his birthplace in Boadilla, a return still remembered by a few aged villagers fifty years later, in 1636, when his grandson Pedro had to provide similar evidence for his elevation to the Order of Santiago.[12]

Pedro's marriage to Isabel Ruiz produced five children: Diego, the eldest, whom a document of 1592 describes as 'secretario del consejo de contaduria mayor del Rey nuestro señor'; Juan Bautista; María and Isabel, who became nuns in Toledo; and Ana, who had died, apparently recently, by the time her elder brother Diego made his will in 1615.[13] Although probably not yet forty at the time of her death, Ana had five children, and was the only member of the family to produce any cousins for her nephew Pedro, the poet.

Pedro the elder would have reached the age of forty-four in 1592. The document just referred to, of 26 October 1592, shows that by that date, and possibly some time previously, he had obtained royal permission for his son to succeed to his Treasury post.[14] Since holders of such posts needed to be at least twenty-five, we must assume that Diego was born in 1567, when his father was nineteen, or even before. Cotarelo argues that Pérez Pastor's '1592' should be '1595', but 1592 is correct.[15] There are perhaps three explanations for this unexpectedly early retirement: that Pedro was already dead; that he was suffering from an illness from which he did not expect to recover, or that he was sufficiently well off to facilitate an advantageous marriage for his son. The last possibility receives some circumstantial support from the document of 26 October, which shows Diego buying household silver and silver-gilt ware for 3,971 *reales*.

Diego married Ana María de Henao y Riaño, the daughter of Diego González de Henao, another notary, and Inés de Riaño y Peralta. As often happened, Ana María suppressed the plain paternal surname, González, retaining the more exotic one, Henao. Cotarelo suggests that the marriage took place shortly before 2 April 1595, the date of a document which refers to Ana María as Diego's wife.[16] However, the year after the *Ensayo* appeared, Alonso Cortés published the dowry agreement, signed by Diego and his father-in-law in Madrid on 24 September 1593.[17] This document refers to the signing of the marriage contract on 7 September, 'deste presente mes de septiembre de quinientos y noventa y tres' (p. 158), i.e., just over two weeks earlier. The dowry agreement is effectively a receipt: the total is 7,000 ducats or 2,625,000 *maravedís*,[18] most of it in paper money (annuities and bonds), but including furniture and furnishings, linen and silverware; 44,321 *maravedís* 'en dineros de contado' ('in cash', p. 163) make up the round sum. Diego's *arras*, the bride-gift, was 1,000 ducats. It is important to note that Diego refers to himself as 'secretario del Consexo de la contaduria mayor de hacienda del rrey nuestro señor hijo lexitimo de Pedro Calderon de la barca difunto secretario que fue del dicho consejo e doña Isabel Ruiz blasco defuntos questen en gloria' ('secretary of the royal Council of the Treasury, legitimate son of the late Pedro Calderón de la Barca, former secretary of the aforesaid Council, and of the late Isabel Ruiz Blasco, may they be in glory', p. 158): both parents are dead. The dowry and the bride-gift are both substantial sums: no doubt they reflect the fact that Diego had come into his inheritance. If Diego was planning to marry Ana María at least a year before he did, and Pedro was still alive then, the father may have transferred his post to his son to increase his eligibility, but it seems possible that Diego had simply succeeded to his father's Treasury post by October 1592 because Pedro had died.

Pérez Pastor discovered an entry in the parish records of San Ginés which noted the death, on 2 January 1600, of a Pedro Calderón, *escribano de rentas* in the Calle de las Hileras: he left no will and was buried in San Ginés.[19] Perhaps not surprisingly, both he and Cotarelo assumed that this was the poet's grandfather. In particular, Cotarelo concluded that, having ceded his Treasury post to his son, Don Pedro had decided to live off his income as an *escribano de rentas*, a civil servant whose job it was to arrange for the collection of rents paid to the Crown by towns and cities.[20] The deduction is plausible, but this Pedro Calderón cannot have been the grandfather of the dramatist. Nor can we conclude that the real grandfather, like this homonym, left no will. Even if he did not, since it was the practice among *hidalgo* families to pass on the inheritance as intact as possible to the eldest son (under the system called *mayorazgo*),[21] and since this had effectively happened to Diego, the lack of a will would not have affected his prosperity.

Unusually, both the mother-in-law and the father-in-law of Diego Calderón were *madrileños* (see Figures 2.1 and 2.2). They were also wealthy and well connected: the father-in-law, Diego González de Henao, was a *regidor* of the city, and possessor, like his son-in-law's father, of an *ejecutoria*. The researches of Guerrero Mayllo have demonstrated that the *hidalgos* were by far the most numerous group in Madrid's municipal ruling class, and also that many of the *regidores* were related by marriage.[22] One of her tables shows that, by the marriage contract of Diego González de Henao and Inés de Riaño, the bride brought a dowry of 487,500 *maravedís*, while the groom's contribution was 37,500 (1,000 ducats).[23] Compared with many other *regidor* families, these were not huge sums; but some idea of the growth in prosperity (and, it must be admitted, of inflation) can be gleaned from the same table, which shows that another Henao son-in-law, Juan Bautista de Sosa, the husband of Juliana, sister of the poet's mother, received a dowry of 2,937,200 *maravedís*, while Ana Calderón, the sister of Diego Calderón, brought 1,500,000 to her marriage with Martín de Montalvo. The fortune of the poet's maternal grandfather Diego González de Henao was reckoned in 1613, after his death, at 17,560,656 *maravedís* (the purchasing power of 10 *maravedís* in 1600 is roughly equivalent to that of £1 in 2009).[24] His widow, Inés de Riaño, funded a chaplaincy for one of her Calderón grandsons, the chaplaincy which Don Pedro availed himself of when he was ordained in 1651. Diego's second son, and eventual heir, Andrés Jerónimo, would also play an important part in the life of his nephew, as would Juan Bautista de Sosa.

The codicil of Diego Calderón's will of 1615 reveals a premarital relationship with a very well-born woman ('una muger muy bien nacida'), whom he does not name because she is dead. A son whom he calls Francisco González was born of the relationship. This suggests – but does not prove – that the mother's surname was González. When the will was made, Diego had no idea where Francisco was, but the child had been brought up in his household, acting as a servant when he was old enough, until, as the codicil puts it, 'él a sido tan trabieso ... que me obligó a hecharle de mi casa' ('he has been so wayward that he forced me to eject him from my home').[25] The news that their former servant was their half-brother apparently came as a surprise to the younger members of the family. Possibly Ana María knew of, or guessed at, the relationship, although we do not know when Francisco entered the Calderón household. The age of six or seven, when children whose parents could afford it would begin their primary education, would be usual enough. Instead of learning the 'three Rs', such children would be educated by the senior household employees in the duties of a servant: literacy and numeracy were considered superfluous in the serving classes. It is just possible that the anonymous Ms González was a relative of Ana's, and that Diego's sense of responsibility was sharpened by her death. As we shall see, there was a Calderón servant called Francisco, aged eighteen in April 1608. If this was he, he was born in 1589 or 1590, two or three years before Diego's marriage.

Guerrero Mayllo has devoted a section of her book on the *regidores* of Madrid to the *regidores*' illegitimate children: in the group studied, there were only eleven of these, or 3.6 per cent of the total number of offspring, and seven of the eleven were accounted for by only two fathers. The law entitled illegitimate children to claim up to one twelfth of the father's estate, but some fathers went further than this requirement: most of the illegitimate sons became civil servants, like their fathers, while the daughters ended up in convents, with dowries supplied by the fathers.[26] Diego Calderón's stipulation that if Francisco should return, his brothers should give him 'lo que le tocare conforme a las leyes del reyno' ('what he is entitled to according to the laws of the kingdom') seems less than generous.

Two and a half years after his marriage to Ana María, on 21 April 1596, Diego Calderón's first legitimate son was christened in the parish church of San Martín. The church of San Martín was then housed in the Benedictine monastery of St Martin, in the Calle de San Martín, but the building was pulled down in 1809. The street still carries the same name, however, and runs up from the Calle del Arenal to the Plaza de San Martín, not far from the famous convent of the Descalzas Reales. The address of the family during this period is not known, but they had clearly moved from the Calle del Lobo, which was in the parish of San Sebastián, to a dwelling in

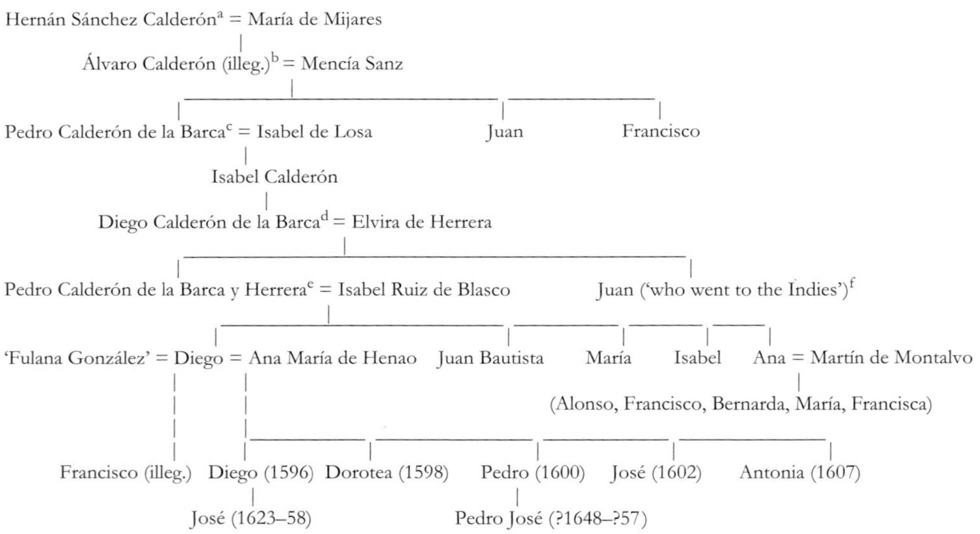

Hernán Sánchez Calderón[a] = María de Mijares

Álvaro Calderón (illeg.)[b] = Mencía Sanz

Pedro Calderón de la Barca[c] = Isabel de Losa | Juan | Francisco

Isabel Calderón

Diego Calderón de la Barca[d] = Elvira de Herrera

Pedro Calderón de la Barca y Herrera[e] = Isabel Ruiz de Blasco | Juan ('who went to the Indies')[f]

'Fulana González' = Diego = Ana María de Henao | Juan Bautista | María | Isabel | Ana = Martín de Montalvo

(Alonso, Francisco, Bernarda, María, Francisca)

Francisco (illeg.) | Diego (1596) | Dorotea (1598) | Pedro (1600) | José (1602) | Antonia (1607)

José (1623–58) | Pedro José (?1648–?57)

Figure 2.1 Simplified family tree of the Calderón family (male line)

The early ancestry is based on Narciso Alonso Cortés, 'Genealogía de D. Pedro Calderón', *BRAE* 31 (1951), 299–309. He notes that the first Diego Calderón de la Barca specified in his will (23 June 1573) that he should be buried in the village church in the grave of his mother Isabel Calderón. He concludes that this Isabel Calderón was probably the daughter of the first Pedro Calderón (p. 305). If she was, Diego's lack of reference to a father and his use of his mother's surname imply that he was illegitimate and not acknowledged by his father. It is just possible, however, given that the wife of the first Pedro was Isabel de Losa, that the notary mistakenly wrote the mother's forename and the father's surname.

This tree excludes two of the poet's sisters, the first Antonia María, baptised in September 1605, and the girl born in October 1610, both of whom died in infancy. Don Pedro's brother Diego married Beatriz Núñez de Alarcón, who died young in 1631; their only child, José, married Agustina Antonia Ortiz y Velasco, but he died childless in 1658. The name of the mother of Diego Senior's illegitimate son, González, is conjectural. Of Calderón's siblings, Diego died in 1647, Dorotea in 1682, José in 1645, and Antonia between March 1613 and November 1615; Francisco was still alive in April 1655.

[a] Resident in Viveda (Santillana).

[b] Resident in Aguilar de Campoo; 'Siendo moço havía venido de la montaña de santillana' ('He had come from La Montaña, Santillana, as a young man'); allegedly died around 1520–5.

[c] Resident in Sotillo (Reinosa).

[d] Resident in Boadilla del Camino; died 1573.

[e] Baptised 31 January 1548; procurador en cortes de Su Majestad, 1575; secretario de Su Majestad en el Consejo y Contaduría Mayor de Hacienda, 1582.

[f] According to Constancio Eguía Ruiz, 'Cervantes, Calderón, Lope, Gracián: nuevos temas crítico-biográficos' (Madrid: Instituto 'Miguel de Cervantes' de Filología Española, 1951) (*Anejos de Cuadernos de Literatura* 8), pp. 56–61 (p. 50).

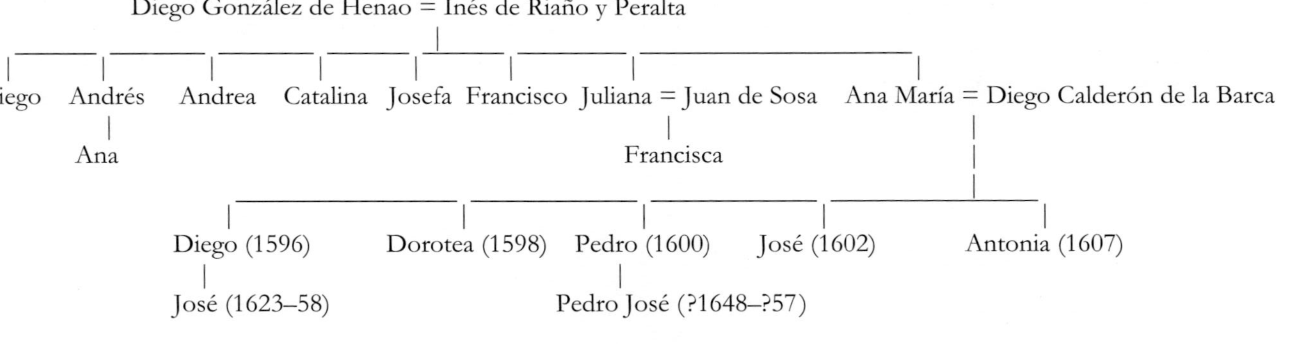

Figure 2.2 Simplified family tree of the Calderón family (female line)

the parish of San Martín. San Martín was the largest parish in Madrid, but a house in the southern end would have been closer to Diego's place of work, and correspondingly more expensive.[27] When the baby was christened – also Diego – the godfather was his uncle Juan Bautista, while the godmother was Juana Dantisco, widow of the writer and royal secretary Diego Gracián. The witnesses were his uncle Juan Bautista de Sosa (another *regidor* of Madrid); his maternal grandfather, Diego González de Henao (as we have seen, also a *regidor*); Tomás Gracián Dantisco, son of Juana Dantisco and an author as well as a royal secretary; Juan Francisco Correa de Acosta; and Pedro de Riaño, another notary, who was probably the child's great-uncle.[28]

The picture is of a rising young civil servant, anxious to give influential relatives and colleagues a role in the life of his new son and heir. At a different time or in a different place, the family would have been provincial gentry who had progressed to the capital city, and were making their way up to the top of its middle class. In Spain, then, it was more complicated. The difference between nobles and non-nobles was still important, as Guerrero Mayllo's researches show, but the rigid structures of early modern Spanish society were beginning the long process of disintegration, helped by the regime's increasing willingness to sell minor titles for ready cash, and by the rapid growth of the new capital. Some members of the old provincial aristocracy resented and resisted change, defending their values in ways which even then seemed ridiculous and amusing. Don Mendo in *El alcalde de Zalamea* is an impoverished provincial *hidalgo*, partly based on the *escudero* in *Lazarillo de Tormes*, too proud to remedy his poverty by marrying a commoner. In this context, Cotarelo mentions *El agua mansa*'s Don Toribio Cuadradillos, a country cousin chosen by a Madrid-based *hidalgo* as a husband for one of his daughters.[29] The first draft of *El agua mansa* probably dates from the 1640s, possibly from 1649. Don Toribio is a nobleman from La Montaña (i.e., the Santander area, like the Calderón family), but such a chauvinistic boor that even the girls' father eventually notices. We should not assume, though, that Calderón's familiarity with the type came from his own family members. Perhaps what should impress us most here is the discomfiture of supporters of absurd old values, which include, in Don Toribio's case, a ridiculous *pundonor*. In this context, we should note the action of the *regidor* Miguel de Cereceda, the husband of Anastasia de Cos, daughter of the *regidor* Alonso Martínez de Cos, who ran off with her lover Diego Alonso Velázquez. Far from plotting some dire secret vengeance, the aggrieved husband went to law (29 January 1583), accusing the pair of adultery and theft, which led to their arrest and imprisonment in Bilbao.[30]

* * *

More Calderón children followed at regular intervals. Two years after that of Diego, on 4 March 1598, the baptism of Dorotea took place. This time the godparents were Martín de la Peña and Juana Dantisco, the witnesses Juan Bautista Calderón and Felipe Lozano.[31] As we shall see, Diego Calderón had seven legitimate children, but not all of them survived.

These births, deaths and successions had their parallels at the highest level. In September 1598 Philip II's *mayorazgo*, the Spanish empire, passed to his only surviving son, Philip III, who was aged just twenty. In the course of his forty-year reign, Philip II had expanded state bureaucracy enormously. Most of the councils on which his system of government was based had been established under his predecessors (the Council of Finance, for example, in 1525), but under Philip the councils met increasingly frequently, generating correspondingly more paperwork. Philip's manner of rule had been to handle as much as possible of the bureaucracy himself, but the prosperity of civil servants like the Calderón family was indirectly his doing, especially since his 'hands-on' style of government declined greatly during the last few years of his life, as his various ailments, notably his gout, made it increasingly hard for him to write, to walk, and even to get a comfortable night's rest. Philip III was incapable of ruling as his father had done, and surrendered the reins of government to Don Francisco Gómez de Sandoval y Rojas, Marquis of Denia (Plates 5, 6).

In *Miau*, Pérez Galdós describes how a change of regime in nineteenth-century Spain affected the livelihood of all government employees. At the close of the sixteenth century, no such momentous change took place among the lower echelons of the civil service, since those who 'owned' their jobs, like Diego Calderón, could not be turned out without financial compensation. Momentous changes were about to take place, however, their nature indicated by the first significant event of the new reign: the king's marriage to his cousin Margarita, celebrated in Valencia on 18 April 1599. The festivities lasted for months. The austerity of Philip II had ended: it was replaced by the heavy, and public, royal expenditure which was to become a feature of Calderón's lifetime, as well as an enabling factor in his career.

The new favourite (*valido* or *privado* in Spanish: the term 'prime minister' had still to be invented) was forty-five. Philip II had done what he could to minimise his influence over the crown prince, but as soon as the prince was king, the marquis was made Duke of Lerma. His pedigree was impeccable, if 'impeccable' is the right word for a pedigree which included a pope, Alexander VI, Rodrigo Borja. Apart from Rodrigo Borja, Lerma's ancestors included King Ferdinand of Aragón, who was the uncle of his great-grandmother, Juana de Aragón; he was a great-grandson of the Marquis of Denia who had been put in charge of Queen Juana la Loca during the revolt of the *comuneros* in 1520–1, and a grandson of St Francis Borja, the Duke of Gandía who took holy orders after the death of his wife, and on whose life Calderón based a play, now lost.[32] Unlike his more famous successor, the Count-Duke of Olivares, Lerma could not be denigrated for his modest ancestry. Unlike Olivares, too, he was a friendly, affable man, driven not by a passion for power, but by a simple love of money; he recognised that the way to obtain money was through patronage. Since no individual could keep track of every piece of patronage, or collect every bribe and gift for a favour granted or a position found, Lerma's technique was to delegate, by placing members of his large extended family around him, and around the king, which had the additional advantage of preventing Philip III from coming in contact with Lerma's enemies and detractors. His greatest virtue was his belief that war was an impediment to making money, although this view was not one which his enemies shared. On the contrary, this difference of opinion about the role of war was a major contributory factor in Lerma's fall. However, thanks to his policy of filling important posts with his family and supporters, Lerma was able to remain in power for twenty years, from 1598 until 1618, when the king finally yielded to pressure and invited him to retire.[33] This was the period during which Calderón the dramatist grew to adulthood.

CHAPTER 3

Childhood and early adolescence

Bien como víbora humana,
nació reventando el seno
de las maternas entrañas. (*Apolo y Climene*)

(Just like a human viper, she was born bursting her mother's womb.)

Calderón's first biographer, Don Juan de Vera Tassis y Villarroel, stated that the poet was born on 1 January 1601, the feast of the Circumcision, but Cotarelo has drawn attention to this error, not without some sarcasm.[1] Gaspar Agustín de Lara, a reliable witness, gives the date as 17 January 1600,[2] a date supported by Álvarez Baena, who was the first scholar to reproduce the details of the poet's baptism four weeks later:[3]

En la villa de Madrid en catorce dias del mes de Hebrero de mil y seiscientos yo Fabian de San Juan Romero tiniente de cura de San Martin bautice a Pedro yjo del secretario Diego Calderon de la Barca y de doña Ana Maria de Enao fueron sus padrinos el contador Antolin de la Cerna [*sic*] y doña Ana Calderon, fueron testigos Lucas del Moral y Juan de Montoya, lo firmé. – Fabian de San Juan Romero.

(In the town of Madrid, on 14 February 1600, I, Fabián de San Juan Romero, substitute priest of San Martín, baptised Pedro, son of the secretary Diego Calderón de la Barca and Doña Ana María de Henao; his godparents were the accountant Antolín de la Serna and Doña Ana Calderón; the witnesses, Lucas del Moral and Juan de Montoya; I signed it. Fabián de San Juan Romero.)

The date 17 January was the feast of St Anthony of Egypt (San Antonio Abad), but Pedro was evidently named after his paternal grandfather, not after the saint. The four-week gap between birth and baptism implies that he was a healthy baby. As for the godparents, it will be remembered that Ana was the poet's aunt; Antolín de la Serna was another civil-servant colleague (and friend) of the father; he would figure as one of the executors in his friend's will in 1615, but there is no other record of his role as the poet's godfather.

Pedro was the third Calderón child to be baptised in San Martín. Perhaps Diego imagined a secure and stable future stretching before him. If so, the stability did not last long. Before Pedro was two, the family had to move nearly 120 miles north to Valladolid. The person responsible for the move was the Duke of Lerma, who persuaded Philip III to move his capital, despite the lack of an appropriate royal palace. The conclusive argument was that prices were substantially lower in Valladolid. Lerma's true reason for the move may have been to get the king away from his influential grandmother, the Empress María, then living as a nun in the Descalzas Reales: her hatred of Lerma was well known. But Lerma also had properties in Valladolid, from which he was able to profit, not to mention the large bribes he received from Valladolid's wealthy merchants for bringing about the transfer.

The announcement that the court was to move was made on 10 January 1601, and the royal family set out the next day. The move was assumed to be permanent. There was talk of some government departments remaining in Madrid, the Treasury among them; but the Treasury eventually moved in the summer. Just as a modern businessman might do, if his company decided to transfer him to another city, Diego Calderón had to leave for Valladolid, while his family remained in their old Madrid home. Once there, he had to live in what accommodation he could find, while simultaneously getting on with his job and searching for a new family home. Valladolid was a larger city than Madrid had been in 1561, but it was unable to cope with the influx of courtiers, civil servants, artisans and providers of services, all of whom had servants of their own, as well as all the hangers-on that every court attracts. Everything was in short supply and, predictably (as it must seem now, to us), prices rose. Five years went by before Lerma conceded that he had made a mistake; accepting further bribes, this time from the wealthy citizens of Madrid, he persuaded Philip to return to his father's capital. According to González Dávila, Madrid offered the king 250,000 ducats (93,750,000 *maravedís*) to bring the court back.[4]

At the time of the first move in 1601, the cost of accommodation in Madrid must have fallen at the same time as it rose in Valladolid, forcing those who depended on the government for their jobs to sell cheap and buy dear. Some fortunate government employees may have been the equivalent of 'insider dealers', possessed of important information before it was generally released, but this is only speculation. All we know for certain is that by the time Pedro's younger brother José was baptised in October 1602, Diego had brought the family to the new capital, and found accommodation for them in the Calle de Imperial:

Yo Juan Ruiz de Ladesma [*sic*], cura propio de la yglesia parroquial [de San Benito] desta ciudad de Balladolid, según horden y forma de la santa madre yglesia católica romana, bavtiçé a Jopsepe hijo leximo [*sic*] de Diego Calderón, secretario del Consejo, y de doña Ana María del Nao [*sic*], su muger, y mis parroquianos, que biben en la calle de Ynpirial; fueron sus padrinos Antolín de la Serna y doña Juliana Henao y lo firmé en Balladolid a tres días del mes de otubre de mill y seiscientos y dos, siendo testigos Pedro Gutiérez [*sic*] sacristán y Pedro Vceta. – Juan Ruiz de Ledesma.[5]

(I, Juan Ruiz de Ledesma, priest of the parish church of San Benito in this city of Valladolid, according to the order and form of the holy Catholic mother church of Rome, baptised José, legitimate son of Diego Calderón, secretary of the Council, and of Doña Ana María de Henao, his wife, and my parishioners, who live in the Calle de Imperial; his godparents were Antolín de la Serna and Doña Juliana Henao, and I signed it, in Valladolid on 3 October 1602; the witnesses were Pedro Gutiérrez, sacristan, and Pedro Uceta. – Juan Ruiz de Ledesma.)

It is hardly surprising that the civil servant Antolín de la Serna should also have moved to Valladolid. Juan Bautista de Sosa, who had been a *regidor* of Madrid since 1594, gave up the post in 1602, presumably in order to move to the new capital with his wife Juliana, sister of Ana María and aunt of the Calderón children.[6] Nowadays, a luxury bus takes the traveller from Madrid to Valladolid in two hours and fifteen minutes. The trip gives us little idea of what it was like then, even for a small and well-to-do family like Calderón's, to travel 120 miles across northern Castile (including the Guadarrama mountains), whatever the season. We do not know exactly when Diego brought his family north to join him, but we can assume that it was in the latter half of 1601, before Ana María's fourth pregnancy; that is, when her children were aged one, three and five. Even with servants to help, it cannot have been pleasant to travel with three small children for a week, enjoying the notoriously primitive food and lodging of Castile's rural inns.

While still in Valladolid, the Calderón parents had a fifth child:

En dicho día [8 September 1605] bapticé a Antonia María, hija del secret.° Diego Calderón de la Barca, sr.° en el c.° de Hacienda y de doña Ana María de Nava [*sic*]. P. [= padrinos] el c°r Antolín de la Serna y doña Luysa Castellana de Bargas, y lo firmé. – Luis de Çedillo.[7]

(On the same day I baptised Antonia María, daughter of the secretary Diego Calderón de la Barca, secretary in the Council of Finance, and of Doña Ana María de Henao; godparents, the accountant Antolín de la Serna and Doña Luisa Castellana de Vargas, and I signed it: Luis de Cedillo.)

The baptism took place in the parish of Santiago, indicating another change of address. This Antonia María cannot have survived, since less than two years later, on 10 July 1607, another daughter was baptised with the same names in the parish church of San Ginés in Madrid. The present San Ginés, standing on the Calle del Arenal roughly opposite the Calle San Martín, scene of earlier Calderón family baptisms, dates from 1645, but the building in which Antonia María was baptised was much older. Her godparents were her uncle Andrés de Henao and her cousin Francisca de Sosa, daughter of Juan Bautista de Sosa and Juliana de Henao. Francisca was hardly more than a child herself. One of the official witnesses present at the ceremony was also very young: the baby's eldest brother Diego, aged eleven; the other was her uncle Diego, elder brother of her godfather Andrés.[8] The lack of any mention of Diego González de Henao, the child's maternal grandfather, may indicate that he was dead by this time. The second Antonia María was still listed as one of Diego Calderón's children on 5 May 1613,[9] but she had died before her father made his will in November 1615.

By the time of the second Antonia's baptism, the family was living in the Calle de las Fuentes, which runs from the Plaza de Herradores down to the Calle del Arenal, where it enters the Plaza Isabel II: the Calderón house was at the bottom end. As this was only a few hundred yards from the palace, we can imagine that the proximity was a reflection of the family's continuing social ascent, or at least of its aspirations. A document dated in Madrid, 13 March 1606, shows that on that day Diego promised to pay Juan de Medina, a merchant, 1,500 *reales* he had borrowed from him.[10] We can guess that the move back to Madrid caused Diego to be short of ready cash; the document also shows that he at least had returned to Madrid by that date. However, we should not read too much into a loan made in a society with no credit cards or automatic cash dispensers.

Another document, a receipt dated Madrid, 19 July 1607, shows that Diego, described as an 'escribano de Cámara de S[u] M[ajestad]', a notary of the royal exchequer, acknowledged a payment of 12,600 *maravedís* from Jerónimo de Barrionuevo, a Treasury employee, for the time he had spent checking cases of fraud in the income from customs posts between Castile and Portugal.[11] As Barrionuevo worked in the Treasury, he was no doubt an acquaintance of Diego's. The fact that Diego dealt with the matter as a notary (and was paid for it) rather than as a Treasury official may mean that Don Jerónimo was putting some extra business in his direction. The existence of the receipt suggests that they were doing nothing illegal, but its content reminds us that fraud was more or less endemic in Spanish government offices during the Lerma administration, and that there were many cases when officials engaged in activities which, while not actually illegal, would certainly now attract the interest of the tax authorities at least.

Less than a year after Antonia's baptism an extraordinary event occurred in the Calderón household: Diego Calderón petitioned the king for permission to send his eldest son Diego to Mexico City, with four servants:

Diego Calderon de la Barca scriu° de Camara de V. mag^d^. en su Cons° y Cont^a^ de Hazd^a^. = diçe que queria ymbiar A la çiudad de mexico a Diego Calderon de la Barca su Hijo y de Doña Ana Maria de Henao su muger y Para Poderlo Hacer = Supp^ca^ A V. mag^d^. le haga mrd de Darle liçençia Para ello y Para que Pueda llebar quatro criados en su serui° que en ello Reciuira mrd. / Diego Calderon.[12]

(Diego Calderón de la Barca, notary in Your Majesty's Council of Finance, states that he would like to send to Mexico City Diego Calderón de la Barca, his son, and that of his wife Doña Ana María de Henao; and in order to do so he asks Your Majesty to do him the favour of giving him permission, and for him to take four servants: by this he will receive a favour: Diego Calderón.)

The request was granted on 30 April 1608, but with permission for one servant only. The verso of the same sheet of paper gives us the only surviving physical description of any member of the Calderón family:

Diego Calderon de la Barca de hedad de doce años blanco de Rostro una señal en la frente el pelo castaño claro y fran^co^ su criado de 18 años moreno y el rostro largo.

(Diego Calderón de la Barca, aged twelve, pale-faced with a mark on his forehead, light brown hair, and Francisco, his servant, aged eighteen, dark-haired, with a long face.)

Of course, children matured earlier then than now. They had to, given that life expectancy was around forty. In addition, one of the father's uncles, Juan Calderón, had apparently emigrated to the New World, although there is no evidence that the twelve-year-old Diego was going to make contact with him, or that he did so.[13] The fact remains that a trip to Mexico in 1608, whether a return journey was planned or not, was a pretty hazardous affair. Peace had been made with England in 1604, by the Treaty of London, and hostilities with the Dutch were halted in March 1607 by the governor of the Netherlands, Archduke Albert, who arranged a ceasefire which was confirmed by the truce of 1609. But agreements made in Europe were not always respected in the Caribbean, where, if nothing else, the unpredictable weather meant that every voyage carried a significant risk.

Diego was still in Mexico when his grandmother, Inés de Riaño y Peralta, signed her will on 5 January 1612, and Doña Inés at least had no reason to suppose that he was planning to return soon.[14] By November 1615, however, he had returned to Spain, as his father's will shows. Cotarelo suggests that Diego had done something of which his father disapproved.[15] Given that the normal practice at the time would have been for him to inherit his father's post in the Treasury, we can only agree that the suggestion is plausible: there was no training for such a post in Mexico that was not also available in Spain. Moreover, as we shall see, the will does indeed suggest that Diego had done some things that did not meet with his father's blessing, apparently contemplating marriage to women his father did not want him to marry. It may seem unlikely that he was thinking of such a thing at the tender age of twelve, although nobles regularly married off their offspring in their mid teens during this period. Diego's banishment, if it was a banishment, and his father's relationship with him, are part of a larger picture, of which all the parts are best examined together later.

The Mexico document raises another question: could the eighteen-year-old servant named Francisco have been Francisco González Calderón? The answer is: possibly; Diego's household evidently had a number of servants, if he could contemplate the expense of sending four to Mexico for an indefinite period, and Francisco was a common name. However, surviving portraits of the poet show that he had a long face, like his putative half-brother Francisco. If this Francisco was Diego's son, he would have been born in 1589 or 1590, when Diego himself was in his early twenties, a plausible age for an amorous adventure; and if this Francisco *were* his illegitimate son, living unidentified in his household, it might have seemed a good idea to let him go to Mexico to avoid possible future embarrassment.

***

In seventeenth-century Spain, it was reckoned that it took a year to teach a child literacy. With no state education system, however, there were no rules about when a child's formal education should begin, or what level he should reach at any particular age (we need to say 'he', since the formal education of girls was still in the distant future). All we can be reasonably sure of is that a family such as Calderón's must have prized the skills of literacy and numeracy. Calderón's younger brother José was given lessons in 1616, from January to July, when he was thirteen, by Pedro Díaz Morante, one of the most notable teachers of fine handwriting of the period. Morante was later to become the first of what we might now call 'His Majesty's inspectors for schools'.[16] Since José's father had died the previous year, the bill, at 8 *reales* per month, a total of 56 *reales*, was paid by Andrés Jerónimo de Henao, his maternal uncle.[17] If we are to judge from the fact that he had just published a book on the subject (*Nueva arte de escreuir inventada con el fabor de Dios por el maestro P. Diaz Morante*, 1615), Morante must have been one of the more expensive teachers available. The intention cannot have been to teach José *to write*: it must have been a question of teaching him the finer points of the different kinds of handwriting used by civil servants. Picatoste is probably correct in saying of Don Pedro that 'basta ver su letra y conocer algo de la historia del arte de escribir en España para decidir que le enseñó Pedro Diaz Morante ó alguno de sus discípulos. A mayor abundamiento hemos consultado á dos calígrafos, y ámbos son de nuestra opinion' ('it is enough to see his handwriting and to know something of the history of the art of writing in Spain to decide that he was taught by Pedro Díaz Morante or one of his disciples. In confirmation, we have consulted two calligraphers, and both agree with us'),[18] but Cotarelo is right to point out that the poet could not have been taught literacy by Morante in person: Morante remained in his native Toledo until 1612, opening his school in Madrid's Plaza del Ángel in that year.[19] Conceivably Don Pedro was given additional lessons, as José was, sometime between 1612 and 1616.[20]

Calderón's schooling may have begun in Valladolid. In January 1606 he would have been six, an age when bright children were considered old enough to go to school. Vera Tassis says that he spent his first years 'con la educacion de sus Nobles, y Virtuosos Padres' ('with the education/upbringing of his noble and virtuous parents').[21] If this is true, it may mean that one of his parents taught him to read before he attended school.[22] Even primary education was a luxury which only the better-off minority could afford. Town councils, when granting licences, often insisted that teachers accept a few poor pupils without charge in every class, but Calderón's family would not have qualified for such charity.[23]

However Calderón's education began, most of his formal primary education must have taken place in the parish of San Ginés, after the family's return to Madrid. Some *cartillas* (reading primers) and teachers' instruction books have survived from this period. They show how pupils had to learn by rote hundreds of syllables, some of them not even encountered in Spanish, so that they could recognise any complete word. When they had done this, they were taught the Lord's Prayer, the Hail Mary, the Creed and the Salve Regina. Only then were they taught to form letters themselves, and only after that, to count.[24]

As an old man, at his birthday party, Don Pedro told his friends 'graciosisimos cuentos, que con festiva gracia referia de sus niñezes; y en particular, el de que no sentia tanto los azotes del Maestro, como que los muchachos de la Escuela le llamasen el Peranton, por llamarse Pedro y haber nacido el dia de San Anton' ('very funny stories, which he told of his childhood with droll humour; and, in particular, the fact that he did not feel the teacher's beatings as much as the schoolboys calling him Perantón, because his name was Pedro and he was born on St Antony's day').[25] Correas quotes a jingle which may have formed part of the teasing:

Perantón, comé de las uvas,
Perantón, que no están maduras.[26]

(Perantón, eat the grapes, Perantón, they're not ripe.)

As a *Perantón* is a tall person, able to reach up for grapes on an overhead vine, we may also surmise that Pedro was taller than his fellow pupils, but a teasing nickname is little enough in comparison with some of the brutalities inflicted on their classmates by children. Don Pedro remembered it, however, and remembered being beaten, although he could joke about it much later. Since he is not likely to have been beaten for being stupid, we may suspect that he was beaten for disobedience.

According to Vera Tassis, the young Calderón showed such early promise that, before he was nine, he was sent to the Jesuit college in the Calle de Toledo (a site now occupied by the Instituto de San Isidro).[27] There had been a Jesuit college in Madrid since 1572, but the title Colegio Imperial (so called because it was endowed by the Empress María, daughter of Charles V and wife of the Emperor Maximilian II) was not conferred until 1603. Lope de Vega and Quevedo had been pupils at the college, but the Jesuits' reputation as educators had still to be established. Indeed, the *regidores* of Madrid (who numbered relatives and colleagues of Diego Calderón among them) complained that among the Jesuits 'no se enseñauan en ellas letras sólidas y que todo eran deuociones con que criauan los hombres cobardes' ('there was no solid learning there, it was all devotions, which bred men to be cowards').[28] In the circumstances, it is not clear why Diego Calderón chose them for Pedro. Cotarelo suggests that Francisco de Henao, a Jesuit brother of the poet's mother, may have influenced the choice, but this is speculation.[29] Father Francisco was in Madrid in 1631, when he witnessed the will of the poet's sister-in-law, but we do not know what contact he had with the family around 1609.[30] If Vera Tassis is right about the date (and his details of Calderón's early life are unreliable), Pedro began his secondary schooling shortly after his elder brother had been despatched to Mexico. It would be idle to speculate about possible connections between the two events.

Claudio Acquaviva, General of the Order, had set out the curriculum for Jesuit colleges in 1599. A slightly later document lists the 'estudios menores' in the Colegio Imperial:

Primera Classe: para decorar el Arte Latino, declinar, y conjugar.

Segunda Classe: Para el conocimiento, y vso de las partes de la oracion; y para leer el Genero de los nombres.

Tercera Classe: Para leer Preteritos, y Supinos de los Verbos, y algunos principios de la syntaxis Latina; y para leer, y declinar la Lengua Griega.

Quarta Classe: Para leer mas cumplidamente la syntaxis, y componer congruentemente en Latin: y para leer las conjugaciones de la Lengua Griega.

Quinta Classe: Para aprender estilo, leer la sylaba, hacer Versos Latinos, y enseñar la syntaxis, y prosodia de la Lengua Griega, y componer congruentemente en ella.[31]

(First class: to learn Latin grammar by heart, to decline and conjugate. Second class: for knowing and using the parts of speech, and studying the gender of nouns. Third class: for studying preterites and supines of verbs, and some principles of Latin syntax; and for studying and declining Greek. Fourth class: for studying syntax more fully, and congruent Latin composition; and for learning the conjugations of Greek. Fifth class: for learning style and studying syllabification, writing Latin verse, and teaching the syntax and prosody of Greek, and congruent Greek composition.)

The grounding was clearly in Classical languages, but not via Classical authors only: they began with Cicero's letters, then Ovid, more Cicero, Virgil's *Eclogues* and *Georgics*, Seneca, Catullus, Propertius, Plautus and Terence, but they also studied fathers of the church and humanistic authors such as Sannazaro (d. 1530) and Erasmus (d. 1536).[32] Suitable extracts from most of these were available in Father Cosme Magallanes's anthology, *Sylvae illustrium autorum, qui ad usum collegiorum Societatis Iesu selecti sunt* (1598).[33] Higher studies included rhetoric, 'divine and human' history, natural philosophy (i.e., physics), metaphysics, mathematics, ethics, politics and economics (all from Aristotle), natural history, philosophy, moral theology and scripture. The first professor of rhetoric at the college had been Pedro de Acevedo (1522–73), who wrote plays for his pupils to perform, since school drama, in Spanish and in Latin, was also part of the curriculum.[34] It is easy to suppose that Pedro's interest in the theatre began at this point.

Some Jesuit-educated children rebel against what they are taught (James Joyce springs to mind), but much of what he learned in college remained with Pedro all his life. On 2 February 1614 (Candlemas), in his final year, he joined the Congregación de la Anunciata.[35] The *congregación* was established 'para fomentar entre los alumnos el culto y devoción a Nuestra Señora ... iniciándoles a la vez en algunas obras de celo y caridad' ('to promote among the pupils the worship of and devotion to Our Lady, while initiating them in works of zeal and charity').[36] The adult Calderón's devotion to the Virgin is reflected in his lost plays *Nuestra Señora de la Almudena* (two parts), and *Nuestra Señora de los Remedios,* as well as in the surviving *Origen, pérdida y restauración de Nuestra Señora del Sagrario* (?1629). He also wrote Marian *autos* such as *La hidalga del valle* (?1634), *El cubo de la Almudena* (1651), and *A María el corazón* (1664), but perhaps most significant is his *auto Las órdenes militares / Las pruebas del segundo Adán,* written for 1662 and banned by the Inquisition. Using as a metaphor the genealogical tests which had to be passed by aspirants to membership of military orders (like Calderón himself, for Santiago), it deals with the doctrine of the Immaculate Conception, a doctrine of particular interest to the Jesuits, but one which did not receive its official form until 1854. It was precisely this lack of official form which embarrassed the Inquisition, which was even more embarrassed by Don Pedro's reluctance to accept that he had been too specific, as the surviving documents show.[37] As for works of charity, in the 1650s Calderón was an active member of the *Congregación y Hermandad del Refugio de Pobres* in Toledo, later transferring to Madrid. While in Toledo, he participated in running a hostel for the poor, an experience which may have inspired the *loa* he wrote for *Las órdenes militares*: *Loa para el auto sacramental intitulado las órdenes militares, en metáfora de la Piadosa Hermandad del Refugio, discurriendo por calles y templos de Madrid.*

Other works which point to the influence of Calderón's Jesuit education are his poems written for the canonisations of St Ignatius ('Con el cabello erizado', 1622), St Francis Xavier ('Tirana la idolatría', 1622) and St Francis Borja ('Al que nace glorioso' and 'Joven arrojo mal precipitado', 1671). He also wrote two plays on notable Jesuits: *San Francisco de Borja* (1671, on St Francis Borja, now lost) and *El gran príncipe de Fez* (1669, on Muley Mahomet, who took the name Baltasar de Loyola after his baptism; St Ignatius Loyola appears in the play).

Not long after Pedro had entered the Colegio Imperial, his mother died, on 22 October 1610, as a result of complications developing from childbirth. In the seventeenth century, when being born and giving birth presented serious threats to health, the Calderón family was more fortunate than many in having a mother who had four of her seven children reach adulthood, and who survived parturition six times before dying of problems involved in her seventh. We may suspect that the members of the family are unlikely to have felt very fortunate, but the truth is that we know nothing of what they felt. In particular, we know nothing of the feelings of the ten-year-old Pedro. People have claimed that there are few mothers in Calderón's plays, but male roles simply outnumber women's roles in plays of the period. This is borne out by a careful analysis of 316 plays by Lope, which reveals that they include only forty-eight characters classified as 'mothers' (15 per cent). On the other hand, a similar study of 114 Calderón plays lists only two mothers (1.8 per cent).[38] These are not Calderón's only mothers, however, since some are classified under other headings, such as Catalina (*La cisma de Ingalaterra*), Semíramis (*La hija del aire*), Tetis (*El monstruo de los jardines*), Liríope (*Eco y Narciso*), Dánae (*Andrómeda y Perseo*) and Climene (*El hijo del sol*). Even if we add these, the figure reaches only 7 per cent, still less than half of Lope's total, which may be under-recorded in the same way. As for stepmothers, Lope has a modest total of eight (2.5 per cent); Calderón, perhaps significantly, has none at all, unless we include Ana Bolena, at whose death her stepdaughter María rejoices (*La cisma de Ingalaterra*). It may be noted that Semíramis, Tetis and Liríope have baleful effects on their sons' lives, but while all three are domineering, the over-protective Tetis and Liríope are very different from the power-hungry Semíramis. If there was a model for such women in Calderón's own family, we cannot say who it was. On the other hand, the plays have significant numbers of examples of death in childbirth. Thus Admeto, the father of Climene in *Apolo y Climene*, tells his subjects, and his daughter, that

Bien como víbora humana,
nació reventando el seno
de las maternas entrañas,
falseándome en que una muera,
el gozo de que otra nazca. (I, 1878b)[39]

(Just like a human viper, she was born bursting her mother's womb, the death of one adulterating the joy of the birth of the other.)

Other examples include other daughters, Semíramis (*La hija del aire*, ?late 1630s), and Anajarte (*La fiera, el rayo y la piedra*, 1652), as well as sons: Don Lope the younger (*Las tres justicias en una*, ?1630–7), Heraclio and Leonido (*En la vida ...*, 1659), and Calderón's most famous character, Segismundo (*La vida es sueño*, ?1630).

The will of Pedro's mother has survived.[40] After the conventional opening, she asks to be buried with her parents in San Salvador. She then refers to some gold buttons, a string of pearls and other objects which she gave her mother as security for a loan of 1,900 *reales* (64,600 *maravedís*); and to an additional 50 ducats (18,750 *maravedís*) loaned by the mother 'cuando el secretario mi marido salio desta villa' ('when the secretary my husband left Madrid', to go to Valladolid, presumably; if so, still not repaid nine years later). Her daughter Dorotea, she says, has 500 *reales* which are to be given to the rector of Santa Catalina de los Donados, to be distributed according to orders which she has already given him (and he is to get receipts). As executors she names her mother and her husband. In particular, she adds, 'pido y suplico a mi madre por el amor de Dios ... se apiade y favorezca y ampare a mis hijos pues que siempre fue el amparo de ellos' ('I ask and beg my mother, for the love of God, to have pity on my children, since she was always a support for them'). Finally, she names as heirs for the remainder of her estate, in equal shares, her children Diego, Dorotea, Pedro, Jusepe, Antonia and 'la niña que ahora pari, que no está christiana' ('the girl I have just borne, who is not Christian': that is, she had not been baptised; she died soon after her mother). The witnesses were Doctor Gabriel de Riaño (an uncle?), Juan Bautista de Sosa (brother-in-law), Andrés Jerónimo de Henao (brother; all three were *regidores* of Madrid), Domingo de Gómara (surgeon, citizen of Madrid) and Pedro de Vivanco (citizen of Madrid). The last of these signed the will for her, since she was too ill to sign it herself. She died soon afterwards, apparently during the night of 21–22 October 1610, since her death and burial certificates contradict each other on the date.[41]

What should we make of this will? It was quite normal that nothing should be left to the husband. The borrowings from the mother, of substantial sums, together with the plea that she should 'have pity', are more striking. Was Diego Calderón a squanderer or a miser? Had he borrowed too heavily to achieve his position, or was he a bad businessman? Had he been financially damaged by the need, twice within six years, to sell his property cheap in one city while buying dear in another? Whichever it was, he was apparently short of money, and contrived to keep his wife short of it. We can read between the lines the mother-in-law's disapproval, a disapproval that the daughter was afraid might be extended to her children. Doña Inés, however, was a pious and charitable woman, although we can sense that, in her eyes at least, her son-in-law's shortage of cash was a fault which it was in his power to mend.

In 1611, the year after her mother's death, Diego Calderón's daughter Dorotea entered the convent of Santa Clara la Real, in Toledo, as a novice.[42] Dorotea's fourteenth birthday was in the spring of 1612, so she was still only thirteen. Why Toledo? Why so young that she would need over two years of noviciate before she reached sixteen, the canonical age of consent? Parker has suggested that the combination of Dorotea's age, the choice of Toledo and the role of her godparents points to paternal retribution for a sexual offence.[43] There are plenty of examples, even recent ones, of pregnant teenage girls being packed off to relatives or handed over to religious organisations, in order to 'hide their shame' and make them suffer for their 'crime', but is this one of them? Toledo was the home town of Dorotea's grandmother, Isabel Ruiz. Two of Dorotea's aunts, María and Isabel Calderón, sisters of her father, were nuns in Santa Clara.[44] This certainly makes the choice of Toledo much less sinister. Also, it was then perfectly normal for the daughters of Madrid civil servants to become nuns: working from an admittedly small base of seventy-one daughters of *regidores*, Guerrero Mayllo found that 55.5 per cent got married and 42.2 per cent became nuns.[45] (The other 2.3 per cent, presumably, remained spinsters.) Three of Dorotea's other aunts, on the maternal side, Andrea, Catalina and Josefa, were also nuns: in particular, Andrea had entered the Madrid Convento de la Concepción Jerónima at the age of sixteen.[46] Finally, but not irrelevantly, convents required smaller dowries than husbands; and since the dowry in this case remained unpaid for some time, her father was saving the cost of Dorotea's upkeep at no cost to himself. On the other hand, Diego's possible previous example of child banishment (his son Diego, aged twelve, to Mexico) confirms the need to examine his credentials as a father, particularly in the context of other events to be discussed in the next chapter.

One more death marks the end of this period of Calderón's adolescence, that of his mother's mother, Inés de Riaño. Doña Inés was already a widow when she made her will on 5 January 1612; she lived on until 26 March 1613.[47] She begins by setting aside 200 ducats (75,000 *maravedís*) for her granddaughter Dorotea, to pay her dowry to the convent of Santa Clara, in which she is a novice, since her father still owed this money. (It is worth noting that when Doña Inés's daughter Andrea joined her convent, she brought 525,000 *maravedís* in cash plus an income of 37,500 *maravedís* a year.)[48] She goes on to found a chaplaincy in the church of San Salvador. To endow it, she leaves her house in the Calle de Platerías.[49] (Don Pedro was living in this house at the time of his death, and had done for some years. The site is now no. 61 in the Calle Mayor: the ground floor is a bar, the Bar de la Villa, and the upper floors are divided into flats: Plate 7.)[50] As first chaplain, she nominates her grandson Diego Calderón, if he is ordained by the time he is twenty-four. If not, the chaplaincy is to pass to his brothers Pedro or José, if they are ordained, 'prefiriendo el mayor [Pedro] al menor [José]' ('the elder taking precedence over the younger'); but she goes on to say that as long as Diego is in Mexico, Pedro is the first choice. In the interim, the chaplaincy should be administered by Diego González de Henao, her eldest son: she prohibits 'en absoluto' that Diego Calderón Senior should have any role in administering the chaplaincy. She names as her heirs her children Diego, Andrés Jerónimo and Juliana, as well as her grandchildren from the marriage of her late daughter Ana, that is, the Calderón children. She makes no bequests to her other four children, Andrea, Catalina, Josefa and Francisco, all of them members of religious orders, since she has already paid their dowries. She ends by naming as executors her sons Diego and Andrés Jerónimo, her sons-in-law Diego Calderón and Juan Bautista de Sosa, and the Rector of the Company of Jesus in Madrid, as well as Father Cetina, her confessor, also a Jesuit. Finally, as if in an afterthought, she leaves 300 ducats to her Calderón granddaughter Antonia, together with some linen, chests, crimson velvet cushions and a carpet; and charges her daughter Juliana to look after these things on her behalf, making it clear that she would prefer Antonia to live with her.

Once again we are left trying to read between the lines. Mothers not infrequently distrust their daughters' husbands. Given what we already know (which is little enough), her prohibition of Diego's involvement in the administration of the chaplaincy suggests that she believed that the money was not safe in his hands, for whatever reason. Although she named him as an executor, he was only one of six; and although an executor, he was evidently not trusted to look after Antonia's heritage either. At the time when the will was made, Antonia was four and a half. At the time of the second codicil (19 March 1613, in which she was left a gold necklace and earrings), she was approaching six. As we have seen, Juliana had a daughter, Francisca, who was Antonia's godmother, although she was possibly still a teenager. Perhaps Doña Inés simply thought that being brought up by Juliana, still a young woman, and by her cousin/godmother, would be best for her. However, we are left with the impression that she believed that Diego was an unsuitable father, one who would fail to provide adequately for his daughter. We also have the impression, perhaps fainter, that Pedro was the favourite among her grandsons.

One other contemporary event from this period should be mentioned here: the expulsion of the Moriscos. Moriscos are usually regarded as descendants of the conquered Moorish invaders of Spain; in practice, many were descended from pre-invasion inhabitants who adopted Islam to avoid the taxes to which non-Muslims were subject. The highest concentration was in the kingdom of Valencia, since those once resident in the former kingdom of Granada had been forced to disperse throughout Castile after the abortive rebellion of the Alpujarras in 1568–70. All of them, in theory, were Christians. Many of them genuinely were, although others had not quite shaken off some of the rites of Islam. In April 1609 the government announced its decision to expel them, a move welcomed by many non-Morisco Spaniards as the culmination of the Reconquest, although the official announcement was cynically timed to sweeten the unpopular news of the Dutch truce.[51] The actual expulsion took place over several years (1609–14) and caused immense suffering. Velázquez, who was only a year older than Calderón, produced in 1627 a large canvas, now lost, entitled *La expulsión de los moriscos por Felipe III*.[52] This was planned for the Hall of Princely Virtue in the *alcázar*, that is, to bolster official propaganda about the Christian actions of the Catholic King. However, we can imagine, examining *La rendición de Bredá* (another 'propaganda' canvas painted later than the events, i.e., around 1634–5), and remembering Palomino's description of the canvas's 'host of tearful men, women and children', that the Moriscos were treated with the same compassion that the painter extended to the defeated Breda garrison.[53] Calderón wrote no play about the expulsion, but his portrayal of the Morisco leaders of the Alpujarra rebellion in *El Tuzaní de la Alpujarra* (*c*. 1631?) is remarkably sympathetic. His only personal experience of Moriscos could have been of the small Madrid community in the few years before and after the expulsion order of 1609.[54]

* * *

According to Vera Tassis, Don Pedro wrote his first play, *El carro del cielo*, 'de poco mas de treze años' ('at the age of little more than thirteen').[55] No play of this title has survived, and, given some of Vera Tassis's errors, we may feel inclined to dismiss his claim. Calderón did write a play of this title, however, since it appears in the Veragua and Marañón lists; and Juan Acacio Bernal had a manuscript copy in Valencia in March 1627.[56] The *carro del cielo* suggests that the subject-matter was Elijah, as do the remarks of Eleno in *El José de las mujeres* (I, 890b), although there was a St Elias (= Elijah) of Egypt (d. 309).[57] As we shall see, Vera Tassis was in possession of information about Calderón's plays that must have come from Don Pedro himself, so it is just possible that the first draft of this play was completed while the author was still at secondary school. Successful writers often begin early: it would be surprising if the first recorded plays of 1623, which were considered good enough for royal performances, were Calderón's first attempts at drama.

CHAPTER 4

A turning-point

> En este tiempo
> murió mi padre: yo, triste
> y alegre en un punto, viendo
> ya mía la libertad ... (*La cisma de Ingalaterra*)

(At this time my father died: I, at once sad and joyful, seeing that I was now free ...)

While the death of their grandmother, Inés de Riaño, may have deprived the Calderón children of some emotional comfort, it improved their financial situation considerably. The amount of her estate which was allotted to them totalled 3,641,532 *maravedís*, a considerable sum.[1] Cotarelo points out that each one of the other principal legatees, Diego de Henao, Andrés Jerónimo de Henao and Juliana de Henao, received the same amount, so that the total estate of Don Pedro's grandmother was close to 15 million *maravedís*, the equivalent of some £1.5 million today.[2] It may have been his share of this sum, or the provisions made regarding the chaplaincy funded by Doña Inés, that enabled (and persuaded?) Don Pedro to enrol as a *sumulista* (a freshman studying logic and rhetoric) at the University of Alcalá on 18 October 1614, three months short of his fifteenth birthday: he signed himself 'P° Calderon. de Madrid. 14.' in the matriculation book.[3] The age of fourteen seems young for a student to begin his university studies, but it was not unusual for this period;[4] it was certainly young enough for paternal wishes to play a major part in the decision. As we shall see, Don Diego was anxious, after Pedro had begun his university studies, that he should continue them. Presumably he encouraged them in the first place: a degree in canon law would be the first step towards ordination and a secure future in Doña Inés's chaplaincy. Apart from the lessons in handwriting given to José in 1616, after his father's death, we know nothing of the education of the other Calderón sons. There is no evidence that they attended the Colegio Imperial, or that they went to university.

The fact that the students were younger than freshmen today meant that student pranks were at least as numerous and even less subtle, particularly where the treatment of the new intake was concerned. Most former students look back fondly on their time at university, but some of Calderón's contemporaries, such as Ruiz de Alarcón, Mateo Alemán and Quevedo, refer to less pleasant aspects. In *El buscón* in particular, Quevedo describes, no doubt with artistic exaggeration, the disgusting indignities perpetrated upon Pablos de Segovia on his arrival at the University of Alcalá. *El buscón* was published in 1626, but Quevedo's personal experience as a student at Alcalá dates from the period 1596–1600, that is, around fifteen years before Calderón's matriculation there.[5] Ruiz de Alarcón refers in particular to the cost of university education, and virtually all writers refer to the financial hardship suffered by students. Interestingly, while some Calderón characters refer to university studies, there is none specifically described as an 'estudiante', unless we count Cipriano in *El mágico prodigioso*, which is set in early Christian Antioch. Lope has nearly ninety 'students' in his plays, and even Cervantes, who never went to university, could create a character like Lugo in *El rufián dichoso*, or write an *entremés* round a Salamanca student (*La cueva de Salamanca*). Students are even rarer in Calderón's plays than mothers, which suggests, at the very least, that his years at university did not supply him with dramatic raw material.

The best evidence for the true financial standing of Calderón's father is provided by two events in Pedro's early teens, a year and a half apart: Don Diego's second marriage and his death. On 12 May 1614, Martín de Villarroel, priest of the parish of Santiago (the bride's parish, adjacent to that of San Ginés), officiated at the marriage of Diego Calderón and Juana Freyle Caldera. We can imagine how much Diego's first mother-in-law would have disapproved, but of course she had died in March 1613. The bride was to bring a dowry of 2,400,675 *maravedís*, while Don Diego's contribution (the *arras*), was 1,000 ducats, or 375,000 *maravedís*. Diego was in his late forties; the age of the bride is unknown. The marriage produced no children. It was common enough for a bridegroom possessed of social status and financial difficulties to marry his way out of trouble (out of financial trouble, at any rate), but Cotarelo suggests that that was not the case here: according to him, Doña Juana was 'no muy rica de bienes pero sí de parentela' ('not very rich in property, but rich in family connections').[6] As evidence of her lack of wealth and of her 'parentela', he adds that she belonged to the family of 'the famous Dr Gaspar Caldera, author of several books'. This will hardly do as evidence; even the relationship is unproved. Nor is Cotarelo's reference to Gallardo's entry on Caldera immediately helpful.[7] Gaspar Caldera was an *indiano*, that is, someone who had returned from the Spanish Indies (in his case, to Seville, his native city). His books include three printed editions (two of them published in Leyden) and one, still unpublished, in manuscript. One item (four folio pages, hardly a book) appears to be by someone else: it examines whether Spanish monarchs, by virtue of their royal blood, could cast out devils and cure those possessed of evil spirits.[8] This is scarcely encouraging, but another book, on the genealogy of the author, includes a reference to 'el señor L. Melchor Caldera Freyre'. Since Caldera is not a common surname, and since the spellings Freyre and Freyle are interchangeable, this is more auspicious. It seems likely that Melchor Caldera Freyre was the brother of another author whose name is recorded as Fernando Caldera Freile.[9] Fernando was a member of the order of St Francis of Paola (the Order of Minims) and a preacher who wrote on mystic theology. One of his books, the *Sermon predicado en … Santa Ana de los Minimos* (1622), is dedicated to his brother, 'D. Melchor Caldera, oidor de la Chancillería de Granada' ('judge in the Granada court of chancery'). Álvarez Baena lists Fernando as a *madrileño* who was a preacher in Nuestra Señora de la Victoria, in his home city.[10] It was common enough for males to use their paternal surname first and their maternal one second, while females would reverse them, so there is a reasonable chance that Fernando Caldera Freile of Madrid was the brother of Juana Freyle Caldera, particularly since Fernando seems to have been about the right age: he died in 1633. Moreover, the will of Diego Calderón refers to a 'licenciado don Fernando Caldera', who was evidently a relation of his wife. And if this Fernando's brother, *Don* Melchor Caldera, the Granada magistrate, is the Licentiate Melchor Caldera Freyre (which seems likely), then Juana's social status is confirmed: she came from a family of *hidalgos*, two of whom had university degrees. It would be normal enough to find some members of a Seville family in Madrid, with another in Granada (returning to Andalusia?). What is not confirmed is Cotarelo's claim about Juana's lack of wealth. *Indianos* were proverbially wealthy, like Filipo de Carrizales in Cervantes's *El celoso extremeño*. No doubt some émigrés returned precisely because they had failed to get rich, but we do not know which category the Caldera family belonged to. It seems reasonable to suppose that Diego Calderón believed that Juana's family *was* wealthy, and that the large dowry would be forthcoming, although it had not been paid at the time of his death. Whatever else he and Juana shared, it seems that they may have had in common an ability to promise much and deliver little: not quite *El casamiento engañoso* of Cervantes, but enough to recall it.

Several other documents relating to Diego demand our attention at this point. The first is a receipt, dated 8 August 1612 in Madrid, issued by Diego to Alonso Gutiérrez, described as a *clérigo*, for 1,100 *reales*.[11] This is the only reference in any Calderón family document to a priest of this name.[12] The money might be a loan, but it is more likely to be payment for a service performed by Diego in his capacity as a notary.

The second document, dated 29 January 1613 in Madrid, is an IOU issued by Diego to Don Juan de Alcocer, who had lent him 2,000 *reales*.[13] Once again, we have no idea who this is, although the title Don points to someone of the same social status, perhaps a friend or colleague.

The third document, dated Madrid, 24 January 1614, is a formal request by Diego that, as 'padre y ligitimo administrador de las personas y bienes de mis hijos' ('father and legitimate administrator of my sons and their property'), he be allowed to redeem an annuity which had formed part of his mother-in-law's bequest to his children. The annuity, valued at 2,400 *reales*, dated back to August 1586. For reasons which are not entirely clear, Diego could claim only half of the amount, the other half going to a María de Herrera, widow of Pedro de Aleas. The request was granted.[14]

The fourth document is the sale contract of a house, by Diego to Pedro de Tapia, on 15 September 1614. Pedro de Tapia had been promoted to a judgeship among the accountants in the Council of Finance in 1596, and in the Council of Castile in 1598; in 1617 he would become chairman of the Plaza Mayor Committee.[15] The house was in the Calle de los Tintoreros, and the price was a modest 600 ducats.[16] This was not the tiny street which now bears the name, and which runs from the Calle de Toledo to the Plaza de Puerta Cerrada: Pedro Texeira's plan of 1656 marks Tintoreros as the street immediately behind Fuentes, where Diego's principal property stood; it is now the Calle de la Escalinata. When Diego died a year later, he was still owed 120 of the 600 ducats. In 1618, as part of the outcome of their protracted lawsuit with their stepmother, the Calderón brothers agreed that she could collect the rest of the debt.[17]

The last document is later, dating from 3 September 1618. In it, Juan Bautista de Sosa agrees to give up the lawsuit he has been undertaking against his nephew, Diego Calderón Junior, for the recovery of 41,000 *maravedís*.[18] The document indicates that on 3 December 1600, Diego Calderón Senior borrowed 200 ducats (71,400 *maravedís*) from one Tomas Carpa, a Fugger agent. Sosa stood as guarantor for the loan, more than half of which was still owing when Diego died. Pursued by the Fuggers in the person of another agent named Segismundo Hinderhofen, Sosa paid out 41,000 *maravedís* on 6 July 1617. To recover this sum, Sosa went to law (one hopes that he tried gentle hints and then persuasion first); the law responded by attaching the Calderón house in the Calle de las Fuentes. Since the house would have been worth far more, the action had the desired effect of catching young Diego's attention: he agreed to repay the money at 60 *reales* (2,040 *maravedís*) a month, and the case was dropped.

These different documents, together with the revelations from the wills of his first wife and mother-in-law, show that for the last fifteen years of his life, Diego Calderón was regularly trying to raise money by selling property, redeeming annuities and borrowing. Debts incurred in 1600 and 1601 had still not been repaid in full fifteen years later. His wife had effectively used her own mother as a pawnbroker. It is true that in the days before bank accounts, such transactions between friends and acquaintances were common; what is significant about Diego's transactions is their one-way nature.

The most important document left by Diego is his will, of 18 November 1615. The will is an unusually long (around 4,000 words) and often fussy document.[19] After the usual devout preliminaries and less usual instructions about his coffin (which has to be 'very well nailed'), he asks to be buried in the Henao family chapel (in San Salvador, as we have seen, which was pulled down in 1842). This is a temporary arrangement, until the fulfilment of his plan to endow his own chapel, dedicated to Nuestra Señora de los Peligros, whereupon his remains are to be transferred, and, if agreed, those of his first wife. The image of this Virgin was then in the chapel of a Benedictine convent ('de las monjas de Vallecas', 'of the Vallecas nuns') which stood at the corner of the Calle de Alcalá and the Calle de Nuestra Señora de los Peligros, which runs north to the Gran Vía, but Diego does not say where his new chapel is to be, and nothing came of the plan.[20] (Nor is there an obvious explanation for Diego's devotion to a Virgin who was invoked in moments of danger.) The first bequest is that the Licentiate Cristóbal Vaca is to be given 914 *reales* so that he may do with them what Don Diego has asked him to, 'as discreetly and speedily as possible'. A very precise amount (oddly, 913 *reales* was exactly 83 ducats), and a need for both discretion and haste: we do not know who Cristóbal Vaca was, but the bequest is strange, not to say suspicious.[21]

Only then does Diego turn to the property making up his estate, which is: his post as secretary, which he values at 20,000 ducats, since he has been offered this amount for it; the house in the Calle de las Fuentes, 'esquina de la Vajada del Arroyo' ('the corner where the stream comes down'), which, 'con los mexoramientos que yo he hecho en ellas valdrán seis mill ducados' ('with the improvements I have made in it must be worth 6,000 ducats'); a *censo*, that is, an annuity of 1,000 ducats against Don Martín de Montalvo, *regidor* of Madrid, and his late wife, Ana Calderón (i.e., Diego's brother-in-law and sister: it was evidently a life annuity);[22] a 500-ducat *juro* (a debenture bond) from the Espartinas salt-works,[23] and several smaller annuities worth 300 ducats in all, 'porque los demás se bendieron para pagar a doña Catalina de Henao ciento y veinte ducados y los gastos que se hicieron en la entrada de doña Antonia Calderón y del velo de doña Dorotea Calderón, mis hijas, y de la dicha doña Ana María, mi muger' ('because the others were sold to pay Doña Catalina de Henao 120 ducats and the expenses of the "entry" of Doña Antonia Calderón and the taking of the veil of Doña Dorotea Calderón, my daughters, and of the aforesaid Doña Ana María, my wife'); a lot in the Calle de la Madera, with a house on it, originally part of his first wife's dowry, valued at 6,000 *reales* at the time of his marriage, but now worth more, he claims. (The Calle de la Madera runs north-east, one of the network of small streets in the area between San Bernardo and Fuencarral; then, it was in the poor suburbs. In August 1643, after thirty years of inflation, the Calderón brothers sold 'trece casillas y un corral', 'thirteen shacks and a yard', in the Calle de la Madera to Don Jerónimo de Villanueva, who may have been the protonotary of Aragón, for only 9,475 *reales*.)[24] In addition, there were twelve *fanegas* of land (about 20 acres) in the town of Barajas (near the modern Madrid airport) and the village of Rejas,[25] which were given to him as being worth 2,000 *reales*, but they too are worth more; and the furnishings of the family home, rated at 500 ducats. The total is 11,077,000 *maravedís* by Diego's valuation, but his reiterated claims that the properties are 'worth more' may arouse suspicion. Over two thirds of the apparently impressive total of the estate is accounted for by the secretaryship (20,000 ducats = 7,500,000 *maravedís*). When the Calderón brothers sold the post in 1623, it fetched only 15,500 ducats.[26] As for the house in the Calle de las Fuentes, when the brothers had it valued in August 1623, the *alarifes* (surveyors) Juan de Aranda and Miguel de Santana rated it at only 52,000 *reales* (4,727 ducats).[27] In spite of the improvements Diego referred to only eight years previously, by 1623 'las dhas cassas estaban muy malparadas y nezesitadas de rreparos y con gran riesgo de caerse si no se fortificassen luego' ('the house was badly damaged and in need of repair, and in danger of falling down if it were not reinforced immediately').[28] The true value of Diego's assets was at least 63,500 *reales* (2,159,000 *maravedís*) less than he claimed.

Apart from concealing Diego's true financial worth, the will hides other information from us. Catalina de Henao was the sister of Diego's first wife. Since her mother Inés de Riaño paid her dowry when she took the veil, it is hard to know why her brother-in-law had to sell bonds to give her 120 ducats, unless this was in part payment of the debts Diego had owed to his mother-in-law. The expenses incurred in the 'entrada' of his daughter Antonia are another mystery: entry into what? Antonia would have been eight in the summer of 1615, but she died between March 1613 and November 1615; and since Ana María is also dead, what is being referred to here must be the cost of the funerals of Antonia and her mother.

From Diego's assets various bequests and debts were to be paid. First, the Crown was still owed 2,000 ducats (750,000 *maravedís*) of the charge payable for permission to transfer his post as secretary;[29] this left 2,581,750 *maravedís* to each of his four children. Since Dorotea had renounced any claim on his estate when she took the veil, as was usual, the younger Diego was to get her share and his own, with the proviso that Diego pay 700 ducats (262,500 *maravedís*) still owing for her dowry, and give her 100 ducats a year for the rest of her life (she was to live another sixty-five years!). In lieu of the *arras* of 1,000 ducats promised his wife by the marriage agreement, and evidently never paid, Diego was to give her, out of the extra share, an annuity with a principal of 2,000 ducats, with the yield to be paid from the date of the father's death until the date of its redemption (at 5 per cent, the yield would be 100 ducats a year); if necessary, the younger Diego's earnings from the secretaryship were to be attached to ensure payment! The father adds that his son 'me dará mucho gusto en disponello de manera que ella cobre esta miseria sin pleytos ni diferencias' ('he will give me great pleasure in arranging for her to collect this pittance without lawsuits or disagreements'). He was evidently aware of the bad feeling that already existed between his children and their stepmother, but his exhortations did not prevent a long legal wrangle; and 'this pittance' of 100 ducats was to be one of the sticking-points. Diego Junior was also to give his cousin Alonso de Montalvo, son of Martín de Montalvo and the father's sister Ana, 100 ducats to help finance his studies ('y quissiera poder mandar cien mill': 'and I wish I could bequeath 100,000'). Two of the father's cousins, María and Francisca, 'que están en Toledo' ('who are in Toledo': they were probably nuns), were also to have 100 ducats. From the remainder young Diego was to pay all debts that might arise, including those owed by his grandfather (who had been dead for well over twenty years); he was to come to arrangements with the creditors to pay by instalments. And if the total amount of debts exceeded the amount of money remaining from the extra share, Pedro and José should pay equal portions. Those whose mourning wear was to be paid for (a normal practice) were Don Manuel de Paz and his wife Doña Felipa Caldera (sister-in-law), the Licentiate Don Fernando Caldera (brother-in-law?), Doña Leonor Caldera (sister-in-law), Ortiz (a principal servant, perhaps housekeeper), 'the other maid', and 'the servants', as promised.

The bequests to his sons were made with the proviso that the secretaryship be sold, except that if Diego should want it, he should be allowed to have it for 2,000 ducats less than the alleged market value, provided that he worked at the job in person for ten years. Pedro and José were to have 6,000 ducats each; Pedro's 6,000 was to be made up of 1,965,500 *maravedís* (5,241 ducats), plus the land at Rejas and Barajas, 'las casas' ('the houses' – in the Calle de la Madera), 'y lo demás en algunos vienes muebles u algún censo' ('and the rest in furnishings or an annuity'). Excluding the last items, this brought the total to only 5,968 ducats, accepting Diego's valuation of land and houses (727 ducats), which makes his claim that they were worth more sound dubious. José's bequest of 6,000 ducats was to be made up of the house in the Calle de las Fuentes (supposedly worth 6,000 on its own) and the Espartinas bond (500 ducats).

If we combine the 2,000 ducats for the stepmother's annuity, 700 to Dorotea and 100 each to Alonso, María and Francisca, and the mysterious 914 reales to Cristóbal Vaca, we see that Diego was expecting that his son would have to find 1,153,000 *maravedís* in ready cash, or even more: one can see why he was told to pay creditors by instalments. Ostensibly, the estate was worth enough to cover these bequests and to leave substantial sums to the three sons, but this happy outcome depended on the fact that Dorotea had already been taken out of the equation, and on the sale of the secretaryship. With debts dating back to his father, and debts of his own dating back to 1600 and 1601, we can see why Diego may have been anxious to have Dorotea take the veil so early: some figures suggest that the dowry paid to a convent was as little as a tenth of that expected by a husband.[30] We cannot so easily see how Diego's eldest son could have found 12,000 ducats to compensate his brothers should he decide to buy out their shares in the Treasury post: 200 ducats a year each for thirty years?

Diego was a bad businessman, and his marriage to Juana Freyle Caldera, which he no doubt hoped would improve his fortunes, was his worst deal of all. Not only did it fail to do as he had hoped (at the time of his death, all he had received of the promised dowry was an annuity for 4,000 *reales*, which he had redeemed on his wedding day), but it brought legal, financial and – arguably – emotional problems to his sons. At least his failure as a businessman implies that he was honest. While his contemporaries in government, led by Lerma himself, and including his unrelated namesake, Rodrigo Calderón, as well as civil-servant colleagues like Pedro Franqueza and Alonso Ramírez de Prado, were lining their pockets at the expense of their fellow countrymen, Diego Calderón simply muddled his way into debt.[31]

There is another, less attractive side to Diego, however. In the sections of the will referred to so far, there is a hint of bluster in the reiterated claims that his property has increased in value. Presumably he accepted a couple of fields at Barajas and Rejas in lieu of 2,000 *reales* which he was owed; now, to prove how wise he was to do so, he claims they are worth more. In several European countries, northerners have the reputation of being hard-headed businessmen. Some of them are, but some of them merely try to live up to the reputation. Diego was evidently one of the latter. In *La dama duende* (1629), we learn that the late husband of the widowed heroine Ángela was a civil servant, an *escribano de rentas*, as the homonym of Diego's father had been (see above, p. 18):

Su esposo era
Administrador en puerto
de mar de unas rentas reales
y quedó debiendo al Rey
grande cantidad de hacienda. (II, 241b)

(Her husband was a royal revenue administrator in a seaport, and he finished up owing the king a great deal of wealth.)

A system in which government employees bought their jobs by instalments was bound to lead to hardship for dependants when the purchaser died prematurely.

Some of the other dispositions of the will are much more striking, though not necessarily more revealing. Diego charges Antolín de la Serna with the protection of his younger sons Pedro and José, a reasonable request, since he was their godfather. He adds:

A Pedro le mando y rruego que por ningún caso deje sus estudios, sino que los prosiga y acaue, y sea muy buen capellán de quien con tanta liueralidad le dejó con qué poderlo hacer. (p. 48)

(I order and request Pedro on no account to abandon his studies, but to continue and complete them, and to be a very good chaplain of the person who so generously left him the means to do so.

Since Doña Inés de Riaño was dead, and since he believed – correctly – that he was dying himself, he could afford to speak generously of her; anyway, her distrust of him might not have been mutual. By itself, this recommendation that Pedro continue his studies would not be remarkable. The next clause is, however:

Yten mando expressamente a Diego Calderón, mi hijo, no sse casse ni disponga de su persona sin licencia y acuerdo de los señores mis testamentarios [they were

Antolín de la Serna, Martín de Montalvo, Andrés Jerónimo de Henao, and his wife Juana Freyle], o de la mayor parte dellos, y en particular le proybo de que no sse casse con vna persona con quien me dijeron trataua dello, ni con ninguna prima suya, de que él y los señores mis testamentarios tienen noticia porque se la e dado yo, y si todavía lo hiciere o tomare otro estado sin la dicha prevención, por la pressente revoco y anullo y doy por ninguno todo lo que por este testamento tengo hecho en su favor, y desde luego como hijo ynobediente le desheredo en todo aquello que puedo conforme las leyes del reyno, y desde luego mejoro en el tercio y quinto de los dichos mis bienes de suso declarados a los dichos Pedro y Jusepe Calderón, a los quales les mando y encargo no sse comuniquen ni traten con él, pues a banderas desplegadas a querido ser afrenta de sus agüelos y padres, y esto se cunpla ynbiolablemente en cualquiera de los dichos casos. (p. 48)

(Moreover, I expressly order my son Diego Calderón not to marry or dispose of his person without the permission and agreement of my executors, or of the majority of them, and in particular I prohibit him from marrying a person with whom I was told he was negotiating marriage, or any of his cousins, concerning which he and my executors have knowledge because I have provided them with it; and if he still does so or makes another marriage without telling them, as of this moment I revoke and annul and consider as nought all that I have done in his favour in this will, and from that moment I disinherit him in all that I can according to the laws of the kingdom, and from that moment I increase by one third and one fifth the amount of my above-listed property bequeathed to the aforesaid Pedro and José Calderón, whom I order and charge not to communicate or have dealings with him, since he has overtly sought to be an affront to his grandparents and parents; this should be carried out without fail in any of the aforesaid contingencies.)

Behind this tirade, one suspects, there is more than one example of what the father considered to be his son's disobedience. Literature and history supply us with plenty of examples of fathers disinheriting children who dared to marry someone of their own choice, but the prohibition on marriage to cousins is strange. Diego had three female cousins: Bernarda de Montalvo (daughter of his father's sister Ana), whose brother had been bequeathed 100 ducats, and whose father was an executor;[32] Ana González de Henao, daughter of his mother's brother Andrés Jerónimo, whom the will also named as an executor; and Francisca de Sosa, daughter of his mother's sister, who had been chosen by Diego Senior as the godmother of his youngest daughter. The prohibition, in other words, cannot readily be explained away by theories about a family feud. It seems equally unlikely, given the splendid example of the house of Habsburg, that Diego should have had some anachronistic idea that marriage to cousins was genetically unwise. Perhaps there were illegitimate cousins of whom we know nothing. However, one brother-in-law was not named as an executor: Juan de Sosa, husband of Juliana and father of Francisca. If this omission reflects a rift, the disagreement presumably took place after Antonia Calderón was baptised in 1607.

The will's codicil, of 20 November, in which Diego admitted the existence of his illegitimate son Francisco, also made it clear that Francisco was not to marry the person of his choice:

> Él a sido tan trabieso y de mal [illegible] que me obligó a hecharle de mi casa, y anda perdido por el mundo; quiero que si pareciere en algún tienpo, que mis hixos de la parte que les toca de mi hacienda y herencia le dé cada uno lo que le tocare conforme a las leyes del reyno, sin que sea necessario que el dicho Francisco Calderón tenga necesidad de probar si es o no mi hijo, y a él le mando expresamente no sse casse con aquella muger con quien trató de cassarse, y si lo hiciere y conforme a las leyes le puedo desheredar de todo, lo ago. (p. 50)

> (He has been so wayward and of bad … that he forced me to eject him from my home, and his whereabouts are unknown; should he ever appear, I wish each of my sons to give him, from his share of my property and heritage, what he is entitled to according to the laws of the kingdom, without it being necessary for the aforesaid Francisco Calderón to prove whether he is my son or not; and I order him expressly not to marry that woman with whom he was negotiating marriage, and should he do so and I am able to disinherit him entirely according to the laws, I do so.)

He too was threatened with being disinherited, if he ever returned to claim his inheritance. We may well think that any father who, to our knowledge, never admitted to the son that he was his father, and who threw him out of his house for being disobedient, had forfeited any right to a say in choosing the son's wife, but not all of Diego's contemporaries might have agreed with us. One who would is Calderón's friend Juan Pérez de Montalbán: in Act I of *El monstruo de la fortuna*, Don Pedro described how Queen Juana of Naples had been instructed in her father's will to marry King Carlos of Hungary (her cousin, interestingly). '¿Quién ha visto | mandar en un testamento | como alhaja un albedrío?' ('Who ever saw someone's freedom of choice bequeathed in a will, like some jewel?'), she asks, outraged, in Act II (Pérez de Montalbán's). However, what is perhaps more important is that these parts of the will point to a father who was so anxious to impose his wishes on his children that he tried to use his last testament to do so: even the injunction to Pedro, which might have seemed innocent on its own, takes on another significance in the light of his father's other prescriptions.

When fathers in the plays try to impose their will in the choice of their offspring's marriage partners, the victims are usually daughters, although not always. In *La cisma de Ingalaterra* (1627), when Carlos wants to marry Ana, his father has different ideas, so that his death prompts a mixed reaction in Carlos:

> En este tiempo
> murió mi padre: yo, triste
> y alegre en un punto, viendo
> ya mía la libertad,
> el tratado casamiento
> dije al Rey. Dióme licencia. (I, 578b)

(At this time my father died: I, at once sad and joyful, seeing that I was now free, told the king of the planned marriage. He gave me permission.)

It is easy to imagine that this mixture of sorrow and joy was not confined to Don Diego's eldest son.

Young Diego did not marry any of his cousins. We cannot tell whether Doña Beatriz de Alarcón, whom he married in February 1623, was the anonymous woman he was thinking of marrying over seven years earlier; it may seem unlikely, although there is a long tradition in Spain of young people becoming *novios* (fiancés) years before they can afford to marry. We do not know if Francisco ever married. We cannot conclude that Diego Senior was a reasonable man trying desperately to bring order to an unruly family. The sending of his son Diego to Mexico, at the age of twelve, can be seen at best as a half-baked scheme for the boy to make a fortune by himself; at worst, as a punishment for some disobedience. The ejection of Francisco, which has no favourable alternative explanation, suggests the latter. As for the treatment of Dorotea, which can almost seem normal in its contemporary context, it shows, at the very least, an indifference to her sensibilities. No thirteen-year-old girl could know her mind, as even the Church recognised. The possibility remains that she, like Diego and Francisco, had done something to displease her father. This is not to say that the elder Diego was a tyrannical father who tried to impose the discipline of his own life on others: this is too 'modern' a view, one which Diego's contemporaries would not have shared. Rather, he seems to have been a person who tried to compensate for the chaos of his own life by forcing his vision of order on those whom he could control.

Many years ago, Alexander Parker tried to examine the Calderón children's relationship with their father in terms of some of Don Pedro's plays. A substantial number of Calderón plays portray sons – or, less frequently, daughters – whom their father has abandoned, or failed to love. Segismundo and Rosaura (*La vida es sueño*) are perhaps the most obvious, but Parker, referring to and correcting an essay by Blanca de los Ríos, cited others:

La devoción de la cruz	Eusebio
Las tres justicias en una	Lope de Urrea Junior
Eco y Narciso	Narciso
En la vida todo es verdad …	Leonido
El monstruo de los jardines	Aquiles
El hijo del sol	Faetón
Andrómeda y Perseo	Perseo
La hija del aire	Semíramis
Apolo y Climene	Climene
Los tres afectos de amor	Rosarda
Hado y divisa …	Marfisa[33]

To these we can add Adonis, from *La púrpura de la rosa*, and Irífile, from *La fiera, el rayo y la piedra*, and even Justina (*El mágico prodigioso*), whose mother was killed by her father, a total of eight sons and six daughters. We can exclude characters such as Heraclio (*En la vida …*), whose father was killed in battle, and even Irene (*Las cadenas del demonio*), on the grounds that this last play is of doubtful authenticity. Even if we do not include them in the list, we should not overlook characters such as Siquis (*Ni Amor se libra de amor*) and Andrómeda (*Andrómeda y Perseo*), whose fathers Atamas and Fineo abandon them to a monster (or to what they think is a monster), in order to avert divine wrath.

Parker suggested, first, that Francisco González Calderón was the inspiration for the fatherless son, in particular for characters such as Eusebio and Lope de Urrea. Going further, he suggested, arguing from the Eusebio–Julia and Lope–Violante relationships in *La devoción de la cruz* and *Las tres justicias en una* (where the couples fall in love without realising that they are brother and sister), that there was a sexual incident between Francisco and his half-sister Dorotea, aided and abetted by her brother Diego. The incident would have taken place in 1611. This would account for Diego's banishment to Mexico, Dorotea's being sent to the convent in Toledo and Francisco's ejection from the household. It could even account for the father's strange objection to Diego marrying any of his cousins.

We now know that the dates do not fit the second hypothesis. The plan to send Diego to Mexico was set in motion in April 1608, when Dorotea (baptised 4 March 1598) had just turned ten. The eighteen-year-old Francisco who accompanied him may have been Francisco González Calderón, in which case he was not yet being ejected from the household. It might still be argued that something was thought by the father to have taken place around March 1608, causing Diego and Francisco to be sent to Mexico immediately, and Dorotea to be despatched to Toledo when it became clear that they were thinking of returning, but it stretches our imagination too much to suppose that an eighteen-year-old Francisco really had designs on the nine-year-old Dorotea, with the connivance of her eleven-year-old brother (Diego was baptised on 21 April 1596). Perhaps the safest explanation is that years later, as he constructed plots from problematic family relationships, the poet became aware of the potential for disaster which had existed in his own family, and developed in his imagination a situation which had not come about in reality.

We are on firmer ground with the suggestion that Francisco is the starting-point for the fatherless-son character in general. It seems almost as plausible to suppose that the father (or substitute father) who tries to prevent a young woman from having any sexual relationship (Curcio/Julia in *La devoción de la cruz*, Admeto/Climene in *Apolo y Climene*, Tiresias/Semíramis in *La hija del aire*), or who surrenders his daughter to appease divine anger (Atamas/Siquis in *Ni Amor se libra de amor*, Fineo/Andrómeda in *Andrómeda y Perseo*) was inspired by what Pedro's father did to Dorotea. It will not do to argue that these views are modern anachronisms, or that seventeenth-century families expected fathers to be dominant: *dominant* does not have to imply *destructive*. Calderón's plays have too many fathers whose domination blights or destroys their children's lives. The theme is almost an obsession. Dominant mothers are rarer than those who die in childbirth or soon afterwards (the mothers of Segismundo, Semíramis, Rosarda, Leonido, Heraclio, Adonis, Justina), so it seems possible that the young Pedro subconsciously blamed his mother for dying in this way, and so leaving the way free for at least some of the family's misfortunes, notably the hostile stepmother and the ensuing lawsuits. He would not be a unique example of this kind of subconcious blame.

Whatever the long-term effects of Calderón's relationship with his father, the short-term one was straightforward: no sooner had he enrolled for his second-year course in logic at Alcalá (18 October 1615) than he had to return home to deal with the consequences of his father's death. Diego Senior died on Saturday 21 November. That same day Pedro and his elder brother, acting on their own behalf and on that of their younger brother José, appointed Martín Preciado to represent them in the anticipated legal wrangle over their father's estate.[34] Presumably word had been sent to Pedro in Alcalá when the father's condition became serious. In the slightly longer term, the father's premature death apparently resulted in his decision to hedge his bets in career terms: instead of returning to Alcalá and a degree in canon law, he matriculated in December in Salamanca, where civil law was also available. Financial considerations may have influenced him, but the possibility that Pedro was reacting to the end of what he saw as his father's oppressive tutelage should not be disregarded. After all, the father had certainly assumed in his will that his death would not leave Pedro without the money to continue his university education. If this was not another of his financial miscalculations – and the continuation of those studies a fortnight later, in Salamanca, would suggest that it was not – then Pedro's failure to return to Alcalá for his second term looks like a deliberate rejection of his father's wishes.

Our childhood perceptions of how our parents dealt with certain situations may influence our reactions as adults. If we approved of what our parents did, we are likely to try to imitate them; if not, we are likely to attempt to do something very different. When Pedro's own son, Pedro José, was born, like Francisco, out of wedlock, he acknowledged him, and, in the 1650s, made him the legal beneficiary of his own and his brother José's army pensions, valued at 30 *escudos* a month. It is easy to suppose that Pedro, faced, like his father before him, with the question of how to deal with his illegitimate son, took a conscious decision to reject his own father's solution.

CHAPTER 5

A talent discovered by accident

Al ruido de las espadas
llegó la justicia luego,
y yo, apelando a los pies
de la ejecución que hicieron
las manos, me puse en salvo.

(*Mañanas de abril y mayo*)

(Then the law officers arrived at the noise of the swords, and I, appealing to my feet against the execution carried out by my hands, got to a place of safety.)

Had Diego Calderón Senior lived for another decade, the lives of his children would have been very different, although not necessarily free from financial difficulties. As we have seen, two of the executors named in his will were his brothers-in-law Martín de Montalvo and Andrés Jerónimo de Henao. The second, according to the death certificate, 'vive en las casas del difunto' ('lives in the house of the deceased').[1] The others were Antolín de la Serna, Pedro de Piña and the widow Juana Freyle Caldera. A week after she was widowed, Doña Juana moved out of the family home, and their maternal uncle, Andrés Jerónimo, remained in charge of the boys, temporarily taking over the secretaryship on behalf of his nephew Diego.[2] The lawsuit between Doña Juana and her stepchildren was finally settled, after appeal, in March 1618, in a judgement which largely favoured the stepmother.[3] The experience seems to have marked Don Pedro deeply. In *Los tres mayores prodigios* (1636, when his stepmother had ten more years to live), his character Friso describes the feelings towards him and his sister of his father's second wife:

o como ambiciosa, o como
cruel, o como madrastra
(que en esto lo digo todo),
a los dos aborreció
con tal rencor, con tal odio,
que estaban de nuestra sangre
hidrópicos sus enojos. (I, 1641b)

(Either because she was ambitious or because she was cruel, or because she was a stepmother – for in this I say it all – she abhorred the two of us with such rancour, with such hate, that her anger was thirsty for our blood.)

Young Diego would not be twenty-five (old enough to take over his father's post) until April 1621. There is no evidence that the government asked questions about his fitness for the post, or about the ability of his uncle to act as stand-in. What the government did care about was collecting the fee for making the post transferable. On 3 October 1615, less than seven weeks before his death, Diego had received the authorisation for this, in return for a fee of 2,800 ducats, of which he paid 800 ducats down:

Trato con su mag^{d} que el dho off^{o} se le hiciesse renunciable y se le hizo y dio titulo para ello y hecha dello merced por cedula que para ello le dio su mag^{d} firmada de su rreal mano fecha en burgos en tres dias del mes de otubre del dicho año passado de seis^{tos} y quinçe siruio a su magd por ello dos myll y ochocientos ducados de los quales en vida pago ochocientos ducados el dho diego calderon de la barca quedando a deuer los dos mill ducados.[4]

(He dealt with His Majesty for the aforesaid post to be made transferable, and it was done and he was given a certificate for it; and the favour having been granted by warrant which His Majesty gave him, signed by his royal hand, dated in Burgos on 3 October 1615, he presented to His Majesty 2,800 ducats for it, of which the aforesaid Diego Calderón paid 800 ducats in his lifetime, leaving 2,000 ducats still owing.)

In February 1616 the second instalment, of 1,000 ducats, fell due, and the brothers' representative, Martín Preciado, asked permission for them to sell an annuity for that amount. This was not the 1,000-ducat annuity mentioned in the father's will (the life annuity against Don Martín de Montalvo and his wife Ana Calderón), since the father's estate was still *sub judice*. This was a life annuity inherited from their mother, in the names of Don Lorenzo de Olivares and Francisco de Montoya and their wives.[5] Lorenzo de Olivares y Figueroa was a *regidor* of Madrid, whose name is linked to Diego's in a document of 1630,[6] and Francisco de Montoya had been a notary. The annuity was bought by Antonio de Espinosa, a silversmith. The document was signed by Diego, by Martín Preciado and by Don Pedro, using the form 'P^{o} Calderon Riaño'. The use of the surname of his maternal grandmother may mean that he still regarded her chaplaincy as a career option, or that he was continuing to reject his father.

The accounts kept by their uncle are the best source of information for the Calderón family during the period from January 1616 to June 1619.

They indicate that by 12 August 1619 the missing half-brother Francisco had returned, and that, like his siblings, he had engaged the services of Martín Preciado to help him obtain his share of the father's estate. They also show that there was enough money for the Calderón boys to attend bullfights every year from 1616 to 1619 inclusive, including three in 1618: one 'para probar la plaza', to try out the square; the second, in the *fiesta* of St John; the third, 'la de Santa Ana que se hizo en la plazuela de la Cebada' ('that of St Anne, which took place in the Plazuela de la Cebada').[7] The feast of St John the Baptist (24 June) is still widely celebrated in Spain, while the first reference reminds us that the new Plaza Mayor was being laid out at this time.[8] St Anne, mother of the Virgin, was one of Madrid's patron saints, and her feast day fell on 26 July: the whole city marked the occasion. Once the Plaza Mayor was finished, the Santa Ana bullfights were normally held there. The cost of each bullfight was 116 *reales*, spent on 'colación y ventana', lunch and the rent of a window overlooking the events (Plate 8). We can compare this sum with the 8 *reales* for woollen stockings for Don Pedro (February 1617), or the 336 *reales* spent on food for the three brothers in the same month. During this period Diego was seriously ill, with a total of 13,110 *maravedís* (386 *reales*) spent between 3 January 1617 and the end of May. Another 108 *reales* are recorded in July 1618, with no indication of what the illness was, unless it is indicated by the eye treatment Diego received in 1619. It is worth noting that the cost of feeding the three brothers averaged a modest 4 *reales* each a day, and that they had only two servants, a maid Ortiz (presumably the Ortiz named in the father's will in November 1615), and Sedano, who is sometimes refered to as 'criado, oficial del escriptorio' ('servant, office clerk'): he must have been employed to carry out the mechanical tasks of the secretaryship, the seventeenth-century equivalent of a photocopying machine. In the will the father had referred to Ortiz, 'la otra moza' and 'los criados', a total of at least four. It may be that the number of servants – four to be sent to Mexico with Diego in 1608, perhaps as few as four in all by November 1615, only two by 1616 – is a barometer of the family's financial decline. Another indicator of decline is also revealed by the accounts: by this time the brothers were letting part of the house in the Calle de las Fuentes. This is confirmed by a document of 4 February 1624, which shows that a *cuarto* (which probably meant a flat) was being let to another civil servant, Francisco Gómez de Olivera, for 1,300 *reales* a year.[9]

The accounts also indicate a degree of uncertainty about how Pedro's university career should continue. Eventually, on 5 December 1615, with the first term already well advanced, he left for Salamanca, returning on 15 March 1616. The intention seems to have been that he should study both canon and civil law (civil law was not available at Alcalá), but the studies did not proceed straightforwardly. Instead of returning to Salamanca that autumn, he matriculated in Alcalá on 18 October 1616. Cotarelo has confused matters by stating that he matriculated in Salamanca at the same time.[10] He reproduced the matriculation book entry correctly enough ('Pedro Calderon Riaño, n[atura]l de M[adri]d, dioc[esis] Toledo, del 3° año': Plate 9), but the matriculation details for 1616 and 1617 are recorded in a single volume, and the date at the top of the page in question is 'a 21 de otu[br]e 1617' ('Pedro Calderón, native of Madrid, diocese of Toledo, in the third year; 21 October 1617').[11] In the event, Calderón did not study in Alcalá in 1616–17, since the accounts from November until the following July refer to him in particular or to the three brothers as being in Madrid. We might suppose that this change of plan was caused by shortage of funds, except that during this period (see p. 30 above) José benefited from a seven-month course in handwriting, at the cost of 56 *reales*, from the calligrapher Díaz Morante, while in July 1616 Pedro received an 8-*real* lesson from 'el Licenciado Muñoz'.[12] Cotarelo suggests that this licentiate was Luis Muñoz, author of some eight biographies of religious notables, male and female, including St Charles Borromeo (1626), Luisa de Carvajal (1632), Juan de Ávila (1635) and Luis de Granada (1639). Since Luis Muñoz was a *madrileño*, clerk of the Council of Finance and its chief cashier, he would have been a colleague of Pedro's father: the suggestion is probably correct.[13] Muñoz's interest in Luisa de Carvajal extended to her religious poetry, and in his *Corona de Nuestra Señora en alabança de su purissima concepcion* (1642) he published some religious poetry of his own. Unfortunately, we can only guess at how much Pedro was influenced by his ostensibly brief contact with this poet-biographer, none of whose books had yet appeared in print.

Pedro's university studies continued at Salamanca from October to May in 1617–18 and 1618–19. As just noted, he matriculated there on 21 October 1617. Eight days previously, on 13 October, Pedro, his cousin Francisco de Montalvo and a Gaspar Arias de Reinosa had rented a house between what is now the Calle Ancha and the Capuchin convent.[14] The house belonged to the Convent of the Eleven Thousand Virgins, but it was administered for them by the steward of the Colegio Menor de San Millán. Two instalments of rent were paid, but by May 1618, when Francisco and Pedro returned to Madrid, they owed 150 *reales*, plus 50 *reales*' charge for damage. When approached by the convent's agent in Madrid, Pedro refused to admit that he owed the extra 50 *reales* (and so tacitly admitted liability for the 150); Francisco said he did not owe the money. Gaspar Arias was not mentioned. Since the money was owed to a convent, the nuns took the normal course of having both young men excommunicated. Pedro and Francisco were back in Salamanca by 5 November 1618, but the debt was still unpaid, and the excommunication still in force. The university judge therefore ordered that their goods should be seized, and that if the value of the goods was not sufficient, they should be imprisoned in the *cárcel del maestrescuela*, the chancellor's prison. As a result, Calderón spent two nights in gaol, where he signed an admission that he owed the 150 *reales*, 'i los pagare' ('and I shall pay them'), but denied that he owed the extra fifty. He was released when he offered a *manteo* (his student's cloak: it was November) and 70 *reales* in cash, and was given thirty days to pay the rest.[15] At the end of the thirty days, he was unable to pay what was still owed, although he was allowed to matriculate on 22 December. The nuns' administrator continued to demand 132 *reales*, the amount having presumably been augmented by legal expenses. On 30 January 1619 another order was made for this sum, with the same sanctions – seizure of goods and prison – as before.

We do not know what happened next. Vera Tassis says Don Pedro left Salamanca in 1619 after five years of study, a remark that appears to match our scanty facts. Francisco eventually completed his degree, and remained on good terms with the Calderón brothers: on 21 November 1624, he set up an annuity with 600 ducats given him by Don Pedro from the sale of the father's secretaryship, from which Pedro would receive 330 *reales* a year. In the document, Francisco described himself as 'abogado en los consexos de su mag^{d}', 'a lawyer in His Majesty's councils'; he signed himself 'Licen^{do} don fran^{co} de montalbo', while Calderón used the plain 'Don P^{o} Calderon de la Barca' (Plate 10).[16]

The little information we have makes it hard to be certain about who was at fault in this dispute, but we can glimpse the same obstinacy, the same reluctance to admit to being wrong, as Don Pedro was to display in his encounter with the inquisitors in 1662. If the debt was ever paid, presumably it was settled by Francisco's father Martín de Montalvo or Pedro's other uncle, Andrés Jerónimo, or both. Unfortunately, Diego lost or had stolen from him Andrés's account book for the period July 1619 to August 1621, when Pedro should have finished his studies and graduated.[17] Such evidence as we have indicates that Pedro's university career never recovered from this setback; it is certainly true that by the spring of 1621 the three brothers were in serious financial trouble.

Although his time at Salamanca seems to have ended badly, there is evidence from the plays that Calderón looked back fondly on some of his experiences there:

Bien os acordáis de aquellas
felícisimas edades
nuestras cuando los dos fuimos
en Salamanca estudiantes. (*Casa con dos puertas*, II, 276b)

(You remember well those happy days of ours when we two were students in Salamanca.)

On 24 October 1621 'P° Calderon, de Madrid. 21 [años]' matriculated as a *sumulista* at Alcalá. The age given matches that of our Pedro, but it is not clear why he should wish to enrol for a course he had already taken. Two years later, on 18 October 1623, 'd. P° Calderon, de Madrid. 24 [años]' registered as a canonist.[18] Here the age is one year (or, strictly, three months) out, a discrepancy which by seventeenth-century standards is inconclusive. There is no record of the name among those who matriculated for the academic year 1622–3. If these two records refer to our Don Pedro, there is no corroborating evidence that he attended the courses. On the contrary, our Don Pedro was definitely in Madrid on several occasions during these periods. If the Pedro Calderón, *escribano de rentas*, who died in 1600, had male descendants, the odds are that one would have been named after him. It does seem just possible, though, that our Pedro still had thoughts, as late as his early twenties, of completing his degree, and therefore, presumably, of taking up his grandmother's chaplaincy; and there is plenty of evidence in the plays for his knowledge of the law: his characters make accurate use of legal metaphors, allusions, arguments and principles, and the conflicts they face are often expressed juridically.[19]

Since Calderón's first published poetry dates from 1620, it seems reasonable to assume that he had experimented with writing verse in his teens. One attributed poem, a ballad with the title 'A un río helado' ('Salid, ¡oh Clori divina!') invites Clori to tread on the frozen river Tormes and turn winter into spring. On occasions the style resembles that of unquestioned Calderonian works. As the text makes clear, it was written at Christmas, arguably in Salamanca, and most plausibly during the severe winter of 1619. Francisco de la Torre y Sevil published it as Calderón's in 1670, but it had been published in 1654 as by García de Porras.[20] Conceivably De la Torre, a poet and playwright who in 1670 was one of Calderón's circle of friends,[21] wished to restore the poem to its original author, but we may question whether Don Pedro, had he been asked, would have consented to the printing of a poem he had written fifty years previously. If it were his, it would suggest that he had enrolled for the course of 1619–20, and had spent at least the first term in Salamanca. Since there is no documentary evidence that he did so, we must suspect that the poem is not authentic.

Another ballad ('¿No me conocéis, serranos?') invites 'Filis', who already has a relationship with someone else, to share her favours with the writer. It has the same publication history as the previous one (attributed to Porras in 1654, to Calderón in 1670), but the Salamanca connection is more tenuous: the author's reference to himself as a 'huésped en vuestras riberas' ('a guest on your banks') could have been penned by any visitor to a riverside site.[22] We may doubt, as Cotarelo did, whether a seventy-year-old priest would have consented to its publication under his name, even if it were his. A third ballad ('Curiosísima señora'), ostensibly written much later, but with a reference to a degree completed in Salamanca ('Bachiller por Salamanca | también me hice luego', 'I also took my BA in Salamanca then') was once attributed to Calderón, but modern scholarship has assigned it to Carlos Alberto de Cepeda y Guzmán, who was born in 1640.[23] The evidence that Calderón never completed his degree certainly suggests that he was not the author.

The first undeniably authentic Calderón poems date from 1620. In May of that year Madrid celebrated the beatification of San Isidro (d. 1130, canonised 1622, feast day 10 May) with a poetry competition, and Don Pedro submitted a sonnet ('Los campos de Madrid, Isidro santo') and thirty-two lines of *octavas* ('Túrbase el sol, su luz se eclipsa cuanta'). The proceedings were described and published by Lope de Vega, the competition secretary, who also bestowed some conventional praises on the competitors, including Don Pedro, who was still using the surnames Calderón y Riaño:[24]

> A don Pedro Calderón
> admiran en competencia
> cuantos en la edad antigua
> celebran Roma y Atenas.

(All those whom Rome and Athens celebrate in antiquity admire in rivalry Don Pedro Calderón.)

We do not know who won the prizes, but the praise must have pleased a twenty-year-old.

Philip III had been taken ill as he was returning from Lisbon to Madrid in 1619, and attributed his recovery to the intercession of Ignatius Loyola, Francis Xavier, Philip Neri and Teresa of Ávila, and in particular to that of

Isidro, whose body was brought to him in Casarrubios. Accordingly, he asked Pope Gregory XV to canonise all five of them, and although he died on 31 March 1621, the five were canonised on 12 March 1622. To mark the event, the Colegio Imperial, Calderón's old school, organised a poetry competition on 25 June, while the municipal authorities organised another on the following day. Calderón submitted two poems for the first and five for the second. At the college competition, the poems were preceded by a dumb-show relating to their subject-matter, which was prescribed by the competition organisers. Don Pedro's *quintillas* on St Francis ('Tirana la idolatría') brought him second prize ('cuatro cucharas y cuatro tenedores de plata', 'four spoons and four forks in silver', valued at 10 ducats); the first prize was won by Juan Pérez de Montalbán. His other submission, a *romance* on the penitence of St Ignatius at Manresa (the inspiration of the *Ejercicios espirituales*), was preceded by a procession of barefoot, bleeding and sackcloth-clad penitents, among them the poet himself, who, 'dando muestras en tan cortos años, como lo ha hecho en muchas ocasiones' ('giving indications at such a tender age, as he has done on many occasions'), then delivered his *romance* ('Con el cabello erizado').[25] Several of Calderón's *autos* or *loas* include a character called Penitencia, who, when garb is specified, wears sackcloth and a hairshirt, and carries a scourge.[26] We cannot be certain that the little piece of theatre which preceded his poem was planned by the poet, but it seems likely. In any event, it worked: Don Pedro won the first prize, a chased silver-gilt *pomo* (a container for pomander) valued at 15 ducats. He may have kept this little trophy for sixty years, since his effects at his death included a silver *pomo*, then valued at 148.5 *reales* (11.5 ducats).[27]

Although only one of the five poems submitted for the municipal competition won a prize (third, an ornate hat-band valued at 30 ducats), the result was arguably even better. As before, the poems were published by Lope de Vega: a *glosa* ('Aunque de glorias reviste'), *décimas* ('Ya el trono de luz regía') and a *canción* ('Coronadas de luz las sienes bellas') to San Isidro; *tercetos* ('¡Oh tú, temprano sol, que en el oriente ...!') to Philip IV; and a *romance* ('En la apacible Samaria') to St Teresa.[28] The *canción* won third prize, with Lope himself and Francisco López de Zárate taking the first two. Since Lope and López de Zárate were thirty-eight and twenty years older respectively, the twenty-two-year-old cannot have been too disappointed. Lope also published an elaborate sonnet by Don Pedro on the Carmelite altar set up for the festivities ('La que ves en piedad, en llama, en vuelo'), and, in the preliminaries of his published account, a *décima* dedicated to him by the young poet ('Aunque la persecución'), who, flatteringly, and elegantly, suggested that those who envied Lope were really admirers. In return Lope congratulated

> a don Pedro Calderón
> que merece, en años tiernos,
> el laurel que con las canas
> suele producir el tiempo. (fol. 149)

(Don Pedro Calderón, who deserves, at a tender age, the laurel which, along with grey hair, time usually produces.)

The young Don Pedro unquestionably admired Lope, but poems like the altar sonnet show the influence of Góngora, one of Lope's greatest rivals (though not to be numbered, presumably, among those who envied him). Even in the other poems we can detect Gongorine echoes in phrases such as 'Eran, con belleza suma, | al campo flores de pluma, | cuando al viento aves de flores' ('They were, with the greatest beauty, feathered flowers to the field, while they were flowery birds to the wind'), or 'Campos de estrellas son, cielo de flores' ('They are fields of stars, a sky of flowers'); and the ending of 'Con el cabello erizado' ('al fin | fuego, y humo, tierra y polvo': 'at last fire and smoke, earth and dust') is an obvious echo of the last line of Góngora's sonnet 'Mientras por competir con tu cabello' (1582): 'en tierra, en humo, en polvo, en sombra, en nada' ('to earth, to smoke, to dust, to shadow, to nothing'). Góngora would remain an abiding source of inspiration throughout Calderón's career. Evidently this influence began at an early stage.[29]

The influence of Góngora is also evident in the prefatory sonnet ('No fatal te construya mauseolo') written for the *Sossia perseguida. Sueño y pregunta de Cassio, a Prudencio. En que se trata del honor paterno y amor filial* (1621), of Juan Bautista de Sosa, who was married to Juliana, the sister of Don Pedro's mother (Juliana, we may remember, was the godmother of Pedro's brother José; the book – a rather odd book – was written for Sosa's daughter Francisca, who had been the godmother of Pedro's younger sister Antonia). Here too, as he would the following year, Don Pedro used the surnames Calderón y Riaño. During all this period his elder brother was signing himself with the surnames Calderón de la Barca, so the difference is significant.

Don Pedro's growing reputation as a writer concealed a number of family difficulties. On 22 March 1621, while the text of *Sossia perseguida* was in press, the three Calderón brothers requested permission to sell a life annuity valued at 109 ducats because they were destitute and ill. Until then, as the document makes clear, the three brothers had lived together. Within a week the necessary witnesses (including Juan Bautista de Sosa and a doctor) had vouched for them, and on 6 April the annuity was sold to their other uncle, Andrés Jerónimo de Henao.[30] Since the preliminary pages of a book were printed last, the prefatory sonnet may have been as much an expression of thanks as an opportunity to appear in print.

The second 'difficulty' was even more serious. That summer Nicolás de Velasco, son of Diego de Velasco, a servant of Don Bernardino Fernández de Velasco y Tovar, Constable of Castile and sixth Duke of Frías, was killed. The three Calderón brothers were involved in the death, and took refuge 'en las casas del embajador de Alemania': as we would now say, in the Austrian embassy. The document prepared in connection with the missing account book referred to earlier shows that they were there on 3 August.[31]

In 1621 Pedro entered the service of Don Bernardino as an *escudero*: in April or May, says Cotarelo. The correctness of this date cannot be proved, but a document of 21 December (referred to below) seems to confirm that 1621 is the correct year.[32] Although born in 1610, and therefore still a child by our standards, the duke was the nephew by marriage of Don Gaspar de Guzmán, Count of Olivares.[33] Olivares was not yet the Count-Duke or the king's first minister, but since 1615 he had been a gentleman of the chamber of Crown Prince Philip (since 31 March 1621, King Philip IV) and was the nephew of Baltasar de Zúñiga, who had supplanted Uceda as first minister on 31 March. Olivares was evidently on the rise, and joining the household of his nephew was a tremendous opportunity for an impoverished would-be writer with no formal qualifications. It is reasonable to assume that Don Pedro's duties brought him, and perhaps also his brothers, into contact with Nicolás de Velasco, whose surname suggests some kinship with the Duke of Frías himself; that someone insulted someone else; that swords were drawn; that Nicolás was fatally injured; and that no one was uniquely at fault. In fact we do not know what happened. But a scenario of this kind would fit other facts: Calderón remained in the duke's service; in 1636 his brother José would dedicate the dramatist's *Primera parte de comedias* to the duke; Nicolás's family settled for compensation, and did not press charges. We can find similar situations in several Calderón comedies, in which the hero, or his friend, is guilty of a similar offence. Thus in *Mañanas de abril y mayo* (?*c*. 1632–3), Don Juan, having killed a would-be rival suitor, has to leave Madrid; he is something of a hothead compared with his sensible friend Don Pedro, but he eventually wins the heroine, Ana. In *También hay duelo en las damas* (?1652–3), the cause of the quarrel is less romantic:

fué fuerza ausentarse Félix,
porque en la casa del juego
dio a un caballero la muerte,
y su padre retraído
en un convento le tiene
fuera de aquí, por temor
de muchos nobles parientes
del muerto, y por la justicia. (II, 1491)

(Félix had to leave because he killed a gentleman in the gaming-house, and his father has him secluded in a monastery away from here, for fear of the dead man's many noble relatives, and because of the law officers.)

The authorities come second to the dead man's relations, and although in the plays relatives tend to seek vengeance rather than compensation, the family of the perpetrator could negotiate a pardon, as happens in this example. Don Félix is another hothead, far less sensible than his beloved Violante, but plays of this kind suggest that society then had a more lenient attitude to certain types of killing. To assume that characters like Don Juan and Don Félix owe their origin to self-analysis is to go too far; it seems reasonable, though, to associate them with personal observation.

Calderón would argue, in other plays, that when a victim had more than one suspected assailant but only one wound, it was better that the guilty person should escape than that the innocent should be punished:

Las políticas leyes,
que establecieron césares y reyes,
dicen que si una herida
en un cadáver se halla, y de homicida
contra dos el indicio
resulta igual, no deben ser en juicio
condenados los dos; porque prudente
tuvo la ley piadosa
por mejor que en sentencia tan dudosa
se libre el delincuente,
que no que la padezca el inocente. (I, 1195b)

(The political laws established by emperors and kings state that if one wound is found in a corpse, and the evidence of murder is the same against two people, the two should not be found guilty; for the merciful law prudently held it better, in such a doubtful verdict, that the perpetrator should be freed than that the innocent should be condemned.)

This example is from *En la vida todo es verdad y todo mentira* (1659). To claim a close relationship between this passage and the Velasco case would be fanciful, especially since we have no idea how many wounds Nicolás may have had: we do not know who struck the fatal blow, or blows. Perhaps only the brothers knew, even then. There is plenty of evidence that Don Pedro was a stubborn man (his refusal to admit to the debt in Salamanca will do as an example for now). He was capable of stating his case forcefully, even irascibly, or even of taking revenge – with the pen (the Paravicino affair, the sonnet to Antonio Sigler de Huerta, the letter to the Patriarch of the Indies, the prologues of his *Cuarta parte de comedias* and *Primera parte de autos sacramentales*, or his dealings with the Inquisition in 1662). As evidence for his involvement in the death of Nicolás de Velasco, these examples are ambivalent: a writer does not need a sword to retaliate, but the revenge on Paravicino, although only a pen was used, was certainly hot-headed, and got the writer into trouble. In the event, the brothers' pardon was secured on 13 October, in exchange for 600 ducats' worth of compensation, plus 3,000 *reales*' costs, a total of 9,600 *reales*. It will be remembered that on 15 September 1614 Diego Calderón Senior had sold a house in the Calle de los Tintoreros for 600 ducats; in his will, he had valued another, in the Calle de la Madera, at the same amount. This was no trivial sum.

Coming within seven months of the brothers' sale of an annuity to raise 109 ducats (a mere 1,199 *reales*), the judgement was a financial catastrophe. At the time of their father's death, the family owned only three items which could have paid off this amount: the post as secretary, which the father had valued at 20,000 ducats; the house in the Calle de las Fuentes, which he had valued at 6,000 ducats; and the life annuity of 1,000 ducats against Don Martín de Montalvo and his late wife, Ana Calderón. Additional debts included the claim of Juana Freyle Caldera, Diego's widow, for 2,700 ducats against her husband's estate, the capital (600 ducats) for a life income for their sister Dorotea, and 120 ducats for their aunt Catalina de Henao (the father's will had referred to selling bonds to raise this money, but it had evidently not been handed over). All this reduced the brothers' options. As an *escudero* of the Duke of Frías, Calderón might have been expected to live in the ducal household, but his uncle's accounts show that all three brothers were living in the family home until 30 November 1622.[34] Diego and José in particular must have wanted to retain the house. In any case, as noted above (p. 45), the building was in such urgent need of repair by 1623 that it was more in danger of collapse than of fetching 6,000 ducats. The only remaining option was to sell the secretaryship. Eventually, on 24 April 1623, the post would be bought by one Duarte Coronel Enríquez for 15,500 ducats, 4,500 less than the father had claimed it was worth: one suspects that all the assets of Diego Calderón the elder were overvalued by him in this way.[35] It is also possible, of course, that the recommendations of the *Junta Grande de Reformación*, published on 20 October 1622, which included suggestions that *escribanos* and rent-receivers be reduced by two thirds in an effort to cut back expenditure, not to mention the ongoing corruption trials of those who had profited from the reign of Philip III, had made the civil service a less attractive career option than it had been under Lerma.[36]

In December 1621 Don Pedro successfully petitioned the king for a *venia*, that is, leave to manage his own estate, although he would not reach the legal age until January 1625; it was granted on 24 December.[37] The use of the surnames Calderón de la Barca, rather than Calderón y Riaño, might suggest that he had abandoned thoughts of his grandmother's chaplaincy in favour of the new post with the Duke of Frías. The request may reflect the independence conferred by this post, but it would also save him the expense of paying a manager. It may also reflect the recognition that the future held a long vista of legal action resulting from the father's disputed estate and the death of Nicolás de Velasco. The first legal action took place only three weeks later, on 14 January 1622, when the brothers requested that their uncle Andrés Jerónimo, still acting temporarily in the secretaryship, should provide accounts.[38] There is nothing to suggest that Don Andrés thought the manner of the request unfriendly, and he duly supplied the accounts, although not until December 1622. The period covered ran from 1 July 1619 until 30 November 1622, and the accounts show that the household still consisted of the three brothers, the *criada* and the *criado oficial del escriptorio*. There is no reference to expenses incurred for Francisco, or to Pedro's absence at university. However, the money paid out for Pedro included 64 *reales* for three pairs of shoes, two of stockings, and 'botica' (the apothecary's), as well as 'quatro reales que dio á Pedro Calderon, que los pidió' ('4 *reales* which he gave to Pedro Calderón, who asked for them').[39] One imagines that the father would have asked what the money was for. Don Pedro was present on 12 December, with Martín Preciado, to 'hear' the accounts.

The same period shows that Duarte Coronel was beginning to advance some of the money to be paid for his purchase of the father's post. On 7 November 1622 Don Pedro signed a receipt for 200 *reales* from Coronel, and a month later for 500 *reales* 'para un vestido' ('for a suit').[40] It would not do for the *escudero* of the Duke of Frías to be dressed in rags.

* * *

Don Pedro's formal education may have ended in 1619 or soon afterwards, but young gentlemen of noble family, debarred by their status from a whole series of activities, always had time on their hands. Becoming an *escudero* in a great household would not have altered this. Dabbling in literature was acceptable for nobles, and many, including Olivares, tried their hand at poetry, and also possessed important libraries.[41] It was not uncommon for great nobles to employ writers as keepers of their libraries: thus Olivares's librarian was the poet and chronicler Francisco de Rioja, while Lope de Vega, after being in the employ of various noblemen, became secretary and librarian of the Duke of Sessa. Don Pedro's new post would have left him time not only to write, but time to read, as well as giving him access to books which he could never have purchased on his own: González Dávila tells us of Don Juan Fernández de Velasco, the father of Calderón's employer, that 'fue tan hõrador de las letras, que las professò con particular estudio ... Los tesoros que dexò en su Casa, fueron los mejores y mas eruditos libros que pudo juntar en los Reynos donde estuuo' ('he held letters in such esteem that he exercised them with particular study ... The treasures that he left in his house were the best and most erudite books he could collect in the kingdoms he was in'); the kingdoms in question included England, where he was ambassador extraordinary, and France, as well as various parts of Italy.[42]

***

In 1718, referring to the *autos El divino Jasón* and *La cena del rey Baltasar*, the bibliographer Juan Isidro Fajardo wrote:

Y aunque se duda sean suyos, creo que estos autos son de los primeros que hizo, y que despues nego, o enmendo, pues en las comedias que imprimio siendo mozo con el nombre de don Pedro Calderon y Riaño hizo lo mismo, declarando no eran suyas las que tenian este nombre; y que solo conocia por propias las que estaban con el de don Pedro Calderon de la Barca.

(And although there is some doubt about their being his, I believe that these *autos* are among the first which he wrote, and which he later rejected or altered, since he did the same in the plays he printed as a young man under the name of Don Pedro Calderón y Riaño, declaring that those which had that name were not his; and that he recognised as his own only those which carried that of Don Pedro Calderón de la Barca.)[43]

No plays have survived, printed or not, under the surnames Calderón y Riaño, and since the first surviving editions of his plays were not attributed to Don Pedro at all, we may be inclined to doubt this suggestion. Moreover, the earliest surviving autograph manuscript, of *La selva confusa* (1623), is signed only 'Don P. Calderon'. However, Fajardo owned or had seen printed editions of plays which are now lost, such as *San Francisco de Borja* or *Nuestra Señora de la Almudena*; and Calderón did publish poems under the name Calderón y Riaño between 1620 and 1630. It is possible, then, that some of Don Pedro's plays were first printed earlier than the surviving evidence might lead us to suppose; some of them may even be concealed in Fajardo's list of titles, which does not go into great detail about authorship.[44] Some circumstantial evidence in support of Fajardo's claims is provided by Germán Vega García-Luengos, who has collected evidence to show that Calderón was capable of rejecting plays he had written, if the text had been tampered with; thus *Cómo se comunican dos estrellas contrarias*, expressly rejected by Don Pedro, shows signs, in its imagery and language, of having started life as an authentic Calderón play, based on one of Lope's.[45]

As we have seen, Don Pedro's early poems show that he had encountered the poetry of Góngora. Góngora's collected works were not printed until 1627, after his death, but his work circulated extensively in manuscript. It is perhaps worth noting that when Calderón quotes at length from Góngora (for example, from 'Entre los sueltos caballos' in *El príncipe constante*), his context sometimes obliges him to alter the text, while at other times he gives a different reading – different from the printed versions, that is – for no obvious reason. Thus line 2 of the ballad, 'de los vencidos Cenetes' ('of the defeated Cenetes') in all printed versions, appears in the play as 'de los vencidos jinetes' ('of the defeated riders': line 612), while line 4, 'entre la sangre lo verde' ('the green among the blood') appears as 'entre lo rojo lo verde' ('the green among the red': line 614). Thanks to a study by Luis Iglesias Feijoo, we can be almost certain that Calderón used (possessed?) manuscript versions which are now lost, but which must have been very similar to some which have survived. It is also possible in some other cases that he knew his Góngora well enough to quote from memory, but not quite perfectly. In the case of *El príncipe constante*, however, the extensive quotation suggests a deliberate homage to Góngora, who had died only two years previously.[46]

That Calderón had also read and been inspired by Cervantes is beyond dispute: most obvious, perhaps, is the lost play *Don Quijote de la Mancha* (1637), but the earliest example may be the closing scene of *El astrólogo fingido* (*c.* 1625), which is adapted from Cervantes's Clavileño episode. Other successful inspirations include *La púrpura de la rosa* (1660, from *La casa de los celos*, printed in 1615) and *La mojiganga de las visiones de la muerte* (?*c.* 1673–5, from *Don Quijote*, II, xi, also printed in 1615).[47] Debts to the chivalresque novel, to Lope, to Tirso and to numerous other earlier and contemporary writers are also beyond question.[48] In July 1635, when Calderón was invited to approve for publication the *Quinta parte* of the plays of Tirso, he did so in conventional enough terms, but used one significant phrase when he referred to the relationship between writers of his own generation and that of Tirso: 'ha dado que aprender a los que más deseamos imitarle' ('he has given those of us who most desire to imitate him something to learn from'). Wilson has referred to the 'voraz apetito literario', the voracious literary appetite of the young Calderón, a phrase which is completely justified by the evidence. One suspects that this voracity was very soon accompanied by a desire to imitate. The post in the Frías household provided increased access to books and, arguably, encouragement of the wish to write, but also, and perhaps most important, potential patronage. It was a tremendous opportunity, but a dangerous one, for the potential patrons were the rulers of Spain. Tirso in particular would fall foul of them four years later, in 1625. The remark that he had taught a lesson to those who most wished to imitate him is full of meaningful ambiguity: whatever the precise significance of 'deseamos imitarle', it implies that Don Pedro had learned from Tirso's fall.

While those who incurred the enmity of the Olivares regime might find their careers impeded, those whom he favoured could prosper. Being a *sevillano* helped, since Olivares preferred to promote those from his own region of Spain, giving rise to a 'Seville connection'. Thus, on 6 October 1623, thanks to the intercession of Juan de Fonseca, an art-loving cleric who had left Seville in 1609, and who had the ear of Olivares, Diego Velázquez was appointed royal painter.[49] Velázquez was less than a year older than Calderón, and their careers have much in common, including that crucial starting-point: catching the eye of Olivares.

CHAPTER 6

Letters, not arms

> No volví el rostro a las armas
> por inclinarme a las letras. (*Nadie fíe su secreto*)

(I did not turn to arms, because I was inclined towards letters.)

The changes in family fortunes which took place in Don Pedro's teens and early twenties were parallelled by major changes on a national scale. In October 1618, after twenty years as royal favourite and effective prime minister, during which his personal fortune supposedly increased by 44 million ducats, the Duke of Lerma was ousted by a group which included his own son, the Duke of Uceda. Whatever his faults, Lerma had realised that the main obstacle to a nation's prosperity was war. Accordingly, when Bohemia's rebellion against the Empire began in May 1618 with the Defenestration of Prague, he resisted Spanish military involvement. By July, his hawkish opponents had convinced the king that Spanish interests, and not merely blood ties, were at stake. On 4 October he was forced into exile from the court, and Spain's involvement in the Thirty Years War began. As for Uceda, he remained in power only as long as the king lived. Philip III died on 31 March 1621, and within hours the Guzmán family had taken over. Ostensibly in charge was Baltasar de Zúñiga, a former counsellor of Philip II, but real control was shared with his nephew, Gaspar de Guzmán, Count of Olivares.

The new regime was anxious to dissociate itself from the financial corruption of the old, and set up a show trial of Rodrigo Calderón, Marquis of Siete Iglesias and the favourite of the former favourite. There is no evidence of any relationship between our Calderón family and Rodrigo, but the attitude of Don Pedro and his brothers is not likely to have been indifference. Lerma's waning power had been unable to prevent an earlier trial in 1614, but Calderón had been acquitted. The dubious legality of the retrial, the closeness of the verdict (two judges against one) and, in particular, the courage he displayed in his public execution (October

1621) made the marquis a subject of fascination: loathing and dislike, or at best indifference, were turned to admiration. We can glimpse this reaction in Velázquez's portrait (?*c.* 1631) of Diego de Corral y Arellano, the single judge who stood up for due process against political pressure: Don Diego's erect stance and keen gaze proclaim his upright principles and alert legal mind, and remind us that attitudes to the new regime were mixed (Plate 11). Zúñiga died in office a year after the execution, and Olivares took over overtly as first minister. In spite of the propaganda fiasco of the Calderón trial, he was determined to change the way in which Spain was ruled.

Some changes had already been initiated by the short-lived Uceda regime. Although Spain was already committed to the imperial war, neither Uceda nor Spanish public opinion was eager to renew the twelve-year truce with the Dutch, which was due to end in April 1621. This attitude was shared by Zúñiga and Olivares. Both of them were convinced of the need to maintain Spain's imperial standing, despite the cost in money and men: in Flanders, this meant resisting Dutch independence. Resistance to the Dutch, who were seen as fomenters of Lutheran and Calvinist heresies, was more than a question of religious dogma, however: as the birthplace of Philip III's grandfather, the Emperor Charles V, Flanders still had emotional ties for Spain, and these were complemented by important commercial links. Flanders was the main market for Spanish wool, the main source of imported manufactured goods, and a vital staging-post for grain and timber from the Baltic. Finally, there was the apparent logic of the domino theory, which claims that if an unwelcome ideology is allowed to take over one area, whether it be the northern Netherlands or North Vietnam, then neighbouring areas will fall in turn. Yet Flanders was much more than Spain's Vietnam, and the consequences of the war were also much more serious. Bullion that might have revitalised Spanish industry went straight to Antwerp, as did men, at the rate of 3,000 a year from Castile alone.[1] In the eighty-eight years between 1566 and 1654, the Military Treasury in the Netherlands received at least 218 million ducats from Castile. In the same period, the Crown received from the Indies only 121 million ducats, a little over half.[2] Castilian taxpayers made up the difference. Eventually, the horrendous cost of the war, in men and materials, would bring down Olivares (January 1643), while the treaties of Westphalia (1648) and the Pyrenees (1659) would bring Spain's pre-eminence in Europe to a definitive end. Lerma had been right, but no one living or writing in the 1620s could have guessed the extent of the disasters that lay ahead, especially since the war went well until 1628, when the Dutch captured the Indies fleet; but Flanders loomed hugely in the

Castilian mind during this period, a fact which is often reflected in Castilian literature.[3]

***

The first unambiguous documentary evidence relating to a Calderón play involves *Amor, honor y poder*, which was performed by the company of Juan Acacio Bernal on Thursday 29 June 1623, in Madrid's old royal palace.[4] *Amor, honor y poder* deals with Eduardo, *rey de Inglaterra* (Edward III), and his passion for Estela, daughter of *el conde de Salveric* (the Earl of Salisbury).[5] Apart from *La cisma de Ingalaterra*, *Amor, honor y poder* is the only Calderón play with a setting in England. Since Charles Stuart, Prince of Wales, was in Madrid from 17 March 1623 until 9 September, the setting alone presents *prima facie* evidence of a connection with his visit. The plot provides even more: it portrays a foreign prince, Teobaldo, who has come to the court of the young King Eduardo to woo Eduardo's sister. The parallel with Charles is obvious. The courtship is unsuccessful, and the princess marries one of her own young nobles. Charles saw many plays during his stay, and probably saw this one in the recently adapted *salón de palacio*. Hanging in the *galería de mediodía*, only an anteroom away from the *salón* (Plate 12), was Titian's *Diana and Actaeon*; when Charles saw the painting and expressed admiration, Philip immediately presented it to him: it was taken down and packed. We cannot tell whether Charles appreciated that a reference in the play suggested that he was Actaeon, the prince who looked on an unattainable beauty and paid a dire penalty.[6]

More surprisingly, perhaps, the play also presents the young king's dishonourable pursuit of Estela, *condesa de Salveric*. Don Pedro's source for his plot was probably a translation of Bandello's *Novelle* (1554), which also provided the sources of Lope's *El castigo sin venganza* and *Castelvines y Monteses* (or Capulets and Montagues, the Romeo and Juliet story),[7] but every courtier would see a parallel with Philip IV, whose nocturnal escapades had given rise to scandal as early as 1621 (Plate 13).[8] In *Darlo todo y no dar nada* (?1651), which re-creates the relationship between Alexander the Great and his court painter Apelles, Calderón spells out how the artist should portray his royal employer's warts. The artist should not lie; unpalatable messages should not be avoided, but must be presented delicately. Whether or not Don Pedro had thought out this view as early as 1623, it does not seem likely that he would have jeopardised a career opportunity by giving possible offence to the monarch without the approval, perhaps even encouragement, of Olivares. Olivares was unhappy when gossip named him as an abettor of the king's adventures, and since he is known to have persuaded Quevedo to write *Cómo ha de ser el privado* (1629), in which he appears, thinly disguised as the anagrammatic Marquis of Valisero, to discourage an 'inappropriate relationship' on the part of the king, it seems likely that he was involved in this case, suggesting a message not merely to Philip, but also to Charles. Allowing two weeks for rehearsal, Calderón must have begun work on the play in May or even April, when the marriage negotiations were still at an early stage.

What was the mechanism, we may wonder, of Olivares's involvement? As we have seen, Calderón's employer, the Duke of Frías, was the nephew of Olivares. As Constable of Castile, the duke had an important place in court protocol, but at the age of only thirteen, he would not have contributed to policy decisions. He could have conveyed a commission to Calderón from Olivares, but such a commission is not likely to have been given to an unknown: Don Pedro must have come to the notice of the first minister before *Amor, honor y poder* was written, and, arguably, must have shown his competence as a playwright.

Amor, honor y poder may come first in terms of unambiguous documentary evidence, but the preceding argument adds to the likelihood that it really comes second. The royal accounts show that a play entitled *Las selvas de amor* was performed by the company of Manuel Vallejo between 5 October 1622 and 8 February 1623 (i.e., before Charles Stuart's arrival in Madrid). On 7 May 1623 there was a performance by Vallejo of a play listed as *Selvas y bosques de amor.*[9] Six weeks later, on 21 July 1623, Juan Acacio Bernal received payment for a performance of *La selva confusa.*[10] As royal accounts were usually in arrears, we cannot make assumptions about the date of this third performance; but if all three references are to one play, as seems almost certain, then it was written before the royal visit, and most probably in 1622. Doubt has been cast on the authorship of *La selva confusa,* which was printed as by Lope, but an original manuscript survives, in Calderón's own hand.[11] Don Pedro's opinion of the two plays may be deduced from the fact that *Amor, honor y poder* was chosen to appear as the eleventh play in his *Segunda parte* of 1637;[12] *La selva confusa* appeared in none of his *partes,* and was never printed as his during his lifetime. However, there is a possible reference to it in *Peor está que estaba* (?1630): Camacho says that his master, Don César (the protagonist), has got him so enchanted 'que ando en las selvas de amor' ('that I'm wandering in the woods of love': II, 336b).

La selva confusa is a comedy of intrigue set in Mantua and Milan, with a complex plot which so confuses several characters that they are believed to be mad. Northup (pp. 174, 176–7, see n. 11) suggests, no doubt correctly, that although the type of plot shows a debt to Tirso, the depiction of the 'mad' characters, and the manner of treating them by humouring them, is inspired by Cervantes. The principal characters are dukes and duchesses, and we can easily imagine that the play was written in 1622 by the new *escudero* of the Duke of Frías to entertain the members of the ducal household or even to allow them to perform it, as happens in *Las manos blancas no ofenden* (?1640), in the household of Princess Serafina of Ursino. Someone with influence (perhaps the duke's uncle) saw the play, and thought it good enough for a performance in the palace. Since we know from palace accounts that there were more than fifty royal performances between October 1622 and February 1623 inclusive, it is easy to suppose that this need for suitable plays reminded some person with influence (perhaps the same one) that Calderón was among those who could be invited to submit material. When Charles's arrival stimulated the royal theatre even more, it was played again, twice.[13] This scenario is all surmise, but it is quite plausible.

Payment for a royal performance of a third Calderón play, *Judas Macabeo*, also known as *Los Macabeos*, was made on 30 September to Felipe Sánchez de Echavarría; that is, it may have been performed during Prince Charles's stay.[14] The account in the Apocrypha, on which *Judas Macabeo* is based, tells how, in the second century BC, three Jewish brothers, Judas, Simon and Jonathan, successfully defended Judaism from Seleucid oppression. In the play, the chaste warrior values of Judas, the leading brother, triumph over the decadent and sybaritic Assyrians; the plot shows how those who fight to defend their religion should be governed by that religion's values. The court would have seen a parallel between the three Maccabee brothers and the three Habsburgs, Philip, Carlos and Ferdinand, whose corresponding role was to be defenders of Catholic values in the Thirty Years War; in particular, they would have noticed the importance of chastity among the virtues of the eldest brother. Jingoism and triumphalism are not part of the picture: the theme of respect for the defeated enemy (shown by Judas in the funeral organised for the dead Gorgias) is striking. We see the theme here in Calderón for the first time, but its regular recurrence shows the importance he attached to it. Significantly, 1 and 2 Maccabees do not mention the death or burial of Gorgias; on the contrary, what is described is Judas' mutilation of the body of the defeated Nicanor. When his sources did not suit Calderón's artistic purpose, he changed them.

Other striking features of these early plays involve the role of the funny character, the *gracioso*: even when ignoble, in keeping with his ostensibly low social status, he offers a sometimes valid antidote to the rigid, honour-bound views of his social superiors. In addition, when he jokes about the theatrical process (Tosco's reference to the implausibility of the plot in *Amor, honor y poder*, or Chato's anachronistic play with the terms *tragedia, comedia, mosqueteros, tercera jornada* in *Judas Macabeo*: 'tragedy, comedy, groundlings, third act'), he creates irony, which in turn promotes 'audience distancing'. Distancing (or 'alienation effect', as it was called when developed by Brecht) is a feature also found in Lope and Tirso, where Calderón probably encountered it first, and in other contemporary dramatists.[15] His more extensive use and development of it suggest that he was fully aware of its potential to encourage increased reflection, rather than only laughter, in his audience.[16]

These early plays provide circumstantial evidence for Don Pedro's presence in Madrid in the summer of 1623. This presence is confirmed by documentary sources. On 24 January 1623 he and his brother José signed a receipt for 500 *reales* advanced by Duarte Coronel, the purchaser of the father's post, to buy clothing and other necessities (this was less than seven weeks after Don Pedro had received 500 *reales* for the same purpose). On 22 March Don Pedro signed for another 300 *reales*.[17] On 24 April 1623 he and his brothers signed the documents relating to the sale of the father's post.[18] His brother Diego had contracted marriage with Doña Beatriz de Alarcón on 26 February 1622, and although the religious ceremony was delayed until 19 February 1623,[19] the couple set up house together, and their first child, José, was baptised on 30 April 1623; Don Pedro and his uncle Juan Bautista de Sosa were witnesses.[20] When Pedro and José 'sold' their share of the house in the Calle de las Fuentes to Diego (a way of allowing them to share in the sale of the father's secretaryship), Pedro was present to sign the document on 25 August 1623;[21] and while documents relating to financial transactions involving Pedro, of 18 April and 20 November 1624, do not carry his signature,[22] that of 21 November 1624 does.[23] These last three documents relate to the setting up of annuities in favour of Don Pedro, using his share of the money from the sale of the secretaryship: annuities were a safe form of investment. Together, the three annuities brought in 715 *reales* a year, or not quite two *reales* a day, a pretty modest sum. The total amount of capital tied up (but redeemable) in the annuities was 14,300 *reales*. Vera Tassis cannot have known of these documents, but they seem not to contradict his assertion that

> El [año] de [16]25 passò, por su natural condicion, à servir à su Magestad al Estado de Milàn, y despues à los de Flandes ... Mucho se huviera adelantado en este honroso exercicio, à no averse servido su Magestad de llamarle para el de sus Reales Fiestas, honrandole el año de [16]36. con vna merced de Abito.

(In 1625 he went, because of his natural disposition, to serve His Majesty in the state of Milan, and afterwards to Flanders. He would have excelled greatly in this honourable activity, had not His Majesty been pleased to summon him to that of his royal fiestas, honouring him in 1636 with the favour of a knighthood.)[24]

However, if this is taken to mean that Don Pedro served abroad with the army from 1625 until 1636, it is untrue: he was in Madrid to sign a document on 16 April 1626,[25] and at regular intervals subsequently. Given the lack of signed documents between 21 November 1624 and 16 April 1626, we might suppose that Vera Tassis was correct about the military service, but that it lasted less than eighteen months. The most convincing evidence that he was completely wrong is provided by Don Pedro's application, dating from about 1648, for a military pension. In the application, Don Pedro gives details of his service in Cataluña in 1640–2, as well as of the service of his brother José, killed in action in 1645.[26] When it would clearly have been in his interest to do so, Don Pedro makes no reference to an earlier period of service in the 1620s.

Pedro and José are likely to have moved out of the house in the Calle de las Fuentes in 1622, or at least by August 1623, when they gave up their share of the house to Diego and his new wife. As Cotarelo points out, the employment of Antonio Coello (later to become one of Calderón's collaborators) in the service of the Duke of Alburquerque brought with it accommodation in the ducal palace.[27] We do not know if Don Pedro moved into the palace of the Duke of Frías; if not, the likelihood is that he and José moved into the grandmother's house in Platerías, since her will had given them until the age of twenty-four to take up her chaplaincy. This could explain why our Pedro Calderón might have registered as a canonist in Alcalá in October 1623. If he did, the continuing success of his dramatic productions may have helped him to change his mind.

Although there is no firm evidence for dramatic production in 1624, there is circumstantial and documentary evidence for plays written about this time, or soon afterwards. Indeed, since there may be over twenty plays from the eight years between 1622 and 1629 inclusive, they provide evidence for the author's presence in Madrid for most, if not all, of the 1620s, although there are no dated documents between 16 April 1626 and 23 March 1630.

The other plays which date from or have been attributed to the 1620s are as follows: *Nadie fíe su secreto* (?1623–4),[28] *El astrólogo fingido* (1624–5),[29] *Lances de amor y fortuna* (1624–5),[30] *La gran Cenobia* (1625),[31] *El sitio de Bredá* (1625),[32] *El alcaide de sí mismo* (1627),[33] *La cisma de Ingalaterra* (1627),[34] *El hombre pobre todo es trazas* (1627),[35] *La cruz en la sepultura* (= *La devoción de la cruz*) (?by 1627),[36] *El purgatorio de San Patricio* (?1627–8),[37] *De un castigo tres venganzas* (*c*. 1628),[38] *Saber del mal y del bien* (1628),[39] *El príncipe constante* (1628–9),[40] *El médico de su honra* (?1628–9),[41] *Luis Pérez el gallego* (1628 or 1629),[42] *Casa con dos puertas* (1629),[43] *La dama duende* (1629),[44] *La Virgen del Sagrario* (?1629).[45] Not all of these dates are equally reliable, as we shall see. On the borderline between the two decades we may place *La vida es sueño*, 'de fecha probablemente anterior a 1630' ('probably prior to 1630'), or no later than the latter part of 1630, according to the most recent research;[46] *Peor está que estaba*, which one source dates to May 1630 (detailed below); *La puente de Mantible*, which had a royal performance on 7 July 1630;[47] and *Con quien vengo, vengo*, which was apparently written before 25 September 1630.[48]

Nadie fíe su secreto deals with the historical Alejandro/Alessandro Farnese, Prince of Parma, and his supposed passion for Ana de Castelví, who loves and is loved by his secretary Don César. After hindering the relationship of César and Ana by various ruses, the prince finally remembers his namesake Alexander the Great (who gave up Campaspe to Apelles, a subject examined in the plot of *Darlo todo y no dar nada*) and leaves for Flanders:

> Yo he de partir luego a Flandes
> a servir el gran Filipo
> Segundo, donde Mastrique
> venga a ser el blasón mío. (II, 122b)[49]

(I shall leave at once for Flanders to serve the great Philip II, for Maastricht to become my glory there.)

Given that the historical Parma's first military success as governor of the Low Countries was the capture of Maastricht on 22 June 1579, it is unnecessarily fanciful to see in these lines a reference to the author's own plans to leave for Flanders. It is more plausible to see an autobiographical comment in César's lines

> No volví el rostro a las armas
> por inclinarme a las letras. (II, 117a)

(I did not turn to arms, because I was inclined towards letters.)

The reference to Maastricht reminds us that the city was recaptured by the Prince of Orange in 1632, and that in November of that year Philip IV's brother Prince Ferdinand was named governor of the Low Countries. If this reference is a way of suggesting that Ferdinand may be a worthy successor to Parma, the play must date from late 1632 or early 1633. It is also possible to argue that Parma's remark points to composition in the period 1623–8, before disillusionment over the Flanders war began to set in.

The play contains a less developed version of a joke about a lady who wanted to give up her house for a coach (found in *Mañanas de abril y mayo*, *c.* 1632–3), and makes use of the *hombre = breve mundo / mujer = breve cielo* argument that we find, placed more effectively in the mouth of Segismundo, in *La vida es sueño*. Similarly, Segismundo's observation that 'presidía entre comunes flores | la deidad de la rosa' ('the goddess of the rose presided over common flowers': I, 516b) is parallelled by Alejandro's 'presidía entre comunes flores | la rosa hermosa y bella' ('the lovely, beautiful rose presided over common flowers': II, 98b). Again, the passage of which these lines form part is arguably better expressed in *La vida es sueño*. However, the argument that Calderón's writing consists of a uniform process of improvement is a dangerous one. Nor is it safe to assume that the use of similar material in other plays is proof of near-contemporary composition; evidence, perhaps, but not proof. All we can be sure about is that Calderón's method of writing involved the reworking of material of all kinds, from turns of phrase, through images and jokes, to entire plots. Thus the plot (and some of the characters, such as the Prince of Parma) of *Nadie fíe su secreto* finds echoes in *Amigo, amante y leal* (?1630–1) and *Basta callar* (?first drafted in 1639–40), while the theme that a ruler must *vencerse a sí mismo*, that is, that he must curb his desires precisely because he has the power to get what he wants, was one to which Don Pedro returned regularly throughout his career. Perhaps the best evidence for the date of *Nadie fíe su secreto* is the remark that a new play is worth 800 *reales* (II, 102a). Compared with the 460 *reales* paid in 1625 to Guillén de Castro (an established writer whose *Segunda parte* was published that year) for *Las maravillas de Babilonia*, this is a substantial sum.[50] The figure suggests that a better guess-date might be *c.* 1629, since this was the amount Calderón received for *El príncipe constante* in 1628/9. Don Pedro did not include the play in his Veragua or Marañón lists, conceivably because he regarded it as an early version of *Amigo, amante y leal*.

El astrólogo fingido is certainly an early play, since it appeared in *Parte veynte y cinco de comedias de diferentes autores* (1632; second edition, 1633). We cannot safely assume that the play was written several years before it was printed, as often happened, although Pedro Escuer's dedication of the play to Francisco Jiménez de Urrea implies that composition was not recent.[51] The early printing almost certainly helped it to become one of the first Calderón plays to attract interest abroad, inspiring Thomas Corneille's *Le Feint Astrologue* (1648) and – indirectly – Dryden's *An Evening's Love, or the Mock Astrologer* (1668), as well as Carlo Costanzo Costa, *L'astrologo non astrologo o gli amori turbati* (1665) and Raffaello Tauro, *La falsa astrologia, ovvero el sognar vegghiando* (1669).

Don Diego de Luna is not a real astrologer, but his servant Morón claims he is, to avoid giving the real reason for his apparently extraordinary knowledge of the relationship between Don Juan de Medrano and Doña María de Ayala. The true explanation is a prosaic one: indiscretion on the part of María's maid Beatriz. Juan has courted María for two years without apparent success, and claims that he is leaving for Flanders:

mañana a Flandes me parto
a servir al gran Felipe …
Don Vicente Pimentel,
mi señor, hoy apercibe
su jornada. (II, 130a)

(I leave tomorrow for Flanders to serve the great Philip. My master Don Vicente Pimentel is preparing his journey today.)

Once again, there is no reason to regard this remark as autobiographical. Rather, it is a simple dramatic device, using current events to enable the character to provide a plausible way of provoking a declaration on the part of a virtuous and discreet young woman. Gratefully promising to be equally discreet, Juan uses an unusual image:

Yo seré
el ave que el viento rompe
con una piedra en el pie
y otra en el pico, advirtiendo
que soy vigilante y fiel. (II, 131b)

(I shall be the bird which pierces the wind with one stone in its foot and another in its bill, indicating that I am vigilant and true.)

Don Gutierre ('Seré el pájaro que fingen | con una piedra en la boca': 'I shall be that bird they imagine with a stone in its mouth') gives a more concise version in *El médico de su honra* (?1628–9). There are emblem-books in which Don Pedro could have seen this, but it goes back to Pliny, was used by Cervantes in the *Persiles*, and so on.[52] A more certain borrowing from Cervantes is the trick played on the fussy old *escudero* Otáñez, which, as we saw, comes from the Clavileño episode in *Don Quijote* (II, xlii). Another scene, in which Juan and María's father discuss a jewel which the father thinks Juan has stolen from his daughter, has been linked to Plautus' *Aulularia*.[53] As we have seen, Don Pedro's familiarity with Plautus may have begun at school.

Don Diego may be no astrologer, but he is happy to pretend to be, if it will get him what he wants, namely María. His pretence involves him in much lying and deception, and, in the closing scene, the other characters, among them María (who happily marries Juan), are scathing in their rebukes. His fate reminds us of Ruiz de Alarcón's García in *La verdad sospechosa* (?written by 1623), whose lying is blamed for his failure to marry the girl he wanted. Like García, though, Diego attracts some sympathy, since he is the main source of our amusement when we laugh at credulous believers of liars or in the powers of astrologers. At the same time, Calderón's mention of Giambattista della Porta (author of *Magia naturalis*, 1561) and Ginés Rocamora (author of *La esfera del universo*, 1599) suggests that when he created Basilio in *La vida es sueño*, he had at least encountered the names of contemporary writers on astrology, and, possibly, that he had read their works.[54]

The reference to Don Vicente Pimentel, 'mi señor', is significant but not quite conclusive. The Pimentel family had several branches, and its members included María Pimentel de Fonseca, the mother of Olivares, and the counts of Benavente. The fifth count, Don Alonso, had married Ana Herrera de Velasco, daughter of Bernardino de Velasco, Constable of Castile and the first Duke of Frías (Calderón's employer was the sixth duke). The ninth count of Benavente, Juan Francisco, was the queen's *mayordomo mayor*, and in October 1622 he married his relative Leonor Pimentel, who was one of the maids-of-honour of the Infanta María. Leonor in turn was the sister of Don Antonio Pimentel y Toledo, Marquis of Távara, who happened to be married to the niece of the Duke of Lerma. In detailing these complex relationships, Ruth Lee Kennedy has drawn attention to the Pimentel family feud which turned some members into critical opponents of their relative Olivares. Tirso de Molina had close links with some of the anti-Olivares members of the family.[55] The family continued to be prominent throughout the seventeenth century: Vera Tassis would dedicate Calderón's *Verdadera quinta parte* (1682) to the twelfth Count of Benavente, Francisco Antonio Casimiro Alfonso.

Don Vicente Pimentel is a character in *El sitio de Bredá*. The siege of the city began in July 1624 and lasted until June 1625. The text of the play gives us some details about Vicente, mostly in his own words. He was a cavalry officer, the youngest of a family whose military deeds he was striving to emulate; and he had just brought a cavalry squadron from Lombardy. Had he gone to Lombardy expressly to take troops to Breda, he might have left Madrid in 1624 or 1625. If we take the *Astrólogo* reference to his imminent departure at face value, then the play could have been written in 1624–5.

The text says nothing about Lombardy, however, and the possibility remains that Don Vicente returned to Madrid after the triumph in Breda, in order to raise more troops for Flanders. Calderón may have known him personally as a relative of his patron, the Duke of Frías, and his brother José, another cavalry officer who served in Milan and Flanders, could have encountered him, although José's military career began only in 1627.[56] Another possibility is that Vera Tassis's undoubted familiarity with the text of *El sitio de Bredá*, together with some knowledge of the careers of José and Don Pedro himself (who served with the cavalry in Cataluña in the 1640s), led him to make assumptions about the military career of the poet.

Don Vicente was not a prominent Pimentel, and we do not know how he felt about Olivares. The only traceable Pimentel with this Christian name was the grandson of Juan Alonso, the eighth Count of Benavente, who had fourteen children. One of these was Vicente's father Jerónimo, who, despite being a patron of Tirso (who was censured by the Olivares regime in March 1625), was a member of the Council of War, and in May 1625 was created Marquis of Bayona by the king. Vicente's mother was Clara Lucadelli, a Milanese noblewoman, and Vicente, who was born in Vigevano, became a knight of Santiago in 1628.[57] For a young author seeking patrons, there were potential risks in taking sides, but a brief reference to a young nobleman who was doing his patriotic duty was unlikely to attract anyone's disapproval. It is worth noting, too, that Olivares is twice recorded as expressing surprise that sensible men should consult astrologers, an attitude that the play certainly seems to endorse.[58] If it is as early as 1624–5, then it is Calderón's first character comedy (*comedia de figurón*).

Lances de amor y fortuna is set in Barcelona at an indeterminate time, and involves members of the Catalan nobility. The heroine Aurora's admission that she has fallen in love with the portrait of the hero recalls Serafina in Tirso's *El vergonzoso en palacio* (written by July 1611, printed 1624). The themes of truth and falsehood, and of constancy in love (of the hero Rugero) versus good fortune (of the 'villain' Lotario) recur frequently in Calderón. Unexpectedly, and implausibly, the ending pairs Lotario off with Diana, Rugero's sister. This is different from the ending of *El astrólogo fingido*, but the difference does not allow any conclusions about date of composition. The play was printed in the *Primera parte* (1636).

In September 1624 Calderón's employer, the Duke of Frías, married Isabel de Guzmán, the sister of the Marquis of Toral, who was the titular head of the house of Guzmán, and a relative of Olivares. On 5 January 1625 Olivares received his dukedom, and four days later his only daughter María, aged fourteen, married the Marquis, who was even younger.[59] Since the

Duke was already the nephew by marriage of Olivares, these matches allied the families even more closely. The ceremonies were lavish, involving all of Spain's aristocracy from the royal family downwards, and certainly affected the *escuderos* of the ducal household. While there is no indication that Don Pedro wrote anything to mark the occasions, he must have been conscious of being close to the centre of political power, even as a mere observer.[60]

On 6 March 1625 one of the new regime's committees, the *Junta grande de reformación de las costumbres*, having ostensibly concluded that public morals were being corrupted by the reading of plays and novels, recommended that they should not be granted printing licences in Castile; the kingdom of Aragón, juridically separate, was not affected. The same extraordinary decision also singled out Tirso for the 'comedias que hace profanas y de malos incentivos y ejemplos' ('the profane plays which he writes, and which set bad incentives and examples'), and recommended that he be banished and forbidden to write plays. Since Tirso was an active critic of the Olivares regime, we can guess that the target of the recommendations was as much political opposition as alleged moral corruption. Effectively unenforceable, the printing licence ban nevertheless remained part of government policy for ten years, seriously damaging the Castilian book trade and encouraging piracy.[61] We can guess, too, from the approbation of Tirso's *Quinta parte* which he wrote immediately after the end of the ban, where Don Pedro's sympathies lay.[62] The ban's effect on genre needs further investigation, since during it Lope produced his *Dorotea*, 'acción en prosa' ('an action in prose', i.e., neither a novel nor a play), while Pérez de Montalbán wrote his *Vida y purgatorio de San Patricio*, 'novela a lo divino', a novel disguised as hagiography – and the source for Calderón's *El purgatorio de San Patricio*. For the time being, the ban had little effect on a young writer who, to our knowledge, was not yet seeking to print his small number of plays. The publication of Calderón's plays would be affected, however.

On 23 June 1625 Andrés de la Vega was paid for a royal performance of *La gran Cenobia*. The historical Zenobia became Queen of Palmyra (in central Syria) after the murder of her husband Odenathus in about 267 AD. Within a few years, she had conquered Egypt and much of Asia Minor, but she was finally defeated by the emperor Aurelian and brought back for a Roman triumph. She eventually married a Roman senator. Calderón's most likely sources were the *Historia imperial y cesárea* of Pedro Mexía (first printed in Seville, 1545) or the *Epístolas familiares* of Antonio de Guevara (first printed in Valladolid, 1539–41), but he introduces an anachronistic Decio, who kills the tyrannical Aureliano and marries Cenobia (a Decius, mentioned by Guevara, was emperor from 249 to 251 AD).

The play has two royal audience scenes involving Cenobia and Aureliano. These are earlier and arguably cruder versions of the more subtly revealing audience scene in *El médico de su honra*. The most controversial scene, however, is the last, in which four characters, including Decio, await their opportunity to murder the emperor. Some modern critics have argued that only Decio has pure motives, but others, including the play's editor, Juan Manuel Gómez, disagree, quoting Decio's reference to 'la venganza que esperé'.[63] What is certain is that the most striking character is Cenobia; arguably, she is the only one without moral blemish.

For over a century, since Machiavelli's *Il principe* (1513, printed 1532), political theorists had debated the role of the ruler, some of them dealing with the possibility that rulers might be female. Thus John Knox, in *The First Blast of the Trumpet against the Monstrous Regiment of Women* (1558), had argued that a female ruler was 'a thing most odious in the presence of God'. Castilians, with Queen Isabella as a shining precedent, were not so prejudiced. In his *De rege* (1595), Juan de Mariana reminded his readers that the laws of Castile made no distinction between male and female where succession to the monarchy was concerned, and he saw no reason why they should be changed.[64] Don Pedro evidently agreed. And yet, while we can see how the Cristerna of *Afectos de odio y amor* (?1658), modelled on Queen Christina of Sweden, might be a plea for the independence of the Infanta María Teresa, and how the virtuous Queen María and the womanising King Pedro, protagonists of *Gustos y disgustos son no más que imaginación* (?1638), can be linked with Queen Isabel and Philip IV's then current infatuation with the Duchess of Chevreuse, the events that might have inspired *La gran Cenobia* are less obvious.[65] Philip and Isabel were married in 1616, when Philip was only eleven, although they did not live together until 1620. By the summer of 1625 they had produced only two daughters, both of whom had died, but the queen was pregnant again, and there was no immediate prospect of a female monarch, especially since Philip had two brothers (one of them admittedly a cardinal). Given this fact, and given also the moral rectitude of the completely invented Estela in *Amor, honor y poder*, we have to conclude that Calderón chose to portray upright and effective queens out of principle. Cenobia is courageous, intelligent, a successful military leader and a lawgiver, and, perhaps most important, she reacts stoically to the reverses of Fortune.

In 1625 the Spanish government, after several setbacks, had two significant military successes: the capture of the city of Breda in Flanders by Spanish troops under the Genoese Ambrogio Spinola, and the expulsion of the Dutch from the colony of La Bahía in Brazil. The story of the first is told in Calderón's play *El sitio de Bredá*, while the second is the subject of Lope de Vega's play *El Brasil restituido*. In both plays Spain's enemies are mostly Dutch. The siege of Breda ended in June 1625. Logic would suggest that the play was written and performed later that year, although 1628 has also been proposed.[66] Composition must be earlier than 1628, however, since Juan Acacio Bernal had a copy of *El sitio de Bredá* on 13 March 1627, in Valencia. The twenty-nine plays in Acacio's repertoire included other early Calderón plays: *Amor, honor y poder*, *Selvas y bosques de amor* and *Los Macabeos*.[67] The argument that the two plays were commissioned by the government soon after the events is supported by *La fe no ha menester armas, y venida del inglés a Cádiz* and *El socorro de Cádiz*, which were written to mark the containment of the Anglo-Dutch attack on Cadiz (November 1625). The first, by Rodrigo de Herrera, was apparently written between November 1625 and January 1626; and while the *auto El socorro de Cádiz* (Juan Pérez de Montalbán) is lost, we know that it was dated 6 April 1626, and that its characters included La Fe (Faith, the Infanta María), El Error (Error, Charles Stuart) and El Engaño (Deceit, Buckingham). To judge from *El caballero del sol*, commissioned by Lerma from Luis Vélez de Guevara in 1617 as an early commentary on the proposed Spanish Match, the government of Philip III was aware of the propaganda value of drama. Under Olivares, this awareness went as far as policy.

One way of looking at *El sitio de Bredá* is as a kind of war film, made to celebrate a victory early in the fourth year of what promised to be a long war: El Alamein, perhaps, in October–November of 1942. War films are likely to glorify military personnel, or to give relatively minor deeds an exaggerated importance; and they may try to introduce a 'love interest' that was absent from the original events. However, those produced during the conflict are rarely complimentary about the enemy. It comes as no surprise to find that Calderón heaps praise on the 'Allied' commanders, or even that he depicts a mutual attraction between Don Fadrique Bazán and Madama Flora, a young Dutch widow, or between Don Vicente Pimentel and Laura, who is also Dutch. Equally unsurprising is the response of the Marquis Balanzón to the news of the death of the Dutch leader, Maurice of Nassau: 'El primero es que me ahorró | de deçir: ¡Dios te perdone!' ('He's the first that saved me the trouble of saying, God forgive you': 2639–40).[68] What is unusual is the sympathetic portrayal of the enemy, from Justin of Nassau down, and including the remarks of Flora ('Confieso que en la defensa | de su rrelijión murió', 'I confess that he died in the defence of his religion': 495–6, made of her late husband) and of her son ('Mi padre perdió la vida | en defensa de su patria', 'My father lost his life defending his homeland': 639–40). Officially, the Dutch were rebels and heretics.

The most famous depiction of sympathy for the defeated Breda garrison is Velázquez's huge canvas, *La rendición de Bredá*, in which Spinola lays a comforting hand on Justin's shoulder, as he accepts from him the keys of the city. One might suppose that the painter inspired the poet, except that the canvas dates from 1634–5: the link ran from the poet to the painter.[69]

This capacity for empathy, which Calderón shared with Velázquez, is even more striking if we compare *El sitio de Bredá* with *El Brasil restituido*. As Spinola accepts the keys, he tells Justin:

Justino, yo las reçibo
y conozco que baliente
sois; quel balor del benzido
haze famoso al que benze. (3213–16)

(I accept them, Justin, and I recognise that you are valiant; for the valour of the vanquished makes the victor famous.)

In Lope's play, the Spanish general tells a colleague: 'No dan, Enrique, ocasión | de honor, enemigos viles' ('Base enemies give no opportunity for honour, Enrique').[70] While both plays were commissioned to mark victories, no instructions were given, presumably, about how to portray the Dutch. Calderón presents them with tolerance and respect. Lope portrays them with contempt, perhaps because he recalled that in 1621 the Olivares regime had ignored Spinola's advice to renew the twelve-year truce of 1609. Calderón's closing lines present him as the regime's obedient servant:

Y con esto se da fin
al *Sitio*, donde no puede
mostrarse más quien a escrito
obligado a tantas leyes. (3231–4)

(And with this the *Siege* comes to an end, in which he who has written it, constrained by so many laws, cannot show himself under more of an obligation.)

But he reminds the jingoistic that those who cannot show pity or respect for their opponents do not deserve to win.[71] A few years later, in *Mejor está que estaba* (?1631), the heroine's father, Don César, refers briefly to his youthful exploits involving a combat with two relatives of 'el gran príncipe de Orange' ('the great Prince of Orange': II, 405b), i.e., Maurice of Nassau. The ability to see the world from another point of view, to put oneself in the position of someone whom others see as a contemptible enemy, is a useful one for a dramatist.

CHAPTER 7

Blasphemy, sacrilege and lèse-majesté

Una oraçión se fragua
fúnebre, que es sermón de Berbería:
panegírico es que digo al agua,
y en emponomio horténsico me quejo.

(*El príncipe constante*)

(A funeral oration is being brewed, which is a Barbary sermon: it's a panegyric I'm saying to water, and I'm complaining in a hortensian emponomy.)

In 1627, as we know from Don Pedro's own account, his younger brother José joined the army: 'Siruiò a V. Magestad en los estados de Milan, Italia, y Flandes desde el año de seiscientos y veinte y siete' ('He served Your Majesty in the states of Milan, Italy and Flanders from 1627').[1] The same account indicates that the poet maintained a keen interest in his brother's career, with names and dates: he evidently missed him.

If 1627 marked a considerable change in the life of Don Pedro, it was to be a momentous year for the Spanish monarchy, in several ways. On 25 July 1626 Olivares had published the decree inaugurating his ambitious Union of Arms project, which was intended to distribute more equitably the cost of Spain's involvement in the Thirty Years War; that is, to relieve the burden on Castile. Predictably, the plan had attracted much opposition in Aragón, especially in Cataluña, where the Cortes had agreed to provide neither money nor men, a fact which the inauguration simply ignored. On 31 January 1627, the Crown suspended payments to its bankers, technically a declaration of bankruptcy, but in reality a way of changing from expensive Genoese bankers to cheaper Portuguese ones. Olivares then turned his attention to the *vellón* problem. *Vellón* was a copper-silver alloy which had been used in previous regimes to mint 'silver' coins with a higher face value than the intrinsic value of the metal: it was legal tender in Castile, but unacceptable anywhere else. To make matters worse, it was the target of counterfeiters. In February, jurisdiction in the trials of counterfeiters was turned over to the Inquisition, a piece of theological sleight-of-hand which was justified in *El monte de la piedad*, an *auto* written by Mira de Amescua, who was soon to collaborate with Calderón in *Polifemo y Circe*. At the same time, the favourite devised a scheme to 'consume' *vellón* coinage, that is, to withdraw it from circulation, since it was blamed for the fall of the real value of wages (20 per cent since 1622), although others thought the cause lay in the rumours that the government was planning to devalue *vellón* by as much as 50 per cent.[2]

On 23 August, at the height of the crisis, the king fell ill, so ill that there was talk of the succession, and a royal will was prepared. While the will stipulated that Olivares should continue in his position, and even that he would be responsible for the education of the queen's unborn child, he must have remembered how he and his uncle had seized power from Uceda as Philip III lay dying. As he did during some other crises, Olivares too fell ill. Stress and depression were almost certainly factors, but there is room for the belief that he exaggerated his symptoms to gain sympathy, and in the hope of making his opponents feel guilty. Significantly, the king's recovery – in the week of 4–10 September – coincided with his own. And while the sympathy, what there was of it, did not extend to the Council of Castile's agreement to devalue *vellón*, Philip at least felt guilty: he refused to accept Olivares's devious offer to resign, and summoned up a burst of bureaucratic energy; although, being Philip, he did not extend his efforts to his personal morals.

Sometime in 1627 (or, if not in 1627, the following year), Philip encountered Inés Calderón, another unrelated namesake of Don Pedro. Both Inés and her sister María, with whom she is sometimes confused, were actresses. A sobriquet, the prosaic La Calderona, and a portrait, now preserved in the Descalzas Reales, have survived, but these are a consequence of notoriety gained as the royal mistress, rather than of her fame on the stage, which she was too young to have acquired (Plate 14).[3] Deleito y Piñuela lists some of the extraordinary stories that have attached themselves to her, stories which lead us to doubt even the relatively plausible one that Philip first saw her while attending, incognito, a performance in the Corral de la Cruz in 1627, when she was sixteen.[4] The truth is that we have no reliable data about where Philip first saw her, but since companies performed frequently in the *alcázar*, usually in the *salón de palacio*, he may well have seen her there; she may even have been taking a role created by Don Pedro, since the accounts regularly refer to his plays.

The first record of Calderón's name in the palace accounts for 1627 is on 22 February, when Tomás Fernández was paid for a performance of *El alcaide de sí mismo*, a date which suggests that composition, and perhaps even the performance, could go back to 1626. Set in Naples, it tells how Federico, Prince of Sicily, who has killed Pedro Esforcia/Sforza in a joust, takes refuge, disguised, from the vengeance of Pedro's uncle, the King of Naples, and his sister Elena. Unaware of his identity, Elena makes him warden of the Castle of Belflor, to which is brought Benito, the peasant who found Federico's abandoned armour and put it on, only to be arrested as Federico. Federico, playing the warden, becomes the gaoler of Benito, forced to play Federico: hence the play's title. The play shows Calderón's interest in the process of 'putting on a performance', and how he could re-use and adapt situations, scenes, characters, jokes. Federico had won the affection of Margarita, Pedro's cousin, by pretending to be a jewel merchant and using his wares to tell his story (as Luis would do with Leonor in 1635, in *A secreto agravio*). Benito, wrongly taken for a prince, like Clarín in *La vida es sueño*, decides, as Clarín would put it, that 'fuerza es hacer mi papel' ('I must play my role'). Roberto, Federico's servant, even reports of Benito that 'dice que sueña | cuanto ve' ('he says he dreams all he sees': II, 820a). The plot is pretty implausible, but Calderón turns even this problem to advantage, as in other plays, by having Federico draw attention to it:

porque sepas
la novela más notable
que en castellanas comedias
sutil el ingenio traza,
y gustoso representa. (II, 821a)

(so that you may know of the most remarkable novel which was ever cunningly contrived among Spanish plays by inventive faculty, and pleasingly performed.)

Margarita, thinking that Federico is the imprisoned one, visits him, bringing a horse, weapons and money for his escape, as Flérida did for Enrico in *Amor, honor y poder*. Like Enrico, Federico has made a promise he will not break. Eventually, Federico's identity is revealed, and her father sanctions their marriage. The play is set in a sort of 'non-time', but the characters differ little from the minor nobles we find in plays with a contemporary Spanish setting: thus the King of Naples is the gruff father, anxious to find a suitable husband for his daughter; Federico is the young nobleman whom the daughter loves, but who has killed someone in a duel. Re-use of earlier material, adapted, extended to plot structures.

For a long time *La cisma de Ingalaterra* was considered a late play, inspired by the English Civil War and the execution of Charles I in January 1649.

The discovery that a royal performance was paid for in March 1627, and the conclusion, given the tardiness with which royal accounts might be settled, that it could have been written several months earlier, when Calderón was only twenty-six, prompts fresh consideration of his development. The 1627 performance could be of an early draft, but *La cisma* is an extraordinary play in several ways. First, it is an astonishingly sympathetic portrayal of Henry VIII, normally demonised in Spanish history for leading England away from the Church of Rome. For example, Calderón's source for the play was Pedro de Rivadeneyra, whose book on the schism was first published in 1588, the year of the Armada. Rivadeneyra is extremely hostile to Henry, Thomas Wolsey and Anne Boleyn, but Calderón's Enrique is a tragic character, the more so because he realises that his treatment of Catalina has inspired the fanaticism of their daughter María. The play ends with María recognised as heir, thanks to Enrique's assurance that

> Ella es cuerda, y sabrá bien
> moderarse, como cuerda. (2970–1)

(She is prudent, and she will know how to restrain herself, like a prudent woman.)

Any educated spectator knew that Mary was not prudent, and that even the counsel of her famously prudent husband had not made her moderate. *La cisma*, then, is the first play in which Calderón creates a powerfully ironic situation by allowing the audience's knowledge of history to contradict what the characters think has taken place.[5] Far from taking the orthodox Spanish line that Mary and her Catholic zeal could have been a solution to the situation, Calderón implies that she was part of the problem. The visit of Charles Stuart to Madrid in 1623 had led to war with England, and sensitive Spanish observers came to realise that English antipathy to Catholic rule had begun with Mary's religious persecutions.

One Rivadeneyra feature which Calderón retains in his portrayal of Anne and Wolsey is his warnings to kings against illicit relationships with women and against favourites. When the performance of *La cisma* was paid for, the illicit relationship with Inés Calderón was still in the future; but the relationship with the royal favourite was very much in the present.

There are other significant features in this play. The *octavas* in which Carlos describes his love and successful courtship of Ana (Anne Boleyn) constitute one of Calderón's finest (and most technically skilful) pieces of poetry. One of the images, a moth bewitched by a deadly flame, was used by Diego in *El astrólogo fingido*:

Sin que su riesgo tema,
mariposa iluminada,
de aquel fuego enamorada,
cercos hace, hasta que quema
las alas de tornasol. (II, 138a)

(Without fearing its peril, the brightly coloured moth, in love with that fire, flies in circles, until it burns its iridescent wings.)

In *La cisma* the adjective *iluminada* is transferred to a bee approaching a flower, while the moth image was developed into a rhetorical question:

¿No has visto enamorada mariposa
dar cercos a la luz, hasta que deja
en monumento fácil abrasadas
las alas de color tornasoladas? (409–12)

(Have you not seen a moth in love fly round the light, until its iridescent wings are burned to a fragile monument?)

Carlos is not one of those lovers whose fondness is diminished by possession: in a later scene (760–833), he and Ana tenderly proclaim their ostensibly undying affection. These sentiments, and these scenes, may be the product of a poetic imagination, but they must be modelled on real relationships, even if they were merely observed, not felt. However, when Don Pedro portrays these relationships, our only evidence for their basis in reality is the intensity with which they are depicted in the plays.

El hombre pobre todo es trazas (payment on 29 May 1627 to Roque de Figueroa for a royal performance) presents a con-man, Don Diego de Osorio. Like his namesake in *El astrólogo fingido*, Don Diego is ready to lie and deceive to get what he wants, but he is even less scrupulous, becoming entangled with two young women simultaneously, and lying about his financial prospects in order to borrow money. However, his view that 'engañarlas [= las damas] con industria | es más buen gusto que infamia' ('deceiving ladies by a ruse is more good taste than infamy': II, 230a) is flung back in his face, and, as the play ends, the other characters leave him alone on the stage; he is forced to admit that his experience will have a point if people learn a lesson from what has happened, 'mirando en mí castigadas | estas costumbres' ('seeing this behaviour punished in me': II, 231b).

This second experiment with character comedy presents a less sympathetic protagonist and spells out the consequences of his behaviour, and the play's moral, more clearly. While the author's impoverished family circumstances were probably in his mind as he wrote the play, there are two 'autobiographical' references. One involves an intelligent young noblewoman,

Beatriz de Córdoba, who writes verse, 'con que acabo de decir | que es pobre; porque a estas gracias | no se les sigue un cuatrín' ('with which I've just said that she's poor; for these gifts don't attract a penny': II, 203b); the other mentions taking sanctuary in an embassy after wounding a rival in a sword fight (II, 202a). There are also references to Mira de Amescua's play *Amor, ingenio y mujer* (published in 1640, composition date unknown) and to the bridge of Mantible (not necessarily to Calderón's play, first recorded in July 1630), as well as jokes about the philosopher Nicomedes (*ni comedes = ni coméis*, nor do you eat) and the Concilio Niceno (*ni ceno*, nor do I dine) which are also made by the hungry Clarín in *La vida es sueño* (II, 224b, 228b, 222a).

In 1628, the collection entitled simply *El cancionero de 1628* included an elegy by Calderón, *En la muerte de la señora doña Inés Zapata, dedicada a doña María Zapata* ('Sola esta vez quisiera'). It is easy to imagine, given the poem's lyricism and apparently genuine feeling, that Don Pedro had some degree of personal fondness for Inés, but we do not know if he knew her well, or slightly, or at all, or even when he wrote the poem; Zapata is too common a name for María and Inés to be identified with certainty. It contains a memorable epitaph:

> Aquí debajo de esta losa dura
> la hermosura naciera,
> si naciera sembrada la hermosura.[6]

(Here beneath this hard slab beauty would be born, if beauty were born when sown.)

There is also, in line 93, a noteworthy literary allusion, to *Nise* (= Inés) *laureada*, the tragedy of Jerónimo Bermúdez (alias Antonio de Silva), which tells the story of the famously beautiful Inés de Castro, who died (was killed) prematurely, but who was raised from beneath her *losa dura* to be crowned Queen of Portugal. Since *Nise laureada* was printed in Madrid in 1577, Calderón would not have had difficulty in laying hands on the text.[7]

The following year, 1629, there was published a volume which claimed to be Lope's *Veinte y tres parte de sus comedias, y la mejor parte que hasta oy se ha escrito*. The printer was ostensibly Miguel Sorolla of Valencia, and production was allegedly 'A costa de Luys de Soto Velasco vezino de Seuilla', 'at the expense of Luis de Soto Velasco, resident of Seville', but the preliminary leaves with this imprint are typographically different from the rest of the book, which is made up of twelve plays, each with separate pagination and signatures.[8] The date 1629 may be genuine, but the preliminaries were printed in Seville, and the plays had been printed there by Simón Fajardo a couple of years earlier; only three of them are indisputably by Lope. Two of the other nine are entitled *La industria contra el poder, y el honor contra la fuerza* and *La cruz en la sepultura*. The first of these is Calderón's *Amor, honor y poder*, which we know to have been written by the summer of 1623, and the second is an early version of *La devoción de la cruz*. These may be the first surviving prints of Calderón plays, and both have head-titles attributing them to Lope, quite apart from their appearance in a volume of 'Lope's plays'. Don Pedro would eventually develop a reputation for complaining about the publication of the plays of others under his name, and vice versa. *Parte 23* may have provided the starting-point for his resentment: it would be a strange author who would remain indifferent when his first printed plays were attributed to someone else, even if the someone else was Lope de Vega. One must say 'may have', since Lope was not the only author to have Calderón's work attributed to him: the library of the Hispanic Society of America has an apparently unique copy of a *suelta* of *La cruz en la sepultura* attributed to Juan Ruiz de Alarcón (Plate 15). The typography suggests production by Manuel de Sande of Seville, around 1628.

In the 1620s, Lope's reputation was at its height, and his was the name to guarantee sales. The publication of others' plays under his name had begun long before this, in 1603, with a volume ostensibly produced in Lisbon, entitled *Seis comedias de Lope de Vega Carpio y de otros autores*. The reference to 'other authors' concealed the fact that only two of the plays were by Lope. In 1612 his *Tercera parte de comedias* was printed in Seville by Gabriel Ramos Bejarano, using a false imprint ('Barcelona'). The refusal of licences to publish plays in Castile certainly led to a proliferation of these false imprints, and thus, arguably, to a greater degree of irresponsibility among printers and publishers, when it came to attributing texts to their real authors. As for Alarcón, if it now seems extraordinary that a printer should have credited such a 'minor' playwright with a work by Calderón, we need to remember that Alarcón's *Primera parte* was published in 1628, eight years before Don Pedro's.

La cruz en la sepultura was probably written some time before its approximate printing date of 1627–8, perhaps as early as 1623:[9] it is a forerunner of Calderón's 'wife-murder' plays, in that the husband has murdered his wife before the play opens. It is the first of his plays in which the selfish pride of a father blights the life of his children. In *Los comendadores de Córdoba* (written about 1597), Lope had turned honour-vengeance into a black farce, but this play adopts a different approach: Curcio's wife Rosmira is innocent, and although Curcio survives the catastrophe he has created, the remainder of his life will be very bleak. Curcio's children, Eusebio and Julia, are twins who do not know of their relationship (folklore held that male–female twins had different fathers). The fact that they almost have an incestuous affair has led to suggestions that this episode was inspired by real-life relationships in the Calderón family, such as between Calderón's sister Dorotea and his half-brother Francisco. These suggestions are unprovable. Delgado has quoted with approval John Varey's remark that the play, full of episodes based on contemporary theatre conventions, is the work of 'un escritor joven que está buscando su propio estilo' ('a young writer searching for his own style'), and has shown how the play has debts to Mira de Amescua's *El esclavo del demonio*, *Nardo Antonio, bandolero* and *La mesonera del cielo*, as well as to Luis Vélez's *La serrana de la Vera*; there are also parallels with Tirso's (?) *El condenado por desconfiado*, with the anonymous *La estrella de Sevilla* and Castro's *Las mocedades del Cid*.[10] Whatever the sources, the play contains themes to which Calderón returned again in later work: the Oedipus myth, the honour-obsessed husband, the father with a need to control his children's lives. When Curcio tells Julia that she is to become a nun, and that he has already said 'yes' on her behalf, her reply is that if he is to live her life for her, he can take the veil: 'Pues si tú vives por mí, | toma también el estado' ('Well, if you're living my life for me, take the status [= the veil] as well': 596–8). The middle-aged fathers in the audience cannot have liked this, but Curcio is a wretched man, unworthy of admiration. It is hard to believe that some thought of Dorotea – or of himself – did not cross Calderón's mind as he wrote these lines. The fact that the version which he published in his *Primera parte* is a revised one shows how the themes of the play continued to occupy his thoughts, and that he wanted to refine his expression of them.

There is no early record of a palace performance of *El purgatorio de San Patricio*, but the play was closely based on Pérez de Montalbán's *Vida y purgatorio de San Patricio*, the first edition of which appeared in 1627. The *Primera parte* tells us that the play was performed by Andrés de la Vega, and a poem of 1628 indicates that María de Córdoba, then Andrés's wife, took the role of Polonia.[11] This must have been sometime between mid 1627 and mid 1628. Many of the details of St Patrick's life are disputed, and Montalbán's book, which avoided the Castilian ban on the printing of novels because it was ostensibly hagiology, is inventively novelesque, as well as full of endearing anachronisms and inaccuracies.

Another possible influence on *El purgatorio* is *El condenado por desconfiado*, one of the first plays to juxtapose saint and sinner, although we cannot be sure about its date (or even about the identity of its author). The Enrico of *El condenado* has much in common with Ludovico Enio in *El purgatorio*: both are ostensibly Christian believers, but both have committed such horrific crimes that salvation seems impossible. Calderón had already explored this type of character with Eusebio and Julia in *La devoción de la cruz*, but here he invites comparison with both the saint Patricio and the atheist Egerio. Patricio is his first depiction of a saint, although plays about the lives of saints were an established genre. Here, as often happens, the sinner Ludovico is a much more interesting character. He also has a much larger role: the two speeches in which he describes, first, his life and crimes ('a mis delitos | ya les viene el mundo estrecho', 'the world is too narrow for my crimes', he says, in a phrase later used by Semíramis to quantify her ambition), and, later, his experiences in the cave total 750 lines, almost a quarter of the play. Ludovico is the major character, since he best illustrates the significance of the purgatory of the play's title.

La devoción de la cruz had explored the use of comic relief provided by Gil and Menga, a squabbling peasant/*gracioso* couple, who speak *sayagués*, the stylised language of stage rustics. Here, the exploration involves a possibly triangular relationship with a third character (Paulín and Locía, plus Filipo, a soldier). In *La hija del aire I* (?late 1630s) the relationship between Sirene, her husband Chato and the soldier Floro is developed further, although most of the commentary and parallels relating to the main characters are provided by Chato, particularly in Part II, after he is widowed. Perhaps the most accomplished use of this triangular situation is in *La púrpura de la rosa* (premiered 17 January 1660), where the Chato / Celfa / soldier Dragón threesome parodies and mocks the relationship between Adonis, Venus and Marte.

Although the play relies heavily on Pérez de Montalbán, to the extent of reproducing two of his errors, the play's modern editor has noted lesser debts to Góngora, Cervantes and Garcilaso. Calderón improves on Montalbán's curious (and tame) description of Ludovico seeing an image of himself on a piece of paper, replacing it by a lifesize phantom: the inspiration here may be Lope's *El caballero de Olmedo*, which probably dates from the early 1620s.

As noted in the previous chapter, *De un castigo tres venganzas* was printed in a collected volume which was licensed for printing on 27 October 1633. The surviving manuscript has been assigned to the period 1628–32.[12] Like *El alcaide de sí mismo*, it has a foreign setting (this time, Burgundy) in the indefinite past; and like that play, its plot, with an elderly father whose beautiful daughter attracts the attentions of several young nobles, has much in common with that of some cloak-and-sword comedies – until one of the nobles kills another.

The Duke of Burgundy, Carlos, 'lord of the house of Austria', inevitably recalls Charles V, who referred to Burgundy as 'nuestra patria' ('our homeland'), and who brought the title of Duke of Burgundy to the Crown of Spain. Carlos's ruse, to pretend to want Federico garrotted secretly in the castle of Torreblanca for his alleged treason, just as inevitably recalls the Baron de Montigny, garrotted secretly for alleged treason in the castle of Simancas by order of Philip II. There are other, more literary relationships: the drug given to Federico in his wine produces the same effect, apparent death, as the 'distilled liquor' taken by Juliet: no doubt Calderón, like Shakespeare, found it in Bandello. As we shall see, an *entremés* which can be dated to Carnival 1631 mentions five play titles, four by Calderón and *De un castigo dos venganzas*, which is by Pérez de Montalbán. The word 'dos' may be a slip for 'tres', since one guess dates the Montalbán play to 1625–6.[13] It seems likely, in any case, that 'dos venganzas' preceded 'tres venganzas', and the titles may have influenced Lope in choosing the title of *El castigo sin venganza*, which he completed in August 1631.[14]

As noted above (Chapter 6, n. 39), Roque de Figueroa received payment in March 1628 for a royal performance of *Saber del mal y del bien*. The setting is the reign of Alfonso VII of Castile (1105–57), and the source has been identified as Lope's *Las mudanzas de la fortuna y sucesos de don Beltrán de Aragón*.[15] Alfonso was proclaimed king as a child, and eventually acquired a considerable reputation in the Reconquest. As a young man, he had to wrest his kingdom from his widowed mother, Urraca, and her 'friend', the Conde de Lara, Don Pedro González. Of the count, the principal historian of Calderón's time tells us that 'la soberuia de sus costumbres, y su arrogancia, tenia alterados los coraçones de muchos, que publicamente le odiauã' ('the haughtiness of his behaviour and his arrogance changed for the worse the hearts of many, who publicly hated him'). His enemies first imprisoned him, then released him, but 'los de Castilla ... tanto le aborrecian' ('the Castilians hated him so much') that he had to take refuge in Barcelona.[16] In the play the king is young, but old enough to have dishonourable intentions with regard to Hipólita, the younger sister of Don Pedro. Don Pedro is the royal *privado*, and although he admits that 'está Castilla | deshecha en parcialidades | con mi privanza' ('Castile is divided into factions because of my position as favourite': 1, 120b), his only wish is to serve the king and the kingdom faithfully. The parallels between the lecherous young Alfonso with his older *privado*, the count, and the real-life Philip IV and his Conde-Duque (about whom opinions were also divided) seem obvious now. In the play, the *privado* is disgraced when his enemies forge an incriminating letter. The king suspects that the letter is a fake, but decides to teach the count a lesson: 'Yo soy rey, y yo puedo | vivir sin vos' ('I am king, and I can live without you': 1, 129b); his property is confiscated, and he has to leave court.[17]

Ostensibly, the play deals with the rise and fall of several twelfth-century characters (including servants), as their fortunes change, and they experience both 'bien' and 'mal', as well as realising that things are not what they seem (in this context Calderón quotes Leonardo de Argensola's famous line about the sky: 'ni es cielo ni es azul', 'it is not heaven and it is not blue').[18] The count's position is eventually restored, but he admits to having learned from his experience. The king learns that 'más quiere | quien llega a querer de veras, | el honor de lo que ama, | que el fin de lo que desea' ('he loves more who really wants the honour of what he loves than the end of what he desires': I, 138b). The play could be represented as a commentary on the regimes of Lerma and Uceda, but the parallels between that of Philip IV and Olivares are far more obvious: most interesting is the suggestion that both *privado* and king should realise that the *privado* is not indispensable. If Olivares knew or checked the facts about 'his' character, he cannot have enjoyed being reminded that the Conde de Lara's *privanza* not only provoked dissension, but also ended in failure and exile; and that once exiled, he was not recalled.

Curiously, the 'manifesto of the nobles' which was circulated in June 1629 expresses a number of the themes of the play: the favourite's loyalty and good intentions on the one hand, and, on the other, the opposition, not to say enmity, which his policies and *arrogancia* aroused.[19] The play cannot be inspired by the manifesto, which was produced over a year later. It is tempting to suppose that the manifesto was inspired by the play, but opposition to his regime had been of concern to Olivares for several years previously, reaching a high point in 1627, the year before the play was performed. Don Pedro must have known of this, but this play should not tempt us to conclude that he had joined the opposition. Rather, we should see it as an early example of what his Alexander the Great character later called 'knowing how to speak to the king': that is, of making unpalatable facts palatable, of presenting constructive criticism without seeming disloyal: hence the alteration of history to portray the reinstatement of the favourite. Once we are aware of this, we can see numerous other examples throughout Calderón's career.

El príncipe constante was apparently written in late 1628 and early 1629, to judge from events connected with it. The events are referred to in an undated letter from Lope de Vega to his patron, the Duke of Sessa, in a memorial written by Fray Hortensio Paravicino, royal preacher (Plate 16), to the king, and in the comments on the memorial which were written by Cardinal Don Gabriel de Trejo y Paniagua, president of the Council of Castile.[20] In January 1629 an actor named Pedro de Villegas stabbed one of Don Pedro's brothers and took refuge in the church of the Convento de las Trinitarias Descalzas in the Calle de Cantarranas (now Lope de Vega). The convent, founded in 1612, was the burial-place of Cervantes in 1616, the year his daughter Isabel took her vows there; Lope's daughter Marcela joined her there in 1623 as a novice. More useful information, such as where the stabbing took place, why, and which brother was involved, is elusive. Cantarranas, however, was in the theatre quarter, so the crime is likely to have taken place there or nearby. Lope's letter gives more information: postponing a meeting planned for that evening, he refers to

> la reboluçión de nuestras Monjas, la molestia de los Alcaldes, la prisión de nuestro sacristán y las diligençias para librarle … Grande la sido el rigor buscando a Pedro de Villegas: el Monesterio, roto, la clausura, y aun las imágenes; que hay alcalde que se traga más excomuniones que vn Oydor memoriales. Ana de Villegas con guardas, el mozo en Osuna y la justicia buscándole entre las Monjas, a quien sacrílegamente han dado los golpes que pudieran a Cristo, si le hallaran en defensa de sus esposas …

> (the disturbance of our nuns, the bother of the law officers, the imprisonment of our sacristan and the efforts to release him … There has been a relentless search for Pedro de Villegas: the convent, the cloister, even the images damaged; for there are law officers who can cope with more excommunications than a judge can briefs. Ana de Villegas under guard, the lad in Osuna and the police looking for him among the nuns, who were sacrilegiously struck the blows the officers might have bestowed on Christ, had they found him defending his brides …)

The Villegas family were probably acquaintances of Calderón, since most of them were involved in the theatre. The parents were the actors Antonio de Villegas and Ana Muñoz, and Ana de Villegas had been baptised on 19 September 1602.[21] Ana, her sister María and her brother Juan were all actors, while Juan also wrote plays; their brother Francisco was a poet.[22] Plays like *La dama duende* (written later that year) depict brothers who are prepared to use violence against their sisters or their supposed male friends, in defence of what they believe to be their honour. Young Pedro ('el mozo') possibly considered that his sister or the Calderón brother had said or done something inappropriate. Since José Calderón was serving abroad and Diego recently married, the half-brother Francisco is the likely brother; whichever it was, he survived, as did the acting career of Pedro de Villegas. Since the stabbing was done 'alevosamente', 'treacherously', canon law gave the aggressor no right to sanctuary. In Paravicino's words, 'siguióle la Iustiçia, el hermano, parientes y otra muchedunbre grande, y él, buscando su natural defensa, halló medio como ocultarse, dicen que dentro de la clausura' ('he was followed by the law officers, the brother, relatives and a large crowd, and he, seeking his natural defence, found a way to hide, allegedly inside the cloister'). The *alcaldes*, Don Pedro, the 'relatives' (who were they?) and the crowd followed into the cloister. Doors were allegedly burst open and nuns' veils removed in the search. In particular, he claimed, Calderón was moved 'a profanar entre la sangre de su hermano la de las Religiossas Trinitarias' ('to profane amid his brother's blood that of the Trinitarian nuns'). Paravicino was himself a Trinitarian. 'Informado de Relijiossos graues' ('informed by important men of the cloth') (one of them his friend Lope de Vega, an interested party?), he was suitably outraged, and chose to refer to the event in a sermon preached to the king on 11 February at a royal memorial service. We cannot be sure when *El príncipe constante* was completed, but after the play was approved for performance by Pedro de Vargas Machuca, Don Pedro added some lines at the point when the *gracioso* Brito is voicing his relief at having survived the sea voyage to North Africa. Asked what he is saying, he replies, as quoted by Paravicino:

Vna oraçión se fragua
fúnebre, que es sermón de Berbería:
panegírico es que digo al agua,
y en emponomio horténsico me quejo;
porque este enojo, desde que se fragua
con ella el vino, me quedó, y ya es viejo.

(A funeral oration is being brewed, which is a Barbary sermon: it's a panegyric I'm saying to water, and I'm complaining in a hortensian emponomy, because, since the wine got watered, I was left with this anger, and now it's old.)

The exact meaning of the lines was disputed. *Emponomio* is not in the dictionaries, but it was clear that the hyperbolic rhetoric of Fray Hortensio's sermons was being mocked.[23] The preacher was incandescent with rage, and produced a document of six folio leaves, in which he accused Calderón of blasphemy, defamation, sacrilege and *lèse-majesté*, not to mention the initiation of the destruction of religion in Spain, as Luther had done in Germany. All this was made worse by the fact that Calderón had not acted in the heat of the moment, but 'después de muchos días', 'después de una quaresma de amenaças y palabras indignas' ('after many days', 'after a Lent full of threats and disgraceful words'). Plays were not performed in Lent. Ash Wednesday had fallen on 28 February, Easter Sunday on 15 April, so that the performance of 'last Friday' to which Paravicino refers was possibly on 20 April. What was worse, not only did Calderón refuse to delete the offending passage after one performance, but also 'se arrojó él a que se representase a V^a^. M. el domingo en la noche' ('he was determined to have it played to Your Majesty on the Sunday night': 22 April, the first Sunday after Easter?). The 'amenaças y palabras indignas' were apparently a reference to a visit paid to Paravicino by a Calderón uncle (we cannot tell which),[24] presumably in an attempt to persuade Paravicino to drop the matter. Although action had been taken by the time the memorial was written, with Calderón under house arrest, it was far too little to satisfy Paravicino: he protested that house arrest was 'tratamiento de vn Gran Señor en vn hombre particular' ('treatment of a private individual like a great lord'). We cannot be certain what the king's view was, but Paravicino himself gives a hint: 'si V^a. M. … se a diuertido con mi dolor …' ('if Your Majesty … was entertained by my suffering …'). Perhaps Philip was seen to be amused at the relevant point during the royal performance: he had only just turned twenty-four. Whether or not he was diverted by Paravicino's discomfiture, he did the proper thing, and passed the memorial to Cardinal Trejo, president of the Council of Castile.

Trejo, born in Plasencia in 1562, educated at Salamanca University, was both a knight of Alcántara and bishop of Salerno. Ironically enough, he owed his post as president of the Council (to which he was appointed in March 1627) to a recommendation by Paravicino.[25] He was thorough. He called for the manuscript text of the play, and noted that the offending lines were later additions, made – in his view – by the same hand as had written the rest, namely, Calderón's. The censor, Vargas Machuca, and the actors, were not to blame. On the other hand, the police had been doing their job; they had every right to enter the convent, and the nuns might have been punished for not ejecting the fugitive immediately. Fray Hortensio should be told that those who objected so strongly to their words being criticised should themselves abstain from inappropriate criticism. As for Calderón, who had broken the law by tampering with the text of a play after it had been approved, 'se castigará al Poeta en la forma q[ue] [V.]M. lo mandó, o en la q[ue] agora fuere seruido' ('the poet will be punished in the manner which Your Majesty ordered, or in that which may now please Your Majesty'). This order presumably involved the house arrest; so far as we know, the king took no further action. The claim that the police – and Calderón – had used excessive force had already been investigated: 'El consejo informó de la uerdad de todo i de los casos en q[ue] se auía hecho lo mismo; con q[ue] V. M. quedó satisfecho' ('The Council investigated the truth of the whole matter, and of the cases in which the same had been done: with which Your Majesty was satisfied').[26] Clearly this complaint was also dismissed. Another claim by Paravicino, which had nothing to do with the case, that Calderón 'en los Ángeles este mismo Año dio un bofetón, diçen, a vn honrrado caballero' ('they say that this very year he slapped the face of an honourable gentleman in los Ángeles'), was not even referred to.[27]

Calderón had perhaps been fortunate, or perhaps he knew Philip IV well enough to be sure where his sympathies would lie. Born in 1580 in Madrid, Paravicino was by 1629 a considerable literary figure, whose friends included, or had included, El Greco (d. 1614), Valdivielso, Góngora (d. 1627, whom Calderón greatly admired) and Lope, whom no young playwright would readily antagonise. Some of his poetry now seems unusually erotic for a celibate; he had even written a play, *La Gridonia, o cielo de amor vengado*. Linguistic extravagance had helped make his reputation as poet and preacher. In his memorial, however, extravagance became ridiculous overstatement, which greatly damaged his case; and he did himself no good by implying that the Council of Castile was neglecting its duties. Calderón's own resentment is significant. We cannot assume that he knew as much about the laws of sanctuary as he did when he wrote *La inmunidad del sagrado* in 1664, but the episode provides further evidence that his belief that he was in the right could make him act unwisely. The fact that his vengeance (Paravicino's word) took literary form casts doubt on the claim about the slap in the face. The claim, corroborated only by Paravicino's 'diçen', would be laughed out of any modern court. Constandse's assertion, made with no supporting evidence, that the 'chevalier honorable … sans doute lui avait rappelé le père' ('the honourable gentleman no doubt reminded him of his father'), is one that Paravicino himself might have made, had he ever heard of the Oedipus complex.[28] However, it is thanks to Paravicino that we know that *El príncipe constante* was performed by the company of Bartolomé Romero, who paid Don Pedro 800 *reales* for the play. The role of Brito was taken by 'Thomas, Representante graçiosso'; he can be plausibly identified with Tomás Enríquez, who was regularly with Romero's company between 1626 and 1643.[29]

The text of *El príncipe constante* survives in two versions: that printed in Calderón's *Primera parte* in 1636, and a seventeenth-century manuscript copy.[30] The main sources of the play were an older play, *La fortuna adversa del infante don Fernando de Portugal*, possibly written by Tárrega in the late 1590s, and surviving only as a *desglosada* of unexplored date, and Manuel de Faría e Sousa's *Epítome de las historias portuguesas* (1628).[31] Writing in 1940 about Calderón's historical drama, Lucy Weir stated that 'he sometimes loses sight of the historical facts for the sake of the dramatic situation, or carries his technique to a point where the story must be readjusted in order that the technique may not suffer'.[32] Precisely, we might now say, adding that the dramatic situation, for Don Pedro, clearly took precedence over the historical facts – as Aristotle had said. The historical Ferdinand was a minor figure compared with his famous brother, Henry the Navigator. In the play, 'the historical Henry, intrepid and cool, is converted into an anxious earthbound second to his brother Fernando: Enrique's diffidence sets into relief Fernando's confidence'.[33] All of the other major characters, in fact, are foils for Fernando: Muley, the 'noble Moor', and Fénix, the melancholy princess, prone both to an Islamic fatalism; or the King of Fez, a generous opponent until his wishes are thwarted. The remark of the *gracioso*, Brito ('ainda mortos, somos portugueses': 'even dead, we're Portuguese'), prepares us for Fernando's triumph in death. The triumph extends to the fulfilment of Fernando's wish that his friend and opponent Muley should be united with Fénix, despite the desire of her father, the king, to marry her to Tarudante, King of Morocco.

One casualty of the Paravicino affair was Calderón's relationship with Lope de Vega. Lope had noticed Don Pedro in 1620, and printed two of his poems. Two years later he published more, and was warm in his praise. In July–September 1628 (?) he had written a letter to Antonio de Mendoza in which he described a friendly dramatic competition:

Estos dias se decretó en el senado comico que Luis Velez, don Pedro Calderon y el dotor [Antonio Mira de] Mesqua hiciesen vna comedia, y otra, en conpetençia suya, el dotor [Juan Pérez de] Montalban, el dotor [Felipe] Godinez y el liçenziado Lope de Vega, y que se pusiese vn xarro de plata en premio. Respondi que era este año capellan mayor de la Congregacion, y que para el que viene açetaua el desafio.[34]

(In these last few days it was decreed in the comic senate that Luis Vélez, Don Pedro Calderón and Doctor Mira de Amescua should write a play, and that Doctor Pérez de Montalbán, Doctor Godínez and the Licenciate Lope de Vega should write another in competition, and that a silver jug should be put up as a prize. I answered that this year I was chief chaplain of the congregation, and that I accepted the challenge for the following one.)

Vélez was one of Calderón's collaborators in *Enfermar con el remedio* (date unknown), and Mira in *Polifemo y Circe* (1630), but no play involving all three has survived; one suspects that the plays were never written because of the Paravicino affair. Lope mentioned Calderón again only once, in Silva VII of his *Laurel de Apolo* (1630), and that with no reference to any plays:

Con decirte las señas,
aunque callase el nombre celebrado,
desde las tuyas a las altas peñas
del alto Pindo, del licor bañado
a cuya orilla los ingenios nacen,
que las doctas vigilias satisfacen,
que era don Pedro Calderón dirías:

verdades son, que no lisonjas mías,
que en estilo poético y dulzura
sube del monte a la suprema altura.[35]

(With my giving you the description [he is addressing Apollo], though I do not give the name which is celebrated from your crags to the high crags of tall Pindus, bathed in the liquid on whose shore are born the talented individuals who honour learned nocturnal study, you will say that it is Don Pedro Calderón; these are truths, not my flatteries; for in poetic style and sweetness he climbs to the mountain's supreme height.)

Conceivably Lope was reluctant to offend Paravicino by saying more, but since the *Laurel de Apolo* omitted no one who had ever written verse, the inclusion proves little. We may compare these vague praises with those of Lope's disciple Pérez de Montalbán, in his *Para todos* (1632):

Don Pedro Calderon, florido, galante, heroico, lirico, comico, y bizarro poeta, ha escrito muchas comedias, autos y obras sueltas, con aceptacion general de los doctos. En las Academias ha tenido lugar primero: en los certamenes ha ganado los mejores premios, y en los teatros la opinion mas segura, y tiene tambien empezado a escribir para dar a la estampa un elegantissimo poema que llama El diluvio general del mundo.[36]

(Don Pedro Calderón, an elegant, polished, heroic, lyric, comic and spirited poet, has written many plays, *autos* and separate works, with the widespread acceptance of the learned. In the academies he has taken first place; in competitions he has won the best prizes; in the theatres, the most unfaltering reputation; and he has also begun to write for the press an extremely elegant poem called *The Flood*.)

Despite these generous remarks (so generous that they referred to a poem which, to our knowledge, was never published separately), Don Pedro did not contribute to the *Fama póstuma* poetry collection published by Montalbán in 1636 in honour of Lope.[37] While Calderón had nursed his grievance against Paravicino for the six weeks of Lent, it may be that the seven years between the affair and the *Fama póstuma* were not enough for him to forgive Lope's role in the matter. This argument is supported by the fact that Don Pedro wrote two contributions for the *Lágrimas panegíricas* published to mark the premature death of Montalbán in 1638.[38]

As for *vellón*, Olivares finally got his way in August 1628, when it was devalued by 50 per cent. Despite months of rumour, many *vellón*-holders suffered substantial losses, while people with connections benefited from advance warning. We cannot say whether the son of a former treasury official still had the right connections, or had been wise enough to foresee the devaluation, but it does not seem likely that our Don Pedro had substantial savings in any type of coin.

CHAPTER 8

Lessons for controlling personalities

Sirva de ejemplo este raro
espectáculo, esta extraña
admiración, este horror,
este prodigio. (*La vida es sueño*)

(May this extraordinary spectacle, this singular cause of wonder, this horror, this marvel, serve as an example.)

Two of Philip IV's sons were born in 1629. The first, by La Calderona, was christened Juan José on 21 April; the surname, de Austria, was added in 1642, when Philip recognised him officially, the only one of his allegedly numerous illegitimate children to enjoy this status. The second son, by Queen Isabel, was born on 17 October and christened Baltasar Carlos.[1] For Isabel, it was a momentous event: this was her fifth pregnancy, but no child still survived from the previous four. As for Juan José's mother, she supposedly begged the king to be allowed to take the veil; there is evidence that she eventually became abbess in Valfermoso de las Monjas in the Utande valley, some 55 miles to the north-east of Madrid.[2] For a royal playwright who already had a history of drawing attention to chastity as a kingly virtue, a royal bastard was something of an embarrassment, although Juan José's recognition and political ambitions would turn him into a figure who could not be ignored. A crown prince was another matter: his birth and deeds were fitting subjects for mention; and his fatal accident on 9 October 1646, with the resulting closure of the public theatres, was one of the factors which led to Calderón's ceasing to write for them.

A play entitled *El médico de su honra* was performed on 8 October 1629 (or, just possibly, 1628).[3] It now seems likely that this performance was of Calderón's version of the drama. Set in the reign of Peter of Castile (1350–69), in the immediate aftermath of the Black Death, his play portrays a sick society obsessed with honour and reputation, ruled over by a king whose concern for his position eventually detaches him from reality. While the main plot deals with an excessively punctilious husband whose imagination convinces him of his wife's infidelity, the omnipresent obsession with reputation is bound to remind us that this was the driving force of the foreign policy of the Olivares regime. It is possible to see in this play and its later companion piece, *A secreto agravio, secreta venganza* (1635), the implication that too great a concern for *opinión* might be mistaken, especially if it were sought on a foreign battlefield, as is foreseen with King Sebastián in the second play.

The vocabulary we use in the context of prose fiction includes the expression 'unreliable narrator'. Just as the novelist needs to curb the reader's natural tendency to identify with the first-person storyteller, so the dramatist may need to find ways in which members of the audience can become aware of the unreliability of the character who addresses them directly, either in a soliloquy or in an aside. In *La cisma de Ingalaterra* Calderón had presented a flawed but tragic king, but this was a historical personage whom the audience had expected to be flawed. In *El médico de su honra*, he could make use of audience awareness of the ambiguous reputation of King Peter (the Cruel, the Justicer), but a fictional character like Gutierre is different. Gutierre has several soliloquies, including the longest speech in the play, so we can guess at Calderón's concern to give the character the opportunity to reveal his traits, and his thought processes, through his imagery. The audience needs to be alert, though, to detect the flaws in Gutierre's rhetoric, and to draw conclusions about the flawed mind that produces it.

Luis Pérez el gallego is an unusual play, not to say a strange one. The confused palace accounts indicate a performance on 21 December by Antonio de Prado in 1628 or 1629, probably the latter.[4] The plot is supposedly based on the deeds of a real person; references to the fleet, to England, to the role of the duke in Sanlúcar (the Duke of Medina Sidonia) place the events in early 1588. An exchange with the *gracioso*, Pedro ('Humor | gastáis … gasto lo que tengo', 'You are lavish with your joviality. – I spend what I have': I, 152a), recalls a similar one involving Becoquín in *De un castigo tres venganzas* ('Vos gastáis buen humor … cada uno gasta lo que tiene', 'You are lavish with your joviality … Everyone spends what he has': I, 193a–b); and some of the wording of Luis's opening *silvas* of Act III ('Este monte eminente, | cuyo arrugado ceño, cuya frente | es dórica coluna', 'This lofty mountain, whose wrinkled frown, whose brow is a Doric column': I, 165a) looks ahead to lines 14–16 of the first version of *La vida es sueño* ('la aspereza enmarañada | deste monte eminente, | que arruga al Sol el ceño de su frente', 'the tangled ruggedness of this lofty mountain, which wrinkles its frowning brow in the sun').[5] At the same time the words 'mejor está que estaba' ('it is better than it was': I, 154b) remind us to be careful: the phrase is proverbial, and *Mejor está que estaba* had yet to be written.

Luis Pérez is best described as a principled anarchist. He reminds us of E. M. Forster: 'If I had to choose between betraying my country and betraying my friend, I hope I should have the guts to betray my country.' If a friend comes to Luis and says, as he puts it himself, 'Luis Pérez, | un hidalgo dejo muerto, | conmigo traigo una dama | y a vuestra casa me vengo' ('Luis Pérez, I've killed a nobleman, I've got a lady with me, and I've come to your house': I, 148a), he will help the friend, even against the forces of the law. As a consequence, his property is seized by the authorities and auctioned off to the local peasants, and he is reduced to genteel banditry: '¡Bueno es querer reducir | a estilo noble y cortés | el hurtar!' ('It's a fine thing to reduce theft to a noble and genteel way of behaving!': I, 168a), as his friend Manuel puts it. We have all seen Westerns like this, or modern cops-and-robbers films, in which an honourable person is sucked into crime and personal disaster by a combination of bad luck and the unreflecting application of an otherwise laudable code of behaviour. Short of a royal pardon, there is no road back for Luis (such pardons were sometimes granted, conditional upon enlistment in the army). The play ends in a rush, with Luis rescued at sword-point from the authorities. That this could be only a temporary respite is acknowledged by the promise of a second part, which Don Pedro never wrote.[6]

In 1629 Calderón also wrote *Casa con dos puertas mala es de guardar* and *La dama duende*, his first efforts in what would be one of his most successful genres: the situation comedy. These first attempts are arguably his best and almost certainly his most successful. The exact nature of the obvious relationship between the two plays has been complicated by Don Pedro's habit of tinkering with his texts. *Casa con dos puertas* is set in Ocaña, which is about 10 miles south-east of Aranjuez, 'admirable | dosel de la primavera', where the king and queen are on holiday ('a wonderful canopy of spring': II, 279b). However, Laura, one of the female protagonists, is so depressed that even seeing the queen has failed to cheer her up:

> ni el ver la Reina,
> que infinitos siglos viva,
> para que flores de Francia
> nos den el fruto en Castilla ... (II, 297b)

(not even seeing the queen, may she live for infinite centuries, so that the flowers of France may give us fruit in Castile ...)

1 Anon., *Alcázar* [top left] *and Puente de Segovia*, seventeenth century (Caylus Anticuario, Madrid / Bridgeman Art Library)

2 The Puente de Segovia today (author)

3 The *mudéjar* archway of the Torre de los Lujanes (author)

4a The ancestral home, Viveda, seen from the west (author)

4b The coat of arms on the ancestral home (author)

5 Juan Pantoja de la Cruz, *Philip III*, 1606 (Museo Nacional del Prado, Madrid)

6 Peter Paul Rubens, *Duke of Lerma*, 1603
(Museo Nacional del Prado, Madrid)

7 Calderón's house, now in the Calle Mayor, Madrid (author)

8 Anon., *Fiesta in the Plaza Mayor*, seventeenth century (Caylus Anticuario, Madrid / Bridgeman Art Library)

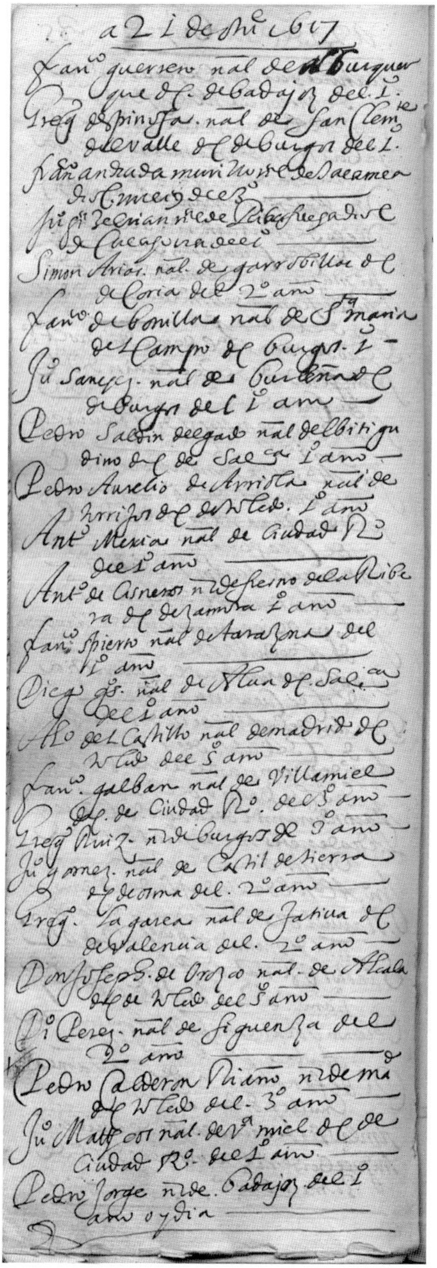

9 Entry of 'Pedro Calderon Riaño' in University of Salamanca matriculation book, 21 October 1617 (third name up) (Archivo Histórico, Universidad de Salamanca)

10 Signatures of Licenciado Francisco de Montalvo and Calderón, 21 November 1624 (Archivo Histórico de Protocolos Notariales, Madrid, tomo 5049, fol. 475v)

11 Velázquez, *D. Diego de Corral*, ?*c.* 1631 (Museo Nacional del Prado, Madrid)

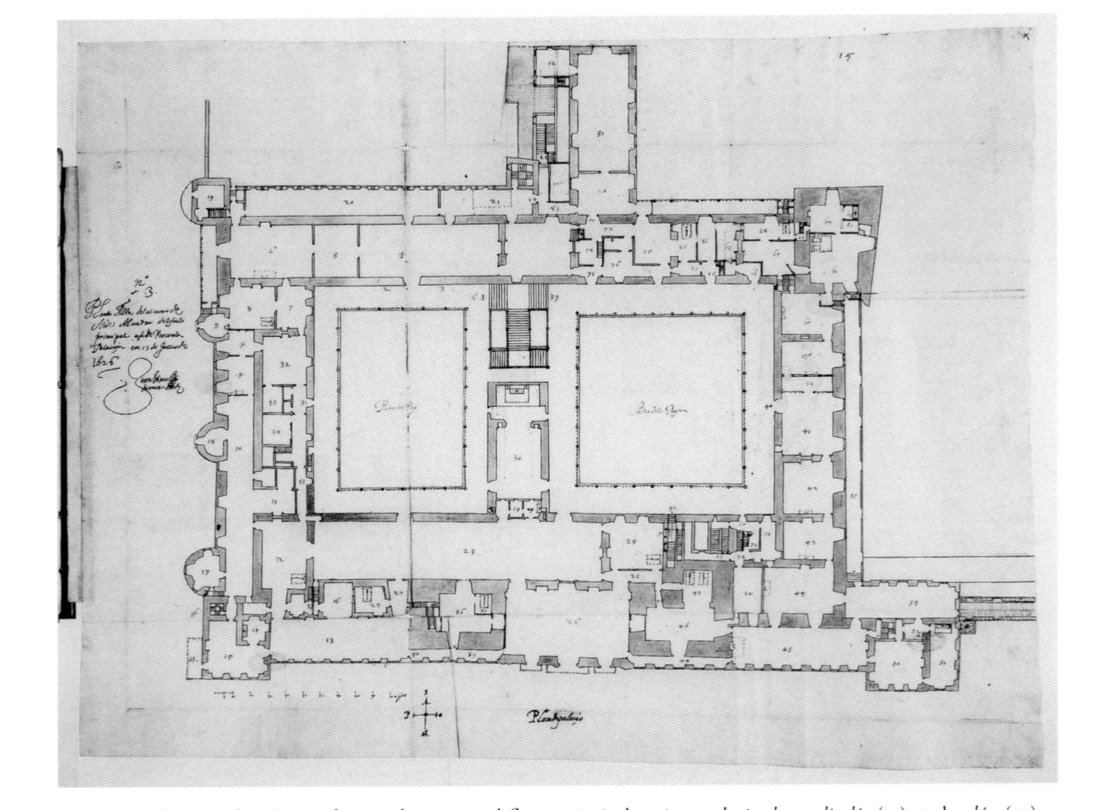

12 Juan Gómez de Mora, *alcázar* plan, second floor, 1626, showing *galería de mediodía* (13) and *salón* (23) (Biblioteca Apostolica Vaticana, Rome)

13 Velázquez, *Philip IV*, 1623 (Museo Nacional del Prado, Madrid)

14 Anon., *Alegoría de la vanidad* (*La Calderona*), *c.* 1629
(Monasterio de las Descalzas Reales, Madrid: © Patrimonio Nacional)

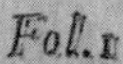
Fol. 1

LA CRVZ EN LA SEPVLTVRA.

COMEDIA FAMOSA

DE DON IVAN DE ALARCON.

Representòla Auendaño.

Hablan en ella las personas siguientes.

Menga.	*Teresa.*	*Ricardo.*
Gil.	*Iulia.*	*Alberto.*
Lisardo.	*Arminda.*	*Leonelo.*
Eusebio.	*Curcio viejo.*	*Vn Pintor.*
Bras.	*Otauio.*	*Vn Poeta.*
Vato.	*Celio.*	*Vn Astrologo.*

IORNADA PRIMERA.

Salen Menga y Gil.
Men. Merà por do va la burra.
Gil. Io dimuño, jo malina,
Men. Ya verà por do camina,
arre aca, el diabro me aburra.
Gil. No ay quien de la cola tenga,
pudiendo tenerla mil.
Men. Buena haziēda as hecho Gil;
Gi. Buena haziēda as hecho Mēga
que tu la culpa tuuiste,
que como yuas cauallera,
que en el lodo le cayera

A al

15 'Juan [Ruiz] de Alarcón', *La cruz en la sepultura* [Seville: Manuel de Sande, *c.* 1628] (Courtesy of the Hispanic Society of America, New York)

16 El Greco, *Fray Hortensio Paravicino*, 1609
(Photograph © 2009 Museum of Fine Arts, Boston)

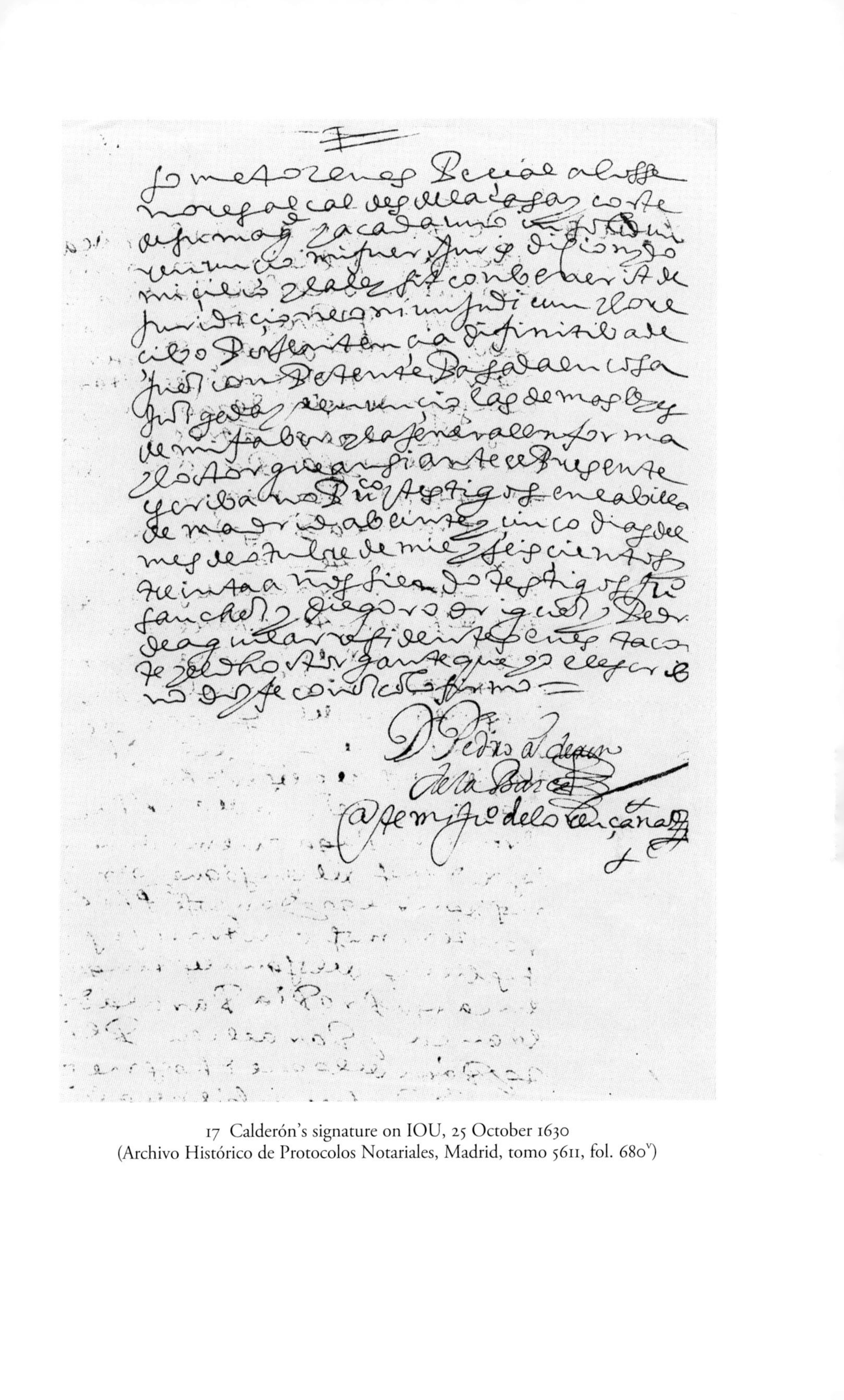

17 Calderón's signature on IOU, 25 October 1630
(Archivo Histórico de Protocolos Notariales, Madrid, tomo 5611, fol. 680v)

18 Francisco de Herrera, el mozo, *Salón dorado*, *c.* 1672 (Austrian National Library, Vienna, Picture Archive)

Fol. 1.

LA PVENTE DE MANTIBLE.

COMEDIA FAMOSA.

DE LOPE DE VEGA CARPIO.

Repreſentòla Granados.

Hablan en ella las perſonas ſiguientes.

El Emperador Carlomagno.	*Fierabras.*
Guido de Borgoña.	*Guarin.*
Floripes.	*Roldan.*
Oliueros.	*Ricarte.*
Yrene.	*Y otros Caualleros*
Arminda.	*Franceſes.*

IORNADA PRIMERA.

Salen Guido, y Oliueros, de Franceſes galanes, con vandas en los roſtros, Fierabras, y Moros deteniendole, Floripes, Yrene, y Arminda, de Turcas, y han ſonado primero caxas y trompetas.

Gui. Solo el valor merece
de mi braço eſta vanda, ſi os parece,
bizarros Caualleros,
que la podeys cobrar, ſean los azeros

A arbitrios

19 'Lope de Vega', *La puente de Mantible* [Seville: Simón Fajardo, *c.* 1632] (Austrian National Library, Vienna)

LA VIDA ES SVEÑO

COMEDIA FAMOSA.

DE LOPE DE VEGA.

Hablan en ella las perſonas ſigientes.

Baſilio Rey, viejo.	*Crotaldo viejo.*
Aſtolfo.	*Sigiſmundo.*
Roſaura.	*Eſtrella.*
Clarin.	*Criados.*

Repreſentòla Chriſtoual de Auendaño.

IORNADA PRIMERA.

Suena ruydo dentro, ſale Roſaura en habito de hombre, como que ha cayd[o].

Roſ. Hipogriſo violento,
que corriſte parejas con el viento,
donde rayo ſin llama,
paxaro ſin matiz, pez ſin eſcama,
y bruto ſin inſtincto
al fragoſo, al deſierto laberinto
quedate en eſte monte
donde tengan los brutos ſu Factonte,
que yo ſin mas camino,
que el que me dan las leyes del deſtino.
Sola, y deſeſperada,
baxarè la aſpereza enmarañada

A deſte

20 'Lope de Vega', *La vida es sueño* [Seville: Francisco de Lyra, *c.* 1632–4]
(By courtesy of the University of Liverpool Library)

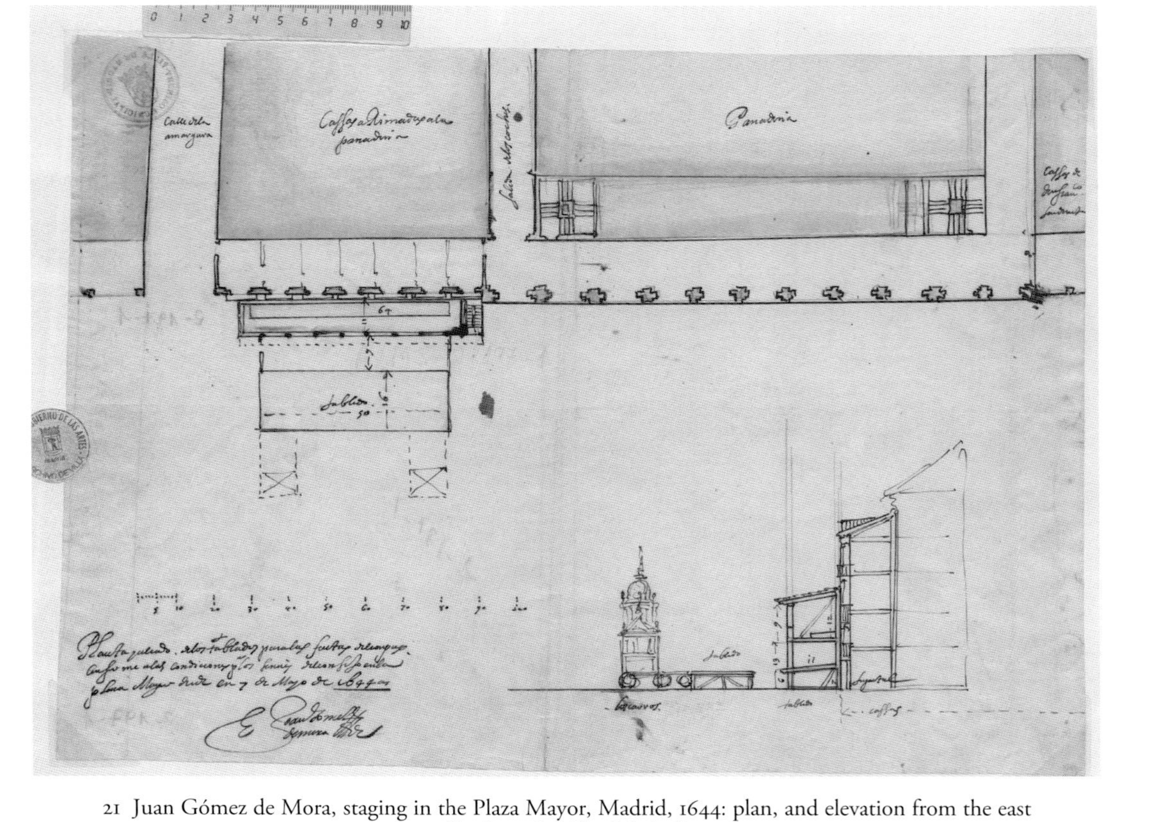

21 Juan Gómez de Mora, staging in the Plaza Mayor, Madrid, 1644: plan, and elevation from the east (Archivo de Villa, Madrid)

PRIMERA

PARTE DE COMEDIAS DE DON PEDRO CALDERON DE LA BARCA.

RECOGIDAS POR DON IOSEPH CALDERON de la Barca su hermano.

AL EXCELENTISSIMO SEÑOR DON Bernardino Fernandez de Velasco y Tobar, Condestable de Castilla, Duque de la ciudad de Frias, Conde de Haro, Marques de Verlanga, Señor de la Casa de los siete Infantes de Lara, Camarero, Copero, y Montero mayor, y Gentilhombre de la Camara del Rey nuestro señor.

75.

Año 1636.

CON PRIVILEGIO.

En Madrid, Por Maria de Quiñones.

A costa de Pedro Coello, y de Manuel Lopez, Mercaderes de Libros.

22 Calderón, *Primera parte de comedias*, 1636
(Bayerische Staatsbibliothek, Munich)

Genealojia de

Don Pedro Calderon de la Barca a quien Su Mgd. a hecho md. del Abito de S. Tiago natural de Madrid En la Parrochia de S. Martin.

Padres

Diego Calderon de la Barca natural de Madrid y doña Anamaria de Henao natural de Madrid y su Muger lijitima

Abuelos paternos

Pedro calderon de la Barca natural de boadilla del camino en campos y su Muger doña Ysabel Ruiz natural de Toledo.

Abuelos Maternos

Diego Gonzalez de Henao natural de Madrid y su Muger doña Ynes de Riaño natural de madrid

Don Pedro Calderon de la Barca

23 Calderón's autograph 'Genealojia', July 1636 (Archivo Histórico Nacional, Madrid)

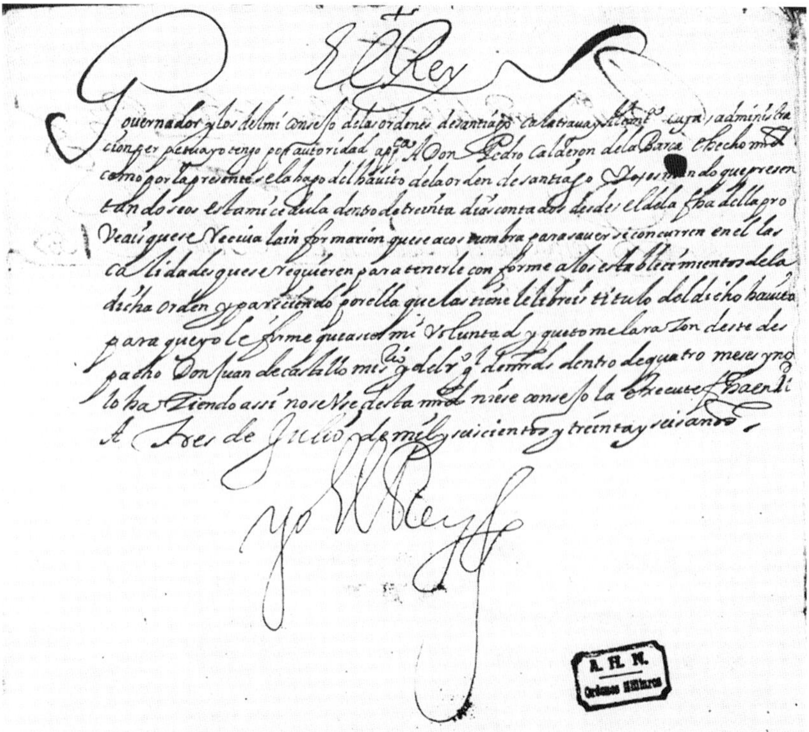
El Rey

Governador y los del mi consejo de las ordenes de Santiago Calatrava y Alcantara cuya administracion es perpetua yo tengo por autoridad apostolica. A Don Pedro Calderon de la Barca he hecho merced como por la presente se la hago del havito de la orden de Santiago. Yo os mando que presentando os esta mi cedula dentro de treinta dias contados desde el de la fecha della agro veais que se reciva la informacion que se acostumbra para saver si concurren en el las calidades que se requieren para tenerle conforme a los establecimientos de la dicha orden y pareciendo por ella que las tiene le librreis titulo del dicho havito para que yo le firme que asi es mi voluntad y que tome la razon deste despacho Don Juan de Castillo mi contador del registro general dentro de quatro meses y no lo haziendo assi no se use desta merced ni ese consejo la execute. Fecha en Madrid a tres de Julio de mil seiscientos y treinta y seis años.

Yo el Rey

Por mandado del Rey nuestro señor
Don Francisco de Calatayud

Tome la razon en 15 de Julio 1636
Don Juan de Castillo

A. H. N.
Ordenes Militares

A Don Pedro Calderon de la Barca, del havito de la orden de Santiago

24 Philip IV's warrant, signed 'yo El Rey', 3 July 1636 (Archivo Histórico Nacional, Madrid)

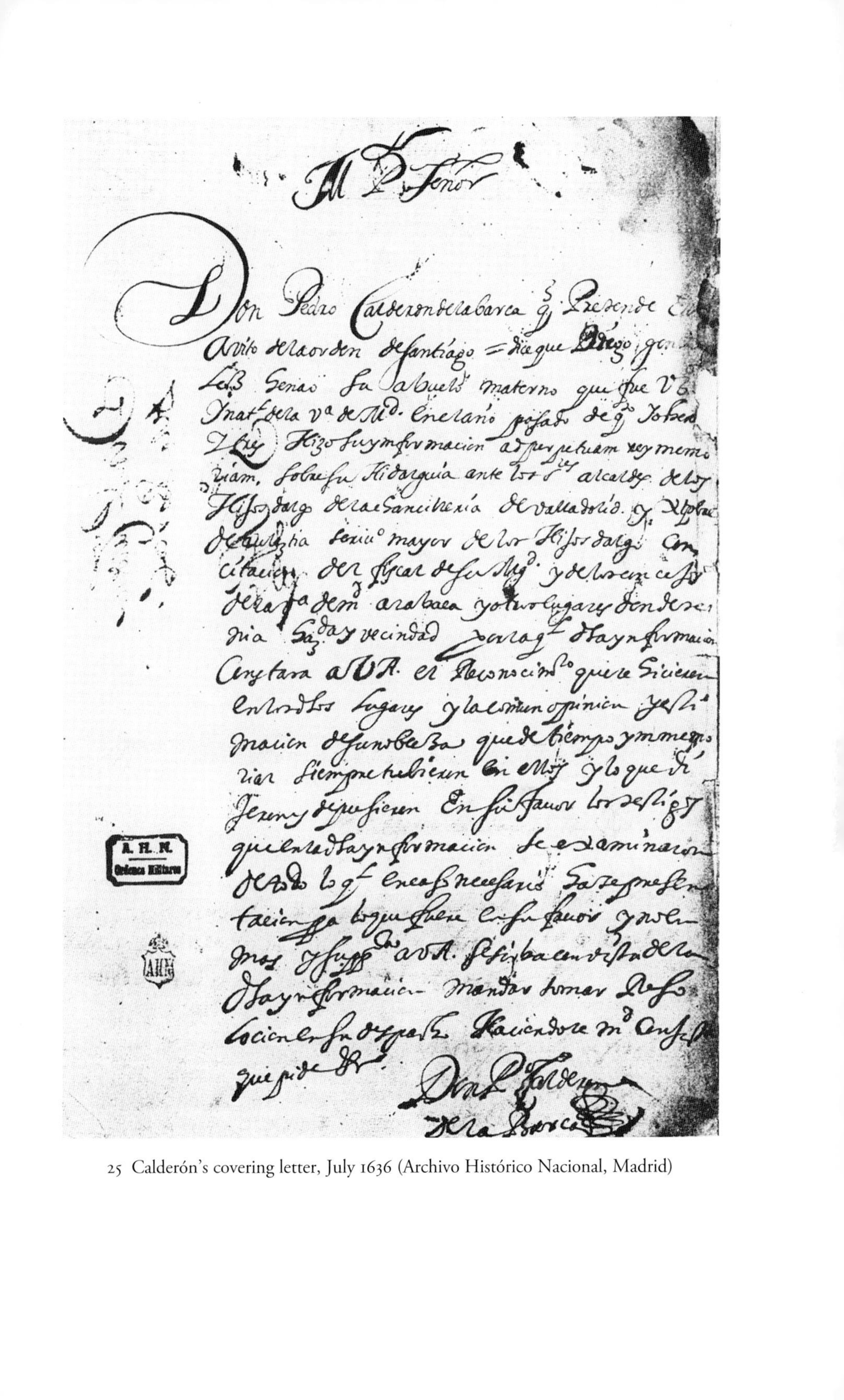

25 Calderón's covering letter, July 1636 (Archivo Histórico Nacional, Madrid)

SEGVNDA

PARTE DE

LAS COMEDIAS DE DON PEDRO CALDERON de la Barca, Cauallero del Abito de Santiago.

RECOGIDAS

Por don Ioſeph Calderon de la Barca ſu hermano.

DIRIGIDAS

AL EXCELENTISSIMO SEÑOR DON Rodrigo de Mendoça, Rojas, y Sandoual de la Vega y Luna, ſeñor de las Caſas de Mendoça, y Vega, Duque del Infantado, Marques del Cenete, Marques de Santillana, Marques de Argueſo, y Campoò, Conde de Saldaña, Conde del Real de Mançanares, y del Cid, ſeñor de la Provincia de Liebana, ſeñor de las Hermandades en Alaba, ſeñor de las villas de Ita y Buitrago, y ſu tierra, ſeñor de las villas de Tordehumos, Sanmartin, el Prado, Metrida, Arenas, y ſu tierra, ſeñsr de las villas del Seſmo, de Duron, y de Iadraque, y ſu tierra, ſeñor de la villa de Ayora, y de las Baronias de Alberique en el Reino de Valencia, Comendador de Zalamea Orden de Alcantara, &c.

72. y medio.

CON PRIVILEGIO.
En Madrid, *Por Maria de Quiñones,*
Año M. DC. XXXVII.

A coſta de Pedro Coello Mercader de Libros.

26 Calderón, *Segunda parte de las comedias*, 1637 (Reproduced by kind permission of the Syndics of Cambridge University Library)

Diez marauedis

SELLO QVARTO, DIEZ MARAVEDIS, AÑO DE MIL Y SEISCIENTOS Y QVARENTA

27 Calderón's signature on authorisation to Juan Martínez de Roitegui, 23 August 1640, on *papel sellado* (Archivo Histórico de Protocolos Notariales, Madrid, tomo 7718, fol. 311v)

28 Velázquez, *Conde-Duque de Olivares*, ?*c*. 1626
(Varez-Fisa Collection / Bridgeman Art Library)

29 Pedro de Villafranca, *Don Pedro Calderón*, 1676 (author)

30 Gregorio Forstman / Fosman, *Don Pedro Calderón*, 1682 (author)

31 Antonio Pereda y Salgado, *Don Pedro Calderón*, c. 1670
(Private Collection, Madrid / Bridgeman Art Library)

32 Velázquez, *Caballero desconocido*, ?1640s
(Wellington Museum, Apsley House, London; © English Heritage)

Queen Isabel was pregnant in the spring of 1629 (Baltasar Carlos was born on 17 October), and these lines could be a discreet reference to her condition, or simply an expression of the general desire that she would produce heirs. Earlier in the play, Calabazas suggested, referring to Marcela, that

> La Dama Duende habrá sido,
> que volver a vivir quiere. (II, 276a)

(It must have been the Fairy Lady, who wants to come back to life.)

This would indicate that *Casa con dos puertas* was the second of the two plays, except that *La dama duende* opens with these lines:

> Por una hora no llegamos
> a tiempo de ver las fiestas
> con que Madrid generosa
> hoy el bautismo celebra
> del primero Baltasar. (II, 236a)

(We're too late by an hour to see the fiestas with which generous Madrid celebrates the baptism today of the first Baltasar.)

The baptism was on 4 November. A few lines later, amid a series of literary allusions, there is one that can be dated precisely: the performance, during Carnival 1629 (4–6 February), of Mira's *Hero y Leandro*, 'tan bien escrita comedia' ('such a well-written play': II, 236b). What seems to have happened is that the first version of *Casa con dos puertas* was indeed written in the spring of 1629, and that its success prompted Don Pedro to re-use the plot for *La dama duende*, which was even more successful. In those days, before professional theatre critics or regular newspapers, dramatists had to get their feedback by word of mouth. There is plenty of documentary and inferential evidence to show that Don Pedro was in regular contact with theatre-company managers like Bartolomé Romero and Antonio de Prado, and they were almost certainly a major, if not the major, source of information, as such men had been from at least the early days of Lope de Vega. Company managers certainly urged authors to 'write another one like your last one, or even better, a sequel', and Tirso's references to *El castigo del penseque* in *Quien calla otorga* (sometimes called *La segunda parte del penseque*) show that it was quite acceptable for authors to engage in self-advertisement, or in advertisement for their friends, such as Mira de Amescua. In this case, when Don Pedro revised *Casa con dos puertas* (at some point after 4 July 1632, as John Varey has demonstrated), he added an advertisement for *La dama duende*, which was originally written several months later.[7]

A common career for young noblemen in Calderón's time was a university education followed by military service, often in Flanders. As a reward for appropriate service, the noble could then apply for membership of a military order. Such membership brought no income, but the status it conferred might open up other possibilities. This is the route chosen by Lisardo in *Casa con dos puertas*. Having followed the court to Aranjuez to further his application, he meets Félix, who reminds them of their university days:

Bien os acordáis de aquellas
felicísimas edades
nuestras cuando los dos fuimos
en Salamanca estudiantes. (II, 276b)

(You remember well those happy days of ours when we two were students in Salamanca.)

As we know, Calderón's time at Salamanca was not uniformly happy. His personal experience was a source on which he drew when creating characters, but we cannot assume that these details are autobiographical. For evidence that they are no more than a commonplace, the passage may be compared with one from *Con quien vengo vengo* (?1630, set in Italy):

Bien os acordáis, don Juan,
de aquel venturoso tiempo,
que en las escuelas famosas
de Bolonia, patria y centro
de las artes y las ciencias,
fuimos los dos compañeros. (II, 1133a)

(You remember well, Don Juan, that happy time when we two were companions at the famous university of Bologna, the home and centre of arts and sciences.)

Lisardo and Félix may have been friends, but Félix never said he had a sister. Now, with Lisardo coming to stay with Félix in Ocaña while he pursues his business at Aranjuez, the sister Marcela not only has to surrender her room to the guest, but must lock herself away, supposedly to avoid giving rise to gossip. The segregation of females by their male relatives was normal among those with social pretensions, but it must have been counterproductive, increasing not only the women's curiosity in individual cases (as Marcela points out), but possibly their susceptibility. Certainly both Marcela and Ángela, her locked-away counterpart in *La dama duende*, readily fall for their brothers' eligible guests and pursue them with ingenuity and determination, causing both plays to move from crisis to crisis with breathless speed. A house with two doors is hard to guard, but the moral goes further, suggesting that the attempts of one person to control the lives of others can lead to the very situation that the controller wished to avoid, as in *La vida es sueño* and numerous other plays.

While Ocaña is the setting of both *Casa con dos puertas* and Lope's *Peribáñez,* the two authors portray the town differently. Lope's Ocaña is very unlike Madrid, but Calderón's setting gives little feel of a rural community, despite regular references to the local geography. Knowing that Lope had spent time in Ocaña, we might assume that Calderón had never been there, except that the local castle belonged to the Dukes of Frías, that is, to Calderón's employer, Don Bernardino Fernández de Velasco. Furthermore, Calderón's plot makes it clear that young noblemen like Lisardo were in the habit of following the court to Aranjuez to further their careers, although he insists that this was not strictly necessary,

porque de ministros tales
hoy el Rey se sirve, que
no es al mérito importante
la asistencia, porque todos
acudir a todo saben;
gracias al celo de aquel
con quien el peso reparte
de tanta máquina, bien
como Alcides con Atlante. (II, 279b)

(because these days the king employs such ministers that being present is not important for getting what one deserves, since all of them know how to attend to everything, thanks to the zeal of him with whom he shares the weight of such a vast structure, just like Hercules with Atlas.)

In his *Tardes del alcázar,* Juan de Robles asks a friend – a priest – if kings should have favourites. After some thought, the friend recalls how Atlas asked Alcides (Hercules) for help in moving the celestial globe from one shoulder to the other. The *Tardes,* perhaps written in 1631, cast Philip IV as Atlas, and Olivares as the helper Hercules, although Luis de Córdoba had referred to Olivares as a 'new Atlas' as early as 1624.[8] In Don Pedro's passage, the zealous 'aquel' is Olivares, with whom the king (Hercules) can share his burden. That is, the association of the kings of Spain with Hercules allows him to present both king and minister favourably. The reference to Olivares and his effect on the civil service is a significant aspect of Calderón's relationship with those in power, or close to it: where he felt that praise was due, praise was bestowed; where criticism was necessary, it should be discreet as well as constructive. Although he was several years away from seeking his own membership of a military order, it seems likely that he visited both Ocaña and Aranjuez in the spring of 1629, probably in the company of Don Bernardino, the nephew of Spain's Atlas.

Casa con dos puertas and *La dama duende* may have similarities in plot, but the inspiration for *La dama duende* seems to be a short passage in Tirso's *Quien calla otorga*. This Tirso play is a *comedia palaciega* which is superficially unlike either of the Calderón plays, except that at the end of Act I, one of the young noblemen (Don Rodrigo) receives a mysterious and anonymous letter from a female admirer. His servant Chinchilla remarks that

> mujer ilustre ha sido
> esta nuestra dama duende,
> si crédito hemos de dar
> al modo con que te escribe.[9]

(This fairy lady of ours is a noblewoman, if we are to give credit to the way in which she writes to you.)

Quien calla otorga was written as early as 1615, but first printed in Tirso's *Primera parte* of 1627, just two years before Doña Ángela, Don Pedro's *dama duende*, took a similar initiative in her relationship with Don Manuel.[10]

There are other debts, however. An examination of the ostensibly supernatural events of *La dama duende* has led to the conclusion that, in constructing his plots, Calderón was influenced by the Cervantine technique of showing all the links in the chain of causality. It has been suggested that this rationalistic approach to plot-making is one of Cervantes's most important legacies to Calderón and his generation, and that it is inseparable from the rationalism which judges behaviour: debts could be demonstrated here too.[11] Indeed, we can see how the philosophy of the obsessive controller Carrizales ('Casarme he con ella; encerraréla, y haréla a mis mañas, y con esto, no tendrá otra condición que aquella que yo la enseñare': 'I shall marry her, keep her shut up, and mould her to my ways; with this, the only disposition she will have is the one I teach her') not only is the cause of his own undoing, but also provided a model for Calderón's numerous variations (male and female, but mostly male) on the would-be controlling personality.[12]

Doña Ángela is a young widow, but her brief experience of marriage does not prevent her brothers (especially Luis) from trying to control (that is, eliminate) her social life. Since the Calderón brothers were too young, in 1611, to have decided the fate of their sister Dorotea, the situation of Ángela cannot be straightforwardly autobiographical. However, since Calderón so frequently depicts a young woman denied fulfilment (of whatever kind) by males, we must consider the possibility that this obsession is inspired by personal experience; and his own father, with his treatment of Dorotea, is our first suspect. The father's will suggests that he was a would-be controller, but it might seem unwise to assume that he was the stimulus for his son's recurring treatment of this aspect of social life. However, as if to support the view that the writer was making some mental connection, he describes how Ángela's civil servant husband had failed to bequeath her financial independence:

Su esposo era
Administrador en puerto
de mar de unas rentas reales
y quedó debiendo al Rey
grande cantidad de hacienda. (II, 241b)

(Her husband was a royal revenue administrator in a seaport, and he finished up owing the king a great deal of wealth.)

Calderón could hardly have written those words without thinking of the consequences of the death of his own father.

Don Manuel knows almost nothing of the spirited Ángela, but he is a gentleman: faced with the choice of aiding a lady in distress or seeming to betray the trust of a friend, he opts for the lady. One of the play's remarkable features is the way in which it reverses the supposed real-life male/female roles of the seventeenth century, in which males made the running and females were not consulted. Ángela had begun by complaining 'que yo | entre dos paredes muera, | donde apenas el sol sabe | quién soy' ('that I should die between two walls, where the sun hardly knows who I am': II, 240a), but she discovers that her enforced 'anonymity' allows her to make those around her dance to her tune. The honour-obsessed Luis has pursued Beatriz for most of the play, quite unable to see this 'courtship' from the point of view of her male relatives. The penalty for his hypocrisy is that he ends up without her, reminding us of the two Don Diegos in *El astrólogo fingido* and *El hombre pobre todo es trazas*. In this case the moral is not spelled out, but it does not have to be.

The success of *La dama duende* in its turn prompted Don Pedro to use its plot again soon afterwards, with male/female parts reversed, for *El galán fantasma*, which also refers to *La dama duende* by name. Since *La dama duende* was written soon after the baptism of Baltasar Carlos, Cotarelo suggested that this must also be true of *El galán fastasma*, if the reference was to have a point.[13] The argument seems plausible, but we have enough information about the dates of plays in which such references occur to know that it is not infallible.

Although Calderón had found a formula which worked for him, he continued to experiment with other kinds of play. Thus *La Virgen del Sagrario* is a triptych, three chronologically disparate acts united by a theme, the image of Our Lady of the Sanctuary. Act I begins in the Visigothic capital, Toledo, ruled by King Recisundo (Recceswinth), where Ildefonso (Ildefonsus, d. 667, later canonised) is archbishop. Questioned about the image, Ildefonso admits that its origins are uncertain, although he mentions that the image of La Almudena in Madrid was brought to Spain by St James the Greater. Tradition held that the Virgin herself presented Ildefonso with a chasuble as a reward for his treatise on her virginity,[14] and the act ends with this scene. Act II is set in the immediate aftermath of the battle of Guadalete and the defeat of King Rodrigo (Roderic, d. 711) at the hands Tarif (Tariq). Since Toledo surrenders to overwhelming numbers without a fight, Tarif is willing to let Toledan society continue as it was, with Christian churches and priests; but the Toledans nevertheless hide their image of the Virgin, in a scene full of echoes of Israel's Babylonian captivity. Act III is set immediately after the recapture of Toledo in 1085. Thanks to the zeal of Costanza, queen of Alfonso VI, the image is rediscovered. The subject-matter (the defeat of Rodrigo, the career of Alfonso VI) permits numerous references to the King Rodrigo and Zamora cycles of ballads, including Alfonso's alleged complicity in Vellido Dolfos's murder of his brother Sancho, culminating in the legendary *jura en Santa Gadea* ('En Santa Gadea de Burgos') in which Alfonso denied that complicity, as he also does in this play. Calderón evidently knew these ballads, and so it is interesting to find echoes of Góngora's *Polifemo* as well, in Recisundo's description of the cave as 'esta boca, | por donde melancólico bosteza | el monte: sea mordaza dura roca' ('this mouth, through which the mountain yawns in melancholy: let a hard rock be its gag').[15] Finally, Selín's remark about 'la novedad más grave | que el tiempo, archivo confuso, | calificó en sus anales' ('the gravest news that ever time, that confused archive, attested in its annals'), with its echo of *El médico de su honra*'s 'la novedad | del suceso más notable | que el vulgo, archivo confuso, | califica en sus anales' ('the news of the most notable event that the mob, that confused archive, attests in its annals'),[16] offers some support for the view that the two plays are contemporary, that is, written about 1629.

La Virgen del Sagrario represents Calderón's most cavalier treatment of Aristotle's Unity of Time. That he was familiar with this 'rule' is evident from *El maestro de danzar*. As the situation in that play becomes more complicated, the maid Inés turns to the audience and asks:

Señores,
¿en qué ha de parar aquesto,
y más en veinticuatro horas
que da la trova de tiempo? (II, 1560b)

(Sirs, where is this going to end, especially in the twenty-four hours that the poem allows?)

While this may be false modesty, Don Pedro evidently felt that the strict application of Aristotle's rules would exclude stories which should be dramatised for good religious reasons, although there is evidence that he was conscious of having produced a defective play:

Y perdonad al poeta,
si sus defectos son grandes,
y en esta parte la fe
y la devoción le salve. (I, 280b)

(Forgive the poet if his defects are great, and in this aspect let faith and devotion save him.)

We do not know the date of the lost two-part play *Nuestra Señora de la Almudena*, but it may have been an attempt to treat a similar subject in a more dramatically satisfactory way. The play confirms that Calderón's devotion to the Virgin, referred to in Chapter 3, took a practical form, but also that it involved him in historical research, which may even have extended to Ildefonsus's treatise.

Two documents of this period indicate Don Pedro's presence in Madrid. On 23 March 1630 he stood as guarantor for a Francisco de Arantey y Quintana, who was being held for debt in the Cárcel Real. Calderón stood to lose 659 *reales* (the amount of the debt) if Arantey did not return to prison in thirty days.[17] There is no evidence, in the indexes of recently published theatre documents, that Arantey had anything to do with the theatre, but Calderón clearly knew him and trusted him. Perhaps he was a domestic.

Seven months later, on 25 October, Calderón signed an IOU for 400 *reales* lent him by Bernardino González (Plate 17).[18] A document referred to earlier (Chapter 6, n. 25) indicates that this González was a secretary in the Council of Finance (i.e., an ex-colleague of the Calderón father), and that the father's heirs (his children and his widow) were dividing up the yield (225 ducats p.a.) on an annuity against Don Bernardino's secretaryship. The widow's share was 100 ducats, so the remaining 125 (1,375 *reales*) were due to Don Pedro and his brothers. The 400 *reales* were an anticipation of the poet's share of this amount.

* * *

At this point we should note the text of an *entremés*, *La maestra de gracias*, printed as by Belmonte Bermúdez in 1657, which has a close textual relationship with *Las Carnestolendas*, another *entremés* printed as by Calderón in 1661. Juan Bezón, the *gracioso* in the company of Cristóbal de Avendaño, and Bernardo de Medrano, who had the same role with Andrés de la Vega, are on stage together:

Bezón ¿Qué haremos, señor Bernardo?
Ber Que con su autora se vaya,
que yo, *con quien vengo, vengo.*
Bezón *Aún peor está que estaba.*
Ber ¿No ve que *la vida es sueño*?
Bezón Yo pensé que te mostraras
amigo, amante y leal.
Ber Entre los suyos se vaya,
que ansí tomaré mejor
de un castigo, dos venganzas.[19]

(Bezón: What shall we do, señor Bernardo? Bernardo: You go off with your manageress, because *I'm with whom I'm with.* Bezón. *It's even worse than it was.* Bernardo. Don't you see that *Life is a dream*? Bezón. I thought thou wouldst show thyself *friend, lover and loyal.* Bernardo. Go off among your own lot; that way I'll take *Two vengeances from one punishment* better.)

Four titles by Calderón, one by Pérez de Montalbán: whether or not Calderón's *De un castigo, tres venganzas* was intended, the likelihood is that all five plays are roughly contemporary, and that they were recent. Alfredo Rodríguez López-Vázquez suggests that the original *entremés* text was performed at Carnival 1631 (9–11 February).[20]

We may look at *La vida es sueño* first. By 1833 (the death of Ferdinand VII, and the usual cut-off date for the *comedia suelta* era), *La vida es sueño* had been printed at least fifty-five times.[21] Almost certainly, it is the most-printed Spanish play, and has also generated a correspondingly large amount of literary criticism. Until recently, however, it was believed to have been written in 1635, and to be a refinement of *Yerros de naturaleza y aciertos de la fortuna*, which was written in collaboration by Antonio Coello and Calderón, and sent to the censor on 4 May 1634.[22] In the last fifteen years, the researches of José M. Ruano, Germán Vega and Alfredo Rodríguez, aided by the discovery of a *suelta* which can be dated to Seville, 1632–4, have brought the first version back to no later than the latter part of 1630.[23] Since Suárez de Mendoza's *Eustorgio y Clorilene; historia moscovica* (Calderón's likely source for those two names) was published on

30 April 1629, it seems probable that the first draft of the play dates from 1629–30.[24] The date of the revised version is less exact, but it was licensed for printing in the author's *Primera parte* on 10 November 1635. Not only does this mean that the most famous play in the classical theatre of Spain was written while the author was no more than thirty; it also shows that Calderón's methods of re-using earlier material did not always result in improvement. The early *suelta* tells us that the play was performed by Cristóbal de Avendaño, who must have died soon after he attended the chapter of the Cofradía de la Novena, the actors' guild, on 4 April 1634: his company was taken over, apparently in May, by Salvador de Lara, who also married his widow, the actress María Candado.[25] It is easy to imagine that another *autor* close to Don Pedro (as we shall see, Antonio de Prado is a candidate) persuaded him, during Lent 1634, to try to return to a successful formula. The attempt was a failure: *Yerros* remained unpublished until 1930.

Basilio, one of two fathers in *La vida es sueño*, is another controlling personality, who has to be told that his attempted management of his son Segismundo's life is self-defeating:

> ... quando yo
> por mi nobleza gallarda,
> por mi sangre generosa,
> por mi condicion vizarra
> huviera nacido docil
> y humilde, solo bastàra
> tal genero de vivir,
> tal linage de criança,
> à hazer fieras mis costumbres;
> que buen modo de estorvarlas!
>
> (*La segunda versión*, lines 3176–85)

(When I, through my high birth, my noble blood, my generous nature, should have been gentle and meek, all that was needed was such a way of life, such a kind of upbringing, to make my behaviour wild; what a fine way to hinder it!)

The humiliation of Basilio is echoed by that of Clotaldo, his chief assistant in the imprisonment of Segismundo. Clotaldo puts loyalty to the king before loyalty to his daughter and her mother. He does not even acknowledge the daughter, Rosaura, until he is forced to do so, although it would have cost him no more than embarrassment to follow Basilio in admitting the existence of a previously unsuspected child. We cannot help remembering Francisco González Calderón, while the treatment of Segismundo is bound to recall the Calderón father's treatment of his legitimate children Diego and Dorotea.

Apart from *La maestra de gracias*, the evidence for the date of *Peor está que estaba* is second-hand and unverifiable. The German hispanist Ludwig Tieck once owned a *suelta* of the play which attributed it to 'Luys Alvarez', a name not associated with any other text. The heading stated that 'representóla Francisco López' ('Francisco López played it'); at the end were the words 'acabóse esta Comedia por el mes de mayo de 1630, y la representó Josef de Salazar el mismo año' ('this play was finished in May 1630, and performed by José de Salazar the same year'). The edition can no longer be consulted because it was lost during World War II.[26] However, the references to *autores de comedias* are plausible. For example, Francisco López was present at the chapter, in Madrid, of the actors' guild, on 3 February 1632. José de Salazar attended that on 16 March 1633; at the 1634 meeting he was recorded as having died in the interval.[27] The attribution to Luis Álvarez can be explained as an attempt to conceal an illegal act such as the theft and sale to a printer of a text that still had an active performing life. This explanation is supported by the fact that the text apparently differed from that printed in the 1636 *Primera parte* (i.e., the changes might have been made to conceal the theft).

Peor está que estaba is set in Gaeta, in the Spanish viceroyalty of Naples, mostly in the house of the governor. An old Flanders army friend has written to the governor from Naples to say that a young gentleman, identified by the letter-bearer as Don César Urbino, has run off with his daughter Flérida, after fatally wounding a rival; the friend wants the governor to stop them if they try to board a ship for Spain. In reality, César, believing that Flérida was a willing party to the rival's advances, has left separately. The governor also has a daughter, Lisarda, who is betrothed to Don Juan, another Flanders soldier, whom she has never met. Lisarda, perhaps wishing subconsciously to choose her own husband, becomes emotionally involved with César. César responds, prompting his servant Camacho to ask:

¿Vive Flérida ausente, o la señora,
que tapada pretende
tener futura sucesión de duende? (II, 319a)

(Does absent Flérida live in your heart, or the veiled lady, who's hoping to have future fairy heirs?)

This is certainly another reference to *La dama duende*, and judicious use of a veil on Lisarda's part creates similar confusion in this play. César explains his feelings in painting terminology:

Cuando un pintor procura
linear una pintura,
si está lisa la tabla
fáciles rasgos en bosquejo entabla;
mas si la tabla tiene
primero otra pintura, le conviene
borrarla, no confunda
con la primera forma la segunda. (II, 327b)

(When a painter is trying to outline a painting, if the board is smooth, he begins easy brushstrokes in a sketch; but if the board already has a painting on it, it's better for him to blot it out so that he doesn't mix the second shape with the first.)

There is plenty of evidence, throughout Calderón's life, of his interest in painting. The best-known pieces of evidence are, first, his reference in 1677 to the 'natural inclinación que siempre tuvo a la pintura' ('the natural bent he always had for painting');[28] and second, the inventory of his collection of paintings made after his death in 1681. There were 119 of these, including seven landscapes and thirty-four vases of flowers, and they were assessed by Claudio Coello, who valued them at 17,000 *reales*.[29] The figures are striking, both in terms of numbers and of value. They included Calderón's most valuable possessions: an Italian painting of St Francis in ecstasy, 3,300 *reales*, and a Last Supper, 3,000 *reales*. In contrast, four small landscapes were rated at only 11 *reales* each, and four flower-vases, at only 12 *reales* each. One explanation for the quantity and modest value of the flower-vases, and perhaps of the landscapes, is that they were Calderón's own work. The César passage could be taken to support this explanation; it certainly confirms that the interest in painting had a practical side.

There are other allusions in the play. Camacho is reminded of damsels in distress requesting succour from knights-errant, and refers to three knights, Esplandián, Belianís and Beltenebros, in a parody of the language of the novel of chivalry (II, 327b). Calderón's comic servants regularly mock their masters in this way: for example, Chacón and Don Enrique in *El maestro de danzar*:

Mira, pues, si razón tengo,
cuando locuras me mandas
dejar, en dejarte, puesto
que con dejarte a ti, en ti
todas las locuras dejo
de Esplandián y Belianís,
Amadís y Beltenebros,
que, a pesar de don Quijote,
oy a revivir han vuelto. (II, 1539a)

(See whether I'm right, then, when you tell me to leave folly behind, to leave you, since in leaving you, I leave behind all the follies of Esplandián and Belianís, Amadís and Beltenebros, who, in spite of Don Quixote, have come to life again today.)

Later, Juan tells César that

Escriben los naturales
de dos plantas diferentes
que son venenos, y estando
juntas las dos, de tal suerte
se templan, que son sustento. (II, 328b)

(Physicians write of two different plants which are poisons, and which together temper each other in such a way that they are sustenance.)

Calderón would refer to this again in *A secreto agravio, secreta venganza* (?1635), *La hija del aire II* (?late 1630s) and *Agradecer y no amar* (by 1650), but the source is unknown. Rather later, the scheming Lisarda, thinking that things are going from bad to worse, uses the phrase 'Peor está que estaba' and quotes the 'Portuguese Virgil' (Camões): 'Vi el bien convertido en mal, | y el mal en otro peor' ('I saw good turned to bad, and bad to worse': II, 335b).[30] Indeed, things do turn out disappointingly for her: César is united with his Flérida, while she has to settle for Juan.

Peor está que estaba, like *El astrólogo fingido*, attracted interest abroad. On 20 July 1664 (OS) Samuel Pepys saw *Worse and Worse*, a lost adaptation made from a Spanish play by George Digby, Earl of Bristol, whose father, Sir John, had been the ambassador in Spain at the time of the Spanish Match.[31] *Peor está* is the best candidate for the source, particularly since the same writer also produced *'Tis Better than it Was* (?by 1665, printed London, 1708) from *Mejor está que estaba*. Other seventeenth-century versions include de Brosse's *Les Innocens coupables* (1645) and Le Métel de Boisrobert's *Les Apparences trompeuses* (1656).

In the same year (1630), Don Pedro felt confident enough to experiment with another sub-genre, one which he knew might be frowned on by discerning critics. In Chapter 48 of Part I of *Don Quixote*, the priest and the canon discuss literature, including plays. In particular, the canon tells his colleague how he abandoned the novel he was writing, partly because of his reflections on the current state of drama:

Si estas [comedias] que ahora se usan, así las imaginadas como las de historia, todas o las más son conocidos disparates y cosas que no llevan pies ni cabeza, y, con todo eso, el vulgo las oye con gusto, y las tiene y las aprueba por buenas, estando tan lejos de serlo, y los autores que las componen y los actores que las representan dicen que así han de ser, porque así las quiere el vulgo.

(All or most of these plays which are now in fashion, both invented and historical, are notorious nonsense, a complete jumble, and despite all this, the mob watches them with pleasure, and considers them good, when they are so far from being so, and the authors who write them and the actors who perform them say that that is how they have to be, because that is how the mob wants them.)

In the following chapter, the pair take on the knight himself, trying to persuade him that, rather than absurd novels of chivalry, he should have read books which were 'más verdaderos y que más deleitan y enseñan' ('more true to life and which delight and instruct more'). Don Quixote is outraged and incredulous:

¿Qué ingenio puede haber en el mundo que pueda persuadir a otro que no fue verdad lo de la infanta Floripes y Guy de Borgoña, y lo de Fierabrás con la puente de Mantible, que sucedió en el tiempo de Carlomagno, que voto a tal que es tanta verdad como es ahora de día?[32]

(What writer can there be in the world capable of persuading another that the story of Princess Floripes and Guy of Burgundy was not true, or the story of Fierabras and the bridge of Mantible, which happened in the time of Charlemagne, which I swear is as true as it's daylight now?)

We can be sure that Calderón had read these passages, and that he was perfectly familiar with the Horatian precepts of delighting and instructing, although he may have chosen not to recall either the passages or the precepts in the early summer of 1630, when *La puente de Mantible* was probably written. We certainly have no idea what the actors in the troupe of Roque de Figueroa thought of the piece they performed. The likeliest sources were the *Orlando furioso* of Ariosto (1516) and the *Historia del emperador Carlo Magno y de los doce pares de Francia, y de la vatalla que hubo Oliveros con Fierabrás, rey de Alexandría*, a translation from the French of Jean Baignon made by Nicolás Gazini (or 'de Piamonte'), a Piedmontese printer who worked in Spain and Portugal between 1511 and 1518; there was an edition by Sebastián Martínez (Alcalá, 1589), and there were regular reprints into the eighteenth century.

La puente de Mantible does indeed tell the story of the love affair of Princess Floripes and Guido de Borgoña (who, it is implied, is an ancestor of the house of Burgundy/Austria). Carlo Magno, Fierabrás and Oliveros take part, as do Roldán and other peers. The verse is exceptionally sonorous, the imagery especially striking. One image in particular, the swimming horse as ship, was an image Calderón would return to:

siendo la frente la proa,
remos los pies, los estribos

costados, las ancas popa,
las guedejas jarcias, yo
la vela que el viento azota,
y el timón que nos gobierna
sobre la espuma la cola. (II, 1881a)

(the forehead being the prow, the feet oars, the stirrups sides, the haunches stern, the mane rigging, I the sail lashed by the wind, and the tail which steers us on the foam, the rudder).

A similar passage in Act I of the collaboration play *El privilegio de las mujeres* (?1634) is a good reason for supposing that Calderón wrote that act:

Al abreviado piélago se entregan,
donde por rumbos fáciles navegan
en los brutos bajeles y vivientes:
que, espolones las frentes,
el cuello proa, viento las espuelas,
remos los brazos y las clines velas,
jarcia el arzón más alto de la silla,
el jinete piloto, el vientre quilla,
jarcias las riendas y timón la cola,
y por si el Tíber crespo se enarbola,
áncoras breves siendo los estribos … (1359b)[33]

(To the mini-ocean they commit themselves, where they sail by easy courses on the living beast-ships: for, the foreheads cutwaters, the neck prow, wind the spurs, oars the forelimbs and the manes sails, rigging the saddle-tree, the rider pilot, the belly keel, rigging the reins and rudder the tail, and should the Tiber lift itself in waves, the stirrups brief anchors …)

One line ('corriendo parejas en el viento', 'matching the wind', II, 1851b) recalls line 2 ('que corriste parejas con el viento', 'that matched the wind') of *La vida es sueño*, which we now know to be contemporary, but another ('Etna el corazón, volcán el pecho', 'Etna the heart, volcano the breast', II, 1852a), which Calderón used again and again, reminds us not to set too much store by verbal similarities.

We cannot tell if contemporary audiences reacted with pleasure to *La puente de Mantible*, although both Simón Fajardo and Francisco de Lyra of Seville printed *sueltas* of it about 1632, attributing the play to Lope.[34] Nearly twenty years went by before Calderón based another play on a novel of chivalry (*El jardín de Falerina*, ?1649).

* * *

On 26 December 1627 the Duke of Mantua died, leaving Charles, Duke of Nevers, as his heir. The lands of tiny Mantua, sandwiched between the republic of Venice and the duchy of Milan, included the marquisate of Monferrato, which lay between Savoy and Milan, with Genoa to the south. Richelieu saw the succession as a way for France to gain a toehold in northern Italy, a toehold that the government in Madrid saw as a threat to their Milanese territory: Milan was an imperial fief, as were both Mantua and Monferrato, but the Duke of Milan was Philip IV. Since Nevers had not asked the permission of the emperor, Ferdinand II, to take up his inheritance, Olivares tried to persuade Ferdinand to declare Mantua and Monferrato sequestered, but he delayed until 1 April, giving Nevers time to prepare his resistance. Spanish troops occupied Monferrato, with the important exception of the fortress of Casale, on the Po, near the Milan border. Eventually, on 10 August 1629, Ambrogio Spinola, the Marquis de los Balbases, left Barcelona to lead the Spanish troops in the capture of Casale. Also on board his ship, on his first visit to Italy, was the painter Diego Velázquez. Spinola, aware of what it would cost Spain to fight on two fronts, had hoped to delay further commitments in Italy until the signing of a Dutch truce; by 19 September, he was still only in Genoa.

Octavio, one of the characters in *Con quien vengo, vengo*, describes how, while he was studying at Bologna, he got a letter from his father telling him to leave his studies and join the army. He did so, joining

el tercio
del señor Duque de Lerma,
aquel Escipión mancebo
en quien Adonis, Mercurio
y Marte tienen imperio. (II, 1131b)

(the regiment of the Duke of Lerma, that youthful Scipio ruled by Adonis, Mercury and Mars.)

This is Francisco Gómez de Sandoval, the nephew of the minister of Philip III, and the second duke.[35] Octavio goes on to tell how Spinola gave orders for the *tercio* to march to Casal de Monferrato (Casale), how they took Pontostura (Pontestura), Rofinar (*sic*, Rosiñán, Italian Rosignano), San Jorge (San Giorgio) and other towns (II, 1132b). When Octavio's regiment reached San Jorge, they were attacked by French cavalry, but beat them off and forced them to take refuge in Casal (II, 1133a). At this point Octavio turns to the events which allowed him to go back to Milan, and his account of the Mantuan war is suspended, with Spinola still alive. In the autumn of 1630, however (25 September), Spinola died. More evidence about the fighting around Casale comes from Calderón himself. When Don Pedro made his case for a military pension in the late 1640s, he described himself as the brother of Don José Calderón:

Es hermano de Don Ioseph Calderon de la Barca, que siruiò a V. Magestad en los estados de Milan, Italia, y Flandes desde el año de seiscientos y veinte y siete: y en este tiempo se hallò en la empressa de Nisa de la Palla, y en el sitio y toma de Pontestura, y toma del castillo de San Iorge, sitio y toma de Rosiñan, y en el sitio de la Ciudad del Casal, en la qual, y en las demas assistiô continuadamente, peleando con mucho valor. Y el dia veinte y seis de Octubre de seiscientos y treinta, quando el enemigo fue a socorrer la Ciudadela [del Casal], se hallo en la primera hilera del esquadron de los Españoles: y auiendo seruido a su costa hasta veinte y quatro de Iulio de seiscientos y treinta y vno vino a España.[36]

(He is a brother of Don José Calderón de la Barca, who served Your Majesty in the states of Milan, Italy and Flanders from 1627; during this time he was present in the Nisa de la Palla campaign, at the siege and capture of Pontestura, and the capture of the castle of San Giorgio, the siege and capture of Rosignano, and in the siege of the city of Casale, in which and in the others he was continuously present, fighting very bravely. And on 26 October 1630, when the enemy went to relieve the citadel of Casale, he was in the front rank of the Spanish squadron; and having served at his own expense until 24 July 1631, he came back to Spain.)

Pontestura was taken in May, and Casale was besieged from the end of May until 3 September, when a truce was agreed. A new French army arrived in late October, and the Spanish forces abandoned Casale. Octavio's story must belong to the period June–August 1630, before the Mantuan war began to go badly for Spain, so badly that Octavio's optimistic references to it would be inappropriate. It seems reasonable to conclude that some of Don Pedro's information came from José's letters home, letters that allowed Don Pedro to be precise about places and dates nearly twenty years later.

Con quien vengo, vengo is another situation comedy, in which mistaken identity is compounded by darkness. In the end the sisters Leonor and Lisarda manage to be united to Juan and Octavio, despite the efforts of their honour-obsessed brother Sancho, who reminds us of Ángela's brother Luis in *La dama duende*.

Since Calderón's own relations with his brothers were good, we can imagine his distress at the death of his sister-in-law, Beatriz de Alarcón, in September 1631. Her will shows that her only beneficiaries were her husband Diego and her son José, aged eight. Her executors were her husband and her 'cousin', the Licentiate Francisco de Montalvo.[37] Francisco was her husband's cousin: it was normal for a wife to refer to her husband's relatives as if they were her own. If he had been her true cousin, then presumably her husband Diego would have been her cousin as well, and he would have defied his father's will. There is no evidence that this is the case. Years later, it would be José, grown up and married, who would bring up Calderón's own son.

***

What is most striking about this first decade of Don Pedro's literary production is its quantity and variety. While his first known literary works, his poems, had been relatively well received, he decided at an early stage that his true talent lay in drama. Drama also paid better. In his writing life of sixty years he would write some 120 plays (excluding those written in collaboration), an average of two per year. Allowing for the fact that from the 1630s onwards he was also writing *autos sacramentales*, we can see that the couple of dozen plays he wrote in the nine years from 1622 to 1630 inclusive represent what for him was a typical rate of production. Compared with Lope, who averaged around fifteen plays a year for fifty years, the rate was modest enough; compared with Shakespeare or Corneille, it was prodigious. The sum of money earned was not quite so prodigious: even the 800 *reales* a play he was getting by the end of this period would produce an average of just over 41 *reales* a week. The income from the annuities referred to above (p. 76) would have brought this to 55 *reales*. In 1631, Miguel Caxa de Leruela wrote that rising prices had made it impossible for a day-labourer to survive on the standard daily wage of 8 *reales*, i.e., 48 *reales* for a six-day week.[38] We have seen that a civil servant could pay 1,300 *reales* a year in rent, or 25 *reales* a week, for a flat, while it had cost 28 *reales* a week to feed such a person more than ten inflation-filled years previously. Had he had no other income, a production rate of three plays a year would have left Calderón slightly worse off than an unskilled labourer. While we do not know how much he received from the Duke of Frías, we can be sure that no nobleman, even a minor one, could afford an appropriate lifestyle for himself on the 55 *reales* a week he could earn from plays and annuities.

Categorisation of Calderón's plays is fraught with problems, but we can safely say that the largest group among these early plays were those with a historical or factual background, ranging from ancient history (*La gran Cenobia*, *Judas Macabeo*) to recent events (*El sitio de Bredá*), and often centring on a particular character (Cenobia, Judas Macabeo, Ludovico Enio, Prince Fernando, Luis Pérez, Henry VIII). While shortage of factual detail will always force historical dramatists to be inventive, Don Pedro was evidently familiar with Aristotle's distinction between poetry and history: he would change the facts to make a better play, or to make a point (*La cisma de*

Ingalaterra, *El príncipe constante*); he could also place a fictitious drama in a historical setting (*Nadie fíe su secreto*, *El médico de su honra*). However, while we can describe the subject-matter of five of the plays as 'fictional court intrigue', it seems unlikely that either Calderón or his audience regarded *Nadie fíe su secreto* and *Amor, honor y poder* as very different, although Edward III's passion for the Countess of Salisbury was recorded as fact, while the passion of Alessandro Farnese for his secretary's lady-friend was not. These plays, though, are obviously different from the character comedies (*El astrólogo fingido* and *Hombre pobre todo es trazas*), which pre-date the first situation comedies (*La dama duende* and *Casa con dos puertas*), both of 1629, and similar in plot. While the moral is frequently quite clear, even to the point of explicitness in the character comedies, this clarity is absent from a 'wife-murder' play like *El médico de su honra*. When a moral is not controversial, an author can state it clearly; when he wants to be critical of hypocritical values which a society still prizes, he must be more subtle, demonstrating without commentary how the proponent of those values ends unhappily, or even in catastrophe. If Calderón saw or read Lope's *Los comendadores de Córdoba* (1596–8), he is unlikely to have missed the element of black farce which contradicts the 'happy outcome' of the protagonist's actions; his own solution was different, and involved the feature described as 'diffused responsibility', where all the major characters contribute to the disaster.[39] Whether or not Calderón was as systematic in this matter as Parker's analysis implies, it was a feature he would use repeatedly in later plays, and one which he may be said to have invented. Another characteristic, already referred to and much in evidence, and which appears for the first time in *La devoción de la cruz* and *La vida es sueño*, is the parent–child conflict, where the parent's actions blight the future of the child. Another kind of play which makes its first appearance in this early period is the chivalresque romance, represented by *La puente de Mantible*. Don Pedro wrote a number of plays in this category, including his last, *Hado y divisa de Leonido y de Marfisa*. Chivalresque romances are not popular with modern audiences or critics, but these plays remind us that Cervantes did not kill them off with *Don Quixote*. It may be noted, finally, that there are no mythological works during this period, unless we include the *auto El divino Jasón*, which may have been written by 1630 (although Don Pedro never claimed it as his), and the collaboration play *Polifemo y Circe*.[40]

Polifemo y Circe is usually attributed to Mira, Pérez de Montalbán and Calderón. When it was first printed in 1647, with the title *El Polifemo*, in *Doze comedias las mas grandiosas que asta aora han salido ... Segunda parte*, it was attributed only to Don Pedro. That he did not write the play alone is demonstrated by his own words, in his own hand, at the end of Act III of manuscript Res. 83 of the Biblioteca Nacional:

Y tres
poetas vn perdon os piden
porque lo que dos merecen
el vno consiga humilde.

(And three poets ask you for pardon, so that one may humbly obtain what two deserve.)

Act II is signed by Juan Pérez de Montalbán in 'Madrid y Martes [ ] de Abril de 1630' ('Madrid, Tuesday [ ] April 1630'), but Act I is a copy in which Andalusian spellings like Cirse and Ulices are common. Since Mira was born in Guadix in 1574 and studied in Granada, it seems quite probable that he really did write Act I, and that his odd spelling was retained by the copyist.

Collaboration was a means for writers who were short of cash to write a play in a little more than a third of the usual time (assuming three collaborators, the most usual number) – a little more, because, if the three acts were to be written simultaneously, an extra amount of planning was needed to produce a consistent plot and characterisation. And since the profits had to be divided between the three, it is hard to see what was gained, except for ready cash, quickly. In Don Pedro's case at least, these collaborations were not long-term arrangements like that of Beaumont and Fletcher. In the thirteen plays in which he was involved (including one which has been lost), he had ten different collaborators: Antonio Coello (five times), Rojas Zorrilla (four), Pérez de Montalbán (three), Juan de Zabaleta (three), Cáncer y Velasco and Solís (two), and Belmonte Bermúdez, Mira de Amescua, Moreto and Vélez de Guevara (once each).[41] In eleven of the thirteen, he wrote either the first or the last act, usually the last (on eight occasions); in one case (*Yerros de naturaleza*) his single collaborator, Coello, wrote both the opening and closing lines. We cannot tell whether he preferred to write the last act, or whether his colleagues believed that his skills lay in dénouement.

The stories of Polyphemus and Circe were told by Homer and Ovid. In 1573 Cristóbal de Castillejo's *Obras* were published; they included his version of the Polyphemus/Galatea/Acis story, an acknowledged source of Góngora's *Fábula de Polifemo y Galatea*. Góngora completed his *Fábula* in 1613, and allowed it to circulate in manuscript, although it was not printed until 1627. That it was one of the sources of this play is beyond question. Other sources include Lope de Vega's *La Circe* (1624) and Pérez de

Montalbán's own *auto sacramental*, *El Polifemo* (1628). We do not know who first thought of the play, but a comparison with Pérez de Montalbán's *auto* suggests that if he was the instigator, his co-authors suggested improvements.

The importance of *Polifemo y Circe*, from a literary historian's point of view, is that it is Calderón's first mythological play. Five years later, he used this play as a basis for *El mayor encanto, amor*, performed in July 1635 on the lake of the Buen Retiro. He also dealt with the Circe/Ulysses story in his *auto Los encantos de la culpa* (1636–8 or 1643–5), and portrayed Ulysses in *El golfo de las sirenas* (performed 1657 and printed in his *Quarta parte* of 1672; the Scylla and Charybdis episode) and in *El monstruo de los jardines* (?*c.* 1650–3, also printed in the *Quarta parte*; the discovery of Achilles).

Polifemo y Circe is more than the dramatisation of a myth. In his *Philosofía secreta* Juan Pérez de Moya had pointed to the moral significance of the story of Circe and Ulysses:

> Circe es aquella pasión natural que llaman amor deshonesto, que las más veces transforma a los más sabios y de mayor juicio en animales fierísimos y llenos de furor, y algunas veces los vuelve más insensibles que piedras, acerca de la honra y reputación que conservaban con tanta diligencia … Mas la razón, entendida por Ulises, permanece firme sin ser vencido, contra estos halagos del apetito.[42]

> (Circe is that natural passion which they call illicit love, which usually transforms the wisest and most sensible into the fiercest and most furious animals, and sometimes makes them more insensitive than stones regarding the honour and reputation they preserved so diligently … But reason, represented by Ulysses, remains steadfast against these blandishments of appetite, without being overcome.)

At least some of this message was present in Calderón's part of the 1630 play:

	Polifemo y Circe		*El mayor encanto, amor*
Ulises	Altos montes de Sicilia, cuya hermosura compite con el cielo, pues sus flores con las estrellas se miden, yo fui de vuestros engaños triunfador; Teseo felice fui de vuestros laberintos, y Edipo de vuestra esfinge.	Ulises	Ásperos montes del Flegra, cuya eminencia compite con el cielo, pues sus puntas con las estrellas se miden, yo fui de vuestros venenos triunfador; Teseo felice fui de vuestros laberintos, y Edipo de vuestra esfinge. *Del mayor encanto, amor*, la razón me sacó libre, trasladando esos palacios a los campos de Anfitrite.

	Polifemo y Circe		*El mayor encanto, amor*
TODOS	¡Buen vïaje! ¡Buen vïaje!	TODOS	¡Buen vïaje!
		FLÉRIDA	Buen vïaje, todos los vientos repiten.
		CIRCE	Escucha, tirano griego,
CIRCE	Escucha, engañoso Ulises, pues te habla, no crüel, sino enamorada, Circe.		espera, engañoso Ulises, pues te habla, no crüel, sino enamorada, Circe.
ULYSSES	Lofty Sicilian mountains, whose height competes with heaven, since their flowers with the stars are measured, I was triumphant over your deceptions; I was the fortunate Theseus of your labyrinths, Oedipus of your sphinx.	ULYSSES	Rugged mountains of Phlegra, whose beauty competes with heaven, since their tips with the stars are measured, I was triumphant over your venom; I was the fortunate Theseus of your labyrinths, Oedipus of your sphinx. From *Love, the greatest enchantment*, reason brought me out, free, moving those palaces to the fields of Amphitrite.
ALL	¡Good journey! ¡Good journey!	ALL	¡Good journey!
		FLÉRIDA	Good journey, all the winds repeat.
		CIRCE	Listen, tyrant Greek, wait,
CIRCE	Listen, deceitful Ulysses, since Circe addresses you, not cruelly but in love.		deceitful Ulysses, since Circe addresses you, not cruelly but in love.

These passages illustrate, once again, an important characteristic of Calderón's writing, one which is evident from the beginning: his use of earlier material, both his own and others'. 'Material' covers everything from vocabulary to turns of phrase, jokes, situations, entire plots. He re-used his own jokes, his own images, rewrote his own plays (*La cruz en la sepultura / La devoción de la cruz, Casa con dos puertas, La vida es sueño*), re-used his own plots (*La dama duende* and *Casa con dos puertas*), or rewrote the plays of others (*El médico de su honra, La fortuna adversa / El príncipe constante*). Writing in an age when existing literature was seen as a quarry for literature to be written, he may have made no clear distinction between what he and what others had written, if it could be improved on. It would be quite wrong, on the other hand, to see him as incapable of invention. His only sources for *El sitio de Bredá* were contemporary accounts; for *La gran Cenobia*, *La cisma de Ingalaterra* and *El purgatorio de San Patricio*, brief details in history books; for *La vida es sueño*, his own imagination.

When the re-use of material extends to whole passages, as in the example quoted, an important question is raised: how did Calderón manage? So far as we know, *Polifemo y Circe* was not printed until 1647, but in 1635 Don Pedro incorporated lines from it in *El mayor encanto*; and this case is only one such example. A group of autograph *auto* manuscripts preserved in Madrid's Biblioteca Histórica y Municipal are fair copies, possibly made with a view to publication, but the poet's attitude to the texts of his *autos* was different, because of the nature of the material. There is no evidence that he retained copies of his *comedias* when he sold them; copying the 15,000 words of an average play would be a tedious day's work. However, one of the tasks of a company's prompter was to make fair copies of the plays bought by his manager, especially if the authors' originals were untidy, which was generally true of Calderón's manuscripts. A writer who was on good terms with *autores*, as Calderón was, may have had his originals returned, and it would be a foolish *autor* who would refuse to lend a manuscript which would help an author to write a new play for him.

CHAPTER 9

Only poetry, not precious stones

> Hace versos, canta, juega,
> con que acabo de decir
> que es pobre; porque a estas gracias
> no se les sigue un cuatrín.
>
> (*El hombre pobre todo es trazas*)

(She writes verse, she sings, she plays, with which I've just said that she's poor; for these gifts don't attract a penny.)

As the title of Chapter 11 of his biography of Olivares, J. H. Elliott chose 'A Régime under Pressure', with the first section-title 'The great depression (1629–31)'.[1] By 1631 the *annus mirabilis* of 1625 (words from an earlier section-title) was a distant memory. It was obvious that Spain was doing badly, and not only in military terms. A major contributory factor in the decline was the loss, in September 1628, of the Mexican silver fleet. The squadron of the Dutch admiral, Piet Heyn, had surprised the fleet in the bay of Matanzas in Cuba with superior forces, but the loss was made worse by the lack of Spanish resistance. The Crown lost a million ducats' worth of silver and 3 million in ships and guns, while the *consulado* in Seville reckoned private losses at as much as 6 million.[2] The loss of face, of 'reputation', was at least as damaging. The immediate consequences were that there was no money available for the campaigns in Flanders and Italy, and that the Dutch and French were encouraged into postponing any agreement, in the expectation that the disaster would reduce Spain's bargaining power. Another, longer-term, consequence was the increase of opposition to Olivares. The most coherent example of this opposition was the 'manifesto of the nobles' which was circulated in June 1629 (referred to above, p. 97), and Olivares was so conscious of his unpopularity that he recalled Quevedo from his rural exile to act as propagandist on the regime's behalf.[3] One of the first pieces of propaganda was his play *Cómo ha de ser el privado*.

Olivares was also greatly troubled by a growing independence on the part of the king. He managed to persuade Philip to abandon his plan to lead his troops in Italy in person, but the monarch insisted that he would accompany his sister María on the first part of her journey to Vienna. María had been married by proxy to the emperor's son (the King of Hungary, later the Emperor Ferdinand III) on 25 April 1629, in an effort to encourage the emperor to provide Spain with more military support. In due course the emperor, believing that his interests would best be served by intervention in Italy, sent large numbers of troops there, rather than to Friesland, where they might have been used to induce the Dutch to accept another truce. On 19 August 1629 came the unexpected capture of Wesel (in Germany, on the Rhine), and, four weeks later, the long-expected fall of Hertzogenbosch, only some 25 miles from the great victory at Breda in 1625. There were both hawks and doves among the Dutch, but Spain's repeated losses (which included the Dutch capture, in March 1630, of Olinda and Recife in Brazil) gave the hawks the upper hand, and the Dutch abandoned peace negotiations, further encouraged by news of the arrival in Pomerania, in June, of King Gustavus Adolphus, with 55,000 troops. To make matters worse, Ferdinand's investment in Italy meant that eventually he felt able to decide the Italian terms himself, by the treaties of Cherasco (April/June 1631), which gave Spain no return for her considerable investment in men and money.

When the former Infanta María, now the Queen of Hungary, finally began her move to Vienna (28 December 1629), the journey gave rise to an additional embarrassment for Olivares. It had been supposed that Philip would accompany her only to Alcalá, but he gradually extended his journey as far as Zaragoza, where he alarmed Olivares even more by summoning the Duke of Alba, who was known to be no friend of the chief minister. In the event, it emerged that Philip had sent for the duke only to escort his sister to Italy, where he had recently served as viceroy of Naples; but Philip must have known that his unexpectedly prolonged journey, and prolonged absence, would be seen as a snub to Olivares: indeed, this was probably his intention. One wonders if Philip recalled the performance he had seen, in March 1628, of *Saber del mal y del bien*, in which the young king had decided to teach his favourite that 'Yo soy rey, y yo puedo | vivir sin vos' ('I am king, and I can live without you').

If the absence of the king was one problem Olivares had to face, the cost of maintaining the royal entourage on the road was another. The main royal party was away from Madrid for just over three weeks (28 December to 19 January), and included both the king's brothers and two dukes (of Frías and Medina de las Torres), as well as various marquises and counts. There is no evidence to confirm or to deny that Frías's *escudero* Don Pedro was present: that several of his plays have settings in Zaragoza proves nothing.

Perhaps not surprisingly, Olivares was ill during this period, treated for gout by bleedings and purgings, but also, almost certainly, suffering from what we would now call depression, or what his contemporaries called melancholy, or *hipocondría*, the dejection which afflicts Coquín in *El médico de su honra*. Eventually the infanta left Barcelona for Naples, where, however, she remained from August until December of 1630: it was here that Velázquez painted her.[4] At least peace was signed with England (15 November), ending the hostilities which had resulted from the failure of the Spanish Match; a peace which might, in due course, bring an alliance against the Dutch. And, rather like someone engaging in 'retail therapy' as a means of cheering up, Olivares encouraged Philip to extend the modest royal apartments which adjoined the monastery of San Jerónimo, in what was then open country to the east of Madrid. On 10 July 1630, conscious of the need to find a suitable venue for the swearing of the oath of fealty to Prince Baltasar Carlos, planned for 1632, Olivares had himself appointed governor of the Royal Apartment of San Jerónimo.[5] The first building works, of 1630–1, were modest, but they became increasingly ambitious, and were eventually to result in the palace of the Buen Retiro. The complex would include the Coliseo, Spain's first purpose-built royal theatre; the Hall of Realms, where plays were staged more privately; and a large artificial lake, which would also be used as a performance area.

* * *

For the printers and booksellers of Castile, the great depression started early, and was followed by a series of reverses: beginning around 1620, Seville, Spain's major trading city, had suffered a slump. From 1625 onwards, licences had been refused for the printing of plays and novels; on 13 June 1627 a new law required preliminary approval for the printing of 'memoriales de pleitos, informaciones en derecho, relaciones, cartas, apologías, panegíricos, gacetas, noticias, sermones, discursos, coplas y otros papeles menores' ('lawsuit briefs, legal reports, accounts, letters, apologias, panegyrics, gazettes, newsletters, sermons, discourses, verses and other minor documents');[6] and the loss of the silver fleet in 1628 severely limited the amount of money available for investment in any long-term business such as publishing. The book trade reacted in various ways, one of which, piracy, has been mentioned. Another response was to switch from larger books to ephemera. There are several varieties of ephemera, but all of them are more affordable than large books, and need little or no long-term capital investment. One variety, a lawful one, was the newsheet. The earliest Spanish newsheets go back to before 1500, but a huge growth in numbers can be detected from the mid 1620s onwards. Newsheets must have increased public awareness of events at home and abroad, hence the government's desire to control them. Another variety, less lawful (as long as licences to print plays were not being issued in Castile), was the *comedia suelta*, a single unbound play, rather like a quarto play in England. The earliest *comedias sueltas* were produced in the first decade of the sixteenth century, but it seems likely that the beleaguered book trade of the 1620s saw them as another means of survival, since it was hard to prove where they had been produced when they had no imprint.

For a playwright like Calderón, writing with performance in mind, these changes in the nature of the book trade would have had little immediate impact. In the longer term, however, the literate members of his audience would have an increased political awareness, as well as a better chance to become familiar with the *comedia*, including those which they had not managed to see. Spain might be doing badly on the battlefield and with the bankers, but the opportunities for a dramatist were still good: the thirties were by far Calderón's most productive decade.

As long as the Coliseo remained unbuilt (it was opened only in 1640), royal play performances remained somewhat improvised. Several of the rooms in the old *alcázar* were used, but only in the *salón*, the largest room in the palace at 35 by 170 feet, were modifications made (Plate 18).[7] Even so, no seating was installed: a small dais with armchairs was provided for the king and his brothers, but court ladies (including the queen) had to sit on cushions (a normal domestic arrangement in early modern Spain), while male courtiers had to stand. Occasionally, as Patacón explains in *Las manos blancas no ofenden*, an elderly male aristocrat might be provided with an *apartado*, an enclosed space containing a chair. Others might well envy him, says Patacón,

Porque se excusaran
del de detrás que rempuja,
del del lado que le aja,
del del otro que le aprieta,
del de delante que parla;
redimiendo de camino
la liga que ya le mata,
el callo que ya le duele …
Y lo peor destas andanzas
es que su incomodidad,
es la fiesta quien la paga,
diciendo que es larga. Pues,
hombre, en pie, ¿no ha de ser larga? (II, IIIIb)

(Because they'd avoid the fellow behind shoving, the fellow at one side crushing, the one at the other squashing, the one in front chattering, easing in passing the garter which by this time is killing him, the corn which is hurting him. And the worst thing about these adventures is that it's the play that pays the price for his discomfort, when he says it's long; for a man standing, why shouldn't it be long?)

The spectators must have laughed ruefully at this description, since this performance was probably taking place in the *salón*: getting the members of the audience to laugh at themselves is one of Calderón's comic techniques. Here, he also takes the opportunity to suggest that more comfortable arrangements would allow the audience to appreciate plays better. Some ten years later, in *El conde Lucanor*, which refers in a stage direction to performance in the *salón*, the *gracioso* Pasquín uses a shorter version to make a general complaint about standing around and waiting:

Así atendiera al que ya
la liga aprieta y le duele
el callo, y está diciendo:
'¿Adónde estaba lo breve?' (II, 1996a)

(If only the person would pay such heed whose garter is tight and whose corn is hurting, and who's saying, 'Whatever happened to brevity?')

Unfortunately, we cannot make conclusive assumptions about dates or intended performance venues on the basis of the staging which a play requires: the arrival of the Italian stage-designer Cosme/Cosimo Lotti in 1626 made stage machinery possible even in temporary stages. What we can tell is that Calderón's output increased. While he wrote about twenty-six plays in the period 1622 to 1630, he wrote around fifty-two in the next decade (including those in collaboration), or an average of five per year. 'You do not write thirty-six plays in less than twenty-five years', says Peter Ackroyd of Shakespeare, 'without being driven.'[8] If we are to measure being driven by sheer numbers (close to eighty plays in twenty years in Don Pedro's case) or by the playwright's obsessive concern for his texts, Calderón is the more driven of the two. However, there is another factor that began to operate in Calderón's career, once he had decided not to take up his grandmother's chaplaincy: the need to write enough to survive.

During the 1630s, or perhaps earlier, Calderón began to write *autos sacramentales*, eventually composing two of them every year for Madrid Town Council, which paid him 300 ducats (3,300 *reales*) for them. The greater output and the move into a new genre meant a significant increase in income; but even if we add that from plays, *autos* and annuities together, the poet's average weekly income from these sources in his most productive period, his thirties, is not likely to have been more than 150 *reales*, or 5,100 *maravedís*. If we converted at the same rate as in a previous chapter, we could reckon this at the equivalent of £26,500 a year nowadays: not a fortune, but enough to live on, while the salary and perquisites of an *escudero* would have helped. In fact, though, the purchasing power of 150 *reales* in 1635 was far short of what it had been twenty years earlier. Calderón had found a livelihood, but it was not one which could support a wife and family in the style expected of an *hidalgo*.

As Calderón's output increased, so do the problems of chronology. One play which can be dated approximately is *Amigo, amante y leal*, since it is one of those named in *La maestra de gracias* (i.e., probably no later than 1631). As noted above, the plot of *Amigo, amante y leal* is very similar to that of *Nadie fíe su secreto*: Alejandro, Prince of Parma, has seen and desires Aurora, lady-friend of the protagonist Don Félix. Félix is one of those people for whom the glass is always half-empty, lacking in self-confidence, lacking in the willingness to confide in others: his friend Arias, who has loved Aurora from afar, has no idea that he has two rivals, and strives to protect her from the prince's dishonourable intentions, while Félix, placing loyalty to the prince higher than any other, is willing to hand her over. In the hierarchical society of the seventeenth century, we might think, loyalty to one's superior took precedence. Perhaps, but the spirited Aurora is quick enough to call Félix 'villano' ('peasant') and Arias 'caballero' ('gentleman'), and remarks, sarcastically, when she has taken Félix's sword to defend herself, 'Mas no corta, por ser tuya' ('But it doesn't cut, because it's yours': II, 380b); yet she marries him anyway. Calderón returned again and again to the topic of the self-discipline that men in power must exercise, but it is perhaps improbable that the prince in this play should have been inspired by the 'self-discipline' of a courtier who was willing to give up his fiancée: 'como él se vence, podré | vencerme yo' ('I shall be able to overcome myself as he overcomes himself': II, 380a). We are left with the suspicion that Félix's character has been sacrificed to make a point, and that Ángela's Don Manuel (in *La dama duende*) might have seen matters differently.

Another play named in *La maestra de gracias* is *Mejor está que estaba*, which was performed by Antonio de Prado on 29 March 1633.[9] The setting is in Vienna, and the text refers to the confirmation of the marriage there of the Infanta María on 26 February 1631, and to her progress along the river Danube in a decorated barge. News of the event would have reached Madrid a few weeks later, and Cotarelo suggests that the play was written then, that is, in March/April 1631.[10] The argument is plausible, except for the joke of the *gracioso* Dinero about a *guardainfante* (II, 413b). Hannah

Bergman suggested that references to *guardainfantes* in dramatic works are most numerous in the mid 1630s, beginning, she argued, with Quiñones de Benavente's *El guardainfante*, Parts I and II, which were apparently written in the autumn of 1634.[11] Unless more evidence becomes available, it would seem that Dinero's joke is the first, perhaps even in March 1633, and certainly in March 1631.

Dinero's joke is not his only significant feature: to his own surprise (and, probably, that of the audience), he draws his sword on the honour-obsessed Fabio, who is about to take vengeance on a veiled young woman he thinks is his sister:

No es hombre noble y cortés
el que tan groseramente
atropella una mujer. (II, 416a)

(He who so roughly bullies a woman is not a noble, courteous man.)

We do not know whether the Calderón brother who was stabbed by the brother of Ana de Villegas two (or four) years previously had tried to defend her in this way, although this scene prompts us to consider that he might have. The moment heightens the significance of the actions of Dinero's master Carlos, whose tribulations are the result of defending the same young woman, at her request, from unwanted male attentions. There are a number of jealous brothers in Calderón's plays, and they are almost invariably thwarted. Here, the sister marries the man she wanted to, while Flora, the veiled young woman, marries her rescuer Carlos; to add insult to this injury, Fabio had himself had his eye on Flora.

Cotarelo suggests the date of 1630 for *El galán fantasma*, on the grounds that it must have been composed soon after *La dama duende*.[12] That it was composed later seems clear enough, since the *gracioso* Candil suggests that the *galán fantasma* would make a suitable husband for the *dama duende* (II, 653b). This remark apart, there is no evidence that Don Pedro considered the plays a pair: *El galán fantasma* was published in his *Segunda parte* (1637) and *La dama duende* in the *Primera parte* (1636), and the plots and settings (Madrid and 'Saxony') are quite different. The phrase *Para vencer a amor, querer vencerle* (II, 648a) is also used. The comment which introduces it ('Ovidio dice, hablando del remedio | de amor, cuál es el medio: | oye el verso': 'Ovid, speaking of the cure for love, says what the way is: listen to the line') suggests that this might be a quotation rather than a reference to the play, except that Ovid does not give the advice in these precise words.[13] In *La banda y la flor*, Enrique quotes the 'quererle vencer' remedy ('wanting to overcome it'), and adds 'Así lo dice, señor, | Garcilaso' ('That's how

Garcilaso says it, sir': II, 444a). Since Garcilaso does not say this in so many words either, these references must be examples of self-advertisement.[14] All we have for the date of *Para vencer a amor* are guesses, but *La banda y la flor* refers to the swearing of the oath to Baltasar Carlos (March 1632).[15] All three plays probably date from 1630–3.

The most interesting feature of *El galán fantasma* is the tunnel through which the lover enters the garden of the beloved. As Parker argued, Calderón used this motif as an erotic symbol in *Apolo y Climene* (1661).[16] There is no evidence that he thought of it in that way in this case. Were it not for *Amigo, amante y leal*, in which the lack of scruples of Alejandro Farnese (the nephew of Philip II) extend to ordering the kidnapping of a young woman and planning to use force on her, we might suppose that the setting in Saxony could be explained by the need to portray a head of state – the Duke of Saxony – with a similar lack of scruples (when the play was composed, the head of state of Saxony was the Elector, John George, who was not a duke). As it is, the plays are sufficiently similar in plot and date of composition to prompt the suspicion that they were inspired by some contemporary event.

La banda y la flor is set in Florence in May, and the protagonist Enrique describes in detail, ostensibly for the duke of Florence, the oath of allegiance offered to Prince Baltasar Carlos (Madrid, 7 March 1632): the play probably dates from May 1632. Enrique describes the king and queen, the prince, and the infantes Carlos and Ferdinand; on the left side, the princes of the Church, the ambassadors of Rome, France and Venice, with the Councils (i.e., of State, Castile, Aragón, etc.) behind them; on the right, titled nobles and grandees ('a nadie nombro, | que aquí es la lisonja ofensa', 'I name no-one, for flattery here is an offence': II, 426a). Indeed, one suspects that many aristocrats would have been offended had the organiser of the ceremony been singled out for mention. The organiser, Olivares, would probably not have objected: one of the several contemporary newsletters points out that after the prince's uncles had taken the oath, followed by the princes of the Church, he was the first of the grandees to do so.[17] Another account mentions that the festivities ended with three plays performed in the palace, and gives their authors as the Prince of Esquilache (Francisco de Borja y Aragón), Antonio Hurtado de Mendoza and Diego Jiménez de Enciso.[18] We cannot say whether Don Pedro was describing his own view of the ceremony, seen from a vantage-point among the entourage of the Duke of Frías: he could have got the information from a newsletter.

Enrique closes Act II of *La banda y la flor* with the lines 'ofender con las finezas, | y hacer del amor agravio' ('to give offence with compliments, and make an injury of love': II, 444b). The first is the title of a play by Jerónimo de Villaizán, performed in the *salón* of the *alcázar* on 5 February 1632, by the company of Manuel Vallejo,[19] while the second is an alternative title for this play. The alternative title refers to the attitude of Clori, who is jealous of the attentions paid to her sister Lísida by Enrique, and tries to come between them, with the help of her devious cousin Nise, whose lukewarm response to her earnest suitor Octavio is expressed by her casual comment 'divierto así su esperanza' ('thus do I entertain his hopes': II, 438b). For a time, Nise looks as if she may be an Emma Woodhouse, but her role of would-be matchmaker is a minor one. Clori convinces herself that she loves Enrique, spurning even the duke who, as in other plays, complicates the love-life of his loyal servants Enrique and Octavio, even though he is not a rival. In the end, Enrique and Octavio are rewarded with the hands of Lísida and Nise (although we do not learn what Nise thinks of this); Clori is left, disappointed, to pronounce the moral.

In 1632 the Duke of Frías, Calderón's employer, would have reached twenty-two. He was married, of course (since September 1624), but there would have been plenty of unattached young men and women in the ducal court. Many of these aristocrats, attached or not, must have had little else to do but engage in, or imagine, emotional entanglements with one another: they would have supplied plenty of models for a dramatist. In this case the dramatist's lesson is that love is something that deserves to be treated in a genuine way: those who are manipulative or casual may come to regret it.

The other way in which the moral is presented is through Ponleví, who mocks the sentiments and the language of the upper classes (and the language and plot-construction of the poet). When he has to hide, he likens himself to a king caught in his lady-friend's house by her father:

Rey parezco de comedia,
cuando en casa de su dama
le halla con ella un padre
tiritón y barba larga. (II, 438b)

(I'm like a play-king when a shaky long-beard of a father finds him in his lady-friend's house with her.)

There is just such a scenario in *Yerros de naturaleza*, which was finished by May 1634, too late for an audience to connect with this reference; but there is a similar one in *Amor, honor y poder* (1623), although it involves a king hiding from a lady's brother, not a long-bearded father. Later, he cries, in Gongoristic fashion, as Nise lets fly at him with both hands:

¡Ay, que me matan
diez puñales de cristal,
con diez remates de nácar! (II, 441b)

(Ouch, I'm being killed by ten crystal daggers with ten tips of nacre!)

Calderón's admiration for Góngora is not in dispute, but we can only speculate about Don Pedro's relationships with some of the writers, like Villaizán, whose works are mentioned in his plays. In his *Coronas del Parnaso* (licensed 1630, printed 1635), Alonso de Salas Barbadillo refers, as it were in a single breath, to the 'insignes ingenios Doctor Mira de Amescua, Doctor Iuan Perez de Montaluan, Don Pedro Calderon, Dõ Geronimo de Villaizan' ('the distinguished wits Doctor Mira de Amescua, Doctor Juan Pérez de Montalbán, Don Pedro Calderón, Don Jerónimo de Villaizán').[20] Although Mira, born around 1574, belonged to an older generation, Calderón had collaborated with him and Pérez de Montalbán (b. 1602), and his references to plays and other works by these men suggest that all four of them were friends. This is partially confirmed by Sebastián Francisco de Medrano's *Favores de las musas*, an edition produced in Milan in 1631 by Castillo Solórzano.[21] In the preliminaries Medrano refers to his 'condiscípulos' ('fellow pupils') Juan Pérez de Montalbán, Don Pedro Calderón and Joseph [*sic*] de Villaizán. Villaizán, the son of a *boticario* (a pharmacist), was baptised in Madrid on 9 June 1604. Having studied law, he became a lawyer in the Reales Consejos (*c.* 1630). As early as 1624 he had contributed a prefatory poem to Pérez de Montalbán's *Orfeo en lengua castellana*. When Pedro de Castro y Anaya published his *Las auroras de Diana* in 1630(?), Pérez de Montalbán, Calderón and Villaizán were contributors (as was Lope; oddly, given the date, Don Pedro used the surnames Calderón y Riaño); the publisher was Alonso Pérez, Juan's father.[22] All four men contributed poems to José Pellicer y Tovar's *Anfiteatro de Felipe el Grande*, a strange collection assembled to celebrate Philip IV's shooting dead of a bull at a fiesta on 13 October 1631 (the contributors also included Lope, Antonio Coello, Luis Vélez de Guevara and Francisco de Rojas Zorrilla).[23] Calderón's poem, an epigrammatic sonnet ('Si viste, o Licio, material Esfera', 29^{v}), compares and contrasts the unfortunate bull with the one which carried off Europa, that is, Jupiter. It ends with a clever nod in the direction of the opening lines of Góngora's first *Soledad*:

Pero que importa que el Ladrón de Europa
mentido triunfe, como el Sol de España
contra su frente esgrima el primer Rayo?

(But what does it matter if Europa's disguised abductor should triumph, as long as the Sun of Spain wields the first thunderbolt against his brow?)

The next year, when Castillo de Larzával published *El Adonis*, the contributors of prefatory verses included Calderón, Mira, Pérez de Montalbán and Villaizán, as well as Antonio Hurtado de Mendoza, Francisco López de Zárate, Tirso and María de Zayas.[24] Finally, in his *Para todos*, Pérez de Montalbán refers to Villaizán's having written 'tres comedias con el mayor aplauso que jamás se ha visto' ('three plays with the greatest acclaim ever seen').[25] If the praise seems excessive, it may be irony: there is reason to believe that the two men fell out about this time. Calderón remained friends with Pérez de Montalbán until the latter's death, but while there is no indication of any personal disagreement with Villaizán, whatever friendship survived was cut short by Villaizán's premature death in 1633; as for Mira, he returned to his native Guadix in 1632 to take up an archdeaconry. What is interesting is the social rank of Villaizán and Pérez de Montalbán: both were university graduates, but were the sons of well-to-do businessmen who kept shops. Villaizán claimed the title Don, but some of his contemporaries delighted in calling him 'el hijo del boticario', the pharmacist's son. Don Pedro's background was very different: a noble, although poor, his degree uncompleted; yet he was clearly no snob, and was indifferent to possible suggestions that his friends were 'beneath him'.

Whatever the state of Don Pedro's relationship with Villaizán, there is no shortage of evidence for friendship with Pérez de Montalbán. When Luis Pacheco de Narváez (a much older man, famous for his books on the skills of swordplay) published his *Historia exemplar de las dos mugeres constantes españolas* in 1635, both Calderón and Pérez de Montalbán contributed laudatory poems.[26] Don Pedro's poem was a sonnet ('Si por la espada es inmortal la gloria'), which took the opportunity to recall Don Luis's other works. To judge by Fernando Pérez Pericón's poem, *Descripción ... de Gibraltar*, the connection between Pacheco de Narváez and the two younger men may have been more than acquaintance, since both of them wrote an approbation for that book, while Pacheco contributed a *décima*.[27] The complete gentleman of Siglo de Oro Spain needed to be able to wield both sword and pen.

* * *

Another of the events of 1632 was the unexpected death, on 31 July, of the Infante Don Carlos, a docile and ineffectual young man who, while Philip IV had no child, could have been Spain's next monarch. Ineffectual he may have been, but he was seen by the anti-Olivares faction as a potential leader, so much so that gossip held that Olivares had had him poisoned. Some of Olivares's opponents would gladly have seen the count-duke poisoned, but he would never have taken such a step with the king's brother, although he had him watched. By the same token, he could not conclude (and nor should we) that a young writer with aspirations at court had joined the opposition, if he wrote an elegy for the dead prince. Calderón's *Elegía en la muerte del señor infante don Carlos*, 307 lines in *tercetos*, was probably written in August 1632 and published soon afterwards.[28] It opens with, and uses as a refrain, the line '¡Oh rompa ya el silencio el dolor mío!', the opening line of a sonnet attributed to the prince himself. The sonnet was printed by Pérez de Montalbán in his *Para todos* that same year, a publication which inevitably drew attention to his friend Don Pedro's elegy.

* * *

Other works which probably date from this period are *El monstruo de la fortuna, la lavandera de Nápoles*, a collaboration play, which was performed (apparently not for the first time) on 22 November 1636 by Pedro de la Rosa, and *De una causa dos efectos*. The evidence for the date of the first is an ostensible reference ('a *Pérez*, la *Lavandera*') in Tirso's *Del enemigo el primer consejo*, published in his *Parte tercera*, 1634, which has an approbation dated 13 September 1633.[29] If this really is a reference to *La lavandera de Nápoles*, of which Pérez de Montalbán wrote only Act II, then the play was completed by 1633 at the latest. Lope's play *La reina Juana de Nápoles* was also entitled *El monstruo de la fortuna*, but there is no reason to believe that it was the one performed in 1636, since it was written nearly forty years previously. Both plays deal with Queen Juana, forced to marry the murderous Andrés, whom she hates, and with his killing; but the heroine of the play by Calderón, Pérez de Montalbán and Rojas is Felipa Catanea, a Neapolitan washerwoman. Felipa kills Andrés because her queen wishes it, and willingly suffers death to save Juana and Naples. Calderón's act, the first, gives Felipa a speech which echoes lines 123–45 of *La vida es sueño*:

> Nace con belleza suma
> el ave …
> Nace el bruto …
> Nace el pez de ovas y lamas,
> tan mudo, que aun no respira. (1290b–1291a)[30]

(The bird is born with sovereign beauty … The beast is born … The fish is born of roe and slime, so mute that it does not even breathe.)

Cotarelo suggested that this must pre-date *La vida es sueño*, since Calderón would not have repeated the *décimas* of that play 'para empeorarlas' ('to make them inferior'),[31] but we know from *Yerros de naturaleza* that this kind of argument is not reliable.

At one point Felipa, describing how she has become habituated to sadness, explains that she read how a king, told by astrologers that he risked being poisoned, gradually accustomed himself to poison by taking small doses, only to become addicted to it (1289a–b). The process of drug dependency is described with uncomfortable accuracy, given that the lines were written by 1636. No doubt Calderón read it as well, but it is not clear where.[32]

De una causa dos efectos is set in Mantua and Milan, the respective dukes of which have a history of enmity. This is not a historical play, but the setting suggests composition during or soon after the period when the Mantuan war (1628–30) loomed large in the Spanish consciousness; the only other textual evidence that casts light on the date is another *guardainfante* joke (II, 467a), but, as we have seen, dating by the use of these jokes is not an exact science. At first sight this play is an early venture into the field of nature and nurture, a field Calderón would explore much later with Heraclio and Leonido in *En la vida todo es verdad y todo mentira* (1659). Carlos and Fadrique are twin sons of Duke Federico of Mantua. Carlos is conscientious, intelligent and caring, while Fadrique is lazy, ostensibly stupid and cruel. The play explores what falling in love with Diana, daughter of the Duke of Milan, does to these two very different young men: both of them are changed completely, although Carlos is able to argue, plausibly, that he has been altered for the worse not by love, but by the belief that Diana prefers his brother.

Para vencer a amor, querer vencerle probably dates from 1630–3. Set in a non-historical Italy, like *La banda y la flor* and *De una causa dos efectos*, it deals with the attempts of César to come to terms with rejection by his cousin Margarita. His efforts to overcome his feelings for Margarita – efforts which are eventually successful – lead to his becoming the emperor's favourite and Duke of Ferrara, as well as to marriage with Matilde, Baroness of Momblanc. Margarita ends up with nothing, despite César's endeavours to secure the dukedom of Ferrara for her. Margarita is less than grateful for these endeavours, whereas Matilde's feelings for César grow out of the gratitude she feels for his having rescued her. Not merely is the ability to control oneself good in itself, but we see it bring rich rewards, while the ungrateful are penalised. While Margarita complains that women are discriminated against:

¡Oh mal haya ley infame
que dice que las mujeres
no son de mandar capaces! (II, 532b)

(A curse on the odious law that says that woman are incapable of ruling!),

we can see that it is not her gender but her lack of gratitude that has prevented her from becoming Duchess of Ferrara.

Mañanas de abril y mayo has no record of an early performance, but the text refers to King Philip and Queen Isabel (died 1644), to *La dama duende*, to *El burlador de Sevilla* (published 1630) and to Pérez de Montalbán's *Para todos* (published 1632). Given Don Pedro's friendship with Pérez de Montalbán, it seems likely that the last reference was made soon after *Para todos* appeared. The setting is Madrid, mostly in the homes of Don Pedro or Doña Ana, or in the gardens (el Parque) of the old *alcázar*. The conventional lovers are Don Juan and Doña Ana, faithful to each other but deceived by others, whose actions make Juan think that Ana is giving encouragement to rivals. The unconventional lovers are Don Hipólito and Doña Clara. Hipólito is a male chauvinist who thinks he is God's gift to women: 'Yo tengo notable estrella con mujeres', 'I have remarkable luck with women', he boasts to his friend Don Luis. He expects Clara to stay indoors in the fine spring weather, while he goes off to the Parque with Luis, to ogle other young women there. Like Don Alonso in *No hay burlas con el amor* (?1635), he is a Don Juan Tenorio type who pursues women, but has no thought of commitment. Unlike Alonso, he finds a match in Clara, who is equally uncommitted, equally devious, and more intelligent; also unlike Alonso, he gets his deserts not by falling in love, but by having his wiles exposed by Clara and Ana. The end of the play brings Ana and Juan together, but not Clara and Hipólito, both of whom are fickle and deceitful. The treatment of the characters is so light-hearted, however, that we have no sense of having been exposed to any great wickedness, or to any powerful moral lesson. We do see, though, that the strongest and most sensible character is a woman: Doña Ana.

On 24 January 1633, in the *alcázar*, the *autor* Luis López Sustaete performed a play listed as *Más puede amor que la muerte*. Cotarelo suggests that this was *Amar después de la muerte*, alias *El Tuzaní de la Alpujarra*. However, he had forgotten the play of that title by Pérez de Montalbán, although there is some circumstantial evidence to put composition of *El Tuzaní* around this time.[33] Despite this evidence, if we set any store, in chronological terms, by Calderón's re-use of material, we need to remember a humorous scene in *El cubo de la Almudena* (1651) in which the Morisco *gracioso* Alcuzcuz decides to commit suicide by drinking a *bota* of poison (i.e., wine) which had belonged to the enemy, just as Alcuzcuz does in this play.

The play is set in the Alpujarra revolt of 1568–70, and the principal source was apparently Ginés Pérez de Hita's *Guerras civiles de Granada*, Part II (1619), although Calderón modified the details considerably.[34] The most striking scene takes place in the aftermath of the capture of the town of Galera. Don Álvaro Tuzaní, the male protagonist, is a Christianised Morisco whom honour obliged to become involved in the revolt. Disguised as a Castilian soldier, he listens to Garcés, a real Castilian soldier, tell of his involvement in the sack of the town. Garcés recounts how he captured, contemplated raping, then stabbed and robbed a young Morisca. With growing horror, Don Álvaro recognises the details: this story is that of the murder of his newly wedded wife. He draws his own dagger. '¿Fué | como ésta la puñalada?', he says ('Was the knife-thrust like this one?': 1, 354b). Dying, Garcés complains bitterly that he has been stabbed treacherously, when unarmed: the irony is not likely to have been lost on the audience. Significantly, Don Álvaro is forgiven for this 'crime', thanks partly to the intervention of Don Lope de Figueroa, the same crotchety but fair general who is kind to Isabel Crespo in *El alcalde de Zalamea*. Not only are the hero and heroine of this play Moriscos, but the author also takes a gentle swipe at the great Spanish military heroes of the past: at one point his Morisco *gracioso*, Alcuzcuz, comes on stage to tell us that

> ya muy cerca dejo
> Don Juan de Andustria en campaña,
> a quien decir que acompaña
> el gran Marqués de Mondejo
> con el Marqués de Luzbel,
> y el que fremáticos doma,
> Don Lope Figura-roma,
> y Sancho Débil con él. (1, 337b)

(I leave nearby Don John of Industria on campaign, they say accompany him the great Marquis of Mondejo, with the Marquis of Lucifer, and the one who tames fregmatics, Don Lope de Snub-nose, and Sancho Devila with him.)

This lack of reverence for figures of the stature of Lope de Figueroa and Sancho Dávila, not to mention Don John of Austria, is unusual, even in the mouth of a *gracioso*, and Ted Bergman has noted that it is not the only example.[35] It needs to be said that the likelihood, in 1570, of a real Morisco leader's being forgiven as Don Álvaro was is also unusual, about as unusual as the possibility that Philip II would have made Pedro Crespo lifetime mayor of Zalamea for executing one of his army officers. When Calderón wanted to make a moral point, verisimilitude took second place.

As we saw previously, Madrid had had its own Morisco community, moved there from the Alpujarra after the end of the revolt. Their final expulsion took place in the years 1609–14, when Calderón was old enough to understand and young enough to be impressionable. *El Tuzaní* may also have been partly inspired by Velázquez's *La expulsión de los moriscos*. The painting is lost, but it was hung in the Salón Nuevo of the *alcázar* in 1628.[36] In showing that the victims of Castilian atrocities in 1568–70 included genuinely Christian Moriscos, Calderón implies that this was also true of the expulsion; and that if conversion is to mean anything, it must be voluntary.[37] Alcalá Zamora has argued that the play is critical of the hard-line attitudes which provoked the rising, and that it implicitly presses for government reform in the 1630s.[38] The play may be Calderón's attempt to educate public opinion, an education which led to the king's confessor, Antonio Sotomayor, suggesting in January 1633 that the Moriscos should be repatriated (although it is unlikely that he made this suggestion without the approval of Olivares).[39] Rather than being a belated expression of sympathy for the expelled Christian Moriscos, the play is arguably an attack on the statutes of *limpieza*.[40] When Don Juan Malec explains how he told Don Juan de Mendoza that

los que fueron caballeros
moros no debieron nada
a caballeros cristianos
el día que con el agua
del bautismo recibieron
su fe católica y santa (I, 324a)

(those who were Moorish gentlemen owed nothing to Christian gentlemen the day they received their holy Catholic faith with the water of baptism),

he implicitly condemns the racist notion that 'Old Christians' are somehow more Christian than those descended from converts. This is entirely in keeping with Calderón's presentation of the convert Muley Mahomet in *El gran príncipe de Fez* (1669).

That Calderón should present a case for Christian Moriscos may seem unexceptional enough, but not all the Moriscos in the play are Christians: the first scene opens on a Friday (the Muslim holy day) amid ceremonies which have to take place behind closed doors because Christian authorities would object to them. However, when Don Juan Malec interrupts them to describe how he remonstrated with Mendoza about the timetable for the application of legislation to eliminate such Morisco traditions, and how he was hit with his own stick for his pains, we can see where we are being invited to place our sympathies. There is no evidence that hitting an elderly nobleman with a stick was the real trigger for the revolt of the Alpujarra: this is a literary device, previously used by Lope in *Fuenteovejuna* to highlight the outrageous behaviour of the *comendador*, as he breaks the staff of office of the village mayor Esteban over his head. It is also clear that Mendoza's arrogant racism makes converts think twice about having become Christians:

Porque me volví cristiano,
¿este baldón me sucede?

(This affront happens to me because I turned Christian?)

asks Don Fernando Válor, who eventually becomes 'king' of the Alpujarra, and leader of the rising;

Porque su ley recibí,
¿ya no hay quien de mí se acuerde? (I, 331b)

(Is there no-one to remember me because I accepted their law?)

This is from Don Álvaro, the hero of the play. What is perhaps most remarkable is that Mendoza's most provocative remark,

Pues los míos [ascendientes], sin ser reyes,
fueron más que reyes moros,
porque fueron montañeses (I, 331a)

(For my forebears, without being kings, were more than Moorish kings, because they were from La Montaña),

makes him share the same Cantabrian ancestry as the person who wrote these lines. In *La devoción de la misa* (1658) one of the closing stage directions calls for La Secta de Mahoma to be portrayed in conventional fashion, at the feet of Philip III, with a reference to the Expulsion, but the noble Moorish general Muley of *El príncipe constante*, and, to a lesser extent, the princess Fénix, show how Calderón learned early to distance himself from conventional views.

In the early 1630s, Calderón was involved in another 'historical' play, one which was potentially more hazardous, in that it dealt with events which were still unfolding. Albrecht von Wallenstein, despite the Germanic name, was a Czech, born in Moravia in 1583, brought up as a Lutheran, but an early convert to Catholicism. By 1623 he had amassed large estates in Bohemia, become Count of Friedland, and made an advantageous marriage (his second) to Isabella von Harrach, daughter of a close adviser of the Emperor Ferdinand (and a member of the family which preserved several Calderón manuscripts in their library at Mladá Vožice). This was not enough; nor were his successes as the leading Imperial general, his dukedom, or his reduction of the Swedish threat with the death of Gustavus Adolphus in November 1632 at the otherwise inconclusive battle of Lützen: what he wanted was a crown, the kingdom of Bohemia, and he was willing to switch sides to get it. Finally convinced of his treachery, the emperor dismissed him in January 1634; a month later, on 25 February 1634, he was assassinated by Imperial mercenary officers – two Scots and an Irishman, according to one account – at Eger. C. V. Wedgwood quotes a graphic contemporary description of his body being dragged down a flight of steps, 'his head knocking on every stair, all bloody'.[41]

Such a rise, such a fall, such a death, were an obvious subject for dramatisation, and several playwrights found inspiration in them. The only surviving work of certain authorship is Cubillo de Aragón's *auto La muerte de Frislán*, probably written in 1634: it presents Wallenstein as El Demonio.[42] The previous year, after the news of Lützen had reached Madrid (26 December 1632), the Florentine envoy in Madrid recorded the performance, on 26 January, of 'una gran comedia nuova che se faceva ne' soliti luoghi publici de' comedianti della battaglia et morte del Re di Svezia' ('a great new play which was performed in the usual public theatres, about the battle and death of the King of Sweden'). The author was said to be 'Lope de Vega Carpio ... il maggior poeta senza dubbio che ha oggi in tutta Spagna' ('undoubtedly the greatest poet in all of Spain today'). It drew the envoy's attention because the Council of State prohibited its performance owing (he said) to lack of decorum in its treatment of royal characters who were still alive, or because it included others who were dead or who had nothing to do with the event, like Don Gonzalo de Córdoba and the Marquis of Santa Cruz, or because the 'Infanta of Flanders' (Isabel Clara Eugenia?) discussed state secrets with a buffoon. A week later he reported that the king asked his secretary Antonio de Mendoza to correct the play's 'mancamenti', its defects. It was then licensed and performed, and also taken to El Pardo, on 1 February, by the company of Antonio de Prado, for the queen to see.[43] This play is lost.

The information supplied by seventeenth-century envoys is not always to be trusted, and we may think it unlikely that an author as experienced as Lope would have written a play which had to be corrected in this way, even by a respected playwright like Mendoza; but even if only the other details are correct, they show the risks that playwrights took.

Another Wallenstein play has been described by Germán Vega García-Luengos.[44] With the title *El prodigio de Alemania*, it survives in a single *suelta*, attributed to Calderón. At first sight this ravaged text (with only 637 lines in Act III) would appear to have no connection with Don Pedro, since the title figures among the forty-one spurious plays which he listed in his *Quarta parte* (1672). However, on 4 March 1634, the Florentine envoy in Madrid wrote that

Si compose per due gran poeti qui unitamente, Calderon e Cuello, una commedia che rappresenta le prodezze del duca di Frisland, e prima di recitarsi, come è già seguito più volte dai comici pubblici, perchè trattava di principi viventi, acciò non si offendesse nessuno e non si narrasse cosa all'uso poetico, troppo lontana dalla verità, fu fatta rivedere dal Consiglio di Stato, e in fine approvata. Ha dato gran gusto per il buon modo con que rappresenta le fazzioni di guerra, e in particolare la rotta del Rè di Suezia, celebrando il suo valore.[45]

(A play showing the prowess of the Duke of Friedland was written here jointly by two great poets, Calderón and Coello; before it was performed, it was ordered to be checked by the Council of State, as has happened on other occasions with actors in the public playhouses, because it dealt with living princes, so that no one would be offended, and nothing would be recounted in a poetic manner too far from the truth; it was finally approved. It has given great pleasure for the excellent way in which it shows the warring factions, and in particular the defeat of the King of Sweden, celebrating his courage.)

This is clearly a different play from that of January 1633, although the authorities ostensibly remembered the problems that one had caused. Henry Sullivan has attempted a 'reconstruction' based on the envoy's report, which also included the phrase 'sempre non dicendo male di nessuno' ('never speaking ill of anyone', i.e., not even of the enemy), a Calderonian characteristic we have noticed as early as *Judas Macabeo* (1623) and *El sitio de Bredá* (1625).[46] Ironically, the news of Wallenstein's treachery and death was *en route* to Madrid at the time of the performance, and another visitor to the city, the German Hieronymus Welsch, wrote that the play had to be taken off the day after the news arrived.[47] Unfortunately, the story is complicated rather than clarified by a reference in *No hay burlas con el amor* (?1635, performed by Prado), in which the *gracioso* Moscatel refers to his master speaking 'con más afectos, que cuando | Prado hizo al rey de Suecia' ('with more passion than when Prado played the King of Sweden').[48] This suggests the Calderón/Coello play, in which case Prado took the Gustavus role twice. Portly and fortyish, he would have been ideal.

Although Welsch does not name the authors, his description of the play is consistent with that of the envoy, and implicitly supports the claim that they were Calderón and Coello. Given this fact, plus the attribution to Calderón of *El prodigio de Alemania*, Professor Vega has gone so far as to suggest that this is the 'lost' Calderón/Coello play, with Act I by Calderón, Act II possibly by Coello, and Act III possibly shared: not a usual way of writing a collaboration play, but similar to what Calderón and Coello would do in *Yerros de naturaleza* a few weeks later. Moreover, Vega is able to present an impressive amount of stylistic evidence to link at least part of Act I to Calderón. As for the rejection in the *Quarta parte*, this is not conclusive, since the same list includes *Los empeños que se ofrecen* (the genuine play *Los empeños de un acaso*) and *El conde Lucanor* (a genuine play which had been tampered with). Vega suggests that the original Calderón/Coello text was subsequently altered by another hand to take account of Wallenstein's disgrace, and that Calderón rejected it for this reason. The arguments are plausible. The alteration may also have included retitling: being overtaken by events is one of the hazards faced by plays which deal with contemporary affairs. What we can be sure of is that Antonio de Prado was one of the company managers who was most involved with Calderón's plays in the 1630s.

The date of the first performance of the collaboration play *Yerros de naturaleza y aciertos de la fortuna* is not recorded, but the play was licensed in Madrid on 4 May 1634 by Jerónimo de Villanueva. Villanueva objected to a joke ('resucitó, como es Pascua', 'he rose from the dead, since it's Easter') made by the *gracioso*, Tabaco, near the end of Act III: the passage was Coello's. The line was changed to 'resucitó, cosa es clara' ('he rose from the dead, obviously'), but the joke tends to confirm that the play was completed shortly before the licence was granted, since Easter Sunday had fallen two weeks previously, on 16 April.

As noted above, *Yerros* was long thought to be an early version of *La vida es sueño*. This is no longer accepted, although there is an obvious connection with that play (the setting in Poland, and the names Rosaura, Segismundo/Sigismundo and Clorilene). We may suppose that this link, plus the fact that Don Pedro's co-author Coello was born in 1610, made Calderón the senior partner in the relationship, although he wrote only 42 per cent of the lines; moreover, the cast-list in Act II, in Calderón's hand in the autograph manuscript, names several actors, as well as making it clear that Polidoro and Matilde were played by one actress, the *autora*. The implication is that the playwrights were in contact with the company before the play was finished, perhaps even before it was begun; again, the likelihood is that Don Pedro, the established author, had made this contact. Neither the *autora* nor the *autor* (who played Fisberto) is named, but the chances are that they were María de Córdoba, *Amarilis*, and Andrés de la Vega.[49]

While *Yerros* may not have inspired *La vida es sueño*, several features anticipate *La hija del aire*, most notably the kidnapping of a prince so that his place may be taken by an indistinguishable female relative, whose ambition to rule could not otherwise be satisfied. Like Semíramis, Matilde is ambitious, audacious and ruthless; Polidoro, at least to Matilde, seems spineless and ineffectual, as Ninias does to Semíramis. In Matilde's view, nature has erred, giving Polidoro the feminine qualities, and bestowing on her the ambition and ruthlessness that she believes a monarch should possess. Outraged that one so lacking in these regal qualities should rule, Matilde plans her brother's kidnapping, so that, wearing his clothes, she can take his place. As Semíramis was to do in *La hija del aire*, Matilde, on taking power, shows her 'strength' by dealing harshly with petitioners. Her subjects are alienated and confused, especially when she is unable to remember what she (i.e., Polidoro) did yesterday. The most striking parallel, however, is with Matilde's plan to force Fortune to right the *yerros de naturaleza*. This matches one of Semíramis's metaphors, 'ladrona me he de hacer de mi fortuna' ('I shall become the thief of my fortune': II, 2102–5), a remark she makes as she contemplates kidnapping her son to recover power. That is, since Fortune did not deal the cards she wished, she will compel Fortune. We can see how Calderón developed the motifs of *Yerros*, plus the ingenious piece of casting that allowed one person to play two roles, to use them to better effect in *La hija del aire*. While there are other examples of manuscripts in which playwrights specify which actors are to play particular roles, there is evidence that Calderón did this regularly. And although he may not be unique in specifying that certain male roles were to be taken by women, he is unusual: there are other examples, the most startling being Héctor in *Troya abrasada*.

It may seem unwise to reapply the arguments that were once used to describe the relationship between *La vida es sueño* and *Yerros*, but if it is true that aspects of *Yerros* were used to produce *La hija del aire*, then *La hija* was written after May 1634; not necessarily soon after, since five years elapsed before *Polifemo y Circe* was turned into *El mayor encanto, amor*.

Another play which gives a significant role to women is *El privilegio de las mujeres*. *El privilegio* was first published in *Parte treynta de comedias famosas de varios autores* (1636), an edition which attributes the play only to Juan Pérez de Montalbán; however, the closing lines, with their reference to 'tres oficios' (*sic*: 'three occupations'; an error for 'tres ingenios', 'three wits', or an unusual equivalent?) suggest that the play was written in collaboration. The suggestion is confirmed by a remark made by Mosquito in *El escondido y la tapada* (November 1635–March 1636):

¡Bien hayan los tres poetas,
que piadosos y corteses
sacaron a luz «los Pri-
vilegios de las mujeres»! (II, 693a)

(Hooray for the three poets, who piously and courteously brought out *Women's privileges*!)

According to Vera Tassis, Calderón wrote Act I or Act III.[50] When Don Pedro reworked the story for *Las armas de la hermosura* (?1678), he borrowed most extensively from Act I, particularly in the speeches where Morfodio describes the new laws; for instance:

El privilegio de las mujeres	*Las armas de la hermosura*
Las flacas, que a puras naguas sacaban para sus huesos cuanta carne ellas querían de en casa de los roperos, volvieron a ser büidas.	Las flacas, que a pura enagua sacaban para sus huesos cuanta carne ellas querían de en casa de los roperos, volvieron a ser büidas.
The thin ones, who, just through petticoats, got all the flesh they wanted for their bones in clothes shops, became skinny again.	The thin ones, who, just through a petticoat, got all the flesh they wanted for their bones in clothes shops, became skinny again.

There are no examples like this in Act II. In Act III, however, there are also extensive borrowings: we can see how Vera Tassis might have been confused. Either Don Pedro was content to use another writer's work (as in *Los cabellos de Absalón*), or parts of Act III were his own work, and he was prepared to use those parts. We might suppose that the play could have been like *Yerros de naturaleza*, the work of only two writers, but the reference in *El escondido y la tapada* surely excludes this explanation, although it does raise the possibility that the play's real title is *Los privilegios de las mujeres*.[51]

The main sources of the story of Gnaeus (or Gaius) Marcius Coriolanus are Dionysius of Halicarnassus (*Antiquitates romanae*), Livy (*Epitome*) and Plutarch (*Vitae*). *El privilegio* compresses the events of these early accounts. Rome has been founded 'cuatro lustros habrá, o cinco' ('it must be twenty or twenty-five years ago'). The seven kings are reduced to two: Rómulo (who has just died) and Numa (who has been expelled). The rape of the Sabine women supposedly took place ten years after Rome was founded, and since then Sabino, king of the Sabines, has been trying to exact revenge. Although hampered by a shortage of troops (the Roman men are too uxorious, too fond of the pleasures of love to want to fight), Coriolano defeats Sabino again, and returns to Rome victorious. There he finds that the Senate, in an effort to prevent future troop shortages, has passed laws banning all cosmetics and female adornment, and restricting women to a domestic role. The Roman women, led by Veturia, Coriolano's wife, are outraged. Coriolano leads a revolt against the unjust laws; but, while two senators are killed in the unrest, the revolt fails; after a trial, Coriolano is exiled. Furious at Rome's ingratitude, he leads the Sabine troops in a campaign of vengeance. Rome is besieged, and the citizens begin to die of hunger. To prevent more deaths, Aurelio, Coriolano's father, and Enio, tribune of the plebs and Coriolano's friend, plead with him to end the siege. He is unmoved, but finally the tears of Veturia persuade him to relent. Rome is spared, but only on condition that the privileges of the women are restored.

Given Calderón's portrayal of strong and independent-minded female leaders in plays such as *La gran Cenobia* (1625) and *Afectos de odio y amor* (1658?), we may conclude that he provided the main inspiration for *El privilegio*, but this conclusion, even if correct, cannot explain which contemporary events may have influenced the plot. Cotarelo suggested that the play was inspired by the pragmatic of 12 October 1636 against *guardainfantes*, which are referred to by Morfodio, but this cannot be correct, since *Parte treynta* was licensed in Zaragoza on 5 May of that year. Even more convincing, if we accept that this play is really entitled *Los privilegios de las mujeres*, is the reference to the performance of a play with that title at Christmas 1634.[52] As we have already seen, references to *guardainfantes* in dramatic works are most numerous in the mid 1630s, possibly beginning with Dinero's in March 1633 (or even 1631): the most probable composition period for this play is 1633–4, with 1634 being the most likely year. It cannot be a response to the October 1636 pragmatic, although it might have been written when rumours began to circulate that the government was planning to introduce legislation against women's dress and cosmetics. It does not seem likely, however, that it was written to persuade the government to change its mind about cosmetics. Since the climax of the play is the moment when Coriolano, driven by the desire to restore his injured honour through vengeance, seeks the death of the city he once loved, it is easy to read the play as a parable about male honour. This view is supported by his closing speech:

> Y que podáis, si ofendidas
> de vuestros maridos fuereis,
> castigar, como los hombres,
> su adulterio con la muerte;

y por mayor privilegio,
más grave y más eminente,
pues yo por una mujer
sin honra me vi, se entregue
todo el honor de los hombres
al poder de las mujeres,
porque han de ser absolutos
dueños de la honra siempre.

(And if you are wronged by your husbands, that you may punish their adultery with death, as men do; and as a greater, more weighty, more outstanding privilege, since I found myself without honour because of a woman, let all male honour be entrusted to women, for they are to be completely in charge of honour always.)

The opacity, or alleged opacity, of Calderón's 'wife-murder' plays becomes clearer when we view them against a background of speeches such as this.

* * *

Don Pedro may not have had Shakespeare's 'incalculable advantage of a stable group of actors for whom to write',[53] but he had contacts with the small group of leading companies, the *compañías de título*, of which there were theoretically only a dozen at any given moment during the period 1615–41.[54] While actors normally contracted with a company manager (the *autor*) for a single acting year (from Easter until Shrove Tuesday of the following year), in practice they often remained with an *autor* for years. Companies went on tour, and sometimes had to abandon the public theatres to give royal command performances, but their movements were largely predictable, and it was in their mutual interests for playwrights and actors to discuss common problems, such as the question of which company member would take a particular role, and to agree on the subject-matter of the plays which were commissioned. Calderón certainly made such contacts in the 1620s, as the episode of *El príncipe constante* makes clear, but there is much more documentary evidence for them in the thirties. As we shall see, the role of the stage-designer Cosme Lotti was also significant. Calderón's plays are not uniquely the product of his own mental processes: he was influenced by the wishes of company managers and designers. In addition, he certainly created characters to fit the talents of specific actors; no doubt, as he visualised a character, he imagined a particular actor in that role. Our difficulty is to identify the individuals involved.

CHAPTER 10

Taking over from Lope

Avnque está trazada con mucho ynjenio, la traza de ella no es representable por mirar mas a la ynbención de las tramoyas que al gusto de la representación; y aviendo yo, Señor, de escriuir esta comedia, no es posible guardar el orden que en ella se me da; pero, haciendo eleción de algunas de sus apariencias, las que yo abré menester de aquéllas, para lo que tengo pensado, son las siguientes ...

(Letter, 30 April 1635)

(Although it's very cleverly designed, its plot is not performable because it's more concerned with the ingenuity of the stage machinery than with the pleasure of the performance; and if I am to write this play, sir, it's not possible to preserve the arrangement I'm given in it; but, choosing some of its discoveries, those I'll need for what I've thought out are the following ...)

Lope de Vega died on 27 August 1635, aged seventy-two. His collected poems (there is no complete collection) would make an impressive life's work for any normal poet.[1] As a young man, he kept lists of the plays he had written; as an old man, he referred to 'mil y quinientas' (1,500), and his disciple Pérez de Montalbán put the total up to 2,000 after his death. Experts now believe that there were between 700 and 800; but since his output tailed off in the 1620s, there must have been periods in his life when he was averaging a play per week: he was not an easy writer to emulate.

As far as we know, Calderón took no conscious decision to attempt to inherit Lope's place. However, there is evidence that some of his contemporaries reckoned that he had done so. In the 1620s and early 1630s, six of Calderon's plays were published as Lope's, in a total of eleven (?) editions:

La industria contra el poder (= *Amor, honor y poder*): Lope, *Parte 23* ('Miguel Sorolla: Valencia, 1629' [= Simón Fajardo, Seville]).

La industria contra el poder (= *Amor, honor y poder*): *Parte 28* (Pedro Blusón: Huesca, 1634).[2]

La cruz en la sepultura (= *La devoción de la cruz*): Lope, *Parte 23* ('Miguel Sorolla: Valencia, 1629' [= Simón Fajardo, Seville]).

La cruz en la sepultura (= *La devoción de la cruz*): *Parte 28* (Pedro Blusón: Huesca, 1634).

La cruz en la sepultura (= *La devoción de la cruz*): Lope, *Parte 28* (Zaragoza, 1639) (see n. 2: this may not be a different edition from both of the preceding two).

La selva confusa: Lope, '*Parte 27*' ('Sebastián de Cormellas: Barcelona, 1633' [= Manuel de Sande, Seville]).

Selvas y bosques de amor (= *La selva confusa*): Lope, *Parte 24* (Diego Dormer: Zaragoza, 1633).

La puente de Mantible: Lope, imprintless *suelta* [Simón Fajardo: Seville, *c.* 1632] (Österreichische Nationalbibliothek, 38.V.4(7)) (Plate 19).

La puente de Mantible: Lope, imprintless *suelta* [Francisco de Lyra: Seville, *c.* 1632–5] (British Library, 11728.h.21(2)).

La vida es sueño: Lope, imprintless *suelta* [Francisco de Lyra: Seville, *c.* 1632–4] (Liverpool University Library, L57.13) (Plate 20).

De un castigo tres venganzas, Lope, *Parte 28* (Zaragoza, 1639) (no copy known, see n. 2).

After Lope's death, this practice ceased and, gradually, the name of Calderón became the booksellers' choice for promoting sales. And while Lope had never been entirely *persona grata* in the court theatre, Calderón's early successes in that area were multiplied in the thirties, especially as the new Retiro palace and its grounds opened up fresh possibilities for lavish performances.[3]

The evidence for the view of Calderón held by his contemporaries is not confined to the book trade, however, or even to Spain. While Pérez de Montalbán was compiling his *Fama póstuma* (1636) for Lope in Madrid, Alessio Pulchi was doing the same in Italy, and dedicating it to Don Juan Antonio de Vera y Figueroa, Conde de la Roca and friend of Olivares. The book included a *Ragguaglio di Parnaso*, which involved requests to Lope's followers to go on writing, beginning with Pérez de Montalbán, with Calderón in second place:

Et à Don Pietro Calderone si comandi far molte Comedie, come quelle della Quinta di Gaeta [*sic*, presumably *Peor está que estaba*], & le Case [con] due Porte ò come qual si voglia di quelle ch'a fatto è sà fare, & se gli laudi, que stringa li suoi argomenti quanto vorrà: poiche quando anche alcuno di essi crepi, non è vguale questo danno, al bene di tanti, come le riescono, & se gli aduertisca quanto le adorni el vestirle, con il sastrarol [*sic*], che si vestiua Lope.[4]

(And Don Pedro Calderón is to be told to write many plays like those of the country house of Gaeta and *Casa con dos puertas*, or like whichever of those he has written and knows how to write, and he is to be praised for tightening his plots as much as he wants; for even if any one of those plots should burst, this harm is not equal to the benefit of as many as are successful, and he is to be advised how much they are adorned by dressing them in the *sastrarol* that Lope wore.)

In more than one sense, Pérez de Montalbán was a truer follower of Lope than Calderón was, but we need to remember that our present view of him as a dramatist of the second rank was not one shared by all of his contemporaries.

In the year Lope died, Calderón may have written as many as ten plays, but there is also evidence that he continued to revise, in some cases for the court, those which he had written earlier. Thus there is a recorded payment to Juan Benito Sánchez, who 'pintó cinco lienzos de arquitectura para la *Casa con dos puertas* (1629) que se puso allí [en el Buen Retiro] el día de la Ascensión de 1635 con la compañía de Andrés [*sic*: Antonio?] de Prado' ('painted five canvases of architecture for *Casa con dos puertas* (1629) which was put on there on Ascension Day in 1635 [17 May] by the company of Andrés [*sic*] de Prado').[5] A manuscript copy of the play contains a lengthy description of a royal bird-hunt, with falcons, which is not present in the *Primera parte* version (1636).[6] This may have been added for the royal performance of 1635. Other plays of this period which were revised between original composition and publication include *El astrólogo fingido* and *La vida es sueño*.

While we may sometimes be startled by the diversity of Calderón's sources, his practice reveals, as Ackroyd says of Shakespeare, that 'To work on existing material … was profoundly congenial to him. That is why he was prepared to revise his own work, as well as that of other dramatists, in the course of his professional career.'[7]

The passage is worth quoting, because it is as pertinent to Calderón as to Shakespeare. All writing, his own or others', was a structure which Don Pedro felt he could improve, add to, rebuild, or pull apart to salvage the bricks for another edifice. The pulling apart, we suspect, was particularly satisfactory, since it revealed others' construction techniques. The period around 1635, perhaps because of the quantity of work produced, is especially illustrative of the different practices Calderón used in composition. We may look first at *Las tres justicias en una*.

Las tres justicias en una is a problem play, since it does not appear in the Veragua or Marañón lists. Bances Candamo offers an explanation:

Don Pedro Calderón deseó mucho recoger la comedia *De vn castigo tres venganzas*, que escriuió siendo mui mozo, porque vn Galán daua vna bofetada a su padre, y, con ser caso verdadero en Aragón y aberiguar después que era el Padre supuesto y no natural, y con hacerle morir, no obstante, en pena de la irreuerencia, con todo eso Don Pedro quería recoger la comedia por el horror que daua el escandaloso caso.[8]

(Don Pedro Calderón very much wanted to withdraw the play *De un castigo tres venganzas*, which he wrote when he was very young, because in it a young man slapped his father's face; and although it was a real event which took place in Aragón, and it was made clear later that the father was supposed, not real, and although he made him die as a punishment for the disrespect, Don Pedro nevertheless wanted to withdraw the play because of the horror caused by the shocking event.)

Bances has mistaken the title, but his description indicates that he is referring to *Las tres justicias*. We cannot corroborate his claim, which is complicated by Hilborn's remark that the metre of Act III is unlike Calderón's practice in any other plays.[9] Hilborn suggests a date of 1636–7, and that someone else was involved in Act III; the play's modern editor suggests 1630–7.[10] The play was certainly written by May 1644, when Ascanio offered to play it in Valencia, describing it as a 'comedia nueva, nunca representada en Valencia' ('a new play, never performed in Valencia').[11]

Las tres justicias presents us with Don Lope Senior, who, as an old man, finally decided to marry to preserve his family *mayorazgo*, and chose Blanca, not yet fifteen. This we are told by their son, Lope Junior, who invites Don Mendo Torrellas to imagine the consequences:

imaginad discursivo
ahora vos de qué humores
compuesto nacería, hijo
que nacía para ser
concepto de amor tan tibio.
Bien pensaron que yo fuera
como otros hijos han sido,
la nueva paz de los dos;
mas tan al revés lo vimos,
que de los dos nueva guerra
fui. (I, 523a)

(Imagine meditatively of what humours a child would be composed, who was born to be an expression of such lukewarm love. They thought indeed that I would be as other children have been, a new peace between them; but the reverse was true, that I was a new war between them.)

Young Lope, however, is illegitimate, a love-child born of Blanca's sister's affair with Don Mendo, a royal adviser. Blanca passed off the baby as her own, hoping that he would bring her and her husband together. The effort failed, and young Lope's life is destroyed by apparent lack of paternal love.

Like Segismundo, young Lope is violent and disobedient: he seduces a neighbouring girl, kills her brother, injures an officer of the law and takes to banditry. Like Basilio, his father belatedly tries to undo the damage: he secures a pardon from the girl for the death of her brother, pays her dowry to a convent and obtains from the king a royal pardon. The dowry and the regular payments he must make thereafter reduce him to such poverty that he has to let part of his home to his old friend Don Mendo, who has returned to court to become Justicia Mayor. As on other occasions, we remember the love-child Francisco Calderón, who left home to return only when the father was dead; the father's difficulties in paying the daughter's convent dowry; the sons' regular payments to her, and their letting of part of the family home to a civil servant. There is another, more controversial strand of the plot: the attraction felt by Violante, Don Mendo's daughter, to the bandit who let her and her father go. She does not know that the bandit, Lope Junior, is her half-brother. The situation recalls Eusebio and Julia in *La devoción de la cruz*; there seems little doubt that Calderón developed aspects of that play to create *Las tres justicias*. But did the model for these incestuous relationships come from his own family, from a relationship between Francisco and Dorotea? As we have seen, Francisco may have been sent to Mexico in 1608, when Dorotea was ten: the inference that might be deduced from this detail is not one that encourages us to contemplate it. On the other hand, if some other Francisco went to Mexico, could something have happened in 1611, when she was thirteen and Francisco was twenty-one? We shall never know, but if so, his half-brothers did not hold it against him. Thirteen was a marriageable age in the seventeenth century.

Don Lope Junior has a rival for the affections of Violante: his friend Don Guillén. When the elder Lope intervenes in their fight and calls his supposed son a liar, the young man strikes him. Old Lope goes to the king and asks him to revoke the pardon. There is some ambiguity about the identity of the king, but Don Lope's address to him as

> Rey Don Pedro de Aragón,
> cristiano Monarca, a quien
> llama el sabio justiciero
> y el ignorante cruel (1, 542a)

(King Peter of Aragón, Christian monarch whom the wise man calls justicer and the ignorant, cruel)

suggests that he is intended to be Peter IV (1336–87), known, like his contemporary in Castile, as 'El Cruel'. Pedro is reluctant to believe that a true father–son relationship could be so bad, and extracts the truth from Blanca. As he sees it, three crimes have been committed: a young man has struck the person he thought was his father; Mendo has betrayed the sister of Blanca; and Blanca has deceived her husband. He punishes all three crimes by garrotting young Lope, without revealing his true parentage.

There is no evidence to support Bances's claim that the story was a 'caso verdadero en Aragón'. Benabu has noted, however, that the events do appear to have taken place in Portugal, under Peter I, the third fourteenth-century Peter to share the epithets '*cruel*' and '*justiciero*', and that they were recorded by Faría e Sousa in his *Epítome de las historias portuguesas* (1628), which Calderón apparently consulted as a source of *El príncipe constante*.[12] As in the play, the king supposedly questioned the mother, who admitted that her husband was not the father, although she was the real mother. In avoiding this scandalous detail, Don Pedro was able to make Blanca more sympathetic: a young woman trying to create a bond with her elderly husband. The play shows how a group of people, none of them evil, can conspire to bring about a catastrophe that deeply distresses all concerned, including the innocent Violante, except the king. Lope is a tragic victim of the guilt of others, and of the king's obsession with justice. The pathos of his fate is heightened by our knowledge that the elder Lope loves not only Blanca, but also his son, as his second-last speech indicates:

Cuanto fué hasta aquí rencor,
es ya lástima y angustia. (1, 553a)

(All that was bitterness until this point, is now anguish and pity.)

Don Lope Senior was unable to display the affection which he genuinely felt. We cannot say whether Diego Calderón shared this inability, but public displays of emotion were not part of the life of the ruling classes in early modern Spain: it was said that Philip IV did not permit himself to smile in public.

Hartzenbusch noted that Lope Junior, being a noble, should have been executed by having his throat cut, not garrotting, and suggested that the ending had been tampered with.[13] Given that the garrotte is inflicted on Don Álvaro de Ataide in *El alcalde de Zalamea*, this is perhaps not significant (although that play provides an explanation for the irregularity). What is more noteworthy is that Lope's feelings of apprehension, first for the knife and then for the sword in the hands of his real father, the Justicia Mayor, do not betoken death by a rope. And while Hartzenbusch suggested that

Act III was not Calderón's, the strange plant that both cures and causes a wound is mentioned there, as it is in *El galán fantasma* (?1630–3; II, 637a):

> Una planta oí que nace
> tan rara y tan exquisita,
> que donde hay llaga, la quita,
> y donde no la hay, la hace. (I, 547a)

(I heard of a plant that grows, so rare and excellent, that where there is a sore, it removes it, and where there is none, it causes it.)

In the same passage, Violante refers to two more extraordinary plants:

> También de dos peregrinas
> yerbas oí, que en sus senos,
> apartadas son venenos,
> y juntas son medicinas.

(I also heard of two exotic herbs which, in their heart, are poisonous when separate and medicinal when together.)

The same two plants are found in *Peor está que estaba* (?1630; II, 328b), *A secreto agravio, secreta venganza* (?1635; I, 596a) and *Agradecer y no amar* (by 1650; II, 1380b). This evidence suggests that, although there may have been some tampering, the text is at least partly authentic, and the play is substantially as Calderón intended; he may well have written it in the early/mid thirties. Bances was born in Avilés in 1662, and did not move to Madrid until after Calderón's death: he cannot have received his flawed information about '*De vn castigo tres venganzas*' at first hand.

One piece of evidence suggests that around this time Don Pedro wrote *La Celestina.* That he wrote a play of this title is confirmed by his Veragua and Marañón lists, but the text is lost. One of the plays offered on 6 November 1634 for performance in Valencia by Manuel Vallejo had this title, and since no other play of the title is known, we must assume that this was Calderón's.[14] The original *Celestina* was written in dramatic form, and so offers itself for adaptation for the theatre, but we have no idea how Don Pedro handled the story.

During the early thirties, the construction of the Retiro complex was proceeding. To judge by what contemporaries wrote, it provided a regular subject of conversation. Calderón would describe *autos* as 'sermones puestos en verso' ('sermons put into verse', III, 427a), and, as a priest might do, he often took current events as their topic. We might think that deciding to become a priest in 1650 meant huge changes in his life, but some aspects of it had been preparing him for the adjustment for years. For one of the Corpus Christi *autos* of 1634, he chose the new palace as his subject: *El nuevo palacio del Retiro*. One of the manuscript copies of the *auto* preserves his closing note, 'En Pedrosa a 28 de mayo de 1634 años' ('In Pedrosa, 28 May 1634'), as well as Agustín de Castro's *aprobación*, 'En este Colegio imperial [Calderón's old school in Madrid] … a 1ºde junio de 1634' ('In this Colegio Imperial, 1 June 1634').[15] Unfortunately, the number of Pedrosas runs into double figures, most of them in the province of Burgos. None of them is near Madrid, but Calderón, or his courier, managed to ride back there in no more than three days.[16] In 1634 Corpus Christi fell on 15 June. With lines to be learned and rehearsals to be held, the rush is understandable.

In *El nuevo palacio*'s allegory, the king appears as God and the queen as the Church. God's favourite, Man, is the king's favourite, Olivares. The *auto* opens with Judaísmo, a wandering Jew, who comes on to find that what was once a field of vines and olives has been transformed into a palace. Olive-groves are *olivares* in Spanish, and Man/Olivares explains to Judaísmo that this is the heavenly city the king/God has created for his spouse/the Church. Faith (Fe) bars Judaísmo's way, and he has to watch the ceremony of the Eucharist from outside: he is a sad figure, not a hateful one. At a time when the Olivares government was relying more heavily on Portuguese financiers, whom many suspected of being crypto-Jews, the *auto* apparently conveyed a message, intended or not, to the Portuguese community: they provided funds for the construction in 1635, within the complex, of a chapel dedicated to Portugal's patron saint, St Anthony of Padua, as proof of orthodoxy. Ironically, Olivares was himself of *converso* origin, as his enemies recalled (see p. 205).

A few years later, life imitated art: one of the financiers, Manuel Cortizos de Villasante, who had constructed a private royal garden in the complex, offered the queen a nosegay when he met her walking there. He had no idea that for courtiers to present flowers to the queen was a serious breach of protocol, but he was refused future access to the Retiro. The beliefs of Cortizos are unknown, but after his death in 1650 the Inquisition produced a dossier on the alleged judaizing activities of his family.[17]

While current events provided raw material for some *autos*, others could be mythological, historical or biblical. Calderón's other 1634 *auto* was possibly *La cena del rey Baltasar*, which is based on Daniel 5, in which Daniel interprets for the king the mysterious words 'Mene, Tecel, Fares' (III, 175b).[18] Baltasar's feast is a sacrifice, but a sacrifice offered to himself, to his own senses, a profane travesty of the Mass, and Muerte, taken for a servant, serves him a cup, one of the vessels carried off in triumph from the temple in Jerusalem. 'Yo de tu mano la acepto' ('I accept it from your hand': III, 174b), says Baltasar. As Daniel explains, this sacrifice to the senses is communing in a state of sin: 'quien comulga en pecado | profana el vaso del templo' ('he who takes communion in a state of sin profanes the temple vessel': III, 176a). At the close, Baltasar exits, struggling with Muerte, and his feast is transformed into the bread and wine of the Eucharist, the true sacrifice. The *auto* is readily comprehensible at this simple level, reminding us that for most of Calderón's audience, the only other source of information about doctrine was what they heard from their priest. For those who can appreciate a different level, the *auto* explains that Baltasar is Man's Soul (III, 166b). Daniel means 'juicio de Dios' ('God's judgement': III, 156b), the *juicio* that God places in every man, his conscience. The complex imagery indicates that all the other characters are aspects of Baltasar; most strikingly, Pensamiento, Baltasar's thought, is dressed as a fool. Pensamiento and Daniel are incompatible, and the relationship between them is 'una lid cruel' ('a cruel struggle': III, 156b), 'the conflict of conscience with disordered thought', as Parker puts it, expressed on a symbolic level.[19] Not only is the construction of the *auto* exceptionally skilful and free from superfluity, but it contains some of Calderón's finest poetry, as most critics acknowledge. Muerte's *octavas* (III, 164a–166b), which convey inexorability with their technically difficult final-syllable rhymes, are among Calderón's most quoted verse. The *auto* reminds us that, while he was still in his early thirties, Calderón's techniques were already mature. Indeed, from the late twenties on, it is difficult to use technical mastery, whether of plot-construction or of verse, as an aid for dating.

* * *

As well as writing plays and *autos*, and managing to do so while visiting Pedrosa, Calderón found time in 1634 to write a poem for Ramírez de Arellano's *Avisos para la muerte.*[20] Entitled *Lágrimas que vierte una alma arrepentida a la hora de la muerte* ('Ahora, señor, ahora'), it survives in two versions and has often been reprinted.[21] The other contributors included Lope, Valdivielso, Pérez de Montalbán, Godínez, Vélez and Rojas Zorrilla. The publisher was Pérez de Montalbán's father. Presumably he did well out of it: over twenty editions are recorded.

One of the few anthologies to which Calderón did not contribute was the *Elogios al palacio real del Buen Retiro*, compiled by Diego de Covarrubias y Leiva, 'Guarda Mayor del Sitio Real del Buen Retiro', and dedicated to Olivares.[22] The contributors included Don Pedro's friend Pérez de Montalbán, as well as Valdivielso, Vélez and Godínez. Perhaps we should not read anything into this omission, apart from Calderón's other commitments.

In spite of the amount he was writing at this time, Don Pedro found himself short of ready cash: in 1633 or 1634 (the municipal accounts are not clear) he borrowed 900 *reales* from the lessees of the public theatres.[23] The lessees were entrepreneurs who rented the theatres from their owners, religious brotherhoods, and then tried to make a profit from hiring companies of actors to perform in them. It was in their interest to lend money to a successful playwright, especially if they did so against the promise of a new play. The sum approximates to the amount usually paid for a new play in the early 1630s.

In 1645 Quiñones de Benavente published his *Jocoseria*, which included the *Loa que representó Antonio de Prado*.[24] In the *loa*, which was written for the start of a new theatre season, after Easter, Prado states that

> Tres comedias tengo nuevas
> de Don Pedro Calderón.

(I have three new plays by Don Pedro Calderón.)

His wife, Mariana Vaca de Morales, the *autora*, adds that

> Y es la primera que hacemos
> *No hay burlas con el amor.*

(And the first we're putting on is *There's no fooling with love.*)

It can be deduced, from other plays and persons named, that the year is 1634 or 1635. Since Prado was on tour in early 1634, and in Madrid from November 1634 until June 1635, we can be fairly sure that *No hay burlas* was new in April 1635, when Lent ended.[25]

No hay burlas deals with the conventional lovers Don Juan de Mendoza and Doña Leonor Enríquez. Juan has a friend, Don Alonso de Luna, a would-be philanderer, while Leonor has a sister, Beatriz, a disciple of *culteranismo* who disapproves of men and of her sister's fondness for one; her reading includes Ovid's *Remedia amoris*. Don Alonso's servant, Moscatel, is cast in a different mould from the normal comic servant: he loves Inés, the maid of Leonor and Beatriz. The audience, of course, can see where this plot is going: Alonso, scornful of love and reluctantly agreeing to help Juan pursue his sincere relationship with Leonor, meets her sister, and they fall for each other (although Alonso is quite happy to try to seduce Inés first). In the end, love changes both of them: Beatriz gives up her *culterano* speech and her abhorrence of men, while the chastened Alonso is left to pronounce the moral:

> No se burle con él [= el amor] nadie,
> sino escarmentad en mí. (II, 525b)

(Let no-one make fun of it, but learn a lesson from me.)

While Calderón began writing character comedies in the twenties, this is his first portrayal of an eccentric woman. His coolness towards Lope did not prevent him from referring to one such character created 'con tanto acierto' ('so successfully') by Lope in *Los melindres de Belisa* (?1606–8), who may inspire some of Beatriz's features (II, 496b). Other Lope plays which present women who have intellectual aspirations, or who reject men, are *La discreta enamorada* (1606), *El mayor imposible* (1615) and *El desprecio agradecido* (*c.* 1633); there are also Tirso's *La celosa de sí misma* (published 1627) and Antonio Hurtado de Mendoza's *El marido hace mujer* (1631–2). However, there are no women who speak like Beatriz. Moreto's fake countess in *El lindo don Diego* (?1650s), significantly named Beatriz, imitates her extravagant language, but Calderón's Beatriz is the first. We might suppose that Quevedo's satirical sonnet, 'Quien quisiere ser culto en sólo un día, | la jeri-(aprenderá)gonza siguiente' ('he who would be *culto* in only a day, the following jar-(shall learn)gon'), provided some inspiration, but while Don Pedro used some of the 'recommended' vocabulary elsewhere, he gives scarcely any of it to Beatriz.[26]

No hay burlas also has lines from Góngora's ballad 'Cuatro o seis desnudos hombros' (lines 1805–6, 1821–2), possible references to Mira's play *Cuatro milagros del amor* (?1629, II, 495a) and Don Pedro's own *Con quien vengo, vengo* (1630; II, 503a).[27] However, one of its most interesting features is the language used by Inés and Moscatel when Alonso forces the latter to convey his advances to her:

> Dile a tu amo, villano,
> que soy quien soy. (Inés, 1257–8)

> Bien podéis, ojos, llorar,
> no lo dejéis de vergüenza. (Moscatel, 1275–6)

> Soy grande para dama
> y para esposa soy chica.
> (Moscatel, supposedly quoting Inés, 1484–5)

(Tell your master, you peasant, that I am who I am. / Well may you weep, eyes, do not refrain out of shame. / I am too great to be a mistress, not great enough to be a wife.)

These responses mimic and mock the words of Don Gutierre and Mencía in *El médico de su honra* (Mencía's 'yo soy quien soy', I, 629a; ballad lines also quoted by Gutierre, I, 644b; Mencía's 'soy para dama más, | lo que para esposa menos', 'I am too noble to be a mistress by as much as I am not noble enough to be a wife': I, 631a). They provide us with another light in which to examine characters who, at first sight, are not at all funny. Don Gutierre is no joke in any normal sense, but we are encouraged to see his posturing for what it is.

Another play which Hilborn at least has assigned to this period is *La sibila de Oriente.*[28] The plot deals with the Queen of Sheba's visit to King Solomon, as does the *auto El árbol del mejor fruto* (1677). Of the play, Hartzenbusch states that 'Es una refundicion del auto sacramental *El Arbol del mejor fruto*. Lo que hay aquí del auto es de Calderon; lo demas no lo parece' ('It is a rehash of the *auto sacramental El Árbol del mejor fruto*. What there is here from the *auto* is by Calderón; the rest does not seem to be.').[29] Perhaps significantly, the title does not appear in the Veragua or Marañón lists, although Vera Tassis accepted it as authentic. The play is not so much about Solomon and Sheba as about the miraculous tree (cedar/palm/cypress) which is brought from Lebanon to build Solomon's temple. The sibylline queen interprets the cedar as father, palm as spirit, and cypress as son, and foresees that it will furnish the wood for the cross. One of the possible sources for this story was Book 3 of Jacobus de Voragine's *Legenda aurea.*[30]

There seems to be no doubt that Calderón wrote at least Act I of this plot. The act is full of Calderonian images, for example:

> En un delfín que es pájaro sin pluma,
> en un águila que es pez sin escama,
> monte de velas, huracán de pino,
> selva de jarcias, vecindad de lino,
> aré los campos de cristal y nieve. (I, 707b)

(On a dolphin which is a featherless bird, on an eagle which is a scaleless fish, a mountain of sails, a hurricane of pine, a forest of rigging, a neighbourhood of canvas, I ploughed the fields of crystal and snow.)

> En veloz caballo, cuyo aliento
> jeroglífico ha sido de la guerra,
> sierpe del agua, exhalación del viento,
> volcán del fuego, escollo de la tierra,
> caos animal ... (I, 708a)

(On a speedy horse, whose spirit was a hieroglyph of war, serpent of the water, exhalation of the wind, volcano of fire, reef of earth, animal chaos ...)

After Act I the imagery becomes more prosaic. The most plausible explanation is not that Don Pedro based the play on the *auto*, but that this is a collaboration play of which he wrote Act I; later, as with some other collaboration plays, he adapted it for another work, in this case an *auto*. However, even Act II contains Calderonian phrases like 'la cóncava esfera de la luna' ('the concave sphere of the moon': I, 722a; cf. 'el cóncavo palacio de la luna', 'the concave palace of the moon', in *El nuevo palacio del Retiro*, III, 137a; and in *El pastor Fido*, III, 1585a).

On 1 June 1635 a work entitled *La fábula de Dafne* was played in the Retiro.[31] Perhaps this was the first performance of a version of Don Pedro's *El laurel de Apolo* (premiered 4 March 1658),[32] although the royal reaction to Calderón's *La fábula de Dafne* a year later (see pp. 189–90) suggests that it was a different work: Lope's *El amor enamorado* has been plausibly suggested.[33] Whatever it was, it seems likely that one of the themes of the Calderón version was that of *vencerse a sí mismo*, or self-restraint on the part of those in positions of power: Pérez de Moya, a likely source, explains that the ancients used the Daphne story as a means of praising chastity.[34] What is certainly true is that this was a very busy time for Don Pedro, perhaps the busiest of his life. Even when he re-used old material, as he did with *El mayor encanto, amor*, the period around 1635 was one of creative frenzy.

The frenetic nature of Calderón's composition can be deduced from the handwriting. Everyone's handwriting changes. Slowly, perhaps; within a short interval, imperceptibly; but to the extent that undated writing can be assigned to a particular period, if enough dated material survives. For example, changes in handwriting were used by the editor of Emily Dickinson to date otherwise undatable poems.[35] One of the features of the italic hand used by Calderón and his contemporaries was that certain letters could be formed with a pen-lift or in a single stroke, such as *f* and *p*. In 1630, Calderón was forming these in two strokes, but the single-stroke forms became dominant in the thirties and forties. Later, he reverted gradually to pen-lifts, and, in the sixties, his writing became larger, perhaps because his eyesight was deteriorating. His handwriting is at its least legible in the mid thirties, when a whole line of verse might be written in a single stroke, with *i*'s left undotted and *t*'s crossed without lifting the pen. Calderonian punctuation in this period is almost non-existent; when there is any, it is eccentric by modern standards, and even by the contemporary standards applied by typesetters. This was not unusual: compositors, then, were expected to supply correct accidentals.

If Calderón was dashing off his lines in the thirties, the muse did not supply them in their definitive form. His original manuscripts are full of changes, deletions, additions, *pentimenti*. This is in keeping with the compulsive revision which we now know to have been part of his manner of writing. Some of these alterations were made during composition, as we can tell from their content or the metre. Others, as the different ink suggests, were done later, during revision. Deletions performed during composition were made by a series of pen-loops, as if the writer were reluctant to allow his rejected thoughts to be read; during revision, more cavalierly, he boxed off the lines and drew diagonal strokes through them. Additions of a couple of lines could be squeezed in between the originals. Longer passages were written in the margin, sideways if necessary, with crosses to indicate where they were to be inserted. Sometimes a passage would be rewritten on a fresh piece of paper which would then be glued on top of the old version with flour-paste. Perhaps it seemed too time-consuming to copy the whole sheet, or else the sheets were already bound.

There is evidence that Shakespeare also worked like this.[36] It is normal enough. Anyone who writes, even a biographer, is reluctant to stop when the words are coming; but now the word-processor conceals the procedure. Inevitably, then, copyists and typesetters got confused, including words and even passages which were intended for deletion, as well as omitting some which were meant to be present.

Calderón manuscripts now are bound, sometimes in crushed morocco, the finest leather there is. The bindings, though, are most often of the nineteenth century: we do not know what form they were in two or three hundred years earlier. Apart from the fair copies he made of his *autos*, perhaps in the seventies, which are in folio, Calderón seems always to have written on quarto. Since the standard Spanish sheet was then 44 cm by 30 cm, this means 22 cm by 15 cm. Paper was expensive: even the low-grade, unsized paper used for printed books was reckoned to account for half the cost of an edition, and the finer, lightly sized paper used for writing was too good to waste. We do not know whether Don Pedro bought it in sheets and quartered it himself, then bound it in some way. One autograph manuscript which appears to have survived in something close to its original condition is *Llamados y escogidos* (1643), which consists of fifteen conjugate pairs of leaves (sixty pages). These are roughly sewn together, with no protective covering; as a result, there has been some damage to the edges and to the outside of the last leaf.[37] Some of the later bindings preserve vellum title-pages of the seventeenth century, but the ragged and filthy state of the first and last pages of some manuscripts suggests that the lack of cover of *Llamados y escogidos* is typical. No doubt some *autores* took more care of the manuscripts than others.

* * *

El mayor encanto, amor was performed several times on a floating stage in the lake in the Retiro grounds by Roque de Figueroa in July and August of 1635, although originally planned for St John's Eve.[38] If we are to believe the surviving documents, the play began as an idea of Lotti's: 'Fiesta que se represento en el estanque grande del Retiro, invencion de Cosme Lotti, a peticion de la Excelentisima condesa de Olivares … la noche de San Juan' ('Fiesta performed on the large pond of the Retiro, devised by Cosme Lotti, at the request of the most excellent Countess of Olivares … on St John's eve'). This note, in the past tense, was added to Lotti's proposal document, which was written in the future tense.[39] The proposal was passed to Calderón, who rejected it as it stood, in a letter of 30 April 1635 ('Yo e visto vna memoria que cosme loti hizo', 'I have seen a memorandum made by Cosme Lotti'). The letter has fortunately survived.[40] Don Pedro was firm but also diplomatic, agreeing that some of the suggestions could be used:

> Avnque esta trazada con mucho ynjenio la traza de ella no es representable por mirar mas a la ynbencion de las tramoyas que al gusto de la representacion. Y aviendo yo Señor de escriuir esta comedia no es posible guardar el orden que en ella se me da pero haciendo elecion de algunas de sus apariencias las que yo abre menester de aquellas para lo que tengo pensado son las siguientes … (See the heading of this chapter.)

No doubt the proposal gave him some ideas. Having already collaborated on a play on this subject, he agreed, and presumably wrote the play in May–June; further documents relating to the staging, and signed by Calderón, have since been discovered.[41] Shergold has compared the proposal and the text, noting how Calderón adapted some of the suggestions:

> Calderón uses Lotti's manuscript in much the same way as, elsewhere, he uses plays by other dramatists: as a promising idea, but one which has to be fairly extensively rethought and reworked in order to obtain its maximum dramatic effectiveness.[42]

Sloman has shown how Don Pedro carried out this process in his re-use of *Polifemo y Circe*.[43]

As we saw in Chapter 8, Pérez de Moya saw Circe as representing illicit appetites, Ulysses as reason; indeed, this was how Calderón allegorised them in *Los encantos de la culpa*, which was written between 1636 and 1645 (that is, perhaps soon after this play). In the passages quoted then (pp. 126–7), we see that the text added for *El mayor encanto* includes a specific reference to the reason of Ulysses, as well as to Circe's enchanted palace. With this in mind, Meg Greer has argued that *El mayor encanto, amor* contains a message for Philip IV / Ulysses: do not allow the *engaños*, or the moral labyrinth, of the enchanted palace (= the Retiro) of Circe/Olivares, or your own amorous proclivities, symbolised by Circe's ability to turn men into beasts, to distract you from your duties as a ruler.[44]

Philip IV is not likely to have objected to being seen as Ulysses. He may not have enjoyed the public reminder of his illicit appetites, which had recently borne fruit, but being linked to a Greek hero who triumphed over his enemies would have been flattering enough. It is hard to believe, though, that Olivares would not have objected to being portrayed as Circe, or to his precious Retiro being equated with her palace, had he believed that this was what Calderón was doing. Before we reject Greer's interpretation on these grounds, we should remember that Lotti's proposal had included a giant representing the Buen Retiro: Calderón modified this idea, transforming it into Brutamonte, the giant slave of Circe, which may tell us something about his thought processes, while Circe's use of the phrase 'el retiro | de mi palacio' ('the retreat of my palace': 1, 1606b) certainly prompted the thought processes of the audience.[45]

That the Retiro had its opponents is not in doubt. In the anonymous satire 'La cueva de Meliso', popular in the 1640s, the magician Meliso advises Olivares how to bewitch the king by building a wondrously embellished palace which would be a venue for splendid entertainments. These would so enchant the king that he would leave his favourite to rule.[46] As one of the chief producers of those splendid entertainments, Calderón's views were not the same as those of the satirist, but their shared use of the enchanted palace motif suggests that Greer is right about his message to the king.

* * *

The first *remisión* of Calderón's *Segunda parte* is dated 12 February 1637, which probably means that the twelve plays in the volume had been completed and performed by 1636 at the latest. In the contents list, two of them, *El mayor encanto, amor* and *Los tres mayores prodigios*, are given performance dates of 1635 and 1636 respectively; the others which probably date from this period are *Argenis y Poliarco*, *El mayor monstruo del mundo* and *A secreto agravio, secreta venganza*. The source of the first was the *Argenis* (1621) of John Barclay, whose father, from an Aberdeenshire family, moved to France, where John was born at Pont-à-Mousson in 1582. The characters and events of the plot have been linked to historical events and personages (such as Henry IV of France). While Don Pedro could easily have read the original Latin (there were numerous editions), he is more likely to have worked from one of the two recent translations by José Pellicer and Gabriel de Corral, both of 1626.

Although the play is taken from the *Argenis* (and the complexities of the novelesque storyline must have been hard to follow for an audience which could not turn back to earlier chapters), its plot is surprisingly like that of *Las tres justicias*. Hianisbe, 'Queen of Africa', secretly adopted the son of her sister, who had gone through a form of marriage with a foreigner, who abandoned her. Like Blanca, she hoped to inspire affection in her husband. The foreigner, Meleandro, becomes King of Sicily and has a daughter, Argenis. Hianisbe's adopted son and Poliarco/Manfredo, the 'Dauphin of France', become rivals for the hand of Argenis, who loves only Poliarco. This is the first difference: the other is that all ends well as Meleandro and his son rediscover their relationship; the discovery of his father and his sister console the son for the loss of Argenis to Poliarco/Manfredo. One can see why the plot might have appealed to Don Pedro.

El mayor monstruo del mundo is generally reckoned, without conclusive evidence, to have been written a couple of years before its publication in the *Segunda parte*, that is, in about 1635. Set in the first century BC, it deals with the story of Herod the Great and his wife Mariamne, as told by the Jewish historian Josephus.[47] Herodes sends a letter ordering his wife to be killed in the event of his being executed by Octaviano (later the Emperor Augustus) for his support of Antonio (Mark Antony): Herodes fears that she will fall into Octaviano's hands. Mariene sees the letter and is outraged. She and Herodes love each other, but his jealousy drives them apart and, ultimately, through an accident, causes her death.

One inconclusive piece of evidence for composition in 1635 is Tirso's *La vida y muerte de Herodes*. We can assume that Calderón read this in July 1635, when he wrote his *aprobación* for Tirso's *Quinta parte*, in which it was published. The Tirso play has little enough in common with Calderón's, but it could have triggered his imagination. If it did, he then turned to Josephus, whom he adapted for his artistic purposes. In the play, an astrologer warns Mariene against the dagger of Herodes. Herodes does not realise that murder lies within his own nature, not in an inanimate object. He throws the dagger into the sea, but it is returned to him. When he discovers the truth, he throws himself into the sea: historically false, but poetically appropriate.[48]

The version of the play which was published in 1637 is full of errors, and Calderón apparently revised the text twice, in 1667 and 1672.[49] Critics are not agreed about which is the better version.

A secreto agravio secreta venganza was performed by Pedro de la Rosa before the king and queen on 8 June 1636.[50] However, a manuscript copy, which often offers better readings than the *Segunda parte*, was made by the bookseller Diego Martínez de Mora in 1635.[51] The play may have been written in that year, and performed in the public theatres first. The plot has most in common with *El médico de su honra*, but, like *El médico*, it is distanced from contemporary Spain, this time both temporally and spatially: it is set in Portugal, in the reign of King Sebastian (1557–78). One of the king's nobles, Don Lope, marries the Castilian Leonor, who has reluctantly consented to the marriage because she thinks her fiancé, the Castilian Don Luis, has been killed in Flanders; but Luis comes back. The difference between Leonor and Mencía is that the former plans to run off with her lover while her husband is fighting in North Africa. Lope, guessing what she plans, and believing that, in cases of honour, all publicity is bad publicity, arranges two apparent accidents. In one, he contrives to make it seem that Luis is drowned; in the other, that Leonor is burned to death. Even though Sebastián discovers the truth, he takes no action: he needs a soldier like Lope for his forthcoming campaign, and thinks he acted prudently. The play ends, but everyone knew what happened next: King Sebastian's army was destroyed, at least in part by drowning and burning, on 4 August 1578, at Alcázarquivir.[52] The king's body was never found. Calderón reminds the audience of these events by interrupting Sebastián's speech at the point where the alarm is raised for the fire which supposedly kills Leonor. Sebastián is telling us what he expects to be the outcome of his African expedition: 'Que espero ver …'; the voices offstage cry '¡Fuego, fuego!' ('I hope to see …' 'Fire, fire!': I, 620a).

This is kledomancy in the service of art. The term 'kledomancy' was used by diviners, who made decisions on the basis of words uttered fortuitously by speakers who knew nothing of the situation. The Church disapproved of kledomancy as a means of divination. When used as a dramatic 'accident', it creates irony, telling the audience what to expect later in the play, or, on occasion (such as in this case), after the play has ended. O. H. Green has noted kledomancy as a dramatic device in Cervantes, Lope, Tirso and Mira de Amescua, that is, in older writers with whom Calderón was familiar.[53] In addition to demonstrating this ironic technique, the moment provides another example of how the audience's knowledge of history could be used by Don Pedro to help them understand the play. As Terence May says, the play's title is wittily ambivalent.[54] Don Lope thinks it means that the secret offence of planned adultery should be avenged in secret; but his secret vengeance is a secret offence against God, who takes a secret – unexpected – vengeance at Alcázarquivir: 'Vengeance is mine: I will repay' (Romans 12:19).

Ackroyd says of Shakespeare that 'Despite the apparently orchestrated harmony of his endings, there are in fact very few genuine resolutions of the action. The closing scenes are deliberately rendered ambiguous … That is why some critics have agreed with Tolstoy that Shakespeare really had "nothing to say".'[55] Calderón is arguably different. Although his endings are sometimes ambiguous, and although it can be maintained that in a play like *El médico* he simply presents a series of events and leaves us to make what we will of them, a more plausible interpretation seems to be that we are provided with the means to understand the ambiguities; but we have to work hard to do so. Perhaps we should remember a remark made by Steven Spielberg, to the effect that it would be a poor film that was completely comprehensible in a single viewing. There is evidence, too, that Calderón was aware of, and made use of, an audience's tendency to imagine literary characters, even invented ones, having a life outside the play, or continuing to exist when it was over. Thus in *Mañana sera otro día*, the *gracioso* Roque explains why two characters are missing in the final scene, and adds:

De estos dos
cuentan mil historias largas
que se casaron. (II, 797b)

(A thousand long stories tell us of these two that they got married.)

We also find occasional, very explicit examples of the 'tying up of loose ends', or references to their existence. Since this too is done by *graciosos* (Mosquito in *El escondido y la tapada*, Hernando in *Fuego de Dios en el querer bien*, Barzoque in *No hay cosa como callar*, Hernando in *Los empeños de un acaso*), we can assume that the intention is to amuse; but the audience is also being teased with the notion that details which have little bearing on the plot are important enough to be mentioned, because they are 'real'.

Several other plays have evidence linking them to 1635. These are *La señora y la criada*, with a recorded performance on 20 November 1635 by Roque de Figueroa; *Bien vengas mal, si vienes solo*, performed on 16 December 1635 by Tomás Fernández; and *Mañana será otro día*, with a reference to a death which took place on 11 November.[56]

In the *Verdadera quinta parte* (1682), Vera Tassis tells us that when Calderón gave him permission to publish his plays, 'empezè à vsar della [= de la licencia] en las dos Comedias que puse en la Parte Quarenta y Seis de Varias' ('I began to make use of that permission in the two plays I put in *Parte XLVI*'). The two plays are *La señora y la criada* and *Las armas de la hermosura*. *La señora* does not appear in the Marañón and Veragua lists, but it is not likely that Vera Tassis began his work as editor by publishing a spurious play while Don Pedro was still alive. The close relationship between *La señora* and *El acaso y el error* indicates that one is a revision of the other, and while it has been suggested that *La señora* is the revision, much of the evidence contradicts this.[57] *El acaso y el error* is present in both the Veragua and Marañón lists; it has more than 3,700 lines, 81 per cent of them *romance*. These last two are characteristics of works written after 1650. Calderón naturally put the revised title in his lists, but he was willing to let Vera Tassis publish the original one in 1679.

The play is the story of the lovers Carlos, son of the Duke of Módena, and Diana, daughter of the Duke of Mantua. Without telling each other, they take steps to avoid the marriages their fathers have arranged for them. Diana runs away, while Carlos tries to kidnap her (and mistakenly carries off a young peasant woman, Gileta, to whom Diana has presented one of her dresses). Gileta is given the opportunity to comment sarcastically on arranged marriages, from the point of view of the bride in particular. After locking up his daughter until she reaches marriageable age, a father

> toda la guardada hija
> entrega a un hombre el primero
> día que la ve, y la triste
> doncella, que aún no vio al cielo,
> dentro de la cama al novio
> le escucha el primer resquiebro [*sic*]. (II, 841a)

(hands over all of the carefully preserved daughter to a man on the first day that man sees her, and the poor girl, who has yet to see the sky, hears her bridegroom's first compliment in bed.)

Some of the features of the play are familiar, such as the suitor as jewel merchant (*El alcaide de sí mismo*, ?1626–7; *A secreto agravio*, ?1635), and the rustic taken for a noble and forced to play the role (*El alcaide de sí mismo*). In the end, Carlos and Diana do manage to marry, largely thanks to the ingenuity of Diana, who is able to act the roles of both maid and mistress.

Bien vengas mal, si vienes solo is set in Madrid. The principal male character, Don Juan, kills a rival in the opening scene, and his consideration of his options reminds us of the events of 1621, when the Calderón brothers took refuge in the Imperial embassy:

> Si pretendo que me guarde
> iglesia o embajador,
> es darme luego por parte,
> y culparme yo a mí mismo. (II, 608a)

(If I try to seek refuge in a church or with an ambassador, it's admitting I'm involved, and putting the blame on myself.)

Since the plot presents only two young ladies and three young gentlemen, one of the young men must be disappointed. Significantly, the loser is not Juan, who killed someone in a fair fight, but Luis, who takes an excessively jealous interest in the activities of his sister: we have already noticed that jealous brothers tend to come off badly. The question of which of her suitors Ana should marry is solved by the intervention of Espinel, the *gracioso*: 'Don Diego y Don Luis pretenden | a tu hija', he says to Don Bernardo; 'elija ella | el que mejor le parece' ('Don Diego and Don Luis seek your daughter's hand; let her choose the one she prefers': II, 632b). Ana has never been in doubt about marrying Diego, and pounces on this opportunity before her father can say a word. There may well have been enlightened aristocratic fathers in 1630s Madrid, willing to let their daughters have a say in choosing a husband, but that they should be moved to do so by the prompting of a servant seems unlikely. Once again verisimilitude takes second place to a moral point.

Among the literary references in *Bien vengas, mal* are two to other plays. The first is Rojas Zorrilla's *Entre bobos anda el juego* (printed 1645; II, 606b), a reference which supports the view that Don Pedro's friendship and first dated collaborations with Rojas had already begun: *El jardín de Falerina* (Rojas, Coello, Calderón) was performed by Tomás Fernández on 13 January 1636, only four weeks after *Bien vengas, mal*, while *El mejor amigo el muerto* (Belmonte Bermúdez, Rojas, Calderón) was performed by Fernández on 2 February.[58] If these were first performances, composition presumably took place in late 1635. The second reference is to a play ostensibly entitled *Los favores truecan las desdichas* (II, 615b: 'Deso mismo | he visto yo una comedia', 'I've seen a play about that', says Ana), but no play of this title can now be traced.

El jardín de Falerina, a three-act play on which Calderón based his two-act version of the same title (?1649), survives only in manuscripts and in a doctoral thesis.[59] The sources are Boiardo's *Orlando innamorato* (1486) and Ariosto's *Orlando furioso* (1516; definitive version, 1532). In *El peregrino en su patria* (1604), Lope had listed *El jardín de Falerina*, but this play is lost; it seems unlikely that the text was available to a trio of collaborators over thirty years later. This being so, it is impossible to be certain that Chevalier is correct when he argues that the collaboration play is a forerunner in its presentation of magic and music, since previous adaptations of Italian epic had used the heroic or romantic elements only.[60] In fact, the play is more of a burlesque than anything else, because of the major role played by Brunel, Orlando's *gracioso* squire, who is mistaken for Orlando himself because he found it easier to carry his master's armour by wearing it, rather like Benito in *El alcaide de sí mismo*, for which the same Tomás Fernández was paid for a performance in February 1627. In Calderón's act, Brunel makes a reference to *Peor está que estaba* (1630; line 2728) and paraphrases the song which is used in *La niña de Gómez Arias* (?1637–9) and elsewhere ('Que soy niño y solo, | y nunca en tal me vi', 'I'm a child and alone, and was never in such a situation': 2391–4).[61] One of the most striking debts to another play is the scene where a supernatural table descends on the hungry Brunel, and his questions '¿Es comida o es culebra?' ('Is it a meal or a trick?': 2680) and '¿Beuen vino acaso aquí?' ('Do they drink wine here, by chance?': 2686) recall, and parody, the words of Catalinón in *El burlador de Sevilla* at the supernatural meal provided by the stone guest.

El mejor amigo el muerto survives in a manuscript with the title *El mejor amigo el muerto, y fortunas de D. Juan de Castro, y gloria de Lemos* (BNE, MS Res. 86). Most of the manuscript is autograph in the hands of the three authors, and the full title reminds us that the source of the plot is Lope's *Don Juan de Castro I* and *II* (1597–1608), two novelesque plays set in England, as this is. Tomás Fernández performed it on 2 February 1636, the last Saturday before Lent.[62] Lope had written his play to flatter Pedro Fernández de Castro y Andrade, the then Count of Lemos, nephew and son-in-law of Lerma. By 1636 the holder of the title was the ninth Count, Francisco Fernández de Castro, who took it in 1629 when his father joined the Benedictines, so that the 1636 version presumably did not have the same adulatory intent.

The play deals with the attempt of 'Prince Roberto of Ireland' to marry his cousin 'Queen Clarinda of England', by force of arms if necessary, so that he can become king. The situation recurs in *El monstruo de la fortuna*, written a few months later.[63] In the end, because of a kindness done to a dying man, who miraculously returns to help him, Don Juan de Castro defeats Roberto and marries the queen. Despite the improbable story, the play ran to at least eight editions before 1780, and there are four surviving manuscripts. We should remember that acts of charity played a huge role in early modern Spanish society, and that the plots of some modern films are just as short of verisimilitude.

Mañana será otro día is also set in Madrid, and involves the son (Juan) and daughter (Beatriz) of Don Luis de Ayala. As is so often the case in Calderón plays, there is no mother: she has died. Don Luis explains in the opening scene:

> Tu hermano, muerta tu madre,
> fué con mi gusto a las guerras
> del Monferrato, en servicio
> del señor Duque de Lerma

...
hasta que pasando a Flandes,
que es de la milicia escuela,
murió el Duque. ¡Oh, quién aquí
tocar de paso pudiera
tal lástima, sin que el llanto
embarazase a la lengua! (II, 755)

(After your mother died, your brother went with my approval to the Mantuan war, in the service of the Duke of Lerma ... until, going over to Flanders, the school of soldiering, the duke died. Oh, if only one could touch in passing on such a sad event, without tears hindering the tongue!)

The duke, nephew of Philip III's minister, died on 11 November 1635. It seems likely that these words were written soon after the news reached Madrid. Calderón's brother José had also served with the duke in the north of Italy, although he was given leave to return to Madrid on 24 July 1631. Don Pedro does not describe his brother's activities in Flanders, but Don Juan de Ayala accompanied the duke there, coming home on leave only after his general's death. Since then, his behaviour has displeased his father: young women of dubious reputation have come looking for him at his father's house, to which he also brings his rowdy soldier friends, coming and going at all hours. After a quarrel, he has left home.

When Calderón portrays or refers to Spanish soldiers who were historical figures – in *El sitio de Bredá*, for example – he is complimentary, but imagined soldiers are often portrayed differently, as in *El Tuzaní de la Alpujarra*, or in *El alcalde de Zalamea*: they are guilty of anything from rowdyism to criminal acts. We have no idea whether he felt that military life had changed his brother for the worse, but he must have had ample opportunity to meet young men who had been hardened by soldiering. As for young Don Juan, having left home, he has now initiated a lawsuit against his father for the income from a *mayorazgo* he inherited from his mother. For Don Luis, this is an annoyance, but

para más ofensa,
en todas las peticiones
que da en el pleito que intenta,
no se firma mi apellido
de Ayala, sino el de Leyva,
materno. (II, 756a)

(To give more offence, in all the pleas he presents in the case he's bringing, he does not sign himself with my surname, Ayala, but with his mother's, de Leyva.)

We know from Calderón's own practice that the use of a maternal surname in the context of an inheritance was normal, and Don Luis accepts this, but adds that 'es por hacerme pesar', 'it's to cause me grief'. Don Pedro did not go quite as far. Between February 1616 and 1630 he made intermittent use of the names 'Calderón y Riaño', abandoning part of his father's surname for that of his mother's mother; and, of course, his father could no longer be offended. And while the Calderón brothers never mounted a legal challenge against their father in person, they certainly challenged his will.

Don Juan may no longer be prepared to do what his father tells him, but Don Luis continues to treat his daughter as if she had no will of her own. It emerges that he has chosen a husband for her, Don Fernando Cardona, whom she has never met. This time it is the *gracioso*, Roque, Fernando's servant, who is bold enough to ask the question that must occur to many bystanders in arranged marriages:

Qué la dice a una mujer,
saber quisiera, un marido,
que sin haberla mirado,
ni hablado, señor, ni escrito,
se entra en la cama con ella. (II, 772b–773a)

(I'd like to know, sir, what a husband says to a wife when he gets into bed with her without ever having looked at her, talked to her or written to her.)

Gileta's comment about arranged marriages in *La señora y la criada* is not present in *El acaso y el error*, an omission which supports the view that *La señora* is contemporary with *Mañana será otro día*. It seems likely that Carlos's remark that 'Para hacer lo que no quieren | no tienen más privilegio | los hombres que las mujeres' ('For doing what they don't want to, men have no more rights than women': II, 846) is the writer's deliberate or subconscious recollection of the title of *El privilegio de las mujeres* (?1634), but since these lines are present in both *El acaso* and *La señora*, the allusion does not help us to determine which came first.

In the event, Beatriz meets Fernando by accident, when her willingness to help a friend puts her in a compromising situation. She warms to his gallantry and consideration (and his good looks), and is immensely relieved, as well as very happy, to discover that he is her father's choice. Don Juan, despite becoming entangled with two young women (he loves the poor one, Elvira, but is willing to marry Leonor for her money), settles down with the one he loves, persuaded, perhaps, by her calling herself his *dama*. This happy ending is denied Don Diego in *El hombre pobre todo es trazas*; and, as if he felt sorry for Leonor, Calderón has Roque announce her marriage to Diego, another minor character who was dropped when he had served his purpose. Among the literary references are one to *Peor está que estaba* (?1630, II, 796b) and another to the 'cielo azul' ('blue sky') of Leonardo de Argensola's *A una mujer que se afeitaba* (II, 784a).

Sometime around 1634, at least in the view of the most recent scholarly editor, Calderón wrote the *auto sacramental El gran teatro del mundo*, which likens human life to taking part in a play.[64] To appreciate the metaphor, we need to remember what performing a play was like in seventeenth-century Spain. Most early modern theatres had an apron stage, 4–6 feet high, jutting out into the audience, who surrounded it in a circle, as in the Globe in London, or on three rectangular sides, as in many Spanish theatres. Public theatres were often open to the elements, so that night scenes, for example, were played in daylight. The relationship between actor and audience was physically close. On a psychological level, though, it was arguably more distant. There was no front curtain to divide the real-life space, where the audience were, from the make-believe space, so that, between scenes, stage-hands had to work in full view; the scenery was often rudimentary, when it existed; and costumes were often flamboyant, but 'authentic' is not an appropriate word in this context, although only the educated few would know the difference.[65] The audience had to use a great deal of imagination to suspend its disbelief. The *autos* were played in these public theatres, but because of their religious importance, they were first performed on Corpus Christi Thursday, or on the day following, in town squares, admission free; on a similar kind of high apron stage, but also involving carts, which processed through the streets to the town square before the performance. In Madrid in the 1630s, there were two carts and four *autos*; from 1647 there were two *autos* and four carts. The carts were part scenery (including mechanical scene changes), part performance area, and when they reached the town square, they were parked immediately behind the temporary stage. A drawing for the Madrid *autos* of 1644 shows that the stage, which was 50 by 16 feet, was placed just to the left of the Panadería, the main building in the Plaza Mayor (Plate 21). It was 6 feet high, and faced a temporary grandstand which had two levels. The dignitaries sat in this grandstand, which was only slightly wider than the stage; the vast majority of the audience stood in the square, surrounding the stage on the other three sides.[66] By the 1650s, when Calderón was writing all the *autos* for Madrid Town Council, he was also composing detailed memos, *memorias de apariencias*, on the design of the carts, and what each one had to do and when.

In seventeenth-century Spain, the actor's profession was not quite respectable, but it was open to both sexes, unlike in pre-Restoration England. From 1631, there was an actors' guild, and each company was run by a manager, the *autor de comedias*.[67] When the *autor* made contracts with his actors, they signed up to play 'primer galán' (leading man) 'primera dama' (leading lady), and so on, down to 'apuntador' (prompter), 'guardarropa' (wardrobe-keeper) and 'cobrador' (the one who took the money at the door). The *autor* was also responsible for obtaining the texts of the plays the company would perform. As we have seen, the leading ones dealt directly with playwrights. The author's manuscript was passed to the prompter, who made a fair copy, and copied out the parts for each character. Only the prompter had the whole text: each actor had only his own lines, with each speech preceded by a cue-line spoken by the previous speaker, so that he would know when it was his turn. Roles were assigned by the *autor*, or, perhaps in consultation with him, by the author. The wardrobe-keeper would supply the actor with a suitable costume, and any props his role required. Actors would then learn their lines (with a literate helper, if they could not read), and met for rehearsals.

These activities are turned into an allegory in the *auto*, which opens with the *autor*, who is soon joined by the character Mundo (the World), to whom he identifies himself as the *autor soberano*, the sovereign author. This is a double word-play: this *autor* is the author who wrote the play, as well as the manager of the company; and these are metaphors for the Creator. The character Mundo is the stage on which the play will be performed. In due course the actors are summoned, and the *autor* distributes the roles: the king (Rey); the leading lady (Hermosura, Beauty); Rico, the Rich Man; Labrador, the Peasant; Discreción (Discernment, actually a religious); Pobre, the Poor Man; and Niño, the stillborn child. Pobre protests that everyone else got better roles than he, and is told that in the eyes of the *autor*, all the roles are equal: what matters is the quality of the performance, and all of human life is a performance: 'Que toda la vida humana | representaciones es' (III, 208a). The play is to be called *Obrar bien, que Dios es Dios*. The actors are impressed by this title, and discuss the need to rehearse, in order to produce a good performance. However, as one might expect, when acting in a play is an allegory for the roles individuals have in life, there is to be no rehearsal, and the actors are given no lines: they have to improvise, to 'adlib'. Instead of the series of cues which would normally accompany their lines, they are given only one, the title of the play: 'Obrar bien, que Dios es Dios' ('Do good, for God is God'). However, they are allowed a prompter, which the *autor* describes as 'mi Ley', 'my law'.

Before they begin, the actors are given their costumes and props by Mundo, here acting as wardrobe-keeper. The king demands purple and laurel, and gets them, after Mundo has inspected the document assigning this role to him. Hermosura is given symbolic flowers, Rico receives jewels, Discreción is given a hair shirt and a scourge, and Labrador is given a mattock. When Pobre comes forward, last of all, he is given nothing. Indeed, Mundo takes away what clothes he has.

We know that, after a successful first-night performance, a theatre company might have a celebration. On at least one occasion, there was a dinner party, attended by all the company and by the author, that is, Calderón. This happens in *El gran teatro*, where the guests are served with bread and wine. The first to be invited to sit at the table are Pobre and Discreción. Rey, Labrador and Hermosura are told they must wait (that is, they have to spend time in Purgatory). Discreción intercedes for Rey, and the *autor* accepts him. Before the *auto* ends, Hermosura and Labrador are also accepted. Rico is ejected from the *autor*'s company: that is, sent to hell.

The sources of this allegory are obviously Christian doctrine, but also pre-Christian philosophy, especially the Stoics, and among them, Epictetus in particular. The only surviving work of Epictetus (?50–?125 AD) is the *Enchiridion* ('handbook'), a collection of maxims. The most significant passage reads:

> Remember that, being a mere actor, you are performing a play as the author wants it to be performed. If your role is short, you will play it short; if it is long, you will play it long. If the author wants you to perform the part of a Poor Man, play this part naturally. If in the play you have to be a cripple, a prince, an ordinary man, it does not matter: perform your part as well as you can, because your duty is to play your character well. As for the role that you are to perform, that is for someone else to choose.[68]

While we cannot be sure that Calderón knew this passage, it seems likely. Quevedo published a translation of Epictetus in 1635, that is, about the time of *El gran teatro*'s composition.[69]

El gran teatro was first printed in 1655.[70] However, it reached Mexico, to be translated into Nahuatl by the Jesuit Bartolomé de Alva for the use of pupils in the Colegio de San Gregorio in Mexico City, perhaps as early as 1641, and certainly during the 1640s.[71]

Other Calderón *autos* of this period also travelled: two of them, *El veneno y la triaca* and the Marian *auto La hidalga del valle*, were performed in Valencia in 1634.[72] These may have been among the 'muchas comedias, autos y obras sueltas' which Pérez de Montalbán attributed to Don Pedro in

1632 (see p. 103 above). The dating and even the trustworthy attribution of early Calderón *autos* presents considerable problems.

***

For a playwright to take over from Lope as 'national dramatist', his plays needed to appear in *partes*. In 1635 the Castilian authorities had begun once again to issue licences for the printing of plays, and sometime in 1635 Don Pedro began to assemble texts for his *Primera parte* (Plate 22). 'Assemble' meant borrowing or buying them back from the *autores* to whom they had been sold; not an unfriendly process, since none of the plays was new, and since Calderón was not a writer whom an *autor* would wish to antagonise. The texts, though, were not necessarily unmodified: they needed to be checked and corrected. Ostensibly the editor of the volume was his younger brother José, who signed the dedication to Calderón's employer, the Duke of Frías, but the privilege (a ten-year copyright) was in the name of the author. Some of the plays, like *La vida es sueño* and *La cruz en la sepultura* / *La devoción de la cruz*, were revised, conceivably for publication, but neither brother took consistent pains to present correct texts: *El príncipe constante*, for example, is full of errors, perhaps because it is the last in the volume.[73] The first *aprobación*, by Juan Bautista de Sosa, the poet's uncle, is dated 6 November 1635; the second, by Valdivielso, refers to 'mucha doctrina moral para la reformacion, muchos avisos para los riesgos, muchos escarmientos para la juventud, muchos desengaños para los incautos, y muchos sales para los señores' ('much doctrine for moral improvement, many warnings for dangers, many lessons for the young, many admonitions for the unwary, much wit for gentlemen'): a fellow writer could be expected to comment on the moral value of plays in particular. Once approved, the volume received its religious and civil printing licences, the second of them incorporated in the privilege (10 December). Printing took six months, and publication day (the date of the Tasa, the price certificate, which specified a price of 8 *reales* and 28 *maravedís*) was 15 July 1636.[74] Just two weeks earlier, the king had recommended Don Pedro for a knighthood of Santiago.

CHAPTER II

Knight of Santiago

Porque hay quien presume
que es oficio el que es ingenio,
sin atender que el estudio
de un arte noble es empleo
que no desluce la sangre …

(*La fiera, el rayo y la piedra*)

(Because there are those who presume that what is creativity is merely a job, without heeding the fact that the study of a noble art is an occupation that does not discredit one's ancestry …)

The mechanics of seventeenth-century book production in Spain were such that any author who wanted to read proofs had to do so in the printing-house while the book was being produced. Examination of the handful of surviving copies of Calderón's *Primera parte* reveals, from a small number of press variants (differences between copies), that corrections were made during printing. This was normal procedure, carried out by the compositors themselves, and should not be taken to mean that Don Pedro saw his plays through the press. On the contrary, the numerous remaining errors, to say nothing of the amount of evidence for the writing of new plays while these others were being printed, suggest that the poet left everything to the typesetters and pressmen of María de Quiñones. In any case, if the fiction that writing was merely a pastime were to be maintained, no *hidalgo* could be seen to show too much interest in the printing of his works. The title-page of the *Primera parte* also tells us that the book was produced 'A costa de Pedro Coello, y de Manuel Lopez, Mercaderes de Libros'. These 'book merchants' were the equivalent of modern publishers. They would have had a contract with Don Pedro, whereby they gave him a lump sum (Cervantes got 1,600 *reales* for his *Novelas ejemplares* in 1613)[1] and a small number of copies for distribution to friends and patrons (we know that the Marquis of Astorga, the dedicatee of the *Tercera parte* of 1664, received a copy bound in gilt vellum). There would possibly have been a clause allowing for a second edition, if the market required it. As book merchants, Coello and López would have had premises where customers could buy single copies, and would have distributed copies in bulk, at wholesale rates, to other merchants, some of them in other cities.

Getting into print oneself meant being called on to write approbations for the books of others: it was another sign that one had arrived as a writer. Don Pedro's first *aprobación*, of Tirso's *Quinta parte*, dated from July 1635, before the publication of his own first *parte*, although it may have given him the idea. His second, for Pérez Pericón's *Descripción de … Gibraltar*, was written in February 1636, while his own first book was in press. His third, for Pedro de Oña's religious epic on St Ignatius, was dated 30 July 1636, although the book took another three years to appear.[2] The approbation assured the authorities that the poem 'està escrito con el decoro, la agudeza, el zelo, y la atencion que requirio tan grande assumpto … debaxo de la numerosa suavidad de los versos, està mas apacible la exemplar enseñanza de sus virtudes' ('is written with the propriety, the wit, the zeal and the care required for such an important subject … the exemplary teaching of its virtues is more gentle under the harmonious sweetness of its verse'). All three approbations are signed in Madrid.

Calderón's exceptional mid-thirties output included plays written in collaboration. To our knowledge, he was involved in thirteen plays of this kind, four of them apparently written in the period 1634–6: *Yerros de naturaleza* (1634, with Antonio Coello); *El privilegio de las mujeres* (?1634, Calderón and, according to some editors, Pérez de Montalbán and Antonio Coello); *El jardín de Falerina* (1635, Rojas, Antonio Coello, Calderón); *El mejor amigo el muerto* (1635–6, Belmonte Bermúdez, Rojas, Calderón). As usual, our information about dates is incomplete, but it seems quite likely that Don Pedro's methods of composition did not preclude the possibility of working on several plays at once.

The six weeks of Lent, when plays were not performed, gave writers and actors the opportunity to prepare for the new season. Easter Sunday 1636 fell on 23 March, and on Thursday 3 April *El escondido y la tapada* was performed by Antonio de Prado, who had returned to Madrid with his company.[3] In the text there is an allusion (II, 679a) to the siege of Valenza del Po by French troops (20 September – 28 October 1635). Since the siege was not of lasting military importance, we can assume that the play was written soon after the news of its raising reached Madrid, that is, between November 1635 and March 1636. The text also refers to the collaboration play *Los privilegios* [*sic*] *de las mujeres*, as we have seen, to *La dama duende* (1629; II, 691b) and to Cervantes's *El celoso extremeño* (published 1613, II, 684a).

Since *El privilegio / Los privilegios* is hardly in the same category, in terms of reputation, as *La dama duende* or Cervantes's story, the odds are that it pre-dates *El escondido* only slightly.

At one point Lisarda, who has apparently been hiding a man in her room, exclaims:

> Si así teme una inocente,
> ¿cómo teme una culpada? (II, 706a)

(If an innocent woman is so afraid, how does a guilty one fear?)

These are exactly the words of Beatriz in *Mañana será otro día* (II, 766a), which was almost certainly written at the same time as *El escondido y la tapada*. There is one difference between the plays, however: *El escondido* was written in fulfilment of a promise, as the final lines indicate: 'con que acaba, | por empeño escrito, *El* | *Escondido y la Tapada*' ('with which ends *El escondido y la tapada*, written in fulfilment of a pledge': II, 707b). The promise may have been made to Prado, who performed the play, but the carrying out of a request from the royal household is a more likely explanation.

Another probable Prado performance during this period is of *El alcalde de Zalamea*. For a long time it was thought that *El alcalde*, first printed in 1651, was the product of the author's own experience of war, and that the brutalities of Castilian troops billeted on Catalan peasants in 1640–2 gave him a model for the behaviour of the troops led by Don Álvaro de Ataide in Zalamea de la Serena in the summer of 1580. The discovery that there was a performance of '*El alcalde de Zalamea*' by Antonio de Prado on 12 May 1636 did not immediately change this view, since it was assumed that the performance was of the other version of the play, attributed to Lope.[4] However, the growing awareness of Don Pedro's relationship with Prado in the 1630s, plus the realisation that it would have been insensitive, in the immediate aftermath of the Portuguese rising of December 1640, to portray unfavourably the Castilian troops who took over the country in 1580–1, led to a reconsideration. Victor Dixon has argued convincingly that the 1636 performance was of Calderón's version, and that the roles of Crespo and Isabel were written with Prado and his much younger third wife Mariana Vaca in mind.[5]

Spain's best-known exposition of the joys of living in the country was the *Menosprecio de corte y alabanza de aldea* (1539) of the bishop of Mondoñedo, Antonio de Guevara, which had considerable influence, even on the drama. Literature everywhere, from Horace to Gray's *Elegy*, often wears rose-tinted glasses to examine rural life, and Lope's peasant plays, *Peribáñez* (?1605–13), *Fuenteovejuna* (1612–14), *El villano en su rincón* (1611–15), *El mejor alcalde el rey* (1620–3), and *Los Tellos de Meneses*, I and II (1625–30), are no exception. The peasant heroes suffer, they face crises, but their values are upheld, and happy futures stretch before them. Pedro Crespo's values survive, but they do not bring him happiness: he has lost his son and his daughter, neither of whom fully understood his attachment to those values. Crespo has just brought in his wheat harvest, described as a mountain of gold against the blue sky of Extremadura. If this valuable grain represents Crespo, then the useless chaff is the local nobleman Don Mendo, whose only blue and gold is that of his worthless *ejecutoria*. There is clearly something wrong with a system which gives rights to the Mendos of this world while denying them to the Pedro Crespos, but it is not a system which can be changed. *El alcalde de Zalamea* is Don Pedro's only play about rural life, but it is not an optimistic one.

On 23 June, some six weeks after the performance of *El alcalde*, there took place the premiere of what was arguably the most ambitious play Calderón had written so far, at least in terms of performance requirements: *Los tres mayores prodigios*. The venue was the Retiro, and the specially constructed performing area (in the patio of the new palace) involved three stages. One of the models for this three-part play was *La Virgen del Sagrario* (?1629), which, as has been noted, was a kind of triptych held together thematically by an image of Our Lady. There is no evidence, however, that *La Virgen del Sagrario* was played by anything but a single company, whereas each act of *Los tres mayores prodigios* was played by a separate company on a separate stage; the companies were those of Tomás Fernández, Pedro de la Rosa and Antonio de Prado.[6] We are presented with only the culminating heroic deeds of the three protagonists: Jason's winning of the golden fleece, Theseus' killing of the Minotaur, and Hercules' rescue of Dejanira from Nessus. Those who saw the play, such as the English ambassador, were certainly impressed by the staging, 'the invention whereof was soe good, the place where it was acted sett out with three seuerall sceanes of soe much ostentation and the disposition of the lights soe full of nouelty and delight, that I am hugely tempted to giue your honour a larger description of it'.[7] The plots are less impressive. There is no time for character development, and little enough for the deeds of Jasón and Teseo, most of which happen offstage. Although the three heroes – the three prodigies – are brought together in the end, the common theme in *Los tres mayores prodigios* is less obvious, at least until the final scene, when the death of Hércules reminds us that all three of the heroes are flawed, and that their triumphs are hollow.

At one point Ariadna refers to the way in which music intensifies the emotions, whether they involve joy or sorrow:

> Pues la armonía,
> como al alegre alegría,
> así da al triste tristeza. (I, 1663b)

(For harmony gives sadness to the sad as it gives joy to the joyful.)

This notion had already been described in *De una causa dos efectos* (?*c.* 1632; II, 466b) and *El mayor monstruo* (?1635; I, 476a). There is also another version of the image of the swimming horse as ship, which was previously used in *La puente de Mantible* (1630) and *El privilegio de las mujeres* (?1634); Neso, the 'centaur', is carrying off Deyanira, and his horse takes to the water:

> Animosamente boga,
> siendo los remos los pies,
> siendo la frente la proa,
> vela al [= el?] manto de la ninfa,
> árbol Neso, el anca popa,
> buco el pecho, y el timón,
> sobre la espuma, la cola. (I, 1674a)

(He rows in spirited fashion, his feet being oars, his forehead the prow, the nymph's mantle a sail, Nessus the mast, the haunches stern, the breast hull, and his tail, on the foam, the rudder.)

In *El mayor encanto, amor*, likening a heron to a ship, Ulises used the same metaphors:

> hechos remos los pies, proa la frente,
> la vela el ala y el timón la cola. (I, 1618b)

(the feet made oars, the forehead prow, the wing the sail and tail the rudder.)

Some images or turns of phrase were used and re-used throughout his career by Don Pedro, but others appear to cluster in particular periods, like these. We cannot afford to rely on them for dating evidence, but they can provide support.

The other plays which Calderón may have composed at this time are *Los cabellos de Absalón*, which was probably written soon after *La venganza de Tamar* was published in Tirso's *Parte tercera* (1634), *Antes que todo es mi dama* and *Los dos amantes del cielo*, both of which Hilborn has assigned to 1636.[8] There is some evidence that they are slightly later, and they are examined in the next chapter.

While Tirso's play, *La venganza de Tamar*, was published in his *Parte tercera* in 1634, the first draft may date from 1621–4.[9] Calderón took the third act of this play and used it, very slightly modified, for Act II of *Los cabellos de Absalón*. Nowadays he might be sued for plagiarism. He may have been under pressure to complete his own play, but an equally likely explanation is that it was a compliment to a writer he admired, as well as a kind of *tour de force*, a demonstration of a new way of using existing material.

On 16 November 1819, in a letter to Maria Gisborne, who had taught him to read Spanish, Shelley wrote that he had been reading Calderón without her help: 'The Cabellos de Absalon, is full of the deepest and the tenderest touches of nature ... The incest scene of Amon and Tamar is perfectly tremendous.'[10] Other critics have complained of the play's lack of unity, but, perhaps, rather than a tragedy of a single individual, it is an example of a tragic event, born of the dissensions and rivalries among David's children, and enveloping Amón, the innocent Tamar, the ambitious and vain Absalón, and David himself.[11] Calderón followed 2 Samuel closely, but he also knew what had gone before: the starting-point of David's removal of Uriah so that he could enjoy the latter's wife Bathsheba (mentioned, I, 675a).

The song sung by the musicians in Act I to drown the cries of Tamar derives from a poem attributed to both Hurtado de Mendoza and Quevedo,[12] while David's lament in Act III uses the refrain 'Salid sin duelo, lágrimas, corriendo' ('Run in abundance, tears') from Garcilaso's first eclogue. Joab's reference to how 'la real púrpura de Amón | manchó de Absalón la mesa' ('the royal purple of Amnon stained the table of Absalom': I, 687a) recalls the words of Muerte in *La cena de Baltasar*: 'yo mancharé las mesas de Absalón | con la caliente púrpura de Amón' ('I shall stain the tables of Absalom with the warm purple of Amnon': III, 166a).

***

While Antonio de Prado's company was mocking Zalamea's destitute nobleman, the character's creator was thinking of *ejecutorias* in a different context. Destitute noblemen had been ridiculed since Lazarillo's *escudero* (1554), but the mockery always held an ambivalence. Early modern Spain was obsessed with status, with the measurement of it, and with the documents which were used to measure it. If even impoverished rural nobles could use toothpicks to give observers the impression that they had eaten a meal, we can easily imagine that servants of the most protocol-conscious court in Europe might be obsessive about how their fellows perceived them. This was true of all of Calderón's contemporaries, especially if they had to earn an income to survive. One of the best examples is Velázquez.

Diego de Silva y Velázquez was seven months older than Calderón; like Calderón's, his court career began in the summer of 1623. His desire to become a knight of one of Spain's military orders (Santiago, Calatrava, Alcántara) goes back, in terms of taking action to further his wish, to 1650.[13] No doubt the knighthoods awarded to Rubens (d. 1640) and Van Dyck (d. 1641) were a factor. In theory the rules operating in Spain should have excluded him from any such pretension, since he had practised a 'base occupation': he had painted for a living. The rules specifically excluded such painters, not to mention silversmiths and clerks (except for royal secretaries). It is tempting to think that about this time he confided in a fellow courtier who had also made a livelihood from his art, and who had been a knight of Santiago for over a decade. Tempting, that is, given the circumstantial evidence of two of Don Pedro's most explicit statements about the nobility of art and of the artist: *Darlo todo y no dar nada* (performed for the queen's birthday, 22 December 1651) and *La fiera, el rayo y la piedra* (performed May 1652). In the first of these, after a three-way painting competition recalling that which Velázquez won in 1627, Apeles is appointed Alejandro's *pintor de cámara* (Velázquez's title), with the additional ruling that only he may paint the king in future (a concession granted to Velázquez).[14] The unsuccessful rivals are paid for their paintings, because 'no se han de pagar | los estudios con desprecios' ('study must not be rewarded with contempt': II, 1028a), while the amount finally paid to Apeles for his portrait, 40,000 *escudos*, is huge (II, 1028b). Philip IV was presumably flattered to be identified with Alexander the Great as a patron of the arts, but Calderón also let him know how short he fell of that model in financial terms. In addition, as if Calderón wanted to emphasise the 'brotherhood of artists', Apeles twice refers to the relationship between music, poetry and painting, while Alejandro himself refers to painting as 'el mejor arte, | más noble y de más ingenio' ('the best, noblest and most creative art': II, 1027a, 1029b, 1046a).

At the time of his becoming a priest, Calderón had intended to give up writing. Concern over his status as a writer, and over the status of his writings, never left him entirely, but after 1651 he was no longer an ordinary courtier, with an ordinary courtier's preoccupations about how his fellows perceived him: the need to argue his own case had diminished. It seems likely that he was arguing on behalf of a fellow artist, in whose discipline he had always had a keen interest, especially since Apeles and Pigmaleón, the two protagonists, are both practitioners of the plastic arts, as opposed to writing.

The danger was that an applicant for a knighthood might draw attention to aspects of his family which, in the prejudice-ridden society of seventeenth-century Spain, might be better kept quiet. One such was Calderón's friend and collaborator Francisco de Rojas Zorrilla, who applied for membership of the Order of Santiago in 1643, only to be said to have both *converso* and *morisco* ancestry.[15] The accusations were apparently malicious, and eventually he received the knighthood in late 1645. Although not an applicant for a knighthood, Calderón's other friend Juan Pérez de Montalbán was also 'suspected', while another dramatist, Felipe Godínez, who was reconciled at an *auto de fe* in 1624, was maliciously said by Quevedo to excel in Old Testament subjects.[16] The most famous case is Antonio Enríquez Gómez, who also wrote under the name Fernando de Zárate. Born in 1600 in Cuenca in a Portuguese *converso* family, he was living in Madrid by 1629, but left to reside in France about 1637. His epic poem *Sansón Nazareno* (another Old Testament subject; luckily, Quevedo was dead) was published in Rouen in 1656.[17] In the prologue he referred flatteringly to Antonio de Mendoza, Pérez de Montalbán, Calderón, Villaizán, Godínez and Luis Vélez, another Calderón collaborator. Enríquez Gómez was burned in effigy, and eventually fell into the hands of the Inquisition, dying in one of its prisons in 1663. No one ever charged Don Pedro with having Jewish ancestry, but the accusation was made of his friends and acquaintances.

While Velázquez's ancestors were not said to be Jewish, he had to suffer two humiliating rejections, both of them made on the grounds of 'genealogy', since no witnesses could be found to declare that he had ever accepted money for his paintings (which, of course, he had). Finally, on 28 November 1659, his knighthood was approved. In comparison, Calderón's acquisition of a knighthood of Santiago was painless.

The acquisition process ostensibly began on 3 July 1636, when the king signed a warrant authorising the collection of information about Don Pedro's suitability for elevation to the knighthood. A lengthy investigation had to take place, financed by the candidate, to determine whether he met all the criteria. Ancestry was the most important of these, and Don Pedro presented a one-page 'Genealojia' in his own hand:

Genealojia de

Don Pedro Calderon de la Barca a quien su Mg^d a hecho mr^d del Avito de S.Tiago natural de Madrid En La Parrochia de S Martin

Padres

Diego Calderon de la Barca natural de Madrid y doña Ana Maria de Henao natural de Madrid y su Mujer Lijitima

Abuelos paternos

Pedro Calderon de la Barca natural de boadilla del camino en campos y su Mujer doña Ysauel Ruiz natural de Toledo

Abuelos Maternos

Diego Gonzalez de Henao Natural de Madrid y su Mujer Doña Ynes de Riaño natural de Madrid

Don P° Calderon de la Barca

(Genealogy of Don Pedro Calderón de la Barca, native of Madrid in the parish of St Martin, on whom His Majesty has bestowed the favour of the habit of Santiago. / Parents / Diego Calderón de la Barca, native of Madrid, and Doña Ana María de Henao, native of Madrid, and his lawful wife. / Paternal grandparents / Pedro Calderón de la Barca, native of Boadilla del Camino in Campos, and his wife Doña Isabel Ruiz, native of Toledo. / Maternal grandparents / Diego González de Henao, native of Madrid, and his wife, Doña Inés de Riaño, native of Madrid. / Don Pedro Calderón de la Barca.)

An official added the note 'En M[adri]d A diez y siete de Julio de 1636. Deposite ducientos du[cad]os y de La fi[anz]a' ('In Madrid, 17 July 1636. Let him deposit 200 ducats and give the guarantee').

This document was probably accompanied by the poet's maternal grandfather's *ejecutoria*, with a covering letter beginning with the words 'Don Pedro Calderon de la Barca q[ue] pretende el avito de la orden de Santiago …' ('Don Pedro Calderón de la Barca, who seeks the habit of the Order of Santiago …') (Plates 23, 24, 25).[18] In documents of 1637 and 1647, there is a reference to his redeeming a *censo* worth 1,000 ducats on 9 July 1636, no doubt in anticipation of the expenses referred to by the official.[19] The earlier document acknowledges that only Don Pedro benefited from the redemption of this annuity, which was owned by all three brothers; it also refers to the sale of the Espartinas saltworks *juro* of 500 ducats, which was divided between Don Pedro and his brother José. No date is given for this sale. The first of the poet's expenses was the deposit of 200 ducats referred to in the note above. On 25 August he had to borrow the *fianza* from two *regidores* of Madrid, Don Pedro González de Armunia (father-in-law of his uncle Andrés de Henao) and Don Pedro Romero.[20] We can regard a bond as a kind of savings account, but these were joint accounts: in his most productive period, Don Pedro was reduced to borrowing from his brothers money inherited from his father, as well as borrowing from more distant family and colleagues. The reference to the parish of San Martín is evidently to the place of birth, not to the parish he was living in in 1636.

It seems likely that Calderón had indicated before July that he would like to become a member of the Order of Santiago, but the favourable royal response was not made public until 29 July:

Por la noche … se representó en el Retiro la comedia de la fábula de *Dafne*, con notables tramoyas de grande costa y artificio, que ordenó Cosme Lot, peregrino ingenio para estas invenciones.

(At night there was performed in the Retiro the play of the fable of Daphne, with noteworthy stage machinery of great cost and artifice, arranged by Cosme Lotti, a singular talent for these inventions.)

In the words of another account,

Este día en la noche [29 July] tuvieron Sus Majestades en el Retiro una gran comedia heroica, también hecha de don Pedro Calderón … Y por el gusto que se dieron por servidas Sus Majestades, se le hizo merced a dicho don Pedro Calderón de un hábito de Santiago, cosa que ha parecido bien a toda la corte.[21]

(This evening Their Majesties had a great heroic play in the Retiro, also written by Don Pedro Calderón … And because Their Majesties were so pleased, Don Pedro received the favour of a habit of Santiago, something of which the whole court approved.)

Philip IV was the Master of Santiago, but his public wish to confer the knighthood was not quite law. On 2 September 1636 two investigators, Don Juan de Orellana Pizarro, a knight of the Order, and the licenciate Flores Osorio, were appointed to make enquiries, and the dossier they compiled ran to 182 pages. The enquirers needed to ask the acquaintances of the candidate and his family a fixed series of questions, many of them quite inadmissible in a modern court, as they involved hearsay: about the candidate and his forebears, and the jobs they had had (merchants, or holders of an 'oficio vil, bajo o mecánico', 'a base, mean or mechanical job', would be disqualified), and whether any of them had been in trouble with the Inquisition in matters of faith.

In addition, to be a *caballero*, one needed to own a *caballo* and be able to ride it: one witness, Don Luis de Vargas Andrade, himself a knight of Santiago, assured the enquirers that he knew Don Pedro personally, and that 'sabe andar a caballo y que le tiene y con qué le sustentar' ('he can ride a horse and owns one and has the wherewithal to maintain it'). He added that 'sabe que es caballero de muy buena opinión y bien quisto' ('he knows that he is a gentleman of very good reputation and much liked'); he was also able to say that Calderón had never been challenged: being challenged and backing down would be dishonourable.[22] The tendency of friendly witnesses to have imperfect memories means that this statement cannot help us to draw any conclusions about Don Pedro's involvement in the Nicolás de Velasco affair of 1621. In *Cada uno para sí* (first version 1653), Don Enrique de Mendoza, a knight of Santiago, is charged with discovering whether Don Carlos de Silva, a Santiago candidate, has any declared enemies, that is, whose honour he might appear to have damaged, and who might challenge him. Ironically, he has an enemy: Don Enrique.

Among those questioned, naturally enough, were Don Pedro's relatives, but the list also provides the names of acquaintances, his own or his family's: they included Gregorio López Madera, professor at the university of Alcalá, knight of Santiago, secretary of state and author of *Excelencias de la monarquía de España* (1597); Don Luis Ramírez de Arellano, former secretary of the Duke of Lerma and the compiler of the *Avisos para la muerte*, to which Calderón had contributed two years earlier; Gabriel de Alarcón, a royal secretary; Don Pedro Zapata, another royal secretary; and Don Diego Zapata, Count of Barajas.[23] The most striking name is that of Don Jerónimo de Villanueva. However, this cannot have been the protonotary of Aragón, one of Olivares's inner circle and the second most powerful member of the government, since he would have been forty-two in 1636: this homonym was aged sixty-seven.

Having made enquiries in Madrid, the investigators turned to the country cousins: they made their way to Boadilla del Camino (7–9 October), where the paternal great-grandfather had died in 1573 (some witnesses remembered the grandfather Pedro, who had returned fifty years previously to gather evidence for his *ejecutoria*); and to Sotillo (10–12 October), the former residence of the great-great-grandfather Pedro. This was too far back in time, and they got little information there, or in Reinosa (14 October), Cardeñosa (15 October), Valdeprado (16–17 October, so evidently the one in Cantabria, not Soria) and Celada (i.e., Celada-Marlantes, 17 October, near Reinosa).[24] In Toledo (29 October–1 November), following up the maternal grandmother Isabel Ruiz, they interviewed seventeen people, including a second cousin, Tomás de Salazar: all assured them that the Ruiz family were *cristianos viejos*. Tomás, aged forty-seven, stated that he was brought up in the home of the candidate's father Diego. Sometimes provincial families would send a child to be brought up, 'criado' (i.e., as a 'servant', the other meaning of the word), by prosperous relatives in the capital; the relationship of Tomás, unlike that of the illegitimate Francisco, had presumably not been concealed.[25]

The investigators did not go to Aguilar de Campoo or to Viveda. Since they were presumably told by the poet where to seek statements, we must wonder how far back his information went, as relatives possibly still lived in Aguilar de Campoo.[26]

All this reminds us of Don Toribio Cuadradillos, the eccentric and boorish 'nobleman' in *El agua mansa*, whose *casa solariega* supposedly stands in the Toranzos valley: Santiurde de Toranzos is less than 15 miles from Viveda. 'Real' Calderonian noblemen have surnames like Mendoza and Guzmán, but Cuadradillos means 'gussets', while Toribio then conveyed rustic old fashion, or worse.[27] (The investigators took a statement from a Toribio Estébanez in Valdeprado.) Toribio never travels anywhere without his *ejecutoria*, which he believes may be possessed of special powers; he is also obsessed about 'pundonor'. So while Don Juan de Mendoza could boast of his Cantabrian ancestry in *El Tuzaní*, we note Calderón's awareness of another kind of Cantabrian *hidalgo*: one whose boasts are unsupported by good taste, good manners, or even by literacy.[28] Like Shakespeare with his father's coat of arms, Calderón was able 'to parody his pretensions to gentility at the same time as he pursued them with the utmost seriousness'.[29] Perhaps this ability to stand back and be the dispassionate observer, even of oneself, and to be amused to the point of self-mockery, is one of the traits that a great dramatist needs. It should be remembered that while commanderies in the military orders produced revenue for those who held them, mere membership yielded no income, only status. It was a status, though, which was widely sought after, as the Olivares regime was well aware: between 1621 and 1625 it bestowed 515 *hábitos* of the Order of Santiago alone, compared with 168 in the preceding five-year period.[30]

Don Pedro's maternal great-grandfather, Francisco Ruiz, had been a sword-maker, but if the investigators discovered this, they did not see it as a problem. Their only difficulty was with the father's (and grandfather's) posts as civil servants. This is doubly puzzling, since the rules excluded mere craftsmen like silversmiths, while allowing royal secretaries; perhaps the problem was that both of them had acted as *escribanos*, notaries, a category specifically excluded, conceivably because some of them were supposedly of *converso* origin. However, since it was not uncommon for civil servants to seek membership of military orders, there was a standard way of dealing with the irregularity: a dispensation, from Rome. The dispensation was dispatched on 17 February 1637, and on 28 April final approval was granted.[31]

Approval came in time for Don Pedro to refer to his new honour on the title-page of his *Segunda parte de comedias* (Plate 26). As we have seen, there is evidence that all twelve plays in the *Primera parte* were written no later than 1630, although there were over a dozen plays from the period 1631–5 which could have been chosen. The contents of the volume may have depended to some extent on availability of texts as well as on the author's views on their quality, but we can see that chronology of composition may also have been a factor: even as he assembled his first volume for the press, Don Pedro was probably thinking of the second. The dates support this view, since the second volume was ready for its first approbation to be granted (once again, by Juan Bautista de Sosa) on 20 February 1637. Once again, also, Valdivielso provided the second (22 April). The religious licence was forthcoming in the interval (2 March). By the time the king had signed the privilege (3 May), Don Pedro was free to describe himself as 'Cauallero del Abito de Santiago' on the title-page, and the volume was ready for sale on 28 July.

While we cannot be certain that Calderón planned the layout of the volume, it seems most unlikely that he did not: he began with *El mayor encanto amor* (1635) and ended with *Los tres mayores prodigios* (1636), the only plays to have the dates and circumstances of their premieres provided in the contents. Between these, there was a mix of old and new plays: *Argenis y Poliarco* (?*c.* 1634), *El galán fantasma* (?*c.* 1630), *Judas Macabeo* (1623), *El médico de su honra* (?1628–9), *La Virgen del Sagrario* (?1629), *El mayor monstruo* (?1635), *El hombre pobre todo es trazas* (1627), *A secreto agravio* (?1635), *El astrólogo fingido* (?1623–5), and *Amor, honor y poder* (1623).

José Calderón's dedication – once again Don Pedro was pretending to have no role in the publication – reveals another change in the poet's circumstances: the new patron is Don Rodrigo Díaz de Vivar Hurtado de Mendoza Rojas y Sandoval, seventh Duque del Infantado, grandson of the Duke of Lerma, born in Madrid on 3 April 1614; the godparents at his baptism were King Philip III and his daughter, the Infanta María.[32] The family was one of the wealthiest in Spain, with a reputation for spending its money on the arts. Don Rodrigo contributed to this reputation, acquiring numerous works of art while serving as ambassador to Rome in the early 1650s, but in 1637 he was only twenty-three, and his reputation was for nocturnal escapades.[33] José Calderón's reference to the duke's being 'dueño de ... su persona' ('master of ... his person'), could be taken as a 'faithful servant' metaphor, but a document of 23 August 1640 shows Don Pedro authorising a Juan Martínez de Roitegui to collect for him a payment of 1,500 *reales* as he terminates his employment with the Duke, prior to his military service in Cataluña (Plate 27).[34] The timing of the change of employer seems to coincide with his change of status, but there is no evidence to help us to conclude that the two events are connected. Nor is there evidence that Calderón was consciously joining the opposition. In 1644, after the Count-Duke's nephew, Luis Méndez de Haro, had replaced him as favourite, Infantado would join a group attempting to remove Haro and all other 'creatures' of Olivares from power.[35] Marañón implies that the Duke was one of those behind Olivares's fall,[36] but we have no reason to believe that he was an active opponent as early as 1637.

CHAPTER 12

Discordant voices

VOCES	¡Al arma, celos, al arma, que agravios obligan, y para venganzas, oh Marte, despierta, alienta y anima! …
NINFAS	No al arma, celos, no al arma, que ofensas se olvidan; y al letargo adormida la queja, ni llore ni gima. (*La púrpura de la rosa*)

(VOICES: To arms, jealousy, to arms, for wrongs compel; and for vengeance, Mars, awake, be inspired, take heart! … NYMPHS: Not to arms, jealousy, not to arms, for offences are forgotten; lulled with lethargy, let complaint neither weep nor moan.)

While we need not assume that Calderón's change of employer is evidence that wealthy aristocrats engaged in overt competition to employ people with talent, it is certainly true that the court of Philip IV was a competitive environment, in which opportunities were provided for the demonstration of abilities, sometimes in formal contests, such as Don Pedro had taken part in when he was a young man, sometimes less formally in literary academies, or in amateur performances of plays, often in a spirit of fun, although on occasion these were taken quite seriously. In *Las manos blancas no ofenden* (?1640), for example, the Princess Serafina of Ursino decides that her courtiers are going to put on a play, and much of the plot revolves around this planned performance, with characters rehearsing their roles, or using the pretext of rehearsing to try to convey genuine feelings to each other.

Court performance by amateur actors – ladies and gentlemen courtiers, *meninos*, pages, or other less aristocratic servants – was an innovation introduced early in the reign of Philip III.[1] Sometimes, as in Lope's *El premio de la hermosura* (1614), even members of the royal family took part.

The number of such entertainments increased with the accession of Philip IV, among the most spectacular being the three works performed in May–July 1622: Villamediana's *La gloria de Niquea*, in which Queen Isabel played the Goddess of Beauty (she had no lines), Lope's *El vellocino de oro*, and Hurtado de Mendoza's *Querer por solo querer*; all of these were played by the queen's ladies. Because of the element of spectacle, none of them was a standard *comedia*, although Lope had adapted his from one of his plays; but they were all serious drama, based on mythology or novels of chivalry. The arrival of Cosme Lotti from Florence in 1626 gave a new impetus to this spectacular form of entertainment, and also to the greater involvement of professional performers. The amateurs continued to take part in other activities, both serious and burlesque: academies, pageants, cavalcades, masques, *saraos*, bullfights and *juegos de cañas* (reed-spear jousts): public celebration was part of the style of the Olivares regime.

State visits were an obvious excuse for celebration. On 16 November 1636 the Princess of Carignan, married to Thomas of Savoy, Philip IV's cousin, came to Madrid with three of her children, and stayed for weeks. While she was there, news was brought (13 January 1637) that Philip's brother-in-law, the King of Hungary, had been elected King of the Romans (emperor-elect) at the Diet of Ratisbon on 22 December. Celebrations became almost frenzied, especially as Carnival approached. In the week of Carnival itself (17–24 February), events were taking place on a daily basis, as a contemporary account describes:

Martes [17 February] tuuo Pedro Martinez [chief clerk of the Ayuntamiento?[2]] en su Hermita gran merienda, y dos Comedias. Miercoles Christoual de Medina [a *regidor* of Madrid] en la suya quatro entremeses ... El Sabado fue la Reyna a Nuestra Señora de Atocha y se preuino vna Moxiganga de los Secretarios, y Ministros de Estado, Hazienda, Indias, y Camara, que alegró mucho el Domingo con la graciosa variedad de trajes, inuenciones, carros, motes, y letras en que salieron mas de 300 personas. Lunes corrieron de gala los señores, y Caualleros, y jugaron alcancias [earthenware balls filled with flowers or ash and used as missiles], y corrieron dos toros; y a la noche se representó la Comedia de don Quijote, con lindos bayles, y entremeses [the writer has confused the day: see below]. Martes por vltimo festejo, sacó el Corregidor la Moxiganga de la villa, de Alguaziles, Escriuanos, y otros hombres, que fueron mas de 400 con graciosos disfrazes, y inuenciones: y aduuieron muchos Caualleros, Damas, y otras gentes con mascarillas.[3]

(On Tuesday Pedro Martínez had a great luncheon at his hermitage [the Ermita de la Magdalena], and two plays. On Wednesday Cristóbal de Medina had four interludes at his [the Ermita de San Isidro]... On Saturday the queen went to Our Lady of Atocha and a parade was organised, involving the secretaries and members of the councils of State, Finance, the Indies, and the Royal Council, which caused much merriment on Sunday with the amusing variety of costumes, devices, carts, riddles and poems, in which more than 300 people took part. On Monday the lords and gentlemen rode out in their finery, and played *alcancias*, and two bulls were fought; and in the evening there was a performance of the Don Quixote play, with pretty dances and interludes. On Tuesday as a final entertainment, the *corregidor* led out the town parade, consisting of constables, notaries and other men, more than 400 of them, with amusing disguises and devices; and many gentlemen, ladies and others wore masks.)

Not quite Rio de Janeiro, perhaps, but these were festivities on an extravagant scale, partly sponsored by municipal officials such as the *corregidor* and the *regidores*. The word *mojiganga* (which came to be a synonym for *entremés*) at this time was still used for a fancy-dress parade, with dances, rather as in modern-day Rio. Civil servants from government departments (including the Treasury) were evidently expected to take part in these, as were even relatively minor officials such as the 'police' and notaries public.

The two plays put on by Pedro Martínez were in addition to the three main plays of the festivities, which were *El amor en vizcaíno* (Sunday 22 February, Vélez) and *El robo de las sabinas* (Monday, Rojas Zorrilla, Juan Coello, Antonio Coello), while *Don Quijote de la Mancha* was Don Pedro's, performed on Shrove Tuesday.[4] The performance was described the next day in a newsletter: 'La [comedia] desta vltima [noche fue] del gran don Pedro Calderon, en quien assienta bien qualquier alabança: y la representò [Pedro de la] Rosa con su compañia, no de menores y luzidos personages: y el assunto fue la novela de don Quixote' ('Last night's play was by the great Don Pedro Calderón, for whom any praise is appropriate; it was performed by Pedro de la Rosa and his company of no less brilliant personages; and the subject was the novel of Don Quixote').[5] The reference, in the accounts, to the title *Los disparates de don Quijote*, suggests that the play, now lost, was a burlesque. The novel had been dramatised before by Guillén de Castro, with the title *Don Quijote de la Mancha*, and published in his *Primera parte* (1618).

In addition to writing one of the plays, Calderón was involved with Lotti in the design of the carts which took part in one of the processions. The carts were drawn by forty-eight oxen, themselves wearing fancy dress, 'transformados de aparentes pieles de diferentes animales' ('transformed by the apparent skins of different animals'):

Desde alli [= the house of Carlos Stratta, Genoese merchant-banker, and Comendador of Santiago, in the Carrera de San Jerónimo] fue introduzido el paseo de la mascara, y a lo vltimo dos carros, cuya disposiciõ, significacion, y grandeza, es tal q[ue] me asseguro no passe el describirlos por enfadosa digression [a long description follows]. Y si, Marciales, y belicos instrumētos de musica, en el vno, acordadas y apacibles citaras, y biolones en el otro: y ambos cō tres cōpañias de Comediantes ricamente vestidas para representar à la Reina nuestra señora, Principe nuestro Señor, Señora Princesa de Cariñan, damas, Cōsejos, y Embaxadores (como se hizo despues de la mascara) lo significado dellos en vn dialogo de aquel luzidissimo ingenio, q[ue] por su Cortesano juicio, y Palaciega atenciō, entre los llamados, es de los escogidos D. Pedro Calderō.[6]

(From there the masque procession was begun, followed by two carts, the arrangement, meaning and grandeur of which were such that I feel sure that describing them will not pass for an annoying digression … And if there were martial and warlike musical instruments in the one, there were harmonised and sweet zithers and viols in the other; and both had three companies of actors richly dressed to perform before the queen, the prince, the Princess of Carignan, the ladies, the councils and the ambassadors (as was done after the masque), with their meaning in a dialogue by that brilliant wit, Don Pedro Calderón, who, for his courteous wisdom and courtly civility, is one of the chosen among those who are called.)

The text of the *diálogo* has not survived. Presumably it provided further income for the writer.

On Friday 20 February, there was a burlesque academy in the Retiro.[7] Vélez de Guevara was president; Alonso de Batres (minor poet and playwright) was secretary; Francisco de Rojas Zorrilla was *fiscal*, and the *vejamen*, the closing speech which made fun of the competitors, was by Batres and Rojas. The judges included the Prince of Esquilache (poet and author of at least one play), Don Luis de Haro (nephew of Olivares), Don Antonio Hurtado de Mendoza, Don Jerónimo de Villanueva (protonotary of Aragón) and Francisco de Rioja (the secretary-librarian of Olivares, also a poet). The king was expected to attend, according to an account written that morning:

Hoy fecha es esta, que es viernes, hay en el Salon, en presencia de S. M. Academia de Poetas, que de repente incitados de un furor poetico han de hablar versos sobre las materias propuestas; refieren que dos de ellas es: por que pintan a Judas con barba rubia? Y por que, a las mujeres o criadas de Palacio llaman mondongas, no vendiendo mondongo? Esperase que Luis Velez y don Pedro Calderon seran los que mas se señalaran.[8]

(Today, Friday, there is in the *salón*, in His Majesty's presence, an academy of poets, who, suddenly aroused by poetic fury, are to utter verses on the subjects proposed; they say two of them are: 'why is Judas painted with a red beard?', and 'why are the palace maidservants called *mondongas* [kitchen wenches], when they don't sell *mondongo* [tripe]?' It is expected that Luis Vélez and Don Pedro Calderón will distinguish themselves most.)

If Don Pedro was present, his contributions were not transcribed in the account of the proceedings. The *vejamen*, composed in advance but printed later, does suggest that he was there, however, or expected to be there:

Venía don Pedro Calderón en medio, probándose a un espejo mi cabellera; pero, viendo que no le asentaba, la arrojó diciendo así:

No me la quiero poner;
que a mi desgracia recelo
que no la ha de cubrir pelo.

Hizo para el carro de la mojiganga Andrés de Borgoña con un papel del señor Protonotario en que le encargaba hiciese una comedia de capa y espada para el servicio de su Majestad y que tuviese grandes pasos; y don Pedro Calderón respondió con esta redondilla:

Si pasos de más primores
buscáis para tales casos,
yo escribiré vuestros pasos,
que no pueden ser mayores.

Querían cenar una olla podrida que había guisado don Antonio de Solís.

(Don Pedro Calderón was in the middle, trying on my hairpiece in a mirror; but, seeing that it didn't suit him, threw it away, saying: 'I won't put it on, for I fear it won't cover a hair of my misfortune.' Andrés de Borgoña made for the parade cart with a note from the Protonotary in which he requested him to write a cloak-and-sword play for His Majesty, and that it should have major events; and Don Pedro Calderón answered with this quatrain: 'If you seek events of greatest skill for such cases, I'll write your events/steps, which cannot be greater.' They wanted to dine on a stew cooked by Antonio de Solís.)[9]

Some of the jokes are a little obscure to us now, but the dig at Don Pedro's thinning hair is clear enough. Rojas's reference to 'my hairpiece' (this part of the *vejamen* was his) may seem odd, but Rojas regularly made jokes about his own baldness: the suggestion that Don Pedro was trying on Rojas's own hairpiece took the sting out of the barb.[10] In fact, as the likenesses made in his old age show, Don Pedro never entirely lost his hair; the question of his appearance as he approached middle age will be examined later. For now, perhaps, it is enough to remember the words of Pedro Crespo, probably written the previous year:

Es calvo un hombre mil años,
y al cabo dellos se hace
una cabellera. Éste,
en opiniones vulgares,

¿deja de ser calvo? No,
pues ¿qué dicen al mirarle?
"¡Bien puesta la cabellera
trae Fulano!"[11]

(A man is bald for a thousand years, and at the end of them he gets himself a hairpiece made. Does he stop being bald in the popular view? No, because what do they say when they look at him? 'So-and-so's hairpiece fits him well!')

Another of Rojas's victims in this *vejamen* was the poet and playwright Antonio de Huerta. His unmerciful mockery may have had consequences which will be examined later.

Writing of the performance of *El amor en vizcaíno*, Sánchez de Espejo described Vélez as '[e]l Principe de los Poetas comicos, Maestro de los Liricos, Presidente meritisimo de los Iocosos, honra de nuestra Andaluzia, antiguo morador de la Corte' ('the prince of comic poets, master of lyric poets, most deserving president of the jocular poets, honour of our Andalusia, long-time resident in Madrid').[12] Flowery language was Sánchez's style, but this passage reminds us that Vélez (born 1579) had had a reputation as a playwright since Calderón was a child, and that Don Pedro was not yet universally regarded as the foremost dramatist in Spain. Don Pedro had collaborated, or would collaborate, with Vélez in *Enfermar con el remedio* (date uncertain), and there is no reason to suppose that he might have stayed away from the proceedings out of pique at not being given a formal role. Those who were absent, like Quevedo and Pérez de Montalbán, had reason to be: Quevedo's relationship with Olivares was already in decline, and Pérez de Montalbán was almost certainly suffering from his final illness.

The palace accounts which refer to *Los disparates de don Quijote* also show that Cosme Lotti was paid over 22,000 *reales* 'por el teatro, pintura y tramoyas y adorno que hiço para la comedia de Auristela y Clariana, que esta preuenida' (presumably as one of the Carnival plays), but another entry records that 'la comedia, mascara y fiesta … se dejo de haçer por orden de S.M.' ('for the stage, painting, machinery and décor he did for the play *Auristela y Clariana*, which is planned'; 'the play, masque and celebration … did not take place, by order of His Majesty').[13] The Calderón play usually entitled *Auristela y Lisidante* has a character called Clariana (Auristela's sister), but, according to Hilborn, the verse seems to indicate a date between 1653 and 1660.[14] Either this guess is wrong, or perhaps Calderón kept the version which was not performed in 1637 (for whatever reason), and revised it twenty years later. The fact that the masque was also cancelled suggests that the text of the play was not considered at fault.

Cotarelo argues that in the course of this Carnival Vélez and Calderón took part in a *comedia de repente* entitled *La creación del mundo*.[15] The date of Vélez's serious version of *La creación del mundo* is unknown, but it would make sense if he were asked to become involved in a humorous version of a play he had already written. Because of his age, he took the role of God, while Calderón played Adam, and Moreto, Abel. Moreto was only nineteen: he was baptised in April 1618, and would not complete his university degree until 1639. Eve is not identified. Adam/Calderón protested at his punishment:

Padre eterno de la luz,
Porque en mi mal perseveras?
PADRE ETERNO *Porque os comistes las peras,*
Y juro a Dios, y a esta Cruz
Que os he de echar a galeras.

When even the threat of being a galley-slave failed to silence Adam, God interrupted him:

Por el cielo superior,
Y por mi mano formado,
Que me peza [*sic*] *haver criado*
Un Adan tan hablador.

When Adam finally turned to Eve:

Heva mi dulce plazer,
Carne de la carne mía,

and she responded:

Mi bien, mi dulce alegría,

Moreto stuck his head round the rear curtain and completed the *redondilla*:

Estos me quieren hazer.[16]

(ADAM: Eternal father of light, why do you persevere in my harm? ETERNAL FATHER: Because you ate up the pears, and I swear to God, and by this cross, that I'll send you to the galleys … By the heavens above, formed by my hand, I'm sorry I created such a talkative Adam … ADAM: Eve, my sweet delight, flesh of my flesh … EVE: My darling, my sweet joy … *Abel*: These two want to make me.)

We can imagine the audience's reaction to this saucy irreverence, typical of Carnival. Similar celebrations took place in 1638, but since Calderón's name does not figure in Rojas's *vejamen* for that year (the omission is not conclusive), perhaps Cotarelo's guess of 1637 is the more likely.[17] One account of the Carnival academy of 1638 records then that

> Hubo ... comedias que hicieron los poetas, habiéndoles dado poco antes el tema de lo que habían de tratar. Dicen fué de las cosas más ingeniosas que se han visto, porque todos se esmeraron con emulación, procurando echar el resto por salir con la gloria y aplausos de los circunstantes, que era la nata del reino la que allí asistía.[18]

> (There were plays the poets wrote, having been given their subject-matter a short time previously. They say that it was one of the cleverest things ever seen, because they all did their best to emulate one another, trying to do their utmost to get the glory and applause of the audience, for it was the cream of the kingdom which was present.)

As this passage indicates, *comedias de repente* were not quite improvised. There was also a 'comedia ... de disparates', a play of absurdities, a description which could have been applied to *La creación del mundo*, and for which Vélez received 1,100 *reales*.[19]

One of the items to which the 1638 account refers is the *Mojiganga de la boda*, a skit performed in the Retiro on Shrove Tuesday. While there is no evidence for the participation of our Don Pedro, the cast did include Velázquez, who played the Condesa de Santiesteban (he had a single line); Olivares played the porter; Diego de Covarrubias, the warden of the Retiro, famous for his paunch, played the king, while the queen's part was taken by Alonso Carbonel, the master of works, whose appearance was particularly unprepossessing.[20] There was also a poetic competition, and a 'Juicio final de todos los poetas españoles muertos y vivos' ('Last judgement of all living and dead Spanish poets'), which Bergman attributes to Vélez.[21] She also lists some of the poets whose contributions have not been identified: it includes the dramatists Pedro Rosete and Juan Coello, the poet Bocángel, and 'D. José Calderón' (p. 564). We might suppose that this was an error for Pedro, rather than that his brother was in Madrid, trying his hand at verse; but Don José is referred to in Rojas's *vejamen*: Antonio Coello, says Rojas, is so scruffy that 'Don José Calderón le solía cantar: ¡Ay!, ¿qué lleva, señor Esgueva?, | don Antonios de Coellos lleva' ('Don José Calderón used to sing to him: "Alas, Señor Esgueva, what is it you bear? You bear Don Antonio de Coellos"').[22] The reference is to Góngora's *letrilla* 'Lleva este río crecido', which describes the unsavoury items carried by one of Valladolid's rivers. Since *vejámenes* involved exaggeration and poetic licence, we cannot assume that this passage means that José Calderón shared his brother's familiarity with Góngora's poetry, but it does suggest that he took part in this academy. According to a contemporary account, one of the victims was so enraged by the *vejamen*'s barbs that he (or a hired assassin) attempted to kill the writer.[23]

One commentator suggested that one reason for the conspicuous expenditure was 'para que el cardenal Richelieu nuestro amigo sepa que aun hay dinero en el mundo que gastar y con que castigar a su Rey' ('so that our friend Cardinal Richelieu may know that there is still money in the world to spend, and to punish his king with').[24] Not everyone was convinced. Despite the bread and circuses – or the circuses, at any rate – dissent was growing, dissent which would culminate in the Catalan and Portuguese rebellions of 1640. The diarist who referred to the burlesque academy of 20 February 1637 noted that one of the participants in a Carnival procession was dressed in sheepskins, with the wool inside, and carried a placard which read:

Sisas, alcabala, y papel sellado
me tienen desollado.

(Excise duty, sales tax and stamped paper have me skinned alive.)

Another, wearing habits and crosses of military orders, bore a sign saying, 'Estas se venden', 'These are for sale', while a person in a Jesuit's hat was pursued by a devil carrying a placard which read:

Voy corriendo por la posta
tras el Padre Salazar,
y juro a Dios y a esta Cruz
que no le puedo alcanzar.[25]

(I'm chasing post-haste after Father Salazar, and I swear to God and by this cross that I can't catch him.)

The idea of raising revenue by requiring *papel sellado* (stamped paper) to be used for legal documents was attributed to Father Salazar, a Jesuit; it was introduced early in 1637.[26]

While all this was going on, Don Pedro must have been working on the *autos* for 1637, due for Corpus Christi (11 June). At this date there were still four *autos*, with two companies of actors performing two each. The companies selected for 1637 were those of Tomás Fernández and Pedro de la Rosa: Rosa was to perform two written by Calderón. The documents show that the dress rehearsal was planned for 28 May, and that on 5 May Rosa had still not received the texts.[27] To make matters worse, he was ill, although he assured the anxious *comisarios* that his company could manage without him, and that as long as he got the *autos* twelve days before the dress rehearsal, they would be ready. He seems to have received them on time, although we do not know which they were. Ángel Valbuena Prat suggested (III, 243) that one of them may have been *La devoción de la misa*, but this is now reckoned to date from 1658. The average *auto* was about half the length of a play, so the rehearsal time required for a new play was presumably no more than for two *autos*, that is, about two weeks.[28]

Don Pedro certainly took on numerous commitments in early 1637. The heading of the autograph manuscript of *El mágico prodigioso* tells us that the play was 'Compuesta para la villa de Yepes en las fiestas del SS^mo^ Sacramento año de 1637' ('Composed for the town of Yepes in the feast of Corpus Christi, 1637'). Yepes is on the far side of Aranjuez, some 37 miles from Madrid. Thanks to recent investigations, we know that at this period the inhabitants of towns even further afield were making agreements with companies from Madrid to perform plays for them.[29] No formal agreement made by Don Pedro to write the play has been discovered: the archives in Yepes record only that in the period 1636–8, Corpus Christi was celebrated with bullfights, not with plays.[30] It has sometimes been supposed, since the manuscript is incomplete, that the author did not finish the play in time, causing the agreement to fall through. However, Charles Davis has discovered documents in Toledo which relate to the construction of a stage in the Yepes town square in the four years from 1636 to 1639; in particular, one document deals with carts and fireworks for the performances on 11 June 1637, Corpus Thursday.[31] While no titles are given, the details correspond with the *auto La torre de Babilonia* (performed in the morning) and with *El mágico* (performed in the afternoon). Davis suggests plausibly that this may have been the premiere of the *auto*, which is otherwise of uncertain date. In any event, the documents show how the playwright's Toledo connections extended beyond the provincial capital. By mid September Calderón had found time to revise *El mágico* for performance by Bartolomé Romero in the public theatres in Madrid. There is evidence, though, that Romero did not undertake the Yepes performance.[32]

The play's protagonist Cipriano should not be confused with the third-century St Cyprian who was bishop of Carthage: Cipriano and Justina never existed, but several lives of saints recount their martyrdom: their story is a variant on the Faustian devil-pact theme. Calderón probably worked from Alonso de Villegas's *Flos sanctorum*, of which there were various editions prior to 1637, but he was probably influenced by Mira de Amescua's *El esclavo del demonio* (printed 1612), particularly since he seems to refer to it in line 3469 ('¿Esclavo yo del demonio?', 'I, a slave of the devil?').[33] He is not at all likely to have known Marlowe's *Tragicall History of Doctor Faustus* (printed 1604), but the story of the historical Faust was known in Spain:

in Salamanca, students gave the name Fausto to a particularly studious professor. The fact that Don Pedro used the name Faustina for Justina in the autograph manuscript points to some mental connection, perhaps an unconscious one. The play also has obvious links with Calderón's own *La devoción de la cruz* (which also owes a debt to Mira's play): Justina's innocent mother was killed by her father, as a result of which she was brought up by someone else. In *La devoción* Curcio killed his innocent wife, so that his son Eusebio was brought up by someone else. To a degree, this scenario is a dramatic cliché, but it provides another example of a father who abandons his child. Unlike Eusebio, or, for that matter, the adult Segismundo, Justina commits no crimes, although the devil contrives to make her adoptive father think she has.

Among the play's most interesting features are the stage directions, which refer to the staging in the town square. The play opens with the devil arriving on a painted cart, from which he leaps to the stage; unlike in the *autos*, in which the cart remained as part of the performance area, this one then leaves. Later, when the devil pretends to be shipwrecked, his black-painted ship enters the square; when he has got close enough to swim ashore (i.e., to the stage) with the help of a plank, the ship leaves. The audience has to use its imagination, since this was not like a staged Roman sea-battle in the Coliseum: the town square in Yepes could not have been flooded. Unable to force Justina to yield to Cipriano, the devil must conjure up a simulacrum instead. A long direction (3196*) indicates that the young woman who played Justina was to come on, dressed in black; when Cipriano pursued her off the stage and ostensibly caught her, he was to carry back 'una persona', also dressed in black, but painted as a skeleton under the clothes. When Cipriano drew back the clothes to see her, he would find the skeleton, which would immediately vanish by dropping through the trapdoor on which he had placed her. A stage skeleton might have been used, except that this one has a line: 'Así, Ciprïano, son | todas las glorias del mundo' ('Thus, Cyprian, are all the glories of the world': 3243–4). Yepes is only 8 miles from Ocaña, which Calderón may have visited, but we need not assume that he had inspected the performance area: he knew enough about town squares to adapt his staging to what was available.

Other plays can be assigned to this period. *Antes que todo es mi dama* is one of the most skilfully constructed of Calderón's comedies. Set in Madrid, it deals with two friends, Laura and Clara, who live next door to each other. Laura is watched over by her father, Don Íñigo, and Clara by her hot-headed brother, Antonio, who also has his eye on Laura. Despite their difficulties, Laura and Clara manage to marry their lovers Félix and Lisardo:

once again a zealous brother is disappointed. Unfortunately, despite allusions to *El celoso extremeño* (II, 877a = Don Íñigo), to Boscán and Garcilaso (II, 874b), and quotations from Góngora's *romance* 'Entre los sueltos caballos' (II, 889b), there are no conclusive references to help us date the play. One remark by the maid Beatriz ('No hay cosa como vivir', 'There's nothing like living', II, 902a) could be an oblique reference to *No hay cosa como callar* (1638), while Hernando, a comic servant, repeats the pun used by Nuño in *El alcalde de Zalamea* (?1636): 'Puesto que es rucio el que le trae, rodado, | ¿qué he de hacer?' ('Since it's a dapple grey that brings him, what am I to do?': II, 905b). The play's modern editor suggests 1637–40, a date which these two details support.[34]

In the summer of 1638, the English ambassador reported of Olivares that 'Of late he hath wholly left the recreations he was wont to take in the field and in the Buen Retiro, and that upon some shows of unruliness in the people towards him.'[35] To our knowledge, Don Pedro never attacked Olivares explicitly in anything he wrote, even after his fall (unlike some others); while he was in power, it was dangerous. But Calderón did come to present situations which could be taken to reflect those which existed in government, and did allow his *graciosos* to make critical comments, as we shall see. Others were less circumspect. The maternal great-grandfather of Olivares was Lope de Conchillos, an Aragonese of *converso* origin, and when Quevedo wrote his satire *La isla de monopantos* (?1638), he gave the governor of the island the name of Pragas Chincollos, that is, Gaspar Conchillos, an allusion to the Conde-Duque's *converso* ancestry. Among Pragas's wise men was Arpio Trotono (= Protonotario, Jerónimo de Villanueva). This would have been bad enough, had it been published, but in December 1639 the king allegedly found under his table-napkin a verse *Memorial* which viciously attacked the government. Quevedo was arrested on 7 December and imprisoned for three and a half years, until the fall of Olivares. The many variant versions of the *Memorial* have not made the task of investigators easier, but it is now accepted that Quevedo was the author.[36] The person who denounced him was his friend, Calderón's employer, the Duke of Infantado, although he may have done so under pressure. We can only guess what Calderón thought of this, or how much he knew, especially since he was in Valencia for part of 1638. His apparent absence from Carnival in Madrid may mean that he was in Valencia then.

As the remarks about *sisas*, *alcabala* and *papel sellado* suggest, one of the objections to government policy centred on taxation to finance military campaigns, while the regime was perceived to have no shortage of funds for lavish celebration and for the building of the Retiro itself. The 'unruliness in the people' went as far as tax riots in Evora, beginning in the summer of 1637, and prompting preparations for a royal expedition to Portugal, which would include the knights of the military orders. Neither the king nor the knights were required, although troops were sent to Portugal, and the potential revolt petered out the following spring. However, shortage of funds for military purposes led to losses elsewhere, culminating in the recapture of Breda (10 October 1637) by Frederick Henry, Prince of Orange. In a letter of December 1637, Olivares remarked that no recent year had been as disastrous for Spain as 1637.[37]

The royal order for the knights to stand by for a campaign in Portugal was issued on 16 November 1637. Apparently anticipating that he might have to take part, Don Pedro began to put his affairs in order. On 2 October he signed a document making his brothers Diego and José his heirs, naming them his proxy testators, and requesting that he be buried in the church of San Salvador, as he eventually was, forty-four years later.[38] At the same time, he signed a second document giving them the right to continue with the division of the brothers' inheritance, including the sale of any of his possessions.[39] In a third document of the same date, he acknowledged that only he had received the 1,000 ducats from the sale of the *censo* in 1636, although all three brothers should have been beneficiaries, and that the Espartinas saltworks *juro*, valued at 500 ducats, had also been sold and that he and José had shared the principal, with none going to Diego.[40] The other brothers were to be given their share of these amounts.

Spain continued to do badly in the war. Although he was always prone to exaggerate his feelings when things were going badly, a letter of 31 March 1638 suggests that Olivares was close to the end of his tether.[41] But matters began to improve: Frederick Henry was defeated at Kallo in June, while Piccolomini and Prince Thomas of Savoy forced the French to abandon the siege of St Omer. Olivares, in typical manic-depressive fashion, now (31 July) wrote of 1638 being the happiest year in the history of the monarchy.[42] He planned to invade France through Cataluña, blissfully unaware of Richelieu's invasion of Spain at the other end of the Pyrenees, which was already in progress. In July the troops of the Prince de Condé crossed the border at Irún and laid siege by land and sea to the frontier fortress of Fuenterrabía (marked on some modern maps as Hondarribia, facing Hendaye across the mouth of the Bidasoa). The text of the 1634 map refers to fine bronze artillery, but also to a garrison of only 'duzientos y mas soldados' ('over 200 soldiers').[43] Olivares had assumed that relations between the prince and Richelieu were too bad for him to be entrusted with such a campaign, but he was taken by surprise. The Spanish naval commander, Don Lope de Hoces, ordered to break the blockade, could summon up only twelve seaworthy ships, and lost eleven of them on 22 August, with 3,000 men, to the French at Guetaria/Getaria, some 20 miles to the west.

The news of the siege had reached Madrid while the Cortes was sitting in what had promised to be a difficult session for the government. The potential complaints changed to patriotic fervour, as the delegates approved the renewal of the *millones* for another six years, as well as the raising of 6,000 troops for six months. Finally, on 7 September, the land troops, under the Admiral of Castile and the Marquis of Mortara, broke through the French lines, and Condé's men fled to their boats. The news reached Madrid on the night of 9–10 September, and the minor triumph was celebrated as an overwhelming victory.

Among the troops who broke through on 7 September was the poet's brother:

> Y el dia siete de Septiembre, quando se dio la rota al enemigo, se hallo [Don José Calderón] en el Esquadron de su Tercio [the Admiral of Castile's], que guiaua el Conde Geronimo Ro, Maestre de Campo General, y en la segunda hilera del, siendo de las primeras picas que ocupauan las fortificaciones del enemigo.[44]
>
> (On 7 September, when the enemy were routed, Don José was in the squadron of his regiment led by Field-Marshal Count Jerónimo Ro, in the second rank, and was one of the first pikemen to occupy the enemy fortifications.)

As a result of his exploits, Don José was 'given a company' (promoted to captain) and sent to Madrid on leave, where he arrived in November. On 13 March 1639 the king granted him a pension of 25 *escudos* a month, but a document dated eight days later shows that his treatment for a wound had only just ended.[45] The same day he signed a document authorising his brothers to share his estate,[46] as Don Pedro had done some eighteen months earlier; on 26 March he joined the regiment of Spanish guards.[47]

Calderón referred to the relief of Fuenterrabía in several passages of *No hay cosa como callar*, as well as writing his *Panegírico al Excelentíssimo Señor Don Juan Alfonso Enríquez de Cabrera y Colona, Almirante de Castilla* (220 lines of *tercetos*). Cotarelo supposed that these items could only have been written by someone who was present, but the lack of any reference in the memorial quoted in note 44 shows that Don Pedro cannot have been there; he got the information from his brother, who was an eyewitness and a participant.[48] It should be recalled, perhaps, that the Admiral, whose wife was one of the Lerma family, had a history of enmity with Olivares, and was furious when the favourite was seen as the saviour of Fuenterrabía.[49]

No hay cosa como callar is set in Madrid in the late summer and autumn of 1638, during the siege of Fuenterrabía and immediately after the arrival of the news of the victory. In Act I, Don Juan de Mendoza, a knight of Santiago and a soldier who has served with the Duke of Lerma in Italy and Flanders, is brought news by his father Don Pedro that all those with previous military service have to attend:[50] he has to abandon his attempts to discover the identity of a beautiful young woman he has just seen at mass, and leave for the north. He has no idea that she lives across the street.

No sooner has Juan gone than there is a fire in the house opposite. Little damage is done, but Leonor, whose house it is, accepts Don Pedro's offer of a room (Juan's). When Juan returns unexpectedly in the middle of the night for his service papers, he is astonished to find the unknown young woman who caught his fancy asleep in his room. Perhaps the audience wonders what will happen next, but Juan's servant Barzoque has given them a clue with the suggestion that his master must have made a pact with the devil (as Cipriano did in *El mágico prodigioso*, written the previous year): when she faints, he rapes her and leaves, unidentified.

Taken aback by this unexpected event in what we thought was a comedy, we have an advantage over the audience: we can retrace Juan's character traits. Juan is like Don Alonso in *No hay burlas*, or Don Hipólito in *Mañanas de abril y mayo*: a would-be philanderer with no thought of commitment. He already has a 'dama de respeto' ('spare lady-friend'), as he calls her, the unfortunate Marcela, who thinks he is madly in love with her. And yet, as he compares Leonor with the other women he has known, he likens her to a perfect piece of writing, for which the others were mere drafts:

> Así como un ingenio
> cuidadoso se desvela,
> cuando a públicas censuras
> dar algún estudio piensa,
> que hecho fiscal de sí mismo,
> un pliego rasga, otro quema,
> y mal contento de todo,
> esto borra, aquello enmienda,
> hasta que ya satisfecho
> del cuidado que le cuesta,
> da el borrador al traslado,
> y le da el traslado a la imprenta. (II, 998b)

(Just as a writer takes great care when he plans to submit a piece of work to public censure, and becomes his own prosecutor, tearing up one sheet of paper, burning another, and, displeased with everything, erases this and alters that, until, satisfied at last with the care it has cost him, he hands over the draft for a fair copy to be made, and gives that copy to the press.)

She was a perfect fair copy, a printed edition free of typographical errors:

> fué una impresión sin errata,
> y un traslado sin enmienda. (II, 999a)

It is so common for Calderón comedies to open with the 'hero' and his servant that we may think that these speeches, at the start of Act I, are invitations to identify Juan with the writer of the lines, especially since he had recently become a knight of Santiago himself, not to mention the fact that his brother had served in Italy and Flanders with Lerma. At first we may suspect that Juan will be like Félix in *El agua mansa*, an essentially nice young man who is scornful of love until he falls for Clara. The rape indicates otherwise, and is made even worse by the fact that Leonor and Juan's friend Luis were planning to marry, although Juan knew nothing of this relationship. We are subjected to a cleverly insidious dramatic technique: having identified with this author-character, we discover that he is a criminal.

In parenthesis, the passages just quoted tell us something about how Calderón wrote. We know from surviving autograph manuscripts, and the remarks of Cardinal Trejo about *El príncipe constante*, that the text he gave to the actors was the *borrador* rather than the *traslado*, which would be made by the company's prompter. The *borrador* would not do for printing. The normal practice was to give the author's draft to a professional copyist, as the words 'da el borrador al traslado' may imply. The author could check the copyist's work, but the act of copying would introduce a layer of errors: there must have been few 'traslados sin enmienda'.[51]

As the play progresses, the unpleasant aspects of Juan's character are developed. As he and Luis return to Madrid, Luis speaks of the lady he loves (i.e., Leonor). Juan's response is to ask if Luis has been sleeping with her:

> Esa dama que adoráis,
> ¿poseéis o deseáis? (II, 1015b)

(That lady you adore, do you possess her or desire her?)

For Juan, possession is the antidote to desire, and he has already lost interest in Leonor: he has no wish to know who she is or how she came to be in his house. All he wants in Madrid is his own bed, which makes no demands on him, and does not complain if he enjoys it every night,

Que es la más hermosa dama
y más cómoda, pues no
pide pollera ni coche,
y en un rincón cerrada
todo el día está, y no enfada
con gozarla cada noche. (II, 1018a)

(She is the most lovely lady and most comfortable, since she doesn't ask for skirts or coaches; she spends all day shut up in a corner, and doesn't get annoyed if I enjoy her every night.)

Leonor's first reaction is deep depression and guilt, although she is completely innocent. Her thoughts then turn to revenge, but when she corners Juan with proof that she knows it was he, she decides that silence is the best remedy. Even then, he is unwilling to do what society then saw as the honourable thing: agree to marry her. Only when his father seems to guess what has happened, and Leonor seems about to tell all, does he offer her his hand.

The play ends in sober fashion, with only one marriage, which scarcely promises to be successful. Juan has destroyed the happy relationship between Luis and Leonor, and blighted even the potential relationship between Diego and Marcela. One critic has suggested that the psychological portrayal of Leonor and Juan is so authentic that it must be drawn from life:

La violación en *El alcalde de Zalamea* fue sólo de teatro; ésta ha sido real y Calderón la ha presenciado de cerca.[52]

(The rape in *El alcalde de Zalamea* was only a piece of theatre; this one was real and Calderón witnessed it from close up.)

This is plausible but unprovable, and the same may be said of the relatively minor character Marcela, whom Juan also treats badly; her remark that 'basta tratarme mal | para que le quiera bien' ('his treating me badly is enough for me to love him': II, 1018b) suggests accurate observation. However, it seems certain that Cervantes's *La fuerza de la sangre* (1613) provided a literary source. In Cervantes, Leocadia is kidnapped by Rodolfo and raped after she has fainted, like Leonor. Both young women manage to preserve a piece of evidence: in Leocadia's case, a crucifix; in Leonor's, a *venera*. A *venera* was a kind of locket in the shape of a scallop shell (the symbol of Santiago), adorned with the cross pattée of the saint. At the time of his death, Calderón had five of them, valued at a total of almost 2,200 *reales*, and portraits show him wearing one of them round his neck.[53] Leocadia at least tells her parents, but like Leonor herself, they keep the offence secret. Cervantes's story ends happily, with Leocadia and Rodolfo achieving some semblance of the divine love symbolised by the crucifix. There is no clear evidence that Calderón intended to suggest this in the play. If this is a comedy, it is a black one: Calderón's blackest. What is perhaps most significant is that, as in so many other plays of Calderón, the most admirable character is a woman.

While *No hay cosa* has no apparent references to other plays, there is one to a Lope ballad:

> ¡Qué bien el Fénix de España
> dijo: 'En mi pena se infiere
> que el que piensa que no quiere,
> el ser querido le engaña!'[54] (II, 1027b)

(How well the Phoenix of Spain said, 'In my suffering is inferred that he who thinks he does not love is deceived by being loved.')

Calderón had evidently recovered from his feelings of resentment toward Lope.

* * *

In 1238 the city of Valencia, conquered from the Moors in 1094 by the Cid and abandoned again after his death, was definitively taken by King Jaume el Conqueridor of Aragón (1213–76). The celebrations held 400 years later, on 9 October 1638, to mark the event, were described by Marco Antonio Ortí in his *Siglo quarto de la conquista de Valencia*. He explains that the intention was that a local playwright should write a historical drama dealing with the conquest, but since they thought of this too late,

> Se huuo de elegir la Comedia que se intitula,
>
> *El gusto y disgusto son*
> *no mas que imaginacion.*
>
> Porq[ue] esta trata parte de la historia del Rey don Pedro, que fue padre del Rey don Iayme, y es vna de las q[ue] han ayudado a estender por España la noticia del vnico ingenio de don Pedro Calderon, q[ue] pocos meses antes auia estado en Valencia, y dexado en ella muchos aficionados a la nobleza de su proceder, y muchos imbidiosos de su milagroso caudal. Para parecer (como parecio) prodigiosa esta Comedia, no necessitaua de otra circu[n]stancia mas, que auerla escrito don Pedro Calderon.[55]

(The play entitled *El gusto y disgusto son no más que imaginación* had to be chosen, because it deals with part of the story of King Peter, father of King James, and it is one of those which have helped spread throughout Spain the news of the unique mind of Don Pedro Calderón, who had been in Valencia a few months previously, and left there many who were enthused by the nobility of his behaviour, and many who were envious of his wonderful resources. For this play to seem marvellous (as it did), it needed nothing else but that Don Pedro Calderón should have written it.)

Ortí goes on to name some of the performers: Antonia [Manuela Catalán], wife of the *autor* Bartolomé Romero; [Alonso de] Osuna, his male lead; [Diego de] Robledo and [Diego de] Mencos, his *gracioso*. In 1619 the old playhouse in Valencia had been transformed into the Casa Nova de la Olivera.[56] We cannot be certain, though, that the play was not performed on a temporary stage erected in a suitable place, although the address of one of the characters in *Primero soy yo*, set in Valencia, seems to echo the name of the theatre:

> Vive en una casa nueva
> que hace esquina, como vamos
> a salir a la Olivera. (II, 1182a)

(He lives in a new house on the corner, as we go out into La Olivera.)

The date of Calderón's visit is vague, but it was long enough to make a favourable impression. The play was evidently not written for the commemoration, although the visit may have inspired it in part; and it seems to have been sheer good fortune that the repertoire of Romero's troupe included a play which was more or less appropriate. In theory the play could have been written years earlier, but Blue has suggested that the other inspiration was the visit to Madrid (1637–8) of the Duchess of La Chevreuse, supposedly a refugee from Richelieu, and Philip IV's alleged infatuation with her.[57] In May 1644, offering a performance, Ascanio described the play as a 'comedia nueva, nunca representada en Valencia' ('a new play, never performed in Valencia'), but we need not take his claim too seriously.[58]

King Peter II of Aragón (1196–1213) married María of Montpellier in 1204, but supposedly neglected his bride to pursue a young woman of the city. Concerned, his counsellors devised a plan whereby, as they told Peter, the young woman would offer herself to him if he came to her in total darkness. The king agreed, and spent the night with her; in the morning it was revealed that he had slept with his queen. Nine months later Prince Jaume was born.

This quaint story was published by Bandello and used by Lope for a play, *La reina doña María* (1604–8). Calderón's version is much more decorous. When the king gets the husband of the lady (Violante) out of the way by sending him to the wars, she takes refuge with the neglected queen on her estate. When the king follows her there, he speaks through a window to the queen, taking her for Violante. The queen recognises him, and encourages him to return, charming him with the wit and intelligence of her conversation. When his mistake is revealed, he realises that he has fallen in love with his queen.

Even if the inspiration for Violante was not La Chevreuse, it is possible to argue that there was a lesson here for Philip IV, a lesson which is all the more tactful because the king never gets as far as the bed of his intended mistress.[59] But it is also possible that the play is a discreet celebration of the fact that Philip never reached the bed of the duchess. It may be no coincidence that it became known, about the time that La Chevreuse was leaving Madrid (February 1638), that Queen Isabel was pregnant: the Infanta María Teresa was born on 20 September 1638. If this suggestion is correct, the play may have been written in the spring and summer of 1638, some of it while the author was in Valencia; and Romero took it back to the city in the autumn, in the expectation that it would go down well with audiences there.

There are references in the text of *Gustos* to *Peor está que estaba* (1630; II, 982a) and to 'la puente de Mantible' (not necessarily to the play, which is also of 1630; II, 982a), while 'Don Vicente Para-todos' (II, 982a) is probably a reference to Pérez de Montalbán's *Para todos* (1632). Violante repeats the rhetorical question asked by Lisarda in *El escondido y la tapada* and Beatriz in *Mañana será otro día*, both of which can be dated to late 1635 / early 1636 ('Si así teme una inocente, | ¿cómo teme una culpada?', 'If an innocent woman is so afraid, how does a guilty one fear?': II, 990a). None of this is inconsistent with the suggested date of early 1638, although composition a couple of years earlier is also possible. In the end, the *gracioso* spells out the moral clearly:

> Esta es verdadera historia,
> de que saque el pío lector
> que se estime lo que es propio;
> que lo ajeno no es mejor. (II, 993a)

(This is a true story, from which the merciful reader may conclude that one should esteem one's own; for other people's is not better.)

The expression 'pío lector' was common in printed books: here, it suggests pastiche rather than the desire to address a reading audience.

While we might deduce from such plays as *Primero soy yo* and *El maestro de danzar* that their author was familiar with Valencia, the only documentary evidence for a visit is Ortí's book. Cotarelo suggests that *Primero soy yo* was written during the visit,[60] but *El maestro de danzar*, with its 85 per cent of *romance*, must date from around 1650, despite its Valencia setting: the suggestion is not conclusive. However, a reference in *Basta callar* (?1638–9) to an event in *Primero soy yo* supports his guess (see below, p. 232). A possible reference to *Primero soy yo* in *El secreto a voces* (autograph manuscript signed 28 February 1642) does not contradict him.

Primero soy yo has features from, and makes references to, other Calderón plays. Unlike *El maestro de danzar*, however, it is not set in the present: the protagonist, Don Gutierre Centellas, while serving with the Duke of Alba in Germany, led the Spanish infantrymen who famously swam the river Elbe with their swords in their teeth, paving the way for the imperial victory at Mühlberg (1547). The references are to *Peor está que estaba* (1630; II, 1193b) and *La vida es sueño* (?1629–30; II, 1198b), while there is an underground passageway (a dry water conduit) similar to the one in *El galán fastasma* (?c. 1630). The passageway has little importance to the plot, and is used only in the final scene. Since it is used by Don Gutierre to enter the country house of Hipólita, the rival of the heroine, we may suspect that Don Pedro played it down because he was conscious of its symbolism.

Perhaps the best evidence that the play may be contemporary with *No hay cosa como callar* is the accident involving Hipólita and her maid Juana. Hipólita faints, and the gentlemen present fuss around her, leaving Juana to fend for herself:

> Ve aquí por lo que no puede
> caer una doncella honrada
> el día que cae su señora. (II, 1171b)

(See here why an honest maid cannot have a fall on the same day as her mistress.)

When the coach carrying Marcela and her maid Inés overturns in *No hay cosa*, and the gentlemen present rescue the fainting Marcela, Inés has to limp on without assistance:

> Ninguna criada honrada
> caer donde cae su ama puede,
> pues todos se duelen della
> y nadie de mí se duele. (II, 1013a)

(No honest maid can have a fall where her mistress does, because they all feel sorry for her and no one feels sorry for me.)

As in *No hay cosa como callar*, the play ends with only one marriage, between Gutierre and his faithful Laura. Gutierre may be a war hero, but

Laura has just as much courage and determination. We are never quite sure that his feelings for Hipólita go no further than those of a gentleman for a lady in distress, but it is Hipólita who gives the lie to the proverbial expression 'primero soy yo' ('charity begins at home') by finally acting in the interests of Laura and Gutierre, despite her own attraction to him.

To the period 1637–40 also belongs the Calderón sonnet 'Si Huertecilla está como le pintas'. The surviving manuscript copy has the heading *Respuesta de Don Pedro Calderon por los mismos consonantes*, and also transcribes the sonnet to which it was an answer:

De Don Antonio de huerta a don P° Calderon. Soneto.

Si calderon esta como le pintas
la culpa tiene el cabalgar a medias
de Baldes el alcaide las eredias
de Cardenas el bueno las Jaçintas
el come y calla sin meterse en quintas
ensaiando fornicios y comedias
tal vez muy prometidas da vnas medias
muy en las del Cajero da vnas çintas.
La Cruz descubre y el dinero emboça
riquissimo de versos perulero
sin perdonar la vieja ni la moça
De verdad es muy poco su dinero
aier era Belasco y oy mendoça
y en su bolsillo se bertio el salero.

(Sonnet by Don Antonio de Huerta to Don Pedro Calderón. If Calderón is as you describe him, the fault lies in his riding half-and-half the Heredias of Valdés the warden and the Jacintas of good old Cárdenas. He eats and shuts up, without getting involved in arguments, rehearsing fornications and plays; on occasion, after much promising, he gives a present of stockings; he gives a ribbon or two, very much in the bought-from-hawkers style. He shows off his cross and muffles up his money, a millionaire in verses, omitting neither old women nor girls. In truth his money is very little; yesterday he was a Velasco, today a Mendoza, and he poured the salt-cellar into his purse.)

Edward Wilson, who first printed the sonnets, has examined the career of Antonio de Huerta, who subsequently called himself Don Antonio Sigler de Huerta; he also assesses his works, as well as quoting some contemporary and more recent evaluations: some of these are very uncomplimentary.[61] Huerta was possibly older than Calderón, and may have died in the later 1640s. A brief remark by Anastasio Pantaleón de Ribera suggests that he was inclined to sing his own praises, and this is confirmed by the 1637 *vejamen* of Rojas Zorrilla:

Yba en este carro el mayor Poeta que ay en el mundo, Don Antonio de Guerta, que esto lo diçe su merçed y basta, estorvando todo el carro de la moxiganga, sin permitir se hablase en él cosa que no fuese de su comedia de *La Virgen de Balbaneda*.[62]

(Travelling in this cart was the greatest poet in the world, Don Antonio de Huerta, because that's what his worship says and that's enough, upsetting the whole cart of the procession, without allowing anything to be talked about in it except his play *La virgen de Balbaneda*.)

Rojas goes on in this vein at some length. *Vejámenes* were intended to amuse an audience at the expense of those who had taken part in a literary academy, but this is not the good-natured teasing of a friend for his thinning hair. This mockery of a writer for his conceit about his writing verges on the antagonistic. We can see why one of Rojas's victims in the *vejamen* of 1638 might have sought murderous vengeance for his jibes.

Wilson speculated that Huerta's revenge took the form of an attack on Rojas's friend Calderón. The speculation is lent credibility by the final line of Don Pedro's sonnet, 'restituiale a Rojas su salero' ('give Rojas back his salt-cellar'), which could refer to a silver salt-cellar given as a prize in some literary competition. These arguments are plausible, but one line of Huerta's sonnet, 'riquissimo de versos perulero', hints at the envy felt by the hack for the writer to whom composition comes easily, and suggests that his feelings included personal animosity. Not all of the insults are entirely clear. 'La Cruz descubre y el dinero emboça' suggests that Don Pedro is ostentatious about his knighthood of Santiago, while hiding his money because he has so little, pouring salt into his purse to make it look full. Only rarely can he afford to give his lady-friends small presents such as stockings and ribbons; and the ribbons are bought from street hawkers.

'Pobreza no es vileza', says a Spanish proverb (although it goes on, 'pero es linaje de picardía': 'poverty is no crime, but it's a branch of roguery'). We knew that much from *El hombre pobre todo es trazas*, and this study has made Don Pedro's lack of financial resources clear; but not even Huerta accused him of dishonesty, or of being quarrelsome. The claim that he is a womaniser, with no woman safe from him, is also clear. The proper names are more of a problem. While there was an *autor de comedias* named Pedro de Valdés, the line 'de Baldes el alcaide las eredias' almost certainly refers to the notorious actress María de Heredia, who was arrested in January 1642 with her lover Don Gaspar de Valdés, 'con quien ha años tiene amistad', 'with whom she has had a friendship for years'. Don Gaspar was a 'Regidor desta Villa i Alcayde de sus Cárceles' ('councillor of this town and warden of its prisons'), according to Pellicer.[63] His fate, and María's, remind us that the authorities could take action against extramarital relationships which were deemed to cause public scandal. We need not suppose that Don Pedro was another of María's lovers, although she was to take the role of the heroine Beatriz in *La desdicha de la voz* (1639): Huerta chose her name because she had already given cause for gossip. As for 'Cardenas el bueno', the surname is too common for identification to be certain. A Diego de Cárdenas, married to the actress María de Balbín, is often mentioned in theatre documents of this period, but there is no evidence to link him with the epithet or with any of the several actresses named Jacinta.[64] The penultimate line, 'ayer era Belasco y oy mendoça', refers to Don Pedro's change of employer from the Duke of Frías (surnamed Velasco) to the Duke of Infantado (surnamed Mendoza). Since he was with the second duke from 1637 until the summer of 1640, both sonnets must date from that period.

We know that Don Pedro's illegitimate son was born around 1648, but we know nothing else about the relationship involved, or about possible previous relationships. Given his professional connections with actresses, however, he must have had the opportunity, at the very least, to find some of them attractive. Wilson is sceptical about this part of Huerta's accusations, but since the other details are correct (Calderón's poverty, his knighthood, his change of employer), we must suspect that the jibe had some foundation, even if the basis was no more than a long-term relationship with one particular actress.

As for the quality of the verse, neither sonnet could be called poetry, although in choosing to write an answer with the same rhymes, Calderón showed his superior technical ability. He also stepped up the insult level: Huerta's wife is a slut, and he is a cuckold and a thief. Those who took on Don Pedro with the pen were likely to come off worst.

CHAPTER 13

The storm gathers

> Suenen idiomas de Marte,
> y en voces altivas
> confundid un ruido con otro,
> y viva el que viva. (*La púrpura de la rosa*)
>
> (Let the languages of Mars ring out; mingle one noise with another in arrogant voices, and let live who may.)

The claim of Olivares that 1638 was Spain's happiest year was premature. Despite Fuenterrabía, the year ended badly for Spain. Breisach, now a modest town on the Rhine between Basel and Strasbourg, was then a key fortress on the road from Spain's Italian possessions to Flanders, and when the Duke of Feria relieved the siege on 16 October 1633, his exploit rated a huge canvas in the Retiro's Hall of Realms.[1] But Feria died of typhus, that bane of wintering armies, the following February, and there was no one to stop Breisach's capture in December 1638 by the Duke of Saxe-Weimar, who died in his turn, also of fever, two months later, at thirty-five. His death was as convenient for Richelieu as it was for Olivares.

Worse was still to come. In the late summer of 1639 Olivares devised a plan for sending men and money to Flanders in a fleet so large that it would destroy the Dutch navy on the way. At around a hundred ships, the fleet was almost as big as the Armada of 1588, and it fared almost as badly: after a running battle with Tromp, in which it came off worse, it was trapped in the Downs, off the coast of Kent. Oquendo, the commander, managed to break out with a number of ships, and the Cardinal-Infante may have got 70–80 per cent of his troops, but losses of ships and seamen were heavy.[2]

As events abroad strengthened the resolve of the government's enemies at home, Don Pedro suffered a personal calamity in the illness and death of one of his closest friends, Juan Pérez de Montalbán. When Pedro Grande de Tena brought out his posthumous homage volume to the dead writer in 1639, Don Pedro contributed two poems, in one of which he called him 'nuestro Terencio español, | nuestro Plauto castellano' ('our Spanish Terence, our Castilian Plautus'): coming from another playwright, high praise. The fifth stanza describes the illness:

> No furioso frenesí,
> no delirio riguroso
> su ánimo turbó piadoso;
> un blando letargo sí.[3]

(No furious frenzy, no cruel delirium upset his gentle spirit, only a mild lethargy.)

There is another brief reference to the symptoms, which apparently began early in 1637, and which proved fatal on 25 June 1638: 'Enviar delante previno | a todo su entendimiento' ('He took the precaution of sending on ahead all his understanding').

The other poem, in the preliminaries, is dedicated to the compiler, and identifies him as a friend of Pérez de Montalbán, with a pun on his surname:

> que aun mas allá de las aras
> amigo Grande aueis sido.[4]

(You have been a great friend, even beyond the usual limits of friendship).

A friend of one writer is likely to have been a friend of the other, but we know nothing of Don Pedro's relationship with Grande.[5]

One of those who did not share Calderón's admiration for Pérez de Montalbán was Quevedo. Pérez's father, the bookseller Alonso Pérez, was responsible for producing a pirate edition of Quevedo's *Buscón* in 1626, and when the young writer produced his *Vida y purgatorio de San Patricio* in 1627, Quevedo took his revenge on the father by attacking inaccuracies and anachronisms in the work of the son. However, it was the *Para todos* of 1632 which provoked one of the most savage literary attacks ever written, the *Perinola*, dedicated 'Al Doctor Juan Pérez de Montalbán, graduado no se sabe dónde; en lo qué, ni se sabe ni él lo sabe' ('To Dr Juan Pérez de Montalbán, graduate of where is not known; in what is not known, nor does he know').[6] In fact, Pérez de Montalbán had graduated in theology at Alcalá, Quevedo's university, as Quevedo well knew. There were also dark hints at the *converso* ancestry of the young doctor and his father, and friends such as Felipe Godínez and Jerónimo de Villaizán were not spared. Don Pedro was not among those who were attacked, however; Quevedo ended his assault by giving his victim some advice: 'Deje las novelas para Cervantes; y las comedias á Lope, á Luis Velez, á D. Pedro Calderón y á otros' ('Leave novels to Cervantes and plays to Lope, Luis Vélez, Don Pedro Calderón and others': p. 363). Quevedo would not have been Quevedo if he had not thought to heap additional humiliation on Pérez de Montalbán by praising his mentor and his friend, but it is perhaps significant that he mentions Don Pedro with two playwrights of the old generation, as authors to be emulated.

* * *

Los dos amantes del cielo is a play which might belong to almost any period of Don Pedro's career. It opens with Crisanto puzzling over St John's Gospel, like the prince in *El gran príncipe de Fez* (1669), but also recalling Cipriano in *El mágico prodigioso* (1637). Hilborn suggests that it was written around 1636, but there is now so much documentary evidence for us to reject some of his guesses that this one requires support from other sources.[7] The song sung by Nísida, 'Ruiseñor, que volando vas' (I, 776a) has surviving music by Juan Vado, who is known to have been a violinist in the Capilla Real in 1635,[8] but the same song is found in Calderón's act of *La fingida Arcadia* (1663) and *Fieras afemina Amor* (1671). Daría's reference to a cave as

> una horrible boca
> ...
> por donde con pereza
> el monte melancólico bosteza (I, 787b)

(a horrible mouth through which the melancholy mountain lazily yawns)

with its echoes of the sixth stanza of Góngora's *Polifemo*, is used so often, from *La selva confusa* (1623) to *Hado y divisa* (1680), as to be of no help. One remark, by Crisanto's father Polemio,

> bien dice quien dice que es
> un hijo muchos pesares (I, 795a)

(he who says a son is many sorrows is right)

recalls that made by the protagonist's father in *El galán fantasma* (?*c*. 1630): 'Ay hijos, quien os desea | no sabe lo que costáis' ('Oh, children, he who desires you knows not what you cost': II, 642a). However, what is perhaps most interesting about these sentiments, in a writer who so often portrays father–son relationships to the father's disadvantage, is this glimpse of the father's point of view; except that Polemio is a typical inflexible Roman father, who would rather see his son dead than insulting Rome's gods.

If there is anything about this play that suggests that it may belong to the period being examined here, it is the regular references to loss of reason, particularly since they are in the context of reading and study:

Tus graves melancolías,
que hayan de quitarte, creo,
el entendimiento, si es
que tienes ya entendimiento. (1, 773b)

(I believe that your grave melancholies will deprive you of your understanding, if you still have understanding.)

This is from Crisanto's father, but, as often happens, the *gracioso* joins in:

Ser músicas y poetas
ya para perderlo [el juicio] basta. (1, 794b)

(Being musicians and poets is enough for losing one's mind.)

This is not to suggest that Don Pedro made literary capital out of his friend's mental illness, but current theories would have held that the affliction and 'tenprana muerte del gran poeta' ('early death of the great poet') sprang from overtaxing of the mind, rather than from the more likely cause of a brain tumour. If these passages reflect that illness, then the play may date from 1637–8. However, we find similar suggestions of mental overtaxing in *El José de las mujeres*, which may be later; and of course there is probably a deliberate echo in both plays of the words of the praetor Porcius Festus when Paul proclaimed Christ's resurrection to him: 'Too much study is driving you mad' (Acts 26:24).

Hilborn assigned the two-part play *La hija del aire* to '*c.* 1637', a guess which a number of scholars found unacceptable.[9] The two parts were first published together in the *Tercera parte* of 1664, but the second part had been published in *Parte quarenta y dos de comedias de diferentes autores* (1650), attributed to Antonio Enríquez Gómez. For many years the first known performance was a royal one, in November 1653, of both parts, in the *alcázar*,[10] but we now know that the two parts were played in Seville on 15 and 16 January 1643.[11] Those dates suggest a *terminus ad quem* of December 1642, and since Don Pedro's military service (1640–2) hampered his literary production, the plays were probably written in the 1630s. Attempts to argue that Enríquez Gómez really did write Part II and that Don Pedro wrote Part I later, cannot now be taken seriously. The text of Part II refers to events in 'la primera comedia' ('the first play'); and metrical and stylistic analysis shows that Part II is entirely consistent with composition by Calderón and much less consistent with composition by Enríquez Gómez.[12]

Semíramis has her origin in a real person, Sammuramat, who ruled Assyria from 811 to 808 BC, after the death of her husband and during the minority of her son. Calderón's main sources were Cristóbal de Virués's play, *La gran Semíramis* (published 1609), and possibly Diodorus Siculus'

Bibliotheca historica. Virués gave Calderón the main outlines of the story, including the Semíramis who retained power by posing as her son (as we have seen, Calderón did this by having a single actress take both roles). However, the young Semíramis, dressed in skins and burdened with a baleful horoscope, is another character like Segismundo or Adonis in *La púrpura de la rosa*. Like Adonis, she is the result of an illicit union; in this case, of a rape. The difference is that she is a woman, excluded from power by male prejudice, but yet so beautiful that men will die for her, or kill for her. She is a truly tragic figure, who has already lost her innocence and who soon learns to be ruthless in what she sees as a ruthless world. The word *fortuna* is constantly mentioned, but the attitudes of the characters to it are very different. Characters like Licas (Part II), Lisías and Arsidas/Lidoro strive to do what is right, whatever fortune may do ('Como yo obre bien | lo demás no importa nada', 'So long as I do good, the rest matters nothing', says Licas); others, like Friso (Part II), are complete opportunists ('Ten tú razón, yo fortuna, | y verás que no te envidio', 'You have reason and I, fortune, and you'll see that I do not envy you', says Friso, since good deeds do not guarantee prosperity: 'Muchos obran bien, y son | sus fortunas desdichadas', 'many do good, and their fortunes are wretched'). Finally, there are characters like Menón and King Nino (Part I), who are initially good, but who are not always able to resist fortune's offers.[13]

Since part of the story deals with a young king (Ninias) and an older statesman/favourite (Lisías), we are bound to remember the Philip/Olivares relationship, especially when some of the imagery assists us, for instance when the young king praises the minister for his prudence:

Tu prudencia,
en el mar de mi fortuna,
piloto ha de ser de aquesta
nave, pues será contigo
serenidad la tormenta. (II, 1388–92)

(Your prudence, in the sea of my fortune, will be the pilot of this ship, since with you the storm will be calmness.)

We cannot help recalling what Elliott has called 'that obsessively recurrent image' used by Olivares of himself: a man labouring at the oar of the ship of state in a storm, and clinging to the oar as the ship went down.[14]

One of the most interesting characters in the play is the *gracioso* Chato. Despite his earlier sympathies with Semíramis, Chato comes to be extremely critical of her. Even when young King Ninias grants him a pension, he is sarcastic about the difficulties of having it paid. He approaches courtier after courtier to discover how to turn royal grants into hard cash, and is rebuffed, giving us another reminder of real life at the court of Philip IV:

Mas, ¿qué me admiro si son
las mercedes palaciegas
jubileo, y no se ganan
sin hacer las diligencias? (II, 1557–60)

(But why should I marvel, if palace favours are a jubilee, and you don't earn them without doing what you have to?)

The phrase 'hacer las diligencias [de cristiano]' ('doing the duties of a Christian') plays on the religious duties which must be performed to gain a plenary indulgence, while suggesting the bribes that must be paid to court officials. The criticism of court corruption under Philip IV is done through a comic character, but it is clear enough. We have moved some way from the remark made in 1629, that

de ministros tales
hoy el Rey se sirve, que
no es al mérito importante
la asistencia, porque todos
acudir a todo saben. (II, 279b)

(These days the king employs such ministers that being present is not important for getting what one deserves, since all of them know how to attend to everything.)

The task of signing trivial money orders did not pertain to Olivares himself. Arguably, though, it was his job to ensure that the officials who did were prompt, and that they did not seek bribes.

Perhaps Chato's most interesting remark is made when he brings his pension document back to the monarch (now Semíramis, in the guise of Ninias) to sign: when she tears it up and hits him with the pieces, he is outraged:

¿Así, cielos, se ofende
a la nieve destas canas?
Para ver estos oprobios,
caduca vejez cansada,
¿duraste tanto? (II, 2630–4)

(Is this, heavens, how the snow of these white hairs is offended? Did you last so long, decrepit and tedious old age, only to see this ignominy?)

When the father of Corneille's Cid has his face slapped by the father of Chimène, and discovers that he is too infirm to avenge the insult with his sword, he curses his age:

> Ô râge! ô désespoir! ô vieillesse ennemie!
> N'ai-je donc tant vécu que pour cette infamie?[15]

(O rage, o despair, o enemy old age! Have I lived so long only for this infamy?)

The resemblance between the last line of Don Diègue and the last three of Chato would be less remarkable if this flowery language were Chato's normal manner of speech, but it is not. However, since *Le Cid* was printed in 1637, that is, about the time when Chato's words were being written (to say nothing of the problem of Calderón's understanding the French), this may be no more than a coincidence. Corneille knew Spanish, but it is hard to imagine him getting his hands on a Spanish play which was not printed until 1650.

Another feature of the play is the 'responses' made offstage to remarks of characters onstage. For example, when Semíramis asks herself,

> ¿No tengo de ver,
> sino imaginar no más,
> cómo es el vivir? (I, 1157–9)

(Am I not to see, but only to imagine, what life is like?)

the offstage argument of Chato and Sirene gives an answer: 'Sí harás'. '¿Quién me ha respondido?', asks Semíramis, and the response is 'Dios, | que en eso el mundo a los dos | oirá.' ('You will' – 'Who answered me?' – 'God, for in this the world will hear us both'). This is the kledomancy referred to in Chapter 10. *La hija del aire* provides one of Calderón's more sustained examples of its dramatic use.

In 1639, Calderón was paid for two works composed for royal performances. One entry in the royal accounts, undated, but probably referring to Carnival 1639, says he received 1,500 *reales* for 'la comedia de la fábula de Narciso' ('the play of the fable of Narcissus'), with a *loa* and an *entremés*. Since his *Eco y Narciso* was performed in the Retiro on 12 July 1661, this was presumably an early version.[16] The mention of a single *entremés* (normally performed between the acts of the play) may mean that the play had only two acts. In June he received 2,200 *reales* for a play (title not given), *loa* and *entremeses*. The play could be one of the undated plays which has survived: the fee indicates that it was new, not a restaging. A newsletter of 12 June refers to a play performed in lavish fashion on the lake with much stage machinery.[17] If this was Calderón's, the staging surely excludes the undated plays *La niña de Gómez Arias* and *Basta callar* which apparently belong to this period. Perhaps the only realistic possibility is *La dama y galán Aquiles*, which Ascanio described in 1644 as a 'new play, never performed in Valencia' (but which could be several years old, like *Gustos y disgustos*).[18] No other surviving undated play seems to fit; but of course the play performed on the lake could have been written by someone else.

Between the Narciso play and the unidentified one comes *La desdicha de la voz*, with an autograph manuscript signed and dated in Madrid on 14 May. The manuscript is a working draft, full of changes and corrections. And yet, on the first page, beneath the title, Calderón has written a list of characters, with an actor's name opposite each one (a tear has removed the latter parts of the names). Thanks to other documents, among them Quiñones de Benavente's *Loa con que empezaron Rueda y Ascanio en Madrid* (1638), we can identify all but one of those involved, members of the company which by May 1639 was being run by Antonio de Rueda, although Pedro Ascanio was still a member.[19] We can imagine a meeting between Calderón and Rueda, perhaps during Lent 1639, in which the writer, armed with a draft scenario, discussed the assignment of roles with the manager, who was commissioning the play. No scenarios in Don Pedro's hand have survived, but given the *memorias de apariencias* he wrote for the *autos*, we can be pretty sure that this was how he worked, although his scenarios may have been rough notes, unlike, for example, Cosme Lotti's plan for *El mayor encanto amor*. There are sufficient similar examples of role assignment in his other autograph manuscripts to indicate that this was often, perhaps normally, his procedure. In any case, there is more circumstantial evidence that Don Pedro was in contact with Rueda in early 1639, since the *autor* was charged with performing the two *autos* Calderón wrote for Corpus that year (23 June): *Santa María Egipciaca* and *El mejor huésped de España*, neither of which has survived.[20] The two men almost certainly met, in other words, and it would be surprising if they did not discuss the comedy Don Pedro was writing as he worked on the *autos*. Even if they did not, we can assume that a scenario of the play, with details of who would take which parts, preceded composition.

The manuscript of *La desdicha* has just under 3,800 lines, almost 1,000 more than *El alcalde de Zalamea*. A total of 444 of these were omitted in the first printed edition of 1650.[21] While not unusual for a palace play, 3,800 lines is very long for a performance in the public theatres, and raises the possibility that Don Pedro wrote more than a normal performance would require because he knew that the practicalities of rehearsal would show up scenes and passages which did not work well on the stage, and which would be cut. We cannot be sure, because a play which was in circulation for a decade before it was printed might be cut by a whole series of *autores*. In addition, as Calderón himself put it, plays were cut by printers to fit a convenient number of pages: 'Donde acaba el pliego, acaba la Iornada, y donde acaba el quaderno, acaba la Comedia' ('Where the page ends, the act ends; and where the gathering ends, the play ends').[22]

The play opens in Madrid on Sunday 12 September 1638, with a reference to King Philip and Queen Isabel going to Atocha to give thanks for the victory in Fuenterrabía. Unusually, it moves in Act II to Seville, where the unfortunate heroine Beatriz takes refuge, believing that her brother Pedro has killed her lover Don Juan de Silva and is now seeking to kill her. As she tells her story to the elderly Octavio, a friend of her late father's, we catch a glimpse of what it was like for single women to travel in seventeenth-century Spain. She sold some jewels she happened to be wearing when she ran from the house, bought some plain clothes, and, by pretending to be a married woman who had to go to Seville over a lawsuit, managed to get a seat on a coach.

Speaking of Calderón's comedies, Wilson remarks that 'the ladies are chaste'.[23] This is true, but perhaps some further explanation is required. It may be remembered that Don Pedro's elder brother Diego contracted marriage with Doña Beatriz de Alarcón on 26 February 1622, and that the religious ceremony took place only on 19 February 1623, by which time Beatriz was six months pregnant. In *El galán fantasma*, Julia is secretly married to Astolfo; in *Gustos y disgustos*, Vicente and Violante are already married in secret when the play opens; the same is true of Don Pedro Torrellas and Doña Violante de Urrea in *El postrer duelo de España* (?1651–3). Marriage in the Catholic Church is a sacrament, but that sacrament depends only on a solemn contract between the two parties: no priest is necessary. The marriage of Diego Calderón demonstrates this, although no secrecy was involved: Diego signed a civil contract before witnesses. If witnesses were not present, abuses were possible, and the Council of Trent (1545–63) prohibited secret marriages for that reason. It may be said that the ones depicted in *Gustos* and *El postrer duelo* pre-date the Council, while the setting of *El galán fantasma* cannot be assigned to a particular time. However, the setting of *La desdicha* is contemporary, and Beatriz's account of her relationship is significant:

Un caballero de ilustre
sangre, de bizarras prendas,
puso los ojos en mí,
y yo a su mérito atenta,

con la palabra de ser
mi esposo (que no pudiera
mi honor con menos fianza
obligarse a tanta deuda)
le favorecí. (II, 928a)

(A gentleman of noble blood, of splendid qualities, laid eyes on me; and I, observing his worth, with his promise to be my husband – for my honour could not bind itself to such a debt with any lesser guarantee – showed him favour.)

Later, she twice refers to Don Juan as her 'esposo' (II, 929b, 930a). There is nothing ambiguous about the word, in the sense that she considered that Don Juan had made a binding agreement to marry her, but the passage is not entirely clear. The words 'le favorecí' may mean that she responded to his offer with a binding promise of her own, or they may be a euphemism for offering herself physically. Whichever it is, secret marriages evidently continued, at least on the stage, no doubt because they could lead to dramatic complications and heightened pathos. We should be wary, though, of reading too much into statements about the liberties permitted by Calderón's comedy heroines. In *Casa con dos puertas* Lisardo admits that the young lady to whom he is attracted 'añadió favores tales, | que me obliga la vergüenza, | por mí mismo, a que los calle' ('she added such favours that embarrassment for myself obliges me not to say what they were': II, 280a). She raised her veil and showed her face!

Little stigma, if any, attached to secret marriages, or to secret promises to marry. They could be revealed, or claimed, as in the case of Laura in *Primero soy yo* ('El hombre que yo, es verdad, | escondí en ese retrete, | es mi esposo', 'The man whom I hid in that closet is my husband, it's true': II, 1192a), in the expectation of defusing a threatening situation. In Laura's case, even with her father present, it works (at least until the man in hiding turns out to be someone else!). Beatriz's situation, however, is pitiable: she has (she believes) no 'esposo' and no witness to say that she was 'married'; she is perhaps not a virgin, but she cannot prove that she is a widow.

In the end, of course, Beatriz's promise is upheld: she was misinformed about the death of Juan. The wounded man was her other suitor, Diego, who recovers. Diego's sister, the more manipulative Leonor, who also loved Juan but encouraged Pedro in order to make Juan jealous, ends up with Pedro. The unfortunate Diego, who was ready to try to save Beatriz even when it emerged that his love for her was hopeless, is left with no one: 'Te hieren y no te casas' ('You're wounded and unwed': II, 951b) says the *gracioso* in ironic congratulation. It is unusual for a murderously jealous brother like Pedro to get the girl he wants, but Diego could not marry his own sister.

Calderón may have felt that it was more important to show how the scheming and self-deluding Leonor had brought her unhappiness on herself ('Esperanza', she says, 'pues ya no tenéis remedio, | disimulad vuestras ansias', 'Hope, since you have no remedy, dissemble your anguish': II, 951b) than to contrive some consolation for the more deserving Diego.

The range of comedy is considerable, and includes slapstick (when Leonor peeps through a keyhole as Pedro opens the door, or when the *gracioso* Luquete has his face slapped by Beatriz and Isabel in quick succession) and self-mockery:

Que debe de ser comedia,
sin duda, esta de Don Pedro
Calderón; que hermano o padre
siempre vienen a mal tiempo.
Y ahora vienen ambos juntos. (II, 936a)

(Doubtless this must be a play by Don Pedro Calderón, because a brother or father always come at a bad time; and now here come both together.)

There are references to *Peor está que estaba* (?1630: II, 944b), *Antes que todo es mi dama* (?1637–40: II, 929b), and perhaps to *Fuego de Dios en el querer bien* (?1640–2: II, 921a) and *El privilegio de las mujeres* (?1634: II, 942a). (It should be remembered, of course, that 'Peor está que estaba' and '¡Fuego de Dios en …!' were common expressions.)[24] There were also several opportunities for the actress María de Heredia (Beatriz) to demonstrate her singing ability. Ms Heredia's reputation for chastity, unfortunately, fell rather short of that of a comedy heroine.

Finally, we may wonder whether the Seville setting is evidence for a visit there on Calderón's part. One street is named in the text, la Calle de las Armas, but this will hardly do as evidence: we cannot assume that a writer who mentions Broadway has been to New York.

* * *

The story of a Gómez Arias who eloped with a young woman who was in love with him, only to sell her to the Moors when he tired of her, may not be true, but numerous writers refer to it. The first to dramatise the legend was Luis Vélez, whose modern editor suggests a composition date of 1600–20, probably 1608–14.[25] With some confidence, Hilborn assigns Calderón's version to 1637–9, but the text offers no confirmation.[26]

The most striking, and indicative, difference between the two versions comes at the end. In both versions Gómez Arias's victim is willing to marry him, and pleads with Queen Isabel for his life. Vélez's queen grants the request: Calderón's does not. His Gómez Arias has the same lack of interest in women whom he has possessed as Don Juan de Mendoza, the rapist. Gómez Arias has made a solemn promise to both Dorotea and Beatriz; he sells Dorotea to a Moorish rebel to get rid of her, but continues to pursue Beatriz because she has not surrendered to him. To justify the execution, Calderón has expanded the character's role and, in particular, that of Dorotea, whose lament as she is sold is extended from sixteen lines to 200. He has also enlarged the role of the *gracioso*, using his cowardice to point up the bravery of Dorotea, and his scruples, unusual in a cowardly *gracioso*, to highlight the ruthlessness of Gómez Arias.[27] The Moor Cañerí is also used for this purpose: although he 'owns' Dorotea and could do his will with her, he wants to gain her affection by his self-restraint, and marry her. Even Gómez Arias's reference to Góngora's 'Apeóse el caballero',

> muchos siglos de hermosura,
> como dice aquella letra,
> en pocos años de edad (I, 1095a)

(many centuries of beauty, as that poem says, in few years of age)

reminds us of another young woman who eloped, in circumstances which seem to promise better things.

In some aspects, the play may be compared with *Fuenteovejuna*: both plays have a historical setting in the reign of Ferdinand and Isabella for an event which had become part of Spanish folklore; most of the characters are inventions. The difference is that in *Fuenteovejuna* 'King' Ferdinand (he was crown prince of Aragón until his father died in 1479) pronounces the final judgement; this despite the fact that the events had taken place in Isabella's kingdom, Castile, and that she was in charge of domestic policy in their partnership. In *La niña* Ferdinand is not present. This is also true of Vélez's version; however, Calderón's Isabel is not only a monarch inflicting exemplary punishment with precedent in mind:

> En cualquier delito, el rey
> es todo. Si parte has sido
> tú [= Dorotea] y le perdonas, yo no,
> porque no quede a los siglos
> la puerta abierta al perdón
> de semejantes delitos. (I, 1125b)

(In any crime, the monarch is everything. If you are an involved party and you pardon him, I do not, so that the door may not remain open in the future to the pardon of such crimes.)

She also acts as a woman,

para que digan los siglos
si hubo una mujer burlada,
que otra la vengue ha habido. (I, 1123a)

(So that the centuries to come may say that, if a woman was deceived, there was another to avenge her.)

Characters like Semíramis and Matilde are as ruthless as any male tyrants; Isabel and Cenobia are models for any male monarchs.

The first recorded edition of *Los empeños de un acaso* is in 1651, but somehow the play got to France before this, to be used by Antoine le Métel d'Ouville for his play *Les Fausses Veritez* in 1643, and by Thomas Corneille four years later for *Les Engagemens du hazard*:[28]

Je faisais dessein [wrote Corneille in his dedication] de n'en permettre jamais l'impression; mais vous vous y opposâtes si fortement, pour l'intérêt du fameux Don Pedro Calderon, qui a traité cette comédie avec tant d'esprit, sous le même titre de *Los empeños de un acaso.*

(I planned never to allow it to be printed; but you were so strongly against that, because of the involvement of the famous Don Pedro Calderón, who dealt with this comedy so wittily, under the same title, *The Obligations of an Accident.*)

In Act III, Hernando, whom Don Félix has already hit on the head while he was trying to deliver a message, is asked by his master Don Juan to deliver another to him. He cannot understand why Juan and Félix now appear to be friends, and fears another blow on the head:

Si fué [mi amo] a reñir con él, ¿cómo de amigo
hace ahora finezas?
¿No fuera el monstruo yo de dos cabezas?
¡Oh, cuánto lo estimara mi fortuna,
pues para discurrir tuviera una,
y otra para aparar! (II, 1067a)

(If my master went off to fight a duel with him, how come he's now paying him the courtesies of a friend? Mightn't I be the two-headed monster? Oh, how my luck would esteem it, because I'd have one for talking and another for getting hit!)

This passage reminded Hartzenbusch of a remark in Pellicer's *Avisos* of 8 November 1639: 'En el condado de Aviñon, en Francia, se dice por cierto que una labradora parió un monstruo con dos cabezas' ('In the county of Avignon, in France, it is reliably said that a peasant woman gave birth to a two-headed monster').[29] The seventeenth century had what we see as a morbid interest in deformity, and this is precisely the kind of 'news' that got printed in newsletters. The fact that the play got to Paris by 1643, most likely in printed form, would indicate that it was written at least a year or two previously, so that Hernando could be referring to the Avignon birth, presumably when the news was still relatively recent. There are complications, however: first, several references indicate that the play is set in early summer:

viendo que ya el mayo,
tiranamente depuesto
del imperio de las flores,
le deja a junio el imperio. (II, 1042b)

(seeing that May, tyranically deposed from her rule over the flowers, leaves the rule to June.)

Second, Profeti records several early *sueltas*, one with an attribution to Calderón, the others attributed to Pérez de Montalbán, with the title *Los empeños que se ofrecen*.[30] For how long after his death in June 1638, we may wonder, did the book trade consider Pérez's name a selling-point?

Another of Hernando's allusions, while providing no help with dating, is nevertheless of interest. He is describing the kind of girlfriend he would like:

Quisiera una dama yo
extravagante, y sujeto
capaz de novela, porque
es mi amor tan novelero,
que me le escribió Cervantes. (II, 1043b)

(I'd like an eccentric lady-friend, a fitting subject for a novel, for my love is so novelettish that Cervantes wrote it for me.)

When Calderón uses a contemporary setting, his characters sometimes allude to the time of year. On occasion, there is information to show that the date of the premiere coincides with that season. Hernando's choice of words, and the extent of his play on the idea of having a spare head for getting hit ('aparar', here, probably has the sense of 'to dress meat', perhaps with a tenderising mallet), do appear to be a reference to the Avignon case. If so, the play was written between November 1639 and the spring of 1640, with the expectation that it would be played in early June. As we shall see, Calderón may also have written at least three *autos* during the same period, not to mention the two unidentified plays he wrote for Carnival, which would have needed to be ready by early February at the latest. During these months, the news from Cataluña was increasingly bad. Circumstantial evidence suggests that Don Pedro may have expected to be called up in the autumn of 1637, to go to Portugal. Perhaps he believed that a time was coming when he would have little opportunity to earn money from his writing, and wrote as much as he could while it was still possible.

Enfermar con el remedio was printed in *Comedias escogidas IV* (1653), but it must have been written by 10 November 1644, the date of the death of Vélez, who wrote Act II. The author of Act III, Jerónimo Cáncer, was born about 1582, three years after Vélez, so Don Pedro was collaborating with two writers of the previous generation. As in *El monstruo de la fortuna* (1636), of which Don Pedro also wrote Act I, the play is set in Italy, with the daughter of a ruler (here, a duke) enjoined by her father's will to marry a particular individual to avoid a war of succession; in this case there is also a younger sister to whom the right of succession will pass if the elder does not obey.

We cannot avoid remembering the will of Calderón's father, although his instructions were about who should not be married, rather than who should, while the passing of succession rights from oldest to youngest recalls the wishes of the maternal grandmother, Inés de Riaño. There is nothing in the text, however, to indicate when the play was written. Calderón is usually reckoned to have been involved in another twelve collaboration plays, ten of them written between 1630 and 1645, and six between 1634 and 1640. This last is the most likely period, a guess weakly supported by the plot similarity to *El monstruo de la fortuna.*

Basta callar has survived in a part-autograph manuscript which reveals that the version published by Vera Tassis in 1682 had been badly cut. The first scholar to examine the manuscript concluded that the play was first drafted in 1635–40 and revised in 1657; one modern editor opts for 1638–9, with a revision date of 1653–4.[31] The evidence for both of these adjustments is contained in the text. Early in Act I, Margarita gives several examples of ladies rescued by gentlemen:

> No ha mucho que las dos
> vimos caer de una ventana
> socorrida una hermosura
> no sé si en novela o farsa. (lines 225–8)

(Not long ago, I don't know whether in a novel or a play, the two of us saw a beauty rescued in a fall from a window.)

As we could tell her, it was in a 'farsa', *Primero soy yo*, which is most likely to date from 1638. The revised text includes a reference to the siege and capture of Barcelona (13 October 1652) by Don John of Austria (lines 1020–48), and a joke about bankruptcy which can be linked to the government bankruptcy of 1653 (3335–41, see Greer edn, pp. 12–14).

If *No hay cosa como callar* was a black comedy, *Basta callar* is a dark one, set in Béarne, on the border between France and Spain, against a background of war and uneasy political allegiances. Serafina, a young noblewoman from Montpellier, loves Ludovico, but she is loved by three men: Federico, Count of Montpellier; Enrique, Duke of Béarne; and Ludovico. The duke has a sister, Margarita, who has fallen in love with Ludovico as a result of nursing him back to health after Federico's men have tried to kill him. Margarita takes Flora (and the audience) into her confidence at the start, with a long speech which is calculated to win sympathy:

¡Mal haya
el primer legislador
que hizo a la mujer vasalla
tanto del hombre, que quiso
que ellos hereden las casas
y ellas las obligaciones …
dejándonos a nosotras
sin el libro y sin la espada
y sin el mando, a ser sólo
la más inútil alhaja
de sus familias …! (36–41, 51–5)

(A curse on the first lawmaker who made women vassals to men, so much so that he wanted men to inherit the estates, and women, the obligations … leaving us without books, swords and authority, to be their families' most useless treasure!)

Many of Calderón's contemporaries, among the males at least, would have shrugged: this was how the world was intended to be, a fact apparently confirmed in the end by Margarita's marriage of convenience to the count. But the count had tried to have his rival murdered, and her fate leaves a sense of disquiet, even as we accept the message that social life forces us to compromise with our desires. The message is also true for the duke and the count, who must give up Serafina to Ludovico. *Nadie fíe su secreto* had offered a similar message, but more lightheartedly, perhaps because *Basta callar*, like the contemporary *No hay cosa como callar*, reminds us that we need to compromise in silence. Even Capricho's watch, the primary source of the play's comedy, is a constant reminder of the passage of time, of *desengaño*.[32] Ten years, perhaps fifteen, separate *Nadie fíe* and *Basta callar*. Much had happened in that time to darken Calderón's view of the world.

* * *

While precise figures are impossible, we can calculate that, up to 1630, Calderón wrote about twenty-six plays. In the 1630s, he wrote around forty-seven, with another four or five in collaboration, perhaps at least ten *autos*, and a significant amount of poetry. While he wrote more *autos* after 1650 than before, around half of his total output is crammed into these twenty years. No doubt some of this frenzy of writing resulted from the need to repay the debts he had incurred in becoming a knight, but we can also draw other conclusions: that his facility of composition was surpassed only by Lope's; and that when his reputation prompted invitations to write a piece of work, he may have found it hard to refuse; and the fear that national events might interfere in his writing life may have added to this pressure.

Calderón would not have wanted to decline to write the two poems required for the Pérez de Montalbán homage volume, but around this time he also accepted invitations to write more occasional poems: 'Cuanto la antigüedad dejó esparcido …', a sonnet (1639) for Rodrigo Méndez Silva's genealogy of the Spanish monarchy;[33] 'Tu sumo ingenio, tu agudeza suma', a sonnet (?1639) for the translator of a life of St Eloy;[34] 'Funestas pompas, y cenizas frías', *octavas* (1640), for another Méndez Silva book, dedicated this time to the tomb of the subject;[35] and 'Hacer una traducción …', *décimas* (1640), dedicated to another translator, Mateo de Prado.[36] All of these must have been acquaintances, and may have been friends.

In his Life of Shakespeare, Ackroyd draws attention to the high proportion of collaboration plays in late Elizabethan England (fifty-five out of eighty-nine in one instance), and to the consequent indifference, on the part of the potential audience, to the identity of the author.[37] Collaboration plays did not reach such proportions in Spain, which may explain why commentators such as Ortí, Sánchez de Espejo or the anonymous writers of diaries and newsletters are more likely to give authors' names, and to refer to them in flattering terms when they do so. That the author may have mattered more than the play is surely suggested by Antonio de Prado, when he tells us he has three new plays by Calderón, and gives us the title of only one (see p. 162 above). Furthermore, there was a tradition in Spain of playwrights complaining about their plays being published under the names of others:

> Ahora han salido algunas comedias que, impresas en Castilla, dicen que en Lisboa …; no crean que aquéllas son mis comedias, aunque tengan mi nombre. (Lope, 1604)[38]

> (Some plays have now come out, printed in Castile, but claiming to be printed in Lisbon; do not believe that those are my plays, although they carry my name.)

> Tambien ha obligado a Lope a dar a luz publica esta fabula, el ver la libertad con que los Libreros de Seuilla, Cadiz, y otros Lugares del Andaluzia, con la capa de que se imprimen en Zaragoça, y Barcelona, y poniendo los nombres de aquellos

Impressores, sacan diuersos Tomos en el suyo, poniendo en ellos Comedias de hombres ignorantes. (Lope, 1632)[39]

(Lope has also been forced to publish this story by seeing the freedom with which the booksellers of Seville, Cadiz and other places in Andalusia, under the guise of their being printed in Zaragoza and Barcelona, and using the names of printers there, bring out [?parts of] different volumes in theirs, putting in them plays by ignorant men.)

Las [comedias] que se han impresso hasta aquí sin mi orden son falsas, mentirosas, supuestas y adulteradas; porque como los que las hurtan no tienen bastante espacio para trasladarlas y quien las imprime las compra de los que las hurtan, salen con mil desatinos, errores y barbaridades, sin atender al agravio que se hace a los ingenios assí en la opinión como en el interés, imprimiendo por una parte lo que no han hecho y por otra quitándoles la acción que tienen a sus cosas propias, daño que no solamente nos viene de otros reinos, sino de Cádiz y Sevilla. (Pérez de Montalbán, 1632)[40]

(The plays which have been printed up to now without my authorisation are false, full of lies, spurious and adulterated; because, since those who steal them have too little room to transcribe them, and those who print them buy them from the thieves, they appear full of nonsense, errors and barbarities, with no regard to the harm which is done to the authors, both in reputation and financially, as on one hand they print what they have not written and on the other they deprive the authors of the right to what is their own, a harm which comes to us not only from other kingdoms, but from Cadiz and Seville.)

V.m. la lea por mia, porque [esta comedia] no es impressa en Seuilla, cuyos Libreros, atendiendo a la ganancia, barajan los nombres de los Poetas, y a vnos dan sietes, y a otros sotas, que ay hombres, que por dinero no reparan en el honor ageno, que a bueltas de sus mal impressos libros venden, y compran. (Lope, 1634)[41]

(Let your worship read it as mine, for it is not printed in Seville, of which the booksellers, with an eye on profit, shuffle the names of poets, and deal out sevens to some and knaves to others, for there are men who, for the sake of money, pay no heed to the honour of others, which they buy and sell along with their ill-printed books.)

… el pesar de aver visto impressas algunas dellas antes de aora por hallarlas todas erradas, mal corregidas, y muchas que no son suyas en su nombre, y otras que lo son en el ageno. ('José Calderón', 1636)[42]

(… the grief of having seen some of them in print before now, because they were full of errors and badly corrected, and many under his name which are not his, and others which are his under someone else's.)

… para se conoscan [estas comedias] por mias, pues todas ellas ó las mas que se imprimen en Seuilla les dan los impressores el titulo que quieren y el dueño que se les antoja. (Antonio Enríquez Gómez, 1654)[43]

(… so that these plays may be recognised as mine, since the printers give the title they want and the author's name they fancy to all or most of those printed in Seville.)

Ay quien assegure, que casi todas quantas se imprimen en Seuilla, para passar à las Indias, las graduan con el nombre de Don Pedro, por interesses particulares que se les siguen à los que hazen cambio de los talentos agenos. (Juan de Vera Tassis, 1682)[44]

(Some assert that almost all those which are printed in Seville for export to the Indies are classified under the name of Don Pedro, because of the private profits which accrue to those who deal in the talents of others.)

***

We are conscious, in Don Pedro's early plays, of how frequently women become men's victims, whether their oppressors are married to them (Catalina/Enrique in *La cisma de Ingalaterra*, Mencía/Gutierre in *El médico de su honra*), related to them (Julia/Curcio in *La devoción de la cruz*, Fénix/Rey de Fez in *El príncipe constante*, Ángela/Luis in *La dama duende*) or simply ready to use force to rob them of their honour or their property (Estela/Eduardo in *Amor, honor y poder*, Clara/Garcés in *El Tuzaní de la Alpujarra*, Leonor/Juan in *No hay cosa como callar*, Dorotea/Gómez Arias in *La niña de Gómez Arias*). That this should be so in plays written in a male-dominated society is no surprise. What is more surprising is the number of women who are either clever enough or strong-willed enough to get what they want. The ruthless (Matilde, Semíramis) eventually come to a bad end, but the more principled, such as Estela (*Amor, honor y poder*), Cenobia (*La gran Cenobia*), Rosaura (*La vida es sueño*), Ángela (*La dama duende*) or Ana (*Mañanas de abril y mayo*), are successful. The last two, with contemporary settings in Madrid, are the most interesting. They can scarcely have been modelled on the poet's immediate family (his mother and his sister Dorotea), and we are left to guess where he might have encountered them.

CHAPTER 14

War and disillusionment

DENTRO UNOS	¡Viva nuestro invicto rey!
DENTRO OTROS	¡Viva nuestra libertad!
CLARÍN	¡La libertad y el rey vivan!
	Vivan muy enhorabuena. (*La vida es sueño*)

OFFSTAGE, SOME	Long live our unconquered king!
OFFSTAGE, OTHERS	Long live our liberty!
CLARÍN	Long live liberty, and the king!
	Long live, and the best of luck to them.

There is evidence, as early as 1634, that Richelieu was considering ways of using to France's advantage the discontent which Castilian rule aroused in many of the inhabitants of Portugal and Cataluña.[1] After the setback at Fuenterrabía, he turned his attention to the eastern end of the Pyrenees: in June 1639 Condé's army marched into Rosellón and besieged the fortress of Salces/Salsas, north of Perpiñán, near the coast. Unlike Fuenterrabía, Salces surrendered within weeks, on 19 July, and Olivares laid the blame on those Catalan *fueros* which, as he saw it, merely impeded the war effort. Salces would have to be retaken, and it duly was, in January 1640, but only at the cost of requisitioning supplies from the local population.

Among the casualties of the recapture of Salces was Don José Calderón, wounded, again in the leg, by a musket-ball, but not so severely that he felt the need to withdraw for treatment. As a result of this courage under fire, Philip IV promoted him to Captain in the Royal Guard, and awarded him a habit of one of the military Orders. The Order would have been Santiago, his brother's, but Don Pedro noted that 'aun para tratar de ponerse su Abito, no vino â la Corte, ni faltò de sus vanderas desde la primera entrada de Cataluña, hasta que murio' ('even in order to try to don his habit, he did not come to Madrid or leave his colours, from the first advance into Cataluña, until he died').[2] Like his brother before him, José would have needed to pay for a dossier to be compiled, but with no home leave, he never got the chance.[3]

When it emerged that Olivares planned to invade France from Cataluña, and that the invasion troops would be billeted on the local population until the campaign was ready, unrest began. The *fueros* stipulated that a billeted soldier was entitled to a bed and a table, with salt, vinegar and water: no food, no wine, no oil. Unable to comprehend that Catalan peasants could refuse to feed their saviours, Olivares demanded that the viceroy, the Count of Santa Coloma, himself a Catalan, should arrest at least one of the members of the *Diputació*. The arrest, on 18 March, and the razing, by the viceroy's order, of a village where a royal official had been killed, served only to mark Santa Coloma as a collaborator, a traitor to Catalan liberties. On 7 June, Corpus Christi, his viceregal palace was attacked and he was murdered while trying to escape. The rebellion might still be stoppable, but Olivares had no idea how to stop it; he was ready to make concessions, but not to the viceroy's killers.

Believing as he did that the Catalans and Portuguese had little reason for complaint, Olivares underestimated the hostility they felt to the government in Madrid and to himself in particular. Even as events were spiralling out of control in Cataluña, he was presiding over more circuses in the capital.

In February 1640 the Coliseo del Buen Retiro, the first Madrid theatre to be built as a theatre, was inaugurated:

> En quatro del dicho mes siguiente [i.e., 4 February] se estreno en el Buen Retiro el Coliseo y corral de comedias nuebo con jente que pago la entrada como en los demas corrales. Asistieron los Reyes y muchos señores. Empezo a representar Romero con la comedia de *Los bandos de Verona*.[4]
>
> (On 4 February was the opening of the Coliseo and new playhouse in the Buen Retiro, with people paying to get in, as in the other playhouses. The king and queen and many lords were present. Romero began performing with the play *Los bandos de Verona*.)

The closing lines of the text, Rojas Zorrilla's version of the Romeo and Juliet story, refer to 'tan grande Coliseo', such a great Coliseum, but there is nothing about the simple staging to indicate that Rojas was trying to take full advantage of the new facilities: the play could as well have been performed in one of the old public theatres, the *corrales*.

The account of the performance does indicate a departure from previous practice, however. Philip IV is said to have watched plays incognito in the *corrales*, the Príncipe and the Cruz; in the Coliseo, the presence of the royal family was official, another court occasion; but the new building was also a public theatre, with paying spectators. Not all the performances took place on the stage: to give the queen an 'authentic taste' of a public theatre, fake quarrels and fights were arranged:

Los Reyes se entretienen en el Buen Retiro, oyendo las Comedias en el Coliseo, donde la Reyna Nuestra Señora, mostrando gusto de verlas silbar, se ha ido haciendo con todas malas i buenas esta misma diligencia. Assí mismo, para que viesse todo lo que pasa en los Corrales en la Caçuela de las Mugeres, se ha representado bien al vivo, mesándose i arañándose vnas, dándose vaya otras, i mofándolas los mosqueteros. Han echado entre ellas Ratones en Caxas que, abiertas, saltavan.[5]

(The king and queen amuse themselves in the Buen Retiro, seeing the plays in the Coliseo, where, when the queen seemed to enjoy seeing them whistled [= booed], the same was done with all of them, good and bad. Likewise, so that she might see all that happens in the women's gallery in the playhouses, there was a very vivid performance, with some women tearing out others' hair, and scratching one another, while others jeered at each other and the groundlings made fun of them. They threw mice among them in boxes; when the boxes opened, the mice jumped around.)

Some of the fights were genuine. On Sunday 19 February, at a rehearsal of one of his plays, Don Pedro was involved in one:

El Domingo antecedente, estando ensayando las Comedias, en vnas Cuchilladas que se levantaron dieron algunas heridas a Don Pedro Calderón, su autor; que parece fue presagio de lo que sucedió el Lunes siguiente.[6]

(The previous Sunday, while they were rehearsing the plays, Don Pedro Calderón, their author, received some injuries in a sword fight which arose; it seemed to presage what happened the following Monday.)

Was Don Pedro trying to come between the combatants? The wording suggests that he could have been, but we are bound to wonder, say, if he could have gone so far as to draw a sword on an actor who refused to play his lines as he wanted. Seventeenth-century society was violent, no matter which country we examine. In Calderón's plays, men try to kill each other after a disagreement in a card game (e.g., *Antes que todo es mi dama*, *No hay cosa como callar*); a master draws a knife on a maidservant he thinks is a thief (*No hay cosa*). We shall never know exactly what happened, but the injuries cannot have been serious.

The remark about what happened the following Monday relates to a fire:

Su Excelencia tenia en el Retiro preuenida vna luzida fiesta, para Lunes, y Martes de Carnestolendas, y en el nueuo Coliseo luzidamente adornado y compuesto de modo, que no pudo la imaginacion alcançar mas, dos grandiosas Comedias, con extraordinarias Tramoyas, que su coste fueron dos mil ducados … A Don Pedro Calderon se dio el lauro deste trabajo … Lunes siguiente de Carnestolendas, este dia por la mañana, a las siete horas, y tres quartos se oyeron voces de incendio, que se quemaua el quarto de su Magestad.[7]

(His Excellency [Olivares] had prepared in the Retiro a splendid entertainment for Carnival Monday and Shrove Tuesday, and in the new Coliseo, so splendidly adorned and bedecked that one's imagination could reach no further, two magnificent plays, with extraordinary stage machines, which cost 2,000 ducats … Don Pedro Calderón received the laurels for this work … On the Monday, at 7.45 in the morning, voices were heard crying 'Fire!', that the king's quarters were burning.)

The queen's ladies were rescued by gentlemen of the court, and there were no human casualties, although the damage to the fabric and furnishings of the royal apartments was considerable. Olivares himself took charge of fighting the blaze, and that day's performance was cancelled. Shergold suggests that Monday's play was staged on Shrove Tuesday, in a performance lasting seven hours, but the phrase 'vieron las comedias prevenidas' ('they saw the planned plays') suggests that both were shown on the Tuesday, which would account for the lengthy performance time. Unfortunately, none of the documents gives any hint of which plays they were. The reference to 'extraordinarias Tramoyas' seems to exclude most of the undated plays which were written about this time: *La niña de Gómez Arias*, *La hija del aire I* and *II*, *Los empeños de un acaso*, *Basta callar*, *Fuego de Dios en el querer bien*. *El José de las mujeres* does require *tramoyas*, particularly involving the saint and the devil, but they do not seem to be extraordinary.

Four plays, now lost, have been associated with 1640. The first is *Certamen de amor y celos*, which Vera Tassis assigned to that year:

El [año] de 40. al salir las Ordenes Militares, le excusô [el rey], mandandole escriuir aquella cêlebre fiesta de, Certamen de Amor, y Zelos, que se representô en los Estanques de Buen Retiro, su honrado espiritu, y viuaz ingenio quiso cumplir con las dos obligaciones; pues en breue tiempo concluyô la Comedia, y tuvo lugar para seguirlas â Cataluña; assentando plaza en la Compañia del Excelentissimo señor Conde Duque de Oliuares.[8]

(In 1640, when the Military Orders left, and the king exempted him, ordering him to write that famous entertainment, *Certamen de amor y celos*, which was performed on the Buen Retiro lakes, his honourable spirit and lively mind wished to fulfil both obligations; for he finished the play in a short time and managed to follow them to Cataluña, enlisting in the company of the Count-Duke of Olivares.)

That is, the king allowed Don Pedro to delay his departure to Cataluña in order to write this play. Cotarelo is often scathing about Vera Tassis, and is so about this passage: 'Todo esto es falso', 'All this is false'.[9] However, Calderón's *memorial* on his military service, written around 1648, begins:

Don Pedro Calderon de la Barca Cauallero de la Orden de Santiago, dize: Que en veinte y ocho de Mayo passado de 640. se presentò montado para el seruicio de V. M. en la Caualleria de las Ordenes: y en veinte y nueue de Setiembre siguiente se agregò y començò a seruir en la Compañia de Cauallos Coraças del Conde Duque de San Lucar.[10]

(Don Pedro Calderón de la Barca, knight of the Order of Santiago, states that on 28 May 1640 he presented himself, mounted, for Your Majesty's service in the cavalry of the Orders; and on 29 September he joined and began to serve in the company of cuirassiers of the count-duke.)

Don Pedro presented himself four months before his service proper began, a delay which might be explained by the writing of a play. And Olivares was the Duke of Sanlúcar, so Vera Tassis is right about that detail; immediately before these lines he mentions how Philip granted Calderón a knighthood of Santiago in 1636, with the conferral taking place in 1637: another accurate detail. If he was also right about the venue of *Certamen*, it cannot have been one of the Carnival plays (in any case, performances on the lake were summer events); and a play ready for its final rehearsal on 19 February should have been completed around the end of January. The word 'cêlebre' is an exaggeration, since the only document to confirm that there was ever a play of this title is Calderón's Veragua list. (The omission from the Marañón list is almost certainly an error, and not significant.) But Vera Tassis is wrong in implying that Don Pedro was given leave to stay after his fellow knights had left: the knights did not leave until 1 October, although the four-month delay would have been quite long enough for the composition of a play.

A play entitled *No hay que creer ni en la verdad* has been claimed to be *Certamen de amor y celos*, but although it has some Calderón resonances, there is no allusion in the text to the supposedly correct title (for example, the contemporary *La desdicha de la voz* has several such references, a common practice, with Calderón and others).[11]

The one play which has documentary evidence for performance in 1640 was a collaboration work by Solís, Rojas and Calderón, performed on the Retiro lake on 2 July, the feast of St Elizabeth and Queen Isabel's birthday.[12] In this case not even the title has survived, since Calderón did not include collaboration plays in his lists, and no collaboration play of this authorship exists. This play cannot have been one of the Calderón plays planned for Carnival.

Cotarelo goes on to suggest that the two-part play *Nuestra Señora de la Almudena* dates from the summer of 1640, and was composed to mark the transfer of the image of the Virgin to the main altar of the church on 26 August.[13] This is plausible but unprovable.

Cotarelo also argues that the fire described by Federico (who rescues Serafina) at the beginning of *Las manos blancas no ofenden* was inspired by the blaze of 20 February, especially since Federico adds that 'dilató este acaso | saraos, justas y torneos' ('this accident postponed soirées, jousts and tourneys': II, 1083b). The claim is reasonable; the contention that the play must have been written in that year, less so.[14]

While the Coliseo was being completed and inaugurated, the *salón* of the old *alcázar* was receiving a major refurbishment: a gilt *artesonado* ceiling was installed, and a stage, also gilt; the walls were hung with thirty-two portraits of the kings of Castile, up to and including Philip IV. Thereafter, the room was known as the *salón dorado*. The contemporary account mentions a cost of 82,000 ducats.[15] When these 1640 accounts refer obsequiously to the 'jeneroso animo' ('generous spirit') of the king (the refurbishing of the *salón*) or to the effort expended by Olivares on the 'entretenimiento licito de su Rey, y señor, justo aliuio de la pesada carga y continuo trabajo, que consigo trae el gouierno de tan dilatada Monarquia' ('licit entertainment of his king and master, a just relief from the heavy burden and continuous toil that the government of such an extensive monarchy entails') (Carnival), they have a ring of 'protesting too much'. The mentions of the huge cost (2,000 ducats for two plays, 82,000 for the *salón*), while ostensibly intended to impress, arguably betray suppressed disapproval, while the detailed account of the damage done by the fire, with an estimated total cost of 'medio millon' (500,000), verges on the prurient.[16]

These extravagances were among the last of the Olivares regime. The Count-Duke would survive as *privado* for another three years, until January 1643, but 1640 was a turning-point, and Carnival of that year was the last of its kind. With the benefit of hindsight, we can see that belts should have been tightened before, perhaps years before, but communications were poor in the seventeenth century, and the government in Madrid was wilfully reluctant to believe that matters had deteriorated so much. Pellicer relates how a peasant harangued the king as he took part in a religious procession in June 1640, telling him that he was being deceived and that his monarchy was approaching its end; Philip's response was that the man must be mad.[17] Mad he was, if only for speaking out. And yet, when even the regime's supporters were revealing their subconcious feelings, we can only imagine what Calderón thought. There is no evidence that the news from Cataluña affected his output, at least until May, when he was called up. After May, his productivity declined and would never recover.

May was the usual deadline for *autos*, although Corpus is a movable feast, dependent on Easter. It is not clear how many *autos* and *loas* Calderón wrote in 1640. The two which he wrote for Madrid were *Los misterios de la misa* and *El juicio final*, which is lost.[18] *La hidalga del valle* was played in Valencia in 1634, but Cotarelo also records a performance in Granada in 1640.[19] His source confirms that the *auto* was not new in 1640, but if the *loa* is Don Pedro's, he wrote it for the occasion.[20] The Archivo de la Villa, Madrid, preserves a manuscript of *Psiquis y Cupido (para Toledo)*, which some scholars obstinately regard as autograph, since the scribe apparently copied the signature and the date, 12 May 1640.[21] Since Corpus fell nearly four weeks later, on 7 June, the *autor* would have had almost twice the twelve days Rosa said he needed to rehearse two *autos* in 1637 – allowing two days to get to Toledo. An examination of the text reveals errors typical of a copyist; the date is not quite as reliable as it would be in the author's own hand, but it is in keeping with the fact that Calderón presented himself for military service on 28 May.[22]

Other documents relating to this *auto* have survived in Toledo: a letter written on 29 April to Alberto de la Palma, one of the *regidores* of that city and a *comisario* (official organiser) for Toledo's *autos*, shows Don Pedro's awareness of the shortage of time, but he sends a copy of the *loa*, and assures Palma that in spite of his 'poca salud' ('poor health') and the need to 'acudir a los bandos de la rrelijión' ('turn up for the proclamations of religion'), he will send the text of the *auto* proper in eight days' time (on 7 May, presumably). The second reference is presumably to the proclamation requiring knights of the military orders to present themselves for service, but there is no other reference to an illness at this time. Calderón adds that 'haré antes la fiesta de Toledo que la de Madrid con estar encargado tanvién de la mitad de ella. Y que de aver por la salida de faltar a algo no será a vuestras mercedes' ('I shall do the Toledo fiesta before the Madrid one, although I'm also entrusted with half of that; and if I have to fail to do something because of leaving Madrid, I will not fail your worships').[23] He was evidently afraid that having to leave Madrid with the troops would prevent the fulfilment of his agreements, so it is worth noting that he puts the Toledo agreement first: there is some evidence, a year or two later, that his relations with the authorities in Madrid were not entirely good. If the surviving manuscript is accurately dated, however, he was not quite able to send the text on the date promised.

The second *auto* and *loa* were to be by Blas Fernández de Mesa, a local writer. Don Pedro does not name the *autor* who would perform his *auto*, apparently because he did not yet know who had been chosen: he warns Palma of the tendency among *autores* to promise more than they can perform ('ellos suelen hablar de sí apasionados', 'they get very enthusiastic when talking about themselves'), and requests a list of the whole company, with indications of which members were taking which parts, and which of them sang and danced.[24]

In October 1640 the Colegio Imperial celebrated the first centenary of the founding of the Jesuit Order. The festivities included a play with 'maravillosas tramoyas' ('wonderful machinery') designed by Cosme Lotti. Pellicer gives no title, but tells us that 'El propósito era los Progresos de la Compañía de Jesús, en estos Cien Años' ('The subject-matter was the progress of the Company of Jesus in the last hundred years').[25] No Calderón play matches this description. If the masters of the college thought of asking their distinguished former pupil to write a play for them, Don Pedro presumably declined because of his military commitments; by the time the play was performed, on Sunday 7 October, he was already on his way to Cataluña.

By 1640, or perhaps earlier, Don Pedro's *Primera parte* was *agotado*, as Spanish booksellers say, 'exhausted', and a second edition duly appeared that year, printed for another 'book merchant', Gabriel de León, by the widow of Juan Sánchez. As usual, the printer copied the preliminary documents from the first edition, including the original dedication. As a result, we have no idea of the publication date, beyond the '1640' on the title-page. We can assume, though, if the new edition took as long to print as the first (six months), that Calderón was still in Madrid when the process began. There is nothing in the texts to indicate that his presence involved corrections.

In 1641 the *Segunda parte* was also reprinted, this time by Carlos Sánchez for Antonio de Ribero. Since the original privilege was in Don Pedro's name, he presumably authorised the new edition, but he left it to Ribero to choose a new dedicatee, Felipe López de Oñate, one of the officials of the queen's household: his family was of Cantabrian origin, according to the dedication. On this occasion an effort was made to correct errors, but by Ribero or his printer, not the author, since some of the corrections are wrong.

The book merchants would have given Don Pedro little more for a reprinted volume of twelve plays than an *autor* would have paid him for a single new one, but he was not indifferent to their publication, or to the manner of it. In 1672, asked by an 'absent friend' to send some books, including volumes of plays, he wrote that

> acudi a buscarlos, y no solo hallè en sus impressiones, q[ue] ya no eran mias las que lo fueron; pero muchas que no lo fueron, impressas como mias, no contentandose

los hurtos de la prensa con añadir sus yerros a los mios, sino con achacarme los agenos.[26]

(I went in search of them, and in their prints found not only that those which were mine were mine no longer, but that many which were not, were printed as mine, and that the thefts of the press were not content with adding their errors to my own, but also attributed to me those of others.)

'O, señor,' he imagined a bookseller saying, 'que son coplas, y no alhajas, y no ay que hazer escrupulo de comprarlas, ni venderlas!' ('Oh, sir, they're poetry, not precious stones, and there's no need to worry about buying or selling them!': 2¶4^r). Nowadays, writers can assert their moral right to be identified as the author of what they have written. In 1616, when Calderón was a teenager, Lope de Vega had decided to publish the plays which he had written with only performance in mind. This was partly to prevent others from profiting from them, and partly because he was offended by the state of the texts which were already in print. At one point he went to law to prevent a publisher from printing texts which he had bought from the theatre-company manager to whom Lope had sold them. The publisher won.[27] The Council of Castile decided that while Lope had written them, he had been paid for them, and the new owner could dispose of them as he saw fit: the notion of intellectual property did not have a legal existence, although it was evidently very real for Don Pedro. However, despite his eloquence and unmistakable anger, we must recognise that some of the wrongs of which he complained were in his power to mend: he may have been obliged to cultivate an aristocratic indifference to the printing of his works, but this pretence need not have extended to a failure to check the texts he gave to the publishers, at least when he was in Madrid.

* * *

As the situation worsened in Cataluña, Olivares and the king planned to hold a session of the Catalan Cortes, beginning on 25 April. Preparations for the king's departure were in hand as early as February, but fears for his safety caused delays. Eventually it was decided that he must have a large military escort, including the 1,400 knights of the military orders, each of whom had to bring horse and saddle, pistols and cuirass: the pay was 20 *escudos* per month. Calderón's description of the first muster is clearly taken from a reference written for him in March 1641 by Don Pedro de Castillo Alvarado, whose job it was to keep the accounts:

Don Pedro de castillo Aluarado, caballero de la horden de s.tiago contt[ador] de la cav^{ia} de las hordenes militares, por el Rey nro señor: Certifico que por el cuaderno de cavalleros de todas las hordenes, que se formó en este oficio consta que Don pedro calderon de la barca, cavallero de la de S.tiago, se presentó montado en la villa de m^{d} en veinte y ocho de mayo pasado de seiscientos y quarenta; y en veinte y nueve de septiembre siguiente se agregó y començó á servir en la compp^{a} de cauallos corazas del señor conde duque de S. Lucar, capp^{n} g.^{l} de la cav^{ia} despaña, donde a continuado en todo lo que se a ofrecido hasta este dia, que lo queda haciendo en este campo, que se halla cuartelada la dha cavalleria, devuelta de barcelona, en el ex.^{to} de su mag.^{d} Y para que dello conste, á su pedimento doy la press^{te} en la villa de Reus del principado de cataluña. – A catorce de Março de seiscts y quar^{ta} y uno = D. P^{o} de castillo Aluarado.[28]

(Don Pedro de Castillo Alvarado, knight of the Order of Santiago and accountant of the cavalry of the military orders, by royal appointment: I certify that according to the record-book of the knights of all the orders which was drawn up in this post, it is on record that Don Pedro Calderón de la Barca, knight of that of Santiago, presented himself, mounted, in the town of Madrid on 28 May 1640; and on 29 September following he enlisted in and began to serve in the company of cuirassiers of the Count-Duke, Captain-General of the Cavalry of Spain, where he has continued in all that presented itself until today, and is still doing so in this camp in which the aforesaid cavalry is quartered on its return from Barcelona, in His Majesty's army. And so that it may be clear, at his request I am issuing the present letter in the the town of Reus in the principality of Cataluña: 14 March 1641: Don Pedro de Castillo Alvarado.)

In the event, the knights kicked their heels in barracks until 30 September, when the Patriarch of the Indies blessed their banners. Don Pedro's presence in Madrid on 23 August, and the absence he was shortly expecting, are confirmed by a document authorising a Juan Martínez de Roitegui to collect for him 1,500 *reales* owed him by the Duke of Infantado, his recent employer.[29] The knights finally set out on 1 October for Cataluña, not as a royal escort, but as part of an army which consisted of 35,000 infantry and 2,000 cavalry – or at least those were the numbers Olivares had planned for in June. The commander was Don Pedro Fajardo Zúñiga y Requesens, Marquis of Los Vélez. The marquis had been Viceroy of Valencia, but he had never commanded an army: he moved cautiously, even slowly, crossing into Cataluña only on 10 December. Once again, Don Pedro's own account is taken from a reference he requested, this time from his commanding officer. However, since he modestly suppressed his commander's praise, it seems best to quote the original, lengthy though it is:

D. Aluaro de quiñones caualllero de la horden de Santiago, del conss^{o} supremo de guerra de su mag^{d} y su theniente g.^{l} de la caualleria de las hordenes militares, gobernador y castellano de Cremona: Hago fe: que conozco á Don pedro calderon de la barca, cauallero de Santiago, soldado de la compañia de cauallos de las hordenes militares del Sr. conde duque, ntro. general. Despues que nuestro exercito entró en este principado de cataluña por el col de balaguer [10 December], allandose en todas las ocasiones que se an ofrecido, particularmente el dia que yo fui á tomar los puestos de cambrills [13 December], y rrompí tres mil hombres que el enemigo tenia emboscados, fuera de la plaça, y en la toma de ssalo [20 December] y villaseca, y quando con dha compp[a] y treinta arcabuceros á cauallo de la del comissario g.[l] Don Rodrigo de herrera fui a reconocer á constanti [21 December],[30] y á la retirada rrompí quinientos hombres, que salian de villaseca para ssocorro de tarragona, degollando la mayor parte dellos, donde dho Don pedro calderon se señaló y peleó como muy honrrado baliente cauallero y ssalio herido de una mano en dha ocassion; y las veces que yo fui á rreconocer á martorell [6–21 January 1641] fué uno de los treinta coraças que nombré para que con la compp[a] del capp[an] don juan de otto cerrasen con tres tropas del enemigo; y en esta ocassion se portó como de su persona y partes se podia esperar. Y lo mismo hizo en la rrota que alli se dio al enemigo, y el dia que nuestro exercito llegó á barcelona [23 January]. Y despues que se retiró á este campo de tarragona se a allado en las que se han ofrecido en él y en el sitio desta ciudad, particularmente el dia que el enemigo tuvo cortados seiscientos cauallos que yban a forragear; se alló en el puesto de las orcas que yo ocupaua con el resto de la caua[ia] [10 June], no faltando jamás á su estandarte, haciendo algunos servicios particulares. Y el dia que el S.[r] marq[s] de villafranca metió el ssocorro en esta plaça [4 July], assistió á la marina sin faltar un punto con mucho rriesgo ayudando á facilitar el saccar el bastimento á tierra. Y en todo lo demas que se a ofrecido a procedido muy a ssatisfaccion de sus superiores y a cumplido con las obligaciones de su sangre: es persona de prouecho en el seruicio de su mag[d], y en quien será muy bien empleada qualquiera mrd que su mag[d] fuere seruido de hacerle. Y a su pedimento doy la presente firmada de mi mano y sellada con el sello de mis armas en tarragona a 19 de ott[e] 1641.[31]

(I, Don Álvaro de Quiñones, knight of the Order of Santiago, member of His Majesty's Supreme Council of War and his lieutenant general of the cavalry of the military orders, governor and warden of the castle of Cremona, bear witness to the fact that I know Don Pedro Calderón de la Barca, knight of Santiago, soldier in the company of cavalry of the military orders of our general the count-duke. After our army entered this principality of Cataluña by the Col de Balaguer, he was involved in all the opportunities which have presented themselves, especially the day when I went to take the positions of Cambrils and broke through 3,000 men whom the enemy had in ambush outside the fortress, and in the capture of Salou and Vilaseca, and when, with the aforesaid company and thirty mounted aquebusiers from the company of the commissary general Don Rodrigo de Herrera I went to reconnoitre Constantí, and during the withdrawal I broke through 500 men who were coming out of Vilaseca to relieve Tarragona, massacring most of them, where the aforesaid Don Pedro Calderón distinguished himself and fought like a very honourable brave gentleman, and on this occasion was wounded in the hand; and on the occasions when I went to reconnoitre Martorell, he was one of the thirty cuirassiers I named to close with the enemy troops, along with the company of Don Juan de Otto; and on this occasion he behaved as might be expected of his person and talents. And he did the same in the rout inflicted on the enemy there, and on the day when our army reached Barcelona. And after the withdrawal to this camp of Tarragona, he was involved in the action which presented itself there and in the siege of the city, particularly on the day when the enemy cut off 600 cavalry who were foraging; he was present at the position of Las Horcas which I was occupying with the rest of the cavalry, never leaving his standard, performing special services. And the day when the Marquis of Villafranca relieved this fortress, he was present on the beach without failing in any way and at great risk to himself, helping to get the supplies ashore. And in everything else which has presented itself, he has proceeded to the great satisfaction of his superiors and fulfilled the obligations of his status. He is a worthy person in His Majesty's service, and one well deserving of any favour which His Majesty may be pleased to bestow on him. And at his request I provide the present letter signed with my hand and sealed with the seal of my arms, in Tarragona, 19 October 1641.)

Don Pedro omitted the references to fighting like an honourable and brave gentleman, to behaving as he might be expected to, and to deserving any favour which the king might see fit to bestow on him, although he did add that, like his brother, he fought on without having his wound treated.[32] The brothers almost certainly had opportunities to meet: both were present in the attack on Montjuic (Barcelona), both formed part of the force besieged in Tarragona, and both were involved in the fighting at Las Horcas. Perhaps the most touching detail is that José was one of the 600 cavalrymen whom Don Pedro helped to rescue when they were cut off by superior forces while foraging: he gives the credit to the diversionary tactics of Don Fernando de Ribera, but adds that his brother 'se retirô sin perder soldado', 'withdrew without losing a man'.[33]

In his reference, Don Álvaro was happy to expatiate on his own successes, and on Don Pedro's role in them, although he glossed over the unexpectedly tame surrender of Tarragona by the Duke d'Espenan on 24 December 1640; and he made no criticism of Los Vélez's equally unexpected withdrawal from Montjuic a month later, when victory was supposedly within the grasp of the royalist troops.[34] By this time Pau Claris, president of the *Diputació*, had formally placed the principality under the protection of Louis XIII, and Portugal had also risen.

On 7 December 1640 news reached Madrid that the Portuguese nobles, or most of them, had proclaimed the Duke of Bragança King John IV. Miguel de Vasconcelos, the chief instrument of Castilian rule in Lisbon, had been murdered, ostensibly because he was planning to introduce a hearth tax which was already causing trouble in Castile. The reaction of Olivares was disbelief, incoherence verging on hysteria, and paranoia which nourished a desire for vengeance. When Pau Claris died on 27 February 1641, he was said to have been poisoned; Bragança's brother, supposedly the chief instigator of the Portuguese revolt, was to be taken dead or alive, and the count-duke even considered arranging for the Portuguese envoy to England to be assassinated. It was while he was in this mood that our poet was entrusted with carrying dispatches to him.

Don Pedro was entitled to some leave, and may have requested Don Álvaro's reference with the intention of seeking permission to return to Madrid. Shortly after the reference was written, Don Pedro was asked by the Marquis of La Hinojosa to take dispatches to the capital. The previous marquis had been a close friend of Olivares;[35] his successor may have chosen the poet because he was known to the minister, and also, presumably, because he trusted him. Not all the details were committed to paper ('se auian de tratar a boca', 'they were to be dealt with verbally', wrote Calderón in his *memorial*), but the mission was not exactly secret:

> Vino Don Pedro Calderón de la Barca, Cavallero del Orden de Sant-Iago, embiado por el Señor Marqués de la Hinojosa desde Tarragona, a dar quenta a Su Magestad del estado de aquel Exército, i de la Forma con que le tenía dispuesto. También de cómo se havía reformada la Cavallería, por estar los soldados desmontados, dejando solos algunos Capitanes de los de más experiencia. Trujo las Listas del Exército que llega a nueve mil Hombres, las Plantas de la Plaça con todo lo concerniente a esta materia. Passó al Escorial donde estava Su Magestad (Dios le guarde), y bolvió en el Coche del Señor Conde Duque, haciéndole Relación de todo con mucha Puntualidad, i del Cange o trueco que piden los Catalanes de Prisioneros de vna parte a otra.[36]

> (There arrived Don Pedro Calderón de la Barca, knight of the Order of Santiago, sent by the Marquis of La Hinojosa from Tarragona, to give His Majesty an account of the state of that army, and of the manner in which he had disposed it; also of how the cavalry had been reformed, because the soldiers were dismounted, apart from only a few of the most experienced captains. He brought the lists of the army, which comes to 9,000 men, and the plans of the fortress with everything relating to that material. He went to the Escorial, where His Majesty was (God preserve him), and returned in the coach of the count-duke, giving him an account of everything with great exactness, including the exchange of prisoners requested by the Catalans.)

The 9,000 men is far short of the 37,000 Olivares had intended to send, although there had been considerable casualties by this time. Pellicer could have got this information from Don Pedro, or from one of the aides who may have been present. However, Calderón could hardly have contributed a sonnet to Pellicer's *Anfiteatro* in 1631 without the two men becoming acquainted: the most likely source of his information about the poet's meeting with Olivares in November 1641 was Don Pedro himself.

Calderón remained in Madrid for several months, as we know from the autograph manuscript of *El secreto a voces*, dated in Madrid on 28 February 1642, and written 'para Antonio de Prado'. Ash Wednesday fell on 5 March, so the play was not licensed until 2 June.

There is no record that Olivares revised any plans on the basis of the information Calderón brought him. The king, on the other hand, apparently working alone, drafted a paper on the state of affairs in Cataluña, and on 27 December sent it to the Junta Grande for consideration.[37] He argued that the time was ripe for him to visit Aragón in person, thanks to the recent successes of royalist troops in Rosellón and Tarragona (he was perhaps thinking of the defeat of the French attempt to retake the city, a defeat of which Don Pedro could have given him a participant's account). But there were other factors at work: Philip had been shocked by the discovery, in August–September, of a plot led by the Duke of Medina Sidonia and the Marquis of Ayamonte. The aims of the plot are not clear. One rumour held that the intention was to make the duke 'King of Andalusia', but a more likely aim was to induce Philip to remove Olivares. The news of the death, on 9 November 1641, of the Cardinal-Infante Ferdinand, Philip's only surviving brother, shocked the king even more: he broke down and wept. Calderón's information may have influenced him, but the principal motivation for Philip's decision to become more involved was probably a combination of grief and guilt, sharpened by the knowledge that if he had taken a more active role in government himself, he could have curtailed that of his unpopular minister.

If Philip was beginning to think of how Spain would be ruled when his minister had gone, Olivares aided the process: his health worsened, and, always a hypochondriac in the modern sense, he complained more: he only wanted to retire, or even to die. If we compare portraits made near the beginning of his ministerial career (Plate 28) with those made towards the end, such as that now in the Hermitage (1637–8), the effects of more than a decade of responsibility are obvious.[38] That he was hated by many of his fellow nobles was common knowledge, and his emotional overreaction to news, good or bad (and most of it was bad) had not gone unnoticed. In December 1642, as he returned from Zaragoza, students in Alcalá would shout insults as the minister's coach passed through the streets.[39] We have no idea whether there were any such incidents on the 27-mile coach trip from El Escorial to Madrid in November 1641, or how Olivares appeared to Don Pedro, closeted with him for two hours or more. What we do know is that the writer described his subsequent military service in the briefest terms:

Y despues quando se formaron las Compañias de la Guardia de V. Magestad por el año de seiscientos y quarenta y dos, para la jornada de Zaragoza, sentò su plaza en la del Conde de Oropesa, y con ella marchò gouernando vna Esquadra, y assistio a las cosas que se le ordenaron, con toda fineza y puntualidad.[40]

(And afterwards, when the companies of Your Majesty's guard were formed in 1642 for the trip to Zaragoza, he enlisted in that of the Count of Oropesa, and marched with it in charge of a squad, and attended to the things he was ordered to, with all nicety and exactness.)

Philip left Madrid on 26 April, but not immediately for Aragón: he went to Loeches, where the Countess of Olivares entertained his party for three days, then to his own palace at Aranjuez. He finally left for Aragón on 23 May, although he did not reach Zaragoza until 27 July.[41] As a member of one of the companies of the royal guard, Calderón accompanied the king, and was given command of an *escuadra* ('25 soldiers', according to Minsheu):[42]

Don Pedro de Porres y Toledo, cauallero del avito de Santiago, gentil hombre de la boca de su mag.[d] y su capitan de caballos coraças españoles, teniente de la compañia del conde de Oropesa, una de las de la nobleça despaña, y guarda de su Mag.[d]

Certifico, que Don pedro calderon de la barca, cauallero del avito de Santiago, a seruido esta campaña con toda puntualidad, y por haberle allado mi capitan por soldado mas meremerito [*sic*] le nombró por cavo descuadra, y sirvió la dha escuadra como muy honrrado y baliente cauallero; y assi le juzgo meremerito [*sic*] de toda la mrd que su mag[d] fuese servido de hacerle... Çaragoça a beinte y ocho de octubre de mil y seiscientos y quarenta y dos años.[43]

(I, Don Pedro de Porres y Toledo, knight of the Order of Santiago, gentleman-in-waiting of His Majesty and his captain of Spanish cuirassiers, lieutenant in the company of the Count of Oropesa, one of those of the nobility of Spain and guard of His Majesty, certify that Don Pedro Calderón de la Barca, knight of the Order of Santiago, has served in this campaign with all exactness, and since my captain found him a most worthy soldier, he put him in charge of a squad, and he served the squad like a very honourable and gallant gentleman; and so I judge him worthy of all the favour which His Majesty may be pleased to show him. Zaragoza, 28 October 1642.)

Like that of Don Álvaro de Quiñones, the reference did not draw unnecessary attention to military failure. When news came of the fall of Perpiñán, on 10 September, to the French, Philip had decided on Lérida for a counter-stroke. The army led by the Marquises of Mortara and Torrecuso (which included Don José Calderón) would move north-west from

Tarragona, while that of the Marquis of Leganés (the cousin of Olivares) would march east from Zaragoza to meet them at Lérida. After initial dawdling, Leganés made his men march all through the night of 6–7 October, in the vain hope of achieving surprise: 20,000 royalist troops encountered the waiting 13,000 French and 1,000 Catalans early in the morning of 7 October. Although they had some initial successes, the exhausted Castilian troops suffered more and more casualties. At nightfall, after twenty-four hours without sleep or food, they withdrew, despite causing heavy French losses. The person blamed was Leganés, although some of the blame was attached to the minister himself, because of their relationship. Philip sacked Leganés, but also blamed himself.

According to Cotarelo, the battle began with the Castilian troops taking up position on the plain of Las Horcas; the first assault on the French, dug in with their guns on a hill called Cuatro Pilares, was led by Don Rodrigo de Herrera with 300 horse, among them Don Pedro: they captured a battery, and even managed to bring it back to their own lines. In his *memorial*, however, Don Pedro attributes this action to his brother, and makes no mention of himself:

Y el dia que el Marques de Leganès peleò en las Horcas de Lerida subio [Don José Calderón] gouernando su Tercio con el del Conde de Basto ... donde puso en fuga el enemigo, y le ganô la artilleria.[44]

(And on the day when the Marquis of Leganés fought at las Horcas de Lérida Don José Calderón went up in charge of his regiment, with that of the Count of Basto ... where he put the enemy to flight, and captured his artillery.)

Perhaps Cotarelo confused Las Horcas (a hill near Tarragona), where both brothers were involved, with Las Horcas de Lérida, the name used by Don Pedro to avoid such confusion.[45]

When Calderón asked Don Pedro de Porres for his reference three weeks after this battle, he was in Zaragoza, 90 miles from Lérida. He may already have been ill, his request prompted by the belief that he would soon have to make another, more momentous one. On 15 November Olivares himself granted the second request and signed a release document:

Por quanto Don Pedro Calderón, Soldado de la compañia de cavallos del batallon de la nobleza de la guardia de su Mag.[d] del duque de Pastrana, nos ha pedido le demos licencia para irse á curar adonde tuviese mas comodidad para ello; atento á hallarse con achaques de calidad que le imposibilitan el continuar el R[l] servicio: Constandonos ser assi lo referido: hemos tenido por bien de concederle, como por la presente le concedemos, la licencia que pide para el dho effecto. Y della se tomará la razon en los libros del sueldo por los ministros á quienes toca. Dada en Çaragoça a 15 de Nov.^{e} de 1642. – Don Gaspar de Guzman.[46]

(Inasmuch as Don Pedro Calderón, soldier in the cavalry company of the Duke of Pastrana's batallion of His Majesty's noble guard, has asked us to give him permission to go for treatment where he may do so with more convenience, mindful that he is suffering from indispositions of a nature which make impossible his continuing in the royal service; verifying that this is so, we have considered it appropriate to grant him, as we hereby do, the permission for the aforesaid. And it will be recorded in the paybooks by those whose job it is. Given in Zaragoza on 15 November 1642: Don Gaspar de Guzmán.)

The illness was never specified, and neither Don Pedro nor his superiors made any reference to taking part in the battle of Lérida. If he was suffering from what we now call 'post-traumatic stress syndrome', the cause cannot have been that battle. Both the Olivares document and Don Pedro's, with its reference to a 'passport', indicate that he was able to travel:

hasta que por hallarse muy enfermo, y impossibilitado del manexo de las Armas, y reconociendolo V. Magestad assi por su Real Cedula de veinte y seis de Nouiembre de seiscientos y quaranta y dos le dio licencia para retirarse a curar a donde mas comodidad tuuiese, y passaporte para los puertos de Castilla.[47]

(until, because he was very ill and unable to bear arms, and Your Majesty, recognising this by his royal warrant of 26 November 1642, gave him permission to withdraw for treatment where he might do so with more convenience, and a passport for passage into Castile.)

Neither document refers specifically to a permanent discharge, but Calderón's military service was over. Presumably he reached Madrid a few days before Olivares and the king, who left Zaragoza on 1 December.

Apart from his *memorial*, the references of his superior officers and the count-duke's letter of permission, there is one other Catalan war document which should be mentioned here: the *Conclusión defendida por un soldado del campo de Tarragona del ciego furor de Cataluña*. This pamphlet was printed anonymously in Pamplona in 1641, but Zudaire presents arguments that it was written by Calderón.[48] The best of these is a sentence in Pellicer's *Idea del principado de Cataluña*:

No merece olvido otro papel que se estampó con Nombre de un Soldado de Cataluña, cuyo Auctor es don Pedro Calderón de la Barca; donde igualó la fuerça de la razón con la delgadeça del Ingenio.[49]

(Another document which was printed under the name of 'a soldier of Cataluña' should not be forgotten: its author is Don Pedro Calderón de la Barca, and in it he equalled the force of reason with the keenness of intellect.)

Pellicer (1602–79) had been appointed *Coronista de Castilla* in 1629, *Coronista de Aragón*, his native kingdom, in 1637, and *Coronista del Reino* in 1640. He took a lively interest in current events, commenting on them as well as recording them. There is good reason to suppose that he and Calderón were acquainted. The text of the *Conclusión* indicates that it must have been written before 26 January 1641, nine months before the Olivares meeting. If the anonymous pamphlet described by Pellicer as written by a 'soldier of Cataluña' is the same as that produced by a 'soldier of the field of Tarragona' (and there are no other candidates), then we have to concede that Pellicer's attribution is probably correct because it is likely to be based on personal information. Pellicer's remarks about the author's force of reasoning and keenness of intellect are accurate: the prose reads like Don Pedro's, and there is a significant reference to books in the opening paragraph: 'Permitasele a un soldado que te escriue [he is addressing the Principality of Cataluña] desde la campaña, más atento a la obediencia militar, que a los libros que olvidé' ('Allow a soldier to write to you from the field, more heedful of military obedience than of the books I have forgotten').[50]

As we have seen, Calderón was among the Castilian troops who occupied Tarragona when the French gave it up in December 1640. We must consider him a strong candidate for authorship of the *Conclusión*. The Pamplona imprint may raise doubts, since Pamplona is over 200 miles from Tarragona, but if Calderón sent the text to his brother Diego, asking him to have it printed anonymously in Madrid, it is quite possible that the printer took similar precautions with a false imprint. This possibility cannot be checked until a copy is traced, but at least one other item written in the 1640s about the struggle with France was given a false Pamplona imprint.[51]

* * *

The Madrid of December 1642 was very different from the Madrid Don Pedro had left in October 1640, and was about to differ even more. Far from planning festivities for Carnival, Philip was summoning up the courage to govern without Olivares. On 17 January 1643, from the safe distance of his hunting-lodge at La Torre de la Parada, on his El Pardo estate, he sent his minister a note saying that he was acceding to the repeated requests to be allowed to retire. At first Olivares remained in Madrid, but on 23 January, the day after Philip's return to the capital, he left for his house in Loeches, some 18 miles east of Madrid. The creator and governor of the Retiro, the venue for so many of Don Pedro's successes, was gone, and with him, effectively, the promotion and sponsorship of court drama, at least for the foreseeable future.

The end of this flowering of court plays deprived Calderón of a major source of income, but not all of his livelihood had gone. He still had the *autos sacramentales* and the public theatres to fall back on. Not surprisingly, Don Pedro wrote none of the four *autos* of 1641: two of them were written by Rojas Zorrilla, who was free to remain in Madrid, since he was not yet a member of a military order.[52] In 1642 Calderón wrote at least one *auto*, *El divino cazador*, for Madrid, to judge from the actors (from Prado's company, which was then in the capital) named in the autograph manuscript, and two *autos* for Toledo.[53]

On 16 March 1643, Don Antonio de Contreras, who was in charge of Madrid's Corpus festivities, wrote that 'Pareceme muy bien que escriba D. Pedro Calderon, que yo lo habia deseado y quise procurarlo como saben algunos caballeros' ('It seems very appropriate to me that Don Pedro Calderón should write, for I had wished it, and tried to arrange it, as some gentlemen know').[54] This wording can be taken to mean that by the middle of March Don Pedro had only just indicated that he was willing to write an *auto* or *autos* for Madrid that year, although Corpus (4 June) was then only ten weeks away. He may have been waiting to be persuaded. While he was waiting, he wrote *Llamados y escogidos*, but not for Madrid: the recently rediscovered manuscript shows that he wrote it to be played in Toledo by Pedro de la Rosa, and that the text was licensed there on 20 May 1643.[55] The licence, granted by Andrés Fernández de Hipenza, bishop-elect of Yucatán, referred to 'estos autos', 'these *autos*', and gave permission 'para que se puedan representar en esta ciudad', 'for them to be performed in this city'. That is, there was at least one other *auto*, although we cannot be certain that it was Don Pedro's, or that it was new. It may be that the illness which prompted his discharge from the army was not entirely physical, and that he found it hard to write two *autos* for Toledo and two for Madrid in the five months from December 1642 to April 1643. Other factors influenced his output, however. There had always been some individuals, most of them churchmen, who disapproved of playhouses in principle. The fact that a portion of the playhouses' income was devoted to maintaining the public hospitals had weakened their arguments, but as the 'excesses' continued while Spain was visibly doing badly in a war of religion, they became more vociferous. Calderón may have been making a point, the same point as he was to make a decade later in his letter to the Patriarch: if the authorities wanted him to write *autos*, they should not make it difficult for him to write plays.

If Don Pedro was making a point in being slow to write for Madrid, the authorities missed it. Ostensibly he allowed himself to be persuaded to write one *auto* for the capital, *La sierpe de metal*, which may have been an early version of *La serpiente de metal* (1676),[56] but in 1644 the Council of Castile recommended

> [q]ue las comedias se reduxesen á materias de buen exemplo, formándose de vidas y muertes exemplares, de hazañas valerosas ... y que todo esto fuese sin mezcla de amores; que para conseguirlo se prohibiesen casi todas las que hasta entonces se habían representado, especialmente los libros de Lope de Vega, que tanto daño habían hecho en las costumbres.[57]

> (that plays should be restricted to subjects which set a good example, consisting of exemplary lives and deaths, of valiant deeds, and that all this should be with no admixture of love affairs; that in order to achieve this almost all those which had been performed so far should be banned, especially the books of Lope de Vega, which had caused such harm to people's behaviour.)

The principal mover of this document was the same Don Antonio de Contreras who had wanted Don Pedro to write *autos* a few months earlier. The curious wording he chose on that occasion could be taken as a desire to indicate that his known opposition to some aspects of the public theatres did not extend to Calderón as a writer of *autos*.

Hilborn has assigned several plays (*Las manos blancas no ofenden*, *El alcalde de Zalamea*, *Primero soy yo*, *El José de las mujeres*, *Fuego de Dios en el querer bien*) to the period 1640–4,[58] but the second of these is probably of 1636, while only *El José de las mujeres* would meet with the full approval of the Council. It seems likely that all the others were composed before May 1642. Those which have not been dealt with already may be examined here.

As noted previously, one of the events described in *Las manos blancas* may have been inspired by the Retiro fire of February 1640. Federico, who believed he would inherit the principality of Ursino, has been passed over by the emperor in favour of his cousin Serafina. The Council of Ursino was willing to accept her as princess, if she married within a year. Believing that his relationship with Lisarda, daughter of the Guelph Enrique, had no clear future, since he was a Ghibelline, Federico visited Ursino and fell for Serafina. After rescuing her, fainting, from a palace fire, he retained one of her jewels, in the hope of using it to reveal himself as her rescuer at a suitable moment.

Described in these terms, the first stages of the plot are unexceptional enough, but Serafina's beauty, and her status, have attracted other suitors. One of them is César, Prince of Orbitelo, shielded from the world by his overprotective mother. Shielded he may have been, but he has seen Serafina, who spent one night as a house-guest of his mother. His meeting with her was brief, but he managed to watch her prepare for bed through a keyhole. He describes at length to his tutor Teodoro how she undid her jet-black hair, describes her overskirt, her underskirt ... This is one of Calderón's most erotic passages: a beautiful young woman undressing. As if conscious of how the censors might react, he has César abbreviate his description out of respect for the elderly Teodoro: next moment Serafina is in bed, but not without a reference to 'nácar' and 'jazmines' ('nacre, jasmines': II, 1088a): euphemisms for bare skin. It is hard to avoid the suspicion that this is a record of personal experience, a record of the excitement felt by a young man watching an attractive woman disrobe. Not seen through a keyhole, perhaps, but seen by the poet, and for his benefit.

The direction to be taken by the plot is hinted at by the song which his mother's ladies sing to César:

> De Deidamia enamorado,
> hermosísimo imposible,
> en infantes años tiernos
> estaba el valiente Aquiles. (II, 1085b)

(The valiant Achilles, unattainably handsome, in his tender years was in love with Deidamia).

It was noted above that a Calderón play entitled *La dama y galán Aquiles* was in existence by 1644, and might date from 1639. As this part of the Achilles myth suggests, César will dress as a woman. He does not intend to maintain his disguise: the intention is merely to escape from his mother, but subsequent circumstances force him to retain his female role in Urbino. By the time he reveals his escape plan, we already know that the rejected Lisarda intends to pursue Federico to Urbino, dressed as a man, and that she has managed to steal Serafina's jewel from him: the theft and her dress cast her in the role of a potential suitor. To be more convincing, she will not be just any man: she chooses a real person, one who she thinks will never reach Urbino, because he will never escape from his protective mother: her cousin César. The stage is set not merely for cross-dressing, but for some very ambiguous relationships, as Serafina is courted by the false César (i.e., Lisarda) and by the real one (i.e., 'Celia'). The plot is further complicated by Serafina's acceptance of a plan to have her courtiers and guests perform a play, which adds a further degree of role-playing, as well as giving César the opportunity to say what he really feels while pretending to act a part.

The plot requires César to sing on several occasions. Serafina finds his singing particularly attractive, and so she is delighted that he should take the lead in a musical play, 'a usanza | de Italia' ('in the Italian fashion': II, 1096a). César too is pleased: taking the lead will mean playing a male role: 'me holgaré me veas | en el traje de galán | cantar amantes finezas' ('I'll be delighted for you to see me singing a lover's compliments in male dress': II, 1096a). This so appeals to Serafina that she promises to choose his costume. This is apparently Calderón's first reference to Italian 'musical plays'. In *El laurel de Apolo* (1658), the character Zarzuela describes the forthcoming performance as 'una fábula pequeña, | en que, a imitación de Italia, | se canta, y se representa' ('a little fable, in which, in imitation of Italy, there is singing and acting').[59] However, his first experiment in the genre was *El jardín de Falerina* (?1649), in which only 7 per cent of the lines are sung.

Since the date of *Las manos blancas* is uncertain, we do not know who took the roles in the first performance. What we do know is that male roles in which singing was required were most frequently taken by women.[60] That this was the case with César is suggested by his reference to his long plaited hair and lack of beard:

presumo que la misma
Naturaleza se agravia,
quejosa de que el cabello
crecido y trenzado traiga,
y por eso no ha querido
brotar, Teodoro, en mi cara
aquella primera seña
que a la juventud esmalta. (II, 1087a)

(I presume that Nature herself is offended, querulous because I wear my hair long and plaited, and for that reason that first sign which adorns youth has not wished to bud on my face.)

Since Serafina is aged twenty ('cuatro lustros': II, 1082b), César is presumably not a beardless aristocrat seeking to marry in his early teens, as often happened in real life. When Calderón was planning the character, he knew an actress would take the role. Far from trying to conceal this from the spectators, he drew it to their attention, thus inviting them to contemplate yet another layer of male–female role-playing. He was also aware that the actress playing Serafina would have very dark hair. That is, he knew, as on other occasions, which company would perform his play; he also knew who his audience would be, as the closing lines suggest:

Ahora harto que hacer tienen [los oyentes]
en perdonarnos las faltas,
y las del que más pretende

> serviros siempre, pues yerra
> a cuenta de que obedece. (II, 1124b)

(Now the audience has enough to do in forgiving our faults, and those of him who most seeks to serve you, since he errs in exchange for obeying.)

The play was probably intended for a royal audience, including the king in particular, as implied by César's metaphor 'descanse un rato la cuerda' ('let the bowstring rest for a little': II, 1095a), used elsewhere by Calderón to suggest the monarch's right to relaxation.[61] We cannot tell whether the obedient author was given instructions about the kind of play that would be found pleasing.

Part of Serafina's 'flirting' with César, an actress playing a man dressed as a woman, involves discussing her suitors: she admits that Federico repels her least, because he hints at having rescued her. But when César rehearses the scene when Hercules wears female attire because of his infatuation with Yole, he does so with such passion that she is embarrassed:

> Calla, calla: no prosigas;
> que ya no puedo sufrir
> de la duda si es aquesto
> representar o sentir. (II, 1107b)

(Hush, hush, don't go on; I can't stand wondering whether this is acting or feeling.)

Calderón would dramatise the Hercules/Yole myth in *Fieras afemina Amor* (played for Queen Mariana in January 1672), but there is no evidence for an early version around 1640. Just as he often referred to plays he had written, however, he sometimes referred to plays which he was thinking of writing, such as the second parts of *Judas Macabeo* and *Luis Pérez el gallego*.

Patacón describes the venue for the performance of Serafina's play in terms which fit the *salón dorado*, which Vera Tassis gives as the venue for this play in the *Octava parte* (1684), although he may have been referring to a later production. However, the venue of the premiere is possibly confirmed by Federico's earlier references to Serafina sitting on a throne in the *salón* of her palace, as well as to a *dorado artesón*. The play introduces an additional complication: Serafina's guests are wearing *máscaras*. When Serafina drops her glove, there is a scramble among her suitors to pick it up. Lisarda, still dressed as a man but unrecognisable in different clothing and her mask, is made furiously jealous by Federico's participation in the scramble. She not only slaps his face but contradicts his claim that he has a right to pick up the glove with the fatal word '¡Mientes!' ('You lie!': II, 1114a). Immediately realising the gravity of what she has done, she lets him glimpse the face behind her mask. Even the bystanders are outraged by the insult to Federico, and ready to take his vengeance for him, as he hesitates. Federico does his best: he will not give Lisarda away, especially since her father is present, but he reveals the delicate female hand which struck him: *Las manos blancas no ofenden*. Even this knowledge is not enough for all of the onlookers: for one courtier to strike another in the presence of the head of state is an offence, and Serafina is offended (and made jealous by the discovery that there is another woman in Federico's life). Federico has to rescue Lisarda, and to continue to protect her. Dramatic plots from *The Taming of the Shrew* to *The African Queen* have been based on situations which throw together a couple who either dislike each other intensely or who are having a furious quarrel: the progress from hate, through toleration, to admiration and fondness, has great dramatic potential, and Don Pedro used such situations in comedy after comedy. Federico's gallantry to one who has done him such damage (although with understandable motives) prepares us for their eventual reconciliation. Even when everyone's identity is revealed, however, Prince Carlos (another Serafina suitor) and Federico are unhappy about the thought that César, in his female disguise, may have seen more of Serafina than was proper for a gentleman:

Traición
más grave es que te atrevieses
a asistir a Serafina
tan de cerca, que pudiesen
familiarmente tus ojos
tal vez … (Carlos, II, 1123b)

No lo digas, tente;
que se ajan los decoros
aun sólo con que se piensen. (Federico, ibid.)

(It is a more serious betrayal that you dared to attend Serafina so closely that perhaps your eyes might familiarly… *Federico*: Don't say it, stop; for proprieties are disparaged just by being thought about.)

Unlike Carlos and Federico, the spectators have done more than merely think these thoughts: César has already told them that he saw more of Serafina than he should. The text does not prove that she guesses this, but she knows that he used his disguise to take liberties, kissing her hand; and anyway, she liked him, even when she thought he was female. She gives him her hand.

A character who pretends to be someone else, and dresses appropriately, is a common feature of plot-making, an extra level of irony in what is already a performance. Calderón had often written roles of this kind, the best example being Rosaura (*La vida es sueño*, ?1630), who plays a young man, a lady-in-waiting, and herself. The exploration of the feminine side of men and the masculine side of women was one of his ongoing preoccupations. But if *La dama y galán Aquiles* and *Las manos blancas* do date from 1639 and 1640, they suggest a desire at this time to explore sexual role-playing in particular. This is partially confirmed by Patacón's joke about 'lo tapado y lo escondido | … | este paso está ya hecho ' ('the veiled and the hidden … that passage has been done already': II, 1079a), an almost certain reference to *El escondido y la tapada* (1635–6), in which the *gracioso* Mosquito dresses as a woman. Unfortunately, we can only speculate about the content of *Certamen de amor y celos*, another '1640' play, which Serafina apparently alludes to in the context of the competition for her hand ('certamen de amor', 'contest of love', II, 1089b). Other literary references are to Góngora's ballads, 'Cuatro o seis desnudos hombros' (1614: 'hurta un poco sitio al mar | y mucho agradable en él'; 'cuatro o seis desnudos hombros | de dos escollos o tres', 'steals a little room from the sea, and very pleasant therein'; 'four or six bare shoulders of two or three reefs': II, 1090b), and 'Según vuelan por el agua' (1602: 'que un aquilón africano | las engendró a todas tres … | si no le da el temor alas, | de plumas calza los pies', 'for an African north wind engendered all three … if fear does not give him wings, it shoes his feet with feathers': II, 1090b). Patacón gives the source of another example:

Y como decir se suele:
'En la silla y en las ancas
suben ambos, y él parece
("textus in Góngora", en el
romance de los Cenetes),
de ninguna espuela herido,
que dos mil diablos le mueven.' (II, 1117b)

(And as they say, 'The two of them mount the saddle and the haunches, and the horse – text in Góngora, in the ballad of the Cenetes – struck by no spur, seems moved by two thousand devils.')

There are also allusions to *Don Quixote* (II, 1113a), a quotation of the line 'arded, corazón, arded' ('burn, heart, burn', II, 1094b), first recorded in Narváez's *El delphin de musica* of 1538, of a couplet from Don Pedro's own poem 'Ya el trono de luz regía' (1622), and of the Comendador Joan Escrivá's *canción* 'Ven, muerte tan escondida' (II, 1097b).

Las manos blancas is one of Calderón's cleverest plays, both in terms of plot and in use of allusion. It could be argued that it has a dark side in its exploration of sexual ambiguity, and because we are left with the suspicion that Serafina has sacrificed her feelings for Federico to her belief that both she and he must do what is proper: he has compromised Lisarda, and César has compromised her. But the play is so funny that we may overlook this.[62]

Fuego de Dios en el querer bien was one of the plays offered by Ascanio in Valencia in June 1644 as a 'comedia nueva, nunca representada en Valencia' ('a new play, never performed in Valencia').[63] Corpus in 1644 had fallen early, on 26 May, and Ascanio's company had been one of those chosen for the Madrid *autos*; Calderón conceivably wrote the play for him in the spring of that year, or it may have been like *El secreto a voces*, written while Calderón was in Madrid on leave, between November 1641 and April 1642. Hilborn's guess of 1641–4 does not contradict these possibilities.[64] However, since Hilborn's calculations have in many cases been overtaken by dating evidence from other sources, we should not exclude the possibility that the play was written in the very productive period which ended in the summer of 1640.

Set in Madrid, *Fuego de Dios en el querer bien* is yet another play in which the plot is advanced by one of the female characters in particular: Ángela, the sister of Don Álvaro. Ángela is attracted to her brother's friend Juan, who rescues her from Álvaro's wrath when circumstances suggest that she has been entertaining a young man. Quick-witted and inventive, especially when she is forced to lie, Ángela can also summon up a fine semblance of outrage when she tells the truth and is not believed; she gets her man in the end. At one point Juan's servant Hernando, the play's *gracioso*, is taken for a gentleman who has killed someone in the street, and, with Ángela's connivance, is arrested. Calderón does not develop Hernando's role as a gentleman, but to a degree, he allows Ángela to share his role as *gracioso*: in one scene she dresses as a maid, and makes the remarks we expect from clever maidservants.

Efforts have been made, on the basis of Calderón's plays, to draw conclusions about social behaviour in seventeenth-century Spain, but these overlook the conventions that operate in cloak-and-sword plays.[65] *Fuego de Dios* opens with Álvaro, who is attracted to Beatriz, his sister's friend, asking Ángela to put in a word for him. The situation gives rise to some good-natured teasing, as we might expect nowadays from a brother and sister. A few hundred lines later, Álvaro is ready to kill his teasing sister. However, her subsequent outrage when proved innocent, largely feigned though it is, suggests that his reaction is to be seen as excessive; and we are conscious of the double standards which operate as we observe Álvaro's interest in his sister's friend Beatriz, and Ángela's interest in her brother's friend Juan: Álvaro can enlist the aid of his sister, but Ángela cannot tell her brother she likes Juan. The text makes a possible reference to *Peor está que estaba* (II, 1273b), but there is nothing to help us date the composition.

Like all of us, dramatists fantasise. Unlike most people, they can enact their fantasies vicariously, through the creation of characters. Calderón created numbers of male characters who try to make women into creatures submissive to their will; but these are not admirable characters, and they do badly. To judge by their success in the fantasy world of his creations, Calderón admired spirited and resourceful women: he may well have been attracted to them. Unfortunately, we are not in a position to deduce that the mother of his son was one such.

El José de las mujeres presents another strong female character, although not a contemporary one. The play was printed in *Escogidas XIII* (1660), but it too has been dated to 1641–4 on metrical grounds.[66] St Eugenia's feast day is 25 December, but almost nothing is known of her life. Early martyrologies (in particular, Jacobus de Voragine in his *Golden Legend*) tell how, in her anxiety to lead a religious life, she dressed as a man and lived in a monastery in Egypt. When a local lady made advances to this 'monk' and was rejected, she accused Eugenia of attempted rape. Eugenia rebutted the charge by revealing that she was a woman. While the Joseph of the Old Testament could make no such devastating response to the accusation of Potiphar's wife, the situations had enough in common to provide the play's title. Calderón supposes that Eugenia is the daughter of Filipo, governor of Egypt under the Emperor Gallienus (AD 253–68), and that she has rescued from the flames one of the Christian books her father has been ordered to destroy: it is Paul's First Letter to the Corinthians, and, like Crisanto in *Los dos amantes del cielo*, or Muley Mahomet in *El gran príncipe de Fez*, she finds a passage which requires further explanation: 'Nihil est idolum in mundo, quia nullus est Deus nisi unus' ('An idol is nothing in the world, for there is no God but one': 1 Corinthians 8:4). Like Polemio in *Los dos amantes*, Filipo thinks his child's 'visions' are figments of a brain deranged by excessive reading; like Escarpín in that play, the *gracioso* Capricho contributes his prejudiced viewpoint:

Una mujer
no ha menester (que es error)
más filosofías que rueca,
almohadilla o bastidor. (I, 892a)

(A woman has no need – for it's a mistake – of more philosophy than a distaff, a sewing cushion or a sewing frame.)

Like Margarita in *Basta callar*, Eugenia complains that her female status denies her a career in both arms and letters, and the play begins by presenting her as if she were a contemporary young aristocrat with intellectual pretensions, presiding over a literary academy attended by young men who are rivals for her attention. Everything changes when one rival kills another, and the devil takes over the corpse. In 1670 the inquisitorial censor Juan de Rueda y Cuebas altered this episode in a manuscript he was asked to read prior to performance, 'por ser eretico y contra el viejo y nuebo testamentos' ('because it is heretical and against the Old and New Testaments'). Wilson, who examined the alterations, described the censor as a humourless pedant, but suggested that he might have a point.[67] In fact the evidence Wilson cites indicates that the point is a debatable one. The devil cannot perform miracles: that is, he cannot raise the dead; but that he can enter the body of a creature, living or not, and bend it to his will, seems not to be in dispute. There is no evidence that Calderón was aware of this intervention, which affected only one performance, but his reaction to the inquisitorial attempts to get him to modify *Las órdenes militares* in 1662 suggest that he would have objected strongly. The play had already been printed with this passage intact, and continued to be so, without objection. The erotic charge of *Las manos blancas* is absent here, or nearly absent: the scene in which Melancia reveals her desire for the young 'monk', Eugenia, is acted, not reported.

Nothing in the text of *El José de las mujeres* aids in dating with confidence. A reference to *La dama duende* (1629: I, 906a) is not helpful; a remark made by Capricho as he describes Eugenia's death, while interesting, is not conclusive:

Ya el verdugo,
rey de comedia enojado
contra algún valido suyo,
la cabeza de los hombros
la ha dividido. (I, 919b)

(Already the executioner, like a king in a play, angered against some favourite of his, has separated her head from her shoulders.)

Since Rodrigo Calderón was a favourite's favourite, the last royal favourite to be executed in Spain was Don Álvaro de Luna, in 1453, although his rise and fall had been chronicled in a pair of plays, *La próspera/adversa fortuna de don Álvaro de Luna* (?1621–4), now usually ascribed to Mira de Amescua. On 10 May 1641 (OS), in England, Charles I had signed the death warrant of the Earl of Strafford, although he was ashamed, not *enojado*; the executioner duly separated the earl's head from his shoulders two days later. As for

Olivares, he would die in his bed in July 1645, although plenty of his rivals, both before and after his fall, would gladly have attended his execution. If this passage was written while the count-duke was still alive, it may have prompted more than wry amusement, but we cannot be certain which *valido* Calderón was thinking of as he wrote it.

Calderón completed *El secreto a voces* on Friday 28 February 1642, four days before Shrove Tuesday, but a reference in the text to 'estas mañanas de mayo' ('these mornings of May', line 52) suggests that he was aware that it could not be performed until Lent was over.[68] Antonio de Prado, for whom he wrote the play, was in Madrid at this time, and his company was one of those nominated for the 1642 *autos*.[69] The play's setting is in Parma, and the duchess, Flérida, is suffering from melancholy. Her courtiers have been trying to cheer her up with the kind of amusements which were such a feature of the reign of Philip IV prior to 1640: her ladies have put on plays and musical evenings, while the gentlemen have organised masques, jousts and tourneys, all without success. Flérida's problem is that she loves her secretary, Federico. She suffers from the knowledge that Federico already has a lady-friend, but she does not know that his beloved is one of her own ladies-in-waiting, Laura. The couple have to keep their relationship secret because Laura's father has other plans for her; however, thanks to a code devised by Federico, they can communicate in public: this is *el secreto a voces*.

Don Pedro may have borrowed the lovers' code from Tirso's *Amar por arte mayor*, which he would have read in the *Quinta parte* of 1636, but the plot as a whole has similarities with several plays: his own *Nadie fíe su secreto* and *Amigo, amante y leal*, in both of which the head of the duchy of Parma takes a fancy to the beloved of the ducal secretary; and Lope's *El perro del hortelano* (?1613–15), which depicts an Italian duchess in love with her secretary. One difference is that Federico, unlike Lope's secretary, has no thought of giving up his Laura; whereas, like the Duke of Parma in *Nadie fíe su secreto* and *Amigo, amante y leal*, Calderón's duchess realises that her position brings obligations.

There are references to *La dama duende* and *El galán fantasma* (lines 527–8) and perhaps to *Primero soy yo* (line 1893); and while the autograph version of the text has over 3,500 lines, it was originally significantly longer: Don Pedro himself deleted scores of lines by all of the major characters. The censor, Juan Navarro de Espinosa, ordered others not to be performed: he objected to Fabio's

haciendo
misterios sin ser rosario,
sin ser cura sacramentos (lines 29–31)

(performing mysteries without being a rosary, sacraments without being a priest) and to a harmless story which involved the Latin of a priest saying mass being misunderstood by his parishioners (lines 2132–71). This must have been particularly awkward, since Fabio refers on subsequent occasions to the 'moral' of this story. As with *El José de las mujeres*, the censors of the printed edition made no objection, and the jokes were included: lines spoken aloud to illiterate groundlings were considered more dangerous than those read in the privacy of someone's home; and the censor may have been reacting to the growing anti-theatre movement.

It may be said that many of Don Pedro's plays, while carefully constructed, are less than original. To a degree, though, the return to plots he had used previously was arguably prompted by the wish to reiterate moral points he had made before: that discretion, especially for lovers, is a key virtue; and that those who wield power must exercise it responsibly.

* * *

The list of plays offered in May 1644 by Pedro Ascanio included *Las cadenas del demonio*: 'comedia nueva, nunca representada en Valencia', 'de D. Pedro Calderon' ('a new play, never performed in Valencia', 'by D. Pedro Calderón').[70] The title does not appear in Don Pedro's Marañón or Veragua lists, and Wilson did not consider it authentic.[71] The plot deals with the supposed exploits of St Bartholomew in Armenia. There are several typically Calderonian features: the king's child, Irene, has been imprisoned from birth because of her baleful horoscope, like Segismundo in *La vida es sueño*; when she sees that birds, beasts and fish have more liberty, she asks the heavens the same rhetorical question as he does:

> ¿Qué delito cometí
> contra vosotros naciendo?
>
> (I, 738a, cf. *La vida es sueño*, lines 105–6)

(What crime did I commit against you by being born?)

Despite his relationship with Calderón, Ascanio is not an unimpeachable source of information. His incorrect claim that *Gustos y disgustos* had never been performed in Valencia may be an error or artistic licence. The same may be argued of his attribution of *Las cadenas*. However, there is another explanation: that his claim is partly true, that he was offering a collaboration play as the work of Don Pedro alone. It was not uncommon for such plays to be attributed to only one of the authors involved, especially to the one who wrote the first act. This explanation has the virtue of accounting for the Calderonian echoes, as well as for the title's omission from Don Pedro's own lists. It is less likely that *Las cadenas* was the collaboration work (Solís,

Rojas, Calderón) performed on the Retiro lake on 8 July 1640: a play about St Bartholomew is not obviously suitable for the feast of St Elizabeth or the queen's birthday, although it is true that *Las cadenas* requires some spectacular staging.

* * *

A document of 11 July 1643 indicates that José Calderón, over nineteen but not yet twenty-five, 'como capellan que soy de la capellania y patronazgo de legos que fundó Doña Inés de Riaño, mi abuela' ('as chaplain of the chaplaincy and entail founded by my grandmother Doña Inés de Riaño'), leased part of the house in the Calle de las Platerías to a Cosme Rodríguez, silversmith.[72] The chaplaincy, with the property as residence of the chaplain, had been founded by Doña Inés for whichever of her grandsons was ordained by the time he was twenty-four. Since none of them had taken this step, the right had passed to Don Pedro's nephew José (born 1623), son of the eldest brother, Diego. Young José had not taken holy orders (he intended to practise law), and was probably living with his father in the Calle de las Fuentes. We can surmise that Don Pedro and his brother José had been living in the Platerías property, apart from their time on active service. A month later, the three brothers sold the Calle de la Madera property for 9,475 *reales*:[73] no doubt it was the poet who was most in need of the ready cash.

Unless the rest of the Platerías house had been let earlier, part of it was still available for Don Pedro to live in; but he moved to Toledo shortly after this. The letting may be explained by his having told his nephew as early as July that he was planning this move. Calderón's paternal grandmother, Isabel Ruiz, was from Toledo, and the poet still had relatives there, including his sister Dorotea. That he already had professional contacts in the city is indicated by the *autos Psiquis y Cupido (para Toledo)* (1640) and *Llamados y escogidos* (1643). The main reason for the move was probably an economic one: Toledo was cheaper than the capital. In 1644 he wrote two more *autos* for the city, *El socorro general* and *La humildad coronada de las plantas*. The autograph manuscript of the second tells us that it was written 'Para La ciudad de Toledo En las Fiestas del ss^{mo} sacra^{to} año de 1644'; at the end it is signed and dated in 'Toledo a 17 de março de 1644 años' ('For the city of Toledo in the festival of Corpus Christi, 1644'; 'Toledo, 17 March 1644').[74] Although Madrid did have *autos* that year, there is no evidence that they were written by Calderón.[75]

There was more to come in the way of catastrophes, personal and national. Although Richelieu had died in December 1642 and Louis XIII a few weeks later, leaving a regency, Spain did not have the strength to take any advantage: on 19 May 1643, at Rocroi, in the north of France, the once invincible Spanish infantry suffered its worst ever defeat. On 6 October 1644 Queen Isabel died, her death certainly hastened by the royal doctors, who bled her eight times in as many hours. The theatres closed in mourning until St John's Day (24 June) of 1645. Ironically, Don José Calderón was killed the previous day, defending the bridge of Camarasa, a village on the river Segre some 25 miles north of Lérida. In May 1644, the king had approved a grant of 500 ducats to enable him to proceed with his knighthood; later that year he was promoted to colonel, and finally to *teniente de maestre de campo general* (brigadier).[76] The death of his favourite brother, and the manner of it, 'hecho pedazos en el campo', 'blown to pieces in the field', to say nothing of the premature end of a brilliant career, must have affected Don Pedro deeply.

While many (among them, Quevedo) rejoiced at the death of Olivares, now exiled to Toro for his attempts at self-justification, on 2 July, the deaths of Philip's sister, the Empress María (13 May 1646), and of his son, Prince Baltasar Carlos (thrown from his horse on 9 October 1646), brought further periods of mourning. Paradoxically, the theatre closure decreed in the spring of 1646 preceded these royal deaths. For the moment at least, Philip yielded, reluctantly, to the 'godly faction' and allowed the ban to go ahead, at least until it began to seem that this attempt to curry favour with God had not worked.[77] Plays did not begin again, as they would normally have done, after Easter 1646 (1 April), and that year there were no *autos* in Madrid. Although there were *autos* in 1647, the public theatres did not begin to get back to normal until 1648.

One probable casualty of the death of José Calderón was Don Pedro's *Tercera parte de comedias*. On 7 March 1645 the poet obtained a licence to publish a volume with this title, and paid for a *privilegio*, which gave him copyright.[78] His *Primera* and *Segunda partes* had been reprinted in 1640 and 1641, but a third part was overdue, given his number of plays; no doubt, too, there had been a significant fall in income from works written for performance. Presumably the plan was for José to lend his name as editor, as he had done for the first two parts; we can easily imagine that his death three months later caused the project to be abandoned. The titles of the twelve plays to be included in the volume are not known. The *Tercera parte* published in 1664 by Sebastián Ventura de Vergara Salcedo is certainly different, since it contains plays which had not been written by 1645.

Don Pedro's career had not ended, but it had certainly changed. He was able to write the Madrid *autos* of 1645, and was paid 300 ducats (112,200 *maravedís*) for them on 23 June, although their titles are unknown.[79] By the end of the year, however, he had given up trying to live on his writing alone, and had moved to Alba de Tormes, the site of the ducal palace of Don Fernando Álvarez de Toledo, sixth Duke of Alba. Don Fernando had family connections with the Dukes of Frías and Infantado, Calderón's previous employers. It is also worth remembering that the Count of Oropesa, Don Duarte Fernando Álvarez de Toledo y Portugal, whose company of Royal Guards Don Pedro had joined in the summer of 1642, was the Duke of Alba's nephew.

The dukes of Alba had never liked Olivares. The sixth duke had led an army to the Portuguese frontier, only to return in February 1641, refusing to serve under the Count of Monterrey, Olivares's brother-in-law. When Monterrey was recalled in disgrace in November, Alba agreed to take his place, only to retire again in 1643, complaining this time of lack of resources. When Calderón joined him in 1645, he was effectively sulking on his estates. Somewhat unexpectedly, however, Philip offered him the viceroyalty of Sicily the following year. He accepted, probably reckoning that the viceroyalty of Naples would follow, and even went to Madrid to thank the king. There is evidence that Calderón would have accompanied him to Sicily, but nothing came of the offer.[80] Calderón remained in Alba, with occasional trips to Madrid in connection with the *autos*, or with the duke's business, apparently until 1650.

In spite of living in Toledo and Alba de Tormes for most of the period from 1644 to 1650, Don Pedro continued to maintain contact with the public theatres in Madrid. The Biblioteca Nacional preserves a manuscript of *Troya abrasada* (Res. 78) of which Acts II and III are in Calderón's hand. The hands of Act I have not been identified, although neither appears to be that of Juan de Zabaleta, Calderón's supposed collaborator.[81] Leaf 70 contains three *licencias*, dated 2 February 1644 (Madrid), 3 August 1644 (Valencia) and 7 January 1645 (Zaragoza). The wording of the first, signed by Juan Navarro de Espinosa, states that 'esta comedia se puede volver a representar', 'this play can be performed again', a clear indication of an earlier performance. A joke by the *gracioso* Biznaga about Aeneas's son Ascanio (who does not appear in the play), the names of the actors in the *reparto* (in Calderón's hand), plus the three licences, all help to show that the play was written for the *autor* Pedro Ascanio in the acting year Easter 1643 to Lent 1644.[82]

Despite films like *Troy*, modern audiences have forgotten the literary importance of the Trojan legend. Unlike some collaboration plays (for example, *Yerros de naturaleza*, which vanished from sight as soon as it was written), *Troya abrasada* continued to be printed and performed for almost 200 years, with the last recorded performances in the Teatro de la Cruz as late as November 1811. The authors took huge liberties with the traditional version of the story. Their Casandra is not the daughter of Priam and Hecuba; she is a Greek, niece of Agamenón and Menelaos. Héctor has no Andrómaque, but loves Helena, like his brother Paris; Helena's marriage to Menelaos is unconsummated (making her much more sympathetic to a seventeenth-century Catholic audience). The one critic to have noticed this play is critical of this relaxed attitude to Homer's account.[83] But the *Iliad* is a poetic invention, not a historical description, and if we see it as a depiction of the tragic futility of war (as many critics think), then we can see that *Troya abrasada*, for all its differences in detail, is a true successor to its sources. The immediate source for the play was most probably Cristóbal de Monroy y Silva's *Epítome de la historia de Troya* (1641), but the fact that it was written so soon after Calderón's personal experience of war is surely significant.

The cast-list reveals that Calderón considered that the leading man was Paris, played by Pedro Manuel de Castilla, Ascanio's *primer galán*, while Helena was played by Antonia Infanta, Ascanio's wife and *primera dama*. We are surprised to discover that Héctor's role was taken by the *cuarta dama*, Doña Beatriz, especially since the part involves no singing. Doña Beatriz is recorded only three times: in the *auto* documents of 1642 (when she was in the company of Juan de Malaguilla), in those of 1644, and in this *reparto*; her surname is unknown. A tiny number of actors, evidently of *hidalgo* parentage, used the title Don/Doña. Perhaps it was someone like this Beatriz, a noblewoman involved in the theatre, whose relationship with Don Pedro in the 1640s resulted in the birth of the poet's son Pedro José.

CHAPTER 15

A time to mourn

A florecer las rosas madrugaron,
y para envejecerse florecieron:
cuna y sepulcro en un botón hallaron.
Tales los hombres sus fortunas vieron:
en un día nacieron y expiraron;
que pasados los siglos horas fueron.
(*El príncipe constante*)

(The roses awoke early in order to bloom, and bloomed in order to grow old: they found cradle and sepulchre in one bud. Thus did men their fortunes see: in a day they were born and expired, for centuries once past are but hours.)

When Don José Calderón was killed at Camarasa on 23 June 1645, he left no will, although in March 1639 he had given his brothers power of attorney to divide up his possessions.[1] If an inventory of these was made, it has not survived. No doubt, as an unmarried professional soldier, absent from Madrid for years at a time, he owned little enough: his only practical legacy was his military pension and the money granted him to help him proceed with his knighthood. On 21 September, the king ordered that Don Pedro receive a pension of 30 *escudos* a month in recognition of his own service and that of his brother.[2] In April 1646, when it looked as if Don Pedro would be leaving for Sicily with the Duke of Alba, Philip signed another document authorising the continued payment of this amount.[3] In practice, when it came to converting the royal order into money, Don Pedro had as many difficulties as Chato in *La hija del aire*; his *memorial* to the king of around 1648 was a response to them. Perhaps when the plan to go to Sicily fell through, the authorities were confused: this, at least, was implied by Don Pedro's polite explanation:

Y por no auer tenido efeto el passar a ella [= Sicilia], no le ha tenido el goze del dicho sueldo, debiendosele del casi todo el tiempo q[ue] ha que se le señalô.[4]

(And since the move to Sicily did not come about, he has not enjoyed the aforesaid salary, and is owed it for almost the whole period since it was awarded him.)

Wearily, one imagines, the king tried again, signing another order on 20 July 1648.[5] This was not the end of the story of the pension.

Apparently anticipating further financial problems, in the closing paragraph of his *memorial* Don Pedro also asked the king for an official court post:

Y assi suplica a V. M. que en consideracion destos seruicios, y otros particulares, de que no haze mencion en este Memorial, por ser menores, y no de esta calidad, ni dignos de ponerse en el, aunque lo sean de traerlos a la memoria de V. M. sea seruido de q[ue] la satisfacion que se le dè sea vna llave de Ayuda de Camara de V. M.[6]

(And so he begs Your Majesty that it may please him that the settlement he should be given should be the key of an assistant in Your Majesty's privy chamber, in consideration of these services and of other special ones not mentioned in this memorial because they are lesser ones and not of this quality, nor worthy of being listed in it, although they are worthy of being brought to Your Majesty's memory.)

Presumably the 'lesser services' referred to were the works written for royal performances.

In 1623 there were no fewer than thirty-two (or, according to another source, forty-seven) *gentileshombres de la cámara*, most of them dukes, counts or marquises. Listing the thirty-two, González Dávila adds that 'tiene el rey en su Camara otros criados, con titulo de Ayudas de Camara' ('in his Privy Chamber the king has other servants, with the title Assistants in the Privy Chamber').[7] The number of *ayudas* is given by the other source as only nine, but the post clearly brought the holder into contact with the highest nobility of Spain: the status of both the 'gentlemen' and their assistants was marked by the symbolic key they carried. Calderón would also have known that he was applying to become a palace colleague of Diego Velázquez. Velázquez had been sworn in as one of Philip's *ayudas de cámara* on 6 January 1643. This was his official position until February 1652, when he became *aposentador mayor*; that is, he was one of the *ayudas* when Calderón's undated *memorial* was written.[8] It is tempting to think that the painter suggested this application to the poet; but while there is no evidence that he did so, it is distinctly possible that the idea came to Don Pedro from his familiarity with Velázquez's career.

If Calderón's application had been successful, his official duties would have interfered with his writing, but the position would have brought him a security which he had never had, at a time when he was finding it harder to live on his writing and, perhaps, finding it harder to write. Moreover, he almost certainly saw Velázquez as a congenial colleague. While a Velázquez/

Calderón friendship is speculation supported at best by circumstantial evidence, Don Pedro's interest in art is undeniable, and extends far beyond plays about painters such as *El pintor de su deshonra* (?1644–6) and *Darlo todo y no dar nada* (1651), in the second of which he makes some very flattering remarks about the art of painting. Other passages suggest that he had watched painters at work:

> Cuando un pintor procura
> linear una pintura,
> si está lisa la tabla
> fáciles rasgos en bosquejo entabla;
> mas si la tabla tiene
> primero otra pintura, le conviene
> borrarla, no confunda
> con la primera forma la segunda.
>
> (*Peor está que estaba*, II, 327b)

(When a painter is trying to outline a painting, if the board is smooth, he begins easy brushstrokes in a sketch; but if the board already has a painting on it, it's better for him to blot it out so that he doesn't mix the second shape with the first.)

> En las acciones
> de un diestro pintor lo advierto,
> pues cuando labra estudioso
> alguna imagen, al lienzo
> arrima el tiento, y descansa
> luego la mano en el tiento:
> cuando no le sale a gusto
> el rasgo que deja hecho,
> lo que la derecha pinta,
> borra la izquierda. (*Las manos blancas no ofenden*, II, 1082a)

(I notice it in actions of a skilful painter, for when he is studiously forming an image, he leans the maulstick on the canvas and then rests his hand on the maulstick; when the brushstroke he has done does not meet with his approval, his left hand rubs out what his right hand paints.)

Are these descriptions of Velázquez in particular? As noted in Chapter II, several of the attributes of the royal painter Apeles in *Darlo todo* match those of Velázquez; and the painter was certainly influenced by the writer in his composition of *La rendición de Bredá*. But while this evidence points to mutual respect, even admiration, it does no more than that. The conclusive evidence, on paper or on canvas, of a closer relationship, appears to be absent. Velázquez had already painted Góngora and Quevedo; others painted Lope, Tirso, Moreto. It is not that artists failed to make likenesses of Calderón: there are several of these, but all show him as an old man, that is, after Velázquez was dead. All but one of them portray him from a similar angle: slightly from his left. Of the engravings, the only one published in his lifetime was made in 1676 by Pedro de Villafranca for the frontispiece of his *autos* (1677) (Plate 29). The best-known was made by Gregorio Forstman/Fosman in 1682 for the frontispiece in the volumes of the Vera Tassis edition of the plays (Plate 30). In both we see a lean face, hollowed at the temples and cheeks. The eyes are still penetrating beneath the impressive forehead; there is a goatee beard and, in the second, a small moustache. The dress is plain, as befits a priest, and would have been black, with the single adornment of the cross of Santiago, which would have been red. In other portraits we see the subject wearing the mantle of this Order.[9] The most frequently reproduced oil painting is that by Juan de Alfaro (1643–80), now preserved in the Biblioteca Nacional (frontispiece); a drawing by Alfaro also survives;[10] both probably date from the 1670s. Alfaro was taught by Velázquez, and is considered to have supplied Palomino with the names of the 'cast' in *Las meninas*. The one portrait which portrays Calderón from his right is attributed to Antonio de Pereda y Salgado (1611–78). The appearance of the subject suggests that it too was produced within a few years of 1670 (Plate 31).

However, an earlier portrait did exist. The inventory of the possessions of Calderón's nephew José lists several portraits of family members, including José's father Diego, his uncle Don Pedro, and two of himself, one of them as a boy.[11] José was baptised on 30 April 1623 and died in February 1658. His father had died in November 1647. The inventory dates from May 1658. If any of the portraits it refers to have survived, they have not been identified. If they were commissioned by Diego, they would presumably date from the period around 1630 to the death of Diego in 1647. That any of them could have been painted by Velázquez is most improbable, although the possibility remains that the portrait of Don Pedro was a copy of a Velázquez original. It may be argued that no such original exists. In fact, there is a possible candidate, a portrait of an 'unidentified gentleman', supposedly dating from the 1640s.[12] As the painting is unfinished, it has been said to be of a friend or colleague, rather than a commission.[13] According to one theory, the sitter could be José de Nieto, the chamberlain whose blurred figure appears in the background of *Las meninas*: but there is no evidence other than an alleged resemblance.[14] The scholar who made this suggestion refers, rather dismissively, to another suggestion that the sitter is Calderón. Like the 'unidentified man', José de Nieto appears to have a large nose and receding hair, but the proportions of the face are arguably different. We know from Rojas Zorrilla's teasing that the poet's hair was receding while he was in his late thirties. It seems distinctly possible that this figure, with its high forehead, lean face, hollow temples and cheeks, goatee beard and penetrating eyes, is Don Pedro. Interestingly, Velázquez's point of view is slightly from the sitter's left (Plate 32).

There are two difficulties about this identification. The first is that the provenance tells us almost nothing. This may be 'another head of a man, with a black beard, unfinished', listed as in Velázquez's possession when he died in 1661,[15] but the first reliable reference is in 1772, in the royal collection. The sitter's exuberant moustache, with its upturned ends, is not a problem: the style was favoured by the king himself, by Olivares and others; there are many examples in portraits painted from the 1630s to the 1650s: Velázquez himself sports one in his self-portrait in *Las meninas*, painted around 1656. It would be natural for an older man, who was also a priest, to abandon this flamboyant style. The second problem is the lack of insignia: most of the other portraits show Calderón as a knight of Santiago, an order he received in April 1637. Calderón was proud of his knighthood: it was referred to on the title-page of his *Segunda parte de comedias*, of July 1637, and again, forty years later, on the title-page of his *Primera parte de autos sacramentales*, the only collection he published himself. Even in his will, while he stipulated that his body was to wear the habit of St Francis, he requested that it be laid on his habit of Santiago.[16] There are four possibilities: one, that the suggested identification is wrong; two, that the portrait, if it is of Calderón, dates from the mid thirties, just before the knighthood, but when his reputation was already established; three, that Don Pedro was not wearing his Santiago insignia when the portrait was painted (no insignia can be seen in the Pereda painting; they are absent in another anonymous portrait);[17] and four, the fact that the portrait is unfinished could account for the absence.

* * *

If Don Pedro had difficulties in obtaining the army pension for his and his brother's military service, the same was true of the 500 ducats granted by the king towards the expenses of José's knighthood. We may feel that the death of the intended recipient had nullified the royal obligation in this matter, but a grant was a grant, and the family had been bereaved. On 16 May 1646 Don Pedro and Diego went through the legal process which was necessary for them to become their brother's heirs. Among the witnesses called to vouch for them were the playwrights Antonio Martínez de Meneses (?1612–61) and Rojas Zorrilla, now sporting on his chest his new cross of Santiago: he placed his hand on it when swearing the oath. Both of them said that they knew the brothers well, and that they had known José likewise. Given these witnesses, we might suppose that it was Pedro who was pressing for this money to be paid, but, as we shall see presently, he was not the only sibling who was in financial difficulties. Eventually Pedro and Diego got 5,000 *reales* (i.e., 500 *reales* less than the original 500 ducats), but not directly, since the crown was apparently too short of ready cash: it was paid them by a Don Manuel Osorio Calvache, Veinticuatro of Granada, who owed the Crown a large sum for the purchase of his post of Veinticuatro. Don Pedro was present in Madrid to sign the document on 16 May 1646. Two days later, he and Diego were authorised to go to Granada for the money, but it was eventually paid in Madrid, in two instalments, on 30 June and 14 August. The documents show that on 25 June, Don Pedro, who was then in Alba de Tormes, authorised Diego to collect the amount.[18]

One of those who suffered from the Calderón brothers' chronic cash shortage was their sister Dorotea. The father's will had stipulated that Diego was to give her an allowance of 100 ducats a year, but documents of 1647 show that she had received nothing for the period 25 June 1632 to 24 June 1646. Good sister that she was, Dorotea had let this go. In March 1646, however, the hated stepmother Juana Freyle Caldera had finally died, and with her the 100 ducats per annum which Diego also had to pay to her. Not surprisingly, Dorotea felt that Diego could now better afford her 100 ducats; and she also asked for the 15,400 *reales* she should have received since 1632, since it was money which she would herself have to pay. Diego and Pedro signed their agreement to do this in Madrid on 4 May 1647.[19]

Don Pedro was still in Madrid, or in Madrid again, in July: he found time to write an approbation for Miguel Cid's *Justas sagradas*, a volume of poems published in Seville by the poet's son.[20] The approbation was strikingly short: forty-six words including date (12 July) and signature. The son may have hoped that Don Pedro's reputation would outweigh the trouble of tracking him down; if so, he must have been disappointed. The *censura* which followed, by Fray Juan Ponce de León, ran to twenty-two and a half pages, and inevitably drew attention to Don Pedro's brevity. Perhaps Calderón did not like the poems; more probably he had other matters to worry about. When his brother Diego made his will on 13 November, he revealed that on the last occasion on which Don Pedro was in Madrid with the Duke of Alba, the two had tried to sort out their finances. Perhaps he was referring to the July visit. Diego had agreed to transfer to Pedro an annuity valued at 2,800 ducats, 'y que con esto se habia de contentar por las dichas sus legitimas por no haber más que poder darle' ('and that with this, for his lawful share, he would have to be satisfied, for there was no more to give him'). For his part, Pedro had agreed to transfer some annuities to Diego's son José. However, although the papers had been drafted, they were never completed because Don Pedro had to leave in a hurry with the duke. Now,

> Le pido quan encarecidamente puedo que con él [= José] se otorguen las dichas escrituras como se habian de otorgar conmigo, pues aunque le tocara por sus legitimas y herencia de nuestro hermano Don Juseph mucha mas cantidad, no hay de donde poder sacalla, y efectos y creditos contra mi no es hacienda para él y puede serlo para su sobrino, al qual le dejo como hijo suyo y le pido quan encarecidamente puedo lo haga con él como padre, que poco falta le haré yo donde él queda.[21]

> (I ask him as earnestly as I can that the deeds should be executed with José as they were to be executed with me, since although he is entitled to much more for his lawful share and the inheritance of our brother Don José, there is nowhere to get it from, and bills and credits against me do not constitute property for him and may be for his nephew, whom I leave him as his son, and ask him as earnestly as I can to deal with him as a father, for my son will not miss me while his uncle remains.)

Although Don Pedro was the only one of the brothers to attend university, the lack of a degree did not prevent Diego from acting as a legal administrator, although it may have hindered him from becoming as wealthy as a qualified lawyer.[22] However, if we add up his debts, they come to a trivial 1,400 *reales*; and while he was owed 2,777 *reales* by the Hospitales General y de la Pasión for work he did for them between April 1643 and December 1646, he was ready to overlook the 777. He could not overlook the whole amount, 'porque muero muy pobre' ('because I die very poor').[23] He may not have been rich, but he had managed to send his son to university: the will describes him as a *licenciado*, and he was an 'abogado en los reales consejos' ('a lawyer in the royal councils'), a secure position. A week after signing his will, Diego died; among his executors he named his brother and his son.[24] Don Pedro did what he could for his nephew, and vice versa: it was José and his wife who brought up the poet's son.

Diego's will and the other documents of the years 1645 to 1647 are very revealing. They confirm the disastrous financial management of the father, the greed of the stepmother, and the catastrophic result of the death of Nicolás de Velasco. And yet, while the Calderón children never recovered in monetary terms, it is clear that each was prepared to suffer hardship for the others, and their mutual affection never diminished, as another paragraph of the will makes clear:

Siempre nos hemos conservado todos tres en amor y amistad y sin hacer particiones de los bienes que quedaron del dicho nuestro padre, en que estaban inclusos los de Doña Ana Maria de Henao, mi señora y madre, y nos hemos ayudado los unos a los otros en las necesidades y trabajos que hemos tenido.[25]

(All three of us have always maintained ourselves in love and friendship, without dividing up the goods which remained from our father, which included those of Doña Ana Maria de Henao, my lady mother, and we have helped one another in the needs and tribulations which we have had.)

Diego's father was a mean-minded man, but the son was a person of generous spirit. If he had made a conscious effort to be different from his father, he had succeeded. Don Pedro had lost another brother whom he loved, but around the same time he gained a son. It has been suggested that the poet might have entered into a 'secret marriage', as some characters did in his plays, because he could not afford to maintain a wife overtly in a manner becoming his status as an *hidalgo*.[26] That such relationships existed is not in question, but no documents exist to confirm or deny that this was the case with Calderón. The name of the mother and the birth-date of the son are also unknown. Pérez Pastor suggested that

De los documentos publicados se infiere que este niño hubo de nacer por los años de 1648 á 1650, y que su madre debió de morir poco tiempo después de haberle dado á luz. Esto supuesto, cabe preguntar: ¿el fallecimiento de la madre pudo ser motivo bastante para que D. Pedro Calderón se decidiera á tomar el estado eclesiástico como lo hizo teniendo cumplidos los cincuenta años?[27]

(From the published documents it can be inferred that this child must have been born around 1648–50, and that his mother must have died soon after giving birth to him. Having supposed this, we may ask whether the death of the mother could be sufficient motive for D. Pedro Calderón to decide to become a priest, as he did when he reached fifty.)

Later scholars have sometimes treated the parts of this mere suggestion as if they were facts. It is easy to condemn them for this, but we should not do so without consideration of those few facts which we do possess. Don Pedro was single, nearing fifty, not wealthy, not his own master: such a man is not likely to be anxious to assume responsibility for the result of a casual fling if the child's mother is still alive. At the very least, we must concede that the mother was still in contact with Calderón when she discovered that she was pregnant. The chances are, then, that the relationship was not a casual one. At the same time, Don Pedro could scarcely have installed his mistress in the ducal palace in Alba de Tormes, although she could have been a lady-in-waiting there. Alba now has about 4,700 inhabitants: it is some 14 miles from Salamanca, a city Don Pedro knew, but 125 miles from Toledo, where he had last lived, and 115 from Madrid. In October 1648, when Calderón was confined to bed with fever in the Duke's palace, he wrote a letter, urging that he be paid the money he was owed for the Madrid *autos*, giving his illness as the reason for his urgency.[28] Doctors and apothecaries did not come cheap, but Don Pedro was paying no rent, at least not for himself. Since he was in receipt of a salary from the Duke, we may suspect that he was anxious on behalf of a mistress, whom he perhaps knew to be pregnant, or whose child had already been born. Even if this suspicion is correct, however, it is carrying surmise too far to guess at where she was living: in Alba, braving small-town gossip; in Salamanca, only an hour's ride away; in Toledo, where she and Don Pedro might have moved in 1643 to find anonymity and a lower cost of living; or in Madrid, two days away, even by normal post-horse. Wherever and whenever the child was born, his mother went out of his life: but we do not know when, or in what circumstances. Given maternal mortality rates in the seventeenth century, she may well have died during or soon after the birth; but since the first documentary evidence that the boy was living with the poet's nephew and his wife dates from April 1655, we cannot be certain, even about this.

The first document to refer to the boy, Pedro José, is of June 1654 (perhaps significantly, his second forename was that of Don Pedro's younger brother). The poet had asked the king to transfer to him his military pension:

> No obstante haberse ordenado de sacerdote, suplicóme le haga merced que el dicho entretenimiento se passe y ponga en caueça de Don Pedro Joseph Calderon, sobrino suyo, y del dicho Don Joseph Calderon, su hermano, que es en quien mas propia y legitimamente pueden recaer los seruicios de los dos, y ser de poca edad sin tener otra cosa de que sustentarse para su crianza.[29]

> (Despite having been ordained as a priest, he petitioned me to do him the favour of transferring the said maintenance to Don Pedro José Calderón, his nephew, and the nephew of Don José Calderón, his brother, on the grounds that he is the person on whom the services of both may most properly and legitimately devolve, and because he is very young, with no other maintenance for his upbringing.)

The boy was indeed the nephew of José Calderón, the poet's brother, but Don Pedro, never married and recently ordained, was reluctant to state, at least at this point, that he was the father. The term 'nephew' was an accepted euphemism, and the king agreed.

Calderón's real nephew, José, married Doña Agustina Antonia Ortiz y Velasco, a young widow, in September 1652; she brought a substantial dowry of nearly 16,000 ducats.[30] The documents reveal a clear picture of genuine affection, but the story of the marriage is a sad one: one of the documents, of 9 September 1656, reveals that Doña Agustina was then administering her husband's affairs, on the grounds that he had been 'loco furioso', 'furiously insane', for more than a year.[31] Luckily, perhaps, on 2 April 1655, while he was still 'en pie, sano de toda enfermedad', 'on his feet, free of all illness', José had made his will. In it he referred to his cousin

Don Pedro Calderon de la Barca, mi primo hermano, hijo natural del dicho Don Pedro Calderon, mi tio, que al presente le tengo y crio en mi casa, y pido y encargo encarecidamente a la dicha señora Doña Agustina Ortiz de Velasco, mi muger, que en su crianza y educacion continue con el cuidado y fineza que hasta aqui lo ha hecho, pues sabe que le hemos criado y tenido hasta agora en lugar de hijo nuestro, y fio lo hara por lo mucho que la estimo y me ha querido y quiere y por la voluntad que sabe tengo al dicho Don Pedro Calderon, mi primo, que conque quede en su poder voy muy consolado fiando de su cariño que no le haré falta para nada.

(Don Pedro [José] Calderón de la Barca, my first cousin, natural son of Don Pedro Calderón, my uncle; at present I am bringing him up in my house, and I request and earnestly charge Doña Agustina Ortiz de Velasco, my wife, to continue his upbringing and education with the care and kindness which she has done so far, because she knows that we have raised him and had him until now in place of a child of our own, and I trust she will do so for the great esteem in which I hold her and for the great love which she has had and has for me, and for the fondness which she knows I have for the aforesaid Don Pedro [José] Calderón, my cousin, for, as long as he is in her charge, I take great consolation, trusting in her affection, that he will not feel the lack of me.

Two other clauses stand out:

Mando a Don Pedro Calderon de la Barca, mi tio … doce laminas que tengo de piedra aobadas, con los misterios de la Pasion de Cristo con sus marcos negros, y le pido me encomiende a Dios, que esta niñeria le dejo porque sé el gusto con que siempre las ha mirado, y que yo quisiera dejarle mucho mas, y le suplico no desampare a la señora Doña Agustina Ortiz de Velasco, mi muger, pues sabe lo que yo la he querido y estimado, y lo que la deseo.

Mando a Francisco Gonzalez Calderon, criado antiguo de mis padres, un vestido de los que dejo, el que eligiere la dicha Doña Agustina, y le pido me encomiende a Dios.[32]

I bequeath to Don Pedro Calderón de la Barca, my uncle, twelve oval stone engravings in black frames, with the mysteries of Christ's passion, and I ask him to commend me to God; I leave him this trivial thing because I know how much he has always liked them, and that I would like to leave him much more, and I beg him not to forsake Doña Agustina Ortiz de Velasco, my wife, since he knows how much I have loved and esteemed her, and how much I want for her … I bequeath to

Francisco González Calderón, former servant of my parents, one of my suits, whichever Doña Agustina may choose, and ask him to commend me to God.)

Don Pedro still had these black-framed stone 'láminas' when he died,[33] but this is the last reference to Francisco Calderón, now aged around sixty, and to how his life had been spent, at least until Diego died in 1647. Young José ends by asking Doña Agustina not to marry again, but to live off their estate, 'sin sujetarse a nueva voluntad y sujecion, que hartas experiencias tiene con lo que ha padecido en esta vida con mis impertinencias' ('without subjecting herself to a new set of wishes, for she has had enough experiences with what she has suffered in this life with my frettings').[34] When José died on 19 February 1658, aged only thirty-four, she followed this request, dying in her turn on 9 October 1694 in the house in the Calle de las Fuentes, which her husband had bequeathed to her. Interestingly, she was buried in the poet's vault in San Salvador.[35]

While José was still well (although his early will, and its reference to his 'impertinencias', suggests that he had suffered attacks before his final illness), his uncle, 'como padre y lexitimo administrador que soy de Don Pedro Joseph Calderon, mi hijo' ('as father and lawful administrator of my son Don Pedro José Calderón'), gave him legal access to all the child's income. With every confidence in his nephew and Doña Agustina, Calderón was able to acknowledge that the child was really his. This acknowledgement is dated 7 May 1655. Two years later, however, on 19 May 1657, he had to make a different acknowledgement: that he was the heir of 'Don Pedro Joseph Calderon, su hixo difunto' ('Don Pedro José Calderón, his late son').[36] The little boy had died in the interval, in circumstances almost as obscure as those of his birth.

One of the factors that made Don Pedro decide to become a priest was almost certainly a financial one; the deaths of his brothers were undoubtedly another; to these we can add the possible death of the mother of his child. Pérez Pastor's suggestion remains a suggestion, but it is not one which should be disregarded.

While the deaths of the queen and the crown prince affected Calderón's livelihood, they are not likely to have had the emotional effect of the deaths of those close to him. There was, however, a third category of deaths in the 1640s: of those who had provided Calderón with inspiration or opportunity, or who had, in the widest sense, collaborated with him in the production of his plays. The first of these was the stage designer Cosme Lotti, who died in late 1643: it was thanks to Lotti that plays such as *El mayor encanto amor* had taken the form they did. Among the writers who had collaborated with Don

Pedro were Mira de Amescua and Luis Vélez, both of whom died in 1644. However, Mira (b. *c.* 1574) and Vélez (b. 1579) belonged to an older generation, and Mira had been living in Guadix since 1632, although he did visit Madrid. Also in 1644 died the royal secretary Antonio Hurtado de Mendoza, at the age of fifty-seven. Calderón had never collaborated with him as a dramatist, but he had often used his songs in his plays, referring to him as 'aquel gran cortesano' ('that great courtier').[37] As for Olivares, there is no proof that his sponsorship and promotion of court plays extended to discussing their content with those who wrote them (with the possible exception of Quevedo and *Cómo ha de ser el privado*): our only evidence for Calderón's dealing with him directly involves the dispatches of November 1641 and possibly Calderón's resignation from the army a year later. Nevertheless, the minister's death in July 1645 marked the end of an era for all those who had once bestowed praise on his regime, including Calderón; even for Quevedo, who rejoiced at his death and who survived him for only a couple of months, his health broken by his imprisonment. Don Pedro, we suspect, cannot have *liked* Quevedo, whose family's origins were only a few miles from his own. Quevedo had cruelly mocked Calderón's friend Pérez de Montalbán as well as his admired Góngora (although Góngora was quite able to look after himself), but he had to be respected as a writer. Another writer whom Calderón admired, and who died at this time, was Tirso de Molina (12 March 1648). Tirso had been living in Soria for years, in charge of one of the houses of his Order, the Mercedarians: rather than plays, he had been writing a history of the Order. In the case of Tirso, we do not know whether admiration extended to friendship; in those of Vélez and Mira, while we have evidence of friendship, we do not know whether it extended beyond a cordial professional relationship. The death which should have affected Don Pedro most was that of Francisco de Rojas, on 23 January 1648. Born on 4 October 1607, Rojas was only forty at the time of his death: the document of May 1646 referred to above points to a degree of closeness that went far beyond professional friendship.

For Calderón, in other words, the forties were his most traumatic decade, involving his military service, and the deaths of several of those closest to him, as well as of those of colleagues, and those who had influenced his career. It is perhaps not surprising that in 1650 he came to the conclusion that events were pushing him towards an entirely different life, a different career.

Don Pedro's personal hardships were reflected on a national scale. When Olivares fell, no *privado* replaced him, at least not officially. His juntas were abolished, and his chief assistant, the Protonotario Jerónimo de Villanueva, was unable to avoid being arrested by the Inquisition in 1644, on suspicion of heresy. The king went so far as to announce that he intended to govern without a *privado*, and began attending meetings of the Council of State. He also began a 600-letter correspondence with a remarkable nun, Sor María de Ágreda, whom he had met in July 1643 on his Aragonese campaign.[38] Sor María provided spiritual consolation and even political counsel, not concealing her opposition to the restoration of Olivares; but Philip needed a confidant who was closer to events, and gradually he began to rely on Don Luis de Haro, the nephew of the former favourite. The Olivares family had plenty of enemies, but Don Luis was a discreet and affable man, who remained in power until his death in 1661. Discreet and affable he may have been, but he was unable to avert the consequences of his uncle's policies: bankruptcy in October 1647, revolt in Sicily and Naples, and fears that Valencia and Aragón would join in. In August 1648 it was discovered that the Duke of Híjar, presumably disappointed in his ambitions to become favourite, had been plotting, with Mazarin's help, to become king of an independent Aragón.[39] All of these revolts and plots were failures. With the benefit of hindsight, we can see that they were not likely to succeed, but some of those who lived through them must have feared the worst. The monarchy survived, although further humiliations awaited.

As early as 1639 negotiations to end the Thirty Years War had begun in Hamburg. By late 1641 agreement had been reached on the conference venues, Osnabrück and Münster, and on the opening date, 25 March 1642. Some of the delegates, though, were determined to come to the table only after one last victory had strengthened their bargaining position. The Emperor Ferdinand let the deadline for his agreement lapse, and the parties came together only on 4 December 1644. The 'one last victory' syndrome continued to delay agreement. Spain's bankruptcy had considerably weakened her position, but at least the revolt of Portugal enabled the Count of Peñaranda, Spain's chief negotiator, to take Brazil out of the Dutch equation. By January 1648 the Dutch and Spanish delegates had reached general agreement, and in October of that year, by the Peace of Westphalia, Spain signed away the United Provinces, which had been *de facto* independent for years. The war with France continued, and the French continued to assist the rebellious Portuguese and Catalans. Portugal, by now an independent country, and sufficiently far from France to rule her own affairs, would never be recovered, although Philip died before he would admit as much; as for Cataluña, while there was increasing dissatisfaction there with the government of the new Count of

Barcelona, Louis XIV, Castile lacked the energy to bring the revolt to an end: it would last for another four years.

* * *

Despite all that happened in his private life in the forties, and despite the regular closure of the public theatres, Calderón was able to write, if not very much in comparison with the previous decade. On 7 July 1645, Francisco Garro de Alegría, the lessee of Madrid's public theatres, signed an agreement with Antonio García de Prado for Prado to begin a run in the city on 24 October.[40] Garro was to give Prado 200 *reales* on account, and to supply three plays, by Calderón, Moreto and Martínez de Meneses. Since Don Pedro had dealt directly with Prado in the past, we cannot be certain that this anonymous play was new.

Another possible play of this period, published as by Rojas, also survives in manuscript, this time in the Institut del Teatre, Barcelona: *La más hidalga hermosura* (Zabaleta, Rojas, Calderón). Once again there is a licence by Juan Navarro de Espinosa, signed in Madrid 'a 4 de Dicienbre de 1645'. Licence dates are not conclusive on their own, but the handwriting of Calderón in Act III is typical of the 1640s, while the untidy appearance of the manuscript is typical of an original draft: the play was probably written towards the end of 1645. The Madrid theatres were functioning normally in the period from Easter 1645 to 14 February 1646 (Ash Wednesday). The play deals with Fernán González (d. 970), Count of Castile, who has defeated and killed in battle King Sancho of Navarre. Sancho's son and heir (García) and daughter (Teresa, married to the King of León) use their sibling Sancha as bait to capture and imprison the count, but Sancha, resentful at having been used in this way, and attracted to the prisoner, sets him free and elopes with him; the play's title refers to Sancha. The ultimate source was the *Poema de Fernán González* (*c.* 1260). The plot would have satisfied the Council of Castile's demand for 'hazañas valerosas' ('valiant deeds'), but it was not achieved 'sin mezcla de amores' ('with no admixture of love affairs'). To judge from the number of early editions, the play was not hugely popular, but it was probably '*La hidalga hermosura*' performed on 14 January 1652.[41]

* * *

Another play of this period may have been inspired by contemporary events. The painter Alonso Cano was born in Granada and studied in Seville. Thanks to the 'Seville connection', he came to Madrid in 1638, where he obtained a court post as painter and architect. Two years later, in 1640, he was involved in repairing the damage done to the Retiro by the fire of

20 February, and his career seemed secure. In June 1644, however, his wife was stabbed to death, and he was arrested and subjected to vigorous questioning, which included torture.[42] Although the investigators were ready to accept that he had not killed her himself, they believed that he had had her killed for infidelity. Public opinion was divided, but Cano maintained his innocence, and he was eventually released for lack of evidence. His career never quite recovered, despite a stay in Valencia (1644–5); in 1652 he returned to Granada.

In the 1640s Don Pedro wrote a play and an *auto* with the same title, *El pintor de su deshonra*. There is no external evidence to date the play, except that it received a palace performance on 29 September 1650;[43] but such performances, especially in the 1650s, need not have been premieres. The plot deals with a painter who kills his wife because he believes she is unfaithful. The wife, Serafina, is innocent, but she is a victim of appearances, and of the powerful imagination of her husband, which is misdirected from his art to his life. Logically, the play should have preceded the *auto*, of which the allegory can be fully appreciated only by those familiar with the play. Since the *auto* is reckoned to have been written shortly before 1647,[44] it would seem that the play was completed sometime before the closure of the theatres in February 1646. It seems reasonable to wonder whether the starting-point for both works was the Cano affair. Given Don Pedro's interest in painting, we can be sure that he followed the case, but this does not prove that he decided to dramatise it. However, the fact remains that, if we can make the connection over three and a half centuries later, an audience of the mid 1640s must also have done so, and the author must have known that it would, unless both play and *auto* pre-date the murder. If the play was inspired by the death of Cano's wife, then it was written between June 1644 and February 1646.

It has been argued, however, that the play was written later, after the *auto*. At one point in the play, the Prince of Ursino explains that

tengo
puesto el gusto en unos cuadros
que para una galería
me hacen los más celebrados
pintores de toda Italia,
y aun España, pues yo he hallado
alguno que a Apeles puede
competir; y tan pagado
desto estoy, que todo el día
sólo en verles pintar gasto. (I, 993b)

(I have taken delight in some paintings which are being done for me, for a gallery, by the most famous painters of all Italy, and even of Spain, since I have found one who can rival Apelles, and I am so pleased with this that I spend the whole day just watching them paint.)

The reference recalls Philip IV's *galería de mediodía* in the *alcázar*, where Spanish and Italian paintings predominated. We remember, too, that Philip liked watching Velázquez at work: there seems no doubt that the passage offers a compliment to the king and his painter, but Regalado goes further, suggesting that the lines were written while Velázquez was in Italy, enhancing his own reputation with portraits of Innocent III and Juan de Pareja, as well as that of the monarch, as a collector.[45] Velázquez had left Málaga in January 1649 in the company of the Duke of Nájera, who was going to collect Princess Mariana; he did not return until 23 June 1651. However, Calderón's normal practice when writing *autos* was to use material familiar to his audience, whether it was a historical event like the king's second marriage, or an existing play: thus the *autos Los encantos de la culpa*, *El árbol del mejor fruto*, *La vida es sueño*, *El jardín de Falerina*, *El pastor Fido* and *Andrómeda y Perseo* are all later than the plays which inspired them.

The play's critics have noted how the play's extraordinary coincidences make it appear 'artificial, theatrical, even operatic'.[46] Paterson in particular has suggested that 'much of [the play's] business lies in contriving "fatalities", certain alignments that prove comically dire when they intersect', and he has described the play as a 'black comedy'.[47] This, then, is another exploration, as in *No hay cosa como callar* and *Basta callar*, of the ways in which comedy and tragedy overlap, of how comical situations leading to the discomfiture of an individual can lead us to laugh – until the discomfiture turns into something worse.

The *auto* version of the story acts as an antidote to the view of critics who have suggested that in his 'wife-murder' plays Calderón was attempting to promote the view that murder was the best way to deal with marital infidelity. In the *auto*, the creator on canvas becomes the Creator. In the play, the innocent wife is courted by a prince, without success. In the *auto* the wife, who is guilty, is Human Nature. She is unfaithful with a prince, the Prince of Darkness. As in the play, the painter tries to paint a portrait of his wife. As in the play, he fails, but for a different reason: when he opens the box of colours, he spills it over his hands. The box contains only red. The scene shows how God the Son takes on himself the guilt of humanity, and the infidelity is forgiven. At the same time the *auto* shows Calderón's vision of the painter as god-like creator, as well as revealing his knowledge of both the theory and the practice of painting.

It is worth noting that Calderón's experiments with black or dark comedy (*No hay cosa como callar*, 1638; *Basta callar*, first version ?1638–9; *Las manos blancas*, ?1640; *El pintor*, ?1646) are confined to a relatively short period, the beginning of which cannot readily be linked with any personal misfortunes; and while he eventually gave up writing comedies completely, the process was a gradual one, not obviously inspired by a single decision: his last comedies with Spanish settings are *Cada uno para sí*, written soon after the fall of Barcelona in October 1652, and *También hay duelo en las damas*, probably written in the winter of 1652–3.[48] His last two comedies were probably *Dicha y desdicha del nombre*, which is referred to in April 1660, and *Mujer, llora y vencerás*, written for Carnival of the same year.[49] Perhaps significantly, both of these are distanced from contemporary Spain, at least spatially, with settings in Italy and Thuringia. As we shall see, though, he did not stop writing humorous material: the most likely explanation for the gradual change of genre involves the royal family's increasing fondness for mythological plays.

CHAPTER 16

Beginning to recover

> Yo estoy en vna cama con vnas grandes tercianas y avnque el duque mi señor me hace mas merced que yo merezco con todo no pueden los señores cuydar tan por menor de los menesteres de vn enfermo que no le hagan soledad quatro Reales a su cabecera.
>
> (Letter, 9 October 1648)
>
> (I'm in bed with very bad tertian fever, and although my lord the duke shows me more favour than I deserve, nevertheless lords cannot care in detail for the needs of an invalid who doesn't have as much as four *reales* by his bedside.)

There is a small amount of circumstantial evidence to suggest that in the late 1640s Calderón was trying to get his output back to what it had been ten years earlier, as if he were making one last attempt to see whether he could survive on his writing. The need to provide for his son, or to be seen to provide for him, may have been a factor. As many as ten plays may belong to the years 1648–50, although none of them can be dated with absolute confidence. *La exaltación de la cruz* is possibly the first. The problem with this title is that it does not appear in the Marañón or Veragua lists, which include instead *El triunfo de la cruz.* No play of this second title survives. However, *La exaltación de la cruz* was printed in *Escogidas I*, a volume which was approved for the press by Calderón himself on 18 May 1652. Given his previous history of hostile reaction to incorrect attribution, it does not seem likely that Don Pedro would have allowed the printing under his name of a play which he had not written: the two titles, *La exaltación* and *El triunfo*, most probably refer to the same play.[1] As for the date, Cotarelo suggests that the Emperor Heraclio's words in Act I,

> esperando cada instante
> ser dueño de la divina
> belleza de mi sobrina
> Eudocia (I, 929b)

(expecting at every moment to be the master of the divine beauty of my niece Eudocia), are an allusion to the expected arrival in Spain of Philip IV's niece Mariana of Austria, who was to become the king's second wife, although she had originally been chosen as the bride of Prince Baltasar Carlos: this would imply a royal performance in 1648 or 1649.[2] The marriage of the character Heraclio is superfluous in terms of the plot, as well as being unchronological: that of the historical Heraclius (610 AD) took place over a decade before his war against the Persians (*c.* 622, portrayed in the play); the unnecessary reference makes the argument more plausible. The apparent mention of the *auto No hay más fortuna que Dios* (I, 934b) might seem to create a problem. The *auto* is reckoned to date from the years 1652 or 1653, probably the former.[3] In 1652 Corpus Christi fell on 30 May. To be approved for printing almost a fortnight earlier, the play must surely have been written before the *auto*, probably some time before it. As on other occasions, the *auto*'s title used an existing phrase, to which it gave a new dimension of meaning.

The play has a historical foundation: the Emperor Heraclio, the patriarch Zacarías of Jerusalem, the magician Anastasio, and the Persians Cósdroas, Síroes and Menardes, are all based on historical figures from the early seventh century, but most of the events portrayed in the play are not historical. The most interesting character is Anastasio, whose search for truth leads him, as it leads Cipriano in *El mágico prodigioso*, from magic to sainthood.

Another of the plays printed in *Escogidas I* is *No siempre lo peor es cierto*. Like *La exaltación de la cruz*, it poses a title problem, since it appears in *Escogidas* as *Nunca lo peor es cierto*. Sometimes the preliminary dates in early Spanish books suggest that printing approval was given for a book that had already been printed, but this is not the case with *Escogidas I*. Calderón apparently approved a manuscript which did not have his original title.[4]

No siempre is set in Valencia, but apart from a reference to galleys leaving for Italy from the port of Vinaroz (II, 1463a), the setting could as well be Madrid. This reference, however, suggests that the play could date from Don Pedro's visit to Valencia in 1638 rather than from the 1648–50 suggested by Hilborn:[5] when Don Carlos decides to enter the king's service as a soldier in order to escape what he thinks is the wreckage of his relationship with Leonor, he speaks of going to Italy, an unnecessarily long journey for any volunteer after the rising of Cataluña in 1640. Pedro Texeira's description of the coasts and ports of Spain (1634) tells us of Valencia that 'su puerto no es capas [= capaz] de grandes baxeles por ser vna plaia abierta y mal segura con los bientos traveçías en la costa' ('its harbour is not capable of taking large ships because it is an open, unsafe beach with crosswinds on the coast'), but the choice of Vinaroz is a strange one: it lies 90 miles north of Valencia, and Texeira dismisses it and Benicarló as possible safe ports: 'Entranbos lugares son de buena población aunque abiertos y sin otra defença que la poca seguridad de su plaia' ('Both places have a good population, although they are open, with no defences other than the insecurity of their beaches'). The port of Denia, on the other hand, 'es el mejor de toda la costa deste reyno' ('is the best on all the coast of this kingdom'), as well as being only 55 miles from Valencia.[6] This vagueness about the topography of Spain's east coast could support the view that the play was written before the author's trip to Barcelona and Tarragona improved his geographical knowledge.

The play's possible reference to Ruiz de Alarcón's *La verdad sospechosa*, 'contra mí hasta la misma | verdad sospechosa tengo' ('against me truth itself is suspect': II, 1452a), is not helpful: that play was written by 1623, and the phrase 'en boca mentirosa es la verdad sospechosa' ('in a lying mouth the truth is suspect') was proverbial. The most interesting comment is one which gives us no help with the date of composition: the maid Inés observes the pleasure and anger in the face of her mistress Beatriz as she reads the words on a piece of paper:

¿De qué nace
ya el agrado y ya el furor?
Sin duda que es borrador
de alguna comedia que hace. (II, 1456b–1457a)

(What makes her pleased one minute and furious the next? It must be the draft of a play she's writing.)

Is Calderón describing himself at work, or one of his colleagues? This is not a question of trying out lines for the sound of them: Beatriz is reacting to words she is reading silently, ostensibly unaware of what she is doing. Whether Don Pedro had caught himself doing this or not, it was a feature of the creative process which he had encountered.

As noted in Chapter 10, *El jardín de Falerina*, a collaboration play by Rojas, Coello and Calderón, was performed by Tomás Fernández on 13 January 1636. Some twelve years later, Don Pedro decided that the plot could be reworked to incorporate more singing. The result was a shorter text (only two acts), which is generally reckoned as the first '*zarzuela*', a peculiarly Spanish variety of musical play named after the intended venue of some early examples of the genre. The Palacio (originally Casa) de la Zarzuela, now the residence of King Juan Carlos, was planned in the early 1630s by the Infante Ferdinand as a hunting-lodge in the grounds of the palace of El Pardo. Construction was completed by the end of the decade and, by the 1650s, it was being used as a winter residence by the king; both *El laurel de Apolo* (1658) and *La púrpura de la rosa* (1660) were planned for performance there (although the second, being entirely sung, was an opera, not a *zarzuela*). The two-act version of *El jardín de Falerina* was apparently not written for the Zarzuela: it was probably the 'comedia cantada' which was performed on 25 June 1649, ostensibly in the *alcázar*.[7] The closing words of the revised text reinforce this probability:

Con que podremos dar fin
todos, a los pies rendidos
de dos vidas, de que el Cielo
nos deje gozar mil siglos. (II, 1912b)

(With which we can all make an end, humbling ourselves at the feet of two lives, which may heaven allow us to enjoy for a thousand centuries.)

The 'two lives' must be Philip IV and María Teresa, born in 1638. The death of Baltasar Carlos on 9 October 1646 had reduced the royal family to only two, and the new queen, Mariana, would not reach Madrid until 15 November 1649. The revised version of the play must have been composed between these dates.

In a drama involving characters with supernatural or magic powers, the question of visions may arise. When the dramatist wishes the audience to participate in these visions, for example by using an image to reveal distant events, contemporary or not, he may encounter technical difficulties. Calderón tried to solve these difficulties in various ways. Early in his career, in *El purgatorio de San Patricio* (?1627–8), he had shown an angel appearing to the saint, carrying a shield with a mirror on it. In the mirror Patricio could see 'viejos, niños y mujeres' ('old men, children and women') begging him to evangelise Ireland, but there is no evidence that the audience could see this small image.[8] At the start of *La exaltación de la cruz*, Anastasio used magic to allow Síroes and Menardes (and the audience) to see their father in Jerusalem while they were in Persia. This was done by means of *apariencias* ('discoveries') and collapsible mountains, but we are given no precise details of the mechanisms used. In *El jardín de Falerina*, Don Pedro was a little more specific, perhaps because he was restricted by the small *alcázar* stage. Once again, he allowed characters on stage to see others who were supposedly hundreds of miles away: the stage direction opens with the words *Con terremoto dentro se corre la cortina y queda con segunda colgadura el teatro* (*With an earthquake offstage, the curtain is drawn, and the stage is left with a second hanging*), and goes on to tell us what can be seen, although the role of the 'second hanging' is not made clear.[9] Perhaps it was meant to provide a frame for the image, but the image involved the actions of real actors. The scene ends with the direction 'corre la cortina' ('the curtain is drawn': II, 1895b), but it is not stated which curtain this is: presumably it was the second curtain, which thus concealed the image seen by the characters on the front of the stage. This device was also used in *El conde Lucanor*, as we shall see presently. A similar scene in *La púrpura de la rosa* (1660) gives us more information, but still not quite enough for us to know exactly how the staging was achieved. Desengaño, the chief inhabitant of the cave of Jealousy, offers to let the jealous Marte see what Venus is doing while he is absent. When he accepts, the stage direction reads *Descúbrese un espejo, y vese en él lo que dicen las coplas* (*A mirror is revealed, and in it can be seen what the lines say*: line 1388*). This is obviously not an example of a situation often encountered in Golden-Age plays, in which a character describes something offstage and invisible to the audience. Here the audience is intended to see what the lines describe. However, no very large piece of glass could have been employed, since seventeenth-century technology could never have created one. One possible explanation is that a large frame was used, representing the frame of the 'mirror', as the 'second hangings' may have done in *Falerina*. Alternatively, a piece of plain glass in a frame, as big (say) as the mirror in Velázquez's *Las meninas*, could have been provided for the characters to look through, while the audience could see round it. Whatever the *espejo* was, the characters it revealed must have been in the upper part of the stage, with the onlookers Marte and Dragón in the foreground, rather as art connoisseurs might stand back to admire a large painting. It is possible to argue that, in the case of *La púrpura*, Calderón had a particular painting in mind, one which would have been familiar to his court audience: Veronese's *Venus and Adonis*, bought for Philip IV in Rome by Velázquez in 1652, and which in 1660 was hanging in the *galería de mediodía* of the *alcázar*.[10]

This desire to recreate a painting on the stage is arguably the result of Don Pedro's interest in art, and in Velázquez in particular. Throughout his career, Velázquez experimented with images within the images of his paintings. The first examples are *Cristo en casa de Marta* (1618) and *La cena de Emaús* (?*c.* 1618), both of which use a 'window' to reveal a scene taking place in an adjoining room. By 1633 – perhaps – he had painted *San Antonio Abad y San Pablo ermitaño* for one of the Retiro chapels, reinventing the medieval technique of showing several scenes from the relationship between the two saints as parts of the main image. Velázquez's source was probably the *Legenda aurea*, and the subject is likely to have been of particular interest to Don Pedro, born on the feast day of St Anthony. However, Velázquez's experimentation reached its height in two works which may have inspired *La púrpura de la rosa*, but which are too late to have influenced *El jardín de Falerina*: *La fábula de Aracne* (*Las hilanderas*) and *Las meninas*, both of them produced around 1656. In the first, the view from one room into another is presented as if we were among the spectators in the pit of a theatre, looking up and through a proscenium arch into the stage, of which the backdrop is Arachne's tapestry; the subject she has chosen is the *Rape of Europa*, as painted by Titian (the original was also hanging in the *alcázar*). In the second, all the features come together: the mythological canvases hung on the walls, the view into another room, and the reflected image of the spectators, Philip and Mariana, in the mirror on the back wall. Don Pedro's use of the word *espejo*, when no literal *espejo* could have been present, recalls *Las meninas* in particular. It has been suggested that Velázquez's use of the mirror to reflect the spectators owes something to Van Eyck's *Arnolfini Family*, another *alcázar* painting.[11] Perhaps Calderón also found inspiration in it.

The inspiration of *Las meninas* at least is evident in the staging of the *loa* of Calderón's last play, *Hado y divisa de Leonido y de Marfisa* (1680).[12] As Charles II and Maria Luisa watched, the curtain was raised to reveal

> un teatro que representaba un salon regio de arquitectura corintia, con la techumbre de artesones de florones de oro ... Desde su primer término hasta el último habia catorce reyes, siete á cada lado ... En la frente del salon, ocupando el medio de la perspectiva, se hizo un trono cubierto de un suntuoso dosel, debajo del cual habia dos retratos de nuestros felicísimos monarcas, imitados tan al vivo, que como estaban frente de sus originales pareció ser un *espejo*.[13]

> (a stage representing a royal drawing-room of Corinthian architecture with a caissoned ceiling of gold rosettes ... From the foreground to the rear there were fourteen kings, seven on each side ... In the front of the drawing-room, occupying half the perspective, was a throne covered by a sumptuous canopy, under which were two portraits of our happy monarchs, so vividly imitated that, since they were opposite their originals, it seemed a mirror.)

The gilt *artesonado* ceiling, the images of the fourteen kings, the canopied throne, combine to indicate that the intention was to re-create a version of the *salón dorado*, the theatre of the old *alcázar*. Melchor de León was paid 1,000 *reales* 'por auer escripto la narratiua de la fiesta para embiar a Alemania' ('for having written the account of the entertainment to send to Germany' (i.e., Vienna)), so this description is likely to be his. However, Don Pedro was paid for the *loa* and for attending rehearsals, so he presumably conceived this situation: the king and queen in a theatre, watching a play which portrayed them in a theatre, watching a play.[14]

* * *

The second version of *El jardín de Falerina* also shows Calderón experimenting with the effects of music on characters. He had often presented characters whose taste for music reflected their sentiments: this had involved songs 'llenas | de dolor y sentimiento' ('full of grief and sorrow': I, 215a) for the melancholy Fénix in *El príncipe constante*, and the preference of the belligerent Segismundo for 'las músicas militares' ('military music': I, 378a) in *La vida es sueño*; now, musical plays provided an opportunity for a more systematic relationship between the characters and their feelings.

On 18 December 1656, Pedro de la Rosa should have performed *El conde Lucanor* in one of the public theatres, but he had to cancel the performance because 'estuvo estudiando y ensayando la fiesta de los años de la reina' ('he was studying and rehearsing the entertainment for the queen's birthday').[15] The queen's birthday was on 22 December, but while it is almost certain that *El conde Lucanor* was not a new play at this time, we have to guess at how old it was. The play was printed in *Comedias escogidas XV* (1661), but this version of the text, rejected by Calderón himself, has been identified as a clumsy rehash.[16] In 1672, when a friend approached Don Pedro to sanction the printing of his *Quarta parte*, the poet reluctantly agreed, 'con condición … que ha de ser la de Lucanor alguna dellas … pues hallarà el que tuuiere curiosidad de cotejarla, con la que anda en la Parte Quinze, que a pocos versos mios, prosigue con los de otros' ('on condition … that that of Lucanor is one of them … for he who is curious enough to compare it with that in the *Parte quince* will find that after a few of my lines, it continues with those of others').[17]

Don Pedro's apparent concern for the text of this play cannot be explained by the suggestion that it was the only one he had noticed: he goes on to provide a list of forty titles of plays which have been wrongly attributed to him. On the other hand, he had not been nursing his resentment since 1661: his prologue suggests that it was only when he went looking for printed texts of his plays to send to a friend who had asked for them that he realised that the text of *El conde Lucanor* had been tampered with.[18]

El conde Lucanor is not a borrowing from Don Juan Manuel's work of the same title, but it has several familiar features. Set in Egypt and Tuscany, it opens with Ptolomeo, the Sultan of Egypt, thrown from his horse in a mountain wilderness. Like Rosaura in *La vida es sueño*, he comes on a dark and isolated building, the prison of Federico, Duke of Tuscany, whose horoscope has threatened Ptolomeo with his overthrow (as Segismundo's threatens Basilio). News is brought to Federico that his subjects are unwilling to be ruled by his daughter Rosimunda unless she marries (in *Las manos blancas no ofenden* Serafina is faced with the same problem). Rosimunda feels the need to consult her father, who knows nothing about two of the three suitors she must choose from. The sibylline figure Irifela, who had warned Ptolomeo of the threat from Federico, is consulted. Irifela, dressed in skins like Segismundo, offers to show what they are like by means of 'la luna | de un espejo' ('the glass of a mirror': II, 1961a). The next scene represents the interior of her cave, where *Corre [Irifela] vna cortina, y en medio del teatro se vè vn espejo* (*Irifela draws a curtain and in the middle of the stage can be seen a mirror*: p. 394).[19] At first, Ptolomeo and Federico look at the mirror and describe what they see; there is no indication that the audience can see any of what is described, and the mirror is covered. When Federico protests, Irifela allows them to look again: one by one, they see the three suitors, Casimiro, Astolfo and Lucanor, as well as Rosimunda and the *gracioso* Pasquín; finally, all of these appear together, along with soldiers and musicians. All the characters have lines, and the audience was clearly able to see them, at least on this second occasion.

As noted previously, if the *espejo* was made of real glass, it cannot have been very large. As with *El jardín de Falerina*, the 'vision' and those seeing it were presumably separated by a 'second hanging' which could be opened and closed. The duration of the 'vision', and the variety of actions portrayed in it, are rather greater in *Lucanor* than in *Falerina*. In addition, at the beginning of Act II, the heroine Rosimunda is required to approach a statue of Venus in a garden. The stage direction suggests that the second curtain was used again at this point:

En medio se corre vna cortina, y vese vna fuente con vna estatua pequeña de marmol, y si no se pudiere executar en el salon, se represente dentro. (p. 405)

(*In the middle a curtain is drawn, and a fountain with a small marble statue can be seen; if this cannot be done in the salón, it should be performed offstage.*

The reference to the *salón* probably means that Calderón knew that the play was to be performed in the *salón dorado* of the old *alcázar* (although there were other *salones* which were sometimes used); if the limitations of this small performance area did not permit a fountain, this part of the scene would have to take place offstage. This more extensive use of the middle curtain suggests that *Lucanor* is later than *El jardín de Falerina*, that is, after

June 1649, but the argument is not conclusive. The evidence is complicated by the ending:

Lucanor Con que el Conde Lucanor
será feliz, si merece …
Todos Que de los que a otros sobraron
algún víctor se le preste. (II, 2000b)

(Lucanor: With which Count Lucanor will be happy, if he earns … All: Being lent a cheer from those which others had to spare.)

Calderón's most frequent closing plea is for pardon. Of all his plays, including collaboration plays in which he wrote the final act, only two end with a request for a *víctor* (the equivalent of a cheer): *Lucanor* and *La niña de Gómez Arias*, both printed in the *Quarta parte*, and neither surviving in autograph form. It seems unlikely that he would make such a request of a courtly audience, and these lines are probably spurious. The anonymous friend who produced the *Quarta parte* presumably tried to ensure that the *Lucanor* text he included was accurate, but Don Pedro's remarks in his prologue suggest that he was not invited to check the texts. Although corrections were made to some plays for the second edition (1674), the closing lines of *Lucanor* were not changed. If the lines were authentic, the play might have been written in the latter part of 1649 or in 1650, while the author was still writing for the public theatres, but the text offers another clue in Federico's remark that

sólo es venturosa la corona
que tiene rey que vence y que perdona. (II, 1962b)

(Only the crown which has a king who conquers and pardons is fortunate.)

This can be taken as a reference to the Catalan rebellion, which ended on 13 October 1652 with the surrender of Barcelona. Three months later, Philip IV granted a general pardon, promising to observe Cataluña's laws and liberties as they had existed when he became king in 1621: that is, before Olivares came to power. It seems probable that 'que vence y que perdona' refers to that military success and the subsequent pardon: the play is likely to have been written in early 1653.

There is a curious resemblance between *El conde Lucanor* and Ana Caro's *El conde Partinuplés*. In the latter, Rosaura, empress of Constantinople, is urged, like Rosimunda, to marry. Like Rosimunda, she is enabled to inspect her suitors by means of a 'discovery': *Vuélvese el teatro, y descúbrense los cuatro de la manera que los nombra* (*The stage turns, and the four are revealed as they are named*).[20] Rosaura is told that

> Este que miras, galán,
> que en la luna de un espejo
> traslada las perfecciones
> del bizarro, airoso cuerpo,
> es Federico Polonio. (lines 341–5)

(This young gentleman you are looking at, who in the glass of a mirror conveys the perfections of his dashing, elegant body, is Federico of Poland.)

Federico's use of an 'espejo' is interesting, but these suitors have no lines, although the editor suggests in a note that the real actors were involved. *Partinuplés* was printed in *Escogidas IV*, of which the approbations date from December 1652 and the *tasa* from 14 May 1653; that is, it probably predates *Lucanor*, but perhaps not by much.[21]

If we regard the plot of a play as a means of creating suspense, *Lucanor* will disappoint us: we know that the eponymous character will be the successful suitor. What the courtly audience was offered instead was the opportunity to experience emotions vicariously. The means involved music. In this case the lyrics were familiar ballads, and the skill of the writer was to adapt them to their new setting. While we can assume from Pedro de la Rosa's planned performance of 1656 that public-theatre audiences were willing to accept this feature, we may suspect that it was the theoretically more cultured audience of the court that most appreciated it, as they did the use of novel staging techniques which were not possible outside the royal theatres. Golden-Age courtiers were cultivated and sophisticated people, or liked to be perceived as such. Don Pedro knew how to gratify their desires by triggering that self-satisfaction which we experience when we recognise an allusion. For example, when he decided to re-create that moment in the Perseus myth when Jupiter descends on Danaë in the form of a golden shower, most of us now might wonder how he could have coped with the staging of 'golden rain'. In 1653 his solution involved real gold coins, which so distracted the *dueña* and other ladies of Dánae that Júpiter was given his opportunity to descend and carry her off.[22] The solution may seem elegant and original, but it is an allusion to Titian's *Danaë and the Shower of Gold* (?1549–50), another of the paintings in the royal collection: the 'dueña' of Titian's Danaë spreads her apron to catch the coins.[23]

* * *

The play usually entitled *Guárdate del agua mansa* should really be called *El agua mansa*, although the two titles conveniently differentiate the two versions of the text. The title *El agua mansa* (AM) is that of the autograph manuscript.[24] The *Guárdate* version (GAM), printed in 1657 in *Escogidas VIII*, includes long descriptions of the arrival of Queen Mariana in Madrid. At one point both versions refer to 'plague guards' (AM, 779; GAM, 1077), whose job it was to prevent possibly infected travellers from entering cities. Madrid was threatened by plague from 1647 to 1649, especially in the last year.[25] The revised version must have been written soon after the events it describes: both versions may well date from 1649.[26] The date is significant, since it shows that Calderón was able to write, or at least to revise, one of his funniest secular comedies a matter of months before he took the first steps towards becoming a priest. The play also presents what was for Calderón a new kind of character.

The title, 'Still water [runs deep]', refers to Clara, in whose mouth butter refuses to melt. Clara is the elder daughter of Don Alonso, who left his family in Spain while he went to Mexico to make his fortune. Returning to care for his daughters when their mother dies, the wealthy Don Alonso's first concern is to find them suitable husbands, particularly when he hears that Eugenia, the younger sister, reads worldly books and writes poetry. (On the stage at least, cultured sophistication did not always extend to older male aristocrats, or, if it did, they saw it as a masculine prerogative.) Don Alonso explains that he has chosen a nephew from the north, the son of his eldest brother and thus the head of the family:

Ved
que es vuestra cabeza, y creo
que será la más dichosa
la que le tenga por dueño. (AM, 645–8)[27]

(Understand that he's your head, and I believe the happier of you will be the one to marry him.)

Postponing the entry of an anticipated character, especially one who may be eccentric, is a standard dramatic technique. Thus, while we hear before line 200 of Don Alonso's plan, the arrival and the full name of the nephew are delayed for hundreds of lines. In line 621 of the manuscript (GAM, 923), he is named as Don Toribio Cuadradillos. Some aristocratic surnames, like Luna and Lara, are place-names, but Cuadradillos means 'gussets', as noted earlier. Saint Toribio of Lima conferred some respectability on the Christian name, but he was canonised only in 1726; in 1649 the name had negative associations.[28]

Don Toribio comes from La Montaña: specifically, from the Toranzos valley. He brings his patent of nobility, and constantly refers to it, and to his *casa solariega*, his family seat. La Montaña was of course Calderón's own ancestral home, and his family's *casa solariega* is less than 15 miles from Santiurde de Toranzos. Because of the shared background of Don Pedro and Don Toribio, there is an element of self-mockery in the dramatist's portrayal of his character, but Toribio is ridiculed in other ways: first, through his name; second, through audience anticipation, increased by the long-awaited arrival; third, through his appearance; fourth, through his manner of speech; fifth, through his actions; and last, through his attitudes. The quaint surname, first mentioned in line 199, is followed by the long delay: the audience knows to expect something extraordinary. As for appearance, the remarks of the sisters ('¡Jesús, qué rara figura!', 'Goodness, what an eccentric character!' – Eugenia; 'Tú tienes razón, por cierto', 'You're certainly right' – Clara, AM, 667–8) confirm that he looks unusual, as does Don Alonso's remark (AM, 783–4; GAM, 1081–2) about their finding Toribio's dress displeasing, although we are given no details.

Toribio's speech offers much more information than the circumstantial evidence regarding his dress. He uses uneducated or archaic pronunciation or word-forms, most of them concealed by regularisation in the printed editions, but clear in the autograph manuscript: 'verdá' (AM, 676), 'nenguna' (AM, 719), 'despensación' (AM, 727), 'estrución' (AM, 772), 'quijeran o no quijeran' (AM, 1010), 'dende' (AM, 1124), 'Engeña' (for Eugenia, AM, 1127), 'envesible' (AM, 1688). There are also malapropisms, or unwitting puns, such as 'sombreros de castrón' (AM, 1120) (he means beaver hats, 'de castor'; 'castrón' is a gelded goat); or, when Don Alonso refers to him as the senior member of the family, he complacently replies that in the valley of Toranzos, he was the 'cabeza mayor' wherever he went (AM, 676–80) ('cabeza mayor' is a head of cattle; 'cabeza menor', of sheep or goats). There are also word-plays or coinings typical of *graciosos*: he refers to his cousins as 'primiesposas' ('cousinywives', AM, 1925), and when he objects to what Don Alonso calls an 'acción cortesana', his response is 'Más me güele a corte enferma' (AM, 977–8).[29] However, although Toribio is permitted these flashes of verbal dexterity, we are more conscious of his maladroitness, for example, the malapropisms, or his unfamiliarity with the word 'filis' ('charm'), which he thinks is a commodity that can be bought.

Toribio's maladroitness extends to social niceties and manners. When he arrives in Don Alonso's house, his uncle invites him to sit. He does so, only then inviting the others to sit as well: the printed edition adds the direction '*Siéntase*' ('*He sits*') before his 'que os sentéis los tres os ruego' ('Please be seated, the three of you': AM, 696). Sitting in the presence of a standing lady was a serious social solecism; his uncle notices, but believes that Madrid will soon teach him better manners (AM, 783–90).

Calderón seems concerned to portray a wide range of Toribio's lack of social graces. His tardy and clumsy compliments (AM, 705–6) fall well short of what would be expected from a cousin and future husband, and his efforts are marred by his rustic imagery: while trying to describe the difficulty of choosing between Clara and Eugenia, he explains how donkeys starve to death when faced with a choice between two lots of barley (AM, 711–20). He is of course unaware that this image casts him as a donkey.

Other aspects of the behaviour of Toribio show him to be no gentleman. He does not think it inappropriate to enter the bedroom of Clara and Eugenia, and when their *dueña* Mari Nuño annoys him by impeding him and later by refusing to give him information, he threatens to hit her. He is suitably astonished when she punches him. Being hit, accidentally or deliberately, is one of the things that happen to *graciosos*. In fact the typical *gracioso*, who is usually a servant or a lower-class rustic – sometimes both – is not present in this play. *El agua mansa* has four servants, three of whom have very minor roles. The fourth is Mari Nuño, the *dueña*, and while *dueñas* are frequent sources of humour, they are normally given a foil, in the form of a *gracioso*. Here, the foil is Toribio. Once we realise this, we see that Toribio has other *gracioso* characteristics, among them hunger and cowardice. The two combine in the scene where Mari Nuño enters to say that the food is ready:

MARI NUÑO La comida está en la mesa.
DON TORIBIO ¡Ay, señor tío! ¿Qué es esto?
¿Trujistis esta alimaña
de las Indias?, que no veo
que es hombre ni mujer y habla.
DON ALONSO Es dueña.
DON TORIBIO ¿Y es mansa?
MARI NUÑO [*Ap.*] (Necio
es el tal primo.)
BRÍGIDA [*Ap.*] (No es
sino tonto por extremo.)
DON TORIBIO ¡No me haga mal! … ¿Dijo algo
de comida, si me acuerdo? (AM, 759–68)

(MARI NUÑO: Dinner is on the table. DON TORIBIO: Oh, uncle! What's this? Did you bring this animal from the Indies? It's neither man nor woman as far as I can see, and it talks. DON ALONSO: She's a duenna. DON TORIBIO. Is it tame? MARI

NUÑO, ASIDE: This cousin is a fool. BRÍGIDA, ASIDE: He's not, he's incredibly stupid. DON TORIBIO: Don't let it hurt me! It said something about dinner, if I recall?)

His preoccupation with food associates Toribio with absurd *hidalgos* like Don Mendo of Zalamea, or Lazarillo's *escudero.*

When Calderón revised the play, he retained all these features, but added a new one, arising out of a note sent to the girls to invite them to see the royal entry. Toribio, suspecting that the note may come from a rival, wants to see it, but he cannot read it (GAM, 2564–6). For an *hidalgo* to be illiterate, even in 1649, must have been at least a little shocking, even though there was always a minority of the 'old school' of aristocrats which considered learning unnecessary.

In one sense, the old school has already figured in the play. When the ostensibly demure Clara upbraids her sister for appearing flighty, Eugenia tells her that things have changed:

Has de saber, Clara, que
los 'non fagades' de antaño,
que hablaron con las doncellas
y las demás deste caso,
con las calzas atacadas
y los cuellos, se llevaron
a Simancas, donde yacen
entre 'magueres' y 'fallos'.
Don Escrúpulo de honor
fue un pesadísimo hidalgo
cuyos privilegios ya
no se leen de puro rancios. (AM, 565–76)

(You must know, Clara, that the 'ye shall nots' of yesteryear, that they said to young women and the rest about this matter, along with buttoned hose and collars, were taken to Simancas, where they lie among albeits and arbitraments. Sir Scruple of Honour was a very boring nobleman whose rights are no longer read, they're so fusty.)

The old vocabulary, and the prohibitions it was used to frame ('non fagades' = 'no hagáis'), has been relegated, along with the old fashions of dress, to the state archives in Simancas.

This conversation airs some of the play's subject-matter. For example, the play deals with a father's right to choose his daughters' husbands. In one sense, this right is not challenged. The lively Eugenia meekly accepts her father's decision that she will marry Toribio, but when she sees the intended bridegroom alone, she makes it clear that she has no intention of marrying him, and tells him that if he reports their conversation to her father, she will deny it (he does, and she does). In the end, neither sister marries a man chosen by the father, but Calderón does not attack these supposed paternal rights: he undermines them by portraying young women marrying the young men they have chosen.

While the words of Eugenia's Simancas speech are obviously applicable to her father, the old-fashioned clothes and vocabulary also suggest a relevance to Toribio, as does the name Don Escrúpulo de Honor: Toribio is very sensitive to the presence of young men anywhere near his cousins, and, like serious men of honour, he believes that his concern for the behaviour of his female relatives allows him to violate their privacy. His first attempt to enter the sisters' room was foiled by Mari Nuño. Later, during a search for a supposed intruder, he gains access and, searching, finds what he thinks is evidence of improper behaviour. Both versions of the text portray his concern, but in the revised version he has a 'soliloquy' in which parts of the body or human sentiments are apostrophised amid syntax broken by exclamations of dismay. This increases the resemblance between him and Calderón's real 'men of honour'. When he finally finds his evidence, he does so 'detrás de la cama ¡ay triste! | de Eugenia' ('behind, alas! Eugenia's bed': GAM, 2879–80).

In *El médico de su honra* Don Gutierre found his evidence, the dagger of Prince Enrique, 'detrás de mi cama' ('behind my bed': 2907); like Toribio, he was searching for a supposed burglar. This was one of the passages Calderón expanded when he revised *El agua mansa*, and the added lines, typical of Gutierre's manner of speech, exemplify Toribio as a caricature of Gutierre. Toribio's evidence, however, is not a dagger: he has found what he thinks is a folding ladder, the elaborate framework of Eugenia's *guarda-infante*, her farthingale. Even when he has been told what the 'ladder' really is, Toribio is none the wiser, and less than reassured: he clearly suspects that Eugenia may have had a child (*infante*) out of – before – wedlock.

* * *

Funny characters existed in the earliest Spanish plays, although Lope de Vega is usually credited with inventing the *gracioso*. The critics who give him this credit are, in general, those who condemn Calderón for stereotyping the role.[30] It is clear, though, that Calderón experimented with various kinds of funny characters during his career, particularly the *figurón*, to the extent that in *El agua mansa* the role of the *figurón* incorporates that of the *gracioso*, who is suppressed. Some of Toribio's risible traits are shared with lower-class *graciosos*, such as cowardice and concern with food. However, others of the traits which are offered for our amusement are shared with men like Gutierre, and expressed in similar vocabulary: this feature has already been noted in *No hay burlas con el amor*. Another aspect of this play, characteristic of Calderón's comedies, is the way in which it demonstrates that categorisation of individuals, whether by themselves or by others, is often incorrect. In Act I of *El agua mansa*, Mari Nuño tells us how agreeable Clara is, while Eugenia is the opposite. As for Don Félix, he has never been in love, and, in his view, is past the stage of ever being so. The play shows that all these character assessments are wrong: this is the kind of moral that we expect from a comedy. More subtly, though, this play provides us with another light in which to examine characters who do not amuse, but who may merit ridicule.[31]

The plot of *El agua mansa* resembles that of Moreto's *El lindo don Diego*. The date of composition of *El lindo don Diego* is unknown. While the first recorded printing was in *Comedias escogidas XVIII* (1662),[32] it has been suggested that the play was written after Moreto became a priest in 1657;[33] there can be little doubt that it was written after Calderón's play. Moreto's debt to Castro's *El Narciso en su opinión* has been examined, but it is evident that his sources also included Don Pedro.[34]

In addition to plays, Calderón continued to write *autos*. The *autos* of 1647 were performed by Prado and Rueda, but we do not know their titles, and the only reference to Don Pedro in the documents relates to a payment of 550 *reales*, a mere third of what he was receiving at this time for a single *auto*: he may have been paid in instalments, a possibility supported by the events of the following year.[35] In 1648 Calderón wrote both *autos*, and came to Madrid from Alba to do so. On this occasion there was considerable documentation generated by Madrid Town Council's shortage of cash and consequent inability to pay the participants, but no one mentioned the *auto* titles. Corpus had fallen on 11 June, but on 9 October Don Pedro, by then confined to bed in Alba with 'tertian fever', was still requesting the money he was owed.[36] Antonio de Prado was eventually given his performance fee on 19 October, but the intervention of José Calderón was required to ensure that his uncle was finally paid, José collecting the money for him on 20 November.[37] Although the Madrid documents refer to *autores* in the plural, another document shows that in August Prado went to Brihuega to perform 'los autos de Madrid' and various plays, one of them *El escondido y la tapada*.[38] Brihuega is over 50 miles from Madrid, on the far side of Guadalajara. These documents, and hundreds of others like them, show that even small towns (modern Brihuega has around 3,000 inhabitants) could see the *autos* a matter of weeks after Spain's leading dramatist had written them. The plays they were offered were rarely very new, but they were performed by one of the country's leading companies. Nowadays, Spanish local and regional authorities spend significant sums bringing cultural events to their areas, but in terms of drama at least, their seventeenth-century counterparts may have done even better.

One of the *autos* of this period is certainly *La segunda esposa y triunfar muriendo*, inspired by the king's second marriage: the *auto* transformed the king into Christ and his second spouse into the Church. However, 1648 seems very early, and it has been suggested that the *auto* was not played at Corpus at all, but for the queen's formal entry into Madrid in November 1649.[39] Another contemporary *auto* is *La primer flor del Carmelo*. In the *loa*, the character Invierno expresses a wish:

> Así, de la nueva esposa
> el día felice llegue,
> y llegue el felice día
> que tu Real familia aumentes.

(So let the happy day of the new bride arrive, and the happy day when you increase your royal family.)

Philip's plan to marry Mariana was announced on 12 January 1647.[40] Three *loas* have been linked with this *auto*, but this is the earliest, printed in 1655 as the 'Loa sacramental que la compañía de Antonio de Prado representó en el auto de la primer flor del Carmelo' ('Sacramental *loa* which the company of Antonio de Prado performed with the *auto La primer flor del Carmelo*').[41] We have seen that from 1647 *autos* used four carts, but the text of this *auto* is not helpful: it mentions only two, although four are possible. Composition was probably in 1647 or 1648: Prado was involved in the *autos* in both years.

The *autos* of 1649 were Don Pedro's *La vacante general*, played by Prado, and *La Magdalena*, played by Diego Osorio.[42] The text and the name of the author of the second have not survived, but the companies used their obligation to perform them as a lever to persuade the king's Council to open the public theatres so that they could earn a living during the preparation period. Only one member of the Council objected.[43]

The accounts of the Cofradía de la Novena (the actors' guild) list a number of the plays and *autos* performed in 1650. Not all the titles are given, but some of those which are are Calderón's, or can be identified as his.[44] On 5 July Antonio de Prado performed an *auto* referred to simply as *Gedeón*. This is presumably Don Pedro's *La piel de Gedeón*, and we can conclude that Prado, whose company was one of the two chosen for that year, had played that *auto* on Corpus Thursday (16 June). The other company was Osorio's and his *auto* was Calderón's *El año santo* [*de Roma*].[45] It was normal for the companies to offer their *autos* to paying spectators for some time after the free Corpus performances. Osorio also performed *El mejor amigo el muerto* (a collaboration play which dated back to 1636) and the lost play *Nuestra Señora de los Remedios*, as well as *Agradecer y no amar*, *Dar tiempo al tiempo* and *Para vencer a amor, querer vencerle*, which was close to twenty years old. Some of the performances were *particulares* (i.e., private), some to the king during Carnival, or at other times unspecified. While the plays given before the king at Carnival were presumably new, there is no evidence that any of the named works were being performed for the first time. On the contrary, they ranged from a few weeks old (the *autos*) to almost twenty years; the accounts do not help us to tell where *Agradecer y no amar* and *Dar tiempo al tiempo* come in this chronology. *Agradecer y no amar* was printed in *Escogidas V* (1653). *La exaltación de la cruz* may have been four years old when printed in this series, *Lucanor* perhaps eight.

Agradecer y no amar is set in Italy. In the contrived plot, Princess Flérida of Bisiniano saves Laurencio from his enemies out of gratitude for his attempt to return a garter she has lost while hunting, and because she feels some sympathy for his declared love for her, although she does not return it. Despite references to *Querer por solo querer* (1622, by Antonio Hurtado de Mendoza; II, 1381a), *El monstruo de la fortuna* (?by 1633; II, 1372a) and *La dama duende* (1629; II, 1404b), there is no textual evidence for the date of composition, unless we consider two similarities. One involves the two plants which, taken individually, are poisonous, and which, when mixed, are beneficial. The other references to these plants are in *Peor está que estaba* (?1630), which is also set in Italy and which also has a reference to *La dama duende*, in *A secreto agravio, secreta venganza* (?1635), and in *La hija del aire II* (?late 1630s). The second similarity involves a scene in which a would-be suitor pretends to be a diamond merchant to gain access to a lady. In *Agradecer* the jewels offered are a Cupid, an eagle, a *firmeza*, *memorias* and an emerald (a *firmeza* was a jewel symbolising constancy, while *memorias* were linked 'memory rings'; green is the colour symbolising hope). In *A secreto agravio* Leonor's lover Luis offers a *firmeza*, a Cupid, a heart and *memorias*, as well as referring to an emerald (= his hope) which was stolen from him.

It has been noted that resemblances of this kind are not sure guides to dates of composition. Hilborn accepts that *Agradecer* was written in 1650, disregarding the evidence that the play was no longer new by then.[46] If we look at his data (23% *redondillas*, 62% *romance*, 5% *décimas*, 7% *silva*) and compare them with those for *El alcaide de sí mismo* (1627: 26% *redondillas*,

53% *romance*, 6% *décimas*, 13% *silva*) or *Mañana será otro día* (1636: 25% *redondillas*, 64% *romance*, 8% *décimas*, 2% *silva*), we may feel that there is nothing in the verse-forms to prevent the play from being contemporary with *Para vencer a amor* (?1630–3), which also appears in the 1650 accounts. It should be noted that Hilborn admits that both *Agradecer* and *Dar tiempo al tiempo* have acts ending in *redondillas*, 'which we have not seen since 1636, in *Mañana será otro día*' (p. 43). In the *Verdadera quinta parte* (1682) Vera Tassis lists the play as a 'fiesta que se representò à sus Magestades' ('an entertainment performed before Their Majesties'), but only the closing request for pardon, 'a vuestras plantas invictas' ('at your unconquered feet'), presents (inconclusive) evidence for this; he may have been aware of the royal performance on 23 April 1680.[47]

Dar tiempo al tiempo, unlike *Agradecer y no amar*, is set in Madrid. Not printed until 1662, in *Escogidas XVII*, it could be said to take its title from Cervantes: 'Será bien dar tiempo al tiempo, que no se ganó Zamora en una hora' ('It will be well to give time time, for Zamora was not won in an hour').[48] These are two proverbial expressions, however, although the Cervantes connection is strengthened by the fact that the play also refers to Zamora: '¿He de tratar del reto de Zamora?' ('Am I to deal with the challenge of Zamora?': II, 1350b).

Dar tiempo offers yet another example of a play in which a zealous brother, Diego, is disappointed in love. Its most interesting feature is the way in which the triangular relationship involving the servants Chacón, Ginés and Juana mimics and mocks those of the main characters; but it also provides a contrast with them. The principal male protagonist, Juan, has been in Seville with his servant Chacón for thirteen months, establishing his right to an inheritance. Since he has been on the move, he failed to get the letter in which his beloved Leonor explained that she and her father had moved house. After several misadventures, they arrive at the old address, where Chacón is given a baby by a woman who immediately re-enters. The arrival of others prevents them from discovering more, and Chacón takes the baby to a 'nursery'. He had evidently been sleeping with Juana, but he knows this child cannot be his. Unlike the steadfast Leonor, Juana believed that out of sight was out of mind, and took up with Ginés, who is the real father of her child. Chacón swears dire vengeance:

Mi venganza sea
más campanuda venganza
que la de aquel Veinticuatro
de Córdoba o de Granada. (II, 1333b; cf. also 1363a)

(Let my vengeance be more high-flown vengeance than that of that Veinticuatro of Córdoba or Granada.)

Using almost the same vocabulary as his master, who wrongly thinks Leonor has not been true to him, he upbraids Juana, but with a humorous twist:

> ¿Puedes negarme, ingrata,
> falsa, aleve, cruel, fiera, mulata
> (perdona el consonante …)? (II, 1350b)

(Can you deny to me, you thankless, false, perfidious, cruel, ferocious, mulatta – excuse the rhyme …?)

The joke implicitly mocks honour-vengeance, especially since Chacón's vengeance involves trying to extract payment from Ginés to give to a supposed astrologer who will locate his child. In the end, this ruse is discovered, and Ginés happily marries Juana. We are not explicitly invited to think about how they will support their baby, but the thought occurs to us. In the seventeenth century the Madrid Hermandad del Refugio, which Calderón would join in 1666, was rescuing 300–400 children per year from the streets.[49]

As often happens, the allusions do not help us to date the play. Lope's *Los comendadores de Córdoba* (of which the Veinticuatro is the protagonist) dates from 1596–8. We may note, though, that in *Cada uno para sí*, written soon after the fall of Barcelona in October 1652, Hernando makes a similar, lengthier allusion to the Lope play, swearing that he will go one further and be the 'veinticinco de honor' (II, 1693b).[50] As for *Primero soy yo*, which may date from 1638–41, the phrase was proverbial, so the reference (II, 1357b) is inconclusive. Finally, there is a quotation from Lope's ballad, '¡Ay, verdades que en amor …!':

> Que en vano llama a la puerta
> quien no ha llamado en el alma. (II, 1335a)

(He who has not knocked on the soul knocks in vain at the door.)

These lines are also found in *El conde Lucanor* (?1653: II, 1979b), but this is equally inconclusive.[51] There is nothing to prevent this play from having been written long before the recorded performance of 1650, for example in the 1630s. If we find the Veinticuatro allusions significant, we may opt for the late 1640s.

Another play which should be examined in the context of *Dar tiempo al tiempo* is *El maestro de danzar*, which has been dated on the basis of its verse to shortly after 1650.[52] The closing lines ('pidiendo a esos reales pies | el perdón de nuestras faltas', 'asking forgiveness for our faults at these royal feet': II, 1571b) have been taken to indicate composition after 1650, when Calderón was writing only for the royal theatre. Neither argument is quite conclusive, although we are on firmer ground with the verse, since *El maestro* has 85 per cent of *romance*: no reliably dated play written entirely by Calderón prior to 1650 reaches the figure of 80 per cent of this metre. What is certain is that the play has nothing in common with Lope's *El maestro de danzar*,[53] and a great deal in common with *Dar tiempo al tiempo*. In *Dar tiempo al tiempo*, Don Juan and Chacón have left Seville to find Leonor, who lives with her father in Madrid. They arrive at night, but as they wander the streets to get to her house, Beatriz, fleeing from her brother's vengeance, begs for Juan's help. In *El maestro de danzar*, Don Enrique and Chacón have left Madrid to find Leonor, who now lives with her father in Valencia. They arrive at night, but as they wander the streets in a search for her new home, Beatriz . . ., etc. One difference lies in Calderón's treatment of the two cities in the two plays. In Madrid the travellers are attacked by thugs in the dark muddy streets, and have filth dropped on them from upstairs windows; interestingly, the thugs are soldiers. In Valencia the apparently clean streets are lit by the moon, and the only unwelcome encounter is with a group of *alguaciles* (which also happens in *Dar tiempo al tiempo*). We might suppose that for a Madrid-born author to draw a Madrid audience's attention to the seamier side of the city was acceptable, especially when they knew that he was often full of praise; but his fellow dramatist Pedro Rosete Niño was physically attacked for being too explicit:

> Hirieron a Don Pedro Rosete-Niño, Poeta de opinion por haver escrito una Comedia intitulada: *Madrid por de dentro*, donde pintava la Vida de Tahures, Rufianes, Mugeres de mal vivir y gallinas con apariencia de Valientes, con otros Interlocutores semejantes.[54]

> (They wounded Don Pedro Rosete Niño, a poet of some repute, because he wrote a play entitled *Madrid por de dentro*, in which he portrayed the lives of gamblers, pimps, women of ill repute, and cowards dressed like toughs, with other similar characters.)

Since this happened in April 1641, while Calderón was in Cataluña, he may not even have heard of it; in any case, his portrayal of the more sordid aspects of Madrid life was incidental. As for the unpleasant features of other Spanish cities, if Don Pedro noticed them, he preferred not to mention them.

Calderón made a good impression during his visit to Valencia in 1638, and the city seemingly made a good impression on him. We should not conclude, though, that the impression was so short-lived that this play must have been written soon after the visit, or that the resemblances between this play and *Dar tiempo al tiempo* must mean that they are contemporary, especially since there are other, less helpful textual parallels. Don Diego's remark that 'la venganza no dirá | lo que el agravio no dijo' ('the vengeance will not say what the offence did not': II, 1562b) is used by Don Juan de Silva in *A secreto agravio, secreta venganza* ('Dijo la venganza | lo que la ofensa no dijo', 'The vengeance said what the offence did not': I, 615a); Chacón's plea for 'sanctuary', 'Guitarra pido, | como iglesia' ('I request a guitar, as I would a church': II, 1565a) is an echo of Moscatel's in *No hay burlas con el amor* ('Alacena como iglesia | pido', 'I request a cupboard, as I would a church': II, 523a); and both Chacón and Moscatel make a joke on the proverb 'Cornudo y apaleado, mandarle que baile' ('Cuckolded and beaten, then tell him to dance': II, 1559a, 517b). *A secreto agravio* and *No hay burlas* were probably written in 1635.

Leonor is an intelligent and resourceful young woman, who does not intend to let the enforced move to Valencia end her relationship with Enrique. The same is true of Enrique, who is devoted to Leonor, although inclined to be jealous. Indeed, Leonor has another suitor: Juan, the punctilious brother of Beatriz, although she gives him no encouragement. As in similar comedies, Leonor is the strongest character in the play. She saves Enrique from discovery by casting him in the role of dancing-master, unites Beatriz with her lover Don Félix (and makes her brother apologise to her), while her quick mind rescues her embarrassed father Don Diego from his conflicting obligations to Beatriz and Juan, whose father was an old friend. Somewhat hypocritically, Diego advises Juan to respect his sister's judgement, and let her marry the man she has chosen, rather than publicise his loss of honour by seeking vengeance on her unauthorised suitor; hypocritically, because, when he finds himself in the same position, he has to be reminded by Juan to take his own good advice. Once again the brother with the suspicious mind and obsessive sense of honour is doubly thwarted: he has to accept his sister's choice of husband, while his own choice for a wife marries someone else.

When we examine the relationship between *La señora y la criada* and *El acaso y el error*, we shall find evidence that while under pressure from his royal patron to produce new plays, Calderón may have been willing to make extensive use of those which he had written many years previously. Perhaps the resemblances between *Dar tiempo al tiempo* and *El maestro de danzar* can be explained in this way. But if they belong to the period running from the late 1640s to the early 1650s, the relationship between them may be like that of *La dama duende* and *Casa con dos puertas*: a successful plot re-used a short time later.

Since *Nuestra Señora de los Remedios* is lost, we cannot examine it to try to guess at its date. In addition to the 1650 performance, Cotarelo notes another in Seville in 1667,[55] but the text got into print as a *suelta*, which was seen by Fajardo (1717).[56] It is also listed in Medel's *Índice* (1735), although this does not prove that he saw a print himself.[57] There is a slim chance that a copy will turn up in some small library.

Another play written about this time is *Los hijos de la fortuna*. The plot derives ultimately from the *Historia aethiopica* of Heliodorus of Emesa (Greek, ?fourth century). The story became very popular throughout Europe, and several editions of two different Spanish translations were published from 1554 onwards. Lope, el Pinciano, Gracián and others allude to it; Gil Polo's *Diana enamorada* (1564), the story of Osmín and Daraza in Alemán's *Guzmán de Alfarache* (1599) and Cervantes's *Persiles y Sigismunda* (1617) owe debts to it. Pérez de Montalbán produced a dramatised version with the same title as Calderón's play; it was probably written in 1634–5, and printed in his *Segundo tomo* (1638). One might suppose that Don Pedro was most inspired by his friend's play, but he appears to owe more to the original story.

If Don Pedro was attracted by Heliodorus' use of flashback, he did not attempt the difficult task of adapting this feature to his play. Other features of the original were familiar to him, however, such as the use of 'lower-class' characters to provide a contrast with those of noble origin, and the way in which the actions of a single character affect the lives of the others. As in *La hija del aire*, the role of Fortune is constantly referred to, particularly with reference to the lives of Teágenes and Cariclea; however, Jebnón's final speech helps us to see that the real causes of the events which complicate their lives are human failings. The play has been dated to 'c. 1651–3' on the basis of the verse-forms it uses, but there is nothing in the text to confirm this.[58]

The last of the plays that could belong to this period is *¿Cuál es mayor perfección, hermosura o discreción?* The verse, with 19 per cent *redondillas* and 80 per cent *romance*, is most unusual, and suggests, if anything, that using metre to date Calderón's plays accurately is not a reliable exercise. Perhaps more useful is the reference to the royal guard clearing the way for 'los reyes' ('the king and queen': II, 1620a). This at least excludes the period 6 October 1644 (death of Queen Isabel) to 15 November 1649 (arrival of Queen Mariana).

If we are to believe old films, gentlemen may prefer blondes, but they marry brunettes. The notion provided Calderón with dramatic capital three centuries earlier. In *¿Cuál es mayor perfección …?* the blonde (with 'hebras de oro', 'golden tresses': II, 1620b) is Ángela; and while the colour of the hair of Leonor and Beatriz is not specified, we can see that they are brunettes, at least metaphorically. Ángela may be blonde and beautiful, but she is worse than dumb. It is hardly her fault if she is so slow-witted that she cannot cope politely with social intercourse; her real problem is that she is so full of herself that she imagines that all of Madrid's young men are besotted by her. To a degree, this is true: those who have not got to know her *are* besotted by her. At the start of the play, Don Félix supposes chauvinistically that 'no tiene una mujer | más que hacer que ser hermosa' ('a woman has nothing else to do but be beautiful': II, 1622a). There is plenty of evidence that Calderón admired intelligent and spirited women, and Félix comes to share this admiration, falling for Beatriz. As the play ends, Ángela turns desperately to those she thinks are her admirers, Luis and Félix, but they have already chosen Leonor and Beatriz. Finally, Don Antonio, whose head was never turned by anyone, is persuaded to take her hand because he is poor and her father is wealthy. Perhaps no one deserves Ángela, but if anyone can put up with her, perhaps it is the sensible, unromantic and somewhat cynical Antonio. Apart from her ability to look attractive, Ángela has much in common with *El agua mansa*'s Don Toribio. Unlike Toribio, though, she finds a marriage partner, showing that there is a grain of truth in Félix's remark, as well as undermining the play's moral.

Antonio provides two of the play's literary references, as he tries to persuade his friend Luis to come down to earth:

> ¿Habéis estado en Teruel?
> ¿Conocisteis a Macías? (II, 1627a)

(Have you been in Teruel? Did you know Macías?)

The first reference is to the lovers of Teruel, whose ancient story was dramatised by Andrés Rey de Artieda (*Los amantes*, printed in 1581), as well as by Calderón's contemporaries Tirso and Pérez de Montalbán (both plays were entitled *Los amantes de Teruel* and printed in 1635).[59] The other is to the fifteenth-century Galician-Portuguese love-poet Macias 'o namorado' ('the enamoured'), whose life was dramatised by Lope in *Porfiar hasta morir* (?1624–8, printed 1638). While Macías is less famous than the lovers of Teruel, we cannot conclude that the reference dates the play to the 1630s. Even less helpful are the other allusions. The line 'clarín que rompe el albor' ('trumpet which breaks the dawn': II, 1649a), from Góngora's *romance* 'Contando estaban sus rayos' (1614), is used in *La vida es sueño* (?1630) and *En la vida todo es verdad y todo mentira* (1659). Lope's ballad lines 'Quien piensa que no quiere | el ser querido le engaña' ('He who thinks he does not love is deceived by being loved': II, 1649a) have been noted in *No hay cosa como callar* (1638), while the words 'con quien vengo, vengo' ('I'm with whom I'm with': II, 1651a) are another proverbial expression used for the title of a play (1630).[60] *¿Cuál es mayor perfección?* was first printed as the opening play in *Escogidas XXI* (1663). Its most probable composition date is about ten years earlier.

One more play, *El acaso y el error*, should be examined here, not so much because there is evidence that it was written by 1650 as because of its close relationship with *La señora y la criada* (1635: see pp. 171–2 above). As in the latter play, *El acaso* deals with the planned kidnapping of the Duchess Diana, who has given one of her dresses to the peasant Gileta, so that Gileta is kidnapped by mistake (the 'error'). Gileta may be only a peasant, but she has evidently seen Calderón's most famous play:

¡Yo mosicas y yo galas!
¡Yo dorados paramentos!
¡Yo cama blanda y mullida!
¡Yo damas! Si bien me acuerdo,
parece [*sic*: ?parecer] quiere este paso
algo de 'La vida es sueño'. (II, 743b)

(Music and finery for me! Gilt hangings for me! A soft and fluffed-up bed for me! Ladies for me! If I remember right, this passage is trying to be like something from *La vida es sueño*.)

Rather than of Segismundo, though, Gileta reminds us of the peasant Benito, forced to pretend to be a prince in *El alcaide de sí mismo*. The reference to *La vida es sueño* tells us little enough, since Calderón often refers to it, but there is also a half-reference to *También hay duelo en las damas* (?winter of 1652–3; II, 747a). To these we can add the closing lines,

A vuestras plantas rendidos
nos ponemos, suplicando
que lo que se escribe aprisa
no lo murmuréis de espacio (II, 752b)

(We place ourselves humbly at your feet, beseeching you not to criticise at leisure what's written in a hurry),

in which the reference to haste implies writing to order. After 1650, the only orders for secular works were coming from Philip IV, and we know that court plays kept Calderón busy in the early 1650s: *Darlo todo y no dar nada* (performed 22 December 1651),[61] *La fiera, el rayo y la piedra* (performed May 1652),[62] *Cada uno para sí* (1653),[63] *El encanto sin encanto* (?1650–2), *El postrer duelo de España* (?1651–3),[64] *También hay duelo en las damas* (?winter of 1652–3), *El conde Lucanor* (?early 1653) and *Andrómeda y Perseo* (performed May 1653).[65] It would be possible to take a play written in 1635, retitle it, perhaps change the names of some characters, alter some scenes, and pass it off as a new work: few of the writer's contemporaries would ever know. This is not what happened in this case, and Don Pedro listed only *El acaso* as his, although his authorship of *La señora y la criada* is certain. He may seem to have cut a corner by modern standards, but revising old plays was normal practice both in general and in his particular case, although not all critics think this revision better than the original. Both versions sacrifice character delineation to the same ingenious and complex plot, although only *El acaso* makes a reference to the complexity, effectively admitting that the audience may have trouble following what is going on:

Si tan desusada cosa
hubiere ningún ingenio
inventado para hacer
alguna fábula, quiero
perder la vida; y si acaso
llegase a escribirse esto,
doy licencia al auditorio
que por aqueste momento
pueda no entenderlo, pues
aun yo misma no lo entiendo. (II, 742b)

(I hope to die if any writer ever invented such an unusual thing to make a plot; and if ever this were to be written, I give the audience permission not to understand it for this moment, because even I don't understand it.)

At this point in Calderón's career, minor items present fewer problems of dating than major ones. In 1650 the calligrapher Joseph de Casanova published his *Arte de escrivir*, a handsome folio illustrated with numerous fine copper engravings of letter-forms.[66] When Don Pedro was in a hurry, as he evidently often was, his handwriting could decline to the semi-legible. When he took his time, his writing is neat, regular, even elegant, something he cared about; so it is not surprising that he wrote a sonnet for the book ('De cuantos artes, cuantas ciencias fueron …').[67] About the same time he wrote an approbation for Jerónimo de Cáncer y Velasco's *Obras varias*, some of which is worth quoting to compare with the bald approval he conceded to Miguel Cid three years earlier:

Y aunque el ingenio de su Autor (tan celebrado en España) es su mas segura aprobación, con todo esso le he leido con cuidado, y no hallo en él inconueniente que reparar; antes bien mucho que agradecer al estilo, en quien se hallan usadas con agudeza y donayre los primores de la lengua Castellana ... Madrid y Noviembre 20 de 1650.[68]

(And although the talent of its author, so famous in Spain, is its most reliable approbation, I have nevertheless read it with care, and find no difficulty to take note of; rather much to be grateful for to the style, in which the beauties of Castilian are used with wit and elegance: Madrid, 20 November 1650.)

While we know nothing of Don Pedro's contacts with Casanova, he and Cáncer had already collaborated with Vélez in *Enfermar con el remedio* (date uncertain, but Vélez had died in November 1644), and they would also collaborate with Zabaleta in *La margarita preciosa*, perhaps at about this time.[69] Cáncer was an inveterate collaborator, writing relatively few plays on his own, although he was famous for his *entremeses*. Interestingly, several of his joint works involved Antonio de Huerta, 'Calderón's enemy', including the notorious *La luna africana*, written by nine playwrights working together. The *Obras varias* included his burlesque play *La muerte de Valdovinos*, as well as a preface by Zabaleta.

* * *

In 1648, negotiations were taking place for the marriage between Philip IV and Princess Mariana, the daughter of his sister the Empress María: a dispensation was required, but was not refused. On 8 November, in Vienna, the fourteen-year-old princess was married by proxy to her uncle. The news brought the opening of the theatres, both for the public and in the court. Once Mariana was installed as queen, the royal theatres returned to something like their heyday of the 1630s, while her arrival was an enormous fiesta in itself. Calderón's descriptions of the royal entry in *Guárdate del agua mansa* have been noted, but it has been suggested that his role in the festivities went far beyond this. There were numerous accounts, but one in particular, the *Noticia del recibimiento i entrada de la Reyna nuestra Señora Doña Maria-Ana de Austria en la muy noble i leal coronada Villa de Madrid*, has been attributed to Calderón, and there have also been claims that he designed the allegorical arches and statues he was describing.[70] The attribution begins with Vera Tassis, who tells us in his life of the poet in the *Primera parte* of 1685 that the king sent word to Alba, summoning Don Pedro to Madrid 'â trazar, y descriuir aquellos cêlebres Arcos Triunfales para la feliz entrada de ... Doña Maria-Ana de Austria' ('to design and describe those famous triumphal arches for the happy entry of Doña Mariana of Austria': ¶7^{v}). The unreliable Vera Tassis is ostensibly supported by Gaspar

Agustín de Lara, a more trustworthy witness, in the preliminaries of his *Obelisco fúnebre*. Lara tells us that the organiser of the festivities, Lorenzo Ramírez de Prado, allowed a text written by Calderón to appear under his name. Not surprisingly, Cotarelo accepts this statement.[71] We now know that Ramírez de Prado commissioned a Juan Antonio Calderón to plan the allegories: the surname may have contributed to the confusion.[72] While Don Pedro did not write all of the *Noticia*, however, he may have played a role in the festivities, as well as writing some of the verse involved, as a manuscript source suggests:

Fabricaronse unas vallas de un lado a otro, desde la puerta dicha hasta poco antes de la Torrecilla de Juan Fernandez, todas de azul y plata ... en la Torrecilla se levantaba en forma de piramide, y en ella, en los cuatro lienzos, muchas pinturas y versos latinos, traducidos por D. Pedro Calderon, asi estos como los demas de toda la fiesta.[73]

(Fences were constructed from one side to another, from the aforesaid gate until just before the Torrecilla de Juan Fernández, all in blue and silver ... on the tower a pyramid shape was raised, and on its four sides there were many paintings and Latin verses, translated by D. Pedro Calderón, both these and the rest of all the entertainment.)

Several poems in the *Noticia* are very Calderonian in imagery and language, and two of them in particular, 'Coronada de esperanzas' and '¡A, d'el Coro de Hymeneo', are probably his.[74] However, the accounts for the festivities show that Don Pedro was paid 400 ducats, a very large sum for translating Latin poems and writing some Spanish ones; Varey and Salazar are at a loss to explain the amount.[75] Whatever Don Pedro's role in the proceedings, it was evidently a significant one: his career as a secular poet seemed to have recovered. With a new young queen, who would surely add to the royal family, the auguries for a successful continuation appeared to be good. And yet, it was precisely at this time, in 1650, that he took the first steps towards giving up the writing of plays.

CHAPTER 17

Epilogue: The glories of the world

> Yo Señor juzguè siempre, dexandome lleuar de humanas y Divinas letras, que el hazer versos era una gala de el alma, ô, agilidad del entendimiento, que ni alzaba, ni vajaba los sugetos, dexandose a cada uno en el predicamento que le hallaua, sin presumir que pudiera nunca obstar, ni deslucir la mediana sangre en que Dios fue seruido que naciese.
>
> (I always felt, sir, when I let myself get involved with secular and religious literature, that writing verse was an adornment of the soul or a nimbleness of the mind, which neither raised up nor brought down those involved, leaving each one in the predicament in which it found him, without thinking that it could ever hinder or tarnish the middling status in which it pleased God I should be born.)
>
> (*Papel al Patriarca*, ?1652)

Calderón never married. A superficial look at his comedies, the majority of which end with they-lived-happily-ever-after marriages, might lead us to suppose that never marrying helped him to retain this rose-coloured view of the marital state. A closer examination, involving his entire output, leads to a different, more complex conclusion. All we know about the relationships between Diego Calderón and Beatriz de Alarcón and between José Calderón and Agustina Ortiz y Velasco indicates that they were good ones. We know little enough about the relationship between Diego Calderón Senior and his first wife Ana, and even less about that with his second wife. In the first there were tensions, at least within the wider family; the second caused a rift, although the extent of the rift before Don Diego's death is not clear. The plays have numerous examples of marital strife among members of the servant class, and while this is a commonplace, exaggerated to amuse, we find it also, in a different social category, and with very different results, in plays like *La devoción de la cruz*, *El médico de su honra*, *Las tres justicias en una*, *A secreto agravio, secreta venganza* and *El pintor de su deshonra*.[1] Even the comedies provide examples in which the auguries for future happiness are at best neutral, at worst unfavourable: we think of the innocent Leonor forced into marriage with Don Juan in *No hay cosa como callar*, or her more conniving namesake in *La desdicha de la voz*, married to someone she does not love, like the various young noblewomen whose position obliges them to do likewise.

Not only does Calderón return constantly to the difficulties faced by women in a male-dominated society; throughout his career he wrote plays in which women are the most sensible, most principled or most intelligent characters. Simple psychology would suggest that he was able to do this because his formative years were spent in contact with such women: his grandmother Doña Inés, his mother, his older sister Dorotea. It would seem likely that such a man would have good relationships with women: it would be a particularly hypocritical writer who treated women very differently from what his plays seem to recommend. There are, of course, real-life women like Marcela (*No hay cosa como callar*), who are attracted to men who treat them badly, but it seems likely that most women prefer the men who treat them well. And while women may well have liked Don Pedro, it seems extremely probable that he liked women; in the circumstances, it is frustrating to have so little information about his relationships with them.

In January 1650 Calderón reached fifty, a fair age for the time, but certainly not one which precluded marriage. Whatever his reasons for not marrying when he was younger, he decided in that year to put the possibility behind him. On 11 October he entered the Third Order of St Francis, and received its habit five days later.[2] On 2 November Pedro Ladrón de Guevara, the husband of the poet's cousin Ana González de Henao, ceded to him the right to enjoy the chaplaincy founded and funded by Doña Inés de Riaño in 1612.[3] When none of the three Calderón brothers had taken up that right by the age of twenty-four, it had passed to José, the son of the eldest brother. In 1647 José had reached twenty-four. He was not yet married, but he had chosen a career in the law. In June of the following year he had passed on the right to Juan Ladrón de Guevara, the son of Pedro and Ana. We might conclude that at the time of this transfer the poet had no immediate plans to enter the priesthood, and perhaps that his son, another possible candidate for the chaplaincy, had not yet been born. However, the agreement had specified that the Platerías house would not be handed over until the end of 1651, three and a half years away.[4] Don Pedro may have asked for this period to consider his future.

Formal qualifications were less important in the seventeenth century. Neither Lope nor Calderón studied in a seminary, and neither had a university degree. By the time they became priests (Lope was almost exactly the same age as Calderón when he did so), both were well versed in theology and scripture; and both had written successful *autos* and religious poetry.

While we do not know exactly when Calderón took orders, it must have been in late September/early October 1651. On 18 September the king signed a document authorising him to 'ordenarse de misa y andar con el hábito de sacerdote en la forma ordinaria' ('to be ordained as a priest and to wear a priest's habit in the usual way').[5] Four weeks later (14 October) Juan del Corral wrote to Andrés de Uztarroz to say that 'Don Pedro Calderón cantó Misa, y yo le besé la mano en ella seis días hace' ('Don Pedro Calderón sang mass, and I kissed his hand at it six days ago'), so he was by then ordained.[6] A meeting of the Third Order on 27 December 1651 elected him as one of the 'discretos eclesiásticos' of that year.[7] An earlier meeting had already agreed to ask him to write a chronicle of the order, a request he accepted, even taking delivery of the archival material. However, he apparently baulked at the size of the task, despite being offered the opportunity to choose two or more research assistants, and eventually it was passed to a Father Francisco de Rojas, a namesake of Calderón's friend;[8] the need to move to Toledo (see below) may have been a factor. As well as the duties prescribed by his chaplaincy (four masses every week in perpetuity, in addition to various others on specified feast days, providing meals for poor women and so on), he was writing two *autos* every year for Madrid Town Council. He travelled to the capital regularly to oversee the *autos*, but presumably he had to arrange for the duties of the chaplaincy to be carried out by someone else when he was not in Madrid. By 1653, when he finally conceded that he would not write the chronicle, he was again writing plays for the king, although his output declined somewhat after the 1650s. Given a choice between history and poetry, he chose poetry.

'Poetry' included non-dramatic works: one of the first after his ordination was a sonnet on the death of Don Martín Suárez de Alarcón, one of the last casualties of the Catalan war,[9] but few, if any, of these poems were written spontaneously: he wrote them because he was asked to. For the next thirty years he wrote *autos* for Madrid and plays for the king, averaging a little more than two plays per year for the first twenty years.[10] At the beginning of the period he continued to write situation comedies of the kind he was writing thirty years earlier, such as *También hay duelo en las damas* (?1652–3) and *Cada uno para sí* (?1653), or *comedias palaciegas* like *Dicha y desdicha del nombre* (by 1660) and *Mujer, llora y vencerás* (for Carnival 1660). After 1660, he wrote no more of these, and more mythological plays, although his revision of *Cada uno para sí* dates from 1665–70. There were also plays from ancient history such as *El segundo Escipión* (1676), *Duelos de amor y lealtad*

(1678) and *Las armas de la hermosura* (1678, rather than the 1652 usually accepted). All of these, mythological and historical, can be associated with current events.[11] Most difficult of all to date are the short humorous pieces. That he continued to write them is without question: for example, the *Entremés del triunfo de Juan Rana* was apparently written to be played with *Fieras afemina Amor* (1671, performance delayed until January 1672); it opens with a trademark self-parody as the *autor* Antonio de Escamilla falls from his steed (an ass), echoing the words of Rosaura in *La vida es sueño* ('Hipogrifo violento, | mira que eres un mísero jumento' ('Violent hippogriff, see that you are a wretched ass').[12] One of the funniest (and in the word of its editors, the most 'calderoniano') is *Las visiones de la muerte*, described below.[13] Gradually his output slowed, and in his last decade he wrote only about seven plays. Thanks to the king, he was still being paid his military pension of thirty *escudos* a month.[14] At first, he had transferred this money to his son, but it had to be transferred back to him when Pedro José died.[15] Early in 1653 the king put forward his name for a chaplaincy of the Reyes Nuevos in Toledo,[16] which brought him an annual stipend of 1,000 *escudos*.

Once again Don Pedro had to submit his genealogy for inspection, since Philip II had decreed that only 'old Christians' could hold such a position: that is, it was subject to the *estatutos de limpieza de sangre*.[17] What the poet thought of these statutes is clear enough from *Amar después de la muerte*, or from *Las órdenes militares*: Christ may have been the Son of God, but having a Jewish mother would have excluded him from a range of posts in Habsburg Spain. Once again, as in 1636, enquiries were made about Calderón's ancestry. The long delay (until 19 June) gave him time to write *Andrómeda y Perseo*, which was premiered on 18 May 1653 in the Coliseo.[18] Like *El conde Lucanor*, the play makes a reference to the achieving of peace: 'con dos monstruos vencidos, | en paz dos reinos' ('with two monsters vanquished, two kingdoms at peace': I, 1860b). Perseus, love-child of Jupiter (Juan José of Austria, love-child of Philip IV) has lived up to his ancestry. The two monsters are ostensibly Medusa and the sea-monster which threatened Andromeda, but Discordia has also been defeated.

For the next ten years, Calderón spent much of his time in Toledo. When he had approved for publication *La vida y hechos de Estevanillo González*, he had signed his approbation in Madrid on 24 July 1652; three years later, his approval of Luis Hurtado's *Imagen del sacro-erario de la muy santa iglesia de Toledo* was signed in that city on 31 July 1655. On 14 September 1653 he joined Toledo's Hermandad del Refugio; three years later he was elected Hermano Mayor, senior brother, which meant that he had to chair the meetings.[19] The brotherhood existed to minister to the poor, which included running a hostel for them, and keeping accounts. One account book gives brief details, mostly in Don Pedro's own handwriting, of the aid he distributed, spiritual and material, in the years 1653 to 1656 inclusive.[20] During this period he also wrote one of his most significant poems, the 525-line *Exortación panegírica al silencio* (1661), sometimes known as *Psalle et sile* from the words which inspired it, engraved on a small metal plate on the screen of the Cathedral of Toledo: 'Ò calla, | O algo di, que mejor que callar sea' ('Either be silent, or say something which is better than silence') it tells us, a significant remark from someone who wrote two million words.[21]

Calderón may have thought that Toledo, the birthplace of his paternal grandmother, would be his home for the rest of his life, but in 1663 the king made him an honorary chaplain, which meant returning to the capital: in May of that year he joined the *Congregación de presbíteros naturales de Madrid.* Three years later he transferred his membership of the Toledo Hermandad del Refugio to its counterpart in Madrid.[22]

By now his reputation had spread abroad. In 1659 a French *abbé,* François Bertaut, a member of the group which had come to negotiate the end of the war with France, made a point of meeting him and talking to him. Bertaut was not impressed, but then little in Spain met with his favour, and he missed a great opportunity.[23]

In the late 1640s Philip IV had not offered Don Pedro the post of *ayuda de cámara,* but in the following decades he had put his name forward for the chaplaincy in Toledo, and then appointed him one of his own chaplains, as well as providing the only market for the writer's plays. Philip died in September 1665, but, apart from the lengthy period of official mourning, Calderón continued to enjoy the patronage of the queen mother and of the new king, Charles II. Charles, the last of Spain's Habsburgs, was handicapped, both mentally and physically, but he liked the theatre, as did his surviving parent, the queen mother. With the advantage of over three centuries of hindsight, we can see that his reign was a cultural nadir: Calderón was the only great writer still living, Murillo the only great painter. And yet, for the first time in his life Don Pedro was comfortably off: in his modest house in Platerías he had four servants; he was able to indulge in his fondness for art, collecting numerous paintings, and perhaps experimenting with the medium himself.[24] He continued to write non-dramatic poetry: his last sonnet was for Cubero Sebastián's *Peregrinación del mundo,* written the year before his death: the heading of the poem calls him an 'intimo amigo del Autor', a 'close friend of the author'.[25] The sonnet that follows is by the playwright Juan de Matos Fragoso, also described as the author's friend: no doubt he was Don Pedro's too. Calderón also continued to write occasional printing approbations. Of the first part of the plays of Matos (b. 1608), he wrote that

no hallo en él inconueniente alguno que desdiga a la pureça y decoro de nuestra santa Fé ... los aplausos que han merecido en los Teatros, traían anticipada la licencia que para su impression pide.[26]

(I find in it no obstacle which might clash with the purity and propriety of our holy faith ... the applause which the plays have deserved in the theatres carries with it, in anticipation, the permission which he seeks for their printing.)

He knew which buttons had to be pressed to satisfy the Council of Castile's God squad, and was happy to press them; but he was also willing to suggest that the Council's implied contempt for the judgement of theatregoers was mistaken.

* * *

If we reckon the duration of Calderón's career at sixty years, his ordination in 1651 comes at the midway point. In the first half of his career, Don Pedro wrote around eighty-five plays (excluding collaboration plays, but not lost ones); in the second half, he wrote only about thirty-five. The implication, clearly, is that one of the factors which made Calderón write was the need to earn money: once he had achieved financial security, his output fell significantly. In fact, his intention had apparently been to stop writing altogether when he became a priest. Referring to his 'gift', he wrote:

Y aunque es verdad que ocioso Cortesano la tratè con el cariño de hauilidad hallada acaso; No dexè de desdeñarla el dia que tomè el no merecido estado en que oy me veo; pues para boluer a ella fue necesario que el S^{r}. D. Luis de Haro me lo mandase de parte de Su Mag^{d}. en el festiuo parabien dela cobrada salud de la Reyna N^{a}. S^{a}. (que Dios g^{de}).[27]

(And although it is true that as a courtier with time to spare, I treated it with the affection of a talent discovered by accident, I did not fail to disdain it on the day when I took on the undeserved status in which I now find myself, since, for me to return to it, it was necessary for Don Luis de Haro to order me on His Majesty's behalf, on the occasion of the festive congratulation for the recovered health of the queen, whom God preserve.)

The ostensible purpose of this letter was to decline to write the *autos*, probably those of 1652. In 1651 Calderón had applied, apparently successfully, for some ecclesiastical post, but the offer was subsequently withdrawn because of an objection on the part of someone who 'juzga incompatibles el sacerdocio, y la Poesia' ('considers priesthood and poetry incompatible'). Cotarelo assumes that this post was one of the twelve chaplaincies of the

Reyes Nuevos de Toledo, and suggests that the 'someone' was the Senior Chaplain himself, the Patriarca de las Indias, Don Alonso Pérez de Guzmán.[28] No document supports this assumption, and it would have been the height of rudeness, in a letter addressed to the Patriarca, to refer to him as 'no sè quien' ('I know not who').[29] At the start of the letter Don Pedro seems to belittle poetry: the ability to write it does not change a person's status, and the words 'ocioso Cortesano' in particular suggest that writing had been for him no more than a leisure activity. When we read on, however, we see that the real purpose of the letter is to defend poetry: if writing is an unworthy exercise, all its products are unworthy:

Dirame V S Y[ll^{ma}] que las fiestas del Corpus no hazen consequencia para otras, y respondere [le] Yo: que si a mi me pusieran la objecion en los asumptos de quanto hasta oy he escrito, con mejorar los asumptos desuaneciera la objecion; pero quien me capitula, no me capitula, ni puede, lo que escriuo, sino el que lo escriuo: y lo digno de un objeto no emmienda lo indigno de todo un exercicio, y mientras no me dieren por digno el exercicio, no me pueden dar por digno ningun objeto suyo; fuera, Señor, de que darme al partido de que en particular es bueno, es darme al partido de que en comun es malo. Declarese si lo es, ô, no; que siendo bueno aqui estoy para seruir, y obedecer toda mi Vida; y no lo siendo ni a su Magestad ni a V S Yll^{ma}. les puede parecer mal que conocido el yerro trate de emmendarle, y aun el mismo Misterio se darà por mas bien seruido, pues lo que se califica indecoro de un Altar, mal puede quedar festiuidad de otro. Y en fin Señor, dexandome a ser primero exemplar del Mundo en que se pudo desmerecer obedeciendo, reduzgamos a dos palabras el discurso; que no es justo que por mi se haga saeta a mayores importancias. O este es malo, ô, es bueno: si es bueno no me obste; y si es malo no se me mande.

(Your lordship will tell me that the Corpus festivities have no consequences for any others, and my answer is that if any objection were made to the subject-matter of what I have written up to now, by improving the subject-matter I would dispel the objection; but those who accuse me do not accuse me, nor can they, for what I write, but because I write; the worthiness of an aim does not mend the unworthiness of a whole exercise, and as long as they do not admit the worthiness of the exercise, they cannot admit the worthiness of any of its aims, apart from the fact that for me to concede that in particular circumstances it is good, is to concede that in general it is bad. Let it be stated whether it is or not; for if it is good, here I am ready to serve and obey all my life; and if not, neither to His Majesty nor to your lordship can it seem bad that, recognising the error, I should try to put it right, and the mystery itself will be better served, for what is described as improper for one altar can hardly be a celebration for another. Finally, sir, leaving me to be the world's first example of loss of merit through obedience, let us reduce this discourse to two words, for it is not right that matters of greater importance should suffer on my account. Either this is bad or it is good: if it is good, let me not be obstructed; if it is bad, let me not be ordered to do it.)

We can see the outrage behind the stated readiness to obey, the outrage of a writer who has been told that writing is not a respectable occupation. Don Pedro might say that writing poetry does not change a person's status, but the fact was that it had already changed his, making him a knight; ten years after he wrote this letter, it would make him one of the king's personal chaplains. Not only that: poetry could raise a humble priest to a height that the greatest of prelates might envy, at least according to the words of Don Luis de Haro, also quoted in the letter, when he persuaded Don Pedro to continue to write for the king: '[¿]Quien le ha dicho a Vm que el mayor Prelado no se holgara de tener una habilidad, y mas que ingenio, que tal vez fuese pequeño aliuio a los cuidados de su Mag[d][?]' ('Who told you that the greatest prelate would not rejoice to have an ability, and more than talent, which might provide a small relief for His Majesty's cares?').

Unusually, Calderón expressed some of these feelings in an *auto*, *No hay más fortuna que Dios*. The musicians have just performed a song in praise of Hermosura, who asks who wrote the words. Mal replies:

MAL Ahí trabajillo es de un cierto
amigo, que aún no ha llegado
a desengañarse cuerdo
de la poca estimación
que tiene ya el hacer versos.
HERMOSURA ¿Por qué?
MAL Porque no los hacen
los que dicen mal de ellos. (III, 625a)

(EVIL: It's a little piece of work by a certain friend, who still hasn't got over the low esteem in which writing verse now is now held. BEAUTY: Why? EVIL: Because those who speak ill of it don't write it.)

The letter achieved its purpose. Don Pedro continued to write two *autos* every year for Madrid, and to write plays for the king until Philip died in 1665. The Patriarca did not oppose his appointment to a chaplaincy of the Reyes Nuevos in 1653; and his reputation grew, both in Spain and abroad. After Philip's death he wrote fewer plays, but his last, *Hado y divisa de Leonido y de Marfisa*, was performed in March 1680. As long as we remain uncertain about his authorship of plays like *Las cadenas del demonio* and *Céfalo y Pocris*, we cannot say exactly how many he wrote. The least misleading figure is about 120, with another thirteen or so written in collaboration. In his Marañón list he gave sixty-five *auto* titles, but the real total, including lost *autos* of which we know the titles, is closer to eighty. For many of the *autos* and plays he wrote *loas*: some for which we know he was paid no longer survive, while some surviving *loas* seem not to be his. Perhaps most problematic are the minor pieces, the *entremeses*, *jácaras* and *mojigangas*. Twenty-four of these have been published by Evangelina Rodríguez and Antonio Tordera, but half-a-dozen others may also be authentic.[30] While there is no complete edition of the poems, around fifty can safely be assigned to him.[31] Finally, there are sixteen *aprobaciones*, a dozen and a half *memorias de apariencias* for his *autos*, many of them autograph, six letters and around a dozen other documents.[32]

***

We may think, given that his first poems were published when he was twenty and that his plays were performed before the king three years later (one of them, perhaps, while he was still twenty-two), that Calderón was unusually precocious. However, he grew up in a literary hothouse, full of young plants struggling towards the light of adulation, competing with the well-established, which, even as they provided models for growth, stood in the way of the sun. While he never chose to present a writer as protagonist, his plays are full of young people striving for recognition, whether their names are Segismundo or Semíramis. We do not know which of the young collaborators chose to tell the story of Felipa Catanea in *El monstruo de la fortuna* (?by 1633), but it was one of Don Pedro's characters, young Prince Luis, who asked the question:

Cuantos los mares transcienden,
cuantos las armas menean,
cuantos varias ciencias leen,
cuantos al trabajo acuden,
¿a qué aspiran? ¿Qué pretenden,
sino hacerse más dichosos
que nacieron? (1292b)

(All those who go beyond the seas, all those who wield arms, all those who study different sciences, all those who turn to work, to what do they aspire? What do they seek but to become happier than they were born?)

In the late 1630s, even after the death of Lope de Vega, Calderón was not immediately recognised as the foremost dramatist in Spain; as long as Pérez de Montalbán and Vélez de Guevara were still alive, at least some contemporaries regarded them as serious rivals. Within twenty years – by which time, paradoxically, his tremendous output of the thirties had dropped – Calderón had become a national institution. In 1662, as we have seen, he wrote *Las órdenes militares*, which used as a metaphor the genealogical tests which had to be undergone by those aspiring to membership of Spain's military orders. He applied the metaphor to the genealogy of Christ to illustrate the doctrine of the Immaculate Conception. Since the details of the doctrine were not yet official dogma, the inquisitors were invited to read the *auto*, and encountered a problem: in their view, Calderón had expressed too explicitly, and for a largely illiterate audience, a doctrine which was not finally formulated until 1854.

Our typical modern image of the Spanish Inquisition, the result of centuries of hostile propaganda (and perhaps of a famous Monty Python sketch), may contain some exaggerations, but it was a powerful organisation, with secret prisons and terrible punishments for those who persisted in what was seen as unorthodoxy. The correspondence generated by the problem perceived in *Las órdenes militares* has survived. When one reads it, it becomes clear, not that Calderón was quaking in his shoes at being investigated by the Inquisition, but that the inquisitors were terrified of Don Pedro, terrified by their presumption in daring to suggest that someone of his status, both as a poet and as an intellectual, might alter his text to suit them.[33] We are left with the suspicion that the inquisitors were as embarrassed by the *auto*'s implication for the statutes of *limpieza* as they were by over-explicit treatment of the Immaculate Conception.

The following year, on 8 and 17 January 1663 (OS), in London, the diarist Samuel Pepys described seeing a play called *The Adventures of Five Hours*, translated from the Spanish by Samuel Tuke. Pepys was a theatre addict, who even imposed penalties on himself in an effort to ration his visits. He reckoned that this was 'the best play that ever I saw, or think ever shall'. Three years later, when it was in print, and he was able to read it at his leisure, it was still 'the best play that ever I read in my life'. In comparison with it, he said, *Othello* was 'but a mean thing'. Pepys and his contemporaries thought that Calderón was the author of the original, *Los empeños de seis horas*, which was printed under his name. The real author was Antonio Coello, but the tight, intricate plot is typically Calderonian. On 20 July (OS) Pepys 'went to a play, only a piece of it; which was at the Dukes house, *Worse and Worse* [Don Pedro's *Peor está que estaba*] – just the same manner of play, and writ I believe by the same man, as *The Adventures of Five Hours* – very pleasant it was.'[34]

While we cannot be sure that 'the same man' was a reference to the original author or to that of the English version, it is certain that, when he managed to visit Spain years later, Pepys bought a couple of dozen printed plays. Calderón's name was the best-represented in the collection, although some of those he bought were incorrect attributions.[35]

In 1664, Don Tomás de Oña, one of those invited to approve for publication Don Pedro's *Tercera parte*, explained that when he called Calderón 'the poet of Spain', he was using antonomasia. Just as the term 'our poet' meant Homer to the Greeks, and Virgil to the Romans, so 'the poet of Spain' was Calderón. There are other references like this, in Spain, from this period. However, few graphs of early modern writers show a steady rise to national eminence. This is true of Shakespeare in England, and even more true of Calderón in Spain. While there are no complete statistics for all authors, those we have leave little doubt that Calderón continued to be admired long after his death. There are far more *suelta* editions of his plays than there are of any other dramatist, and no single play comes near the fifty-five editions of *La vida es sueño* during the *suelta* period. This is also true of *relaciones de comedias*. Those *relaciones*, of which the earliest recorded date from around 1680, were separate prints of famous speeches, sometimes slightly doctored to enable them to stand alone; most were monologues, but a few were dialogues. At least some of those who bought them did so to learn them as 'party pieces', for public performance at *tertulias*, gatherings with literary pretensions:

Estas diversiones consistían en cantar, bailar y frecuentemente recitar trozos de comedias del teatro antiguo español, conocidos con el nombre de *relaciones*. El recitar estaba considerado hasta hace poco como una buena afición en hombres y mujeres, y los que tenían esta habilidad se levantaban a petición de los reunidos para declamar, accionando al estilo de nuestra vieja escuela de oratoria.[36]

(These diversions consisted of singing, dancing and often reciting passages from the classical Spanish theatre, known as *relaciones*. Until recently, reciting was considered a good pastime among men and women, and those possessed of this ability would stand up at the request of those present in order to declaim, acting in the style of our old school of oratory.)

Editions of these *relaciones*, and the public-theatre archives, show that Calderón continued to be performed, by professionals or by amateurs, to an extent unequalled by any of his contemporaries, including Lope. The neoclassical critics of the eighteenth century were often scathing about his high-flown style, or about his apparent indifference to the Rules of Drama and to historical fact. Leandro Fernández de Moratín even suggested banning *La vida es sueño* in 1799, but the theatre archives show that the audiences still merited the confidence placed in them by Don Pedro in 1658.[37]

Ironically, it was thanks to the Franco regime, that bastion of Spanish cultural values, that Calderón's reputation suffered most. Some critics have suggested that the main reason for his deliberate neglect under Franco was his discreet satirising of sexual hypocrisy. Reluctant though one is to credit Franco's censors with so much critical perspicacity, one suspects that the suggestion is correct, and that the censors preferred not to admit that such hypocrisy existed. What this neglect meant, however, was a break in continuity such as Shakespeare never had to suffer, a break exacerbated by the fact that Franco's censors did not object to the *autos*. Modern directors are still reluctant to put on material that the Franco regime found acceptable. The fact is that the *autos* are tremendous theatre, as well as reminding those in power about some of the more uncomfortable aspects of Christian teaching: that God welcomes the poor and consigns the rich to hell, while kings must be purged of their vainglory.

In the twenty-first century, the world's leading language in terms of distribution is English, while Spanish comes second. In Calderón's day, Spanish came first and English came nowhere. This certainly offers some explanation for the fact that, over a lengthy period, Shakespeare lagged far behind Calderón in terms of recognition in other countries. How many of Shakespeare's plays were translated, and into how many languages, while their author was still alive?

Calderón lived almost thirty years longer than Shakespeare, but the first recorded translation of one of his plays was of *La vida es sueño*, into Dutch, in 1636, the same year as it appeared in the *Primera parte*. We should perhaps remember that at this time, twelve years before the Peace of Westphalia, Spain was the arch-enemy of the Dutch. It would be nice to think that the translator had noticed Calderón's critical attitude to corruption or arrogance in government; perhaps he simply felt that a great play was a great play, whatever its origin. During Calderón's lifetime, seventeen of his plays were translated or adapted into French, fourteen into Italian, ten into Dutch, eight into English and seven into German. The total number of translations was seventy-five, some of them by established dramatists like Dryden and Thomas Corneille. The process continues: more and more plays are still being translated, into more languages. Some of the translators he attracted were successful poets, like Shelley, Longfellow, Edward Fitzgerald (best known for his 'translation' of Omar Khayyam) and Roy Campbell. The tercentenary of his death (1981) and the quatercentenary of his birth have confirmed his status.

As recorded in the previous chapter, in 1672 a friend asked Don Pedro to send some books to ease his loneliness, and mentioned plays in particular, as might be expected. In his response the playwright referred to 'el deseo de obedecer en todo, à pesar del dexo con que ya miro esta materia' ('the desire to obey in everything, in spite of the indifference with which I now regard this material'). In spite of this alleged indifference, he went on to complain bitterly and sarcastically about the damage done to his texts, and to his literary reputation, by the greed of the book trade. Twenty years had gone by since the Letter to the Patriarch, but the ambiguity is still present. As a nobleman, he had to play down the importance of what he had written, and this need for disparagement was even more pressing for a priest. However, the obsession with rewriting his work continued long after his ordination. On one level, this involved turning plays into *autos*, as with *La vida es sueño*, which he turned into an *auto* on two occasions, the second in 1673. On a different level, it had involved refashioning plays, producing masterpieces like *El alcalde de Zalamea* or *El médico de su honra* out of promising texts written by others. As frequently, the process involved his own plays. We cannot examine the text of *La fábula de Dafne*, first played in 1636, to compare it with the *El laurel de Apolo* of 1658, but after *El laurel* was printed in 1664, he rewrote it in 1678 for the new king's birthday. We have the same difficulty with *La fábula de Narciso*, which he wrote for Philip IV in 1639 (probably) and turned into the *Eco y Narciso* performed in the Retiro in 1661, but we know that after the play was printed in 1672, he expanded the text in the 1674 edition. His obsession also involved the state of his texts. We have seen the comments he wrote in his *Quarte parte* in 1672. Five years later, when the false *Quinta parte* was published, he wrote furiously of

> vn libro intitulado: *Quinta parte de Comedias de Calderon*, con tantas falsedades, como auerse impresso en Madrid, y tener puesta su impression en Barcelona, no tener licencia, ni remission, ni del Vicario, ni del Consejo, ni aprobacion de persona conocida.[38]

> (a book entitled *Quinta parte de Comedias de Calderon*, with so many falsities, such as having been printed in Madrid and having a Barcelona imprint, having no licence or referral, neither from the vicar-general nor from the Council, nor approbation by any known person.)

Concerned, no doubt, that most of his *autos* were unprinted and circulating in increasingly corrupt manuscript versions, he began to make fair copies at about this time, but could not resist tinkering with the texts.

It has been said before, in this book and elsewhere, that Calderón re-used material. Commissions, many of them royal ones or for Madrid Town Council, put him under great pressure, and there is no doubt that he often wrote quickly, saving time by using what he had written before, perhaps in the hope that the time would come when he could revise and improve what he wrote. On occasion, the time did come; sometimes, though, as with the planned second parts of *Judas Macabeo* or *Luis Pérez el gallego*, it did not. If one reads all of his plays, one can see that some of the comedies are like the old Whitehall farces, technically very clever, superbly funny when well played, but not always crammed with profundities about the human condition. However, Segismundo, Pedro Crespo, King Pedro of Castile and their like give the lie to the claim that Calderón never created complex characters.

No doubt many authors are incorrectly categorised. Apart from the inability to create complex characters, Calderón has been accused of lack of inventiveness, of converting 'la sorpresa en tópico, la forma en molde y lo clásico vivo en académico muerto' ('surprise into a topic, form into a mould and the living classical into the dead academic'),[39] of providing uncritical support for what should have been condemned, whether it was a regime or a set of values (which included the killing of wives suspected of contemplating an affair), and even of writing plays with no 'religious, moral, political, social, or metaphysical content'.[40] Rescuing a pigeonholed author whose writings, from letters to complete plays, number almost 300 pieces, is not easy; it takes more than the stroke of a single critic's pen. But studies of his use of existing material, and of the development and use of his imagery and rhetoric, have shown that he is, above all, a craftsman whose use of imagery needs to be examined in its dramatic context:

> Calderón proves to be a practical dramatist as concerned with the immediate effectiveness of his plays as with subtleties. His use of striking images to link important scenes, to contribute to the creation of suspense, and to draw parallels and contrasts between characters is yet another manifestation of his capacity to subordinate stylistic techniques of many kinds to overtly dramatic ends.[41]

Dramatic ends, we come to realise, were paramount, and not merely stylistic techniques were subordinated to them.

Many years ago, a critic felt the need to ask the question, 'Did Calderón have a sense of humour?' Although later studies provided a positive answer,[42] the fact that the question was asked drew attention to a prevailing image of a humourless intellectual who was more interested in points of theology than in the joys and sorrows of ordinary people. Perhaps this is the time to look briefly at *Las visiones de la muerte*.

In *Don Quijote* II, xi, the knight and Sancho meet a cartload of actors hurrying from one venue to another, still wearing their costumes. Uncharacteristically, Don Quijote asks the carter who they are before launching an attack, and accepts his honest explanation; Cervantes develops the plot by having the company's *gracioso* startle Rocinante and attempt to steal Sancho's ass. When the knight contemplates revenge, Sancho's advice, and the actors' readiness to defend themselves, persuade him otherwise, and he withdraws. Calderón saw another potential in this situation. He begins with the loading of the cart: the actor playing Cuerpo (Body) must not sit next to Alma (Soul), since they are a married couple (enough said); as for the *autor*'s own wife, who plays Ángel, 'echadla con el Diablo' ('bung her in with the Devil', line 47). Meanwhile, a weary traveller stops for a snooze in the heat of the day, fortifying himself with a generous draught of wine. The laden cart overturns in a marsh (i.e., offstage), and the costumed actors stagger on. First comes Diablo with his horns and tail, crossing himself and thanking God for his survival, then Ángel, asking for a handkerchief to use as a bandage. As the terrified and tipsy wayfarer calls on the blessed souls of Purgatory for aid, enter Cuerpo, carrying Alma, followed by Muerte (Death) with his scythe. The last finds the traveller's leather wine-bottle, and the others drink a toast to Muerte for this happy discovery (except for Diablo, for whom none is left). The playlet makes use of stereotypical characters like the threatening gypsies, but also plays with conventions: carters were noted for effing and blinding, but this one is different ('Pero jurar no quiero, | que es impropio el jurar de un carretero', 'but I will not swear, because it's improper for a carter to swear': 10–11); and there is yet another mocking reference to *La vida es sueño* (184).[43] The editors' plausible suggestion is that the *auto* the company is playing is Don Pedro's own *El pleito matrimonial del cuerpo y el alma* (*c.* 1650; the characters all fit, although the Devil in the *auto* is called Pecado, Sin), and that the *mojiganga* may be as late as 1673–5, by which time the author had been a priest for over twenty years. If it was played with the 1673 version of the *auto La vida es sueño*, as it may have been, it would have been even more humorously appropriate.

Frequently, when appreciating Calderón's jokes, we may find that the intellectual approach is useful; but not invariably. However, the alert spectator would have recognised that the *mojiganga*, like the *auto*, illustrates the battle between Flesh and Spirit, as Paul explained to the Galatians: 'If you are guided by the Spirit you will not fulfil the desires of your lower nature. That nature sets its desires against the Spirit, while the Spirit fights against it' (Galatians 5:16–17). Because of the primacy of the spirit ('el alma es lo primero', 'the soul comes first': 41), Alma gets the best seat in the cart; and the traveller's cry, '¡No tuviera el alma cuerpo!' ('If only the soul had no body!': 104), expresses a greater truth than he knows. Only Muerte can stop the fight, by separating Body from Spirit.[44]

Cervantes's scene is amusing, but Calderón saw in it the potential for a very funny situation, which even those innocent of theological knowledge could appreciate. This ability to identify material which could be developed, and to develop it successfully, was perhaps his greatest strength as a dramatic writer. It is clear, too, that he could see the funny side of subjects which society then took very seriously, such as the dogma of the Church and *estatutos de sangre*, or the farcical side of tragic events.[45]

However, accurate observation of the ways in which real people behave was another strong point. How, we may wonder, was a man who never married able to depict female characters with such sensitivity, or the quarrels of lovers? And how was he able to portray the intensity, and the ambiguity, of the relationships that can exist between two young women like Serafina and 'Celia' in *Las manos blancas no ofenden*? Over half a century ago, Gerald Brenan noted of Pérez Galdós's *Fortunata y Jacinta* that 'we cannot help being amazed by the knowledge which this confirmed bachelor had of the intimate life of married people'. A few pages later he answered this implicit question: Galdós had mistresses, by one of whom he had children: 'Readers of his novels will appreciate how much these relations with women of a different social class, each no doubt with her particular bevy of relations and friends, must have given him.'[46] We know nothing of the social class to which the mother of Calderón's child belonged, nothing of her relatives and friends; but while there was more need for the unmarried to be discreet in their relationships in seventeenth-century Madrid, the relationship in itself must have added to his experience of life. And yet, a relationship which, to our knowledge, was enjoyed by a writer approaching middle age could hardly provide material for plays written twenty years earlier. We are bound to suspect that there was a grain of truth in the remark of Antonio Sigler de Huerta, at least to the extent that Don Pedro enjoyed female company, and that he had done so since the beginning of his career.

Some feminists will find plenty to object to in Calderón: jokes about women's inability to keep secrets, about their fickleness, their vanity. But there are also numerous examples of discretion, constancy and humility: Calderón did not generalise about women. On the contrary, his advocacy of the rights of women is exceptionally striking in a bachelor born in the last year of the sixteenth century. For example, the story of Alexander the Great and his painter Apelles tells us that when Alexander discovered that the painter loved Campaspe, the king's intended mistress, he presented her to him; it does not tell us what Campaspe thought of the arrangement. In *Darlo todo y no dar nada* (1651), Campaspe loves Apeles, but will not marry him simply because Alejandro tells her to: she refuses to be treated as an object.

As for the charge of uncritical support for a regime which should have been condemned, the best refutation comes in the same play, which presents another supposed incident from Alexander's life. The character Apeles, Alejandro's *pintor de cámara* (I, 1231a), is modelled on Velázquez, but the writer's insistence on the verb 'hablar', to speak, when dealing with the manner in which a royal artist should portray his employer's warts, real or metaphorical, suggests that Calderón's own verbal arts were as much in his mind as those of the painter. The portrait of one of the rivals of Apeles/Velázquez/Calderón is rejected as too explicit; another, for omitting the defect completely. Describing the approach that should have been taken, Alejandro explains that

ha de buscarse modo
de hablar a un Rey, con tal tiento,
que ni disuene la voz,
ni lisonjee el silencio. (I, 1231a)

(A way must be sought of speaking to a king with such circumspection that words are not objectionable and silence not flattering.)

As for Apeles,

Buen camino habéis hallado
de hablar y callar discreto;
pues sin que el defecto vea,
estoy mirando el defecto. (I, 1231a)

(You have found a good way of speaking and being silent discreetly; for I am looking at the defect without seeing it.)

The truth is that there is no shortage of critical comment in Calderón's works. When he is critical of his rulers, including Philip IV, he brings their defects to their notice by finding a way between saying too much and keeping silent. In *El gran teatro del mundo*, when Pobre is reduced to begging, he approaches Rey:

POBRE Pues a mi necesidad
le falta ley y razón,
atreveréme al rey mismo.
Dadme limosna, Señor.
REY Para eso tengo ya
mi limosnero mayor.
MUNDO Con sus ministros el Rey
su conciencia aseguró. (III, 214a)

(POOR MAN: Since my necessity knows no law or reason, I shall make bold to the king himself. Give me alms, sire. KING: I have my chief almoner for that. WORLD: The king salved his conscience with his ministers.)

The sarcasm is implicit in Mundo's words, however they are pronounced: we remember the deeds that were left undone because Philip entrusted them to his ministers. This remark undermines Rey's list of all that he has accomplished (III, 218b), and his great deeds are put in context when Pobre walks before him to his reward:

REY ¿Tú, también, tanto baldonas
mi poder, que vas delante?
¿Tan presto de la memoria
que fuiste vasallo mío,
mísero mendigo, borras?

POBRE Ya, acabado tu papel,
en el vestuario ahora
del sepulcro, iguales somos.
Lo que fuiste, poco importa. (III, 220b)

(KING: Do you too insult my power so much that you walk ahead of me? Wretched beggar, do you forget so soon that you were my vassal? POOR MAN: Now that your role is over, in the dressing-room of the grave, we are equal. What you were matters little.)

Rey is not Philip IV: he is any monarch; but the message is clear enough.

Several recent critics have drawn attention to Calderón's portrayal of monarchs, and concluded that he 'presents arguments for the necessity of good kingship (as opposed to functioning as servile flattery) and evinces a clear concern for the primacy of law over the arbitrary whim of a ruler'.[47] The critic just quoted suggests that in cases like *Amigo, amante y leal*, *Saber del mal y del bien* or *Gustos y disgustos*, Don Pedro was prepared to sacrifice plausibility in order to show a ruler, late in the day, acting properly. These plays were all written before 1640 and the opening of the Coliseo; it may be argued that as the court theatre grew in importance, the once vocal and unruly audiences of the public theatres found the presence of the king inhibiting.[48] As result, it may be argued further that 'The content of public theater was inherently audience-driven, and by changing the audience, the court effectively removed the ability of the *comedia* to serve as a forum for public discussion of the nature of kings and their relationship with their subjects.'[49] To a degree, this is certainly true. But while the forum may have changed, Don Pedro continued to examine the behaviour of monarchs, in plays written specifically for the court, like *Darlo todo y no dar nada* (1651), or in *autos* like *No hay más fortuna que Dios* (?1652), *El maestrazgo del toisón* (1659) and *El lirio y la azucena* (1660), which he knew would be seen by the king and his court, as well as by the general public. Shergold made this point over forty years ago, when he described *No hay más fortuna* as being 'amazingly and fearlessly outspoken in its dramatic content … and its very unflattering portrayal of crowned Power'.[50] This is not simply a question of a priest sermonising and counting on the immunity provided by his status: Calderón had been making these points throughout his secular career.

***

At this point it may be asked: what was Don Pedro really like? We have a pretty good idea of what Lope was like: he was an emotional extrovert, as has been said already. Calderón was a much more private person, but we can identify some of his traits. He was a man of strong character, marked by apparent contradictions. In spiritual terms, very much a product of his background: deeply religious, profoundly Catholic. Yet his secular side was not at all typical of his environment: he rejected the jingoism and sexism of many of his male contemporaries, understanding and portraying sympathetically the aspirations of what many of those contemporaries saw as 'the other'. We can see that his Jesuit schooling had fostered a preciseness which sat well with a natural obstinacy. He knew that his mind was sharp, and that he had a gift for turning his thoughts into precise expression. There is enough evidence for a quick temper, and he did not suffer slights gladly; if the biting remarks which he committed to paper are echoes of words which were uttered, we can see how he might have made enemies. We may suspect, too, that his dislike of Sigler de Huerta and Paravicino pre-dated what they said about him: despising insincerity and self-delusion, he saw them as vain, self-promoting poseurs; not men he would have attacked, however – unless provoked. But he was loyal to those he cared about, undeterred by Quevedo's slurs about Pérez de Montalbán's learning or his ancestry, happy to write dedicatory poems for Méndez Silva, despite the popular view that any Portuguese was suspect in religious terms. A bad enemy, perhaps, but a good friend, possessed of a sense of humour which did not exclude the bawdy, or self-mockery. Sometimes his self-mockery is just that (e.g., Turín's sarcastic remark in *Afectos de odio y amor* about the length of the plays of 'this author': II, 1759a), but perhaps the most distinctive feature of his writing is irony, the ability to stand back and observe all human activity, even his own, with a dispassionate eye: the kind of man who told jokes about himself, but with a straight face: he would have enjoyed his friend Rojas's witticism about his thinning hair. None of his fellow dramatists refers more often to Cervantes, whose ironic objectivity was undoubtedly an influence. This detachment did not prevent him from enjoying his status, whether as a knight or as a successful writer: why not, if he had worked hard for it? And yet he never lost sight of the impermanence of human accomplishment. While the existential concerns so often voiced by his characters are clearly his own, to such an extent that critics have postulated a crisis of faith in his late twenties and early thirties,[51] he never forgot the answer: human life is meaningless without God. His characters search desperately for meaning in their existence, and contemplation of their struggles induces a profound pessimism, a pessimism which the author himself undoubtedly felt. It has been suggested that Spanish dramatists, including Calderón, do not depict victims of destiny or mischance, but only of wrongdoing, of sin.[52] Perhaps; but of course the consequences of the sins of others can be visited on the innocent, as the stillborn Niño discovers in *El gran teatro del mundo*:

NIÑO Si yo no erré mi papel,
¿por qué no me galardonas,
gran Señor?

AUTOR Porque muy poco
le acertaste; y así ahora,
ni te premio ni castigo.
Ciego, ni uno ni otro goza,
que en fin naces del pecado. (1501–7)

(CHILD: If I did not get my role wrong, why do you not reward me, Lord? AUTHOR: Because you scarcely got it right; and so now I neither reward nor punish you. Enjoy neither in your blindness, for in the end you are born of sin.)

This is perhaps the most truly tragic aspect of mankind's *predicamento*, a predicament which no individual can escape, because it is God's will.

Much has been written about tragedy in Calderón. Some critics have argued that no orthodox Catholic, necessarily believing in the dominant role of divine providence in human affairs, could construct a true tragedy, in which individuals were subject to Fate. Parker argued for a kind of tragedy in which the actions of others took over the role of Fate (the 'diffused responsibilty' referred to above), although he seems to have been reluctant to explore situations where the innocent suffered only because of others' wrongdoing. It is certainly true that Calderón depicted catastrophes created by the actions of a number of characters, but close examination shows that chance events also play a part. Chance, however, is neutral: it is the character's manner of dealing with the chance events that contributes to disaster. The catastrophe of *A secreto agravio* is set in motion by the arrival of a piece of false news: that Leonor's betrothed has been killed in the war in Flanders. Her response is to listen to the well-meaning relatives who persuade her to marry a man she has never met: hardly an example of wrongdoing. But the situation has been created in which the 'dead' fiancé can return and persuade the unhappy wife to run off with him. That Enrique's knife should cut King Pedro's hand in *El médico de su honra* is a chance: if Pedro were not paranoid, he would see the cut as an accident, not an attempted assassination, and Mencía might still be rescued. It is chance that leads Oedipus to meet Laius on the road; if Oedipus were not a hothead, he would not quarrel with and kill the stranger. And if that chance encounter was engineered by Fate, while Pedro's cut was the will of God, the distinction will not bring Mencía back to life. The difference, perhaps, is that Mencía can expect redemption. The play suggests as much, but the degree of comfort extracted by the audience from this suggestion is open to question; and Leonor can expect no redemption for the sin she had yet to commit, and which originated in the chance of a false report. The *autos* may comfort us with the message that *no hay más fortuna que Dios*, but this world is no kinder to individuals than that of Oedipus.

* * *

In the spring of 1681, as usual, Don Pedro worked on that year's *autos*. He completed *El cordero de Isaías*, and he had almost finished *La divina Filotea* when he felt too unwell to complete it. On 20 May he made his will, and three days later added a codicil: Pascual Millán reproduces the two trembling signatures, the first of them misspelled as Caderon.[53] He died on 25 May at around noon. His will is so detailed that it seems likely that he drafted it while he was still able to go through his house, listing his possessions, and who should have them: the beneficiaries are his family, friends, colleagues, servants. Of the last, he states that if he is found to owe them money, it should be paid; if they owe him money, the debt is to be cancelled. Among his possessions, he refers to two bookcases. The books dealing with 'Monarquía eclesiástica' and 'Historia pontifical' are to be given to Don Carlos del Castillo (royal equerry, knight of Santiago and one of the will's executors); the eight-volume set of the *Theatrum vitae humanae* is to be given to Alonso de Cañizares, a fellow Franciscan and royal chaplain; the 'libros del Padre Diana' are to be given to Jerónimo de Peñarroja; the remainder, 'así de lo moral y buenas letras' ('both ethics and literature'), are for Antonio de Padilla, the poet's great-nephew, and also a priest.[54] Father Diana is presumably the moralist Antonino Diana (1586–1663), whose *Resolutiones morales* were often reprinted. Jerónimo de Peñarroja may have been one of several actors of that name. The only book which can be positively identified is Laurentius Beyerlinck's *Magnum theatrum vitae humanae*, a kind of encyclopaedia, first published in Cologne in 1631. This must have been Don Pedro's most valuable book: some of his debts to it have been explored by Alan Paterson.[55]

If the will gives disappointingly few details of its owner's books, it makes no reference to his writings, unless we include the request that he should be carried to his burial 'descubierto, por si mereciese satisfacer en parte las publicas vanidades de mi mal gastada vida con publicos desengaños de mi muerte' ('uncovered, in case I should deserve to make good in part the public vanities of my ill-spent life with the public admonition of my death').[56] In the codicil, written in the third person, there is a more precise reference, however:

> Item declara que algunos papeles con que se hallaba mano-escritos, que no tocan a ninguna cosa de hacienda ni cargo de conciencia suyo, sino solo a algun empleo de su ociosidad, aunque en su estimacion valian poco, fue y es su voluntad hacer donacion de ellos en vida, como con efecto lo ha hecho, en el señor Doctor Don Juan Matheo Lozano, cura de San Miguel, con quien dexa comunicado la forma que ha de usar de ellos, y asi de ellos no se le pida quenta alguna.[57]

> (Next, he declares that some manuscript documents which he had, which have nothing to do with property or charge on his conscience, but only with employment of his leisure, it was and is his will to donate them during his lifetime, as in fact he has done, to Dr Don Juan Mateo Lozano, priest of San Miguel, whom he has told what use he is to make of them, and so he is not to be asked to account for them.)

Despite the claim that they were worth little in his eyes, or because of it, we are reluctant to believe that he had instructed Lozano to destroy them. Calderón had several reasons for choosing to be a writer: he liked it; it gave him the opportunity to say things which he cared about greatly; it provided a livelihood; and it brought him a recognition which he desired, whatever he might say to the contrary. And yet … the knowledge that his life was over may have changed his frame of mind: Así, Ciprïano, son todas las glorias del mundo.

Appendix: Calderón's dramatic works mentioned in this book

A María el corazón (*auto*) : *To Mary, the heart*
A secreto agravio, secreta venganza : *Secret vengeance for secret insult*
El acaso y el error : *The accident and the mistake*
Afectos de odio y amor : *Passions of hate and love*
Agradecer y no amar : *Being grateful and not loving*
El agua mansa / Guárdate del agua mansa : *Still water / Beware of still water*
El alcaide de sí mismo : *His own jailer*
El alcalde de Zalamea : *The mayor of Zalamea*
Amar después de la muerte (*Love after death*), see *El Tuzaní de la Alpujarra*
Amigo, amante y leal : *Friend, lover and loyal*
Amor, honor y poder : *Love, honour and power*
Andrómeda y Perseo : *Andromeda and Perseus*
Andrómeda y Perseo (*auto*) : *Andromeda and Perseus*
Antes que todo es mi dama : *My lady before all*
Apolo y Climene : *Apollo and Clymene*
El árbol del mejor fruto : *The tree with the best fruit*
Argenis y Poliarco : *Argenis and Poliarco*
Las armas de la hermosura : *Beauty's weapons*
El astrólogo fingido : *The fake astrologer*
Auristela y Clariana (= *Auristela y Lisidante*?)
Auristela y Lisidante : *Auristela and Lisidante*
La aurora en Copacabana : *Dawn in Copacabana*
La banda y la flor : *The scarf and the flower*
Basta callar : *Being silent is enough*
Bien vengas mal, si vienes solo : *Welcome, evil, if you come alone*
Los cabellos de Absalón : *The hair of Absalom*
Cada uno para sí : *Every man for himself*
Las cadenas del demonio : *The devil's chains*
Las Carnestolendas (*entremés*) : *Carnival*

Casa con dos puertas mala es de guardar: *A house with two doors is difficult to guard*
La cena del rey Baltasar (*auto*) : *Belshazzar's feast*
La cisma de Ingalaterra: *The schism of England*
Con quien vengo, vengo: *I'm with whom I'm with*
El conde Lucanor: *Count Lucanor*
La cruz en la sepultura (= *La devoción de la cruz*) : *The cross in the tomb*
¿Cuál es mayor perfección, hermosura o discreción?: *Which is greater perfection, beauty or good sense?*
El cubo de la Almudena: *The turret of La Almudena*
La dama duende: *The phantom lady*
La dama y galán Aquiles (= *El monstruo de los jardines*?) : *Achilles, lady and gallant*
Dar tiempo al tiempo: *To give time time*
Darlo todo y no dar nada: *To give all and to give nothing*
De un castigo tres venganzas: *Three vengeances from one punishment*
De una causa dos efectos: *Two effects from one cause*
La desdicha de la voz: *The misfortune of the voice*
La devoción de la cruz: *Devotion to the cross*
La devoción de la misa (*auto*) : *Devotion to the mass*
Los disparates de Don Quijote (see below, 'Calderón, lost works') : *Don Quijote de la Mancha*
El divino cazador (*auto*) : *The divine hunter*
Los dos amantes del cielo: *The two lovers of heaven*
Duelos de amor y lealtad: *Duels of love and loyalty*
Eco y Narciso: *Echo and Narcissus*
Los empeños de un acaso: *The obligations of an accident*
En la vida todo es verdad y todo mentira: *In life, everything is true and everything is false*
El encanto sin encanto: *Enchantment without enchantment*
Los encantos de la culpa (*auto*) : *The sorceries of sin*
El escondido y la tapada: *The hidden lover and the veiled lady*
La exaltación de la cruz: *The exaltation of the cross*
La fiera, el rayo y la piedra: *The beast, the thunderbolt and the stone*
Fieras afemina Amor: *Love tames wild beasts*
Fuego de Dios en el querer bien: *A curse on true love*
El galán fantasma: *The phantom gallant*
El golfo de las sirenas: *The gulf of the sirens*
La gran Cenobia: *The great Zenobia*
El gran príncipe de Fez: *The great Prince of Fez*
El gran teatro del mundo (*auto*) : *The great stage of the world*

Guárdate del agua mansa, see *El agua mansa*

Gustos y disgustos son no más que imaginación : *Liking and disliking are mere imagination*

Hado y divisa de Leonido y de Marfisa : *The fate, emblem and device of Leonido and Marfisa*

La hidalga del valle (*auto*) : *The noblewoman of the valley*

La hija del aire (two parts) : *The daughter of the air*

El hijo del sol : *The son of the sun*

Los hijos de la fortuna : *The children of Fortune*

El hombre pobre todo es trazas : *A poor man is all tricks*

La humildad coronada de las plantas (*auto*) : *The crowned humility of the plants*

La industria contra el poder, y el honor contra la fuerza (= *Amor, honor y poder*) : *Craft versus power and honour versus force*

La inmunidad del sagrado (*auto*) : *The immunity of sanctuary*

El jardín de Falerina : *The garden of Falerina*

El jardín de Falerina (*auto*) : *The garden of Falerina*

El José de las mujeres : *The Joseph among women*

Judas Macabeo : *Judas Maccabaeus*

Lances de amor y fortuna : *Episodes of love and fortune*

El laurel de Apolo : *The laurel of Apollo*

El lirio y la azucena (*auto*) : *The fleur-de-lys and the lily*

Llamados y escogidos (*auto*) : *Called and chosen*

Lo que va del hombre a Dios (*auto*) : *The distance between man and God*

Loa para el auto La protestación de la fe : *Prologue for the* auto *The protestation of faith*

Loa para el auto sacramental intitulado las órdenes militares, en metáfora de la Piadosa Hermandad del Refugio, discurriendo por calles y templos de Madrid : *Prologue for the* auto sacramental *entitled The military orders, in a metaphor of the Pious Brotherhood of the Refuge, roaming through the streets and churches of Madrid*

Loa sacramental que la compañía de Antonio de Prado representó en el auto de la primer flor del Carmelo : *Sacramental prologue which the company of Antonio de Prado performed in the* auto *The first flower of Mount Carmel*

Luis Pérez el gallego : *Luis Pérez the Galician*

Los Macabeos, see *Judas Macabeo*

El maestrazgo del toisón (*auto*) : *The mastership of the Golden Fleece*

El maestro de danzar : *The dancing master*

El mágico prodigioso : *The wondrous magician*

Las manos blancas no ofenden : *Fair hands do not offend*

Mañana será otro día : *Tomorrow will be another day*
Mañanas de abril y mayo : *Mornings of April and May*
El mayor encanto, amor : *Love, the greatest enchantment*
El mayor monstruo del mundo : *The world's greatest monster*
El médico de su honra : *The surgeon of his honour*
Mejor está que estaba : *It's better than it was*
Los misterios de la misa (*auto*) : *The mysteries of the mass*
Mojiganga de las visiones de la muerte : *Masque of the visions of death*
El monstruo de los jardines : *The monster of the gardens*
Nadie fíe su secreto : *Keep your own secret*
Ni Amor se libra de amor : *Not even Love escapes love*
La niña de Gómez Arias : *Gómez Arias's girl*
No hay burlas con el amor : *There's no fooling with love*
No hay cosa como callar : *Silence is golden*
No hay más fortuna que Dios (*auto*) : *There is no Fortune but God*
No siempre lo peor es cierto : *The worst is not always true*
El nuevo hospicio de pobres (*auto*) : *The new poor-house*
El nuevo palacio del Retiro (*auto*) : *The new Retiro Palace*
Nunca lo peor es cierto : *The worst is never true*
Las órdenes militares / Las pruebas del segundo Adán (*auto*) : *The military orders / The second Adam's tests*
Origen, pérdida y restauración de Nuestra Señora del Sagrario : *The origin, loss and restoration of Our Lady of the Sanctuary*
Para vencer a amor, querer vencerle : *To conquer love, desire to conquer it*
El pastor Fido (*auto*) : *The faithful shepherd* (see also below under 'Calderón, collaboration works')
Peor está que estaba : *It is worse than it was*
La piel de Gedeón (*auto*) : *Gideon's sheepskin*
El pintor de su deshonra : *The painter of his dishonour*
El pintor de su deshonra (*auto*) : *The painter of his dishonour*
El pleito matrimonial del cuerpo y el alma (*auto*) : *The matrimonial lawsuit between body and soul*
El postrer duelo de España : *The last duel in Spain*
La primer flor del Carmelo (*auto*) : *The first flower of Mount Carmel*
Primero soy yo : *Charity begins at home*
El príncipe constante : *The steadfast prince*
La protestación de la fe : *The protestation of faith*
Psiquis y Cupido (para Toledo) (*auto*) : *Psyche and Cupid (for Toledo)*
La puente de Mantible : *The bridge of Mantible*
El purgatorio de San Patricio : *St Patrick's purgatory*

La púrpura de la rosa: *The crimson of the rose*
Saber del mal y del bien: *Knowledge of good and evil*
El secreto a voces: *The secret aloud*
El segundo Escipión: *The second Scipio*
La segunda esposa y triunfar muriendo (*auto*): *The second wife and triumph by dying*
La selva confusa: *The confused forest*
Las selvas de amor (*The forests of love*), see *La selva confusa*
Selvas y bosques de amor (*Forests and woods of love*), see *La selva confusa*
La semilla y la zizaña (*auto*): *The seed and the darnel*
La señora y la criada: *The lady and the maidservant*
La serpiente de metal (*auto*; first draft, *La sierpe de metal*?): *The metal serpent*
La sibila de Oriente: *The sybil of the East*
La sierpe de metal, see *La serpiente de metal.*
El sitio de Bredá: *The siege of Breda*
El socorro general (*auto*): *The universal succour*
También hay duelo en las damas: *Women too feel honour's obligations*
La torre de Babilonia (*auto*): *The tower of Babel*
Los tres afectos del amor: *The three emotional effects of love*
Las tres justicias en una: *Three judgements in one*
Los tres mayores prodigios: *The three greatest prodigies*
El triunfo de la cruz (= *La exaltación de la cruz*?): *The triumph of the cross*
El Tuzaní de la Alpujarra: *The Tuzaní of the Alpujarra*
La vacante general (*auto*): *The universal vacancy*
El veneno y la triaca (*auto*): *The poison and the antidote*
La vida es sueño: *Life is a dream*
La vida es sueño (*auto*): *Life is a dream*
La virgen del Sagrario: *The virgin of the sanctuary*

CALDERÓN, COLLABORATION WORKS

Belmonte Bermúdez, Rojas Zorrilla and Calderón, *El mejor amigo el muerto*: *The best friend the dead man*
Calderón, Antonio Coello and Moreto, *La fingida Arcadia*: *The feigned Arcadia*
Calderón, 'Pérez de Montalbán and Antonio Coello', *El privilegio de las mugeres*: *Women's privilege*
Calderón, Pérez de Montalbán and Rojas Zorrilla, *El monstruo de la fortuna*: *The monster of fortune*
Calderón, Vélez de Guevara and Cáncer y Velasco: *Enfermar con el remedio*: *Falling ill with the remedy*

Calderón and Zabaleta, *Troya abrasada*: *Troy in flames*

Coello, Antonio, and Calderón, *Yerros de naturaleza y aciertos de la fortuna*: *Errors of nature and successes of fortune*

Mira de Amescua, Pérez de Montalbán and Calderón, *Polifemo y Circe*: *Polyphemus and Circe*

Rojas Zorrilla, Antonio Coello and Calderón, *El jardín de Falerina*: *The garden of Falerina*

Solís, Antonio Coello and Calderón, *El pastor Fido*: *The faithful shepherd*

Zabaleta, Cáncer y Velasco and Calderón, *La margarita preciosa*: *The precious pearl*

Zabaleta, Rojas Zorrilla and Calderón, *La más hidalga hermosura*: *The noblest beauty*

CALDERÓN, LOST WORKS

El carro del cielo: *The chariot of heaven*

La Celestina: *The Celestina*

Certamen de amor y celos: *Contest of love and jealousy*

Don Quijote de la Mancha / Los disparates de Don Quijote: *Don Quixote of La Mancha / The absurdities of Don Quixote*

La fábula de Dafne: *The fable of Daphne*

La fábula de Narciso: *The fable of Narcissus*

El juicio final (*auto*): *The last judgement*

El mejor huésped de España (*auto*): *Spain's best guest/host*

Nuestra Señora de la Almudena (two parts): *Our Lady of La Almudena*

Nuestra Señora de los Remedios: *Our Lady of the Remedies*

Las proezas de Frislán, y muerte del rey de Suecia [?], with A. Coello: *The prowess of Friedland, and death of the King of Sweden.*

San Francisco de Borja: *St Francis Borja*

Santa María Egipciaca (*auto*): *St Mary of Egypt*

CALDERÓN, ATTRIBUTED WORKS

El consumo del vellón (*auto*): *The consumption of vellón* [silver-copper alloy]

El divino Jasón (*auto*): *The divine Jason*

El gran duque de Gandía: *The great Duke of Gandía*

No hay que creer ni en la verdad: *Not even the truth is to be believed in*

La peste del pan dañado (*auto*): *The plague of the spoiled bread*

El prodigio de Alemania: *The prodigy of Germany*

Notes

PREFACE

1. The posthumous *Noticias y documentos relativos a la historia y literatura españolas*, in *Memorias de la Real Academia Española* 10 (1911), 9–307, devotes only pp. 23–69 to Calderón, scarcely enough to fill a second volume.
2. In the mid 1930s, Wilson and Alexander Parker planned a joint critical volume on the *comedias* and the *autos*. By 1940, when the war interrupted them, Parker had finished the *autos*, while Wilson had completed only two chapters on the *comedias*. Wilson advised him to publish the *auto* section on its own, which Parker did in 1943. Wilson eventually published some of his material as a chapter of *A Literary History of Spain: The Golden Age: Drama 1492–1700* (London: Ernest Benn; New York: Barnes & Noble, 1971) (with Duncan Moir).
3. San Salvador was the burial-place of his maternal grandparents as well as of his parents; it was also the church where his grandmother Inés de Riaño had endowed the chaplaincy which he took up in 1651.
4. Felipe B. Pedraza Jiménez, *Calderón: Vida y teatro* (Madrid: Alianza, 2000), p. 10.

CHAPTER 1. THE BIRTHPLACE: MADRID IN 1600

1. See Henry Kamen, *Philip of Spain* (New Haven and London: Yale University Press, 1997), pp. 180–8; and Jesús Escobar, *The Plaza Mayor and the Shaping of Baroque Madrid* (Cambridge: Cambridge University Press, 2003), pp. 45–52, 'The Hinterland of Madrid'.
2. See especially Francisco Iñíguez Almech, *Casas reales y jardines de Felipe II* (Madrid: CSIC, 1952), pp. 62–100. The *alcázar* was destroyed by fire in 1734; the present palace was built on the same site, beginning in 1738.
3. The date of completion was 1584. The Puente de Toledo was built by Pedro de Ribera, 1718–21.
4. From the sonnet 'Duélete de esa puente, Manzanares' (1588).
5. From the sonnet '¡Quítenme aquesta puente que me mata …!', in the *Rimas de Tomé de Burguillos* (1634). Luis Quiñones de Benavente wrote a two-part *entremés*, *La puente segoviana* (*c.* 1635), which has a fine concentration of Manzanares jokes.

6. *Fuego de Dios en el querer bien*, in Pedro Calderón de la Barca, *Obras completas*, vol. II, ed. A. Valbuena Briones (Madrid: Aguilar, 1956); later references are normally to this edition, in this form. La Florida was the riverside walk area.
7. Just after the passage quoted, there is a reference to a lady bathing.
8. Kamen, *Philip of Spain*, p. 181.
9. Antonio Domínguez Ortiz, *La sociedad española en el siglo XVII*, 2 vols., edn facsímil (Granada: Universidad de Granada, 1992), vol. I, pp. 131–4. Cf. Alfredo Alvar Ezquerra, *El nacimiento de una capital europea: Madrid entre 1561 y 1606* (Madrid: Turner, 1989), p. 33.
10. Martín González de Cellorigo, *Memorial de la politica necessaria, y util restauracion a la republica de España*, ed. José L. Pérez de Ayala (Madrid: Instituto de Cooperación Iberoamericana, 1991), p. 12. (First published Valladolid: Juan de Bostillo, 1600.)
11. That is, some other sites called 'Puerta' (e.g., Puerta de la Vega, Puerta Cerrada) were literally gates, with massive stone gateways, in the remains of the old mud-brick walls. The walls did not extend to the Puerta del Sol, however.
12. See Escobar, *The Plaza Mayor*, pp. 155–71.
13. See John J. Allen, *The Reconstruction of a Spanish Golden Age Playhouse: El Corral del Príncipe 1583–1744* (Gainesville: University of Florida, 1983), especially the sketch facing p. 68 and the model on p. 91; and J. M. Ruano de la Haza and John J. Allen, *Los teatros comerciales del siglo XVII y la escenificación de la comedia* (Madrid: Castalia, 1994); revised as José María Ruano de la Haza, *La puesta en escena en los teatros comerciales del Siglo de Oro* (Madrid: Castalia, 2000).
14. J. E. Varey, 'L'Auditoire du *Salón dorado* de l'*Alcázar* de Madrid au XVIIe siècle', in Jean Jacquot (ed.), *Dramaturgie et Société: Rapports entre l'oeuvre théâtrale, son interprétation et son public aux XVIe et XVIIe siècles: Nancy 14–21 avril 1967* (Paris: Centre National de la Recherche Scientifique, 1968), vol. I, pp. 77–91: see especially pp. 78, 87.
15. See Jonathan Brown and J. H. Elliott, *A Palace for a King: The Buen Retiro and the Court of Philip IV*, 2nd edn (New Haven and London: Yale University Press, 2004), pp. 216–17.
16. Héctor Urzáiz Tortajada, *Catálogo de autores teatrales del siglo XVII*, 2 vols. (Madrid: Fundación Universitaria Española, 2002) (Investigaciones Bibliográficas sobre Autores Españoles 5); W. W. Greg, *A Bibliography of the English Printed Drama to the Restoration*, 4 vols. (London: Bibliographical Society, 1939–59).
17. Alvar Ezquerra, *El nacimiento*, pp. 216–27, 'La limpieza de la ciudad'.
18. Robert Burton, *The Anatomy of Melancholy*, 3 vols. (London: Dent, 1968), vol. I, p. 240.
19. J. H. Elliott, *Imperial Spain* 1469–1716 (London: Arnold, 1963), p. 292.
20. See James A. Amelang (ed.), *A Journal of the Plague Year: The Diary of the Barcelona Tanner Miquel Parets 1651* (New York and Oxford: Oxford University Press, 1991), pp. 99–101. For a general picture, see Vicente Pérez Moreda, *La crisis de la mortalidad en la España interior* (Madrid: Siglo XXI, 1980).

21. Cristóbal Pérez Pastor, *Documentos para la biografía de don Pedro Calderón de la Barca* (Madrid: Fortanet, 1905), p. 161.
22. Alonso López de Corella, *De morbo pustulato, sive lonticulari, quem nostrates Tabardillo appellant* (Zaragoza: Miguel de Güesa, 1574).
23. The list of 'catástrofes' provided by Alvar Ezquerra, *El nacimiento*, pp. 69–70, includes, in central Spain between 1556 and 1603, drought, floods, locusts, bad harvests, food shortages, bubonic plague, influenza, typhus, smallpox and diphtheria.
24. See Margaret Rich Greer, 'Constituting Community: A New Historical Perspective on the *autos* of Calderón', in José A. Madrigal (ed.), *New Historicism and the* Comedia: *Poetics, Politics and Praxis* (Boulder, CO: Society of Spanish and Spanish-American Studies, 1997), pp. 41–67.
25. References are to Pedacio Dioscorides Anazarbeo, *Acerca de la materia medicinal*, ed. and trans. Andrés Laguna (Salamanca: Matías Gast, 1566; reprinted 1570); and to Nicholas Culpeper, *Culpeper's Complete Herbal: Consisting of a Comprehensive Description of Nearly All Herbs with their Medicinal Properties and Directions for Compounding the Medicines Extracted from them* (London: W. Foulsham, [1923]). Culpeper was born in 1616 and died in 1654.
26. One of the first petitions made by the Cortes to Philip IV when he became king in 1621 was that no new convents for men or women should be licensed: J. Deleito y Piñuela, *La vida religiosa bajo el cuarto Felipe* (Madrid: Espasa-Calpe, 1952), pp. 76–7, 83.
27. Others included the essays printed in the *Memorial informatorio por los pintores en el pleyto que tratan con el señor fiscal de S. M. … sobre la exempcion del arte de la pintura* (Madrid: Juan González, 1629), in which Juan Alonso Butrón was one of the authors. Butrón also wrote an *Epistola dirigida al Rey suplicando proteccion para la Academia de los Pintores* (n.p., n.d.). The essays of 1629 were reprinted at the end of Vincencio Carducho's *Dialogos de la pintura* (Madrid: Francisco Martínez, 1633).
28. Richard L. Kagan, *Students and Society in Early Modern Spain* (Baltimore and London: Johns Hopkins University Press, 1974), p. 23.
29. See Claude Larquié, 'L'Alphabétisation à Madrid en 1650', *RHMC* 28 (1981), 132–57; and D. W. Cruickshank, '"Literature" and the Book Trade in Golden-Age Spain', *MLR* 73 (1978), 799–824.
30. The compilers were Pedro López de Arrieta and Bartolomé de Atienza (Alcalá: Andrés de Angulo, 1567).
31. Miguel de Cervantes, *Novelas ejemplares*, ed. Francisco Rodríguez Marín, 2 vols. (Madrid: Espasa-Calpe, 1915–17), vol. 1, p. 45.

CHAPTER 2. THE FAMILY BACKGROUND

1. Emilio Cotarelo y Mori, *Ensayo sobre la vida y obras de D. Pedro Calderón de la Barca* (Madrid: Tipografía de la 'Revista de Archivos, Bibliotecas y Museos', 1924; facsimile reprint, Madrid: Iberoamericana, 2001), pp. 15, 21, 22. Cotarelo's

information about the poet's remote ancestors was corrected by Narciso Alonso Cortés in 'Genealogía de D. Pedro Calderón', *BRAE* 31 (1951), 299–309.

2. Cotarelo, *Ensayo*, pp. 24, 27.
3. Constancio Eguía Ruiz, 'Cervantes, Calderón, Lope, Gracián: nuevos temas crítico-biográficos', in *Anejos de Cuadernos de Literatura* 8 (Madrid: Instituto 'Miguel de Cervantes' de Filología Española, 1951), pp. 56–61.
4. Illustrated by Julio César Izquierdo Pascua, *Rutas del románico en la provincia de Palencia* (Valladolid: Castilla Ediciones, 2001), p. 78. But Ricardo Puente, in *A través de Palencia por el Camino de Santiago* (León: Albanega, 1998), p. 10, refers to an earlier church, still standing in the nineteenth century. I thank Martin Cunningham for drawing my attention to these books.
5. The relevant document was discovered by Ángel de los Ríos y Ríos, who published it in his *Biografía del célebre poeta dramático D. Pedro Calderón de la Barca* (Torrelavega: B. Rueda, 1889), pp. 121, 125–6. Only eighteen cities had the right to send representatives (two each) to the Cortes of Castile, which met only at the invitation of the king: rather than being a legislative body, it was a rubber stamp.
6. Cotarelo, *Ensayo*, pp. 38, 41.
7. Ibid., p. 41.
8. Ana Guerrero Mayllo, *Familia y vida cotidiana de una elite de poder: Los regidores madrileños en tiempos de Felipe II* (Mexico City and Madrid: Siglo XXI, 1993), p. xiv.
9. Cotarelo, *Ensayo*, p. 72.
10. Gil González Dávila, *Teatro de las grandezas de la villa de Madrid corte de los reyes católicos de España* (Madrid: Tomás Junti, 1623), pp. 492–8.
11. Casiano Pellicer, *Tratado histórico sobre el origen y progreso de la comedia y del histrionismo en España*, ed. José M. Díez Borque (Barcelona: Labor, 1975), p. 58.
12. Cotarelo, *Ensayo*, pp. 42–4.
13. Ibid., p. 45.
14. Pérez Pastor, *Documentos*, p. 1.
15. Cotarelo, *Ensayo*, p. 45; but see P. 1311, Juan de la Calle, 1592, fols. 1372–3, AHP, Madrid.
16. Cotarelo, *Ensayo*, p. 45, quoting Pérez Pastor, *Documentos*, pp. 1–2.
17. Narciso Alonso Cortés, 'Carta de dote de la madre de Calderón de la Barca', *Revista Histórica* 2 (1925), 158–67. Alonso Cortés worked from a copy taken to Valladolid for the lawsuit over Calderón's father's will. The original document, signed before Francisco Hernández, should have been preserved in the AHP, Madrid, but the indexes show that none of this notary's documents have survived for 1593.
18. They were reckoning at 375 *maravedís* per ducat, a rate to which the document refers.
19. Pérez Pastor, *Documentos*, p. 4.
20. In his chapter on the Consejo de Hacienda, González Dávila lists 'los Ministros que despachan los negocios que resultan del Consejo, y Contaduria' ('the officials who deal with business originating in the Council and Accounts

Department'), including the 'Escriuano mayor de Rentas': *Teatro de las grandezas*, p. 495.

21. See Guerrero Mayllo, *Familia y vida cotidiana*, ch. 4.1, 'Los mayorazgos', pp. 208–34.
22. Guerrero Mayllo, *Familia y vida cotidiana*, pp. 11–14; see also the family trees on pp. 137–46, in particular that of the Henao family on p. 141.
23. Ibid., pp. 84–5.
24. Ibid., p. 236.
25. The will and codicil were published by Narciso Alonso Cortés, in 'Algunos datos relativos a D. Pedro Calderón', *RFE* 2 (1915), 41–51.
26. Guerrero Mayllo, *Familia y vida cotidiana*, pp. 88–92.
27. For a map of Madrid parishes at this time, see Alvar Ezquerra, *El nacimiento*, p. 24.
28. Pérez Pastor, *Documentos*, p. 2.
29. Cotarelo, *Ensayo*, p. 42 n. 1.
30. Guerrero Mayllo, *Familia y vida cotidiana*, pp. 88–9.
31. Pérez Pastor, *Documentos*, p. 3.
32. The list of his plays which Calderón prepared for the Duke of Veragua shortly before he died included the title *San Francisco de Borja*. St Francis Borja was the Duke of Gandía, and an anonymous manuscript play entitled *El gran duque de Gandía* was discovered in the castle library of Mladá Vožice by Václav Černý, who published it as Calderón's (Prague: L'Académie Tchécoslovaque des Sciences, 1963). I do not think this is Calderón's play. For the Veragua list, see Pedro Calderón de la Barca, *Comedias*, ed. Juan Eugenio Hartzenbusch, 4 vols. (BAE, vols. VII, IX, XII, XIV) (Madrid: Rivadeneyra, 1848–50), vol. I (VII), p. xlii. The list was first printed by Gaspar Agustín de Lara in the *Obelisco funebre, pyramide funesto que construia a la inmortal memoria de D. Pedro Calderon de la Barca … D. Gaspar Agustin de Lara* (Madrid: Eugenio Rodríguez, 1684), 10¶1^{r}–10¶2^{r}.
33. A biography of Lerma has at last been published: Patrick Williams, *The Great Favourite: The Duke of Lerma and the Court and Government of Philip III of Spain*, 1598–1621 (Manchester: Manchester University Press, 2006).

CHAPTER 3. CHILDHOOD AND EARLY ADOLESCENCE

1. Cotarelo, *Ensayo*, pp. 53–4.
2. Lara, *Obelisco funebre*, 2¶1^{r}. The dates are also given in the portrait facing *2^{r}.
3. José Antonio Álvarez Baena, *Hijos de Madrid, ilustres en santidad, dignidades, armas, ciencias y artes*, 4 vols. (Madrid: Benito Cano, 1789), vol. IV, p. 228. See Pérez Pastor, *Documentos*, pp. 4–5.
4. González Dávila, *Teatro de las grandezas*, p. 53.
5. Discovered and published by Narciso Alonso Cortés in 'Algunos datos', 41–2, n. 3.
6. Guerrero Mayllo, *Familia y vida cotidiana*, pp. 117–18.

7. See Alonso Cortés, 'Algunos datos', 42, n. 1; and Eguía Ruiz, 'Cervantes, Calderón, Lope, Gracián', 51.
8. Pérez Pastor, *Documentos*, pp. 5–6.
9. Ibid., p. 20.
10. Ibid., p. 5.
11. Ibid., pp. 6–7.
12. Reproduced by Dorothy Schons, 'A Calderón Document', *RR* 19 (1928), 157.
13. Cotarelo, *Ensayo*, p. 75, n. 1.
14. Ibid., p. 65 and n. 1.
15. Ibid., pp. 74–5.
16. Kagan, *Students and Society*, p. 15.
17. Pérez Pastor, *Documentos*, p. 38.
18. Felipe Picatoste, 'Biografía de Calderón', in *Homenaje a Calderón* (Madrid: Nicolás González, 1881), p. 42.
19. E. Cotarelo y Mori, *Diccionario biográfico y bibliográfico de calígrafos españoles*, 2 vols. (Madrid: Revista de Archivos, 1916), vol. II, p. 46.
20. Cotarelo, *Ensayo*, p. 59. See also D. W. Cruickshank, 'Calderón's Handwriting', *MLR* 65 (1970), 65–77.
21. In his edition of Calderón's *Verdadera quinta parte de comedias* (Madrid: Francisco Sanz, 1682), ¶8^{r}.
22. His mother was apparently literate: when she made her will, it was noted that she was too ill to sign, not that she did not know how to: Pérez Pastor, *Documentos*, p. 10.
23. Kagan, *Students and Society*, pp. 17–18 and n. 53. Kagan estimates fees of 6 ducats (2,250 *maravedís*) a year for teaching literacy and numeracy (p. 14).
24. See, for example, Juan de la Cuesta, *Libro y tratado para enseñar leer y escriuir breuemente y con gran facilidad cõ reta pronunciacion y verdadera ortographia todo Romance Castellano, y de la distincion y diferencia que ay en las letras consonãtes de vnas a otras en su sonido y pronunciacion* (Alcalá: Juan Gracián, 1589).
25. Lara, *Obelisco funebre*, fol. 72^{r}.
26. Gonzalo Correas, *Vocabulario de refranes y frases proverbiales (1627)*, ed. Louis Combet, 2nd edn, revised by Robert Jammes and Maïte Mir-Andreu (Madrid: Castalia, 2000), p. 632. I owe this reference to Edward Wilson.
27. Calderón, *Verdadera quinta parte*, ¶8^{r}.
28. See José Simón Díaz, *Historia del Colegio Imperial de Madrid*, 2 vols. (Madrid: CSIC/IEM, 1952–9), vol. I, p. 16.
29. Cotarelo, *Ensayo*, p. 61.
30. Pérez Pastor, *Documentos*, p. 97.
31. From 'Colegio Imperial de la Compañia de Jesus en Madrid', MS 18183, BNE, fols. 389–92. See also Simón Díaz, *Historia del Colegio Imperial*, vol. I, pp. 45–6; p. 519 shows that Francisco de Henao joined the Congregación de la Anunciata on 20 April 1591, as his nephew would do in 1614 (see below, n. 35): this would suggest that he was born about 1577. See also Simón Díaz's *Los estudiantes de Madrid en el Siglo de Oro* (Madrid: IEM, 1966), pp. 33–5.

32. Cotarelo, *Ensayo*, p. 61 and n. 2.
33. Ibid., p. 62.
34. Simón Díaz, *Historia del Colegio Imperial*, vol. 1, p. 30. Acevedo's *Comoediae, dialogi et orationes* survive in manuscript in the Real Academia de la Historia (9/2564); see also Justo García Soriano, 'El teatro de colegio en España', *BRAE* 14 (1927), 374–411.
35. Simón Díaz, *Historia del Colegio Imperial*, vol. 1, p. 511; the document is reproduced as plate XI (facing p. 145); see also Simón Díaz, 'La congregación de la Anunciata del Colegio Imperial de Madrid', *Revista bibliográfica y documental* 1, no. 2 (1947), 149, and fig. 3. He signed himself 'Pedro Calderon'. His name also appears on a list of 1 March 1614, but not in that of 1615, by which time he had left the Colegio Imperial.
36. Quoted in Simón Díaz, *Historia del Colegio Imperial*, vol. 1, p. 26.
37. See J. M. Ruano de la Haza, 'Historia de los textos dramáticos en el Siglo de Oro: Calderón, *Las órdenes militares* y la Inquisición', in María Cruz García de Enterría and Alicia Cordón Mesa (eds.), *Siglo de Oro: Actas del IV Congreso Internacional de la Asociación Internacional del Siglo de Oro*, 2 vols. (Alcalá de Henares: Universidad de Alcalá, 1998), vol. 1, pp. 5–93.
38. S. Griswold Morley and Richard W. Tyler, *Los nombres de personajes en las comedias de Lope de Vega*, 2 vols. (Madrid: Castalia, 1961), vol. II, p. 685; Richard W. Tyler and Sergio D. Elizondo, *The Characters, Plots and Settings of Calderón's Comedias* (Lincoln, NE: Society of Spanish and Spanish-American Studies, 1981), p. 483.
39. References are to Calderón, *Obras completas*, vol. I: *Dramas*, ed. A. Valbuena Briones (Madrid: Aguilar, 1959).
40. Pérez Pastor, *Documentos*, pp. 7–10.
41. Ibid., pp. 10–11.
42. Cotarelo, *Ensayo*, p. 49.
43. Alexander A. Parker, 'Segismundo's Tower: A Calderonian Myth', *BHS* 59 (1982), 250. His remark that she was taken to Toledo by her godparents, not by her father, does not appear to be supported by documents.
44. Cotarelo, *Ensayo*, pp. 45, 49.
45. Guerrero Mayllo, *Familia y vida cotidiana*, p. 104.
46. Ibid., p. 112.
47. Pérez Pastor, *Documentos*, pp. 11–15, with codicils on pp. 15 and 16, and death certificate on pp. 17–19.
48. Guerrero Mayllo, *Familia y vida cotidiana*, p. 112.
49. This is specified in the death certificate (n. 47 above).
50. See Ramón de Mesonero Romanos, 'La casa de Calderón en las Platerías', *La Ilustración Española y Americana*, Año XXV, 19 (1881), 338; and Pascual Millán's description and plans in 'Iconografía calderoniana', in *Homenaje a Calderón* (Madrid: Nicolás González, 1881), pp. 80–5. The house has five floors plus an attic. Millán corrects the claim that there was only one storey at the time of Calderón's death, and suggests that the poet then lived on the ground floor, with a living-room, a bedroom, an oratory and a 'toilet', as well as a hallway and staircase

to permit communication between these rooms and with the floors above. The bedroom was a mere 8 feet square, and there was a 'patio' which was only slightly larger; at ground level, five floors down, it must have been sunless: not a place for barbecues. It was Mesonero Romanos who rescued the house when it was about to be knocked down in 1859. He tells us that the ground-floor area is a mere 847 square feet and the façade 17.5 feet, with only one balcony on each floor.

51. This interpretation is Lerma's own: see Antonio Feros, *Kingship and Favoritism in the Spain of Philip III, 1598–1621* (Cambridge: Cambridge University Press, 2000), pp. 204–5.
52. Jonathan Brown, *Velázquez: Painter and Courtier* (New Haven and London: Yale University Press, 1986), pp. 56, 111.
53. Quoted in Steven N. Orso, *Philip IV and the Decoration of the Alcázar of Madrid* (Princeton: Princeton University Press, 1986), p. 54.
54. One stage direction in *El gran príncipe de Fez* (1669) calls for '*un Moro de morisco, como andaban en España*' ('a Moor dressed in *morisco* fashion, as they used to go around in Spain': I, 1387a), which suggests that the writer's memory went back sixty years.
55. Vera Tassis (ed.), *Verdadera quinta parte*, ¶7^{v}–8^{r}.
56. Vicenta Esquerdo Sivera, 'Acerca de *La confusa* de Cervantes', in *Cervantes, su obra y su mundo: Actas del I Congreso Internacional sobre Cervantes* (Madrid: Edi-6, 1981), pp. 243–7 (p. 247).
57. See Calderón, *Comedias*, ed. Hartzenbusch, vol. I, p. xlii, for the Veragua list; for the Marañón list, see Edward M. Wilson, 'An Early List of Calderón's *Comedias*', *MP* 60 (1962), 97. Vera's list of plays in his edition of the *Primera parte* (Madrid: Francisco Sanz, 1685) includes, in his projected *Novena parte*, '*El Carro del Cielo, San Elias*' (¶¶5^{r}). The *Novena parte* published in 1691 does not include this title.

CHAPTER 4. A TURNING-POINT

1. Pérez Pastor, *Documentos*, p. 20.
2. Cotarelo, *Ensayo*, p. 67.
3. Ibid., p. 71.
4. Kagan, *Students and Society*, pp. 175–9 and fig. 3.
5. Francisco Gómez de Quevedo y Villegas, *Historia de la vida del buscón, llamado don Pablos*, ch. v.
6. Cotarelo, *Ensayo*, p. 72. For the marriage 'certificate', see Alonso Cortés, 'Algunos datos', p. 43.
7. Bartolomé José Gallardo, *Ensayo de una biblioteca española de libros raros y curiosos*, 4 vols., edn facsímil (Madrid: Gredos, 1968), vol. II, pp. 167–72.
8. Gaspar Caldera de Heredia, *Si los señores reyes de Castilla, por derecho hereditario de su real sangre, tienen virtud de curar energumenos y lançar espiritus*. There is no imprint, but the text is dated Seville, 1655.
9. *Catálogo colectivo del patrimonio bibliográfico español: siglo XVII*, vol. II (Madrid: Arco/Libros, 1989), items 2297–9.

10. Álvarez Baena, *Hijos de Madrid*, vol. II, p. 41.
11. Pérez Pastor, *Documentos*, p. 15.
12. A Carmelite of this name wrote the *censura* in Pedro Barona de Valdivielso, *Hospicio de S. Francisco* (Madrid: Luis Sánchez, 1609); the name is not unusual, however.
13. Pérez Pastor, *Documentos*, p. 16.
14. The original documents are in P. 4437, Juan de Béjar, 1614, unfoliated (24 January), AHP, Madrid. Pérez Pastor, *Documentos*, p. 20, gives no details.
15. Escobar, *The Plaza Mayor*, pp. 81, 153–4.
16. Pérez Pastor, *Documentos*, p. 21.
17. Ibid., pp. 27, 33.
18. Ibid., pp. 30–1.
19. Alonso Cortés, 'Algunos datos', pp. 43–50.
20. See María Isabel Gea, *Guía del plano de Texeira (1656)* (Madrid: La Librería, 2007), p. 334.
21. When the Calderón children finally reached an agreement with their stepmother, she agreed to pay for the masses specified in her husband's will, and to pay off Cristóbal Vaca, 'clerigo', provided that the total did not exceed 1,800 *reales*. By this time it was March 1618: so much for haste! (Pérez Pastor, *Documentos*, p. 27).
22. Although *censos* had at one time yielded as much as 10 per cent, by the early seventeenth century the norm was 5 per cent: Guerrero Mayllo, *Familia y vida cotidiana*, p. 258.
23. Most *juros* yielded from 5 per cent to 7 per cent during the sixteenth century, but in the early seventeenth, some were offering as little as 3.3 per cent: Guerrero Mayllo, *Familia y vida cotidiana*, p. 249. Espartinas is in the province of Seville; 'it is famous for its salt-works', says the Espasa-Calpe *Encyclopaedia*, s.v. Espartinas.
24. Pérez Pastor, *Documentos*, p. 126. Pérez Pastor assumes that this was the protonotary, but Calderón's Santiago papers show that he knew another Jerónimo de Villanueva who was aged sixty-seven in 1636 (see below, p. 191). This homonym is perhaps more likely to have purchased the Madera property in 1643. A Don Jerónimo de Villanueva was the censor in 1634 for *Yerros de naturaleza* (see p. 148 below).
25. Rejas is the name of the brook that flows east into the Jarama, a little to the north of the main airport road, but the village is not marked on modern maps.
26. P. 2671, Francisco Testa, 1623, fols. 461^{r}–482^{v}, AHP, Madrid: see Pérez Pastor, *Documentos*, pp. 71–7. See also Guerrero Mayllo, *Familia y vida cotidiana*, p. 284.
27. Santana was one of the five surveyors who in August 1617 conducted a survey of the Plaza Mayor properties prior to the planned reconstruction: Escobar, *The Plaza Mayor*, p. 152.
28. P. 3597, Francisco Testa, 1623, fols. 1390^{r}–1392^{v}, AHP, Madrid.
29. The document gives contradicting figures of 2,000 and 4,000 ducats, but a later document (27 April 1616) confirms that when Diego died he owed the

Crown 2,000 ducats of this charge: P. 2659, Francisco Testa, 1616, fol. 202[v], AHP, Madrid. See also below, p. 56.

30. See Mauro Hernández, *A la sombra de la corona: Poder local y oligarquía urbana (Madrid 1606–1808)* (Madrid: Siglo XXI, 1995), p. 194. Rafael Ródenas Vilar also refers to this financial incentive in *Vida cotidiana y negocio en la Segovia del Siglo de Oro: El mercader Juan de Cuéllar* (Salamanca: Junta de Castilla y León, 1990), pp. 210–12.
31. Franqueza (?1547–1614) was a younger son from a family of Catalan gentry. He rose rapidly through membership of the Council of Finance to become Count of Villalonga (1603). In 1607 he was arrested and charged with almost 500 offences, mostly of fraud. Found guilty in 1609, he was imprisoned for life and forced to repay 1,400,000 ducats: Guerrero Mayllo, *Familia y vida cotidiana*, pp. 285–6. Ramírez de Prado was another member of the Council of Finance: he was imprisoned and forced to repay 400,000 ducats: R. Trevor Davies, *The Golden Century of Spain: 1501–1620* (London: Macmillan, 1970), p. 256. For Franqueza, see also Julián Juderías, *Los favoritos de Felipe III: Don Pedro Franqueza, conde de Villalonga* (Madrid: Revista de Archivos, 1909).
32. Simón Díaz, *Historia del Colegio Imperial*, vol. 1, p. 524, shows that Pedro's male cousins Alonso, Martín and Pedro de Montalvo all joined the Congregación de la Anunciata in the college on 24 April 1606, 122 (*sic*) February 1603 and 8 December 1606 respectively.
33. The theories were first expressed in 'The Father–Son Conflict in the Drama of Calderón', *FMLS* 2 (1966), 99–113, and developed in 'Segismundo's Tower: A Calderonian Myth'.
34. Pérez Pastor, *Documentos*, pp. 22–3.

CHAPTER 5. A TALENT DISCOVERED BY ACCIDENT

1. Pérez Pastor, *Documentos*, pp. 20–1, 36.
2. Ibid., pp. 35–44, which list the uncle's accounts for the period 1616–19.
3. For example, while she was not held liable for any of her husband's debts, she could claim a fourth part of anything owed to him: ibid., pp. 24–8.
4. P. 2659, Francisco Testa, 1616, fols. 202–13, AHP, Madrid (202[v]).
5. P. 2659, fol. 203[r].
6. Pérez Pastor, *Documentos*, p. 95.
7. Ibid., p. 36. Pérez Pastor devotes pp. 35–44 to these accounts.
8. A 'test' bullfight was recorded as early as 4 December 1617, but the initial layout was too short and narrow: Escobar, *The Plaza Mayor*, p. 157. Escobar does not refer to this second test.
9. Pérez Pastor, *Documentos*, p. 82. Don Pedro's will (pp. 387–8) shows that in 1681 he had four servants.
10. Cotarelo, *Ensayo*, p. 80 and nn. 3, 5.
11. I am extremely grateful to my colleague Dr Jeremy Squires for checking fol. 85[v] of the 1616–17 Salamanca matriculation book.
12. Pérez Pastor, *Documentos*, pp. 38, 39.

13. See Álvarez Baena, *Hijos de Madrid*, vol. III, pp. 405–9, and Nicolás Antonio, *Bibliotheca Hispana Nova*, 2 vols. (Madrid: Joaquín de Ibarra / Viuda e Hijos de Joaquín de Ibarra, 1783–8), vol. II, p. 55.
14. The main source of information here is Florencio Marcos Rodríguez, 'Un pleito de don Pedro Calderón de la Barca, estudiante en Salamanca', *RABM* 67 (1959), 717–31. See also María Jesús Framiñán de Miguel, 'Calderón y la actividad teatral salmantina a comienzos de 1600', in Ignacio Arellano (ed.), *Calderón 2000: Homenaje a Kurt Reichenberger en su 80 cumpleaños*, 2 vols. (Kassel: Edition Reichenberger, 2002), vol. I, pp. 509–24.
15. It is not clear why Don Pedro did not claim exemption from imprisonment for debt, as an *hidalgo*.
16. P. 5049, Mateo de Madrid, 1616–24, fols. 468^{r}, 475^{v}, AHP, Madrid.
17. Pérez Pastor, *Documentos*, pp. 52–5.
18. Joaquín de Entrambasaguas, *Estudios sobre Lope de Vega*, 2 vols. (Madrid: Aldus, 1946–7), vol. II, p. 150.
19. See Heliodoro Rojas de la Vega, *Juicio crítico de las obras de Calderón de la Barca, bajo el punto de vista jurídico* (Valladolid: Agapito Zapatero, 1883).
20. *Delicias de Apolo, recreaciones del Parnaso, por las tres musas Urania, Euterpe y Caliope* (Madrid: Melchor Alegre, 1670), p. 121; *Poesias varias de grandes ingenios españoles, recogidas por Josef Alfay* (Zaragoza: Juan de Ybar, 1654), p. 46.
21. For example, contributors to Pedro Luis Ossorio's *Panegirico al illustrisimo Señor D. Juan Vivas de Cañamas* (no imprint, but before 1676) included Calderón, Diego de Figueroa y Córdoba, Juan de Vera Tassis, Agustín de Salazar y Torres, Matos Fragoso and Torre y Sevil. All wrote plays. Salazar y Torres died in 1675.
22. In this case there is also a manuscript of 1628 with the attribution to Porras. When J. M. Blecua reprinted the *Poesías varias* of 1654 in 1946 (Zaragoza: Heraldo de Aragón), pp. xiii, xiv, he argued cogently that this poem and the previous one should not be attributed to Calderón. See also his edition of the *Cancionero de 1628* (Madrid: Aguirre, 1945), p. 63 (I owe this second reference to Edward M. Wilson). The two poems were printed as Calderón's by Hartzenbusch in his edition of Calderón's *Comedias*, vol. IV, pp. 730–1, and by F[elipe] P[icatoste] (ed.), *Poesías inéditas de D. Pedro Calderón de la Barca* (Madrid: Imprenta de la Biblioteca Universal, 1881), (Biblioteca Universal: Colección de los mejores autores antiguos y modernos, nacionales y extranjeros, vol. LXXI) pp. 13–18.
23. Edward M. Wilson, '¿Escribió Calderón el romance "Curiosísima señora"?', *AL* 2 (1962), 99–118.
24. Lope de Vega, *Justa poetica y alabanzas justas que hizo la insigne villa de Madrid al bienaventurado San Isidro en las fiestas de su beatificacion* (Madrid: Viuda de Alonso Martín, 1620). Calderón's poems begin on 50^{r} and 75^{r}, and were reprinted by Picatoste (*Poesías inéditas*, pp. 19–21) and Hartzenbusch (*Comedias*, vol. IV, pp. 724–5).
25. See 'Fernando de Monforte y Herrera' (= Fernando Chirino de Salazar), *Relacion de las fiestas que ha hecho el Colegio Imperial de la Compañia de Jesus de Madrid en*

la canonizacion de San Ignacio de Loyola, y S. Francisco Xavier (Madrid: Luis Sánchez, 1622), fol. 47^{r}, and Edward M. Wilson, 'Textos impresos y apenas utilizados para la biografía de Calderón', *Hispanófila* 9 (1960), 1–14.

26. See, for example, the *loa* of *La protestación de la fe* (1656), in *Obras completas*, vol. III: *Autos sacramentales*, ed. A. Valbuena Prat (Madrid: Aguilar, 1952), p. 728a.
27. Cf. *Calderón de la Barca y la España del Barroco: Sala de exposiciones de la Biblioteca Nacional del 16 de junio al 15 de agosto de 2000* (Madrid: Sociedad Estatal España Nuevo Milenio, 2000), p. 370.
28. Lope de Vega, *Relacion de las fiestas que la insigne villa de Madrid hizo en la canonizacion de su bienaventurado hijo y patron San Isidro, con las comedias que se representaron y los versos que en la justa poetica se escribieron* (Madrid: Viuda de Alonso Martín, 1622). Picatoste reprinted all nine of the poems written by Calderón on this occasion (pp. 21–39); Hartzenbusch omits the two Colegio Imperial ones (vol. IV, pp. 725–6); for the best texts, see Blanca Oteiza, 'Poesías de Calderón en la justa poética de 1622', in Arellano (ed.), *Calderón 2000*, vol. I, pp. 689–705.
29. See Edward M. Wilson, 'The Four Elements in the Imagery of Calderón', *MLR* 31 (1936), 34–47.
30. Pérez Pastor, *Documentos*, pp. 44–51. For more on Sosa, see Álvarez Baena, *Hijos de Madrid*, vol. III, pp. 144–5.
31. Pérez Pastor, *Documentos*, pp. 52–6.
32. Cotarelo, *Ensayo*, p. 101.
33. For the family connections between Olivares and the Duke of Frías, see D.W. Cruickshank, 'Calderón's *Amor, honor y poder* and the Prince of Wales, 1623', *Calderón 1600–1681: Quatercentenary Studies in Memory of John E. Varey*, *BHS* 77 (2000), 75–99 (77–8).
34. Pérez Pastor, *Documentos*, p. 62.
35. Ibid., pp. 66–77; Cotarelo summarises these tedious documents: *Ensayo*, pp. 100–1.
36. Elliott, *Imperial Spain*, pp. 115–16.
37. Pérez Pastor, *Documentos*, pp. 56–7.
38. Ibid., pp. 57–8.
39. Ibid., p. 61.
40. Ibid., p. 68.
41. See Gregorio Marañón, 'La biblioteca del Conde-Duque de Olivares', *BRAH* 107 (1935), 677–92, and J.H. Elliott, *The Count-Duke of Olivares: The Statesman in an Age of Decline* (New Haven and London: Yale University Press, 1986), pp. 23–6.
42. González Dávila, *Teatro de las grandezas*, p. 466.
43. Juan Isidro Fajardo, *Disertación sobre los autos sacramentales de don Pedro Calderón de la Barca*, MS 209, fols. 8^{r}–8^{v}, Biblioteca de Menéndez y Pelayo, Santander. I owe this reference to Edward Wilson.
44. Juan Isidro Fajardo, *Titulos de todas las comedias que en verso español y portugues se han impresso hasta el año de 1716*, MS. 14706, BNE. Varey has presented

evidence to link Fajardo with Calderón's circle: J. E. Varey, 'An Additional Note on Pedro de Arce', *Iberoromania* 23 (1986), 204–9.

45. Germán Vega García-Luengos, 'Imitar, emular, renovar en la *comedia nueva*: *Cómo se comunican dos estrellas contrarias*, reescritura "calderoniana" de *Las almenas de Toro*', *Anuario Lope de Vega* 11 (2005), 243–64.
46. See Dian Fox, 'A Further Source of Calderón's *El príncipe constante*, *JHP* 4 (1980), 157–66. I thank Professor Luis Iglesias Feijoo for allowing me to read in manuscript his article 'El romance de Góngora en *El príncipe constante de Calderón*'. Quotations are from *El príncipe constante*, ed. Enrica Cancelliere (Madrid: Biblioteca Nueva, 2000). See also Edward M. Wilson, 'La poesía dramática de don Pedro Calderón de la Barca', in *Litterae Hispanae et Lusitanae* (Munich: Max Hueber, 1968), pp. 487–500: 'Entre los predecesores poéticos ninguno tiene mayor importancia que don Luis de Góngora' ('Among his poetic predecessors none has more importance than Don Luis de Góngora': p. 491).
47. For all these examples, see Edward M. Wilson, 'Calderón y Cervantes', in *Hacia Calderón: Quinto Coloquio Anglogermano, Oxford, 1978* (Wiesbaden: Franz Steiner, 1982), pp. 9–19. See also Ignacio Arellano, 'Cervantes en Calderón', *Anales Cervantinos* 35 (1999), 9–35.
48. See, for example, A. Valbuena Briones, 'Los libros de caballerías en el teatro de Calderón', in *Hacia Calderón: Quinto Coloquio Anglogermano, Oxford, 1978* (Wiesbaden: Franz Steiner, 1982), pp. 1–8, and José María Díez Borque, 'Calderón de la Barca y la novela de caballerías', *Calderón 1600–1681: Quatercentenary Studies in Memory of John E. Varey*, *BHS* (Glasgow) 77 (2000), 255–64.
49. Brown, *Velázquez*, p. 44, which also refers to the 'Seville connection'.

CHAPTER 6. LETTERS, NOT ARMS

1. Geoffrey Parker, *Spain and the Netherlands 1559–1659: Ten Studies*, revised edn (Fontana: Glasgow, 1990), p. 186. These figures are for the period 1631–9.
2. Ibid., p. 188.
3. Quevedo's 'No hemos visto de aquellos estados [Flanders] cosa de entretenimiento, sino ojos sacados, tuertos, o brazos quebrados y piernas' is quoted by M. Herrero García, *Ideas de los españoles del siglo XVII* (Madrid: Voluntad, 1928), pp. 440–1 ('We have seen nothing amusing from Flanders, but instead lost eyes and broken limbs').
4. N. D. Shergold and J. E. Varey, 'Some Early Calderón Dates', *BHS* 38 (1961), 276.
5. For the dramatised version, attributed to Shakespeare and others, and the historical sources, see William Shakespeare, *King Edward III*, ed. Giorgio Melchiori (Cambridge: Cambridge University Press, 1998).
6. See Cruickshank, 'Calderón's *Amor, honor y poder*', 88.
7. There was an anonymous Spanish translation, *Historias tragicas exemplares: sacadas del Bandello verones. Nuevamente traduzidas de las que en lengua francesa*

adornaron Pierres Bonistan y Francisco de Belleforest, with recorded editions of 1589 (Salamanca), 1596 (Burgos) and 1603 (Valladolid); and one by Diego de Ágreda y Vargas: *Novelas morales, utiles por sus documentos* (Madrid: Tomás Junti, 1620; Barcelona: Sebastián de Cormellas, 1620 and 1621; Valencia: Juan Crisóstomo Garriz, 1620).

8. Elliott, *The Count-Duke of Olivares*, p. 112.
9. The text of the play printed with this title is the same as that printed as *La selva confusa*: see note 11 below.
10. Shergold and Varey, 'Some Early Calderón Dates', 284–5. On 13 March 1627, in Valencia, Juan Acacio had a copy of '*Selvas y bosques de amor*', as well as of *Amor, honor y poder*: Esquerdo Sivera, 'Acerca de *La confusa* de Cervantes', p. 247.
11. For the doubt, see H. C. Heaton, 'On *La selva confusa*, Attributed to Calderón', *PMLA* 44 (1929), 243–73. The arguments are convincingly refuted by A. E. Sloman, '*La selva confusa* Restored to Calderón' *HR* 20 (1952), 134–48. The editions attributed to Lope are *La selva confusa*, in Lope, *Parte XXVII* ('Barcelona: Sebastián de Cormellas' (= Seville: Manuel de Sande), 1633), and *Selvas y bosques de amor*, in Lope, *Parte XXIV* (Zaragoza: Diego Dormer, 1633). The autograph manuscript was edited by G. T. Northup in *Revue Hispanique* 21 (1929), 168–338.
12. First printed with the title *La industria contra el poder*, under the name of Lope, in *Parte veinte y ocho de comedias de varios autores* (Huesca: Pedro Blusón, 1634).
13. Several contemporary accounts of the prince's stay mention the royal performances, as many as two per week, but without giving titles. Agustín Redondo, in 'Fiesta y literatura en Madrid durante la estancia del Príncipe de Gales', *Edad de Oro* 17 (1998), 132, lists some plays performed in the summer of 1623, but none by Calderón.
14. Shergold and Varey, 'Some Early Calderón Dates', 279–80. By March 1627 the play was listed as part of Juan Acacio's repertoire: Esquerdo Sivera, 'Acerca de *La confusa* de Cervantes', p. 247.
15. See C. A. Jones, 'Brecht y el drama del Siglo de Oro en España', *Segismundo* 3 (1967), 39–54, and Jane Albrecht, *Irony and Theatricality in Tirso de Molina* (Ottawa: Dovehouse, 1994), pp. 25–42.
16. See Hannah E. Bergman, 'Auto-definition of the *comedia de capa y espada*', *Hispanófila* (Especial) 1 (1974), 3–27.
17. Pérez Pastor, *Documentos*, pp. 67–8.
18. Ibid., p. 77.
19. Ibid., pp. 58–9, 62–3.
20. Ibid., p. 78.
21. Ibid., p. 82; P. 3597, Francisco Testa, 1623, fols. 1390^{r}–1392^{v}, AHP, Madrid (see p. 45 above).
22. Pérez Pastor, *Documentos*, pp. 83–5, 86; P. 5049, Mateo de Madrid, 1616–24, fols. 444–51, 452–9, AHP, Madrid.
23. Pérez Pastor, *Documentos*, p. 87; P. 5049, Mateo de Madrid, 1616–24, fols. 468–75 (signed on 475^{v}), AHP, Madrid.

24. Calderón, *Primera parte de comedias*, ¶6r.
25. Pérez Pastor, *Documentos*, pp. 89–90; P. 5611, Juan de Lorenzana, 1630–2, fol. 503, AHP, Madrid.
26. Edward M. Wilson, 'Un memorial perdido de don Pedro Calderón', in A. David Kossoff and José Amor y Vázquez (eds.), *Homenaje a William L. Fichter: Estudios sobre el teatro antiguo hispánico y otros ensayos* (Madrid: Castalia, 1971), pp. 801–17.
27. Cotarelo, *Ensayo*, p. 103.
28. H. W. Hilborn, *A Chronology of the Plays of D. Pedro Calderón de la Barca* (Toronto: Toronto University Press, 1938), pp. 6–8.
29. Hilborn, *A Chronology*, pp. 9–12. The play's modern editor suggests 1623: *Pedro Calderón de la Barca's* The Fake Astrologer, ed. and trans. Max Oppenheimer Jr (New York: Peter Lang, 1994), p. 6; but see also below.
30. Hilborn, *A Chronology*, pp. 9–12.
31. Shergold and Varey, 'Some Early Calderón Dates', 278: payment on 23 June for royal performance by Andrés de la Vega.
32. See Shirley B. Whitaker, 'The First Performance of Calderón's *El sitio de Bredá*', *RQ* 31 (1978), 515–31.
33. Shergold and Varey, 'Some Early Calderón Dates', 275: payment on 22 February for royal performance by Tomás Fernández.
34. Ibid., 277: payment on 31 March for royal performance by Andrés de la Vega.
35. Ibid., 279: payment on 29 May 1627 and 28 March 1628 for royal performances by Roque de Figueroa.
36. Printed in Lope's *Parte 23* ('Valencia: Miguel Sorolla (= Seville: Simón Fajardo), 1629'). This volume was assembled from previously printed *sueltas*, so composition may be a year or two earlier.
37. See the edition by J. M. Ruano (Liverpool: Liverpool University Press, 1988), pp. 20–2.
38. Hilborn, *A Chronology*, pp. 9–12. Printed in *Parte XXVIII* (Huesca: Pedro Blusón, 1634); the volume's printing approval is dated 27 October 1633.
39. Shergold and Varey, 'Some Early Calderón Dates', 284: payment on 28 March for a performance in El Pardo by Roque de Figueroa.
40. Documents, discussed below, show that this play was new in January 1629.
41. Shergold and Varey, 'Some Early Calderón Dates', 281: royal performance on 8 October 1629 or (just possibly) 1628, perhaps by Antonio de Prado. There is another play with this title, however.
42. Shergold and Varey, 'Some Early Calderón Dates', 280–1, performance by Antonio de Prado: the palace accounts are confused, and probably 1629 is meant.
43. See J. E. Varey, 'The Transmission of the Text of *Casa con dos puertas*: A Preliminary Survey', in Francisco Mundi Pedret, Alberto Porqueras Mayo and José Carlos de Torres (eds.), *Estudios sobre Calderón y el Teatro de la Edad de Oro: Homenaje a Kurt y Roswitha Reichenberger* (Barcelona: Promociones y Publicaciones Universitarias, 1989), pp. 49–57.
44. Referred to in the text of *Casa con dos puertas*, while its own text refers to the baptism of Prince Baltasar Carlos (4 November 1629).

45. Hilborn, *A Chronology*, pp. 13–15.
46. See J. M. Ruano de la Haza, *La primera versión de* La vida es sueño, *de Calderón* (Liverpool: Liverpool University Press, 1992), p. 9, and Alfredo Rodríguez López-Vázquez, 'La fecha de "La vida es sueño" y el entremés "La maestra de gracias", atribuido a Belmonte: 1630–31, por la compañía de Cristóbal de Avendaño', in Szilvia E. Szmuk, *Calderón sueltas in the Collection of the Hispanic Society of America: Con un estudio de Alfredo Rodríguez López-Vázquez sobre la fecha de 'La vida es sueño' y otro de Jaroslava Kašparová sobre los manuscritos calderonianos de Mladá Vožice.* Vol. II of *Calderón: Protagonista eminente del Barroco europeo* (Kassel: Reichenberger, 2002) (Teatro del Siglo de Oro, Bibliografías y Catálogos 30; Estudios de Literatura 61), pp. 1–19.
47. Shergold and Varey, 'Some Early Calderón Dates', 284; performance by Roque de Figueroa.
48. The date of the death of Ambrogio Spinola, who is mentioned in the text: see also J. M. de Osma, 'Estudios sobre Calderón de la Barca: notas a la comedia *Con quien vengo, vengo*', *Hispania* II (1928), 221–6.
49. References are to Calderón, *Obras completas*, vol. II.
50. See Cristóbal Pérez Pastor, *Nuevos datos acerca del histrionismo español en los siglos XVI y XVII: Primera serie* (Madrid: Imprenta de la Revista Española, 1901), p. 209.
51. 'Esta Comedia es vna de las que peregrinauan entre los peligros de la ignorancia, he procurado con particular diligencia reduzirla a su primer original' ('This play is one of those that travelled amid the perils of ignorance; I have made a particular effort to restore it to its original version').
52. When the Seville printer Simón Fajardo produced the fraudulent edition entitled *Doze comedias nuevas de Lope de Vega Carpio, y otros autores* ('Barcelona, Gerónimo Margarit, 1630'), his title-page carried a woodblock which showed, with no doubt unconscious irony, a crane standing on one leg with a stone clasped in the other foot, and the legend 'vigilante'.
53. *The Fake Astrologer*, ed. Oppenheimer, p. 7.
54. Della Porta also wrote plays, among them *Lo astrologo*, printed in 1606.
55. Ruth Lee Kennedy, *Studies in Tirso,* vol. I: *The Dramatist and His Competitors, 1620–1626* (Chapel Hill: University of North Carolina Press, 1974), pp. 210–14.
56. Wilson, 'Un memorial perdido', p. 803.
57. See Alberto and Arturo García Carraffa, *Enciclopedia heráldica y genealógica hispanoamericana*, 88 vols. (Madrid: Hauser & Menet, 1919–63), vol. LXX, p. 14.
58. Elliott, *The Count-Duke of Olivares*, pp. 291 and 422, n. 63.
59. See Elliott, *The Count-Duke of Olivares*, pp. 166–8, and the family tree following p. 18.
60. Two accounts are printed in José Simón Díaz (ed.), *Relaciones breves de actos públicos celebrados en Madrid de 1541 a 1650* (Madrid: IEM, 1982), pp. 294–304.
61. Jaime Moll, 'Diez años sin licencias para imprimir comedias y novelas en los reinos de Castilla: 1625–1634', *BRAE* 54 (1974), 97–103.
62. Quoted above, p. 70.

63. 'The vengeance I hoped for' (I, 100b); see Juan Manuel Gómez, 'A Critical Edition of Pedro Calderón de la Barca's *La gran Cenobia*, with Introduction and Notes', unpublished doctoral dissertation (University of Oregon, 1981), p. 35. See also Sandra Clarke, 'Queens in Calderón: A Study of the Figure of the Queen in Selected Plays by Calderón de la Barca', unpublished MA dissertation (University College Dublin, 2000), pp. 50–6.
64. Juan de Mariana, *Del rey y de la institución real* (Madrid: Atlas: 1950) (BAE, vol. XXXI), vol. II, p. 475: 'En Castilla, que es la mas noble region de España ... vemos seguida desde los tiempos primitivos la costumbre de no distinguir para la sucesion varones ni hembras; no creemos que puedan ser vituperadas con razon las disposiciones de nuestras leyes respecto á este punto' ('In Castile, which is the noblest region of Spain, we see that the custom of not distinguishing between males and females for the succession has been followed from earliest times; we do not believe that the dispositions of our laws with regard to this point can be rightly condemned'). His circumlocution may point to reservations, however.
65. See William R. Blue, 'Calderón's *Gustos y disgustos no son más que imaginación* and Some Remarks on New Historicism', in José A. Madrigal (ed.), *New Historicism and the* Comedia: *Poetics, Politics and Praxis* (Boulder, CO: Society of Spanish and Spanish-American Studies, 1997), pp. 29–39.
66. See n. 32 above, and S. A. Vosters, 'Again the First Performance of Calderón's *El sitio de Bredá*', *RCEH* 6 (1981), 117–34.
67. See Vicenta Esquerdo Sivera, 'Acerca de *La confusa* de Cervantes', p. 247. While Juan Acacio Bernal is associated with early performances of *Amor, honor y poder* and *La selva confusa*, we must assume that he bought *Judas Macabeo* from Sánchez de Echavarría.
68. Quotations are from the edition of Johanna Rodolphine Schrek (The Hague: G. B. van Goor Zonen, 1957).
69. See Everett W. Hesse, 'Calderón and Velázquez', *Hispania* 35 (1952), 74–82. In his *Zurbarán: 1589–1664* (London: Secker & Warburg, 1977), p. 61, Julián Gallego suggests that Juan Bautista Maíno's *The Recapture of Bahía* depicts a scene from Lope's *El Brasil restituido* (1625).
70. *Obras de Lope de Vega*, vol. XXVIII: *Crónicas y leyendas dramáticas de España* (Madrid: Atlas, 1970) (BAE, vol. CCXXXIII), p. 285.
71. See also Brown and Elliott, *A Palace for a King*, pp. 185–99, especially pp. 185–93.

CHAPTER 7. BLASPHEMY, SACRILEGE AND *LÈSE-MAJESTÉ*

1. Wilson, 'Un memorial perdido', p. 803.
2. These details owe much to Elliott, *The Conde-Duque*, pp. 295–308. Another *auto* attributed to Calderón, *El consumo del vellón*, was apparently played in Valencia in 1652, although the surviving manuscript dates it to 1660. See also Carmen Sanz Ayán, '*Peor está que estaba*: La crisis hacendística, la cuestión del

vellón y su reflejo teatral en tiempos de Calderón', in José Alcalá Zamora and Ernest Belenguer (co-ordinators), *Calderón de la Barca y la España del Barroco*, 2 vols. (Madrid: Centro de Estudios Políticos y Constitucionales/Sociedad Estatal España Nuevo Milenio, 2001), vol. I, pp. 189–201.

3. *Genealogía* (II, 587) lists María Calderón as the sister of La Calderona, and gives no first name for the latter (II, 644): *Genealogía, origen y noticias de los comediantes de España*, ed. N. D. Shergold and J. E. Varey (London: Tamesis, 1985), pp. 499, 513. See also Hugo Albert Rennert, *The Spanish Stage in the Time of Lope de Vega* (New York: Hispanic Society of America, 1909), pp. 163–4 and n. 1, and p. 186 (Rennert evidently believed that there was only one actress surnamed Calderón), and Cristóbal Pérez Pastor, 'Nuevos datos acerca del histrionismo español en los siglos XVI y XVII: Segunda serie', *BH* 10 (1908), 243–58 (248).
4. José Deleito y Piñuela, *El rey se divierte*, 2nd edn (Madrid: Espasa-Calpe, 1955), pp. 25–9.
5. *La cisma de Inglaterra*, ed. Francisco Ruiz Ramón (Madrid: Castalia, 1981), pp. 55–4, 'La jura'. References are to this edition.
6. The poem is most accessible in Arthur Terry, *An Anthology of Spanish Poetry, 1500–1700*, 2 vols. (Oxford: Pergamon, 1965–8), vol. II, pp. 168–72. See also José Lara Garrido, '*Si naciera sembrada la hermosura*: Discurso del afecto y retórica del dolor en la silva elegíaca de Calderón "Dedicada a doña María de Zapata" ', in Aurora Egido (ed.), *Lecciones calderonianas* (Zaragoza: Ibercaja, 2001), pp. 75–104. Inés and María may have been related to Don Pedro Zapata, a royal secretary, or to Don Diego Zapata, Count of Barajas, both of whom were asked in 1636 about Calderón's qualifications for knighthood, i.e., they knew the writer or his family (see p. 191).
7. 'Antonio de Silva' (= Jerónimo Bermúdez), *Primeras tragedias españolas* (Madrid: Francisco Sánchez, 1577).
8. See D. W. Cruickshank, 'Some Notes on the Printing of Plays in Seventeenth-Century Seville', *The Library* 6, no. 11 (1989), 231–52.
9. See in particular Manuel Delgado's edition of *La devoción de la cruz* (Madrid: Cátedra, 2000), pp. 14–15.
10. See ibid., pp. 24–5, 165, 167, and J. E. Varey, 'Imágenes, símbolos y escenografía en *La devoción de la cruz*', in Hans Flasche (ed.), *Hacia Calderón: Segundo Coloquio Anglogermano, Hamburgo, 1970* (Berlin: De Gruyter, 1973), p. 167.
11. See Pedro Calderón de la Barca, *El purgatorio de San Patricio*, ed. J. M. Ruano (Liverpool: Liverpool University Press, 1988), pp. 20–2.
12. Gary Bigelow, 'Analysis of Calderón's *De un castigo, tres venganzas*: Structure, Theme, Language', in F. de Armas, D. Gitliz and J. A. Madrigal (eds.), *Critical Perspectives on Calderón de la Barca* (Lincoln, NE: Society of Spanish and Spanish-American Studies, 1981), pp. 32–3.
13. Jack H. Parker, 'The Chronology of the Plays of Juan Pérez de Montalbán', *PMLA* 67 (1952), 190.
14. *De un castigo dos venganzas* was performed in 1630 by Manuel Vallejo's company, and printed in Montalbán's *Para todos* (1632): see V. F. Dixon, 'Juan Pérez de Montalbán's *Para todos*', *HR* 33 (1964), 46.

15. Vega García-Luengos, 'Imitar, emular, renovar en la *comedia nueva*', 260.
16. Juan de Mariana, *Historia general de España*, 2 vols. (Madrid: Carlos Sánchez, 1650), vol. I, p. 386 (Book X, viii).
17. The historical Don Pedro also suffered confiscation of property and exile for rebellion against the king.
18. See I, 137a, and Bartolomé Leonardo de Argensola, *A una mujer que se afeitaba y estaba hermosa*, line 13.
19. Elliott, *The Count-Duke of Olivares*, p. 374.
20. All three documents are printed in full by Edward M. Wilson, in 'Fray Hortensio Paravicino's Protest against *El príncipe constante*', *Ibérida: Revista Filológica* 6 (1961), 245–66, from which I quote them. The only dated document is Trejo's (19 May 1629).
21. Cotarelo, *Ensayo*, p. 132 and nn. 1 and 2.
22. Shergold and Varey (eds.), *Genealogía*, p. 215.
23. For Paravicino's sermons, see Emilio Alarcos, 'Los sermones de Paravicino', *RFE* 24 (1937), 162–97, 249–319.
24. The possibilities are Juan Bautista Calderón, Diego González de Henao, Francisco González de Henao, Martín de Montalvo, Juan Bautista de Sosa and Andrés Jerónimo de Henao. The last two are the most likely.
25. See Elliott, *The Count-Duke of Olivares*, p. 305.
26. The documents relating to this investigation have not been traced.
27. Presumably the Calle (or Costanilla) de los Ángeles, running up to the Plaza de Santo Domingo from the foot of the Calle de las Fuentes. The street was named after the convent of Santa María de los Ángeles, at the Santo Domingo end of the street, but Paravicino is less likely to have been referring to the convent church.
28. A. L. Constandse, *Le Baroque espagnol et Calderón de la Barca* (Amsterdam: Jacob van Campen, 1951), p. 63.
29. Wilson, 'Fray Hortensio Paravicino's Protest', 255, 257.
30. The manuscript, no. 15159 of the Biblioteca Nacional, has been edited by Fernando Cantalapiedra and Alfredo Rodríguez López-Vázquez (Madrid: Cátedra, 1996). In the view of Edward M. Wilson, the manuscript is a *refundición*: 'An Early Rehash of Calderón's *El príncipe constante*', *MLR* 76 (1961), 785–94.
31. Albert E. Sloman, *The Sources of Calderón's* El príncipe constante (Oxford: Blackwell, 1950).
32. Lucy E. Weir, *The Ideas Embodied in the Religious Dramas of Calderón* (Lincoln, NE: University of Nebraska Press, 1940) (University of Nebraska Studies in Language, Literature and Criticism, no. 18), p. 40 (quoted – not with approval – by Sloman, *The Sources*, p. 93, n. 1). However, Weir adds that *El príncipe constante* 'is far superior to the other dramas based on history' (pp. 40–1).
33. Sloman, *The Sources*, p. 93.
34. Agustín González de Amezúa, *Epistolario de Lope de Vega*, 4 vols. (Madrid: Aldus, 1935–43), vol. IV, p. 102. The guess-date is Nicolás Marín's, in his edition

of Lope's *Cartas* (Madrid: Castalia, 1985), pp. 271–3. Lope was not a *licenciado*, although the title was often given to priests.

35. Lope de Vega, *Laurel de Apolo*, ed. Antonio Carreño (Madrid: Cátedra, 2007), p. 381.
36. Juan Pérez de Montalbán, *Para todos, ejemplos morales, humanos y divinos* (Seville: Francisco de Lyra, 1645), 'Indice de los ingenios de Madrid', fols. 268^{v}–269^{r}; see also 'Memoria de los que escriben comedias en Castilla solamente', fol. 278^{r}.
37. The poem was not thrown away, however: it is probably the account of the Flood (182 lines) used in both *La cena del rey Baltasar* (?1634) and *La torre de Babilonia* (?1637), and published by Manuel de Montoliu in Calderón de la Barca, *Obra lírica* (Barcelona: Montaner y Simón, 1943), pp. 154–61.
38. Pedro Grande de Tena (ed.), *Lagrimas panegiricas a la temprana muerte del gran poeta, i teologo, doctor Iuan Perez de Montalban* (Madrid: Imprenta del Reino, 1639). Calderón wrote a *décima* to the compiler ('La amistad que celebró', preliminaries), and a poem of six *décimas* ('Aunque nuestro humano ser', fol. 12) to Montalbán.

CHAPTER 8. LESSONS FOR CONTROLLING PERSONALITIES

1. See Álvarez Baena, *Hijos de Madrid*, vol. III, pp. 240–4, and Deleito y Piñuela, *El rey se divierte*, pp. 86–9.
2. Deleito y Piñuela, *El rey se divierte*, p. 28 and n. 2.
3. Shergold and Varey, 'Some Early Calderón Dates', 281.
4. See above, ch. 6, n. 42.
5. J. M. Ruano de la Haza (ed.), *La primera versión de* La vida es sueño, *de Calderón* (Liverpool: Liverpool University Press, 1992), p. 130.
6. Manuel de Anero Puente wrote a second part, apparently first printed in Seville by Francisco de Leefdael, 1717). See Francisco Aguilar Piñal, *Bibliografía de autores españoles del siglo XVIII*, 10 vols. (Madrid: CSIC, 1981–2001), vol. I, pp. 279–80.
7. See Varey, 'The Transmission of the Text of *Casa con dos puertas*', pp. 56–7; and 'Catalina de Acosta and Her Effigy: vv. 1865–68 and the Date of Calderón's *Casa con dos puertas*', in R. O. W. Goertz (ed.), *Iberia: Literary and Historical Issues: Studies in Honour of Harold V. Livermore* (Calgary: University of Calgary Press, 1985), pp. 107–15.
8. Juan de Robles, *Tardes del alcázar, doctrina para el perfecto vasallo*, ed. Miguel Romero Martínez (Seville: Diputación Provincial, 1948), p. 96; Luis de Córdoba Ronquillo (ed.), *Sermones funebres predicados dominica infra octava de todos Stos de 1624 años en la prouincia del andalucia … en las honras de … Enrique de Gusman … y demas progenitores* (Seville: Francisco de Lyra, 1624). The engraved title-page of Juan Antonio de Vera y Figueroa's *El Fernando o Sevilla restaurada* (Milan: Henrico Estefano, 1632) depicts Olivares as Atlas. See also E. Zudaire, 'Ideario político de D. Gaspar de Guzmán, privado de Felipe IV', *Hispania*, 25

(1965), 414, for other Olivares/Atlas references. In *Los tres mayores prodigios* Hércules refers to the help he gave Atlas (I, 1668a).

9. Tirso de Molina (Fray Gabriel Téllez), *Obras dramáticas completas*, 3 vols., ed. Blanca de los Ríos (Madrid: Aguilar, 1969), vol. I, p. 1426a.
10. See A. L. Stiefel, 'Calderons Lustspiel *La dama duende* und seine Quelle', *ZRP* 19 (1895), 262–4.
11. See Anthony Close, 'Novela y comedia de Cervantes a Calderón: El caso de *La dama duende*', in Aurora Egido (ed.), *Lecciones calderonianas* (Zaragoza: Ibercaja, 2001), pp. 33–52 (p. 51).
12. Cervantes, *El celoso extremeño*, in *Novelas ejemplares*, vol. II, p. 94.
13. Cotarelo, *Ensayo*, p. 144.
14. The *Aureus libellus de illibata virginitate Mariae*. Velázquez depicted the bestowal in his *Imposición de la casulla a San Ildefonso*, painted while he was still based in Seville: Brown, *Velázquez*, p. 24.
15. *Obras completas*, I, 253a; cf. *Polifemo*, lines 31–2 ('Allí una alta roca | mordaza es a una gruta, de su boca': 'There a high rock gags the mouth of a cave') and 41–2 ('De este, pues, formidable de la tierra | bostezo': 'Of this formidable yawn of the earth').
16. *Obras completas*, I, 279a; *El médico*, lines 2676–9.
17. Pérez Pastor, *Documentos*, pp. 94–5; P. 2709, Bartolomé Gallo, 1628–30, fol. 631 (23 March 1630), AHP, Madrid.
18. Pérez Pastor, *Documentos*, p. 96; P. 5611, Juan de Lorenzana, 1630–2, fol. 680 (25 October 1630), AHP, Madrid.
19. See Hannah E. Bergman (ed.), *Ramillete de entremeses y bailes nuevamente recogido de los antiguos poetas de España: Siglo XVII* (Madrid: Castalia, 1970), p. 162, lines 189–98.
20. Rodríguez López-Vázquez, 'La fecha de "La vida es sueño"', pp. 3–6.
21. Germán Vega García-Luengos, Don W. Cruickshank and J. M. Ruano de la Haza (eds.), *La segunda versión de* La vida es sueño, *de Calderón* (Liverpool: Liverpool University Press, 2000), pp. 40–118.
22. See in particular Albert E. Sloman, *The Dramatic Craftsmanship of Calderón: His Use of Earlier Plays* (Oxford: Dolphin, 1958), pp. 250–77.
23. See above, ch. 6, p. 78. For the *suelta*, see Vega's list in *La segunda versión*, pp. 44, 76. The *suelta* attributes the play to Lope de Vega, which cannot have pleased Don Pedro.
24. The date of the *tasa* (price) certificate, usually regarded as the publication date. The dedication is dated 6 January 1628. Circulation before publication is a possibility.
25. Shergold and Varey (eds.), *Genealogía*, p. 369.
26. Kurt and Roswitha Reichenberger, *Bibliographisches Handbuch der Calderón-Forschung / Manual bibliográfico calderoniano*, 4 vols. (Kassel: Thiele and Schwarz / Edition Reichenberger, 1979–2002), vol. I, pp. 401–2.
27. Shergold and Varey (eds.), *Genealogía*, pp. 104, 326–7.
28. See Edward M. Wilson, 'El texto de la "Deposición a favor de los profesores de la pintura", de don Pedro Calderón de la Barca', *RABM* 77 (1974), 709–27 (717); and Eunice Joiner Gates, 'Calderón's Interest in Art', *PQ* 40 (1961), 53–67.

29. Pérez Pastor, *Documentos*, pp. 425–7; and Willard F. King, 'Inventario, tasación y almoneda de los bienes de don Pedro Calderón', *NRFE* 36 (1988), 1079–82.
30. 'Vi o bem suceder mal, | e o mal, muito pior', from 'Sôbolos rios que vão', lines 34–5: see Luís de Camões, *Rimas*, ed. Álvaro J. da Costa Pimpão (Coimbra: Coimbra University, 1953); cf. also Garcilaso, 'No ay bien qu'en mal no se convierta y mude' ('There's no good that doesn't turn and change to bad'), *Égloga I*, line 299: see *Obras completas*, ed. Elias L. Rivers (Columbus, OH: Ohio State University Press, 1964), p. 78.
31. R. C. Latham and W. Matthews (eds.), *The Diary of Samuel Pepys*, 11 vols. (London: Bell, 1979–83), vol. v, p. 215.
32. Miguel de Cervantes, *Don Quijote de la Mancha*, edición del Instituto Cervantes, dirigida por Francisco Rico, 2 vols. (Barcelona: Instituto Cervantes/Crítica, 1998), vol. i, pp. 551–2, 565.
33. Don Pedro Calderón de la Barca, *Obras completas (Dramas)*. Textos íntegros según las primeras ediciones y los manuscritos autógrafos que saca a luz Luis Astrana Marín, 3rd edn, revised (Madrid: Aguilar, 1945). There seem to be too many *jarcias* in this passage.
34. British Library, 11728.h.21(2) and Österreichische Nationalbibliothek, 38.V.4 (7); both are unsigned, and attributions and dates use typographical evidence.
35. See Álvarez Baena, *Hijos de Madrid*, vol. i, pp. 126–8, for this Duke of Lerma, b. 1598, d. 11 November 1635.
36. Wilson, 'Un memorial perdido', p. 807.
37. Pérez Pastor, *Documentos*, p. 97.
38. Miguel Caxa de Leruela, *Restauración de la abundancia de España* (1631), ed. Jean Paul Le Flem (Madrid: Instituto de Estudios Fiscales, 1975), pp. 101–2.
39. A. A. Parker, 'Towards a Definition of Calderonian Tragedy', *BHS* 39 (1962), 222–37.
40. See *El divino Jasón*, ed. Ignacio Arellano and Ángel L. Cilveti (Pamplona: Universidad de Navarra; Kassel: Reichenberger, 1992) (*Autos sacramentales completos de Calderón*, vol. i).
41. These figures are approximate, since research on collaboration plays is ongoing: Germán Vega has discovered a *suelta* of *El privilegio de las mujeres* which attributes the play to Antonio Coello, Rojas and Luis Vélez. He argues that Calderón did write Act I, but that the other traditional attributions, to Pérez de Montalbán (Act II) and Coello (Act III), are not to be trusted: 'Sobre la autoría de *El privilegio de las mujeres*', in Álvaro Alonso and J. Ignacio Díez (eds.), *'Non omnis moriar': Estudios en memoria de Jesús Sepúlveda* (Málaga: Universidad de Málaga, 2007), pp. 317–36.
42. *Philosofía secreta* (Madrid: Francisco Sánchez, 1585), iv, xlv, xlvi; see the edition of Carlos Clavería (Madrid: Cátedra, 1995), pp. 540–9 (pp. 547, 548).

CHAPTER 9. ONLY POETRY, NOT PRECIOUS STONES

1. Elliott, *The Count-Duke of Olivares*, p. 409.
2. Ibid., p. 363.

3. Ibid., p. 364.
4. See Enriqueta Harris and John Elliott, 'Velázquez and the Queen of Hungary', *BM* 118 (1976), 24–6. It appears that this portrait is lost.
5. Brown and Elliott, *A Palace for a King*, p. 55.
6. Moll, 'Diez años sin licencias', 99–100.
7. See above, ch. 1, n. 14. For a contemporary (1623) description, see González Dávila, *Teatro de las grandezas*, p. 310.
8. Peter Ackroyd, *Shakespeare: The Biography* (London: Chatto & Windus, 2005), p. 118.
9. Shergold and Varey, 'Some Early Calderón Dates', 282.
10. Cotarelo, *Ensayo*, p. 146.
11. Hannah E. Bergman, *Luis Quiñones de Benavente y sus entremeses* (Madrid: Castalia, 1965), pp. 306–8; see also 172–85. For more on *guardainfantes*, see Rafael González Cañal, 'El lujo y la ociosidad durante la privanza de Olivares: Bartolomé Jiménez Patón y la polémica sobre el guardainfante y las guedejas', *Criticón* 53 (1991), 71–96.
12. Cotarelo, *Ensayo*, p. 144.
13. Cf. *Remedia amoris*, lines 293–6, 785–7.
14. However, Nemoroso explains how he went to Severo to be cured of love, successfully (*Égloga II*, lines 1089–97).
15. For *Para vencer a amor*, see Hilborn, *A Chronology*, p. 22.
16. A. A. Parker, *The Philosophy of Love in Spanish Literature* (Edinburgh: Edinburgh University Press, 1985), pp. 199–201 and 239, n. 38.
17. Simón Díaz (ed.), *Relaciones breves de actos públicos*, p. 413.
18. Antonio Hurtado de Mendoza, *Convocacion de las Cortes de Castilla, y ivramento del Principe nuestro Señor D. Baltasar Carlos* (Madrid: Imprenta del Reyno, 1632), fol. 46^{r}: the first two were 'de capa y espada' ('cloak-and-sword'), the third was entitled *Júpiter vengado*, with décor by Lotti. See also María Cristina Sánchez Alonso, *Impresos de los siglos XVI y XVII de temática madrileña* (Madrid: CSIC, 1981), p. 187; another account is recorded on the previous page.
19. N. D. Shergold and J. E. Varey, 'Some Palace Performances of Seventeenth-Century Plays', *BHS* 40 (1963), 212–44 (232). There was another performance on 13 November 1633.
20. *Coronas del Parnaso y platos de las musas* (Madrid: Imprenta Real, 1635), fol. 34.
21. Sebastián Francisco de Medrano, *Favores de las musas recopilados por Alonso de Castillo Solórzano* (Milan: Juan Baptista Malatesta, 1631), preliminaries.
22. Pedro de Castro y Anaya, *Las auroras de Diana* (Madrid: Imprenta del Reyno, 1632). There may have been editions of 1631 and 1630. Calderón's poem ('Estos útiles verdores') is a *décima*.
23. Joseph Pellicer de Tovar, *Anfiteatro de Felipe el Grande* (Madrid: Juan González, 1631).
24. Antonio del Castillo de Larzával, *El Adonis* (Salamanca: Jacinto Taberniel, 1632): Calderón's poem is a *canción* of twelve lines ('Cantas de Adonis tú, mas tan bien cantas'), and the book contains only forty-eight pages. The only

recorded copy is preserved in the library of the Universidade de Santiago; this copy also contains a handwritten *décima* 'de Francisco de Velasco a D. Antonio del Castillo de Larzával'. The first poem was by Francisco de Eraso, Count of Humanes and a 'close friend and confidant' of Olivares (Elliott, *The Count-Duke*, p. 491), but we cannot assume that all the contributors knew one another.

25. Pérez de Montalbán, *Para todos*, 267r. My main source for Villaizán's biographical details is Victor Dixon, 'Apuntes sobre la vida y la obra de Jerónimo de Villaizán y Garcés', *Hispanófila* 13, no. 3 (1961), 5–22.
26. Luis Pacheco de Narváez, *Historia exemplar de las dos mugeres constantes españolas* (Madrid: Imprenta del Reino, 1635; licensed in 1630); his *Libro de las grandezas de la espada* was published in 1600 (Madrid: Pedro Várez de Castro). The sonnet is reprinted in José Simón Díaz, 'Textos dispersos de clásicos españoles: XVI. Calderón de la Barca', *RLit* 22 (1962), 117–18.
27. Fernando Pérez Pericón, *Descripción de la muy noble, y más antigua ciudad de Gibraltar* (Madrid: Imprenta del Reino, 1636). Calderón's approbation is reprinted in Simón Díaz, 'Textos dispersos' (1962), 120.
28. See Don Pedro Calderón de la Barca, *Obras menores (Siglos XVII y XVIII)*, with *Noticias bibliográficas* by Edward M. Wilson (Cieza: La fonte que mana y corre, 1969) (El aire de la almena, XXIV), and Blanca Oteiza, '*Elegía en la muerte del señor infante don Carlos, al señor infante cardenal*, por don Pedro Calderón de la Barca', in Ignacio Arellano and Germán Vega García-Luengos (eds.), *Calderón: Innovación y legado: Actas selectas del IX Congreso de la Asociación Internacional de Teatro Español y Novohispano de los Siglos de Oro, en colaboración con el Grupo de Investigación Siglo de Oro de la Universidad de Navarra (Pamplona, 27 al 29 de marzo de* 2000) (New York: Peter Lang, 2001), pp. 289–307.
29. Cotarelo, *Ensayo*, p. 147.
30. Calderón, *Obras completas (Dramas)*.
31. Cotarelo, *Ensayo*, p. 148.
32. The king is Mithridates VI, King of Pontus in the first century BC: his name provides English with the noun 'mithridate' and the verb 'mithridatise' ('to habituate to poison').
33. Cotarelo, *Ensayo*, p. 149. There was another performance by Juan Martínez on 5 June 1636: Shergold and Varey, 'Some Palace Performances', p. 230. The first document to refer to a planned performance of 'El Tuzami' (*sic*) is of 12 December 1659, which also lists *La puente de Mantible* (1630): Pérez Pastor, *Documentos*, pp. 265–6.
34. Margaret Wilson, '"Si África llora, España no ríe": A Study of Calderón's *Amar después de la muerte* in Relation to its Source', *BHS* 51 (1984), *Golden Age Studies in Honour of A. A. Parker*, 419–25 (421).
35. Ted L. L. Bergman, *The Art of Humour in the* Teatro breve *and* Comedias *of Calderón de la Barca* (Woodbridge: Tamesis, 2003), p. 135: 'At this moment, the audience is intended to be on Alcuzcuz's side, which consequently means the audience was meant to laugh at the Christian nobles.'
36. Brown, *Velázquez*, p. 111.

37. See Manuel Ruiz Lagos, '*El Tuzaní de la Alpujarra*: Calderón o la singularidad de la memoria histórica', in Alcalá Zamora and Belenguer (co-ordinators) *Calderón de la Barca y la España del Barroco*, vol. II, pp. 767–91, and in particular Margaret Rich Greer, 'The Politics of Memory in *El Tuzaní de la Alpujarra*', in Richard J. Pym (ed.), *Rhetoric and Reality in Early Modern Spain* (London: Tamesis, 2006), pp. 113–30. Greer develops the possibility that the bringing of Granada's famous 'lead books' to Madrid in 1632 was another contemporary event that influenced the composition of the play.
38. J. Alcalá Zamora, 'Individuo e historia en la estructura teatral de *El Tuzaní de las Alpujarras*', in Luciano García Lorenzo (ed.), *Calderón: Actas del Congreso Internacional sobre Calderón y el Teatro Español del Siglo de Oro (Madrid 8–13 de junio de* 1981), 3 vols. (Madrid: CSIC, 1983), vol. I, pp. 343–63.
39. A.A. Parker, *The Mind and Art of Calderón* (Cambridge: Cambridge University Press, 1988), p. 318.
40. Grace Magnier, 'The Assimilation of the Moriscos Reflected in Golden-Age Drama and in Selected Contemporary Writings', unpublished MA dissertation (University College, Dublin, 1992), p. 88.
41. C.V. Wedgwood, *The Thirty Years War* (London: Folio Society, 1999; first published 1938), p. 316.
42. See Álvaro Cubillo de Aragón, *Auto sacramental de la muerte de Frislán*, ed. Marie France Schmidt (Kassel: Reichenberger, 1984).
43. Archivio di Stato, Firenze: Mediceo, filza 4.959: letters from Madrid, 29 January and 5 February 1633. For the El Pardo performance, see Shergold and Varey, 'Some Palace Performances', 236.
44. Germán Vega García-Luengos, 'Calderón y la política internacional: Las comedias sobre el héroe y traidor Wallenstein', in Alcalá Zamora and Belenguer (co-ordinators), *Calderón de la Barca y la España del Barroco*, vol. II, pp. 793–827.
45. Quoted in full in Vega, 'Calderón y la política internacional', 793–4.
46. Henry W. Sullivan, 'The Wallenstein Play of Calderón and Coello, *Las proezas de Frislán, y muerte del rey de Suecia* [?] (1634): Conjectural Reconstruction', *BCom* 52, no. 2 (2000), 93–111.
47. Vega, 'Calderón y la política internacional', 795.
48. See Pedro Calderón de la Barca, *Love is no Laughing Matter (No hay burlas con el amor)*, trans. with an introduction and commentary by Don Cruickshank and Seán Page (Warminster: Aris & Phillips, 1986), lines 1231–2. These lines do not appear in the Aguilar or Vera Tassis editions (1682, 1694), but they are present in the first edition (1650). Vera Tassis may have cut them because they were no longer 'contemporary'.
49. For this couple, see Narciso Díaz de Escovar, 'Comediantes de los otros siglos: La bella Amarilis', *BRAH* 98 (1931), 323–62, and E. Cotarelo y Mori, 'Actores famosos del siglo XVII: María de Córdoba, "Amarilis", y su marido Andrés de la Vega', *RBAM* 10 (1933), 1–33.
50. In the *Séptima parte* (Nn7^{v}) he gives Calderón's act as the first; in the *Novena* (Nn4^{v}), the third.

51. See above, p. 365, n. 41, Vega, 'Sobre la autoría de *El privilegio de las mujeres*'.
52. M. J. del Río, 'Representaciones dramáticas en casa de un artesano del Madrid de principios del siglo XVII', in L. García Lorenzo and J. E. Varey (eds.), *Teatros y vida teatral en el Siglo de Oro a través de las fuentes documentales* (London: Tamesis, 1992), p. 253.
53. Ackroyd, *Shakespeare*, p. 235.
54. Charles Davis and J. E. Varey, *Actividad teatral en la región de Madrid según los protocolos de Juan García de Albertos, 1634–1660: Estudio y documentos*, 2 vols. (London: Tamesis, 2003), p. lxx.

CHAPTER 10. TAKING OVER FROM LOPE

1. The most complete is the *Obras poéticas*, ed. J. M. Blecua (Barcelona: Planeta, 1983), with 1,582 pages.
2. This *parte* also contains *De un castigo tres venganzas*, correctly attributed to Calderón, although Maria Grazia Profeti, in *La collezione 'Diferentes autores'* (Kassel: Edition Reichenberger, 1988), p. 78, cites another edition (Zaragoza, 1639) in which the play is attributed to Lope. The volume also has *La cruz en la sepultura*, also attributed to Lope. No copy is known, but the two plays were probably *sueltas* printed several years earlier.
3. See in particular Germán Vega García-Luengos, 'Cómo Calderón desplazó a Lope de los aposentos: Un episodio temprano de ediciones espúreas', in Ignacio Arellano and Germán Vega García-Luengos (eds.), *Calderón: Innovación y legado: Actas selectas del IX Congreso de la Asociación International de Teatro Español y Novohispano de los Siglos de Oro, en colaboración con el Grupo de Investigación Siglo de Oro de la Universidad de Navarra (Pamplona, 27 al 29 de marzo de 2000* (New York: Peter Lang, 2001), pp. 367–84; and his 'El predominio de Calderón también en las librerías: consideraciones sobre la difusión impresa de sus comedias', in Aurelio González (ed.), *Calderón 1600–2000: Jornadas de investigación calderoniana* (México DF: El Colegio de México: Fondo Eulalio Ferrer, 2002), pp. 15–33; and Felipe B. Pedraza Jiménez, 'De Lope a Calderón: Notas sobre la sucesión en la monarquía dramática', in José Alcalá Zamora and Ernest Belenguer (co-ordinators), *Calderón de la Barca y la España del Barroco*, 2 vols. (Madrid: Centro de Estudios Políticos y Constitucionales / Sociedad Estatal España Nuevo Milenio, 2001), vol. II, pp. 831–53.
4. *Essequie poetiche overo Lamento delle Muse Italiane in morte del Sig. Lope de Vega …: Rime, e prose raccolte dal Signor Fabio Franchi Perugino* [= Alessio Pulchi] (Venice: Ghirardo Imberti, 1636), pp. 76–7. Reprinted in Lope's *Coleccion de las obras sueltas*, vol. XXI (Madrid: Antonio de Sancha, 1779), pp. 1–165 (pp. 66–7). Using his own name, Pulchi had published *Roma festante nel real nascimento del Serenissimo Prencipe di Spagna* (Rome: Lodouico Grignani, 1629). The word *sastrarol* is apparently a coining: see Wido Hempel, '*In onor della fenice ibera*': *über die Essequie poetiche di Lope de Vega, Venedig 1636, nebst einer kommentierten Ausgabe della Orazione del Cavallier*

Marino und des Ragguaglio di Parnaso, *Analecta Romanica*, Heft 13 (Frankfurt am Main: Klostermann, 1964), p. 115. I thank Giulio and Laura Lepschy for this reference.

5. María Luisa Caturla, *Pinturas, frondas y fuentes del Buen Retiro* (Madrid: Revista de Occidente, 1947), p. 34; see N. D. Shergold, *A History of the Spanish Stage from Medieval Times until the End of the Seventeenth Century* (Oxford: Clarendon, 1967), p. 285.
6. G. T. Northup, 'Some Recovered Lines from Calderón', *Homenaje ofrecido a Menéndez Pidal: Miscelánea de estudios lingüísticos, literarios e históricos*, 3 vols. (Madrid: Hernando, 1925), vol. II, pp. 495–500.
7. Ackroyd, *Shakespeare*, p. 241.
8. Francisco Bances Candamo, *Theatro de los theatros de los passados y presentes siglos*, prólogo, edición y notas de Duncan W. Moir (London: Tamesis, 1970), p. 35.
9. Hilborn, *A Chronology*, pp. 40–1.
10. Isaac Benabu, *On the Boards and in the Press: Calderón's* Las tres justicias en una (Kassel: Reichenberger, 1991) (Teatro del Siglo de Oro, Ediciones Críticas 18), pp. 3–5.
11. Vicenta Esquerdo Sivera, 'Aportaciones al estudio del teatro en Valencia durante el siglo XVII', *BRAE* 55 (1975), 429–530 (437–8).
12. Benabu, *On the Boards*, p. 10.
13. *Comedias*, vol. III, p. 416c, n. 1.
14. Esquerdo, 'Aportaciones al estudio del teatro en Valencia', 520–1.
15. Cotarelo, *Ensayo*, p. 151 and n. 1. The manuscript is no. 15298 of the BNE.
16. The largest (now) is Pedrosa de Duero, near Aranda and famous for its wine, some 105 miles from Madrid.
17. Brown and Elliott, *A Palace for a King*, pp. 103–4.
18. José Sánchez Arjona, *El teatro en Sevilla en los siglos XVI y XVII* (Madrid: Alonso, 1887), p. 283, records a performance of an *auto* with this title in 1634.
19. A. A. Parker, *The Allegorical Drama of Calderón* (Oxford: Dolphin, 1943), p. 167. His chapter IV is the main source of this commentary. See also J. E. Varey, 'The Staging of Calderón's *La cena de Baltasar*', in Karl-Hermann Körner and Dietrich Briesemeister (eds.), *Aureum Saeculum Hispanum: Beiträge zu Texten des Siglo de Oro: Festschrift für Hans Flasche zum 70. Geburtstag* (Wiesbaden: Franz Steiner, 1983), pp. 299–311.
20. Luis Ramírez de Arellano (compiler), *Avisos para la muerte* (Madrid: Viuda de Alonso Martín, 1634).
21. *Comedias*, vol. IV, pp. 726b–729a. The elegant 1757 edition is reproduced in Calderón, *Obras menores*. See Edward M. Wilson, 'Un romance ascético de Calderón: "Agora, señor, agora …"', *BRAE* 52 (1972), 79–105.
22. Diego de Covarrubias y Leiva (compiler), *Elogios al palacio real del Buen Retiro* (Madrid: Imprenta del Reino, 1635).
23. Pérez Pastor, *Documentos*, p. 98.
24. Luis Quiñones de Benavente, *Ioco seria: Burlas veras, o reprehension moral, y festiua de los desordenes publicos* (Madrid: Francisco García, 1645), fols. 36^{r}–44^{v}.

25. Bergman, *Luis Quiñones de Benavente*, pp. 332–42. Sadly, the *autora* does not name the other two plays.
26. Francisco Gómez de Quevedo y Villegas, 'Quien quisiere ser culto en sólo un día', in his *Obra poética*, ed. José Manuel Blecua, 4 vols. (Madrid: Castalia, 1969–81), vol. III, pp. 227–8.
27. For the Góngora ballad, see Calderón, *Love is no Laughing Matter (No hay burlas con el amor)*, pp. 114, 116; the lines are present in the first edition, but not in later ones.
28. Hilborn, *Chronology*, pp. 21, 29–30, 34.
29. *Comedias*, vol. IV, p. 199n.
30. The *Legenda aurea* was written around 1260 and first printed in 1470; there were numerous editions. Dramatists quarried it for material, especially about the lives of saints. For other possible sources see Ignacio Arellano, '*El árbol de mejor fruto* de Calderón y la leyenda del árbol de la cruz: Contexto y adaptación', *Anuario Calderoniano* 1 (2008), 27–65.
31. Brown and Elliott, *A Palace for a King*, pp. 214, 215 and n. 70; Sánchez Alonso, *Impresos de los siglos XVI y XVII*, p. 220.
32. Shergold, *Spanish Stage*, pp. 319–20.
33. For the evidence that it was Lope's play, see the edition by Eleonora Ioppoli (Florence: Alinea, 2006), pp. 12–17.
34. Pérez de Moya, *Philosofía secreta*, ed. Clavería, pp. 267–9.
35. T. H. Johnson (ed.), *The Poems of Emily Dickinson: Including Variant Readings Critically Compared with All Known Manuscripts*, 3 vols. (Cambridge, MA: Belknap Press Division of Harvard University Press, 1955), vol. I, pp. xlix–lix. See Cruickshank, 'Calderón's Handwriting'.
36. Ackroyd, *Shakespeare*, ch. 47 (pp. 256–63).
37. Manuel Sánchez Mariana, 'El manuscrito original del auto *Llamados y escogidos*, de Calderón', in Luciano García Lorenzo (ed.), *Calderón: Actas del Congreso internacional sobre Calderón y el teatro español del Siglo de Oro* (Madrid: CSIC, 1983) (Anejos de la Revista *Segismundo* 6), pp. 299–308.
38. N. D. Shergold, 'The First Performance of Calderón's *El mayor encanto amor*', *BHS* 35 (1958), 24–7.
39. Preserved in manuscript in the Biblioteca Nacional and printed by Hartzenbusch (*Comedias*, vol. I, pp. 386–90), mistakenly assigned to 1639.
40. Léo Rouanet, 'Un autographe inédit de Calderón', *RevHisp* 6 (1899), 196–200.
41. Caturla, *Pinturas, frondas y fuentes*, p. 44; see Shergold, *Spanish Stage*, p. 284.
42. Shergold, *Spanish Stage*, p. 283.
43. Sloman, *The Dramatic Craftsmanship*, pp. 128–58.
44. Margaret Rich Greer, *The Play of Power: Mythological Court Dramas of Calderón de la Barca* (Princeton: Princeton University Press, 1991), pp. 87–94.
45. Greer, *The Play of Power*, pp. 89, 92.
46. 'La cueva de Meliso', in Teófanes Egido, *Sátiras políticas de la España moderna* (Madrid: Alianza, 1973), pp. 137–72.
47. Flavius Josephus, *Antiquitates judaicae*, XV, vi–vii, and *De bello judaico*, I, xxii.
48. See Parker, *The Mind and Art of Calderón*, pp. 114–29.

49. See José María Ruano de la Haza, 'Las dos versiones de *El mayor monstruo del mundo*, de Calderón', *Criticón*, 72 (1998), 35–47; and María J. Caamaño Rojo, *El mayor monstruo del mundo de Calderón de la Barca: Estudio textual* (Santiago de Compostela: Universidade de Santiago de Compostela, 2001).
50. Shergold and Varey, 'Some Early Calderón Dates', 276.
51. Edward M. Wilson, 'Notes on the Text of *A secreto agravio, secreta venganza*', *BHS* 35 (1958), 72–82.
52. See E. W. Bovill, *The Battle of Alcazar* (London: Batchworth, 1952), pp. 137, 139.
53. Otis H. Green, *Spain and the Western Tradition: The Castilian Mind in Literature from El Cid to Calderón*, 4 vols. (Madison: University of Wisconsin Press, 1968), vol. II, pp. 237–9, 242.
54. Terence E. May, 'The Folly and the Wit of Secret Vengeance: Calderón's *A secreto agravio, secreta venganza*', *FMLS* 2 (1966), 114–22.
55. Ackroyd, *Shakespeare*, p. 252.
56. Shergold and Varey, 'Some Early Calderón Dates', 285, 276–7.
57. Wolfgang von Wurzbach, *Verzeichnis der Komödien Calderons*, in *Calderons ausgewählte Werke*, 10 vols. (Leipzig: Hesse & Becker, 1910), vol. I, p. 268; and Kurt and Roswitha Reichenberger, *Bibliographisches Handbuch der Calderón-Forschung/Manual bibliográfico calderoniano*, vol. II, 1: *Die Literatur über Calderón und seine Werke 1680–1980 / Los estudios sobre Calderón y su obra 1680–1980* (Kassel: Reichenberger, 1999), p. 183. The only detailed textual study of the two texts is by Ana María Barquín Amezcua, 'Análisis textuales, historia de los textos, estilística y versificación en *La señora y la criada* y *El acaso y el error*', unpublished MA dissertation (University College Dublin, 1999). Ms Barquín is confident that *La señora* came first.
58. Shergold and Varey, 'Some Early Calderón Dates', 279, 281–2.
59. Robert Rudolf Bacalski, 'A Critical Edition of *El jardín de Falerina* by Francisco de Rojas Zorrilla, Antonio Coello y Ochoa and Pedro Calderón de la Barca, with introduction and notes', unpublished doctoral dissertation (University of New Mexico, 1972) (based on MS 17320 of the BNE). Quotations are from this edition.
60. Maxime Chevalier, *L'Arioste en Espagne (1530–1650): Recherches sur l'influence du 'Roland furieux'* (Bordeaux: Féret, 1966), pp. 433–4.
61. Edward M. Wilson and Jack Sage, *Poesías líricas en las obras dramáticas de Calderón: Citas y glosas* (London: Tamesis, 1964), pp. 115–16.
62. Shergold and Varey, 'Some Early Calderón Dates', 281–2.
63. Perhaps its starting-point is the English campaigns in the 1540s to force an English marriage on the infant Queen Mary, campaigns known in Scotland as the 'rough wooing'.
64. Calderón de la Barca, *El gran teatro del mundo / El gran mercado del mundo*, ed. Eugenio Frutos Cortés (Madrid: Cátedra, 1987), p. 21.
65. But see Ruano de la Haza, *La puesta en escena*, pp. 82–4.
66. See N. D. Shergold and J. E. Varey, '*Autos sacramentales* in Madrid, 1644', *HR* 26 (1958), 52–63. Prior to 1644, the much smaller Plazuela de la Villa had been used.

67. For the guild, the Cofradía de la Novena, see Shergold, *Spanish Stage*, pp. 523–5.
68. Quoted in Spanish by Ángel Valbuena Prat in Calderón, *Obras completas*, III, 199b.
69. Francisco Gómez de Quevedo Villegas, *Epicteto y Phocilides en español con consonantes* (Madrid: María de Quiñones for Pedro Coello, 1635). The same printer and bookseller would produce Calderón's *Primera parte* the following year. For Quevedo's version of the passage quoted above, see Calderón, *El gran teatro del mundo / El gran mercado del mundo*, ed. Frutos Cortés, p. 26.
70. In *Autos sacramentales: Con quatro comedias nuevas, y sus loas, y entremeses: Primera parte* (Madrid: María de Quiñones, 1655).
71. See William A. Hunter, 'The Calderonian Auto Sacramental *El gran teatro del mundo*: An Edition and Translation of a Nahuatl Version', *Publication 27* (New Orleans: Middle American Research Institute, Tulane University, 1960), pp. 105–202 (pp. 112–13).
72. Henri Mérimée, *Spectacles et comédiens à Valencia (1580–1630)* (Toulouse: Privat, 1913), p. 80.
73. See Luis Iglesias Feijoo, 'Calderón en la escena y en la imprenta: Para la edición crítica de *El príncipe constante*', *Anuario Calderoniano* 1 (2008), 245–68.
74. Eight *reales* was the minimal daily wage of a skilled labourer at this time.

CHAPTER 11. KNIGHT OF SANTIAGO

1. William Byron, *Cervantes: A Biography* (London: Cassel, 1979), p. 414.
2. Pedro de Oña, *El Ignacio de Cantabria* (Seville: Francisco de Lyra, 1639).
3. Shergold and Varey, 'Some Early Calderón Dates', 278.
4. Ibid., 275–6. Calderón's text first appeared in *El mejor de los mejores libro* [*sic*] *que ha salido de comedias nuevas* (Alcalá: María Fernández, 1651).
5. Victor Dixon, '*El alcalde de Zalamea*, "la nueva": Date and Composition', *BHS* (Glasgow) 77 (2000), 173–81.
6. Shergold, *Spanish Stage*, pp. 285–7.
7. Quoted by Shergold, *Spanish Stage*, p. 285.
8. Hilborn, *A Chronology*, pp. 21, 31–2.
9. A. K. G. Paterson, 'The Textual History of Tirso's *La venganza de Tamar*', *MLR* 63 (1968), 381–91.
10. Frederick L. Jones (ed.), *The Letters of Percy Bysshe Shelley*, 2 vols. (Oxford: Clarendon, 1964), vol. II, p. 154.
11. But see in particular Mike Gordon, 'Calderón's *Los cabellos de Absalón*: The Tragedy of a Christian King', *Neophilologus* 64 (1980), 390–401.
12. Wilson and Sage, *Poesías líricas*, p. 34.
13. Brown, *Velázquez*, p. 251.
14. At least according to his father-in-law, Pacheco: Brown, *Velázquez*, p. 44.
15. E. Cotarelo y Mori, *Don Francisco de Rojas Zorrilla* (Madrid: Imprenta de la Revista de Archivos, 1911), pp. 13–16.

16. Quevedo, *Perinola*, in his *Obras políticas, históricas y críticas*, 2 vols. (Madrid: Viuda de Hernando, 1893), vol. II, p. 340; see also Cecil Roth, *A History of the Marranos*, 4th edn (New York: Hermon Press, 1959), p. 397.
17. Antonio Enríquez Gómez, *Sansón nazareno* (Rouen: Laurenço Maurry, 1656).
18. AHN, Pruebas de Caballeros de la Orden de Santiago, 12/2/1, expediente 1394. The full document is in Pérez Pastor, *Documentos*, pp. 100–1.
19. Pérez Pastor, *Documentos*, pp. 116–17, where the sale is referred to, but without the exact date, and p. 147.
20. Cotarelo, *Ensayo*, p. 173, n. 3. González de Armunia (or Almunia), *procurador en Cortes* for Madrid, was married to a daughter of Pedro Franqueza, the councillor found guilty of fraud in 1609. Don Pedro Romero was one of Diego Calderón's executors in 1647: Pérez Pastor, *Documentos*, pp. 158–9.
21. Cotarelo, *Ensayo*, p. 172 and n. 3, and p. 173. It will be noticed that *Dafne* was apparently played a year earlier (see p. 165 above).
22. Pérez Pastor, *Documentos*, p. 103.
23. Don Diego was the second Count of Barajas. A knight of Santiago since 1585, he died on 18 July 1644: Endika de Mogrobejo, *Diccionario hispanoamericano de heráldica, onomástica y genealogía*, 27 vols. (Bilbao: Mogrobejo-Zabala, 1995–2004), vol. XIV, p. 56.
24. I have not traced a Cardeñosa within a day's ride of Reinosa.
25. Summarised from *expediente* 1394 by Pérez Pastor, *Documentos*, pp. 102–7. Pérez Pastor has misread 'fr. [= fray] Thomas de salaçar' as 'Francisco Tomas de Salazar'. This is not another candidate for the servant Francisco who supposedly went to Mexico with Diego Calderón the younger in 1608.
26. In 1615–18 an Agustín Calderón de la Barca, of Aguilar, was engaged in a lawsuit over the interest on a bond: AHN, Archivo de la Real Chancillería de Valladolid, ES.47186.ARCHV/1.3.2.1// Pleitos civiles. Pérez Alonso (F.), Caja 1802.0002.
27. Pedro Calderón de la Barca, *El agua mansa / Guárdate del agua mansa*, edición crítica de las dos versiones por Ignacio Arellano y Víctor García Ruiz (Kassel: Reichenberger; Murcia: Universidad de Murcia, 1989) (Teatro del Siglo de Oro, Ediciones Críticas 23), p. 401n.
28. There is a tradition of the *montañés* as a figure of fun, as suggested by three *entremeses* listed by C. A. de la Barrera, *Catálogo bibliográfico y biográfico del teatro antiguo español desde sus orígenes hasta mediados del siglo XVIII* (Madrid: Rivadeneyra, 1860), p. 635: *El montañés en la corte*, *El montañés y el estornudo*, *El montañés y el vizcaíno*.
29. Ackroyd, *Shakespeare*, p. 276.
30. Elliott, *The Count-Duke of Olivares*, p. 137.
31. Pérez Pastor, *Documentos*, pp. 108–10; Cotarelo, *Ensayo*, p. 176.
32. Álvarez Baena, *Hijos de Madrid*, vol. IV, pp. 292–4.
33. Cotarelo, *Ensayo*, p. 181.
34. Pérez Pastor, *Documentos*, pp. 122–3; P. 7718, Juan de Pineda, 1640, fol 311, AHP, Madrid. Pérez Pastor misreads the second surname as 'Boitegui'.
35. Elliott, *The Count-Duke of Olivares*, p. 666.

36. Gregorio Marañón, *El conde-duque de Olivares: La pasión de mandar*, 6th edn (Madrid: Espasa-Calpe, 1972), p. 387.

CHAPTER 12. DISCORDANT VOICES

1. Shergold, *Spanish Stage*, p. 250.
2. See Escobar, *The Plaza Mayor*, pp. 14, 82, etc.
3. Sánchez Alonso, *Impresos de los siglos XVI y XVII*, p. 229.
4. Shergold, *Spanish Stage*, pp. 288–9. See also Shergold and Varey, 'Some Early Calderón Dates', 277–8.
5. Andrés Sánchez de Espejo, *Relacion aiustada en lo possible, a la verdad, y repartida en dos discursos* (Madrid: María de Quiñones, 1637), fol. 25^{r}.
6. Sánchez de Espejo, *Relacion*, fols. 17^{v}–18^{r}. For an account of this procession in particular, and of these festivities in general, see J. E. Varey, 'Calderón, Cosme Lotti, Velázquez, and the Madrid Festivities of 1636–1637', *Renaissance Drama* 1 (1968), 253–82. There were two companies, not three, those of Alonso de Olmedo and Pedro de la Rosa.
7. *Academia burlesca en Buen Retiro a la Magestad de Philipo IV el Grande* (MS 10293, BNE, 1637); printed by Antonio Pérez Gómez (Valencia: Tipografía Moderna, 1952), and most recently by María Teresa Julio (ed.), *Academia burlesca que se hizo en Buen Retiro a la Majestad de Filipo IV el Grande de 1637* (Pamplona: Universidad de Navarra; Madrid: Iberoamericana; Frankfurt: Vervuert, 2007). See also Sánchez de Espejo, *Relacion*, fols. 22^{v}–23^{r}, and Cotarelo, *Don Francisco de Rojas Zorrilla*, pp. 46–50.
8. *Noticias de Madrid desde el año de* 1636 *hasta el de 1638, y desde el año 1680 hasta el siglo presente*, por don Juan Francisco de Ayala Manrique, y es su propio original. Recogidas por don Josef Antonio Armona, Corregidor de Madrid, BNE, MS 18447, fols 49^{v}–50^{r} (an eighteenth-century copy of a seventeenth-century original). (I owe this reference to Edward Wilson.)
9. *Academia burlesca* (Julio edn), p. 228.
10. Germán Vega García-Luengos, 'Entre calvos anda el juego': La insistencia de un tema burlesco en Rojas Zorrilla', *RLit* 69, no. 137 (2007), *Número monográfico dedicado a Francisco de Rojas Zorrilla*, 13–34.
11. D. Pedro Calderón de la Barca, *El alcalde de Zalamea*, ed. Peter N. Dunn (Oxford: Pergamon, 1966), pp. 48–9.
12. Sánchez de Espejo, *Relacion*, fol. 24^{r}.
13. Shergold, *Spanish Stage*, p. 289 and nn. 1, 4.
14. Hilborn, *A Chronology*, pp. 61–2.
15. Cotarelo, *Ensayo*, p. 183, n. 1.
16. Pedro Joseph Suppico de Moraes, *Collecçam politica de apophthegmas memoraveis*, 3 vols. in 1 (Lisbon: Officina Augustiniana, 1733), vol. III, pp. 95–6 (from the copy in the Biblioteca Histórica Municipal, Madrid, Par/438).
17. María Teresa Julio, 'El vejamen de Rojas para la academia de 1638: Estudio y edición', *RLit* 69, no. 137 (2007), *Número monográfico dedicado a Francisco de Rojas Zorrilla*, 299–332.

18. Shergold, *Spanish Stage*, p. 290, n. 3.
19. Ibid., p. 290, n. 1, p. 291, n. 1. See also Abraham Madroño Durán, 'Comedias escritas en colaboración: El caso de Mira de Amescua', in *Mira de Amescua en candelero: Actas del Segundo Congreso Internacional sobre Mira de Amescua y el teatro español del siglo XVII (Granada, 27–30 de octubre de* 1994), ed. A. de la Granja and J. A. Martínez Berbel, 2 vols. (Granada: Universidad de Granada, 1994), vol. 1, p. 332.
20. Hannah E. Bergman, 'A Court Entertainment of 1638', *HR* 42 (1974), 67–81.
21. Hannah E. Bergman, 'El "Juicio final de todos los poetas españoles muertos y vivos" (ms. inédito) y el certamen poético de 1638', *BRAE* 55 (1975), 551–610.
22. Julio, 'El vejamen de Rojas', p. 329.
23. Cotarelo y Mori, *Don Francisco de Rojas Zorrilla*, p. 61; Bergman, 'A Court Entertainment', pp. 72–3.
24. Quoted by Shergold, *Spanish Stage*, p. 288, n. 1.
25. *Noticias de Madrid*, fol. 52 (I owe this reference to Edward Wilson).
26. However, Marañón quotes evidence that the idea came from Antonio Hurtado de Mendoza: Marañón, *El conde-duque de Olivares*, pp. 183–4; and see Gareth A. Davies, *A Poet at Court: Antonio Hurtado de Mendoza (1586–1644)* (Oxford: Dolphin, 1971), pp. 37–8.
27. N. D. Shergold and J. E. Varey, *Los autos sacramentales en Madrid en la época de Calderón: 1637–1681: Estudio y documentos* (Madrid: Ediciones de Historia, Geografía y Arte, 1961), p. 2.
28. The same period as in England: Ackroyd, *Shakespeare*, p. 340.
29. Davis and Varey, *Actividad teatral en la región de Madrid.*
30. *Libro de los acuerdos del ayuntamiento de la villa de Yepes*, 1636, 1637, 1638. The official who brought me these *legajos* said he remembered the play being performed in Yepes in – he thought – 1958.
31. Charles Davis, 'Calderón en Yepes: El estreno de *El mágico prodigioso* (1637)', *Criticón* 99 (2007), 193–215.
32. Ibid., 204–5.
33. References are to Pedro Calderón de la Barca, *El mágico prodigioso: A Composite Edition by Melveena McKendrick in Association with A. A. Parker* (Oxford: Clarendon, 1992), which also gives details of Calderón's sources (pp. 36–46).
34. *Antes que todo es mi dama*, ed. Bernard P. E. Bentley (Kassel: Reichenberger, 2000) (Teatro del Siglo de Oro, Ediciones Críticas 106), p. 11; 'rodado' is the past participle of *rodar*, to tumble, as well as 'dappled'.
35. Quoted by Elliott, *The Count-Duke of Olivares*, pp. 558–9, who is my main source for this section.
36. Shirley B. Whitaker, 'The Quevedo Case (1639): Documents from Florentine Archives', *MLN* 97 (1982), 368–79. For the text of the *Memorial*, see Egido, *Sátiras políticas*, pp. 111–15.
37. Elliott, *The Count-Duke of Olivares*, p. 524.
38. Pérez Pastor, *Documentos*, pp. 112–15; P. 5546, Juan Martínez del Portillo, 1637, fol. 1118, AHP, Madrid.

39. Pérez Pastor, *Documentos*, P. 115; p. 5546, Juan Martínez del Portillo, 1637, fol. 1120, AHP, Madrid.
40. Pérez Pastor, *Documentos*, pp. 116–17; P. 5546, Juan Martínez del Portillo, 1637, fol. 1122, AHP, Madrid.
41. Elliott, *The Count-Duke of Olivares*, pp. 532–3.
42. Ibid., p. 537.
43. Felipe Pereda and Fernando Marías (eds.), *El atlas del rey planeta: La descripción de España y de las costas y puertos de sus reinos de Pedro Texeira (1634)* (Hondarribia: Nerea, 2002), map 7 and p. 315.
44. Wilson, 'Un memorial perdido', pp. 804–5.
45. Pérez Pastor, *Documentos*, p. 118; P. 5549, Juan Martínez del Portillo, 1639, fol. 280, AHP, Madrid.
46. Pérez Pastor, *Documentos*, pp. 118–19; P. 5548, Juan Martínez del Portillo, 1638–42, fol. 3, AHP, Madrid.
47. Cotarelo, *Ensayo*, p. 194.
48. Edward M. Wilson, 'Calderón y Fuenterrabía': El *Panegírico al Almirante de Castilla*', *BRAE* 49 (1969), 253–78 (also reprints the text).
49. Elliott, *The Count-Duke of Olivares*, pp. 263–4, 540.
50. This explains why Calderón did not take part, while his brother José did.
51. See in particular Francisco Rico, *El texto del 'Quijote': Preliminares a una ecdótica del Siglo de Oro* (Valladolid: Centro para la Edición de los Clásicos Españoles, Universidad de Valladolid, 2005), especially ch. II, 'Cómo se hacía un libro en el Siglo de Oro', pp. 53–93.
52. David Castillejo, *Guía de ochocientas comedias del Siglo de Oro para el uso de actores y lectores: Con el preámbulo* Tres diálogos (estatal, racional y teatral) (Madrid: Ars Milenii, 2002), p. 573.
53. *Calderón de la Barca y la España del Barroco* (2000), p. 371 (list), p. 85 (*venera*), pp. 52, 53, 64 (portraits).
54. Wilson and Sage, *Poesías líricas*, pp. 100–1.
55. Marco Antonio Ortí, *Siglo quarto de la conquista de Valencia* (Valencia: Juan Bautista Marçal, 1640; facsimile reprint, Valencia: Ajuntament de Valencia, 2005), fol. 19; quoted by Cotarelo, *Ensayo*, p. 197. Ortí (born 1593) was himself a playwright, and wrote a *loa* for the performance of *Gustos*, printed in his book (fols. 19^v–28^r); see also Urzáiz Tortajada, *Catálogo*, p. 491.
56. See Jean Mouyen, 'Las casas de comedias de Valencia', *Cuadernos de Teatro Clásico* 6 (1991), 91–122.
57. Blue, 'Calderón's *Gustos y disgustos*', pp. 29–39. Matos Fragoso's heroic poem on the entry of the duchess is reprinted in Simón Díaz (ed.), *Relaciones breves de actos públicos*, pp. 454–7.
58. Esquerdo Sivera, 'Aportaciones al estudio del teatro en Valencia', 437–8.
59. Blue, 'Calderón's *Gustos y disgustos*', p. 34.
60. Cotarelo, *Ensayo*, p. 198.
61. Edward M. Wilson, 'Calderón's Enemy: Don Antonio Sigler de Huerta', *MLN* 81 (1966), 225–31.
62. Quoted by Wilson, 'Calderón's Enemy', 227.

63. José Pellicer de Tovar, *Avisos: 17 de mayo de 1639 – 29 de noviembre de 1644*, ed. Jean-Claude Chevalier and Lucien Clare, 2 vols. (Paris: Éditions Hispaniques, 2002–3), vol. I, p. 329 (21 January 1642). There is another reference to this Valdés's 'mocedades' ('youthful exploits') as early as 14 June 1639 (I, 20), while María got into more trouble over her relationship with another *regidor*, Don Juan de Ochondiano, in 1644 (vol. I, pp. 549–50: 27 September).
64. The most frequent references are to be found in Davis and Varey, *Actividad teatral en la región de Madrid.*

CHAPTER 13. THE STORM GATHERS

1. See Andrés Úbeda de los Cobos (ed.), *Paintings for the Planet King: Philip IV and the Buen Retiro Palace* (Madrid: Museo Nacional del Prado, 2005), pp. 140–1.
2. Elliott, *The Count-Duke of Olivares*, p. 549–51.
3. Grande de Tena (ed.), *Lagrimas panegiricas*, fol. 12. See Picatoste (ed.), *Poesías inéditas*, p. 48; also José Simón Díaz, 'Textos dispersos de clásicos españoles: I. Bocángel. II. Calderón de la Barca', *RLit* 19 (1959), 110–11.
4. Quoted from Simón Díaz, 'Textos dispersos' (1959), 109.
5. Simón Díaz records a *décima* of his, printed in 1640: *Bibliografía de la literatura hispánica*, 14 vols. (Madrid: Instituto 'Miguel de Cervantes'/CSIC, 1950–93), vol. XI, no. 2491.
6. Quevedo, *Perinola*, vol. II, p. 336.
7. Hilborn, *A Chronology*, pp. 21, 32, 34.
8. Wilson and Sage, *Poesías líricas*, p. 112.
9. Hilborn, *A Chronology*, pp. 36, 38–9, 41.
10. Shergold and Varey, 'Some Early Calderón Dates', 278–9.
11. F. Sureda, 'Algunas tragedias del Siglo de Oro ante el público valenciano del XVIII', 'Datos complementarios', *Criticón* 23 (1983), 117–32 (128 and n. 1). On 13 February there was another performance of '*La hija del aire*', without further details.
12. For the arguments, see Constance Hubbard Rose, 'Who Wrote the *Segunda parte* of *La hija del aire*?', *RBPH* 54 (1976), 797–822 ; 'Again on the Authorship of the *Segunda parte* of *La hija del aire*', *BHS* 60 (1983), 247–8; '¿Quién escribió la *Segunda parte* de *La hija del aire*? ¿Calderón o Enríquez Gómez?', in Luciano García Lorenzo (ed.), *Calderón: Actas del Congreso internacional sobre Calderón y el teatro español del Siglo de Oro* (Madrid: CSIC, 1983) (Anejos de la Revista *Segismundo* 6), pp. 603–15; John B. Wooldridge, 'The *Segunda parte* of *La hija del aire* is Calderón's', *BCom* 47 (1995), 73–94; '*Quintilla* Usage in Antonio Enríquez Gómez: More Evidence against his Authorship of the Second Part of *La hija del aire*', *MLR* 96 (2001), 707–14. See also D. W. Cruickshank, 'The Second Part of *La hija del aire*', *Golden-Age Studies in Honour of A. A. Parker*, *BHS* 61 (1984), 286–94.
13. Part II, lines 2476–7, 1181–2, 2478–9: quotations are from the edition of Francisco Ruiz Ramón (Madrid: Cátedra, 1987). See also D.W. Cruickshank, 'The Significance of *Fortuna* in Calderón's *La hija del aire*', in '*Never-Ending*

Adventure': Studies in Medieval and Early Modern Spanish Literature in Honor of Peter Dunn (Newark, NJ: Juan de la Cuesta Press, 2002), pp. 351–76.

14. Elliott, *The Count-Duke of Olivares*, pp. 231, 628, 643, 651.
15. Pierre Corneille, *Théâtre complet*, ed. Pierre Lièvre and Roger Caillois, 2 vols. (Paris: Pléiade, 1966), vol. I, p. 715.
16. Shergold, *Spanish Stage*, p. 292.
17. Ibid., p. 292 and nn. 2, 3.
18. Esquerdo Sivera, 'Aportaciones al estudio del teatro en Valencia', 438–9. *La dama y galán Aquiles* may be an early version of *El monstruo de los jardines*, or the guesses that the latter is of 1661 may be wrong.
19. Published in his *Ioco seria* (1645), reprinted by E. Cotarelo y Mori (ed.), *Colección de entremeses, bailes, jácaras y mojigangas desde fines del siglo XVI a mediados del siglo XVII*, 2 vols., Nueva Biblioteca de Autores Españoles, vols. XVII, XVIII (Madrid: Bailly & Baillière, 1911), vol. XVIII, pp. 575–8. For full details of the actors, see T. R. A. Mason's edition of *La desdicha de la voz* (Liverpool: Liverpool University Press, 2003), pp. 47–62.
20. Shergold and Varey, *Los autos*, p. 19; and Pellicer, *Avisos*, vol. I, pp. 24–5 (28 June 1639). The other two *autos* for 1639 were *La cárcel del mundo* (Antonio Coello) and *Hércules* (Rojas).
21. Mason edn, p. 31.
22. Pedro Calderón de la Barca, *Quarta parte de comedias* (Madrid: Joseph Fernández de Buendía, 1672), ¶¶2.
23. Edward M. Wilson and Duncan Moir, *A Literary History of Spain: The Golden Age: Drama 1492–1700* (London: Ernest Benn; New York: Barnes & Noble, 1971), p. 105.
24. For the second, see Wilson and Sage, *Poesías líricas*, pp. 117–18.
25. Luis Vélez de Guevara, *La niña de Gómez Arias*, ed. Ramón Rozzell (Granada: Universidad de Granada, 1959) (Colección Filológica XVI), pp. 16, 59; see also Rozzell's 'The Song and Legend of Gómez Arias', *HR* 20 (1952), 91–107.
26. Hilborn, *Chronology*, pp. 36, 39–40.
27. See Sloman, *The Dramatic Craftsmanship*, pp. 159–87.
28. Antoine le Métel d'Ouville, *Les Fausses Veritez* (Paris: Courbé, 1643); Thomas Corneille, *Les Engagemens du hazard* (1647), in his *Poèmes dramatiques*, 5 vols. (Paris: Luynes, 1738), vol. I.
29. Hartzenbusch, *Comedias*, vol. IV, p. 674a. See Pellicer, *Avisos*, vol. I, p. 63.
30. Maria Grazia Profeti, *Per una bibliografia di J. Pérez de Montalbán* (Verona: Università degli Studi di Padova, 1976), pp. 439–40.
31. S. N. Treviño, 'Nuevos datos acerca de la fecha de *Basta callar*', *HR* 4 (1936), 333–41; 'Versos desconocidos de una comedia de Calderón', *PMLA* 52 (1937), 682–704; and Pedro Calderón de la Barca, *Basta callar*, ed. Margaret Rich Greer (Ottawa: Dovehouse, 2000) (Ottawa Hispanic Studies, 26). References are to this edition.
32. See Greer edn, pp. 53–68.
33. Rodrigo Méndez Silva, *Catalogo real genealogico de España* (Madrid: Diego Díaz de la Carrera, 1639).

34. Francisco de Balderrábano (trans.), *Vida y muerte de S. Eloy, obispo de Noyons, abogado, y patron de los plateros. Escrito por San Audeno, y referido por Surio en Latin* (Madrid: Imprenta del Reyno, 1640); the dates in the preliminaries indicate that the book went to press in 1639.
35. Rodrigo Méndez Silva, *Vida y hechos del gran Condestable de Portugal D. Nuño Aluarez Pereyra* (Madrid: Juan Sánchez, 1640).
36. Mateo Prado (trans.), *El manual de grandes, que escriuio en lengua Toscana, Monseñor Querini Arçobispo de Nixia y Paris* (Madrid: Antonio Duplastre, 1640).
37. Ackroyd, *Shakespeare*, p. 311.
38. Lope de Vega, *El peregrino en su patria*, ed. Juan Bautista Avalle-Arce (Madrid: Castalia, 1973), p. 57.
39. 'Al teatro', ostensibly by Francisco López de Aguilar (but really by Lope), in Lope de Vega, *La Dorotea* (1632), ed. Edwin S. Morby (Madrid: Castalia, 1968), p. 54.
40. Pérez de Montalbán, *Para todos*, ¶5^{v}.
41. Lope de Vega Carpio, *El castigo sin venganza* (Barcelona: Pedro Lacavallería, 1634), Prólogo. Quoted in the edition of C. A. Jones (Oxford: Pergamon, 1966), p. 121.
42. Calderón, *Primera parte*, ¶4^{r}.
43. Enríquez Gómez, *Sansón nazareno*, ã4^{v}.
44. Pedro Calderón de la Barca, *Verdadera quinta parte de comedias* (Madrid: Francisco Sanz, 1682), Advertencias a los que leyeren, 6¶1^{r}.

CHAPTER 14. WAR AND DISILLUSIONMENT

1. See Elliott, *The Count-Duke of Olivares*, p. 546.
2. Wilson, 'Un memorial perdido', pp. 804–7.
3. However, on 15 September 1642 his brother Diego acknowledged receipt from the Treasury of 3,000 *reales* to be granted to José towards the expenses of proving his fitness for knighthood: Pérez Pastor, *Documentos*, p. 123.
4. Quoted by Shergold, *Spanish Stage*, p. 298.
5. Pellicer, *Avisos*, vol. 1, p. 93 (14 February 1640).
6. Ibid., p. 95 (28 February 1640).
7. Sánchez Alonso, *Impresos de los siglos XVI y XVII*, p. 246; and the *Relacion general de los sucessos que ha avido en España, Flandes, Italia, y Alemania, y en otras partes, desde 1 de março de 1639 hasta fin de febrero de 1640* [?Madrid, 1640], in Simón Díaz (ed.), *Relaciones breves de actos públicos*, pp. 464–5. See also Pellicer, *Avisos*, vol. 1, pp. 95–6 (28 February 1640).
8. Calderón, *Primera parte* (1685), ¶6^{v}.
9. Cotarelo, *Ensayo*, p. 204.
10. Wilson, 'Un memorial perdido', pp. 801–2.
11. *No hay que creer ni en la verdad*, ed. Václav Černý (Madrid: CSIC, 1968) (Anejos de la Revista *Segismundo* 1).

12. Shergold, *Spanish Stage*, p. 293. See also Pellicer, *Avisos*, vol. I, p. 122 (3 July 1640).
13. Cotarelo, *Ensayo*, p. 205 and n. 3, but the accounts of the celebrations, printed by Hartzenbusch (*Comedias*, vol. IV, p. 675), do not mention plays. Composition in any year for the virgin's feast-day (9 November) is also possible.
14. Cotarelo, *Ensayo*, p. 204. See *Las manos blancas no ofenden (dos textos de una comedia)*, ed. Ángel Martínez Blasco (Kassel: Reichenberger, 1995) (Teatro del Siglo de Oro, Ediciones críticas 60), p. 76.
15. Shergold, *Spanish Stage*, pp. 300–1 and 301, n. 1.
16. The real cost was 'nearly 100,000 ducats': Brown and Elliott, *A Palace for a King*, p. 104. The exaggeration is significant.
17. Pellicer, *Avisos*, vol. I, p. 121 (19 June 1640).
18. N. D. Shergold and J. E. Varey, *Los autos sacramentales en Madrid en la época de Calderón: 1637–1681: Estudio y documentos* (Madrid: Estudios de Historia, Geografía y Arte, 1961), p. 28. Pellicer, *Avisos*, vol. I, p. 119 (12 June) gives the title of the second as '*El Ante-Cristo*'. Valbuena Prat argues that *El juicio final* is an alternative title for an *auto* which has survived, and suggests *Lo que va del hombre a Dios* (*Obras completas*, III, 270–3), but this cannot be right, since the text calls for four carts (ibid., 288b). The other two Madrid *autos* of 1640 were by Rojas.
19. Cotarelo, *Ensayo*, p. 205 and n. 2.
20. Printed by Valbuena Prat in *Obras completas*, III, 113–15.
21. The first was T. Díaz Galdós, 'Un autógrafo de Calderón', *RBAM* 4 (1927), 102–5. Cotarelo (*Ensayo*, pp. 204–5) records the date incorrectly as 24 May.
22. See D. W. Cruickshank and W. F. Hunter, 'Notes on the Text of Calderón's *Psiquis y Cupido* (*para Toledo*)', *Iberoromania* 4 (1970), 282–9.
23. Fernando Martínez Gil, Mariano García Ruipérez and Francisco Crosas, 'Calderón de la Barca y el Corpus toledano de 1640: recuperación de una carta autógrafa en el Archivo Municipal de Toledo', *Criticón* 91 (2004), 93–120.
24. Charles Davis tells me that the *autores* were Francisco Vélez de Guevara, Pedro de Cobaleda and Francisco Álvarez de Toledo.
25. Pellicer, *Avisos*, vol. II, pp. 150 (2 October 1640), 153 (9 October).
26. *Quarta parte de comedias*, 2¶2.
27. Ángel González Palencia, 'Pleito entre Lope de Vega y un editor de sus comedias', *BBMP* 3 (1921), 17–26.
28. Picatoste, 'Biografía de Calderón', p. 18.
29. See p. 193, n. 34.
30. Cambrils, Salou, Vilaseca and Constantí are in the immediate neighbourhood of Tarragona.
31. Picatoste, 'Biografía de Calderón', p. 46.
32. Compare Wilson, 'Un memorial perdido', p. 802.
33. These details come from ibid., p. 805.
34. However, what was presented as a withdrawal was in Catalan eyes a defeat: see Nuria Florensa i Soler, 'La derrota del ejército español en Barcelona: "la batalla

de Montjuïc": Antecedentes y desarrollo de la guerra', in Alcalá Zamora and Belenguer (co-ordinators), *Calderón de la Barca y la España del Barroco*, vol. II, pp. 189–220.
35. Elliott, *The Count-Duke of Olivares*, pp. 348, 383.
36. Pellicer, *Avisos*, vol. I, p. 301 (5 November 1641).
37. Elliott, *The Count-Duke of Olivares*, p. 626.
38. For the Hermitage portrait, see Brown, *Velázquez*, plate 149.
39. Elliott, *The Count-Duke of Olivares*, p. 639.
40. Wilson, 'Un memorial perdido', p. 803.
41. Elliott, *The Count-Duke of Olivares*, pp. 628–9.
42. John Minsheu, *A Dictionarie in Spanish and English* (London: E. Bollifant, 1599), p. 120.
43. Picatoste, 'Biografía de Calderón', p. 20.
44. Wilson, 'Un memorial perdido', p. 806.
45. 'Gallows Hill' would have been the equivalent English name, found in many places. Cotarelo gives no source for Calderón's involvement in the battle (see *Ensayo*, pp. 236–7). In his *memorial* (Wilson, 'Un memorial perdido', p. 802), Calderón cites a reference from Don Rodrigo de Herrera, but it is dated 30 February 1641.
46. Picatoste, 'Biografía de Calderón', p. 20.
47. Wilson, 'Un memorial perdido', p. 803.
48. Eulogio Zudaire, 'Un escrito anónimo de Calderón de la Barca', *Hispania* (Madrid) 13 (1953), 268–93; see also Jean Colomès, 'La Révolution catalane de 1640 et les écrivains espagnols du temps', in *IVe Congrès des Hispanistes Français* (Poitiers: Université de Poitiers, Faculté des Lettres et Sciences Humaines, 1968), pp. 45–58. Zudaire's text is from MS 18717[15] of the Biblioteca Nacional, Madrid. Palau's number 58872 records a copy of the printed version sold in 1949 as a folio, '11 pp.', but this copy has vanished: Antonio Palau y Dulcet, *Manual del librero hispano-americano*, 2nd edn, 28 vols. (Barcelona: Palau, 1948–77).
49. José Pellicer y Tovar, *Idea del Principado de Cataluña* (Antwerp: Jerónimo Verdús, 1642), pp. 5–6.
50. Zudaire, 'Un escrito anónimo', p. 285.
51. 'Hernando de Ayora Valmisoto', *El arbitro entre el marte frances y las vindicias gallicas* ('Pamplona': 'Carlos Juan', 1646). Nicolás Antonio identified the author as the *sevillano* Hernando de Ávila Sotomayor, and gave Seville as the place of printing: Antonio, *Bibliotheca hispana nova*, vol. I, p. 369. The type points to Simón Fajardo of Seville.
52. Shergold and Varey, *Los autos*, pp. 31–2; the others were by Vélez de Guevara and Mira de Amescua.
53. Pedro Calderón de la Barca, *El divino cazador (auto sacramental)*: Edición facsímil del manuscrito autógrafo conservado en la Biblioteca Nacional de Madrid, con introducción y comentario del Prof. Hans Flasche y transcripción del texto por Manuel Sánchez Mariana (Madrid: Ministerio de Cultura, 1981), p. 15; for Prado, see below, n. 69. As for Toledo, a carpenter preparing staging there was told to follow Calderón's *memorias de apariencias* (information from Dr Charles Davis). Presumably he wrote all three *autos* while on leave in Madrid.

54. Pérez Pastor, *Documentos*, p. 124; see also Shergold and Varey, *Los autos*, p. 37.
55. See Sánchez Mariana, 'El manuscrito original del auto *Llamados y escogidos*'.
56. See Shergold and Varey, *Los autos*, p. 41.
57. See Emilio Cotarelo y Mori, *Bibliografía de las controversias sobre la licitud del teatro en España* (Madrid: Tipografía de la 'Revista de Archivos, Bibliotecas y Museos', 1904), p. 164; J. E. Varey and N. D. Shergold, 'Datos históricos sobre los primeros teatros de Madrid: Prohibiciones de autos y comedias y sus consecuencias', *BH* 62 (1960), 286–325; and Alistair Malcolm, 'Public Morality and the Closure of the Theatres in the Mid-Seventeenth Century: Philip IV, the Council of Castile and the Arrival of Mariana of Austria', in Richard J. Pym (ed.), *Rhetoric and Reality in Early Modern Spain* (London: Tamesis, 2006), pp. 92–112.
58. Hilborn, *Chronology*, p. 49.
59. Pedro Calderón de la Barca, *Tercera parte de comedias*, ed. D. W. Cruickshank (Madrid: Biblioteca Castro, 2007), p. 928. This part of the text, the integrated *loa*, is not printed in other modern editions.
60. Louise K. Stein, *Songs of Mortals, Dialogues of the Gods: Music and Theatre in Seventeenth-Century Spain* (Oxford: Clarendon, 1993), p. 134.
61. For example, in the *loa* of *La púrpura de la rosa*, line 345: Pedro Calderón de la Barca and Tomás de Torrejón y Velasco, *La púrpura de la rosa*. Edición del texto de Calderón y de la música de Torrejón comentados y anotados por Ángeles Cardona, Don Cruickshank y Martin Cunningham (Kassel: Reichenberger, 1990). Teatro del Siglo de Oro, Ediciones críticas 9. See the note on p. 226.
62. See in particular T. R. A. Mason, '¿La sexualidad pervertida? *Las manos blancas no ofenden*', in Hans Flasche (ed.), *Archivum Calderoniamum*, Band III: *Hacia Calderón: Séptimo Coloquio Anglogermano, Cambridge, 1984* (Stuttgart: Franz Steiner, 1987), pp. 183–92.
63. Esquerdo Sivera, 'Aportaciones al estudio del teatro en Valencia', 437–8.
64. Hilborn, *A Chronology*, pp. 45–6.
65. See Adolfo de Castro y Rossi, *Discurso acerca de las costumbres públicas y privadas de los españoles en el siglo XVII fundado en el estudio de las comedias de Calderón* (Madrid: Guttenberg, 1881).
66. Hilborn, *A Chronology*, p. 45.
67. Edward M. Wilson, 'Inquisición y censura en la España del siglo XVII', in *Entre las jarchas y Cernuda: Constantes y variantes en la poesía española* (Barcelona: Ariel, 1977), pp. 245–72 (p. 270). See also his 'Calderón and the Stage-Censor in the Seventeenth Century: A Provisional Study', *Symposium* 15 (1961), 165–84.
68. Quotations are from *El secreto a voces, comedia de Pedro Calderón de la Barca, según el manuscrito de la Biblioteca Nacional de Madrid*, ed. José M. de Osma, *Bulletin of the University of Kansas* 39, no. 8 (1938).
69. Shergold and Varey, *Los autos*, p. 42.
70. Esquerdo Sivera, 'Aportaciones al estudio del teatro en Valencia', pp. 437–8.
71. Wilson, 'An Early List', 100.
72. Pérez Pastor, *Documentos*, p. 125. Strictly speaking, she was his *bisabuela*, his great-grandmother.
73. Pérez Pastor, *Documentos*, p. 126.

74. Pedro Calderón de la Barca, *La humildad coronada: Auto sacramental.* Edición facsimilar del ms. Res. 72 de la Biblioteca Nacional (Madrid: Espasa Calpe, 1980).
75. Shergold and Varey, 'Autos sacramentales in Madrid, 1644', 62.
76. For more details, see Cotarelo, *Ensayo*, pp. 239–40, and Wilson, 'Un memorial perdido', pp. 812–14.
77. The chronology of the closures of the 1640s, and the motives and actions of those who engineered them, has been studied by Malcolm, 'Public Morality and the Closure of the Theatres'.
78. Preserved in AHN, Consejos, Libro 649: see Jaime Moll, 'De la continuación de las partes de comedias de Lope de Vega a las partes colectivas', in *Homenaje a Alonso Zamora Vicente: Literatura española de los siglos XVI–XVII* (Madrid, Castalia, 1992), vol. II (III), pp. 199–211.
79. Pérez Pastor, *Documentos*, pp. 126–7.
80. '... en ocasion de pasar a Italia con el Duque de Alba al Reyno de Sicilia por cedula de 2 de Junio de 646' ('on the occasion of travelling to Italy with the Duke of Alba, to the Kingdom of Sicily, by the warrant of 2 June 1646'): Wilson, 'Un memorial perdido', p. 816.
81. Zabaleta's handwriting in his manuscript of *La honra vive en los muertos* (BNE, MS Res. 62, written for Ascanio in 1643, so contemporary), is quite different from those in Act I of *Troya*.
82. See J. E. Varey and N. D. Shergold, 'Sobre la fecha de *Troya abrasada*, de Zabaleta y Calderón', in G. Mancini (ed.), *Miscellanea di studi ispanici* (Madrid: Istituto di Letteratura Spagnola e Ispano-Americana, 1963), vol. VI, pp. 287–97.
83. *Troya abrasada*, de Pedro Calderón de la Barca y Juan de Zabaleta, ed. George Tyler Northup, *RevHisp* 29 (1913), 234: 'A modern reader, familiar with the classics, cannot pardon the strange liberties taken with the story of the fall of Troy.'

CHAPTER 15. A TIME TO MOURN

1. Pérez Pastor, *Documentos*, pp. 118–19; P. 5548, Juan Martínez del Portillo, 1638–42, fol. 3, AHP, Madrid.
2. Pérez Pastor, *Documentos*, pp. 128–9.
3. Ibid., pp. 129–30.
4. Wilson, 'Un memorial perdido', p. 807.
5. Pérez Pastor, *Documentos*, pp. 164–5.
6. Wilson, 'Un memorial perdido', pp. 807–8.
7. González Dávila, *Teatro de las grandezas*, p. 316. The other source is a manuscript, quoted by Elliott, *The Count-Duke of Olivares*, p. 136 and n. 22.
8. Brown, *Velázquez*, pp. 187–8, 215.
9. I should mention the portrait owned by the Marqués de Salvatierra, and preserved in his house in Ronda, since it seems not to have been recorded previously. It appears to be an eighteenth-century copy of an earlier likeness.
10. Reproduced in *Calderón de la Barca y la España del Barroco* (2000), p. 52.
11. Pérez Pastor, *Documentos*, p. 255.

12. See José López-Rey, *Velázquez: A Catalogue Raisonné*, 2 vols. (Cologne: Taschen, 1996), vol. I, p. 147; vol. II, pp. 224–5.
13. Ellis Kirkham Waterhouse, *Eighteen Paintings from the Wellington Gift* (London: Arts Council of Great Britain, 1949), p. 12.
14. Enriqueta Harris, 'Velázquez's Apsley House Portrait: An Identification', *BM* 120 (1978), 304. The portrait was a gift from Ferdinand VII to the Duke of Wellington, who recovered it from Joseph Buonaparte after the battle of Vitoria (1813).
15. See José Gudiol, *Velázquez 1599–1660* (London: Secker & Warburg, 1974), p. 211.
16. Pérez Pastor, *Documentos*, p. 375.
17. This portrait is now in the Museo Lázaro Galdiano, Madrid, but it is of the eighteenth century: see *Calderón de la Barca y la España del Barroco* (2000), p. 281.
18. For all these documents, see Pérez Pastor, *Documentos*, pp. 130–40.
19. Ibid., pp. 140–50.
20. Miguel Cid, *Justas sagradas* (Seville: Simón Fajardo, 1647).
21. Pérez Pastor, *Documentos*, pp. 156–7.
22. See ibid., pp. 93, 152–3, for his administration of the property of Pedro de Porres and Juan Díaz de Bazterra.
23. Ibid., pp. 152–3.
24. Ibid., pp. 158–9 (the death certificate).
25. Ibid., p. 153.
26. Parker, *The Mind and Art of Calderón*, pp. 171–3.
27. Pérez Pastor, *Documentos*, p. 246n.
28. Ibid., pp. 161–2.
29. Ibid., p. 224.
30. Ibid., pp. 197–9.
31. Ibid., p. 241. The same document indicates that Don Pedro was in Toledo at this time.
32. Ibid., pp. 231–2, 233, 235.
33. *Calderón de la Barca y la España del Barroco* (2000), p. 232, although there were fourteen, not twelve, a number confirmed by the inventory of José's possessions of 9 May 1658: Pérez Pastor, *Documentos*, pp. 254–5.
34. The will is in Pérez Pastor, *Documentos*, pp. 226–36. Quotations are from pp. 227, 231–2, 233, 235, 236.
35. Ibid., pp. 252–3, 442–4.
36. Ibid., pp. 237, 246.
37. See Davies, *A Poet at Court*, p. 205.
38. See Francisco Silvela, *Cartas de la Venerable Sor María de Ágreda y del Señor Rey Don Felipe IV*, 2 vols. (Madrid: Sucesores de Rivadeneyra, 1885–6); and T. D. Kendrick, *Mary of Agreda: The Life and Legend of a Spanish Nun* (London: Routledge & Kegan Paul, 1967).
39. Ramón Ezquerra Abadía, *La conspiración del duque de Híjar* (Madrid: Librería Horizonte, 1934).

40. Pérez Pastor, *Documentos*, pp. 127–8.
41. J. E. Varey and N. D. Shergold (with the collaboration of Charles Davis), *Comedias en Madrid: 1603–1709* (London: Tamesis, 1989) (Fuentes para la Historia del Teatro en España 9), p. 129. See also Ana Elejabeitia, 'La transmisión textual de *La más hidalga hermosura*', *Letras de Deusto* 51 (1991), 53–65. The text is most readily available in Francisco de Rojas Zorrilla, *Comedias escogidas*, ed. Ramón de Mesonero Romanos (Madrid: Rivadeneyra, 1849) (BAE, vol. LIV), pp. 507–26.
42. Pellicer, *Avisos*, vol. I, p. 519 (14 June 1644).
43. Varey and Shergold, *Comedias en Madrid: 1603–1709*, p. 186.
44. A. A. Parker, *Los autos sacramentales de Calderón de la Barca*, trans. Francisco García Sarriá (Barcelona: Ariel, 1983), pp. 248–50.
45. Antonio Regalado, *Calderón: Los orígenes de la modernidad en la España del Siglo de Oro*, 2 vols. (Barcelona: Destino, 1995), vol. II, pp. 335–6.
46. Edward M. Wilson, *Spanish and English Literature of the 16th and 17th Centuries* (Cambridge: Cambridge University Press, 1980), p. 66.
47. Pedro Calderón de la Barca, *The Painter of His Dishonour / El pintor de su deshonra*, ed. A. K. G. Paterson (Warminster: Aris & Phillips, 1991), p. 5.
48. See *Cada uno para sí*, a critical edition by José M. Ruano de la Haza (Kassel: Reichenberger, 1982) (Teatro del Siglo de Oro, Ediciones Críticas 1), lines 265–74, and pp. 27, 99; for *También hay duelo*, see Calderón, *Tercera parte de comedias*, ed. Cruickshank, pp. xxviii–xxix.
49. For the reference to *Dicha y desdicha del nombre*, see J. E. Varey and N. D. Shergold, 'Un pleito teatral de 1660', *Hispanófila* 15 (1962), 9–27 (11): the document gives the title as *Dicha y desdicha del hombre*; the play is unlikely to have been brand new. For *Mujer, llora y vencerás*, see Pérez Pastor, *Documentos*, p. 267.

CHAPTER 16. BEGINNING TO RECOVER

1. In any case, there is a possible reference to the play under the title *La exaltación de la cruz* in *La Aurora en Copacabana* (?*c.* 1661): see the edition of Ezra S. Engling (London: Tamesis, 1994), line 1537.
2. Cotarelo, *Ensayo*, pp. 280–1.
3. See p. 392, nn. 27 and 29.
4. The *tasa*, the last preliminary document, is dated 26 August 1652, more than three months after the last approbation, which is of 24 May. This period was just right for the press to set and print one play per week.
5. Hilborn, *Chronology*, pp. 46–7.
6. Pereda and Marías (eds.), *El atlas del rey planeta*, maps 75 and 79 and pp. 353, 354.
7. Shergold, *Spanish Stage*, p. 304, n. 2. For the relationship between the two versions of the play, see Bacalski, 'A Critical Edition of *El jardín de Falerina*'.
8. Pedro Calderón de la Barca, *El purgatorio de San Patricio*, ed. J. M. Ruano (Liverpool: Liverpool University Press, 1988), line 1065. The inspiration for this

mirror in the shield was probably that moment in the Perseus myth when the hero uses Athene's polished shield to avoid looking directly at the Gorgon as he kills her (or, as in some versions, to allow her to turn herself to stone). When Calderón staged the Perseus myth in the play and *auto Andrómeda y Perseo*, Perseo's shield was a mirror, and the sight of herself so weakened Medusa that Perseo was able to kill her. Cf. Caravaggio's *Head of Medusa* (1598–9) in Simon Schama, *Simon Schama's Power of Art* (London: BBC Books, 2006), p. 36 and illustration, p. 37.

9. Calderón, *Obras completas*, II, 1893b.
10. See D. W. Cruickshank, '*Ut pictura poesis*: Calderón's Picturing of Myth', in Isabel Torres (ed.), *Rewriting Classical Mythology in the Hispanic Baroque* (Woodbridge: Tamesis, 2007), pp. 156–70 (pp. 164–8).
11. Jonathan Brown, *Images and Ideas in Seventeenth-Century Spanish Painting* (Princeton: Princeton University Press, 1978), p. 99.
12. Sebastian Neumeister, *Mito clásico y ostentación: Los dramas mitológicas de Calderón* (Kassel: Reichenberger, 2000), pp. 297–311 (first published as *Mythos und Repräsentation* (Munich: Wilhelm Fink, 1978)).
13. Calderón, *Comedias*, ed. Hartzenbusch, vol. IV, p. 358a (my italics). Most editions omit the *loa*.
14. N. D. Shergold and J. E. Varey, *Representaciones palaciegas 1603–1699: estudio y documentos* (London: Tamesis, 1982) (Fuentes para la Historia del Teatro I), p. 133. See also J. E. Varey, '*Andromeda y Perseo*, comedia y loa de Calderón: Afirmaciones artisticoliterarias y políticas', *Revista de Musicología* 10 (1987), 529–45 (542).
15. Pérez Pastor, *Documentos*, p. 243. The theatre is not named.
16. B. B. Ashcom, 'The Two Versions of Calderón's *El conde Lucanor*', *HR* 41 (1973), 151–60; L. Montaral and M. Vitse, 'Para una edición de *El conde Lucanor* de Calderón de la Barca', *Segismundo* 4, nos. 7–8 (1968), 51–70.
17. *Quarta parte* (1672), 2¶4^{v}.
18. One of the forty titles was *Los empeños que se ofrecen*, but this was his own play *Los empeños de un acaso*.
19. Stage directions are quoted from the 1672 edition, since modern editors are inclined to tamper with them.
20. Ana Caro de Mallén, *El conde Partinuplés*, ed. L. Luna (Kassel: Reichenberger, 1993), p. 94.
21. I thank Professor David Hook for reminding me of this play, which, like *El conde Lucanor*, has some features in common with *La vida es sueño*, apart from Rosaura.
22. See Antonio de León Pinelo, *Anales de Madrid (desde el año 447 al de 1658)* (Madrid: IEM, 1971), pp. 351–2, for the premiere (18 May 1653); for this scene, see Rus Solera López, 'El retrete de Dánae en la comedia *Las fortunas de Andrómeda y Perseo*: problemas textuales y escenográficos', in Ignacio Arellano (ed.), *Calderón 2000: Homenaje a Kurt Reichenberger en su 80 cumpleaños*, 2 vols. (Kassel: Reichenberger, 2002), vol. I, pp. 509–24.
23. See Harold E. Wethey, *The Paintings of Titian*, vol. III: *The Mythological and Historical Paintings* (London: Phaidon, 1975), pp. 133–5, for the various rooms

which housed the canvas during Calderón's lifetime. Phyllis Dearborn Massar, 'Scenes for a Calderón Play by Baccio del Bianco', *Master Drawings*, 15 (1977), 365–75, plates 21–31, publishes the drawings made for this performance. For the paintings and other décor of the *alcázar*, see Orso, *Philip IV and the Decoration of the Alcázar*.

24. Available in facsimile: *El agua mansa, edició facsímil del manuscrit autògraf, generalment conegut amb el títol Guárdate del agua mansa* (Barcelona: Diputació de Barcelona / Institut del Teatre, 1981).
25. D. W. Cruickshank, 'Notes on Calderonian Chronology and the Calderonian Canon', in *Estudios sobre Calderón y el teatro de la edad de oro: Homenaje a Kurt y Roswitha Reichenberger*, ed. Francisco Mundi Pedret (Barcelona: Promociones y Publicaciones Universitarias, 1989), pp. 19–36 (p. 30).
26. See *El agua mansa / Guárdate del agua mansa*, edición crítica de las dos versiones por Ignacio Arellano y Víctor García Ruiz (Kassel: Reichenberger; Murcia: Universidad de Murcia, 1989) (Teatro del Siglo de Oro, Ediciones Críticas 23).
27. References are to the Arellano / García Ruiz edition, and to *El agua mansa, edició facsímil*.
28. Calderón's only other Toribio is a peasant in *La devoción de la cruz*. See pp. 191–2 and n. 27 above.
29. An untranslatable pun: 'acción cortesana' means 'courteous act'; the response, 'it smacks to me rather of sickly court' plays on 'corte sana', 'healthy court'.
30. See Américo Castro and Hugo A. Rennert, *Vida de Lope de Vega (1562–1635)* (Salamanca: Anaya, 1969), pp. 342–3; also p. 343, n. 48, quoting Menéndez y Pelayo: 'Los peores son los de Calderón' ('Calderón's are the worst').
31. For the tradition of the *montañés* as a figure of fun, see p. 374, n. 28 above. Compare, however, Gareth A. Davies, 'The Country Cousin at Court: A Study of Antonio de Mendoza's *Cada loco con su tema* and Manuel Bretón de los Herreros' *El pelo de la dehesa*', in Margaret A. Rees (ed.), *Leeds Papers on Hispanic Drama* (Leeds: Trinity and All Saints, 1991), pp. 43–60.
32. E. Cotarelo y Mori, 'La bibliografía de Moreto', *BRAE* 14 (1927), 449–94 (479); see also his 'Catálogo descriptivo de la gran colección de "Comedias escogidas" que consta de cuarenta y ocho volúmenes, impresos de 1652 a 1704', *BRAE* 18 (1931), 232–80, 418–68, 583–636, 772–826 (460–2). The play was printed in Moreto's *Segunda parte* (Valencia: Benito Macé, 1676), a volume often faked by means of collections of *sueltas*.
33. Ruth Lee Kennedy, 'Moreto's Span of Dramatic Activity', *HR* 5 (1937), 170–2 (170–1).
34. Frank P. Casa, *The Dramatic Craftsmanship of Moreto* (Cambridge, MA: Harvard University Press, 1966) (Harvard Studies in Romance Languages 29), pp. 117–44.
35. Shergold and Varey, *Los autos*, pp. 74–5.
36. The complete letter is in Pérez Pastor, *Documentos*, pp. 161–2.
37. Shergold and Varey, *Los autos*, pp. 83–4. See also their 'Un documento nuevo sobre D. Pedro Calderón de la Barca', *BH* 62 (1960), 432–7.

38. Davis and Varey, *Actividad teatral*, vol. 1, p. 306; Pérez Pastor, *Documentos*, p. 159.
39. *Obras completas*, III, 424a.
40. J. E. Varey and A. M. Salazar, 'Calderón and the Royal Entry of 1649', *HR* 34 (1966), 1–26 (4).
41. *Autos sacramentales. Con quatro comedias nuevas, y sus loas, y entremeses* (Madrid: María de Quiñones, 1655), fols. 30–3. There is no modern edition of the *loa*, although a facsimile reprint of the whole volume has been announced by Georg Olms (Hildesheim). I quote from the edition of the *auto* by Fernando Plata Parga (Kassel: Reichenberger; Pamplona: Universidad de Navarra, 1998), p. 13.
42. Pérez Pastor, *Documentos*, pp. 166–8.
43. Shergold and Varey, *Los autos*, pp. 87–8.
44. Cotarelo, *Ensayo*, p. 290, n. 1, gives the details.
45. Shergold and Varey, *Los autos*, p. 94. The 1650 documents do not name the *autos*, but 1650 was a Holy Year.
46. Hilborn, *Chronology*, pp. 42, 49.
47. Shergold and Varey, *Representaciones palaciegas*, p. 239.
48. *Don Quijote*, II, 71, p. 1201.
49. James Casey, *Early Modern Spain: A Social History* (London: Routledge, 1999), p. 122.
50. A play on Veinticuatro (twenty-four) and 'veinticinco' (twenty-five).
51. See Wilson and Sage, *Poesías líricas*, p. 103.
52. Hilborn, *Chronology*, pp. 57–8.
53. T. B. Barclay, 'Dos *Maestros de danzar*', in A. David Kossoff and José Amor y Vázquez (eds.), *Homenaje a William L. Fichter: estudios sobre el teatro antiguo hispánico y otros ensayos* (Madrid: Castalia, 1971), pp. 71–80.
54. Pellicer, *Avisos*, vol. 1, p. 221 (23 April 1641).
55. Cotarelo, *Ensayo*, p. 290, n. 1; p. 322.
56. Juan Isidro Fajardo, *Titulos de todas las comedias que en verso español y portugues se han impresso hasta el año 1716*, MS 14706, BNE.
57. Francisco Medel del Castillo, *Índice general alfabético de todos los títulos de comedias* (Madrid: Alfonso de Mora, 1735); reprinted by J. M. Hill in *Revue Hispanique* 75 (1929), 144–369 (260).
58. Hilborn, *Chronology*, pp. 60–2.
59. See D. W. Cruickshank, 'The Lovers of Teruel: A "Romantic" Story', *MLR* 88 (1993), 881–93.
60. For the Góngora and Lope lines, see Wilson and Sage, *Poesías líricas*, pp. 13, 100–1.
61. Cotarelo, *Ensayo*, p. 290.
62. León Pinelo, *Anales*, p. 348.
63. Pedro Calderón de la Barca, *Cada uno para sí: A Critical Edition, with Introduction, Including a Study of the Transmission of the Text, and Notes*, by José M. Ruano de la Haza (Kassel: Reichenberger), 1982), p. 99.
64. Hilborn, *Chronology*, pp. 58–9. The critical edition, *El postrer duelo de España*, edited with introduction and notes by Guy Rossetti (London: Tamesis, 1979) (Serie B, Textos, 23), does not improve on Hilborn's guess.

65. León Pinelo, *Anales*, pp. 351–2.
66. Joseph de Casanova, *Primera parte del arte de escrivir todas formas de letras* (Madrid: Diego Díaz de la Carrera, 1650).
67. Reproduced in Cruickshank, 'Calderón's Handwriting', p. 66.
68. Printed in Simón Díaz, 'Textos dispersos' (1959), p. 116.
69. The title is a play on the 'precious pearl' and St Margaret, another Christian virgin supposedly martyred in early Christian Antioch. It is just possible that the play was composed to celebrate the birth of the Infanta Margarita (12 July 1651); in Calderón's act, a stage direction reads '*Cae y mantiénese sobre las aguas del estanque*' ('*He falls and is suspended above the water of the lake*'), which suggests that performance took place on or beside the Retiro lake, i.e., before a royal audience.
70. For a summary of the contents, see Sánchez Alonso, *Impresos de los siglos XVI y XVII*, pp. 278–80.
71. Cotarelo, *Ensayo*, pp. 278–80, quoting both Vera Tassis and Lara.
72. Varey and Salazar, 'Calderón and the Royal Entry'; but they reject the possibility that those working out the accounts were confused (23).
73. *Entrada de la Reyna D^{a}. Mariana*, MS 18717^{28}, BNE, fols. 255–61 (fol. 257^{r-v}). I owe this reference to Edward Wilson.
74. *Noticia*, pp. 107–8, 111–14. I owe this suggestion to Edward Wilson. See also Varey and Salazar, 'Calderón and the Royal Entry', p. 25, n. 65a.
75. Varey and Salazar, 'Calderón and the Royal Entry', 23.

CHAPTER 17. EPILOGUE: THE GLORIES OF THE WORLD

1. See Hannah E. Bergman, 'Ironic views of marriage in Calderón', in M. D. McGaha (ed.), *Approaches to the Theater of Calderón* (Washington: University Press of America, 1981), pp. 65–76, which suggests that plays written after 1650 show negative aspects of matrimony (p. 74).
2. Cotarelo, *Ensayo*, p. 285.
3. Pérez Pastor, *Documentos*, pp. 176–82. Ana's father was the poet's uncle Andrés González de Henao.
4. Pérez Pastor, *Documentos*, pp. 163–4.
5. AHN, Letra C, núm. 37, fol. 324: see Cotarelo, *Ensayo*, p. 286 and n. 1.
6. Ricardo del Arco y Garay, *La erudición española en el siglo XVII y el cronista de Aragón Andrés de Uztarroz*, 2 vols. (Madrid: Instituto Jerónimo de Zurita, 1950), vol. II, p. 746.
7. Pérez Pastor, *Documentos*, p. 191.
8. Ibid., pp. 191–5.
9. 'No ya la voz de la sagrada historia', in Alonso de Alarcón (ed.), *Corona sepulcral: Elogios en la muerte de D. Martin Suarez de Alarcon* [Madrid, n. p., tasa dated January 1653], 41^{v}: printed in Cotarelo, *Ensayo*, p. 292 n. 4.
10. There were no *autos* for the years 1666 to 1669 inclusive, the period of mourning for the death of Philip IV. The first court play in this period was planned for Mariana's birthday on 22 December 1669, but the title is not

known. The public theatres opened in 1667, but Calderón was no longer writing for them: J. E. Varey, 'La minoría de Carlos II y la prohibición de comedias de 1665–1667', in Pedro Peira (ed.), *Homenaje a Alonso Zamora Vicente*, 6 vols. (Madrid: Castalia, 1988–96), vol. III: *Literatura española de los siglos XVI–XVII*, I, pp. 351–7.

11. See especially Susana Hernández Araico, 'Coriolanus and Calderón's Royal Matronalia', in *New Historicism and the Comedia: Poetics, Politics and Praxis*, ed. José A. Madrigal (Boulder, CO: Society of Spanish and Spanish-American Studies, 1997), pp. 149–66; and Greer, *The Play of Power*.
12. Pedro Calderón de la Barca, *Fieras afemina Amor*, ed. Edward M. Wilson (Kassel: Reichenberger, 1984), lines 1465–7. Juan Rana (Cosme Pérez) was a famous *gracioso*, for whom numerous parts were written.
13. See Pedro Calderón de la Barca, *Entremeses, jácaras y mojigangas*, ed. Evangelina Rodríguez and Antonio Tordera (Madrid: Castalia, 1982), p. 369 (and, for the text, pp. 371–84); also Rodríguez's 'Calderón se quita la máscara: Teatro cómico breve', in Aurora Egido (ed.), *Lecciones calderonianas* (Zaragoza: Ibercaja, 2001), pp. 105–23 (pp. 122–3).
14. Pérez Pastor, *Documentos*, pp. 210–25.
15. Ibid., pp. 224–5.
16. Ibid., pp. 202–3; Cotarelo, *Ensayo*, pp. 291–2.
17. Pérez Pastor, *Documentos*, pp. 204–5.
18. Antonio de León Pinelo, *Anales de Madrid (desde el año 447 al de 1658)* (Madrid: IEM, 1971), pp. 351–2.
19. Cotarelo, *Ensayo*, p. 295, n. 2.
20. Gallardo, *Ensayo de una biblioteca española*, vol. III, cols. 901–2, quoting the *Libro de entradas desde 1652* of the Toledo Refugio.
21. See fol. 6[r] of the poem in *Obras menores*.
22. For the work of the Madrid Hermandad, see William J. Callahan, *La Santa y Real Hermandad del Refugio y Piedad de Madrid, 1618–1832* (Madrid: CSIC, 1980).
23. François Bertaut, *Journal du voyage d'Espagne, contenant une description fort exacte de ses royaumes et de ses principales villes, avec l'estat du gouvernement et plusieurs traittés curieux* (first published Paris: Denys Thierry, 1669), ed. F. Cassan, in *RevHisp* 47 (1919), 1–308: 'L'aprésdisnée, luy [= the marqués de Heliche] & monsieur de Barriere me vinrent prendre pour aller à une vieille Comedie qu'on avoit rejoüée de nouveau, qui ne valoit rien, quoy qu'elle fust de *D. Pedro Calderon*. I'allay aussi voir cet Auteur que est le plus grand Poëte & le plus bel esprit qu'ils ayent presentement. Il est Chevalier de l'ordre de saint Iacques & Chapelain de la Chapelle *de los Reyes* à Tolède, mais à sa conversation je vis bien qu'il ne sçavoit pas grand'chose, quoy qu'il soit déjà tout blanc' ('After lunch, he and M. de Barrière came to fetch me to go to an old play which had been put on again, and which was worthless, despite being by D. Pedro Calderón. I also went to see that author, who is the greatest poet and the finest wit they have at present. He is a knight of Santiago and a chaplain of *Los reyes de Toledo*, but I saw clearly from his conversation that he knew little, although his hair is already quite white': pp. 151–2).

24. For the servants, see Don Pedro's will (Pérez Pastor, *Documentos*, pp. 387–8); for the paintings, see the inventory (ibid., pp. 425–7), and p. 117 above.
25. 'Si a la Naue de Argos, por primera ...', in Pedro Cubero Sebastián, *Peregrinación del mundo* (Madrid: Juan García Infanzón, 1680); printed in Simón Díaz, 'Textos dispersos' (1962), p. 119.
26. Juan de Matos Fragoso, *Primera parte de comedias* (Madrid: Julián de Paredes, 1658).
27. *Papel de don Pedro Calderón de la Barca, al Patriarcha*. See Edward M. Wilson, 'Calderón y el Patriarca', in Karl-Hermann Körner and Klaus Rühl (eds.), *Studia iberica: Festschrift für Hans Flasche* (Bern and Munich: Francke, 1973), pp. 697–703, which offers the best text. The reference appears to be to *Darlo todo y no dar nada*, performed on 22 December 1651, and for which Antonio de Solís wrote a *loa*: the version published in his *Varias poesías* (1692) has the heading 'Representòse en la fiesta de los años, del parto, y de la mejoria de la Reyna' ('Performed in the celebration for the birthday and delivery of the queen, and the improvement in her health'); it refers to 'Margarita, que naciste | para ser preciosa' ('Margarita, who wast born to be precious'). The Infanta Margarita was born on 12 July 1651. Wilson points out that while this chronology is the most likely, it is just possible that the reference is to *La fiera, el rayo y la piedra*, which would imply that the letter was written a year later, in the spring of 1653. Cf. A. A. Parker's edition of *No hay más fortuna que Dios* (Manchester: Manchester University Press, 1949), p. xiv.
28. Cotarelo, *Ensayo*, p. 287.
29. See Parker's edition of *No hay más fortuna que Dios*, p. xii, n. 2.
30. See n. 13 above. The Fundación Castro plans to publish a volume containing the minor pieces, poems, prose works and letters, edited by Agustín de la Granja.
31. Edward M. Wilson published eight poems in 'Some Unpublished Works by Don Pedro Calderón de la Barca', in *Homage to John M. Hill: In memoriam* (Bloomington: Indiana University, 1968), pp. 7–18. They have not been examined in this book because they are not accurately datable, although all of them, by the subject-matter, precede his ordination. One of them can be dated to 'before 1637'.
32. For the *memorias de apariencias*, see Lara Escudero and Rafael Zafra, *Memorias de apariencias y otros documentos sobre los autos de Calderón de la Barca* (Kassel: Reichenberger; Pamplona: Universidad de Navarra, 2003).
33. See p. 350, n. 37.
34. Latham and Matthews (eds.), *The Diary of Samuel Pepys*, vol. IV, pp. 8, 16; vol. V, p. 215; vol. VII, p. 255.
35. See Edward M. Wilson and Don W. Cruickshank, *Samuel Pepys's Spanish Plays* (London: Bibliographical Society, 1980).
36. José Blanco White, *Cartas de España*, trad. Antonio Garnica (Madrid: Alianza, 1972), pp. 250–1. He is referring to the late eighteenth century. See Jaime Moll, 'Un tomo facticio de pliegos sueltos y el origen de las "relaciones de comedias"', *Segismundo* 12 (1976), 143–67.

37. See Ada M. Coe, *Catálogo bibliográfico y crítico de las comedias anunciadas en los periódicos de Madrid desde 1661 hasta 1819* (Baltimore, MD: Johns Hopkins University Press, 1935).
38. Calderón, *Primera parte de autos sacramentales* (Madrid: José Fernández de Buendía, 1677), ¶7^{v}.
39. Gerardo Diego, *Antología poética en honor de Góngora* (Madrid: Alianza, 1979), p. 37; first published 1927.
40. See in particular Anthony J. Cascardi, *The Limits of Illusion: A Critical Study of Calderón* (Cambridge: Cambridge University Press, 1984), p. 130; and James E. Maraniss, *On Calderón* (Columbia, MO: University of Missouri Press, 1978, p. 87.
41. John V. Bryans, *Calderón de la Barca: Imagery, Rhetoric and Drama* (London: Tamesis, 1977), p. 180. See also in particular William R. Blue, *The Development of Imagery in Calderón's 'comedias'* (York, SC: Spanish Literature Publishing Co., 1983), and Sloman, *The Dramatic Craftsmanship.*
42. Sturgis E. Leavitt, 'Did Calderón Have a Sense of Humour?', in *Romance Studies Presented to William Morton Dey* (Chapel Hill: University of North Carolina Press, 1950) (University of North Carolina Studies in Romance Languages and Literatures 12), pp. 119–21. See also his 'The *gracioso* Takes the Audience into His Confidence', *BCom* 7 (1955), 27–9; and 'Humor in the *autos* of Calderón', *Hisp* 39 (1956), 137–44.
43. 'To swear like a trooper' in Spanish is 'jurar como un carretero', 'to swear like a carter'.
44. See Greer, *The Play of Power*, p. 130; and also Bergman, *The Art of Humour*, pp. 21–7.
45. See Rodríguez, 'Calderón se quita la máscara', p. 118 (*Entremés del reloj y genios de la venta*), or *El pintor de su deshonra.*
46. Gerald Brenan, *The Literature of the Spanish People from Roman Times to the Present Day* (Cambridge: Cambridge University Press, 1951), pp. 398, 407.
47. Jodi Campbell, *Monarchy, Political Culture and Drama in Seventeenth-Century Madrid: Theater of Negotiation* (Aldershot: Ashgate, 2006), p. 12. See also Dian Fox, *Kings in Calderón: A Study in Characterization and Political Theory* (London: Tamesis, 1986); and Stephen Rupp, *Allegories of Kingship: Calderón and the Anti-Machiavellian Tradition* (University Park, PA: Pennsylvania University Press, 1996).
48. Melveena McKendrick, *Theatre in Spain 1492–1700* (Cambridge: Cambridge University Press, 1989), p. 224.
49. Campbell, *Monarchy, Political Culture and Drama*, p. 148.
50. Shergold, *Spanish Stage*, p. 553.
51. For example, Regalado, in his *Calderón*, vol. 1, p. 87: 'No sería temerario aventurar la hipótesis de que, a fines de la década de los veinte y comienzos de la década de los treinta el joven dramaturgo se debatió agónicamente entre la fe y la razón.' ('It would not be rash to risk the hypothesis that, at the end of the 1620s and beginning of the 1630s, the young dramatist struggled agonisingly between faith and reason.')

52. A. A. Parker, *The Approach to the Spanish Drama of the Golden Age* (London: The Hispanic and Luso-Brazilian Councils, 1957) (Colección Diamante 6), p. 11.
53. Pascual Millán, 'Iconografía calderoniana', in *Homenaje a Calderón*, pp. 63–105 (p. 84).
54. His parents were Manuel de Padilla and Bernarda de Montalvo Calderón de la Barca.
55. Alan K. G. Paterson, 'The Great World of Don Pedro Calderón's Theatre and the Beyerlinck Connection', *Calderón 1600–1681: Quatercentenary Studies in Memory of John E. Varey*, *BHS* (Glasgow) 77 (2000), 237–53.
56. Pérez Pastor, *Documentos*, p. 376.
57. Ibid., p. 401. It is just possible that these were manuscript *autos*, although the phrase 'algun empleo de su ociosidad' suggests secular works. In 1682 Madrid Town Council, which had paid for them, asked Lozano to hand over *auto* manuscripts, which he agreed to do (ibid., p. 433). These may be the autograph fair copies now in the Biblioteca Histórica Municipal, Madrid. Pérez Pastor notes that there is no reference in Lozano's will to any Calderón papers (ibid., p. 401, n. 1).

Bibliography

UNPUBLISHED MATERIAL

Acevedo, Pedro Pablo de, *Comoediae, dialogi et orationes*, MS 9/2564, Real Academia de la Historia, Madrid.

Acquaviva, Claudio, 'Colegio Imperial de la Compañia de Jesus en Madrid', fols. 389–92, MS 18183, BNE.

Alcalá, Universidad de, Libros de matrículas, 1616, AHN.

Anon., *Entrada de la Reyna D^a^. Mariana* [1649], fols. 255–61, MS 18717[28], BNE.

Archivio di Stato, Firenze, filza 4.959, Mediceo.

Ayala Manrique, Juan Francisco de, *Noticias de Madrid desde el año de 1636 hasta el de 1638, y desde el año 1680 hasta el siglo presente*, por don – , y es su propio original. Recogidas por don Josef Antonio Armona, Corregidor de Madrid, MS 18447, BNE.

Bacalski, Robert Rudolf, 'A Critical Edition of *El jardín de Falerina* by Francisco de Rojas Zorrilla, Antonio Coello y Ochoa and Pedro Calderón de la Barca, with introduction and notes', unpublished doctoral dissertation (University of New Mexico, 1972) (based on MS 17320 of the BNE).

Barquín Amezcua, Ana María, 'Análisis textuales, historia de los textos, estilística y versificación en *La señora y la criada* y *El acaso y el error*', unpublished MA dissertation (University College Dublin, 1999).

Béjar, Juan de, 1614, unfoliated (24 Jan), AHP, Madrid (P. 4437).

Calderón de la Barca, Pedro, *licencia* and *privilegio* for *Tercera parte de comedias*, 7 March 1645: Consejos, Libro 649, AHN.

Order of Santiago documents: *expediente* 1394, Pruebas de Caballeros de la Orden de Santiago, 12/2/1, AHN.

Psiquis y Cupido (para Toledo), MS m.n.235, Archivo de la Villa, Madrid.

Calle, Juan de la, 1592, fols. 1372–3, AHP, Madrid (P. 1311).

Clarke, Sandra, 'Queens in Calderón: A Study of the Figure of the Queen in Selected Plays by Calderón de la Barca', unpublished MA dissertation (University College Dublin, 2000).

Fajardo, Juan Isidro, *Disertación sobre los autos sacramentales de don Pedro Calderón de la Barca*, MS 209, Biblioteca de Menéndez y Pelayo, Santander.

Títulos de todas las comedias que en verso español y portugues se han impresso hasta el año de 1716, MS 14706, BNE.

Gallo, Bartolomé, 1628–30, fol. 631, AHP, Madrid (P. 2709).
Gómez, Juan Manuel, 'A Critical Edition of Pedro Calderón de la Barca's *La gran Cenobia*, with Introduction and Notes', unpublished doctoral dissertation (University of Oregon, 1981).
Libro de los acuerdos del ayuntamiento de la villa de Yepes, 1636, 1637, 1638.
Lorenzana, Juan de, 1630–2, fol. 503, AHP, Madrid (P. 5611).
1630–2, fol. 680, AHP, Madrid (P. 5611).
Madrid, Mateo de, 1616–24, fols. 444–51, 452–9, AHP, Madrid (P. 5049).
1616–24, fols. 468–75, AHP, Madrid (P. 5049).
Magnier, Grace, 'The Assimilation of the Moriscos Reflected in Golden-Age Drama and in Selected Contemporary Writings', unpublished MA dissertation (University College Dublin, 1992).
Martínez del Portillo, Juan, 1637, fols. 1118, 1120, 1122, AHP, Madrid (P. 5546).
1639, fol. 280, AHP, Madrid (P. 5549).
1638–42, fol. 3, AHP, Madrid (P. 5548).
Pérez Alonso, F., Archivo de la Real Chancillería de Valladolid, ES.47186.ARCHV/1.3.2.1// Pleitos civiles, Caja 1802.0002, AHN.
Pineda, Juan de, 1640, fol. 311, AHP, Madrid (P. 7718).
Philip IV of Austria [authorisation for Calderón's ordination], Letra C, núm. 37, fol. 324, AHN.
Relacion general de los sucessos que ha avido en España, Flandes, Italia, y Alemania, y en otras partes, desde 1 de março de 1639 hasta fin de febrero de 1640 [?Madrid, 1640], fols. 172–81, MS 2370, BNE.
Salamanca, Universidad de: Archivo Histórico, Libros de Matrículas, 1616–17 (AUSA 342).
Testa, Francisco, 1616, fols. 202–13, AHP, Madrid (P. 2659).
1623, fols. 461r–482v, AHP, Madrid (P. 2671).
1623, fols. 1390–2, AHP, Madrid (P. 3597).
Velasco, Francisco de, *A D. Antonio del Castillo de Larzaval, décima*, MS poem in preliminaries of Santiago copy of Castillo de Larzával's *El Adonis*.

PAINTINGS, DRAWINGS, ENGRAVINGS

Alfaro, Juan de, *Don Pedro Calderón*, oil on canvas (?*c*. 1675).
Don Pedro Calderón, charcoal on paper (?*c*. 1675).
Anon., *La Calderona* (?*c*. 1629).
Lope de Vega.
Tirso de Molina.
Caravaggio (Michelangelo Merisi), *Head of Medusa* (1598–9).
Castelló, Félix, *Vista del alcázar* (seventeenth century).
El Greco, *Fray Hortensio Paravicino* (1609).
Eyck, Jan van, *The Arnolfini Family* (1434).
Forstman/Fosman, Gregorio, *Don Pedro Calderón* (1682).
Gómez de Mora, Juan, *alcázar* plan (1626).
staging of *autos* in the Plaza Mayor (1644).

Herrera, Francisco de, the Younger, *Salón dorado (c.* 1672).
Maíno, Juan Bautista, *The Recapture of Bahía* (1633–5).
Pantoja de la Cruz, Juan, *Philip III* (1606).
Pereda y Salgado, Antonio de, *Don Pedro Calderón* (?1670s).
Rubens, Sir Peter Paul, *Duke of Lerma* (1603).
Titian (Tiziano Vecellio di Gregorio), *Danaë and the Shower of Gold* (?1549–50).
Diana and Actaeon (1559).
The Rape of Europa (1559–62).
Velázquez, Diego de, *Caballero desconocido* (Wellington Museum, Apsley House) (?1640s).
La cena de Emaús (*c.* 1618).
El Conde-Duque de Olivares (Hispanic Society of America, ?*c.* 1626).
El Conde-Duque de Olivares (Hermitage, 1637–8).
Cristo en casa de Marta (1618).
D. Diego de Corral (?*c.* 1631).
La expulsión de los moriscos por Felipe III (lost, 1627).
La fábula de Aracne (*Las hilanderas*) (*c.* 1656).
Felipe IV (1623).
Francisco de Quevedo (*c.* 1631) (copies of lost Velázquez original).
Imposición de la casulla a San Ildefonso (?*c.* 1622).
Inocencio X (1649–50).
Juan de Pareja (1649–50).
Juan Martínez Montañés (1635–6).
Marte (1640s).
Las meninas (*c.* 1656).
El poeta don Luis de Góngora y Argote (1622).
La rendición de Bredá (?1634–5).
San Antonio Abad y San Pablo ermitaño (by 1633).
Veronese, Paolo, *Venus and Adonis* (*c.* 1580).
Villafranca, Pedro de, *Don Pedro Calderón* (1676).

PRINTED MATERIAL

Ackroyd, Peter, *Shakespeare: The Biography* (London: Chatto & Windus, 2005).
Aguilar Piñal, Francisco, *Bibliografía de autores españoles del siglo XVIII*, 10 vols. (Madrid: CSIC, 1981–2001).
Alarcón, Alonso de (ed.), *Corona sepulcral, elogios en la muerte de D. Martin Suarez de Alarcon* [Madrid, n.p., ?1652].
Alarcos, Emilio, 'Los sermones de Paravicino', *RFE* 24 (1937), 162–97, 249–319.
Albrecht, Jane, *Irony and Theatricality in Tirso de Molina* (Ottawa: Dovehouse, 1994).
Alcalá Zamora, J., 'Individuo e historia en la estructura teatral de *El Tuzaní de las Alpujarras*', in Luciano García Lorenzo (ed.), *Calderón: Actas del Congreso Internacional sobre Calderón y el Teatro Español del Siglo de Oro (Madrid 8–13 de junio de 1981)*, 3 vols. (Madrid: CSIC, 1983), vol. 1, pp. 343–63.

Alfay, Josef (ed.), *Poesías varias de grandes ingenios españoles* (Zaragoza: Juan de Ybar, 1654).

Allen, John J., *The Reconstruction of a Spanish Golden Age Playhouse: El Corral del Príncipe 1583–1744* (Gainesville: University of Florida, 1983). (*See also* Ruano de la Haza, J. M., and Allen, John J.)

Alonso Cortés, Narciso, 'Algunos datos relativos a D. Pedro Calderón', *RFE* 2 (1915), 41–51.

'Carta de dote de la madre de Calderón de la Barca', *Revista Histórica* 2 (1925), 158–67.

'Genealogía de D. Pedro Calderón', *BRAE* 31 (1951), 299–309.

Alvar Ezquerra, Alfredo, *El nacimiento de una capital europea: Madrid entre 1561 y 1606* (Madrid: Turner, 1989).

Álvarez Baena, José Antonio, *Hijos de Madrid, ilustres en santidad, dignidades, armas, ciencias y artes*, 4 vols. (Madrid: Benito Cano, 1789).

Amelang, James A. (ed.), *A Journal of the Plague Year: The Diary of the Barcelona Tanner Miquel Parets 1651* (New York and Oxford: Oxford University Press, 1991).

Anero Puente, Manuel de, *Luis Pérez el gallego, segunda parte* (Seville: Francisco de Leefdael, 1717).

Anon., *La estrella de Sevilla.*

El montañés en la corte.

El montañés y el estornudo.

El montañés y el vizcaíno.

'En Santa Gadea de Burgos' (ballad).

Lazarillo de Tormes (1554).

La Magdalena (*auto*, 1649) (lost).

La mojiganga de la boda (1638).

Noticia del recibimiento i entrada de la Reyna nuestra Señora Doña Maria-Ana de Austria en la muy noble i leal coronada Villa de Madrid (no imprint, but Madrid: Imprenta Real, 1650).

Antonio, Nicolás, *Bibliotheca Hispana Nova*: vol. I (Madrid: Joaquín de Ibarra, 1783); vol. II (Madrid: Viuda e Hijos de Joaquín de Ibarra, 1788).

Arco y Garay, Ricardo del, *La erudición española en el siglo XVII y el cronista de Aragón Andrés de Uztarroz*, 2 vols. (Madrid: Instituto Jerónimo de Zurita, 1950).

Arellano, Ignacio, 'Cervantes en Calderón', *Anales Cervantinos* 35 (1999), 9–35.

'*El árbol de mejor fruto* de Calderón y la leyenda del árbol de la cruz: contexto y adaptación', *Anuario Calderoniano* 1 (2008), 27–65.

Ariosto, Ludovico, *Orlando furioso* (1516, 1532).

Ashcom, B. B., 'The Two Versions of Calderón's *El conde Lucanor*', *HR* 41 (1973), 151–60.

Astrana Marín, Luis, *Vida heroica y ejemplar de Miguel de Cervantes Saavedra*, 7 vols. (Madrid: Instituto Editorial Reus, 1948–58).

Autos sacramentales. Con quatro comedias nuevas, y sus loas, y entremeses: Primera parte (Madrid: María de Quiñones, 1655). (Facsimile edition in preparation, Hildesheim: Georg Olms, forthcoming.)

Ávila Sotomayor, Hernando de ('Hernando de Ayora Valmisoto'), *El arbitro entre el marte frances y las vindicias gallicas* ('Pamplona': 'Carlos Juan', 1646).

Baignon, Jean, *Historia del emperador Carlo Magno y de los doce pares de Francia, y de la vatalla que hubo Oliveros con Fierabrás, rey de Alexandría*, trans. Nicolás Gazini de Piamonte (Alcalá: Sebastián Martínez, 1589).

Balderrábano, Francisco de (trans.), *Vida y muerte de S. Eloy, obispo de Noyons, abogado, y patron de los plateros. Escrito por San Audeno, y referido por Surio en Latin* (Madrid: Imprenta del Reyno, 1640).

Bances Candamo, Francisco, *Theatro de los theatros de los passados y presentes siglos*, prólogo, edición y notas de Duncan W. Moir (London: Tamesis, 1970).

Bandello, Matteo, *Historias tragicas exemplares: sacadas del Bandello verones. Nuevamente traduzidas de las que en lengua francesa adornaron Pierres Bonistan y Francisco de Belleforest* (Salamanca: Pedro Lasso, 1589).

Novelas morales, utiles por sus documentos, trans. Diego de Ágreda y Vargas (Madrid: Tomás Junti, 1620; Barcelona: Sebastián de Cormellas, 1620 and 1621; Valencia: Juan Crisóstomo Garriz, 1620).

Barclay, John, *Argenis* (Paris: Nicolas Buon, 1621).

Argenis [translated by] José Pellicer (Madrid: Luis Sánchez, 1626).

Argenis [translated by] Gabriel de Corral (Madrid: Juan González, 1626).

Barclay, T. B., 'Dos *Maestros de danzar*', in A. David Kossoff and José Amor y Vázquez (eds.), *Homenaje a William L. Fichter: estudios sobre el teatro antiguo hispánico y otros ensayos* (Madrid: Castalia, 1971), 71–80.

Barona de Valdivielso, Pedro, *Hospicio de S. Francisco* (Madrid: Luis Sánchez, 1609).

Barrera, Cayetano Alberto de la, *Catálogo bibliográfico y biográfico del teatro antiguo español desde sus orígenes hasta mediados del siglo XVIII* (Madrid: Rivadeneyra, 1860).

Belmonte Bermúdez, Luis de, Rojas Zorrilla, Francisco de, Calderón de la Barca, Pedro de, *El mejor amigo el muerto* (1635–6).

(attrib.), *La maestra de gracias* (printed 1657).

Benabu, Isaac, *On the Boards and in the Press: Calderón's* Las tres justicias en una (Kassel: Reichenberger, 1991). (Teatro del Siglo de Oro, Ediciones Críticas 18.)

Bergman, Hannah E., 'A Court Entertainment of 1638', *HR* 42 (1974), 67–81.

'Auto-definition of the *comedia de capa y espada*', *Hispanófila* (Especial) 1 (1974), 3–27.

'El "Juicio final de todos los poetas españoles muertos y vivos" (ms. inédito) y el certamen poético de 1638', *BRAE* 55 (1975), 551–610.

'Ironic Views of Marriage in Calderón', in M. D. McGaha (ed.), *Approaches to the Theater of Calderón* (Washington: University Press of America, 1981), pp. 65–76.

Luis Quiñones de Benavente y sus entremeses (Madrid: Castalia, 1965).

(ed.), *Ramillete de entremeses y bailes, nuevamente recogido de los mejores autores de España. Siglo XVII* (Madrid: Castalia, 1970).

Bergman, Ted L. L., *The Art of Humour in the* Teatro breve *and* Comedias *of Calderón de la Barca* (Woodbridge: Tamesis, 2003).

Bermúdez, Jerónimo ('Antonio de Silva'), *Nise laureada* (by 1575).
Primeras tragedias españolas (Madrid: Francisco Sánchez, 1577).
Bertaut, François, *Journal du voyage d'Espagne* (Paris: Denys Thierry, 1669).
Journal du voyage d'Espagne, contenant une description fort exacte de ses royaumes et de ses principales villes, avec l'estat du gouvernement et plusieurs traittés curieux, ed. F. Cassan, in *RevHisp* 47 (1919), 1–308.
Beyerlinck, Laurentius, *Magnum theatrum vitae humanae* (Cologne: for Antonius and Arnoldus Hierati, 1631).
Bigelow, G., 'Analysis of Calderón's *De un castigo, tres venganzas*: Structure, Theme, Language', in F. de Armas, D. Gitliz and J. A. Madrigal (eds.), *Critical Perspectives on Calderón de la Barca* (Lincoln, NB: Society of Spanish and Spanish-American Studies, 1981), pp. 13–37.
Blanco White, José, *Cartas de España*, trad. Antonio Garnica (Madrid: Alianza, 1972).
Blecua, J. M. (ed.), *Cancionero de 1628* (Madrid: Aguirre, 1945).
(ed.), *Poesías varias de grandes ingenios españoles* (Zaragoza: Heraldo de Aragón, 1946).
Blue, William R., 'Calderón's *Gustos y disgustos no son más que imaginación* and Some Remarks on New Historicism', in José A. Madrigal (ed.), *New Historicism and the* Comedia*: Poetics, Politics and Praxis* (Boulder, CO: Society of Spanish and Spanish-American Studies, 1997), pp. 29–39.
The Development of Imagery in Calderón's 'comedias' (York, SC: Spanish Literature Publishing Co., 1983).
Boiardo, Matteo, *Orlando innamorato* (1486).
Bovill, E. W., *The Battle of Alcazar* (London: Batchworth, 1952).
Brenan, Gerald, *The Literature of the Spanish People from Roman Times to the Present Day* (Cambridge: Cambridge University Press, 1951).
Brosse, [ ] de, *Les Innocens coupables* (Paris: A. de Sommaville, Augustin Courbé, T. Quinet and N. de Sercy, 1645).
Brown, Jonathan, *Images and Ideas in Seventeenth-Century Spanish Painting* (Princeton: Princeton University Press, 1978).
Velázquez: Painter and Courtier (New Haven and London: Yale University Press, 1986).
Brown, Jonathan, and Elliott, J. H., *A Palace for a King: The Buen Retiro and the Court of Philip IV*, 2nd edn (New Haven and London: Yale University Press, 2004). (First published in 1980.)
Bryans, John V., *Calderón de la Barca: Imagery, Rhetoric and Drama* (London: Tamesis, 1977).
Burton, Robert, *The Anatomy of Melancholy*, 3 vols. (London: Dent, 1968).
Butrón, Juan Alonso, *Epistola dirigida al Rey suplicando proteccion para la Academia de los Pintores* (n.p., n.d.).
Byron, William, *Cervantes: A Biography* (London: Cassel, 1979).
Caamaño Rojo, María J., El mayor monstruo del mundo *de Calderón de la Barca: estudio textual* (Santiago de Compostela: Universidade de Santiago de Compostela, 2001).
Caldera de Heredia, Gaspar, *Si los señores reyes de Castilla, por derecho hereditario de su real sangre, tienen virtud de curar energumenos y lançar espiritus* [?Seville, 1655].

Caldera Freile, Fernando, *Sermon predicado en … Santa Ana de los Minimos* (Alcalá: Viuda de Juan Gracián, 1622).

CALDERÓN

Calderón de la Barca y la España del Barroco: Sala de exposiciones de la Biblioteca Nacional del 16 de junio al 15 de agosto de 2000 (Madrid: Sociedad Estatal España Nuevo Milenio, 2000).

CALDERÓN, POEMS

Calderón de la Barca, Pedro, 'Al que nace glorioso', *canción* (1671).

'Aunque de glorias reviste', *glosa* (1622).

'Aunque nuestro humano ser' [décimas a la muerte de Juan Pérez de Montalbán], (1639).

'Aunque la persecución', *décima* (1622).

'Cantas de Adonis tú, mas tan bien cantas', *canción* (1632).

'Con el cabello erizado', *romance* (1622).

(attributable), 'Coronada de esperanzas', various metres, in *Noticia del recibimiento i entrada de la Reyna nuestra Señora Doña Maria-Ana de Austria en la muy noble i leal coronada Villa de Madrid* (1650).

'Coronadas de luz las sienes bellas', *canción* (1622).

'Cuanto la antigüedad dejó esparcido …', sonnet (1639).

'De cuantos artes, cuantas ciencias fueron …', sonnet (1650).

Elegía en la muerte del señor infante don Carlos, elegy in *tercetos* ('¡O rompa ya el silencio el dolor mío!') (1632).

'En la apacible Samaria', *romance* (1622).

En la muerte de la señora doña Inés Zapata, dedicada a doña María Zapata ('Sola esta vez quisiera'), elegy (by 1628).

'Estos útiles verdores', *décima* (?1630).

Exortación panegírica al silencio (*Psalle et sile*), various metres (1661, printed 1662).

'Funestas pompas, y cenizas frías', *octavas* (1640).

(attributable), '¡Ha, del coro de Himeneo', various metres, in *Noticia del recibimiento i entrada de la Reyna nuestra Señora Doña Maria-Ana de Austria en la muy noble i leal coronada Villa de Madrid* (1650).

'Hacer una traducción …', *décimas* (1640).

'Joven arrojo mal precipitado', sonnet (1671).

'La amistad que celebró', *décima* (1639).

'La que ves en piedad, en llama, en vuelo', sonnet (1622).

Lágrimas que vierte una alma arrepentida a la hora de la muerte ('Ahora, señor, ahora'), *romance* (1634).

'Los campos de Madrid, Isidro santo', sonnet (1620).

'No fatal te construya mauseolo', sonnet (1621).

'No ya la voz de la sagrada historia', sonnet (?1652).

Obra lírica, ed. Manuel de Montoliu (Barcelona: Montaner y Simón, 1943).

'¡Oh tú, temprano sol, que en el oriente …!', *tercetos* (1622).

Panegírico al Excelentíssimo Señor Don Juan Alfonso Enríquez de Cabrera y Colona, Almirante de Castilla, tercetos (1638).

Poesías inéditas de D. Pedro Calderón de la Barca, ed. F[elipe] P[icatoste], in Biblioteca Universal: Colección de los mejores autores antiguos y modernos, nacionales y extranjeros, tomo LXXI (Madrid: Imprenta de la Biblioteca Universal, 1881).

Respuesta de Don Pedro Calderón por los mismos consonantes ('Si Huertecilla está como le pintas', sonnet) (1637–40).

'Si a la Naue de Argos, por primera …', sonnet (1680).

'Si por la espada es inmortal la gloria', sonnet (1635).

'Si viste, o Licio, material Esfera', sonnet (1631).

'Tirana la idolatría', *quintillas* (1622).

'Tu sumo ingenio, tu agudeza suma', sonnet (?1639).

'Túrbase el sol, su luz se eclipsa cuanta', *octavas* (1620).

'Ya el trono de luz regía', *décimas* (1622).

CALDERÓN, DRAMATIC PIECES

A María el corazón (*auto*, 1664).

A secreto agravio, secreta venganza (1635).

El acaso y el error (?after 1650).

Afectos de odio y amor (?1658).

Agradecer y no amar (?1630s).

El agua mansa, edició facsímil del manuscrit autògraf, generalment conegut amb el títol Guárdate del agua mansa (Barcelona: Diputació de Barcelona / Institut del Teatre, 1981).

El agua mansa, / Guárdate del agua mansa, edición crítica de las dos versiones por Ignacio Arellano y Víctor García Ruiz (Kassel: Reichenberger/Murcia: Universidad de Murcia, 1989). (Teatro del Siglo de Oro, Ediciones Críticas 23.)

El alcaide de sí mismo (?1626–7).

El alcalde de Zalamea (?1636).

El alcalde de Zalamea, ed. Peter N. Dunn (Oxford: Pergamon, 1966).

Amar después de la muerte, see El Tuzaní de la Alpujarra.

Amigo, amante y leal (?1630–1).

Amor, honor y poder (1623).

Andrómeda y Perseo (1653).

Andrómeda y Perseo (*auto*, 1680).

Antes que todo es mi dama (?1637–40).

Antes que todo es mi dama, ed. Bernard P. E. Bentley (Kassel: Reichenberger, 2000). (Teatro del Siglo de Oro, Ediciones Críticas 106.)

Apolo y Climene (?1661).

El árbol del mejor fruto (*auto*, 1677).

Argenis y Poliarco (?*c.* 1634).

Las armas de la hermosura (?1678).

El astrólogo fingido (?1625).

Pedro Calderón de la Barca's The Fake Astrologer, ed. and trans. Max Oppenheimer Jr (New York: Peter Lang, 1994).

Auristela y Clariana (1637) (= *Auristela y Lisidante*?).
Auristela y Lisidante (?1653–60).
La aurora en Copacabana (?*c.* 1661).
La aurora en Copacabana, edited with an introduction and notes by Ezra S. Engling (London: Tamesis, 1994).
La banda y la flor (?May 1632).
Basta callar (?1638–9).
Basta callar, ed. Margaret Rich Greer (Ottawa: Dovehouse, 2000). (Ottawa Hispanic Studies 26.)
Bien vengas mal, si vienes solo (1635).
Los cabellos de Absalón (?late 1630s).
Cada uno para sí (?1653).
Cada uno para sí: *A Critical Edition, with Introduction, Including a Study of the Transmission of the Text, and Notes*, by José M. Ruano de la Haza (Kassel: Reichenberger, 1982).
Las cadenas del demonio (by 1644).
Las Carnestolendas (*entremés*) (printed 1661).
Casa con dos puertas mala es de guardar (1629).
La cena del rey Baltasar (*auto*, ?1634).
La cisma de Ingalaterra (1627), ed. Francisco Ruiz Ramón (Madrid: Castalia, 1981).
Con quien vengo, vengo (1630).
El conde Lucanor (?early 1653).
La cruz en la sepultura (early draft of *La devoción de la cruz*) (?1623–7).
¿Cuál es mayor perfección, hermosura o discreción? (?early 1650s).
El cubo de la Almudena (*auto*, 1651).
La dama duende (1629), ed. Ángel Valbuena Briones (Madrid: Cátedra, 1989).
La dama y galán Aquiles (by 1644) (= *El monstruo de los jardines*?).
Dar tiempo al tiempo (?late 1640s).
Darlo todo y no dar nada (?1651).
De un castigo tres venganzas (*c.* 1628).
De una causa dos efectos (*c.* 1632).
La desdicha de la voz (1639).
La desdicha de la voz, ed. T. R. A. Mason (Liverpool: Liverpool University Press, 2003).
La devoción de la cruz (revision of *La cruz en la sepultura*, by 1635).
La devoción de la cruz, ed. Manuel Delgado (Madrid: Cátedra, 2000).
La devoción de la misa (*auto*, ?1658).
Los disparates de Don Quijote, see under 'Calderón, lost works', *Don Quijote de la Mancha*.
El divino cazador (*auto*, 1642).
El divino cazador (*auto sacramental*). Edición facsímil del manuscrito autógrafo conservado en la Biblioteca Nacional de Madrid, con introducción y comentario del Prof. Hans Flasche y transcripción del texto por Manuel Sánchez Mariana (Madrid: Ministerio de Cultura, 1981).
Los dos amantes del cielo (?1636).

Duelos de amor y lealtad (1678).
Eco y Narciso (1661).
Los empeños de un acaso (?1639).
En la vida todo es verdad y todo mentira (1659).
En la vida todo es verdad y todo mentira, ed. Don William Cruickshank (London: Tamesis, 1971).
El encanto sin encanto (?1650–2).
Los encantos de la culpa (*auto*, ?1636–8, ?1643–5).
El escondido y la tapada (1636).
La exaltación de la cruz (?1648).
La fiera, el rayo y la piedra (1652).
Fieras afemina Amor (1671).
Fieras afemina Amor, ed. Edward M. Wilson (Kassel: Reichenberger, 1984).
Fuego de Dios en el querer bien (?1640–2).
El galán fantasma (?1630–3; published 1637).
El golfo de las sirenas (1657).
La gran Cenobia (1625).
El gran príncipe de Fez (1669).
El gran teatro del mundo (*auto*, ?1633–5).
Guárdate del agua mansa, see El agua mansa.
Gustos y disgustos son no más que imaginación (?1638).
Hado y divisa de Leonido y de Marfisa (1680).
La hidalga del valle (*auto*, ?by 1634).
La hija del aire (two parts, ?late 1630s).
La hija del aire, ed. Francisco Ruiz Ramón (Madrid: Cátedra, 1987).
El hijo del sol (1662).
Los hijos de la fortuna (?*c.* 1651–3).
El hombre pobre todo es trazas (1627).
La humildad coronada de las plantas (*auto*, 1644).
La humildad coronada: auto sacramental. Edición facsimilar del ms. Res. 72 de la Biblioteca Nacional (Madrid: Espasa Calpe, 1980).
La industria contra el poder, y el honor contra la fuerza (= *Amor, honor y poder*).
La inmunidad del sagrado (*auto*, 1664).
El jardín de Falerina (?1649). *See also* Rojas, Francisco de; Coello, Antonio; Calderón de la Barca, Pedro.
El jardín de Falerina (*auto*, 1675).
El José de las mujeres (?1641–4).
Judas Macabeo (1623).
Lances de amor y fortuna (1624–5).
El laurel de Apolo (1658).
El lirio y la azucena (*auto*, 1660).
Llamados y escogidos (*auto*, 1643).
Lo que va del hombre a Dios (*auto*, ?1647–57).
Loa of *La protestación de la fe* (1656), in *Obras completas*, vol. III, *Autos sacramentales*, ed. A. Valbuena Prat (Madrid: Aguilar, 1952), pp. 725–9.

Loa para el auto sacramental intitulado las órdenes militares, en metáfora de la Piadosa Hermandad del Refugio, discurriendo por calles y templos de Madrid (?1662).
Loa sacramental que la compañía de Antonio de Prado representó en el auto de la primer flor del Carmelo (1647 or 1648).
Luis Pérez el gallego (1628 or 1629).
Los Macabeos, see Judas Macabeo.
El maestrazgo del toisón (*auto*, 1659).
El maestro de danzar (?soon after 1650).
El mágico prodigioso (1637).
El mágico prodigioso: *A Composite Edition by Melveena McKendrick in Association with* A. A. Parker (Oxford: Clarendon, 1992).
Las manos blancas no ofenden (?1640).
Las manos blancas no ofenden (dos textos de una comedia), ed. Ángel Martínez Blasco (Kassel: Reichenberger, 1995). (Teatro del Siglo de Oro, Ediciones Críticas 60.)
Mañana será otro día (1635).
Mañanas de abril y mayo (?1632–3).
El mayor encanto, amor (1635).
El mayor monstruo del mundo (?1635).
El médico de su honra (?1629).
Mejor está que estaba (?1631).
Los misterios de la misa (*auto*, 1640).
Mojiganga de las visiones de la muerte (?*c*. 1673–5).
El monstruo de los jardines (?*c*. 1650–3).
Nadie fíe su secreto (?1623–4).
Ni Amor se libra de amor (1662).
La niña de Gómez Arias (?1637–9).
No hay burlas con el amor (?1635).
Love is no Laughing Matter (No hay burlas con el amor), trans. with an introduction and commentary by Don Cruickshank and Seán Page (Warminster: Aris & Phillips, 1986).
No hay cosa como callar (1638).
No hay más fortuna que Dios (*auto*, ?1652–3).
No hay más fortuna que Dios, ed. A. A. Parker (Manchester: Manchester University Press, 1949).
No siempre lo peor es cierto (by 1652).
El nuevo hospicio de pobres (*auto*, 1668).
El nuevo palacio del Retiro (*auto*, 1634).
Nunca lo peor es cierto, see No siempre lo peor es cierto.
Las órdenes militares / Las pruebas del segundo Adán (*auto*, 1662).
Origen, pérdida y restauración de Nuestra Señora del Sagrario (?1629).
Para vencer a amor, querer vencerle (?1630–3).
El pastor Fido (*auto*, 1678); *see also under* 'Calderón, collaboration works'.
Peor está que estaba (?1630).
La piel de Gedeón (*auto*, 1650).
El pintor de su deshonra (?1644–6).

The Painter of His Dishonour / El pintor de su deshonra, ed. A. K. G. Paterson (Warminster: Aris & Phillips, 1991).

El pintor de su deshonra (*auto*, ?1644–6).

El pleito matrimonial del cuerpo y el alma (auto, ?1636–8, 1643–5, *c.* 1650).

El pleito matrimonial del cuerpo y el alma, ed. Manfred Engelbert (Hamburg: Cram, de Gruyter & Co., 1969).

Polifemo y Circe (1630), *see* Mira de Amescua, Antonio, Juan Pérez de Montalbán, and Pedro Calderón de la Barca, *Polifemo y Circe*.

El postrer duelo de España (?1651–3).

El postrer duelo de España, edited with introduction and notes by Guy Rossetti (London: Tamesis, 1979). (Serie B, Textos, 23.)

La primer flor del Carmelo (*auto*, 1647 or 1648).

La primer flor del Carmelo. Edición de Fernando Plata Parga (Kassel: Reichenberger; Pamplona: Universidad de Navarra, 1998).

Primero soy yo (?1638).

El príncipe constante (1628–9).

El príncipe constante, MS no. 15159, Biblioteca Nacional, ed. Fernando Cantalapiedra and Alfredo Rodríguez López-Vázquez (Madrid: Cátedra, 1996).

El príncipe constante, ed. Enrica Cancelliere (Madrid: Biblioteca Nueva, 2000).

Psiquis y Cupido (para Toledo) (*auto*, ?1640).

La puente de Mantible (?1630).

El purgatorio de San Patricio (?1627–8).

El purgatorio de San Patricio, ed. J. M. Ruano (Liverpool: Liverpool University Press, 1988).

La púrpura de la rosa (1660).

Calderón, and Torrejón y Velasco, Tomás de, *La púrpura de la rosa*: Edición del texto de Calderón y de la música de Torrejón comentados y anotados por Ángeles Cardona, Don Cruickshank y Martin Cunningham (Kassel: Reichenberger, 1990). (Teatro del Siglo de Oro, Ediciones Críticas 9.)

Saber del mal y del bien (1628).

El secreto a voces (1642).

El secreto a voces, comedia de Pedro Calderón de la Barca, según el manuscrito de la Biblioteca Nacional de Madrid, ed. José M. de Osma, *Bulletin of the University of Kansas* 39, no. 8 (1938).

La segunda esposa y triunfar muriendo (*auto*, *c.* 1649).

El segundo Escipión (1676).

La selva confusa (?1622–3).

La selva confusa, ed. G. T. Northup, *RevHisp* 21 (1929), 168–338.

Las selvas de amor, see La selva confusa.

Selvas y bosques de amor, see La selva confusa.

La semilla y la zizaña (*auto*, 1651).

La señora y la criada (1635).

La serpiente de metal (*auto*, 1676; first draft, 1643, as *La sierpe de metal*?).

La sibila de Oriente (?1634–6).

La sierpe de metal, see La serpiente de metal.

El sitio de Bredá (1625).
El sitio de Bredá, ed. Johanna Rodolphine Schrek (The Hague: G. B. van Goor Zonen, 1957).
El socorro general (*auto*, 1644).
También hay duelo en las damas (?1652–3).
La torre de Babilonia (*auto*, ?1637).
Los tres afectos del amor (?1658).
Las tres justicias en una (?1630–7).
Los tres mayores prodigios (1636).
El triunfo de la cruz (= *La exaltación de la cruz*?).
El Tuzaní de la Alpujarra (?*c*. 1631).
La vacante general (*auto*, 1649).
El veneno y la triaca (*auto*, ?by 1634).
La vida es sueño (?1630).
La vida es sueño (*auto*, 1673: second version).
La primera versión de La vida es sueño, *de Calderón*, ed. J. M. Ruano de la Haza (Liverpool: Liverpool University Press, 1992).
La segunda versión de La vida es sueño, *de Calderón*, ed. Germán Vega García-Luengos, Don W. Cruickshank y J. M. Ruano de la Haza (Liverpool: Liverpool University Press, 2000).
La virgen del Sagrario (?1629).

CALDERÓN, PROSE WORK AND LETTERS

'De oy en ocho dias embiare a vuestra merced el auto …' (letter, 29 April 1640).
Deposición a favor de los profesores de la pintura (1677).
'Don Pedro Calderon de la Barca q[ue] pretende el avito de la orden de Santiago …' (letter, 1636).
'Don Pedro Calderon de la Barca Cauallero de la orden de Santiago, dize: …' (*memorial*, ?1647).
'El Dia señor que vese la mano a V Ex[a] para bolverme a alba …' (letter, 9 October 1648).
Papel de Don Pedro Calderon de la Barca, al Patriarcha (letter, ?1652).
'Yo e visto vna memoria que cosme loti hizo …' (letter, 30 April 1635): *see* Léo Rouanet, 'Un autographe inédit de Calderón', *RevHisp* 6 (1899), 196–200.

CALDERÓN, COLLECTIONS

Comedias, ed. Juan Eugenio Hartzenbusch, 4 vols. (Madrid: Rivadeneyra, 1848–50) (Biblioteca de Autores Españoles, vols. VII, IX, XII, XIV.)
El gran teatro del mundo / El gran mercado del mundo, ed. Eugenio Frutos Cortés (Madrid: Cátedra, 1987).
Entremeses, jácaras y mojigangas, ed. Evangelina Rodríguez and Antonio Tordera (Madrid: Castalia, 1982).

Las comedias de D. Pedro Calderón de la Barca, cotejadas con las mejores ediciones hasta ahora publicadas, corregidas y dadas a luz por Juan Jorge Keil, 4 vols. (Leipzig: Fleischer, 1827–30).

Novena parte de comedias (Madrid: Francisco Sanz, 1691).

Obras completas, vol. I: *Dramas*, ed. A. Valbuena Briones (Madrid: Aguilar, 1959).

Obras completas, vol. II: *Comedias*, ed. A. Valbuena Briones (Madrid: Aguilar, 1956).

Obras completas, vol. III: *Autos sacramentales*, ed. A. Valbuena Prat (Madrid: Aguilar, 1952).

Obras completas (Dramas). Textos íntegros según las primeras ediciones y los manuscritos autógrafos que saca a luz Luis Astrana Marín, 3rd edn, revised (Madrid: Aguilar, 1945).

Obras menores (Siglos XVII y XVIII), with *Noticias bibliográficas* by Edward M. Wilson (Cieza: La fonte que mana y corre, 1969) (El aire de la almena 24).

Octava parte de comedias (Madrid: Francisco Sanz, 1684).

Primera parte de autos sacramentales (Madrid: José Fernández de Buendía, 1677).

Primera parte de comedias (Madrid: María de Quiñones, 1636).

Primera parte de comedias (Madrid: Viuda de Juan Sánchez, 1640).

Primera parte de comedias (Madrid: Francisco Sanz, 1685).

Quarta parte de comedias (Madrid: José Fernández de Buendía, 1672).

Quarta parte de comedias (Madrid: Bernardo de Hervada, 1674).

Segunda parte de las comedias (Madrid: María de Quiñones, 1637).

Segunda parte de las comedias (Madrid: Carlos Sánchez, 1641).

Tercera parte de comedias (Madrid: Domingo García Morrás, 1664).

Tercera parte de comedias, ed. D. W. Cruickshank (Madrid: Biblioteca Castro, 2007).

Verdadera quinta parte de comedias, ed. Juan de Vera Tassis (Madrid: Francisco Sanz, 1682; Madrid: Francisco Sanz, 1694).

CALDERÓN, COLLABORATION WORKS

Calderón de la Barca, Pedro, Coello, Antonio, and Moreto y Cabaña, Agustín, *La fingida Arcadia* (1663).

Calderón, 'Pérez de Montalbán, Juan, and Coello, Antonio', *El privilegio de las mugeres* (?1634).

Calderón, and Coello, Antonio, *Yerros de naturaleza y aciertos de la fortuna* (1634), ed. Eduardo Juliá Martínez (Madrid: Hernando, 1930).

Calderón, Vélez de Guevara, Luis and Cáncer y Velasco, Jerónimo de, *Enfermar con el remedio* (by 1644).

Calderón, and Zabaleta, Juan de, *Troya abrasada* (1643–4). See also *Troya abrasada*, de Pedro Calderón de la Barca y Juan de Zabaleta, ed. George Tyler Northup, *RevHisp* 29 (1913), 195–345.

Calderón, Pérez de Montalbán, Juan, and Rojas Zorrilla, Francisco de, *El monstruo de la fortuna* (?1633).

Calderón, Solís, Antonio de, and Coello, Antonio, *El pastor Fido* (by 1652).

See also Belmonte Bermúdez, Luis de; Coello, Antonio; Mira de Amescua, Antonio; Pérez de Montalbán, Juan; Rojas Zorrilla, Francisco de; Solís, Antonio de; Vélez de Guevara, Luis; Zabaleta, Juan de.

CALDERÓN, LOST WORKS

El carro del cielo (by March (1627).
La Celestina (by 1634).
Certamen de amor y celos (?1640).
Don Quijote de la Mancha (1637).
La fábula de Dafne (1636).
La fábula de Narciso (?Carnival 1639).
El juicio final (*auto*, 1640).
El mejor huésped de España (*auto*, 1639).
Nuestra Señora de la Almudena, 2 parts (?1640).
Nuestra Señora de los Remedios (?1650).
Las proezas de Frislán, y muerte del rey de Suecia [?], with A. Coello (1634).
San Francisco de Borja (1671).
Santa María Egipciaca (*auto*, 1639).
Unknown title, with Solís and Rojas Zorrilla (1640).

CALDERÓN, ATTRIBUTED WORKS

'A un río helado' ('Salid, ¡oh Clori divina!'), *romance*.
Conclusión defendida por un soldado del campo de Tarragona del ciego furor de Cataluña. Ninguno de los pretextos que opone este principado, honesta su hostilidad, ni disculpa su atrevimiento, contra la justificación de las armas de la Magestad Católica (Pamplona, 1641). Reproduced from BNE MS 18717[15] by Eulogio Zudaire, 'Un escrito anónimo de Calderón de la Barca', *Hispania* (Madrid) 13 (1953), 268–93.
Consumo del vellón, el (*auto*).
Cómo se comunican dos estrellas contrarias.
'Curiosísima señora', *romance*.
El divino Jasón (*auto*, ?by 1630).
El divino Jasón, ed. Ignacio Arellano and Ángel L. Cilveti (Kassel: Reichenberger; Pamplona: Universidad de Navarra, 1992) (Autos sacramentales completos de Calderón, vol. 1).
El gran duque de Gandía, ed. Václav Černý (Prague: L'Académie Tchécoslovaque des Sciences, 1963).
No hay que creer ni en la verdad, edición y estudio de Václav Černý (Madrid: CSIC, 1968). (Anejos de la Revista *Segismundo* 1.)
'¿No me conocéis, serranos?', *romance*.
La peste del pan dañado (*auto*) (lost).
El prodigio de Alemania.

Callahan, William J., *La Santa y Real Hermandad del Refugio y Piedad de Madrid, 1618–1832* (Madrid: CSIC, 1980).

Camões, Luís de, *Rimas*, ed. Álvaro J. da Costa Pimpão (Coimbra: Coimbra University, 1953).
Campbell, Jodi, *Monarchy, Political Culture and Drama in Seventeenth-Century Madrid: Theater of Negotiation* (Aldershot: Ashgate, 2006).
Cáncer y Velasco, Jerónimo de, *Obras varias* (Madrid: Diego Díaz de la Carrera, 1651).
Cancionero de 1628, ed. J. M. Blecua (Madrid: Aguirre, 1945).
Carducho, Vincencio, *Dialogos de la pintura* (Madrid: Francisco Martínez, 1633).
Caro de Mallén, Ana, *El conde Partinuplés*, ed. L. Luna (Kassel: Reichenberger, 1993).
Casa, Frank P., *The Dramatic Craftsmanship of Moreto* (Cambridge, MA: Harvard University Press, 1966). (Harvard Studies in Romance Languages 29.)
Casanova, Joseph de, *Primera parte del arte de escrivir todas formas de letras* (Madrid: Diego Díaz de la Carrera, 1650).
Cascardi, Anthony J., *The Limits of Illusion: A Critical Study of Calderón* (Cambridge: Cambridge University Press, 1984).
Casey, James, *Early Modern Spain: A Social History* (London: Routledge, 1999).
Castillejo, Cristóbal de, *Obras* (Madrid: Pierres Cosín, 1573).
Castillejo, David, *Guía de ochocientas comedias del Siglo de Oro para el uso de actores y lectores: con el preámbulo Tres diálogos (estatal, racional y teatral)* (Madrid: Ars Milenii, 2002).
Castillo de Larzával, Antonio del, *El Adonis* (Salamanca: Jacinto Taberniel, 1632).
Castro, Américo, and Rennert, Hugo A., *Vida de Lope de Vega (1562–1635)* (Salamanca: Anaya, 1969).
Castro y Anaya, Pedro de, *Las auroras de Diana* (Madrid: Imprenta del Reyno, 1632).
Castro y Bellvís, Guillén de, *Don Quijote de la Mancha* (printed 1618).
Las maravillas de Babilonia (1625).
Las mocedades del Cid (printed 1618).
Primera parte de las comedias (Valencia: Felipe Mey, 1618).
Segunda parte de comedias (Valencia: Miguel Sorolla, 1625).
Castro y Rossi, Adolfo de, *Discurso acerca de las costumbres públicas y privadas de los españoles en el siglo XVII fundado en el estudio de las comedias de Calderón* (Madrid: Guttenberg, 1881).
Catálogo colectivo del patrimonio bibliográfico español: siglo XVII, only 3 vols. published (Madrid: Arco/Libros, 1988–92). (The entire catalogue is now available online.)
Caturla, María Luisa, *Pinturas, frondas y fuentes del Buen Retiro* (Madrid: Revista de Occidente, 1947).
Caxa de Leruela, Miguel, *Restauración de la abundancia de España (1631)*, ed. Jean Paul Le Flem (Madrid: Instituto de Estudios Fiscales, 1975).
Cervantes Saavedra, Miguel de, *La casa de los celos* (printed 1615).
El casamiento engañoso (printed 1613).
El celoso extremeño (printed 1613).
La cueva de Salamanca (printed 1615).

Don Quijote de la Mancha, edición del Instituto Cervantes, dirigida por Francisco Rico, 2 vols. (Barcelona: Instituto Cervantes / Crítica, 1998).
La fuerza de la sangre (printed 1613).
La gitanilla (printed 1613).
Novelas ejemplares (Madrid: Juan de la Cuesta, 1613).
Novelas ejemplares, ed. Francisco Rodríguez Marín, 2 vols. (Madrid: Espasa-Calpe, 1915–17).
Persiles y Sigismunda (printed 1617).
El rufián dichoso (printed 1615).

Chevalier, Maxime, *L'Arioste en Espagne (1530–1650): Recherches sur l'influence du 'Roland furieux'* (Bordeaux: Féret, 1966).

Chirino de Salazar, Fernando (='Monforte y Herrera, Fernando de'), *Relacion de las fiestas que ha hecho el Colegio Imperial de la Compañia de Jesus de Madrid en la canonizacion de San Ignacio de Loyola, y S. Francisco Xavier* (Madrid: Luis Sánchez, 1622).

Cicero, Marcus Tullius, *Epistulae*.

Cid, Miguel, *Justas sagradas* (Seville: Simón Fajardo, 1647).

Close, Anthony, 'Novela y comedia de Cervantes a Calderón: El caso de *La dama duende*', in Aurora Egido (ed.), *Lecciones calderonianas* (Zaragoza: Ibercaja, 2001), pp. 33–52.

Coe, Ada M., *Catálogo bibliográfico y crítico de la comedias anunciadas en los periódicos de Madrid desde 1661 hasta 1819* (Baltimore, MD: Johns Hopkins University Press, 1935).

Coello, Antonio, *Los empeños de seis horas*.

Coello, Antonio, and Calderón de la Barca, Pedro, *Yerros de naturaleza y aciertos de la fortuna* (1634).
See also Rojas Zorrilla, Francisco de, Coello, Juan, and Coello, Antonio, *El robo de las sabinas*.

Coello, Juan, *see* Rojas Zorrilla, Francisco de, Coello, Juan, and Coello, Antonio, *El robo de las sabinas*.

Colomès, Jean, 'La Révolution catalane de 1640 et les écrivains espagnols du temps', in *IVe Congrès des Hispanistes Français* (Poitiers: Université de Poitiers, Faculté des Lettres et Sciences Humaines, 1968), pp. 45–58.

COMEDIAS ESCOGIDAS

Primera parte de comedias escogidas de los mejores ingenios de España (Madrid: Domingo García y Morrás, 1652).

Laurel de comedias: Quarta parte de diferentes autores (Madrid: Imprenta Real, 1653).

Quinta parte de comedias escogidas de los mejores ingenios de España (Madrid: Pablo de Val, 1653).

Comedias nuevas escogidas de los mejores ingenios de España: Octava parte (Madrid: Andrés García de la Iglesia, 1657).

De los mejores el mejor, libro nuevo de comedias varias, nunca impresas, compuestas por los mejores ingenios de España: Parte trece (Madrid: Mateo Fernández, 1660).

Parte quinze: Comedias nuevas, escogidas de los mejores ingenios de España (Madrid: Melchor Sánchez, 1661).

Parte diez y siete de comedias nuevas, y escogidas de los mejores ingenios de Europa (Madrid: Melchor Sánchez, 1662).

Parte diez y ocho de comedias nuevas, escogidas de los mejores ingenios de España (Madrid: Gregorio Rodríguez, 1662).

Parte veinte y una de comedias nuevas, escogidas de los mejores ingenios de España (Madrid: José Fernández de Buendía, 1663).

Primavera numerosa de muchas armonías lucientes, en doze comedias fragantes, parte quarenta y seis (Madrid: Francisco Sanz, 1679).

Constandse, A. L., *Le Baroque espagnol et Calderón de la Barca* (Amsterdam: Jacob van Campen, 1951).

Córdoba Ronquillo, Luis de (ed.), *Sermones funebres predicados dominica infra octava de todos Stos de 1624 años en la prouincia del andalucia … en las honras de … Enrique de Gusman … y demas progenitores* (Seville: Francisco de Lyra, 1624).

Corneille, Pierre, *Le Cid* (1637).

Théâtre complet, ed. Pierre Lièvre and Roger Caillois, 2 vols. (Paris: Pléiade, 1966).

Corneille, Thomas, *Le Feint Astrologue* (1648).

Les Engagemens du hazard (1647).

Poèmes dramatiques, 5 vols. (Paris: Luynes, 1738).

Correas, Gonzalo, *Vocabulario de refranes y frases proverbiales (1627)*, ed. Louis Combet, 2nd edn, revised by Robert Jammes and Maïte Mir-Andreu (Madrid: Castalia, 2000).

Costa, Carlo Costanzo, *L'astrologo non astrologo o gli amori turbati* (Genoa: Pietro Giovanni Calenzani, 1665).

Cotarelo y Mori, Emilio, 'Actores famosos del siglo XVII: María de Córdoba, "Amarilis", y su marido Andrés de la Vega', *RBAM* 10 (1933), 1–33.

Bibliografía de las controversias sobre la licitud del teatro en España (Madrid: Tipografía de la 'Revista de Archivos, Bibliotecas y Museos', 1904).

'Catálogo descriptivo de la gran colección de "Comedias escogidas" que consta de cuarenta y ocho volúmenes, impresos de 1652 a 1704', *BRAE* 18 (1931), 232–80, 418–68, 583–636, 772–826.

Diccionario biográfico y bibliográfico de calígrafos españoles, 2 vols. (Madrid: Revista de Archivos, 1916).

Don Francisco de Rojas Zorrilla (Madrid: Imprenta de la Revista de Archivos, 1911).

Ensayo sobre la vida y obras de D. Pedro Calderón de la Barca (Madrid: Tipografía de la 'Revista de Archivos, Bibliotecas y Museos', 1924; facsimile reprint, Madrid: Iberoamericana, 2001).

'La bibliografía de Moreto', *BRAE* 14 (1927), 449–94.

Cotarelo y Mori, Emilio (ed.), *Colección de entremeses, loas, bailes, jácaras y mojigangas desde fines del siglo XVI a mediados del siglo XVII*, 2 vols. (Madrid: Bailly & Baillière, 1911) (Nueva Biblioteca de Autores Españoles 17, 18.)

Covarrubias y Leiva, Diego de (comp.), *Elogios al palacio real del Buen Retiro* (Madrid: Imprenta del Reino, 1635).

Cruickshank, D. W., '"Literature" and the Book Trade in Golden-Age Spain', *MLR* 73 (1978), 799–824.

'Calderón's *Amor, honor y poder* and the Prince of Wales, 1623', *Calderón 1600–1681: Quatercentenary Studies in Memory of John E. Varey*, *BHS* (Glasgow) 77 (2000), 75–99.

'Calderón's Handwriting', *MLR* 65 (1970), 65–77.

'Notes on Calderonian Chronology and the Calderonian Canon', in Francisco Mundi Pedret (ed.), *Estudios sobre Calderón y el teatro de la Edad de Oro: Homenaje a Kurt y Roswitha Reichenberger* (Barcelona: Promociones y Publicaciones Universitarias, 1989), pp. 19–36.

'Some Notes on the Printing of Plays in Seventeenth-Century Seville', *The Library* VI, xi (1989), 231–52.

'The Lovers of Teruel: A "Romantic" Story', *MLR* 88 (1993), 881–93.

'The Second Part of *La hija del aire*', *Golden-Age Studies in Honour of A. A. Parker*, *BHS* 61 (1984), 286–94.

'The Significance of *Fortuna* in Calderón's *La hija del aire*', in *'Never-Ending Adventure': Studies in Medieval and Early Modern Spanish Literature in Honor of Peter Dunn* (Newark, NJ: Juan de la Cuesta Press, 2002), 351–76.

'*Ut pictura poesis*: Calderón's Picturing of Myth', in Isabel Torres (ed.), *Rewriting Classical Mythology in the Hispanic Baroque* (Woodbridge: Tamesis, 2007), pp. 156–70.

Cruickshank, D. W., and W. F. Hunter, 'Notes on the Text of Calderón's *Psiquis y Cupido (para Toledo)*', *Iberoromania* 4 (1970), 282–9.

Cubero Sebastián, Pedro, *Peregrinación del mundo* (Madrid: Juan García Infanzón, 1680).

Cubillo de Aragón, Álvaro, *Auto sacramental de la muerte de Frislán*, ed. Marie France Schmidt (Kassel: Reichenberger, 1984) (composed 1634).

Cuesta, Juan de la, *Libro y tratado para enseñar leer y escriuir breuemente y con gran facilidad cõ reta pronunciacion y verdadera ortographia todo Romance Castellano, y de la distincion y diferencia que ay en las letras consonãtes de vna a otras en su sonido y pronunciacion* (Alcalá: Juan Gracián, 1589).

Culpeper, Nicholas, *Culpeper's Complete Herbal: Consisting of a Comprehensive Description of Nearly All Herbs with their Medicinal Properties and Directions for Compounding the Medicines Extracted from them* (London: W. Foulsham, [1923]).

Davies, Gareth A., *A Poet at Court: Antonio Hurtado de Mendoza (1586–1644)* (Oxford: Dolphin, 1971).

'The Country Cousin at Court: A Study of Antonio de Mendoza's *Cada loco con su tema* and Manuel Bretón de los Herreros' *El pelo de la dehesa*', in Margaret A. Rees (ed.), *Leeds Papers on Hispanic Drama* (Leeds: Trinity and All Saints, 1991), pp. 43–60.

Davies, R. Trevor, *The Golden Century of Spain: 1501–1620* (London: Macmillan, 1970).

Davis, Charles, 'Calderón en Yepes: El estreno de *El mágico prodigioso* (1637)', *Criticón* 99 (2007), 193–215.

Davis, Charles, and Varey, J. E., *Actividad teatral en la región de Madrid según los protocolos de Juan García de Albertos, 1634–1660: Estudio y documentos,* 2 vols. (London: Tamesis, 2003).

Deleito y Piñuela, José, *El rey se divierte* (Madrid: Espasa-Calpe, 1955).

La vida religiosa bajo el cuarto Felipe (Madrid: Espasa-Calpe, 1952).

Delicias de Apolo, recreaciones del Parnaso, por las tres musas Urania, Euterpe y Caliope (Madrid: Melchor Alegre, 1670).

Díaz de Escovar, Narciso, 'Comediantes de los otros siglos: La bella Amarilis', *BRAH* 98 (1931), 323–62.

Díaz Galdós, T., 'Un autógrafo de Calderón', *RBAM* 4 (1927), 102–5.

Díaz Morante, Pedro, *Nueva arte de escreuir inventada con el fabor de Dios por el maestro P. Diaz Morante* (Madrid: Luis Sánchez, 1615).

Dickinson, Emily, see Johnson, T. H.

Diego, Gerardo, *Antología poética en honor de Góngora* (Madrid: Alianza, 1979).

Díez Borque, José María, 'Calderón de la Barca y la novela de caballerías', *Calderón 1600–1681: Quatercentenary Studies in Memory of John E. Varey, BHS* (Glasgow) 77 (2000), 255–64.

Digby, George, Earl of Bristol, *Worse and Worse* (?1664; now lost).

'Tis Better than it Was (?by 1665, printed London, 1708).

Dionysius of Halicarnassus, *Antiquitates romanae.*

Dioscorides, Pedacius, *Acerca de la materia medicinal*, ed. and trans. Andrés Laguna (Salamanca: Matías Gast, 1566; reprinted 1570).

Dixon, Victor, 'Apuntes sobre la vida y la obra de Jerónimo de Villaizán y Garcés', *Hispanófila*, 13, no. 3 (1961), 5–22.

'*El alcalde de Zalamea*, "la nueva": Date and Composition', *Calderón 1600–1681: Quatercentenary Studies in Memory of John E. Varey, BHS* (Glasgow) 77 (2000), 173–81.

'Juan Pérez de Montalbán's *Para todos*', *HR* 32 (1964), 35–59.

Domínguez Ortiz, Antonio, *La sociedad española en el siglo XVII*, 2 vols., edición facsímil (Granada: Universidad de Granada, 1992).

Doze comedias las mas grandiosas que asta aora han salido de los mejores y mas insignes poetas: Segunda parte (Lisbon: Pablo Craesbeeck, a costa de Juan Leite Pereira, 1647).

Doze comedias nuevas de Lope de Vega Carpio, y otros autores ('Barcelona: Gerónimo Margarit, 1630').

Dryden, John, *An Evening's Love, or the Mock Astrologer* (1668).

Egido, Teófanes, *Sátiras políticas de la España moderna* (Madrid: Alianza, 1973).

Eguía Ruiz, Constancio, 'Cervantes, Calderón, Lope, Gracián: Nuevos temas crítico-biográficos', in *Anejos de Cuadernos de Literatura* 8 (Madrid: Instituto 'Miguel de Cervantes' de Filología Española, 1951), pp. 56–61.

Elejabeitia, Ana, 'La transmisión textual de *La más hidalga hermosura*', *Letras de Deusto* 51 (1991), 53–65.

Elliott, J. H., *Imperial Spain 1469–1716* (London: Arnold, 1963).

The Count-Duke of Olivares: The Statesman in an Age of Decline (New Haven and London: Yale University Press, 1986).

Enríquez Gómez, Antonio, *Sansón Nazareno, poema heroico* (Rouen: Laurenço Maurry, 1656).

Entrambasaguas, Joaquín de, *Estudios sobre Lope de Vega*, 2 vols. (Madrid: Aldus, 1946–7).

Encyclopedia Universal Ilustrada Europeo-Americana, vol. XXII (Madrid: Espasa-Calpe, 1924).

Epictetus, *Enchiridion*.

Escobar, Jesús, *The Plaza Mayor and the Shaping of Baroque Madrid* (Cambridge: Cambridge University Press, 2003).

Escrivá, el comendador, 'Ven muerte tan escondida', *canción*.

Escudero, Lara, and Zafra, Rafael, *Memorias de apariencias y otros documentos sobre los autos de Calderón de la Barca* (Kassel: Reichenberger; Pamplona: Universidad de Navarra, 2003).

Esquerdo Sivera, Vicenta, 'Acerca de *La confusa* de Cervantes', in *Cervantes, su obra y su mundo: Actas del I Congreso Internacional sobre Cervantes* (Madrid: Edi-6, 1981), pp. 243–7.

'Aportaciones al estudio del teatro en Valencia durante el siglo XVII', *BRAE* 55 (1975), 429–530.

Ezquerra Abadía, Ramón, *La conspiración del duque de Híjar* (Madrid: Librería Horizonte, 1934).

Faría e Sousa, Manuel de, *Epítome de las historias portuguesas* (Madrid: Francisco Martínez, 1628).

Feros, Antonio, *Kingship and Favoritism in the Spain of Philip III, 1598–1621* (Cambridge: Cambridge University Press, 2000).

Florensa i Soler, Nuria, 'La derrota del ejército español en Barcelona: "la batalla de Montjuïc": Antecedentes y desarrollo de la guerra', in José Alcalá Zamora and Ernest Belenguer (co-ordinators), *Calderón de la Barca y la España del Barroco*, 2 vols. (Madrid: Centro de Estudios Políticos y Constitucionales / Sociedad Estatal España Nuevo Milenio, 2001), vol. II, pp. 189–220.

Fox, Dian, 'A Further Source of Calderón's *El príncipe constante*', *JHP* 4 (1980), 157–66.

Kings in Calderón: A Study in Characterization and Political Theory (London: Tamesis, 1986).

Framiñán de Miguel, María Jesús, 'Calderón y la actividad teatral salmantina a comienzos de 1600', in Ignacio Arellano (ed.), *Calderón 2000: Homenaje a Kurt Reichenberger en su 80 cumpleaños*, 2 vols. (Kassel: Reichenberger, 2002), vol. I, pp. 509–24.

Franchi, Fabio, *see* Pulchi, Alessio.

Gallardo, Bartolomé José, *Ensayo de una biblioteca española de libros raros y curiosos*, 4 vols., edn facsímil (Madrid: Gredos, 1968).

Gallego, Julián, *Zurbarán: 1598–1664*, with catalogue of the works by José Gudiol, trans. Kenneth Lyons (London: Secker & Warburg, 1977).

García Carraffa, Alberto and Arturo, *Enciclopedia heráldica y genealógica hispano-americana*, 88 vols. (Madrid: Hauser y Menet, 1919–63).

García Soriano, Justo, 'El teatro de colegio en España', *BRAE* 14 (1927), 235–77, 374–411, 535–65, 620–50; 15 (1928), 62–93, 145–87, 396–446, 651–69; 16 (1929), 80–106, 223–43; 19 (1932), 485–98, 608–24.
Garcilaso de la Vega, *Égloga I.*
Égloga II.
Obras completas, ed. Elias L. Rivers (Columbus, OH: Ohio State University Press, 1964).
Gates, Eunice Joiner, 'Calderón's Interest in Art', *PQ* 40 (1961), 53–67.
Gea, María Isabel, *Guía del plano de Texeira (1656)* (Madrid: La Librería, 2007).
Genealogía, origen y noticias de los comediantes de España, ed. N. D. Shergold and J. E. Varey (London: Tamesis, 1985).
Góngora y Argote, Luis de, 'Apeóse el caballero', *romance* (1610).
'Contando estaban sus rayos', *romance* (1614).
'Cuatro o seis desnudos hombros', *romance* (1614).
'Duélete de esa puente, Manzanares', sonnet (1588).
'Entre los sueltos caballos', *romance* (1585).
Fábula de Polifemo y Galatea (1612–13, printed 1627).
'Lleva este río crecido', *letrilla* (1603).
'Mientras por competir con tu cabello', sonnet (1582).
'Según vuelan por el agua', *romance* (1602).
Soledad primera (?1613, printed 1627).
González, Esteban, *La vida y hechos de Estevanillo González* (Madrid: Gregorio Rodríguez, 1652).
González Cañal, Rafael, 'El lujo y la ociosidad durante la privanza de Olivares: Bartolomé Jiménez Patón y la polémica sobre el guardainfante y las guedejas', *Criticón* 53 (1991), 71–96.
González Dávila, Gil, *Teatro de las grandezas de la villa de Madrid corte de los reyes catolicos de España* (Madrid: Tomás Junti, 1623).
González de Amezúa, Agustín, *Epistolario de Lope de Vega,* 4 vols. (Madrid: Artes Gráficas Aldus, 1935–43).
González de Cellorigo, Martín, *Memorial de la politica necessaria, y util restauracion a la republica de España*, ed. José L. Pérez de Ayala (Madrid: Instituto de Cooperación Iberoamericana, 1991). (First published Valladolid: Juan de Bostillo, 1600.)
González Palencia, Ángel, 'Pleito entre Lope de Vega y un editor de sus comedias', *BBMP* 3 (1921), 17–26.
Gordon, Mike, 'Calderón's *Los cabellos de Absalón*: The Tragedy of a Christian King', *Neophilologus* 64 (1980), 390–401.
Grande de Tena, Pedro (ed.), *Lagrimas panegiricas a la tenprana muerte del gran poeta, i teologo, doctor Iuan Perez de Montalban* (Madrid: Imprenta del Reino, 1639).
Gray, Thomas, *Elegy Written in a Country Churchyard* (printed 1768).
Green, Otis H., *Spain and the Western Tradition: The Castilian Mind in Literature from El Cid to Calderón*, 4 vols. (Madison: University of Wisconsin Press, 1968).
Greer, Margaret Rich, 'Constituting Community: A New Historical Perspective on the *autos* of Calderón', in José A. Madrigal (ed.), *New Historicism and the*

Comedia*: Poetics, Politics and Praxis* (Boulder, CO: Society of Spanish and Spanish-American Studies, 1997), pp. 41–67.

The Play of Power: Mythological Court Dramas of Calderón de la Barca (Princeton: Princeton University Press, 1991).

'The Politics of Memory in *El Tuzaní de la Alpujarra*', in Richard J. Pym (ed.), *Rhetoric and Reality in Early Modern Spain* (London: Tamesis, 2006), pp. 113–30.

Greg, W. W., *A Bibliography of the English Printed Drama to the Restoration*, 4 vols. (London: The Bibliographical Society, 1939–59).

Gudiol, José, *Velázquez 1599–1660* (London: Secker & Warburg, 1974).

Guerrero Mayllo, Ana, *Familia y vida cotidiana de una elite de poder: Los regidores madrileños en tiempos de Felipe II* (Mexico City and Madrid: Siglo XXI, 1993).

Guevara, Antonio de, *Epístolas familiares* (Valladolid: Juan de Villaquirán, 1539–41).

Menosprecio de corte y alabanza de aldea (Valladolid: Juan de Villaquirán, 1539).

Harris, Enriqueta, 'Velázquez's Apsley House Portrait: An Identification', *BM* 120 (1978), 304.

Harris, Enriqueta, and Elliott, John, 'Velázquez and the Queen of Hungary', *BM* 118 (1976), 24–6.

Heaton, H. C., 'On *La selva confusa*, Attributed to Calderón', *PMLA* 44 (1929), 243–73.

Hempel, Wido, '*In onor della fenice ibera*': *Über die Essequie poetiche di Lope de Vega, Venedig 1636, nebst einer kommentierten Ausgabe della Orazione del Cavallier Marino und des Ragguaglio di Parnaso, Analecta Romanica*, Heft 13 (Frankfurt am Main: Klostermann, 1964).

Hernández, Mauro, *A la sombra de la corona: poder local y oligarquía urbana (Madrid 1606–1808)* (Madrid: Siglo XXI, 1995).

Hernández Araico, Susana, 'Coriolanus and Calderón's Royal Matronalia', in José A. Madrigal (ed.), *New Historicism and the* Comedia*: Poetics, Politics and Praxis* (Boulder, CO: Society of Spanish and Spanish-American Studies, 1997), pp. 149–66.

Herrera, Rodrigo de, *La fe no ha menester armas, y venida del inglés a Cádiz* (1625–6).

Herrero García, M., *Ideas de los españoles del siglo XVII* (Madrid: Voluntad, 1928).

Hesse, Everett W., 'Calderón and Velázquez', *Hispania* 35 (1952), 74–82.

Hilborn, H. W., *A Chronology of the Plays of D. Pedro Calderón de la Barca* (Toronto: Toronto University Press, 1938).

Homer, *Iliad.*

Odyssey.

Horace (Quintus Horatius Flaccus), *Odes.*

Huerta, Antonio de, *De don Antonio de Huerta a don Pedro Calderón*, 'Si Calderón está como le pintas', sonnet (1637–40).

Hunter, William A., 'The Calderonian Auto Sacramental *El gran teatro del mundo*: An Edition and Translation of a Nahuatl Version', *Publication 27* (New Orleans: Middle American Research Institute, Tulane University, 1960), 105–202.

Hurtado, Luis, *Imagen del sacro-erario de la muy santa iglesia de Toledo* (Toledo: Francisco Calvo, 1655).

Hurtado de Mendoza, Antonio, *Convocacion de las Cortes de Castilla, y ivramento del Principe nuestro Señor D. Baltasar Carlos* (Madrid: Imprenta del Reyno, 1632).

El marido hace mujer (1631–2).
Querer por solo querer (1622).
(attrib.), 'Quien ama correspondido'.

Iglesias Feijoo, Luis, 'Calderón en la escena y en la imprenta: para la edición crítica de *El príncipe constante*', *Anuario Calderoniano* 1 (2008), 245–68.
'El romance de Góngora en *El príncipe constante* de Calderón', in Antonio Sánchez Jiménez (ed.), *Homenaje a Antonio Carreño, RILCE: Revista de Filología Hispánica* (forthcoming).

Ignatius, St, de Loyola, *Ejercicios espirituales.*

Ildefonsus, St, *Aureus libellus de illibata virginitate Mariae.*

Iñíguez Almech, Francisco, *Casas reales y jardines de Felipe II* (Madrid: CSIC, 1952).

Izquierdo Pascua, Julio César, *Rutas del románico en la provincia de Palencia* (Valladolid: Castilla Ediciones, 2001).

Johnson, T. H. (ed.), *The Poems of Emily Dickinson: Including Variant Readings Critically Compared with All Known Manuscripts*, 3 vols. (Cambridge, MA: Belknap Press Division of Harvard University Press, 1955).

Jones, C. A., 'Brecht y el drama del Siglo de Oro en España', *Segismundo* 3 (1967), 39–54.

Jones, Frederick L. (ed.), *The Letters of Percy Bysshe Shelley*, 2 vols. (Oxford: Clarendon, 1964).

Josephus, Flavius, *Antiquitates judaicae.*
De bello judaico.

Juderías, Julián, *Los favoritos de Felipe III: Don Pedro Franqueza, conde de Villalonga* (Madrid: Revista de Archivos, 1909).

Julio, María Teresa, 'El vejamen de Rojas para la academia de 1638: Estudio y edición', *RLit* 69, no. 137 (2007), *Número monográfico dedicado a Francisco de Rojas Zorrilla*, 299–332.
(ed.), *Academia burlesca que se hizo en Buen Retiro a la Majestad de Filipo Cuarto el Grande de 1637* (Pamplona: Universidad de Navarra; Madrid: Iberoamericana; Frankfurt: Vervuert, 2007). (MS 10293 of the BNE.)

Kagan, Richard, *Students and Society in Early Modern Spain* (Baltimore and London: Johns Hopkins University Press, 1974).

Kamen, Henry, *Philip of Spain* (New Haven and London: Yale University Press, 1997).

Kendrick, T. D., *Mary of Agreda: The Life and Legend of a Spanish Nun* (London: Routledge & Kegan Paul, 1967).

Kennedy, Ruth Lee, 'Moreto's Span of Dramatic Activity', *HR* 5 (1937), 170–2.
Studies in Tirso, vol. 1: *The Dramatist and His Competitors, 1620–1626* (Chapel Hill: University of North Carolina Press, 1974).

King, Willard F., 'Inventario, tasación y almoneda de los bienes de don Pedro Calderón', *NRFE* 36 (1988), 1079–82.

Knox, John, *The First Blast of the Trumpet against the Monstrous Regiment of Women* ([Geneva: J. Poullain,] 1558).

Lara, Gaspar Agustín de, *Obelisco funebre, pyramide funesto que construia a la inmortal memoria de D. Pedro Calderon de la Barca … D. Gaspar Agustin de Lara* (Madrid: Eugenio Rodríguez, 1684).

Lara Garrido, José, '*Si naciera sembrada la hermosura*: discurso del afecto y retórica del dolor en la silva elegíaca de Calderón "Dedicada a doña María de Zapata"', in Aurora Egido (ed.), *Lecciones calderonianas* (Zaragoza: Ibercaja, 2001), pp. 75–104.

Larquié, Claude, 'L'Alphabétisation à Madrid en 1650', *RHMC* 28 (1981), 132–57.

Latham, R. C., and Matthews, W. (eds.), *The Diary of Samuel Pepys*, 11 vols. (London: Bell, 1979–83).

Leavitt, Sturgis E., 'Did Calderón Have a Sense of Humour?', in *Romance Studies Presented to William Morton Dey* (Chapel Hill: University of North Carolina Press, 1950), pp. 119–21. (University of North Carolina Studies in Romance Languages and Literatures 12.)

'Humor in the *autos* of Calderón', *Hisp* (Lawrence, KS) 39 (1956), 137–44.

'The *gracioso* Takes the Audience into His Confidence', *BCom* 7 (1955), 27–9.

Le Métel, François, Sieur de Boisrobert, *Les Apparences trompeuses* (Paris: G. de Luyne, 1656).

Le Métel d'Ouville, Antoine, *Les Fausses Veritez* (Paris: Courbé, 1643).

Leonardo de Argensola, Bartolomé, *A una mujer que se afeitaba y estaba hermosa*, sonnet.

León Pinelo, Antonio de, *Anales de Madrid (desde el año 447 al de 1658)* (Madrid: IEM, 1971).

Livius Patavinus, Titus, *Epitome*.

López de Arrieta, Pedro and Atienza, Bartolomé de (compilers), *Recopilación de las leyes destos reynos* [*'Nueva recopilación'*], 2 vols. (Alcalá: Andrés de Angulo, 1567).

López de Corella, Alonso, *De morbo pustulato, sive lonticulari, quem nostrates Tabardillo appellant* (Zaragoza: Miguel de Güesa, 1574).

López Madera, Gregorio, *Excelencias de la monarquía de España* (Valladolid: Diego Fernández de Córdoba, 1597).

López-Rey, José, *Velázquez: A Catalogue Raisonné*, 2 vols. (Cologne: Taschen, 1996).

Machiavelli, Niccolò, *Il principe* (Rome: Antonio Blado, 1532).

McKendrick, Melveena, *Theatre in Spain 1492–1700* (Cambridge: Cambridge University Press, 1989).

Madroño Durán, Abraham, 'Comedias escritas en colaboración: el caso de Mira de Amescua', in A. de la Granja and J. A. Martínez Berbel, (eds.), *Mira de Amescua en candelero: Actas del Segundo Congreso Internacional sobre Mira de Amescua y el teatro español del siglo XVII (Granada, 27–30 de octubre de 1994)*, 2 vols. (Granada: Universidad de Granada, 1994).

Magallanes, Cosme, *Sylvae illustrium autorum, qui ad usum collegiorum Societatis Iesu selecti sunt* (Madrid: Luis Sánchez, 1598).

Malcolm, Alistair, 'Public Morality and the Closure of the Theatres in the Mid-Seventeenth Century: Philip IV, the Council of Castile and the Arrival of Mariana of Austria', in Richard J. Pym (ed.), *Rhetoric and Reality in Early Modern Spain* (London: Támesis, 2006), pp. 92–112.

Maraniss, James E., *On Calderón* (Columbia, MO: University of Missouri Press, 1978).

Marañón, Gregorio, 'La biblioteca del Conde-Duque de Olivares', *BRAH* 107 (1935), 677–92.

El Conde-Duque de Olivares: La pasión de mandar, 6th edn (Madrid: Espasa-Calpe, 1972).

Marcos Rodríguez, Florencio, 'Un pleito de don Pedro Calderón de la Barca, estudiante en Salamanca', *RABM* 67 (1959), 717–31.

Mariana, Juan de, *Del rey y de la institución real* (Madrid: Atlas: 1950). (BAE, vol. XXXI). (First published as *De rege et regis institutione* (Toledo: Pedro Rodríguez, 1599)).

Historia general de España, 2 vols. (Madrid: Carlos Sánchez, 1650); first published as *Historiae de rebus Hispaniae libri XX* (Toledo: Pedro Rodríguez, 1592).

Marlowe, Christopher, *The Tragicall History of Doctor Faustus* (London: V[alentine] S[immes] for Thomas Bushell, 1604).

Martínez Gil, Fernando; García Ruipérez, Mariano; Crosas, Francisco, 'Calderón de la Barca y el Corpus toledano de 1640: Recuperación de una carta autógrafa en el Archivo Municipal de Toledo', *Criticón* 91 (2004), 93–120.

Mason, T. R. A., '¿La sexualidad pervertida? *Las manos blancas no ofenden*', in *Archivum Calderonianum*, Band III: *Hacia Calderón: Séptimo Coloquio Anglogermano, Cambridge, 1984*, ed. Hans Flasche (Stuttgart: Franz Steiner, 1987), 183–92.

Massar, Phyllis Dearborn, 'Scenes for a Calderón Play by Baccio del Bianco', *Master Drawings* 15 (1977), 365–75.

Matilla Tascón, Antonio, *Archivo Histórico de Protocolos de Madrid: Inventario general de protocolos notariales* [Madrid: Ministerio de Cultura, 1980].

Matos Fragoso, Juan de, *Primera parte de comedias* (Madrid: Julián de Paredes, 1658).

May, Terence E., 'The Folly and the Wit of Secret Vengeance: Calderón's *A secreto agravio, secreta venganza*', *FMLS* 2 (1966), 114–22.

Medel del Castillo, Francisco, *Índice general alfabético de todos los títulos de comedias* (Madrid: Alfonso de Mora, 1735); reprinted by J. M. Hill in *Revue Hispanique* 75 (1929), 144–369.

Medrano, Sebastián Francisco de, *Favores de las musas recopilados por Alonso de Castillo Solórzano* (Milan: Juan Baptista Malatesta, 1631).

El mejor de los mejores libro [*sic*] *que ha salido de comedias nuevas* (Alcalá: María Fernández, 1651).

Memorial informatorio por los pintores en el pleyto que tratan con el señor fiscal de S. M. … sobre la exempcion del arte de la pintura (Madrid: Juan González, 1629).

Méndez Silva, Rodrigo, *Catalogo real genealogico de España* (Madrid: Diego Díaz de la Carrera, 1639).

Vida y hechos del gran Condestable de Portugal D. Nuño Aluarez Pereyra (Madrid: Juan Sánchez, 1640).

Mérimée, Henri, *Spectacles et comédiens à Valencia (1580–1630)* (Toulouse: Privat, 1913).

Mesonero Romanos, Ramón de, 'La casa de Calderón en las Platerías', *La Ilustración Española y Americana*, Año XXV, 19 (1881), 338.

Mexía, Pedro, *Historia imperial y cesárea* (Seville: Juan de León, 1545).

Millán, Pascual, 'Iconografía calderoniana', in *Homenaje a Calderón* (Madrid: Nicolás González, 1881), pp. 63–105.

Minsheu, John, *A Dictionarie in Spanish and English* (London: E. Bollifant, 1599).

Mira de Amescua, Antonio, *Amor, ingenio y mujer*.

Cuatro milagros del amor (?1629).

El esclavo del demonio (printed 1612).

Hero y Leandro (1629).

La mesonera del cielo.

El monte de la piedad (*auto*, ?1627).

Nardo Antonio, bandolero.

La próspera/adversa fortuna de Don Álvaro de Luna (?1621–4).

Mira de Amescua, Antonio, Montalbán, Juan Pérez de, Calderón de la Barca, Pedro, *Polifemo y Circe* (1630).

Molina, Tirso de (Fray Gabriel Téllez), *Los amantes de Teruel* (printed 1635).

Amar por arte mayor (by July 1635).

El castigo del penseque.

La celosa de sí misma (printed 1627).

Obras dramáticas completas, ed. Blanca de los Ríos, 3 vols. (Madrid: Aguilar, 1969).

Parte tercera de las comedias del maestro Tirso de Molina (Tortosa: Francisco Martorell, 1634).

Primera parte (Seville: Francisco de Lira, 1627).

Quien calla otorga (= *La segunda parte del penseque*).

Quinta parte (Madrid: Imprenta Real, 1636).

La venganza de Tamar (printed 1634).

El vergonzoso en palacio (by July 1611).

La vida y muerte de Herodes (by July 1635).

(attrib.), *El burlador de Sevilla* (?1621–5).

(attrib.), *El condenado por desconfiado*.

Moll, Jaime, 'De la continuación de las partes de comedias de Lope de Vega a las partes colectivas', in Pedro Peira (ed.), *Homenaje a Alonso Zamora Vicente*, 6 vols. (Madrid: Castalia, 1988–96), vol. III: *Literatura española de los siglos XVI–XVII*, Part 2, pp. 199–211.

'Diez años sin licencias para imprimir comedias y novelas en los reinos de Castilla: 1625–1634', *BRAE* 54 (1974), 97–103.

'Un tomo facticio de pliegos sueltos y el origen de las "relaciones de comedias"', *Segismundo* 12 (1976), 143–67.

Mogrobejo, Endika de, *Diccionario hispanoamericano de heráldica, onomástica y genealogía*, 27 vols. (Bilbao: Mogrobejo-Zabala, 1995–2004).

Monforte y Herrera, Fernando de: *see* Chirino de Salazar, Fernando.

Monroy y Silva, Cristóbal de, *Epítome de la historia de Troya* (Seville: Francisco de Lyra, 1641).

Montaral, L., and Vitse, M., 'Para una edición de *El conde Lucanor* de Calderón de la Barca', *Segismundo* 4, nos. 7–8 (1968), 51–70.

Moreto y Cabaña, Agustín, *El lindo don Diego* (?1650s).

Segunda parte (Valencia: Benito Macé, 1676).

Morley, S. Griswold, and Tyler, Richard W., *Los nombres de personajes en las comedias de Lope de Vega*, 2 vols. (Madrid: Castalia, 1961).

Mouyen, Jean, 'Las casas de comedias de Valencia', *Cuadernos de Teatro Clásico* 6 (1991), 91–122.

Muñoz, Luis, *Corona de Nuestra Señora en alabança de su purissima concepcion* (Barcelona: Lorenço Deu, 1642).

Narváez, Luis de, 'Arded, corazón, arded', in *Los seys libros del delphin de musica de cifra para tañer vihuela* (Valladolid: Diego Hernández de Córdoba, 1538).

Neumeister, Sebastian, *Mito clásico y ostentación: Los dramas mitológicos de Calderón* (Kassel: Reichenberger, 2000). (First published as *Mythos und Repräsentation* (Munich: Wilhelm Fink, 1978).)

Northup, G. T., 'Some Recovered Lines from Calderón', *Homenaje ofrecido a Menéndez Pidal: Miscelánea de estudios lingüísticos, literarios e históricos*, 3 vols. (Madrid: Hernando, 1925), vol. II, pp. 495–500.

Oña, Pedro de, *El Ignacio de Cantabria* (Seville: Francisco de Lyra, 1639).

Orso, Steven N., *Philip IV and the Decoration of the Alcázar of Madrid* (Princeton: Princeton University Press, 1986).

Ortí, Marco Antonio, *Siglo quarto de la conquista de Valencia* (Valencia: Juan Bautista Marçal, 1640; facsimile reprint, Valencia: Ajuntament de Valencia, 2005).

Osma, J. M. de, 'Estudios sobre Calderón de la Barca: Notas a la comedia *Con quien vengo, vengo*', *Hispania* 11 (1928), 221–6.

Ossorio, Pedro Luis, *Panegirico al illustrisimo Señor D. Juan Vivas de Cañamas* (no imprint, but before 1676).

Oteiza, Blanca, '*Elegía en la muerte del señor infante don Carlos, al señor infante cardenal*, por don Pedro Calderón de la Barca', in Ignacio Arellano and Germán Vega García-Luengos (eds.), *Calderón: innovación y legado: Actas selectas del IX Congreso de la Asociación Internacional de Teatro Español y Novohispano de los Siglos de Oro, en colaboración con el Grupo de Investigación Siglo de Oro de la Universidad de Navarra (Pamplona, 27 al 29 de marzo de 2000)* (New York: Peter Lang, 2001), pp. 289–307.

'Poesías de Calderón en la justa poética de 1622', in Ignacio Arellano (ed.), *Calderón 2000: Homenaje a Kurt Reichenberger en su 80 cumpleaños*, 2 vols. (Kassel: Reichenberger, 2002), vol. I, pp. 689–705.

Ovidius Naso, Publius, *Metamorphoses*.

Remedia amoris.

Pacheco de Narváez, Luis, *Historia exemplar de las dos mugeres constantes españolas* (Madrid: Imprenta del Reino, 1635; licensed in 1630).

Libro de las grandezas de la espada (Madrid: Pedro Várez de Castro, 1600).

Palau y Dulcet, Antonio, *Manual del librero hispano-americano*, 2nd edn, 28 vols. (Barcelona: Palau, 1948–77).

Paravicino y Arteaga, Hortensio Félix, *La Gridonia, o cielo de amor vengado* (published in his *Obras posthumas* (Madrid: Carlos Sánchez, 1641)).

Parker, Alexander A., 'Segismundo's Tower: A Calderonian Myth', *BHS* 59 (1982), 247–56.

The Allegorical Drama of Calderón (Oxford: Dolphin, 1943); translated by Francisco García Sarriá as *Los autos sacramentales de Calderón de la Barca*, (Barcelona: Ariel, 1983).

The Approach to the Spanish Drama of the Golden Age (London: The Hispanic and Luso-Brazilian Councils, 1957). (Colección Diamante 6.)

'The Father–Son Conflict in the Drama of Calderón', *FMLS* 2 (1966), 99–113.

The Mind and Art of Calderón (Cambridge: Cambridge University Press, 1988).

The Philosophy of Love in Spanish Literature (Edinburgh: Edinburgh University Press, 1985).

'Towards a Definition of Calderonian Tragedy', *BHS* 39 (1962), 222–37.

Parker, Geoffrey, *Spain and the Netherlands 1559–1659: Ten Studies*, revised edn (Fontana: Glasgow, 1990).

Parker, Jack H., 'The Chronology of the Plays of Juan Pérez de Montalbán', *PMLA* 67 (1952), 186–210.

Parte quarenta y dos de comedias de diferentes autores (Zaragoza: Juan de Ybar, 1650).

Parte veynte y cinco de comedias de diferentes autores (Zaragoza: Hospital Real y General, 1632; 2nd edn, 1633).

Parte veinte y ocho de comedias de varios autores (Huesca: Pedro Blusón, 1634).

Paterson, A. K. G., 'The Great World of Don Pedro Calderón's Theatre and the Beyerlinck Connection', *Calderón 1600–1681: Quatercentenary Studies in Memory of John E. Varey*, *BHS* (Glasgow) 77 (2000), 237–53.

'The Textual History of Tirso's *La venganza de Tamar*', *MLR* 63 (1968), 381–91.

Pedraza Jiménez, Felipe B., *Calderón: Vida y teatro* (Madrid: Alianza, 2000).

'De Lope a Calderón: Notas sobre la sucesión en la monarquía dramática', in José Alcalá Zamora and Ernest Belenguer (co-ordinators), *Calderón de la Barca y la España del Barroco*, 2 vols. (Madrid: Centro de Estudios Políticos y Constitucionales / Sociedad Estatal España Nuevo Milenio, 2001), vol. II, pp. 831–53.

Pellicer, Casiano, *Tratado histórico sobre el origen y progreso de la comedia y del histrionismo en España*, ed. José M. Díez Borque (Barcelona: Labor, 1975).

Pellicer de Tovar, Joseph de, *Anfiteatro de Felipe el Grande* (Madrid: Juan González, 1631).

Avisos: 17 de mayo de 1639 – 29 de noviembre de 1644, ed. Jean-Claude Chevalier and Lucien Clare, 2 vols. (Paris: Éditions Hispaniques, 2002–3).

Idea del Principado de Cataluña, primera parte (Antwerp: Jerónimo Verdús, 1642).

Pepys, Samuel, *see* Latham, R. C., and Matthews, W.

Pereda, Felipe, and Marías, Fernando (eds.), *El atlas del rey planeta: La descripción de España y de las costas y puertos de sus reinos de Pedro Texeira (1634)* (Hondarribia: Nerea, 2002).

Pérez de Hita, Ginés, *Guerras civiles de Granada*, vol. II (Cuenca: Domingo de la Iglesia, 1619).

Pérez de Montalbán, Juan, *Los amantes de Teruel* (printed 1635).

De un castigo, dos venganzas (?1625–6, ?1630).

Más puede amor que la muerte (?1633).
Orfeo en lengua castellana (Madrid: Viuda de Alonso Martín, 1624).
Para todos, ejemplos morales, humanos y divinos (Sevilla: Francisco de Lyra, 1645) (first published 1632).
El Polifemo (*auto*, 1628).
El socorro de Cádiz (1626) (*auto*, lost).
Vida y purgatorio de San Patricio (1627).
(attrib.), *Empeños que se ofrecen, los.*
(ed.), *Fama posthuma a la vida y muerte del Doctor Frey Lope Felix de Vega Carpio* (Madrid: Imprenta del Reyno, 1636).
See also Calderón de la Barca, Pedro; Mira de Amescua, Antonio.
Pérez de Moya, Juan, *Philosofía secreta* (Madrid: Francisco Sánchez, 1585); ed. Carlos Clavería (Madrid: Cátedra, 1995).
Pérez Galdós, Benito, *Fortunata y Jacinta* (1886–7).
Miau (1888).
Pérez Moreda, Vicente, *La crisis de la mortalidad en la España interior* (Mexico City and Madrid: Siglo Veintiuno, 1980).
Pérez Pastor, Cristóbal, *Documentos para la biografía de don Pedro Calderón de la Barca* (Madrid: Fortanet, 1905).
Noticias y documentos relativos a la historia y literatura españolas, in *Memorias de la Real Academia Española* 10 (1911), 9–307.
Nuevos datos acerca del histrionismo español en los siglos XVI y XVII: Primera serie (Madrid: Imprenta de la Revista Española, 1901).
'Nuevos datos acerca del histrionismo español en los siglos XVI y XVII: Segunda serie', *BH* 10 (1908), 243–58.
Pérez Pericón, Fernando, *Descripción de la ciudad … de Gibraltar* (Madrid: Imprenta del Reino, 1636).
Picatoste, Felipe, 'Biografía de Calderón', in *Homenaje a Calderón* (Madrid: Nicolás González, 1881), pp. 7–61.
(ed.), *Poesías inéditas de D. Pedro Calderón de la Barca* (Madrid: Imprenta de la Biblioteca Universal, 1881). (Biblioteca Universal: Colección de los mejores autores antiguos y modernos, nacionales y extranjeros 71.)
Plautus, Titus Maccius, *Aulularia.*
Plutarchus, Mestrius, *Vitae.*
Poema de Fernán González (*c.* 1260).
Porta, Giambattista della, *Lo astrologo* (Venice: Pietro Ciera, 1606).
Magia naturalis (Antwerp: Christophe Plantin, 1561).
Prado, Mateo (trans.), *El manual de grandes, que escriuio en lengua Toscana, Monseñor Querini Arçobispo de Nixia y Paris* (Madrid: Antonio Duplastre, 1640).
Profeti, Maria Grazia, *La collezione 'Diferentes autores'* (Kassel: Reichenberger, 1988).
Per una bibliografia di J. Pérez de Montalbán (Verona: Università degli Studi di Padova, 1976).
Puente, Ricardo, *A través de Palencia por el Camino de Santiago* (León: Albanega, 1998).

[Pulchi, Alessio] (compiler), *Essequie poetiche overo Lamento delle Muse Italiane in morte del Sig. Lope de Vega … Rime, e Prose raccolte dal Signor Fabio Franchi Perugino* [= Alessio Pulchi] (Venice: Ghirardo Imberti, 1636).

Roma festante nel real nascimento del Serenissimo Prencipe di Spagna (Rome: Lodovico Grignani, 1629).

Quevedo y Villegas, Francisco Gómez de, *Cómo ha de ser el privado* (1629).

El alguacil alguacilado (1607).

Epicteto y Phocilides en español con consonantes (Madrid: María de Quiñones, 1635).

Historia de la vida del buscón, llamado don Pablos (Zaragoza: Pedro Verges, 1626).

La isla de monopantos (?1638).

Memorial a S. M. el rey don Felipe Cuarto (1639): printed in Teofánes Egido, *Sátiras políticas de la España moderna* (Madrid: Alianza, 1973), no. 23, 111–15.

Obra poética, ed. José Manuel Blecua, 4 vols. (Madrid: Castalia, 1969–81).

Perinola, in his *Obras políticas, históricas y críticas*, 2 vols. (Madrid: Viuda de Hernando, 1893), vol. II, pp. 335–64.

'Quien quisiere ser culto en solo un día', sonnet (printed 1631).

(attrib.), 'Quien ama correspondido'.

Quiñones de Benavente, Luis, *El guardainfante*, parts I and II (?1634).

Ioco seria: Burlas veras, o reprehension moral, y festiua de los desordenes publicos (Madrid: Francisco García, 1645).

Loa con que empezaron Rueda y Ascanio en Madrid (1638).

La puente segoviana (*c.* 1635).

Ramírez de Arellano, Luis (compiler), *Avisos para la muerte* (Madrid: Viuda de Alonso Martín, 1634).

Redondo, Agustín, 'Fiesta y literatura en Madrid durante la estancia del Príncipe de Gales', *Edad de Oro* 17 (1998), 119–36.

Regalado, Antonio, *Calderón: Los orígenes de la modernidad en la España del Siglo de Oro*, 2 vols. (Barcelona: Destino, 1995).

Reichenberger, Kurt and Roswitha, *Bibliographisches Handbuch der Calderón-Forschung / Manual bibliográfico calderoniano*, 4 vols. (Kassel: Thiele & Schwarz / Reichenberger, 1979–2002).

Relacion general de los sucessos que ha avido en España, Flandes, Italia, y Alemania, y en otras partes, desde 1 de março de 1639 hasta fin de febrero de 1640 [?Madrid, 1640].

Rennert, Hugo A., *The Spanish Stage in the Time of Lope de Vega* (New York: Hispanic Society of America, 1909).

Rey de Artieda, Andrés, *Los amantes* (printed 1581).

Rico, Francisco, *El texto del 'Quijote': Preliminares a una ecdótica del Siglo de Oro* (Valladolid: Centro para la Edición de los Clásicos Españoles, Universidad de Valladolid, 2005).

Río, M. J. del, 'Representaciones dramáticas en casa de un artesano del Madrid de principios del siglo XVII', in L. García Lorenzo and J. E. Varey (eds.), *Teatros y vida teatral en el Siglo de Oro a través de las fuentes documentales* (London: Tamesis, 1992), pp. 245–58.

Ríos y Ríos, Ángel de los, *Biografía del célebre poeta dramático D. Pedro Calderón de la Barca* (Torrelavega: B. Rueda, 1889).

Rivadeneyra, Pedro de, *Historia ecclesiastica del scisma del reyno de Inglaterra* (Madrid: Pedro Madrigal, 1588).

Robles, Juan de, *Tardes del alcázar, doctrina para el perfecto vasallo*, ed. Miguel Romero Martínez (Seville: Diputación Provincial, 1948).

Rocamora, Ginés, *La esfera del universo* (Madrid: Juan de Herrera, 1599).

Ródenas Vilar, Rafael, *Vida cotidiana y negocio en la Segovia del Siglo de Oro: El mercader Juan de Cuéllar* (Salamanca: Junta de Castilla y León, 1990).

Rodríguez Cuadros, Evangelina, 'Calderón se quita la máscara: Teatro cómico breve', in Aurora Egido (ed.), *Lecciones calderonianas* (Zaragoza: Ibercaja, 2001), 105–23.

Rodríguez López-Vázquez, Alfredo, 'La fecha de "La vida es sueño" y el entremés "La maestra de gracias", atribuido a Belmonte: 1630–31, por la compañía de Cristóbal de Avendaño', in Szilvia E. Szmuk, *Calderón sueltas in the Collection of the Hispanic Society of America: Con un estudio de Alfredo Rodríguez López-Vázquez sobre la fecha de 'La vida es sueño' y otro de Jaroslava Kašparová sobre los manuscritos calderonianos de Mladá Vožice.* Vol. II of *Calderón: Protagonista eminente del barroco europeo* (Kassel: Reichenberger, 2002), pp. 1–19. (Teatro del Siglo de Oro, Bibliografías y Catálogos 30; Estudios de Literatura 61.)

Rojas de la Vega, Heliodoro, *Juicio crítico de las obras de Calderón de la Barca, bajo el punto de vista jurídico* (Valladolid: Agapito Zapatero, 1883).

Rojas Zorrilla, Francisco de, *Los bandos de Verona* (1640).

Comedias escogidas, ed. Ramón de Mesonero Romanos (Madrid: Rivadeneyra, 1849). (BAE, vol. LIV.)

Entre bobos anda el juego (?1636).

Rojas Zorrilla, Francisco de, Coello, Antonio, and Calderón de la Barca, Pedro, *El jardín de Falerina* (1635).

Rojas Zorrilla, Francisco de, Coello, Juan, and Coello, Antonio, *El robo de las sabinas* (1637).

Rose, Constance Hubbard, 'Who Wrote the *Segunda parte* of *La hija del aire*?', *RBPH* 54 (1976), 797–822.

'Again on the Authorship of the *Segunda parte* of *La hija del aire*', *BHS* 60 (1983), 247–8.

'¿Quién escribió la *Segunda parte* de *La hija del aire*? ¿Calderón o Enríquez Gómez?', in Luciano García Lorenzo (ed.), *Calderón: Actas del Congreso internacional sobre Calderón y el teatro español del Siglo de Oro* (Madrid, CSIC, 1983), pp. 603–15. (Anejos de la Revista *Segismundo* 6.)

Rosete Niño, Pedro, *Madrid por de dentro* (1641).

Roth, Cecil, *A History of the Marranos*, 4th ed. (New York: Hermon Press, 1959).

Rouanet, Léo, 'Un autographe inédit de Calderón', *RevHisp* 6 (1899), 196–200.

Rozzell, Ramón, 'The Song and Legend of Gómez Arias', *HR* 20 (1952), 91–107.

Ruano de la Haza, J. M., 'Historia de los textos dramáticos en el Siglo de Oro: Calderón, *Las órdenes militares* y la Inquisición', in María Cruz García de

Enterría and Alicia Cordón Mesa (eds.), *Siglo de Oro: Actas del IV Congreso Internacional del Asociación Internacional del Siglo de Oro*, 2 vols. (Alcalá de Henares: Universidad de Alcalá, 1998), vol. I, pp. 75–93.

La primera versión de La vida es sueño, *de Calderón* (Liverpool: Liverpool University Press, 1992).

La puesta en escena en los teatros comerciales del Siglo de Oro (Madrid: Castalia, 2000).

'Las dos versiones de *El mayor monstruo del mundo*, de Calderón', *Criticón* 72 (1998), 35–47.

Ruano de la Haza, J. M., and Allen, John J., *Los teatros comerciales del siglo XVII y la escenificación de la comedia* (Madrid: Castalia, 1994).

Ruiz de Alarcón y Mendoza, Juan, *La verdad sospechosa* (written by 1623).

Primera parte de comedias (Madrid: Juan González, 1628).

Ruiz Lagos, Manuel, '*El Tuzaní de la Alpujarra*: Calderón o la singularidad de la memoria histórica', in José Alcalá Zamora y Ernest Belenguer (co-ordinators), *Calderón de la Barca y la España del Barroco*, 2 vols. (Madrid: Centro de Estudios Políticos y Constitucionales / Sociedad Estatal España Nuevo Milenio, 2001), vol. II, pp. 793–827.

Rupp, Stephen, *Allegories of Kingship: Calderón and the Anti-Machiavellian Tradition* (University Park: Pennsylvania University Press, 1996).

Salas Barbadillo, Alonso de, *Coronas del Parnaso y platos de las musas* (Madrid: Imprenta Real, 1635).

Sánchez Alonso, María Cristina, *Impresos de los siglos XVI y XVII de temática madrileña* (Madrid: CSIC, 1981).

Sánchez Arjona, José, *El teatro en Sevilla en los siglos XVI y XVII* (Madrid: Alonso, 1887).

Sánchez de Espejo, Andrés, *Relacion aiustada en lo possible, a la verdad, y repartida en dos discursos* (Madrid: María de Quiñones, [1637]).

Sánchez Mariana, Manuel, 'El manuscrito original del auto *Llamados y escogidos*, de Calderón', in Luciano García Lorenzo (ed.), *Calderón: Actas del Congreso internacional sobre Calderón y el teatro español del Siglo de Oro* (Madrid: CSIC, 1983), pp. 299–308. (Anejos de la Revista *Segismundo* 6.)

Sanz Ayán, Carmen, '*Peor está que estaba*: La crisis hacendística, la cuestión del vellón y su reflejo teatral en tiempos de Calderón', in José Alcalá Zamora y Ernest Belenguer (co-ordinators), *Calderón de la Barca y la España del Barroco*, 2 vols. (Madrid: Centro de Estudios Políticos y Constitucionales / Sociedad Estatal España Nuevo Milenio, 2001), vol. I, pp. 189–201.

Schama, Simon, *Simon Schama's Power of Art* (London: BBC Books, 2006).

Schons, Dorothy, 'A Calderón Document', *RR* 19 (1928), 157.

Shakespeare, William, *King Edward III*, ed. Giorgio Melchiori (Cambridge: Cambridge University Press, 1998).

Romeo and Juliet (?1594–5).

The Taming of the Shrew (*c.* 1594).

Shergold, N. D., *A History of the Spanish Stage from Medieval Times until the End of the Seventeenth Century* (Oxford: Clarendon, 1967).

'The First Performance of Calderón's *El mayor encanto amor*', *BHS* 35 (1958), 24–7.

Shergold, N. D., and Varey, J. E., '*Autos sacramentales* in Madrid, 1644', *HR* 26 (1958), 52–63.

Los autos sacramentales en Madrid en la época de Calderón: 1637–1681: Estudio y documentos (Madrid: Ediciones de Historia, Geografía y Arte, 1961).

Representaciones palaciegas: 1603–1699: Estudio y documentos (London: Tamesis, 1982).

'Some Early Calderón Dates', *BHS* 38 (1961), 274–86.

'Some Palace Performances of Seventeenth-Century Plays', *BHS* 40 (1963), 212–44.

'Un documento nuevo sobre D. Pedro Calderón de la Barca', *BH* 62 (1960), 432–7.

(eds.), *Genealogía, origen y noticias de los comediantes de España* (London: Tamesis, 1985).

Siculus, Diodorus, *Bibliotheca historica*.

Silva, Antonio de, *see* Bermúdez, Jerónimo.

Silvela, Francisco, *Cartas de la Venerable Sor María de Ágreda y del Señor Rey Don Felipe IV*, 2 vols. (Madrid: Sucesores de Rivadeneyra, 1885–6).

Simón Díaz, José, *Bibliografía de la literatura hispánica*, 14 vols. (Madrid: Instituto 'Miguel de Cervantes' / CSIC, 1950–93).

'La congregación de la Anunciata del Colegio Imperial de Madrid', *Revista bibliográfica y documental* 1, no. 2 (1947), 129–88.

Historia del Colegio Imperial de Madrid, 2 vols. (Madrid: CSIC/IEM, 1952–9).

Los estudiantes de Madrid en el Siglo de Oro (Madrid: IEM, 1966).

'Textos dispersos de clásicos españoles: I. Bocángel. II. Calderón de la Barca', *RLit* 19 (1959), 99–121.

'Textos dispersos de clásicos españoles: XVI. Calderón de la Barca', *RLit* 22 (1962), 117–121.

Simón Díaz, José (ed.), *Relaciones breves de actos públicos celebrados en Madrid de 1541 a 1650* (Madrid: IEM, 1982).

Sliwa, Krzystof, *Cartas, documentos y escritos de Pedro Calderón de la Barca Henao de la Barrera Riaño (1600–1681) y de sus familiares, fénix de los ingenios y lucero mayor de la poesía española* (Valencia: Universitat de València, 2008).

Sloman, Albert E., '*La selva confusa* Restored to Calderón', *HR* 20 (1952), 134–48.

The Dramatic Craftsmanship of Calderón: His Use of Earlier Plays (Oxford: Dolphin, 1958).

The Sources of Calderón's El príncipe constante (Oxford: Blackwell, 1950).

Solera López, Rus, 'El retrete de Dánae en la comedia *Las fortunas de Andrómeda y Perseo*: Problemas textuales y escenográficos', in Ignacio Arellano (ed.), *Calderón 2000: Homenaje a Kurt Reichenberger en su 80 cumpleaños*, 2 vols. (Kassel: Reichenberger, 2002), vol. 1, pp. 509–24.

Solís, Antonio de, Coello, Antonio, and Calderón de la Barca, Pedro, *El pastor Fido* (by 1652).

Sosa, Juan Bautista de, *Sossia perseguida: Sueño y pregunta de Cassio, a Prudencio. En que se trata del honor paterno y amor filial* (Madrid: Diego Flamenco, 1621).

Stein, Louise K., *Songs of Mortals, Dialogues of the Gods: Music and Theatre in Seventeenth-Century Spain* (Oxford: Clarendon, 1993).

Stiefel, A. L., 'Calderons Lustspiel *La dama duende* und seine Quelle', *ZRP* 19 (1895), 262–4.

Suárez de Mendoza y Figueroa, Enrique, *Eustorgio y Clorilene: Historia moscovica* (Madrid: Juan González, 1629).

Sullivan, Henry W., 'The Wallenstein Play of Calderón and Coello, *Las proezas de Frislán, y muerte del rey de Suecia* [?] (1634): Conjectural Reconstruction', *BCom* 52, no. 2 (2000), 93–111.

Suppico de Moraes, Pedro Joseph, *Collecçam politica de apophthegmas memoraveis*, 3 vols. in 1 (Lisbon: Officina Augustiniana, 1733).

Sureda, F., 'Algunas tragedias del Siglo de Oro ante el público valenciano del XVIII', 'Datos complementarios', *Criticón* 23 (1983), 117–32.

Tárrega, Francisco Agustín (attrib.), *La fortuna adversa del infante don Fernando de Portugal*.

Tassis y Peralta, Juan de, *La gloria de Niquea* (1622).

Tauro, Raffaello, *La falsa astrologia, ovvero el sognar vegghiando* (Naples: Novello de Bonis, 1669).

Téllez, Gabriel, *see* Molina, Tirso de.

Terry, Arthur, *An Anthology of Spanish Poetry, 1500–1700*, 2 vols. (Oxford: Pergamon, 1965–8).

Texeira, Pedro, *Topographia de la villa de Madrid* (Antwerp: Joannes and Jacobus van Veerle, 1656).

Treviño, S. N., 'Nuevos datos acerca de la fecha de *Basta callar*', *HR* 4 (1936), 333–41.

'Versos desconocidos de una comedia de Calderón', *PMLA* 52 (1937), 682–704.

Tuke, Samuel, *The Adventures of Five Hours* (?1663).

Tyler, Richard W., and Elizondo, Sergio D., *The Characters, Plots and Settings of Calderón's* Comedias (Lincoln, NE: Society of Spanish and Spanish-American Studies, 1981).

Úbeda de los Cobos, Andrés (ed.), *Paintings for the Planet King: Philip IV and the Buen Retiro Palace* (Madrid: Museo Nacional del Prado, 2005).

Urzáiz Tortajada, Héctor, *Catálogo de autores teatrales del siglo XVII*, 2 vols. (Madrid: Fundación Universitaria Española, 2002). (Investigaciones Bibliográficas sobre Autores Españoles 5.)

Valbuena Briones, Ángel, 'Los libros de caballerías en el teatro de Calderón', in *Hacia Calderón: Quinto Coloquio Anglogermano, Oxford, 1978* (Wiesbaden: Franz Steiner, 1982), pp. 1–8.

Varey, J. E., 'An Additional Note on Pedro de Arce', *Iberoromania* 23 (1986), 204–9.

'*Andromeda y Perseo*, comedia y loa de Calderón: Afirmaciones artisticoliterarias y políticas', *Revista de Musicología* 10 (1987), 529–45.

'Calderón, Cosme Lotti, Velázquez, and the Madrid Festivities of 1636–1637', *Renaissance Drama* 1 (1968), 253–82.

'Catalina de Acosta and Her Effigy: vv. 1865–68 and the Date of Calderón's *Casa con dos puertas*', in R. O. W. Goertz (ed.), *Iberia: Literary and Historical Issues: Studies in Honour of Harold V. Livermore* (Calgary: University of Calgary Press, 1985), pp. 107–15.

'Imágenes, símbolos y escenografía en *La devoción de la cruz*', in Hans Flasche (ed.), *Hacia Calderón: Segundo Coloquio Anglogermano, Hamburgo, 1970* (Berlin: De Gruyter, 1973), pp. 155–70.

'L'Auditoire du *Salón dorado* de l'*Alcázar* de Madrid au XVIIe siècle', in Jean Jacquot (ed.), *Dramaturgie et Société: Rapports entre l'oeuvre théâtrale, son interprétation et son public aux XVIe et XVIIe siècles: Nancy 14–21 avril 1967* (Paris: Centre National de la Recherche Scientifique, 1968), vol. I, pp. 77–91.

'La minoría de Carlos II y la prohibición de comedias de 1665–1667', in Pedro Peira (ed.), *Homenaje a Alonso Zamora Vicente*, 6 vols. (Madrid: Castalia, 1988–96), vol. III, *Literatura española de los siglos XVI–XVII*, Part I, pp. 351–7.

'The Staging of Calderón's *La cena de Baltasar*', in Karl-Hermann Körner and Dietrich Briesemeister (eds.), *Aureum Saeculum Hispanum: Beiträge zu Texten des Siglo de Oro: Festschrift für Hans Flasche zum 70. Geburtstag* (Wiesbaden: Franz Steiner, 1983), pp. 299–311.

'The Transmission of the Text of *Casa con dos puertas*: A Preliminary Survey', in Francisco Mundi Pedret, Alberto Porqueras Mayo and José Carlos de Torres (eds.), *Estudios sobre Calderón y el Teatro de la Edad de Oro: Homenaje a Kurt y Roswitha Reichenberger* (Barcelona: Promociones y Publicaciones Universitarias, 1989), p. 49–57.

Varey, J. E., and Salazar, A. M., 'Calderón and the Royal Entry of 1649', *HR* 34 (1966), 1–26.

Varey, J. E., and Shergold, N. D. (with the collaboration of Charles Davis), *Comedias en Madrid: 1603–1709* (London: Tamesis, 1989). (Fuentes para la Historia del Teatro en España, 9.)

'Datos históricos sobre los primeros teatros de Madrid: Prohibiciones de autos y comedias y sus consecuencias', *BH* 62 (1960), 286–325.

'Un pleito teatral de 1660', *Hispanófila*, 15 (1962), 9–27.

'Sobre la fecha de *Troya abrasada*, de Zabaleta y Calderón', in G. Mancini (ed.), *Miscellanea di studi ispanici*, vol. VI (Madrid: Istituto di Letteratura Spagnola e Ispano-Americana, 1963), pp. 287–97.

See also Davis, Charles, and Varey, J. E.; Shergold, N. D., and Varey, J. E.

Varias poesías (1654), ed. J. M. Blecua (Zaragoza: Heraldo de Aragón, 1946).

Vega Carpio, Lope de, *Las almenas de Toro* (?1610–13).

El amor enamorado, ed. Eleonora Ioppoli (Florence: Alinea, 2006).

'¡Ay, verdades, que en amor ...!', *romance*.

El Brasil restituido (1625), in *Obras de Lope de Vega*, vol. XXVIII: *Crónicas y leyendas dramáticas de España* (Madrid: Atlas, 1970), pp. 357–96. (BAE, vol. CCXXXIII.)

El caballero de Olmedo (?1620–5).

Cartas, ed. Nicolás Marín (Madrid: Castalia, 1985).

Castelvines y Monteses (?1606–12).

El castigo sin venganza (1631, printed 1634), ed. C. A. Jones (Oxford: Pergamon, 1966).
Los comendadores de Córdoba (1596–8).
La Circe (Madrid: Viuda de Alonso Martín for Alonso Pérez, 1624).
Las comedias del fenix de España, Lope de Vega Carpio, parte veinte y siete ('Barcelona: Sebastián de Cormellas', 1633).
El desprecio agradecido (*c.* 1633).
La discreta enamorada (1606).
Don Juan de Castro, parts I and II (1597–1608).
La Dorotea (1632), ed. Edwin S. Morby (Madrid: Castalia, 1968).
Doze comedias nuevas de Lope de Vega Carpio, y otros autores ('Barcelona, Gerónimo Margarit, 1630' (= Seville, Simón Fajardo)).
El fenix de España, Lope de Vega Carpio, veinte y tres parte de sus comedias ('Valencia: M. Sorolla', 1629).
Fuenteovejuna (1612–14).
El jardín de Falerina (lost).
Justa poetica y alabanzas justas que hizo la insigne villa de Madrid al bienaventurado San Isidro en las fiestas de su beatificacion (Madrid: Viuda de Alonso Martín, 1620).
Laurel de Apolo (1630), ed. Antonio Carreño (Madrid: Cátedra, 2007).
El mayor imposible (1615).
El mejor alcalde el rey (1620–3).
Los melindres de Belisa (?1606–8).
Obras poéticas, ed. José Manuel Blecua (Barcelona: Planeta, 1983).
Obras sueltas, vol. XXI (Madrid: Antonio de Sancha, 1779).
Parte veinte y quatro de las comedias del fenix de España, Lope de Vega Carpio (Zaragoza: Diego Dormer, 1633).
El peregrino en su patria (1604).
El peregrino en su patria, ed. Juan Bautista Avalle-Arce (Madrid: Castalia, 1973).
Peribáñez (1605–13).
El perro del hortelano (?1613–15).
Porfiar hasta morir (?1624–8, printed 1638).
El premio en la hermosura (1614).
'¡Quítenme aquesta puente que me mata …!', sonnet, in the *Rimas de Tomé de Burguillos* (1634).
La reina doña María (1604–8).
La reina Juana de Nápoles (1597–1603).
Relacion de las fiestas que la insigne villa de Madrid hizo en la canonizacion de su bienaventurado hijo y patron San Isidro, con las comedias que se representaron y los versos que en la justa poetica se escribieron (Madrid: Viuda de Alonso Martín, 1622).
Seis comedias de Lope de Vega Carpio y de otros autores (Lisbon: Pedro Craesbeeck, 1603).
Los Tellos de Meneses, parts I and II (1625–30).
Tercera parte de comedias [Seville: Gabriel Ramos Bejarano, 1612].

Veinte y tres parte de sus comedias, y la mejor parte que hasta oy se ha escrito ('Valencia: Miguel Sorolla, 1629').

El vellocino de oro (1622).

El villano en su rincón (1611–15).

Vega García-Luengos, Germán, 'Calderón y la política internacional: Las comedias sobre el héroe y traidor Wallenstein', in José Alcalá Zamora y Ernest Belenguer (co-ordinators), *Calderón de la Barca y la España del Barroco*, 2 vols. (Madrid: Centro de Estudios Políticos y Constitucionales / Sociedad Estatal España Nuevo Milenio, 2001), vol. II, pp. 793–827.

'Cómo Calderón desplazó a Lope de los aposentos: Un episodio temprano de ediciones espúreas', in Ignacio Arellano and Germán Vega García-Luengos (eds.), *Calderón: Innovación y legado: Actas selectas del IX Congreso de la Asociación Internacional de Teatro Español y Novohispano de los Siglos de Oro, en colaboración con el Grupo de Investigación Siglo de Oro de la Universidad de Navarra (Pamplona, 27 al 29 de marzo de 2000)* (New York: Peter Lang, 2001), pp. 367–84.

'El predominio de Calderón también en las librerías: Consideraciones sobre la difusión impresa de sus comedias', in Aurelio González (ed.), *Calderón 1600–2000: Jornadas de investigación calderoniana* (Mexico, DF: El Colegio de México: Fondo Eulalio Ferrer, 2002), pp. 15–33.

'Entre calvos anda el juego': La insistencia de un tema burlesco en Rojas Zorrilla', *RLit* 69, no. 137 (2007), *Número monográfico dedicado a Francisco de Rojas Zorrilla*, 13–34.

'Imitar, emular, renovar en la *comedia nueva*: *Cómo se comunican dos estrellas contrarias*, reescritura "calderoniana" de *Las almenas de Toro*', *Anuario Lope de Vega* II (2005), 243–64.

'Sobre la autoría de *El privilegio de las mujeres*', in Álvaro Alonso and J. Ignacio Díez (eds.), *'Non omnis moriar': Estudios en memoria de Jesús Sepúlveda* (Málaga: Universidad de Málaga, 2007), pp. 317–36.

Vélez de Guevara, Luis, *El amor en vizcaíno* (1637).

La creación del mundo (?before 1638).

La niña de Gómez Arias, ed. Ramón Rozzell (Granada: Universidad de Granada, 1959). (Colección Filológica 16.)

La serrana de la Vera (1613).

Vélez de Guevara, Luis (attrib.), 'Juicio final de todos los poetas españoles muertos y vivos'.

Vélez de Guevara, Luis (attributable), *La creación del mundo* (*comedia de repente*, ?1638).

Vera y Figueroa, Juan Antonio de, *El Fernando o Sevilla restaurada* (Milan: Henrico Estefano, 1632).

Vergilius Maro, Publius, *Bucolica* [*Eclogues*].

Georgica.

Villaizán y Garcés, Jerónimo de, *Ofender con las finezas* (?1632).

Villamediana, Conde de, *see* Tassis y Peralta, Juan de.

Villegas, Alonso de, *Flos sanctorum*, 4 vols. (Toledo: various printers, 1578–89).

Virués, Cristóbal de, *La gran Semíramis* (printed 1609).

Vosters, S. A., 'Again the First Performance of Calderón's *El sitio de Bredá*', *RCEH* 6 (1981), 117–34.

Waterhouse, Ellis Kirkham, *Eighteen Paintings from the Wellington Gift* (London: Arts Council of Great Britain, 1949).

Wedgwood, C. V., *The Thirty Years War* (London: Folio Society, 1999). (First published 1938.)

Weir, Lucy E., *The Ideas Embodied in the Religious Dramas of Calderón* (Lincoln, NE: University of Nebraska Press, 1940). (University of Nebraska Studies in Language, Literature and Criticism 18.)

Wethey, Harold E., *The Paintings of Titian*, vol. III: *The Mythological and Historical Paintings* (London: Phaidon, 1975).

Whitaker, Shirley B., 'The First Performance of Calderón's *El sitio de Bredá*', *RQ* 31 (1978), 515–31.

'The Quevedo Case (1639): Documents from Florentine Archives', *MLN* 97 (1982), 368–79.

Williams, Patrick, *The Great Favourite: The Duke of Lerma and the Court and Government of Philip III of Spain, 1598–1621* (Manchester: Manchester University Press, 2006).

Wilson, Edward M., 'An Early List of Calderón's *comedias*', *MP* 60 (1962), 95–102.

'An Early Rehash of Calderón's *El príncipe constante*', *MLR* 76 (1961), 785–94.

'Calderón and the Stage-Censor in the Seventeenth Century: A Provisional Study', *Symposium* 15 (1961), 165–84.

'Calderón y Cervantes', in Hans Flasche (ed.), *Hacia Calderón: Quinto Coloquio Anglogermano, Oxford, 1978* (Wiesbaden: Franz Steiner, 1982), pp. 9–19.

'Calderón y el Patriarca' in Karl-Hermann Körner and Klaus Rühl (eds.), *Studia iberica: Festschrift für Hans Flasche* (Bern and Munich: Francke, 1973), pp. 697–703.

'Calderón y Fuenterrabía': El *Panegírico al Almirante de Castilla*', *BRAE* 49 (1969), 253–78.

'Calderón's Enemy: Don Antonio Sigler de Huerta', *MLN* 81 (1966), 225–31.

'El texto de la "Deposición a favor de los profesores de la pintura", de don Pedro Calderón de la Barca', *RABM* 77 (1974), 709–27.

'¿Escribió Calderón el romance "Curiosísima señora"?', *AL* 2 (1962), 99–118.

'Fray Hortensio Paravicino's Protest against *El príncipe constante*', *Ibérida: Revista Filológica* 6 (1961), 245–66.

'Inquisición y censura en la España del siglo XVII', in *Entre las jarchas y Cernuda: Constantes y variantes en la poesía española* (Barcelona: Ariel, 1977), 245–72. Published in English as 'Inquisitors as Censors in Seventeenth-Century Spain', in Ronald G. Popperwell (ed.), *Expression, Communication and Experience in Literature and Language: Proceedings of the XII Congress of the International Federation for Modern Languages and Literatures* (Cambridge University, 20–26 August 1972) (London: Modern Humanities Research Association, 1973), pp. 38–56.

'Notes on the Text of *A secreto agravio, secreta venganza*', *BHS* 35 (1958), 72–82.

'La poesía dramática de don Pedro Calderón de la Barca', in *Litterae Hispanae et Lusitanae* (Munich: Max Hueber, 1968), pp. 487–500.

'Some Unpublished Works by Don Pedro Calderón de la Barca', in *Homage to John M. Hill: In Memoriam* (Bloomington: Indiana University, 1968), pp. 7–18.

Spanish and English Literature of the 16th and 17th Centuries (Cambridge: Cambridge University Press, 1980).

'Textos impresos y apenas utilizados para la biografía de Calderón', *Hispanófila* 9 (1960), 1–14.

'The Four Elements in the Imagery of Calderón', *MLR* 31 (1936), 34–47.

'Un memorial perdido de don Pedro Calderón', in A. David Kossoff and José Amor y Vázquez (eds.), *Homenaje a William L. Fichter: Estudios sobre el teatro antiguo hispánico y otros ensayos* (Madrid: Castalia, 1971), pp. 801–17.

'Un romance ascético de Calderón: "Agora, señor, agora …"', *BRAE* 52 (1972), 79–105.

Wilson, Edward M., and Cruickshank, Don W., *Samuel Pepys's Spanish Plays* (London: Bibliographical Society, 1980).

Wilson, Edward M., and Moir, Duncan, *A Literary History of Spain: The Golden Age: Drama 1492–1700* (London: Ernest Benn; New York: Barnes & Noble, 1971).

Wilson, Edward M., and Sage, Jack, *Poesías líricas en las obras dramáticas de Calderón: Citas y glosas* (London: Tamesis, 1964).

Wilson, Margaret, '"Si África llora, España no ríe": A Study of Calderón's *Amar después de la muerte* in Relation to its Source', *BHS* 51 (1984), *Golden Age Studies in Honour of A. A. Parker*, pp. 419–25.

Wooldridge, John B., 'The *Segunda parte* of *La hija del aire* is Calderón's', *BCom* 47 (1995), 73–94.

'*Quintilla* Usage in Antonio Enríquez Gómez: More Evidence against His Authorship of the Second Part of *La hija del aire*', *MLR* 96 (2001), 707–14.

Wurzbach, Wolfgang von, *Calderons ausgewählte Werke*, 10 vols. (Leipzig: Hesse & Becker, 1910).

Zabaleta, Juan de, Rojas Zorrilla, Francisco de, and Calderón de la Barca, Pedro, *La más hidalga hermosura* (1645).

Zabaleta, Juan de, Cáncer y Velasco, Jerónimo de, and Calderón de la Barca, Pedro, *La margarita preciosa* (?1651).

Zudaire, Eulogio, 'Ideario político de D. Gaspar de Guzmán, privado de Felipe IV', *Hisp* (Madrid) 25 (1965), 413–25.

'Un escrito anónimo de Calderón de la Barca', *Hisp* (Madrid) 13 (1953), 268–93.

Index of Calderón's works

General index

Spanish people normally use two surnames, paternal followed by maternal, but occasionally, even in Spain, we find Federico García Lorca and Benito Pérez Galdós referred to as Lorca and Galdós. In the seventeenth century males sometimes reversed their surnames or omitted their first (e.g., Góngora), while females regularly put the maternal surname first. In general, this index follows the form favoured by the individual. When there is too little evidence, males are indexed with the paternal surname first. In indexing titles of works of literature, definite articles are disregarded; when a work has more than one title, it is indexed under both or all of them; n and ñ are treated as separate letters, as in Spanish. To facilitate users, Calderón's works have been indexed separately.